WILCOX/WILCOXSON FAMILIES
OF NEW ENGLAND
AND THEIR DESCENDANTS
A Genealogical Dictionary
Revised Edition

Compiled by

Martha Scott Osborne

Heritage Books, Inc.

Copyright 1993 By

Martha Scott Osborne

Published 1993 By

Heritage Books, Inc.
1540-E Pointer Ridge Place
Bowie, Maryland 20716
(301) 390-7709

ISBN 1-55613-802-4

A Complete Catalog Listing Hundreds Of Titles On
Genealogy, History, And Americana
Available Free On Request

Co CT & Newport RI 1675; ch JOHN, AUDLEY, SAMUEL, DANIEL, HANNAH; Ref: Hist of Stonington p658, Austin p423, Wilcox-Brown-Medbery p6, Halifax VT Wilcox Fam mss, Your Ancestors v12 #1 p1405, Wilcox Genealogy p5, See Rhode Island Genealogical Register v2 p93.

HANNAH - b 11 Apr 1684 Portsmouth, Newport Co RI d/DANIEL & HANNAH (COOK) WILCOX; m PHILIP SHERMAN; Ref: Austin p423, Your Ancestors v10 #3 p1267.

HANNAH - b 18 Sep 1685 Stratford, Fairfield Co CT d/TIMOTHY & JOANNA (BIRDSEY) WILCOX; m THOMAS GRIDLEY 31 Oct 1704; Res Farmington, Hartford Co CT; d 19 Nov 1733; Ref: Wilcox-Meigs p24, Desc of Wm Wilcoxson p28, Stratford Gen p1346.

HANNAH - b 04 Oct 1689 d/EDWARD & MARY (HAZARD) WILCOX; m 22 Apr 1704 Westerly, Washington Co RI EZEKIEL GAVITT who was bpt Salem, Essex Co MA 21 Jun 1696 & d 1753/4 [will probated 25 Mar 1754] Westerly RI; ch MARY, HANNAH, EZEKIEL, SAMUEL, JOHN, THANKFUL, PRUDENCE, STEPHEN, JOSEPH, BENAJAH, HEZEKIAH, ESTHER; Ref: Hist of Stonington p658, Austin p423, Gen of RI Families v1 p463, Col Fam of US v3 p226.

HANNAH - b 01 Nov 1692 Simsbury, Hartford Co CT d/SAMUEL & MINDWELL (GRIFFIN) WILCOX; m 23 May 1716 THOMAS NORTON; Ref: Wilcox-Meigs p31, Nutmegger v10 #2 p213, Desc of Wm Wilcoxson p14.

HANNAH - b 16 Jan 1694 Killingworth, Middlesex Co CT d/JOSEPH & HANNAH (KELSEY) WILCOX; m 04 Oct 1733 GERSHOM PALMER; Ref: Bogue Families p394, Wilcox-Meigs pp29,30, Nutmegger v12 #4 p651, v11 #2 p211, Barbour's VR Killingworth v2 p191.

HANNAH - b ca 1705; m CALEB RANDALL who was b 1703 at Scituate, Plymouth Co MA & d be 1761; m poss JOSEPH HOUSE; Ref: Nutmegger v15 #1 p47.

HANNAH - m 07 May 1728 Middletown, Middlesex Co CT MALACHI LEWIS; Ref: Barbour's VR Middletown v1 p39

HANNAH - m 05 Jul 1738 JOHN WILCOX; Res Middletown, Middlesex Co CT; ch JOHN, SAMUEL, HEZEKIAH, HANNAH, JOSEPH, SIMEON, GILES, SUBMIT, COMFORT, SARAH; Ref: Barbour's VR Middletown v2 p94; MUH p747, Your Ancestors v3 #4 p351.

HANNAH - m 09 Jul 1738 Dartmouth, Bristol Co MA THOMAS HATHAWAY; Ref: Dartmouth VR p546.

HANNAH - m 25 Feb 1742 Middletown, Middlesex Co CT [his 3rd wife] BENJAMIN CORNWELL; Ref: Nutmegger v13 #4 p570, Early Marriages of CT v2 p87, Gen of CT Fam v1 p487, Barbour's VR Middletown v1 p81.

HANNAH - b ca 1710 N Kingston, Washington Co RI d/THOMAS & MARTHA (HAZARD) WILCOX; m Mar 1743 Exeter, Washington Co RI ENOCH PLACE; Ref: Arnold v1 pp152,169,177, Austin p423.

HANNAH - b 01 Nov 1715 Dartmouth, Bristol Co MA d/DANIEL & SARAH (-----) WILCOX; Ref: Am Gen. v19 #1 p28, VR of Dartmouth p302, Your Ancestors v10 #3 p1267.

HANNAH - b Oct 1716 Stratford, Fairfield Co CT d/JOHN & DEBORAH (BRINSMADE) WILCOX; m EBENEZER THOMPSON; Ref: Wilcox-Meigs p38, Stratford Gen p1346, Cutter's Northern NY v2 p655.

HANNAH - b 24 Dec 1718 Middletown, Middlesex Co CT d/SAMUEL & HANNAH (SAGE) WILCOX; Ref: Nutmegger v4 #3 p330, NEH&GR v14 p138, Cutter's Western NY v2 p742, Col Fam of US v5 p554, Barbour's VR Middletown LR2 p29 Gen of CT Fam v3 p275.

HANNAH - m 09 Jul 1738 Dartmouth, Bristol Co MA THOMAS HATHAWAY; Ref: Dartmouth VR p546.

HANNAH - b 29 Oct 1720 Westerly, Washington Co RI d/EDWARD & DINAH (BARBER) WILCOX; Ref: Arnold v5 p144.

HANNAH - b 03 Apr 1721 Portsmouth, Newport Co RI d/JOSEPH & SARAH (-----) WILCOX; Ref: Arnold v4 pt1 p104, Your Ancestors v12 #3 p1477.

HANNAH - b 28 Mar 1722 Killingworth, Middlesex Co CT d/JOHN & HANNAH (SHAILOR) WILCOX; m 30 Oct 1740 EPHRAIM BLINN who was b 21 Jan 1715/16 s/WILLIAM & ANNA (COULTMAN) BLINN; Res Lenox, Berkshire Co MA; ch DEBORAH, HANNAH; Ref: Barbour's VR Killingworth v1 p185 v2 p146, ECM p30, Nutmegger v11 #3 p443, Wilcox-Meigs p31, Bogue Families p395, Desc of Wm Wilcoxson pp13,36, NEH&GR v143 p315.

HANNAH - b 26 Jun 1724 or 16 Oct 1725 S Kingston, Washington Co RI d/ROBERT & CATHERINE

HADWIN P - b 20 Sep 1866 s/JAMES PURDY & SABRINA (STANBRO) WILCOX; m 25 Jun 1891 ARMONELLE LOW; 1 ch d in infancy; Ref: Your Ancestors v3 #3 p319.

HALLETT M - b 10 May 1865 Geneva, Ashtabula Co OH s/JOSEPH L & MARY S (IVES) WILCOX; m 15 Sep 1891 FLORA TRUNKEY d/ALBERT & NANCY (BURNS) TRUNKEY; ch GLADYS LOUISE, NEAL ALBERT; d 31 Mar 1838 Geneva OH; Ref: Bogue Families p399.

HAMILTON Lt - b 27 Feb 1786 Guilford, New Haven Co CT s/EDMUND & ELIZABETH (SCRANTON) WILCOX; Res Genesee Co NY 1808; War of 1812; d 27/28 Jan May 1814 Batavia, Genesee Co NY; Ref: Our County & Its People Genesee Co p104, Fam of Early Guilford p1201, Barbour's VR Guilford v2 p198.

HAMILTON Rev - b ca 1814 s/HENRY & EUNICE (-----) WILCOX; m ca 1831 SOPHIA -----; Res Smyrna, Chenango Co NY; ch JOSEPH C, HAMILTON; Ref: Your Ancestors v12 #3 p1462 #4 p1487.

HAMILTON - b ca 1830 s/OLIVER & SALLY (STANTON) WILCOX; Res Norwich, Chenango Co NY; Ref: Your Ancestors v3 #4 p350, Cutter's New England Families v1 p160.

HAMILTON - b 1836 s/HAMILTON & SOPHIA (-----) WILCOX; Res Smyrna, Chenango Co NY; Ref: Your Ancestors v12 #4 p1487.

HAMILTON - b 1845 NY s/ABEL EDWIN & ELIZABETH (SPENCER) WILCOX of Bergen, Genesee Co NY; Ref: 1850 Census Bergen NY p51 Dw# 677, 1860 Census Bergen NY p967 Dw# 248, See Abel Edwin.

HAMILTON C - b 19 Feb 1831 s/SAMUEL GASKELL & SALLY (COOK) WILCOX of Mendon, Worcester Co MA; Ref: Your Ancestors v11 #2 p1346.

HAMILTON M - b 09 Apr 1845 Voluntown, New London Co CT s/MINER & ALICE ANN (-----) WILCOX; Ref: Barbour's VR Voluntown v2 p138.

HAMIT C - b 1844 NY d/HANEY N & AMANDA A (-----) WILCOX of Mexico, Oswego Co NY; Ref: 1850 Census Mexico NY p77 Dw# 1183.

HANANIAH - b 1817 Cortlandville, Cortland Co NY; m NANCY E ----- who was b 1819 NY; taught school in Virgil, Cortland Co NY; Res Dryden Tompkins Co NY 1848; Painter; ch MARY E, MINERVIA;

d ca 1878; Ref: Early Settlers of Virgil NY pp45,46, 1850 Census Dryden NY p101 Dw# 652.

HANEY N - b 1809 NY; m AMANDA A ----- who was b 1810 NY; Res Mexico, Oswego Co NY; ch ALBERT N, SAMUEL M, MARY E, WILLIAM H, HAMIT C, CHARLES A; Ref: 1850 Census Mexico NY p77 Dw# 1183.

HANFORD I - b 1834 Stratford, Fairfield Co CT s/JOEL & PHOEBE (-----) WILCOX; Ref: Desc of Wm Wilcoxson p36.

HANLORD - d 20 Feb 1853; Ref: CT Bible Rec v18 p522.

HANNAH - b ca 1644/5 Stratford, Fairfield Co CT d/WILLIAM & MARGARET (-----) WILCOX; m 17 Mar 1664 Lt DANIEL HAYDEN of Windsor, Hartford Co CT; ch DANIEL, HANNA, NATHANIEL, WILLIAM, WILLIAM, SAMUEL, EBENEZER, MARY; Ref: Wilcox-Meigs p18, Bogue Families p394, Stratford Gen p1346, Cutter's New England Families v1 p159, Records of Windsor, CT from NEH&GR v5 p227, History of Surry NH p943.

HANNAH - b 14 Feb 1664 Stratford, Fairfield Co CT d/JOHN & ELIZABETH (BOURNE) WELLES WILCOX; m 1686 JOSEPH BOOTH; d 10 Jul 1701; Ref: Wilcox-Meigs p22, Desc of Wm Wilcoxson p27, Stratford Gen p1346, Cutter's Northern NY v2 p654, CT Bible Rec v10 pp48,50.

HANNAH - b 19 Jan 1665 Killingworth, Middlesex Co CT d/JOSEPH & ANN (SHEATHER) WILCOX; m 8 Sep/Dec 1686 PETER FARNUM who was b 1660/1 & d 14 Feb 1703/4 Killingworth CT; ch JOANNA, PHEBE, HANNAH, PETER, NATHANIEL, JOSIAH, JOHN; m 24/25 Aug 1707 NATHANIEL ROYCE who d Feb 1726 Wallingford, New Haven Co CT; d 06 Feb 1708; Ref: Nutmegger v11 #3 p390, Wilcox-Meigs p23, Desc of Wm Wilcoxson p28, Bogue Families p394, Desc of Abner & Lucy Hart Wilcox p18, Cutter's Northern NY v2 p656, Cutter's New England Families v1 p159, Fam of New Haven v 7 & 8 p1551, Col Fam of US v5 p207, Your Ancestors v4 #9&10 p586.

HANNAH - m 28 Aug 1692 JOHN RHOADES Philadelphia, Philadelphia Co PA; Ref: Am Marriages p447.

HANNAH - b ca 1672 Westerly, Washington Co RI d/STEPHEN & HANNAH (HAZARD) WILCOX; m SAMUEL CLARKE s/JEREMIAH Jr & ANN (AUDLEY) CLARK of Newport, Newport Co RI; Res Stonington, New London

(LILLIBRIDGE) WILCOX; m 12 Nov 1745 WILLIAM REYNOLDS who was b ca 1720 N Kingston RI s/JOHN REYNOLDS; Res Richmond, Washington Co RI; ch WILLIAM, ROBERT, JESSE; Ref: Your Ancestors v1 pp1,51, v3 #1 p278, Arnold v2 p102, v5 pt3 p35.

HANNAH - b 03 Dec 1724 Middletown, Middlesex Co CT d/THOMAS & ANNA (NORTH) WILCOX; Ref: NEH&GR v14 p138, MUH p747, Nutmegger v4 #3 p330, Barbour's VR Middletown LR2 p10.

HANNAH - b 24 Dec 1726 Stonington, New London Co CT d/WILLIAM & HANNAH (BROWN) WILCOX; m 16 Mar 1758 OLIVER BENTLEY; Ref: Nutmegger v12 #3 p390, Barbour's VR Stonington v2 p48, See William.

HANNAH - b 31 Jul 1731 d/AZARIAH & MARY (FAXTON/SAXTON) WILCOX of W Simsbury, Hartford Co CT; Ref: Your Ancestors v11 #4 p1380, Wilcox-Meigs p49, Barbour's VR Simsbury TM4 p249, Desc of Wm Wilcoxson p23.

HANNAH - b 07 Dec 1731 Killingworth, Middlesex Co CT d/JOSEPH & REBECCA (HURD) WILCOX; m 22 Oct 1761 OLIVER CULLINS; Ref: Wilcox-Meigs p40, Barbour's VR Killingworth v1 p189.

HANNAH - b 15 Sept 1733 E Guilford, New Haven Co CT d/JOSEPH & HANNAH (GOODALE) WILCOX; m 14 Jul 1751 ELI GRAVES/GROVES who was b 20 Jul 1734 & d 29 Jan 1795 s/EBENEZER & MARY (ISBELL) GRAVES; ch GILBERT, MILTON, HANNAH, ELIZABETH, MABEL; d 07 Apr 1786 or 01 Jan 1805; Ref: Wilcox-Meigs p33, Cutter's CT Families v4 p1769, Barbour's VR Guilford v2 pp70,81, Fam of Early Guilford pp513,1208, Gen of CT Fam v2 p85, Desc of Wm Wilcoxson p15.

HANNAH - b 14 Jun 1734 Killingworth, Middlesex Co CT d/DANIEL & HANNAH (BUELL) WILCOX; m MICHAEL SPENCER; Ref: Barbour's VR Killingworth v2 p157, Wilcox-Meigs p44, Desc of Wm Wilcoxson p20.

HANNAH - b 28 Apr 1735 Killingworth, Middlesex Co CT d/JOSIAH & KEZIAH (KELSEY) WILCOX; Res Dutchess Co NY; Ref: Desc of Wm Wilcoxson p43.

HANNAH - b 17 Aug 1735 Dartmouth, Bristol Co MA d/WILLIAM & DOROTHY (ALLEN) WILCOX; Ref: Dartmouth VR p302, Bristol Co Probate Rec v1 p333, v2 p182.

HANNAH - b 10 Mar 1736/7 Middletown, Middlesex Co CT; d 23 May 1772; Ref: Barbour's VR Middletown v1 p86.

HANNAH - b 08 Jul 1738 Killingworth, Middlesex Co CT d/ELISHA & MARY (BEACH) WILCOX; m 27 Oct 1762 SIMON HOUGH; Ref: Wilcox-Meigs p41, See following entry.

HANNAH - b 08 Jul 1738 d/ELISHA & MARY (BEACH) WILCOX; m 22 Oct 1761 Killingworth, Middlesex Co CT OLIVER COLLINS who was b 17 Nov 1738 s/OLIVER & ELIZABETH (HALL) COLLINS; Res Lee, Berkshire Co MA; ch OLIVER, AVIS, ELIAS, JOHN, ISAAC; Ref: Fam of Early Guilford p229, Your Ancestors v3 #3 p321, Barbour's VR Killingworth v2 pp118,162.

HANNAH - m 15 Dec 1751 RI SAMUEL WILBUR Jr; Ref: Arnold v4 pt 5 p71, pt6 p68.

HANNAH - m 22 Jan 1756 Dartmouth, Bristol Co MA THOMAS DENNIS who was b 11 Sep 1734 & d 12 oct 1813 s/JOHN & HANNAH (WILBOR) DENNIS of Little Compton, Newport Co RI; Res Easton, Washington Co NY; 8 ch; Ref: Dartmouth VR p546, Gen of RI Fam v1 p417, Arnold v4 pt5 p71.

HANNAH - m 01 Oct 1767 Portsmouth, Newport Co RI PELEG MANCHESTER who was b 02 Aug 1745 s/THOMAS & JANE (COOK) MANCHESTER; ch JEAN, GEORGE COOK, EUNICE, SUSANNA, HENRIETTA, MARY, JAMES, PHEBE, SARAH, STEPHEN; Ref: Arnold v4 pt1 p48, v7 p372, Your Ancestors v10 #3 p1268, Gen of RI Families v1 p690.

HANNAH - b 12 Nov 1738 Stonington, New London Co CT d/WILLIAM WILCOX; d 11 Feb 1738/9; Ref: Barbour's VR Stonington v2 p48.

HANNAH - b 14 Apr 1740 Dartmouth, Bristol Co MA d/STEPHEN & MARY (RICKETSON) WILCOX; d 1778; Ref: Dartmouth VR p302, Am Gen v19 #1 p30.

HANNAH - b 28 Jan 1748 Middletown, Middlesex Co CT d/JOHN & HANNAH (WILCOX) WILCOX; d 19 Feb 1826; Ref: Your Ancestors v3 #4 p351, Early Fam of Wallingford p331, Barbour's VR Middletown v2 p74, Hist of Wallingford p937.

HANNAH - b 17 Jan 1750 Killingworth, Middlesex Co CT d/ABRAHAM & SARAH (TOOLEY) WILCOX; Ref: Wilcox-Meigs p47, Barbour's VR Killingworth v2 p43.

HANNAH - b Richmond, Washington Co RI d/BENJAMIN & ESTER (SHEFFIELD) WILCOX; m ----- BROWN; Res Nova Scotia, Canada; Ref: Desc of Charles Dyer Wilcox p v, Samuel Gorton Desc v2 p587.

HANNAH - b 10 Sep 1751 Hebron, Tolland Co CT d/EBENEZER & ELIZABETH (DEWEY) WILCOX; m AMOS SMITH of Hebron CT; Ref: Barbour's VR Hebron v1 p57, Desc of Wm Wilcoxson p25.

HANNAH - m 29 Mar 1774 Suffield, Hartford Co CT DANIEL FOWLER; Ref: VR of CT v7 p134.

HANNAH - b 22 Dec 1751 Simsbury, Hartford Co CT d/HOSEA & HANNAH (GRIFFIN) WILCOX; Ref: Wilcox-Meigs p68.

HANNAH - m 15 Feb 1770 Wallingford, Rutland Co VT STANBURY BUTTON; Ref: VT VR.

HANNAH - m 03 Apr 1774 Durham, Middlesex Co CT JOEL ROBINSON who was b 02 May 1753 & d 26 Sep 1835 s/JAMES & AMY (SPELLMAN) ROBINSON; Res Granville, Middlesex Co MA; ch SETH, AMY, ELIZUR; d 15 Jun 1831; Ref: Fam of Early Guilford p995, Barbour's VR Durham v EG p332.

HANNAH - b 17 Dec 1755 W Simsbury, Hartford Co CT d/AMOS & HANNAH (HOSKINS) WILCOX; m EZRA ADAMS; ch MINDWELL, EZRA, ABEL, HANNAH, TRACY, LAURA, DAVID; d 1801 age 46; Ref: Early Settlers of W Simsbury CT pp 133,134, Fiske Card File, Wilcox-Meigs p67, Your Ancestors v12 #4 p1489, v13 #2 p1540.

HANNAH - b 14 Jun 1757 Portsmouth, Newport Co RI d/JOSIAH & ANN (ESTES) WILCOX; Ref Arnold v2 p105, v4 pt1 p105, See Josiah, Your Ancestors v12 #4 p1503.

HANNAH - b 02 Jul 1758 E Guilford, New Haven Co CT d/TIMOTHY & EUNICE (PIERSON) WILCOX; Ref: Wilcox-Meigs p53, Desc of Wm Wilcoxson p27, Fam of Early Guilford p1209, Barbour's VR Guilford v2 p100.

HANNAH - b ca 1760 Exeter, Washington Co RI d/ABRAHAM & LYDIA (HARRINGTON) WILCOX; m WILLIAM SMILEY; Ref: Your Ancestors v4 #7&8 p561.

HANNAH - b 03 April 1764 Stonington, New London Co CT d/EDWARD & ESTHER (-----) WILCOX; m CHAMPLIN LILLIBRIDGE; Ref: Your Ancestors v12 #1 p1405.

HANNAH - b 04 Sep 1767 Sturbridge, Worcester Co MA d/DANIEL & HANNAH (-----) WILCOX who later moved to Bradford Co PA; m 09 Oct 1787 Dudley, Worcester Co MA DAVID MORSE; d be 1794; Ref: Nutmegger v 13 #3 p442, Sturbridge VR p142.

HANNAH - m TIMOTHY WALTERHOUSE Jr who was b 26 May 1765 s/TIMOTHY & CONTENT (WHIPPLE) WALTERHOUSE; Ref: CT Bible Rec v4 pp325,335,336.

HANNAH - m 20 Sep 1781 Dartmouth, Bristol Co MA JOHN DAVIS; Ref: Dartmouth VR p546.

HANNAH - b ca 1770 Exeter, Washington Co RI d/HOPSON & ELIZABETH (HOLOWAY) WILCOX; m JEFFREY GARDNER; Ref: Your Ancestors v3 #1 p278.

HANNAH - b 1771; m 21 Nov 1805 EZEKIEL GAVITT who was b 2 Jun 1773 s/OLIVER & MARJORY (-----) GAVITT; ch LYDIA, JOSEPH; d 03 Jan 1811; Ref: Gen of RI Families v1 p469.

HANNAH - b ca 1772 Halifax, Windham Co VT d/NATHAN & REBECCA (MOON) WILCOX; m 22 May 1800 Marlboro, Windham Co VT DAVID BARTLETT; d 30 May 1870 Guilford, Windham Co VT; Ref: 2nd Boat v5 #2 p76, Halifax Wilcox Fam mss.

HANNAH - b 21 Oct 1772 Middletown, Middlesex Co CT d/SAMUEL & HANNAH (THRASHER) WILCOX; Ref: Barbour's VR Middletown v2 p176, See Samuel.

HANNAH - b 21 Oct 1772 Chester, Hampden Co MA d/ELISHA & ABIGAIL (RANNEY) WILCOX; m 19 Jan 1792 Cromwell, Middlesex Co CT SETH WILCOX s/OZIAS & MABEL (GOULD) WILCOX; ch ERASTUS, MARIETTE, HORACE; Ref: Your Ancestors v3 #9&10 p451, See Seth.

HANNAH - m 16 Jan 1783 Dartmouth, Bristol Co MA JOHN TRIPP; Ref: Dartmouth VR p546.

HANNAH - b 19 May 1776 Killingworth, Middlesex Co CT d/STEPHEN Jr & SARAH (HULL) WILCOX; Ref: Wilcox-Meigs p63, Barbour's VR Killingworth v2 p116.

HANNAH - b 02 Jan 1777 Killingworth, Middlesex Co CT d/JOSEPH & GRACE (WILCOX) WILCOX; d 12 May

1850; Ref: Wilcox-Meigs p64, Barbour's VR Killingworth v2 p149.

HANNAH - d/JOSIAH & ELIZABETH (CURTIS) WILCOX; m 21 Feb 1788 OBADIAH GILLETTE; Ref: Col Fam of US v5 p555.

HANNAH - m 07 Dec 1788 Westport, Bristol Co MA WANTON MACOMBER s/ABIEL MACOMBER Ref: Westport VR p251.

HANNAH - m J---- GOODSILB 05 Oct 1793 Cromwell, Middlesex Co CT; Ref: ECM v2 p97.

HANNAH - b 23 Sep 1779 Simsbury, Hartford Co CT d/ROGER & ELIZABETH (CASE) WILCOX; Ref: Wilcox-Meigs p85, Your Ancestors v12 #4 p1490, Barbour's VR Simsbury TM4 p302.

HANNAH - b 12 Jul 1780 Newport, Sullivan Co NH d/URIAH & HANNAH (WRIGHT) WILCOX; m DAVID ALLEN who was b Killingworth, Middlesex Co CT 13 May 1777 & d 27 Dec 1840 s/GIDEON & PATIENCE (-----) ALLEN; d 13 Oct 1880; Ref: Nutmegger v14 #4 p641, Gen of NH Fam v3 p1509, Your Ancestors v3 #5 p378.

HANNAH - b 1780 d/JACOB & SARAH (BROWN) WILCOX of Mt Holly, Rutland Co VT; m SIMON LAWRENCE; Res Chautauqua Co NY; d 1865; Ref: Early Settlers of NY v3 p96, Fiske Card File, See Jacob.

HANNAH - b 29 Dec 1782 Middletown, Middlesex Co CT d/ELIJAH W & LOIS (WARNER) WILCOX; m 25 Sep 1806 RICHARD BONFEY who was b 10 Feb 1778 & d 08 Jun 1837 s/HENRY & SARAH (-----) BONFAY of Middletown CT; ch ELIJAH WILCOX, HANNAH HEPSIBAH, SETH, DAVID, BENJAMIN F, HENRY, LOIS; d 04 Jun 1873; Ref: Your Ancestors v3 #6 p401, #7&8 p427, Barbour's VR Middletown v2 p108.

HANNAH - d/ELNATHAN & HANNAH (-----) WILCOX of East Bloomfield, Ontario Co NY; m WILLIAM BARRETT; Res Clarence, Erie Co NY; Ref: Your Ancestors v9 #4 p1177, Edward D McCarthy, Desc of William Wilcox p209.

HANNAH - b 1789 d/WILLIAM & HANNAH (-----) WILCOX; m AZON FORSYTH; Ref: Your Ancestors v9 #4 p1178.

HANNAH - b 1789; d 03 Nov 1851 Simsbury, Hartford Co CT; Ref: Rev Allen McLean Rec p15.

HANNAH - b 07 Oct 1794 Exeter, Washington Co RI d/JOB & MARY (GATES) WILCOX; m JONER MOORE or WILLIAM LOTTRIDGE; Ref: Cutter's Western NY v3 p1436, Arnold v3 pp35,63, Your Ancestors v4 #11&12 p610.

HANNAH - b 1795 Harpersfield, Delaware Co NY d/SAMUEL & SALLY (HUNT) WILCOX; m 1817 ANDREW TAYLOR Jr; ch SAMUEL, ALONZO, APOLLOS, LAVINIA, SARAH, HANNAH; d 1887; Ref: Your Ancestors v4 #5&6 pp543,544.

HANNAH - b 26 Jun 1796 RI/NY d/HEZEKIAH & MAHALA (WILCOX) WILCOX; m JACOB TICE; m JAMES DRAKE; Res Orange Co NY & Bradford Co PA; ch 1st husband, JOHN, SAMUEL, ELIZABETH; ch 2nd husband ANDREW JACKSON, REBECCA, AMELIA, EMILY, MAHALA; Ref: Your Ancestors v10 #3 p1248.

HANNAH - b 1798 d/ELISHA & HANNAH (-----) WILCOX Leyden, Lewis Co NY; d 15 Nov 1815; Ref: Tree Talks v7 #1 p36.

HANNAH - m 21 Nov 1804 E Greenwich, Kent Co RI BAILEY MANCHESTER; Ref: Arnold v1 p92.

HANNAH - b 26 Mar 1799 Franklin, New London Co CT d/JOHN CLARK & DORCAS (HARRINGTON) WILCOX; m ca 1814 RUSSELL ROGERS who was b 07 May 1797; Ref: Nutmegger v17 #4 p640, Barbour's VR Franklin v1 p89, Your Ancestors v14 #2 p1658.

HANNAH - b 1799 Simsbury, Hartford Co CT d/ELISHA & ELIZABETH (BABCOCK) WILCOX; m 14 Jun 1838 RUFUS HUMPHREY; d 11 Mar 1875; Ref: Your Ancestors v12 #1 p1407.

HANNAH - b ca 1802 d/AMOS & SARAH (ROGERS) WILCOX of Stockbridge, Windsor Co VT; m DAVID DAVIS; Ref: Your Ancestors v12 #4 p1489.

HANNAH - d/WILLIAM WILCOX of W Mendon, Monroe Co NY; m ----- FORSYTH; Res Schoolcraft, Kalamazoo Co MI; Ref: Desc of Wm Wilcoxson p203.

HANNAH - b 23 Mar 1806 Tiverton, Newport Co RI d/JOSIAH WILCOX; d Jun 1834; Ref: Arnold v8 p514.

HANNAH - m 15 Sep 1833 Norwalk, Fairfield Co CT BENJAMIN FAIRWEATHER; Ref: Barbour's VR Norwalk v1 p17.

HANNAH - b 25 Feb 1809 Charlestown, Washington Co RI d/JOSEPH & HULDAH (SHERMAN) WILCOX; Ref: Arnold v5 pt5 p28, See Joseph.

HANNAH - bpt 06 Jul 1810 d/STEPHEN & HANNAH (HOLMES) WILCOX of N Stonington, New London Co CT; m 22 Sep 1833 W ---- BECK; Ref: Your Ancestors v13 #3 p1565, Barbour's VR Stonington v5 p29.

HANNAH - bpt 21 Jun 1815 N Kingston, Washington Co RI d/NOAH & MARTHA (ALBRO) WILCOX; Ref: Your Ancestors v3 #11&12 p472.

HANNAH - b 06 Sep 1818 Berkshire, Berkshire Co MA d/CALEB & POLLY (BLANDIN) WILCOX; d 16 Apr 1821; Ref: Your Ancestors v3 #7&8 p424.

HANNAH - b 03 Aug 1819 d/WILLARD & HANNAH (GASKELL) WILCOX of Mendon, Worcester Co MA; Ref: Your Ancestors v11 #2 p1345.

HANNAH - m 09 Nov 1823 Providence, Providence Co RI THOMAS FRANCIS; Ref: Arnold v7 p473.

HANNAH - b 1822 d/JOSHUA & ABIGAIL (KELSEY) WILCOX of Newport, Sullivan Co NH; Ref; Your Ancestors v3 #6 p399.

HANNAH - d/ROBERT JOHNSON & LUCY (COLE) WILCOX of Homer, Cortland Co NY; m 22 Mar 1848 AARON ROOT; m 01 Jul 1860 JOHN WEED; ch HELEN; Ref: Your Ancestors v10 #1 pp1199,1200.

HANNAH - b 1825 d/AARON & ELECTA (-----) WILCOX of Bainbridge, Chenango Co NY; Ref: 1850 Census Chenango Co NY.

HANNAH - b 1826 NY; Sister of JOHN & CHARLES WILCOX; Res Ithaca, Tompkins Co NY; Ref: 1850 Census Ithaca NY p234 Dw# 449.

HANNAH - b 20 Oct 1829 d/AMOS & SOPHRONIA (HATFIELD) WILCOX of Wethersfield, Wyoming Co NY; Ref: Your Ancestors v14 #2 p1643.

HANNAH - b 14 Dec 1830 NY d/ELIJAH & SALLY (SHULER) WILCOX; m CHARLES R COLLINS; 3ch; Ref: Your Ancestors v9 #2 p1127, Desc of Wm Wilcoxson p192.

HANNAH - b ca 1830 d/AMOS & RACHEL (-----) WILCOX; m BENJAMIN PORCUPILE; Res OH & Butler MI; ch BENJAMIN; Ref: Bogue Families p400.

HANNAH - b 1834 CT d/SAMUEL & NANCY (-----) WILCOX of Goshen, Litchfield Co CT; Ref: 1850 Census Goshen CT p96 Dw# 116.

HANNAH - b 1836 NY d/HENRY & BETSEY (-----) WILCOX of Concord, Erie Co NY; Ref: 1850 Census Concord NY p54 Dw# 785.

HANNAH - b 1838 NY d/HAZZARD H & MARIAH (PALMER) WILCOX of Sherman, Chautauqua Co NY; Ref: 1850 Census Sherman NY p276 Dw# 67, See Hazzard H.

HANNAH - b 1840 NY d/ISAIAH & POLLY A (-----) WILCOX of Columbus, Chenango Co NY; Ref: 1850 Census Columbus NY p280 Dw# 2131.

HANNAH - b 1842 Harpersfield, Delaware Co NY d/ALONZO BENJAMIN & HANNAH (SWIFT) WILCOX; m ALLEN DeKAMP; Ref: Your Ancestors v4 #7&8 p563, 1850 Census Harpersfield NY p158 Dw# 28.

HANNAH - m 11 Apr 1850 Burrillville, Providence Co RI ESEK [ISAAC] MOWRY; Ref: Arnold v2 pt2 p16.

HANNAH - of Harmony, Chautauqua Co NY m 17 Jan 1853 Jamestown, Chautauqua Co NY CHARLES WEBER/WEBBER; Ref: 19th Cent Marriages Reported in Fredonia Censor p119.

HANNAH - b 1854 NY d/----- & MARY A (-----) WILCOX of Harmony, Chautauqua Co NY; Ref: 1860 Census Harmony NY p660 Dw# 371.

HANNAH - b 13 Apr 1868 d/JOHN HENRY OWEN & MARY (YOUNG) WILCOX; Ref: Your Ancestors v12 #2 p1436.

HANNAH - m 13 Jan 1880 Westerly, Washington Co RI JOHN MOORE; Ref: Arnold v11 p177.

HANNAH ANN - b 1838 CT d/STEPHEN & AMY B (-----) WILCOX of Lisbon, New London Co CT; Ref: 1850 Census Lisbon CT Reel 432 #49 p55.

HANNAH CAROLINE - b 15 Jun 1859 Watch Hill, Washington Co RI d/HORACE & HANNAH (KENYON) WILCOX; m JAMES MOORE who d soon af their dau was born; m JESSE B GREENE; ch by 1st husband JENNIE MAUD; d 18 Oct 1946; Ref: C Douglass Alves Sr.

HANNAH E - b 17 Nov 1818 d/ELISHA & BETSEY (-----) WILCOX; Ref: Your Ancestors v3 #9&10 p451.

HANNAH E - b 1837 NY d/ISAIAH & ARMANDA (-----) WILCOX of Florence, Oneida Co NY; Ref: 1850 Census Florence NY p200 Dw# 144.

HANNAH ELIZA - m 16 Mar 1863 HENRY WHITE WILCOX s/ SAMUEL & ABIGAIL (WHITE) WILCOX; Res Winsted, Litchfield Co CT; ch EDWARD; Ref: MUH p744.

HANNAH G - b 1839 d/WHITMORE & LYDIA/LAURA A (-----) WILCOX of Georgetown, Madison Co NY; Ref: Your Ancestors v3 #6 p401, 1850 Census Georgetown NY p378 Dw# 32.

HANNAH GOULD - b 08 Mar 1850 Rowe, Franklin Co MA d/THOMAS & MARY P (UPTON) WILCOX; Ref: Halifax VT Wilcox Fam mss.

HANNAH J - of Middletown, Middlesex Co CT m 06 Jun 1854 JOHN W MILES of Meriden, New Haven Co CT; Ref: Barbour's VR Middletown v4 p253.

HANNAH JANE - b 13 Apr 1822 Westfield, Middlesex Co CT d/ELISHA BACON & HEPZIBAH (CORNWELL) WILCOX Ref: Your Ancestors v3 #5 p379, Hist of Wallingford p939.

HANNAH L - b 1825+ d/SAMUEL & HANNAH (BAILEY) WILCOX; m J S JENKINS; Res Plains, Luzerne Co PA; Ref: Your Ancestors v3 #5 p1176, Hist of Luzerne Co PA p1456.

HANNAH M - b 20 Au 1842 d/WILLIAM B & IRENE (LARKIN) WILCOX of Putnam, Windham Co CT; m GEORGE E CHANDLER; Ref: Your Ancestors v4 #11&12 p609.

HANNAH M - b 1821 Chautauqua, Chautauqua Co NY m 14 Jun 1845 Mayville, Chautauqua Co NY JOHN WILSON of Westfield, Chautauqua Co NY; d 14 Feb 1893 Laona, Chautauqua Co NY; Ref: 19th Cent Marriages Reported in Fredonia Censor p119, 19th Cent Death Notices Reported in Fredonia Censor p603.

HANNAH M - m 09 May 1850 Cumberland, Providence Co RI FRANCIS W DANIELS; Ref: Arnold v3 pt5 p70.

HANNAH ROGERS - b 01 May 1810 VT d/AMOS BRONSON & SARAH (ROGERS) WILCOX; m 12 Nov 1827 DAVID L DAVIS who was b 10 Nov 1811 & d 13 Jan 1875; ch AMOS BRONSON, MERIDAN W, SIBBEL W, ALVIN C, MELVIN E, HIRAM E, SILAS R; d 21 Sep 1892; Ref: MUH pp745,746.

HANNAH SEABURY - b 28 Dec 1837 Tiverton, Newport Co, RI d/HOLDER NELSON & BETSEY (HART) WILCOX; d 04 Jan 1857; Ref: Cem Inscr, Gen of RI Families v2 p596.

HARLAN - b 1845 VT s/JOSIAH & MARY (-----) WILCOX of Orwell, Addison Co VT; Ref: 1850 Census Orwell VT Reel 920 p41.

HARLIN - b 1836 NY s/STEPHEN PIERSON & ELECTA MARETTA (NETTLETON) WILCOX of Le Roy, Genesee Co NY; Ref: 1850 Census Le Roy NY p39 Dw# 502.

HARLOW - b 29 Nov 1791 Granby, Hartford Co CT s/SEDOTIA/SADOCE & ROXY (HAYSE) WILCOX; Ref: Barbour's VR Granby TM1 p25, CT Bible Rec v18 p520.

HARLOW - b 1818 VT; m SALLY ----- who was b 1823; Res Cambridge, Lamoille Co VT; ch OSCAR; Ref: 1860 Census Cambridge VT p108.

HARLOW EDWARD - b 24 May 1852 s/WILLIAM OLIVER & AMANDA M (ALLEN) WILCOX; Ref: CT Bible Rec v4 p5.

HARLOW G - b 24 Aug 1808 NY s/RIVERIOUS & SOPHRONIA (-----) WILCOX; m MARY J McEWEN d/ZENAS McEWEN; m JEMIMA LEWIS NICHOLSON; Res Big Grove IL; ch by 1st wife SARAH, ELMINA/ALMIRA, MARY E, ALBERT, JAMES B; ch by 2nd wife EDWIN, OLIVE, CHARLES A, ELLEN A, HENRY J; Ref: Your Ancestors, 1850 Census IL; Desc of Wm Wilcoxson p225.

HARLOW MARTIN - b 1831 Cherry Creek, Chautauqua Co NY s/THOMAS WARD & HULDAH PRUDENCE (McMANUS) WILCOX; m 12 Jan 1854 Harbor Creek Erie Co PA EMILINE TERRY who was b 1829 & d ca 1859; m in the south ca 1860 ----- who d soon after marriage; m 05 Aug 1863 MARILLA JAY who was b 09 May 1838 Hamlet, Chautauqua Co NY & d 18 Nov 1914 Silver Creek, Chautauqua Co NY d/JOHN & LUCINDA (TANNER) JAY; Res Chautauqua Co NY, Chicago IL, & Wausau WI; ch by 1st wife EFFIE, ADA, ANNA; ch by 2nd wife THOMAS, FENTON, JAY WARREN, JESSIE, ALTA; d 09 Jun 1885 Wausau WI; Ref: Wilcox History mss pp1,2,4, Obit of Marilla Jay Wilcox.

HARLOW MERLE - b 17 Dec 1895 Chautauqua Co NY s/JAY WARREN & MAY ANGELIA (WILCOX) WILCOX; d in a streetcar accident 09 Nov 1917 Buffalo, Erie Co NY; Res Silver Creek Chautauqua Co NY; Ref: Wilcox History mss, Death Certificate.

HARMON - b 17 Sep 1800 s/DANIEL & ESTHER (MERRIETT) WILCOX; d 29 Aug 1867; Ref: CT Bible Rec v11 p551.

HARMON - b 25 Dec 1805 Madison, New Haven Co CT s/PITMAN & ELIZA (WILCOX) WILCOX; m EUNICE ----- who was b 1806 MA; Res Bergen, Genesee Co NY; ch EUNICE ANN, MARY JANE, SUSAN C, EMMA, EDMUND; Ref: Your Ancestors v3 #2 p302, 1850 Census Bergen NY p45 Dw# 589, 1860 Census Bergen NY p985 Dw# 405.

HARMON - m 14 May 1829 Hartford, Hartford Co CT MARIE FRANCIS both of Wintonbury CT; Ref: Barbour's VR Hartford v1 p71.

HARMON - b 15 Oct 1819 s/ROSWELL & IRENE (NICHOLSON) WILCOX of Lowville, Lewis Co NY; m 30 May 1844 MARTHA SMITH of Gouverneur, St Lawrence Co NY; d 22 June 1846; Ref: Cutter's Northern NY v2 p656, Desc of Wm Wilcoxson p65.

HARMON - b 1842 NY s/----- & CATHERINE (-----) WILCOX; Res Cicero, Onondaga Co NY; Ref: 1860 Census Cicero NY.

HARMON STRATTON - b 16 Dec 1817 Canada s/EBENEZER & JAEL (HANCHETT) WILCOX who later moved to Jackson Co IA; Res Miami Co KS; Ref: Desc of Wm Wilcoxson p124.

HAROLD - b 27 Feb 1883 Geneva, Ontario Co NY s/WILLIAM & NETTIE (HOLMES) WILCOX; d 05 Mar 1883; Ref: Desc of George Holmes p272.

HAROLD - b April 1895 Utica, Oneida Co NY s/ARTHUR RAY & JULIA CAROLINE (SAVAGE) WILCOX; m Marion NY; Res NYC, Port Angeles, Clallam Co WA; d ca 1970's Port Angeles WA; Ref: Judith K Schlitt.

HAROLD - b 06 Apr 1897 Erie Co NY s/LAURA IRENE WILCOX; Adopted by WILLIAM & JULIA L (-----) GLOSS; Ref: 10,000 VR of Western NY p250.

HAROLD A - b 01 May 1890 s/GEORGE W & MINA B (ROE) WILCOX; m 19 Jun 1915 HARRIET GLOVER; ch ALFRED, ELEANOR RUTH; Ref: Denison Gen p506.

HAROLD AUGUSTUS - b 07 Aug 1898 Higganum, Middlesex Co CT s/CHARLES FREDERICK & ELLEN C (CRITTENDEN) WILCOX; m 09 Sep 1919 ROSE DAVIS; no ch; Ref: Your Ancestors p257.

HAROLD CURTIS - b 07 Jan 1889 Meriden, New Haven Co CT s/GEORGE HORACE & NETTIE (BARKER) CURTIS WILCOX; Ref: MUH p761.

HAROLD H - b 09 Jul 1877 Peoria, Peoria Co IL s/ERASTUS S & MARY L (HATCH) WILCOX; Ref: Wilcox-Meigs p119.

HAROLD LEROY - b 09 Apr 1890 Rockdale, Crawford Co PA s/GEORGE NELSON & CLARISSA ADELE (HOTCHKISS) WILCOX; m AMELIA STEINHOFF; Ref: A Wilcox Book p133.

HAROLD W - s/FRANK C & SARAH THERESA (SPENCER) WILCOX; m RUBY AMES; Ref: Your Ancestors v3 #7&8 p427.

HARRIET - b ca 1790 Hartford, Hartford Co CT; m 13 Jun 1813 MERRIL MORSE; Res VT; Ref: Fam of Early Hartford p408.

HARRIET - b 16 Aug 1793 Cornwall, Litchfield Co CT d/ZADOCK & LOIS (-----) WILCOX; Ref: Barbour's VR Cornwall v3 p26.

HARRIET - b 07 Jul 1800 Halifax, Windham Co VT d/STEPHEN & ELINOR (EWING) WILCOX; m 15 Nov 1818 Halifax JOSEPH NYE who d 03 May 1863 Ellington, Chautauqua Co NY; d 29 Nov 1863; Ref: Halifax VT Wilcox Fam mss, Fiske Card File.

HARRIET - m 20 Apr 1825 Franklin Co OH JOHN B BENARD; Ref: OH Marriages p338.

HARRIET/HARRIETT - b 16 Nov 1802 W Winfield, Herkimer Co NY d/JOHN & SYBIL (GOULD) WILCOX; m SHEFFIELD ENOS; Ref: Your Ancestors v3 #1&2 p499.

HARRIET - d/EZRA & REBECCA BROWN (MUNGER) WILCOX; m 02 May 1821 E Guilford, New Haven Co CT JOHN KELSEY of Saybrook, Middlesex Co CT; Ref: Wilcox-Meigs p71, Fam of Early Guilford p1211, Barbour's VR Guilford v2 p290.

HARRIET - m 24 Sep 1828 Berlin, Hartford Co CT JOB PORTER of E Hartford, Hartford Co CT; Ref: Barbour's VR Berlin v1 p32.

HARRIET - m 14 Jun 1838 Simsbury, Hartford Co CT RUFUS HUMPHREY Jr; Ref: Rev Allen McLean Rec p21, CT Bible Rec v11 p375.

HARRIET - b 1802 d/DAVID & SALLY (-----) WILCOX; Res Harpersfield, Delaware Co NY; Ref: Tree Talks v4 #3 p4.

HARRIET - b 1813 NY d/ANTHONY W & HARRIET (-----) WILCOX of Cherry Creek, Chautauqua Co NY; Ref: 1860 Census Cherry Creek NY p150 Dw# 788.

HARRIET - b 06 May 1813 Middletown, Middlesex Co CT d/BENJAMIN & RACHEL (WILCOX) WILCOX; Ref: Barbour's VR Middletown v3 p88, See Benjamin.

HARRIET - b 09 Jul 1813 Benson, Rutland Co VT d/MARTIN & JUDITH (CARTER) WILCOX; Ref: VT VR, See Martin.

HARRIET - b 17 Dec 1814 Sandisfield, Berkshire Co MA d/WILLIAM & LUCINDA (GIBBS) WILCOX; m 26 Jun 1836 CALEB STEELE; Ref: Sandisfield VR p73, Fiske Card File, History of Portage Co OH p635, Desc of Wm Wilcoxson p245.

HARRIET- m 27 Nov 1839 Middletown, Middlesex Co CT GEORGE W KENYON of South Kingston, Washington Co RI; Ref: Barbour's VR Middletown v3 p463.

HARRIET/HARRIETT - b 11 Oct 1820 d/JOHN CLARK & DORCAS (HARRINGTON) WILCOX of Franklin, New London Co CT & Sherman, Chautauqua Co NY; m 12 Sep 1844 ABIATHAR W LAKE of Westfield, Chautauqua Co NY; Ref: Your Ancestors v14 #2 p1658, 19th Cent Marriages Reported in Fredonia Censor p119.

HARRIET - b 12 Sep 1822 Madison, New Haven Co CT d/HEUSTIN & JULIA (CRAMPTON) WILCOX; m 08 Nov 1840 HENRY LORD BUSHNELL; Ref: Fam of Early Guilford p1212, Wilcox-Meigs p87, Desc of Wm Wilcoxson p264.

HARRIET - b 1825 VT d/AARON & MILLIE (-----) WILCOX of Bridport, Addison Co VT; Ref: 1850 Census Bridport VT Reel 920 p8.

HARRIET - m 11 Oct 1848 Farmington, Hartford Co CT LEVI PROSSEE of Bloomfield, Hartford Co CT; Ref: Barbour's VR Farmington LR47 p123.

HARRIET - b ca 1830 d/THURSTON & JANE (LOOMIS) WILCOX Smithville, Chenango Co NY; m AVERY D LANDERS; Ref: Hist of Chenango Co p295.

HARRIET/HARRIETT - b 1830 Lafayette, Onondaga Co NY d/STERLING & PHOEBE (-----) WILCOX; Ref: Your Ancestors v14 #1 p1620.

HARRIET - m 06 May 1850 Portland, Middlesex Co CT CHARLES L SAGE; Ref: Barbour's VR Portland v1 p22.

HARRIET - b 1831 NY d/ABEL & BETSEY (-----) WILCOX of New Hartford, Oneida Co NY; Ref: 1850 Census New Hartford NY p270 Dw# 508.

HARRIET - b 1832 Manlius, Onondaga Co NY d/DAVID & ASENETH (NOBLE) WILCOX; Ref: Your Ancestors v3 #11&12 p474, 1850 Census Manlius NY p28 Dw# 417.

HARRIET - b 1833 NY; Res with JUSTUS HARRIS Fam 1850 Leon, Cattaraugus Co NY; Ref: 1850 Census Leon NY p45 Dw# 134.

HARRIET - b 1834 NY d/EMERY & MARTHA (-----) WILCOX of Newport, Herkimer Co NY; Ref: 1850 Census Newport NY p173 Dw# 289.

HARRIET - b 1834 NY d/OZIAS WILCOX of Utica, Oneida Co NY; Ref: 1850 Census Utica NY p311 Dw# 25.

HARRIET - b 1836 CT d/LUCIUS & BELINDA S (DEMING) WILCOX of Cornwall, Litchfield Co CT; Ref: 1850 Census Cornwall p4 Dw# 61.

HARRIET - b 1836 NY d/CALVIN & ELIZA (-----) WILCOX of Black Brook, Clinton Co NY; Ref: 1850 Census, Florence Arnhart.

HARRIET/HARRIETT - b 1836 CT d/SEYMOUR & SALLY (-----) WILCOX; Ref: Your Ancestors v4 #3&4 p521.

HARRIET - b 1838 OH d/ALANSON & SYLVIA (LAWRENCE) WILCOX of Streetsborough, Portage Co OH; Ref: 1850 Census Streetsborough OH p30 Dw# 21, See Alanson.

HARRIET - b 30 Jan 1839 d/SAMUEL & HANNAH (KNOWLES) WILCOX; m 27 Jul 1862 Dr J E McCLELLAN who was b 03 Oct 1836 & d 24 Nov 1904 De Ruyter, Madison Co NY; ch ROBERT, CARRIE ALBERTA, MABLE M; d 17 Jul 1911; Ref: Your Ancestors v3 #2 p299.

HARRIET - b 1839 NY d/JACOB & CAROLINE (-----) WILCOX of Sherburne, Chenango Co NY; Ref: 1850 Census Sherburne p249 Dw# 1624.

HARRIET - b 1840 d/REUBEN & ORRY (----) WILCOX of McDonough, Chenango Co NY; Ref: 1850 Census Chenango Co NY, Your Ancestors v4 #11&12 p610.

HARRIET - b 1840 NY d/HARRY & HARRIET (-----) WILCOX of Pompey, Onondaga Co NY; Ref: 1850 Census Pompey NY p121 Dw# 1891.

HARRIET - b 1840 NY d/NATHAN & MERCY L (-----) WILCOX of Petersburgh, Rensselaer Co NY; Ref: 1850 Census Petersburgh NY p195 Dw# 310.

HARRIET - b 1841 NY d/ERASTUS & LOUISA (-----) WILCOX of Tully, Onondaga Co NY; Ref: 1850 Census Tully NY p162 Dw# 167.

HARRIET - b 1838 Harpersfield, Delaware Co NY d/ALONZO BENJAMIN & HANNAH (SWIFT) WILCOX; m EDWARD WHEELER; Ref: Your Ancestors v4 #7&8 p563, 1850 Census Harpersfield NY p158 Dw# 28.

HARRIET - b 1843 CT d/ELISHA & MARY (DENISON) WILCOX of Stonington, New London Co CT; Ref: 1850 Census Stonington CT Reel M432 #48 p268.

HARRIET - b 1844 NY d/----- & CATHERINE (-----) WILCOX; Res Cicero, Onondaga Co NY; Ref: 1860 Census Cicero NY.

HARRIET - b 1845 CT d/SILAS A & EMMA (HASKEL) WILCOX of Stonington, New London Co CT; Ref: 1850 Census Stonington CT Reel M432 #48 p256, See Silas A.

HARRIET/HARRIETT - b 1848 NY d/A W & HARRIETT (-----) WILCOX of Arkwright, Chautauqua Co NY; Ref: 1850 Census Arkwright NY p127 Dw# 1764.

HARRIET - b 1849 NY d/JOHN & HANNAH (-----) WILCOX of Jewett, Greene Co NY; Ref: 1850 Census Jewett NY p327 Dw# 117.

HARRIET - b 1850 NY d/HORACE J & RACHEL (-----) WILCOX; Res Collins, Erie Co NY; prob d be 1855; Ref: Alice Wiatr.

HARRIET - b af Sep 1850 Hiram, Portage Co OH d/Dr SYLVESTER K & HARRIET M (STODDARD) WILCOX; m DELOS PECK; Res California; Ref: History of

Portage Co OH p771, 1850 Census Hiram OH p3 Dw# 37.

HARRIET/HARRIETT - b 26 Oct 1864 d/JAMES PURDY & SABRINA (STANBRO) WILCOX; m 30 Apr 1889 WILLIAM P BRIGGS who was b 17 Oct 1854 & d 11 Feb 1921; ch WILLIAM P; Ref: Your Ancestors v3 #3 p319.

HARRIET - b ca 1875 IL d/JOHN & SARA JANE (ROBINS) WILCOX; m ca 1900 HENRY HARVEY; Ref: Wilcox Excerpts v1 p13.

HARRIET - b 17 Apr 1894 d/GEORGE I & GEORGEANNA (DENISON) WILCOX; m 16 Sep 1914 ELMER HEWITT who was b 09 Oct 1892 & d 1978; ch ELIZABETH, GEORGE WILCOX, ALDON; Ref: C Douglass Alves Sr.

HARRIET A - b 1825/6; d 19 Mar 1848 age 22 Middletown, Middlesex Co CT; Ref: Barbour's VR Middletown v4 pp74,75.

HARRIET A - b 14 Apr 1827 Middletown, Middlesex Co CT d/SAMUEL G & SARAH (-----) WILCOX; d 18 May 1827; Ref: Barbour's VR Middletown v3 p111.

HARRIET A - b 1838 NY d/JAMES B & HANNAH H (-----) WILCOX of Alabama, Genesee Co NY; Ref: 1850 Census Alabama NY p320 Dw# 1587.

HARRIET A - b 1840 CT d/RODNEY B & RACHEL (GREEN) WILCOX of Litchfield, Litchfield Co CT; Ref: 1850 Census Litchfield CT p284 Dw# 519, See Rodney B.

HARRIET A - b 1843; d 07 Oct 1848 Tiverton Newport Co RI; Ref: NEH&GR Jan 1963 p19.

HARRIET A "HATTIE" - b 13 Apr 1846 d/HORACE & HANNAH (KENYON) WILCOX of Stonington, New London Co CT; m -----DENISON; ch NANCY, PHOEBE, GEORGEANNA, JUSTIN, GEORGE, OLIVER; d 1884; Ref: 1850 Census Stonington CT Reel 432 #48 p281, C Douglass Alves Sr.

HARRIET ADELIA - b 31 Jan 1817 Bergen, Genesee Co NY d/AUSTIN & CHLOE (NETTLETON) WILCOX; Ref: Fam of Early Guilford p1203.

HARRIET AUGUSTA - b 1848 Saybrook, Middlesex Co CT d/WILLIAM T & MINERVA (GAYLORD) WILCOX; Ref: Saybrook Colony VR p559, See William T.

HARRIET AUSTIN - b 12 Sep 1823 Middletown, Middlesex Co CT d/SAMUEL G & SARAH (-----) WILCOX; d 06 Apr 1826; Ref: Barbour's VR Middletown v3 p111.

HARRIETT B - b 14 Oct 1811 W Springfield, Hampden Co MA d/LEVI & MARY (SPENCER) WILCOX of North Bergen, Genesee Co NY; m ca 1840 Dr THOMAS PIERCE ROGERS of Bloomington Co IL; ch HARRIET JULIA who d age 9 mo; d 1844; Ref: History of McLean Co IL p813, Desc of Wm Wilcoxson p133.

HARRIET C - b ca 1810 d/SHEFFIELD Jr & CHARLOTTE (HINMAN) WILCOX; m JACOB MILLER; Res Albany, Bradford Co PA; Ref: Pioneers of Bradford Co PA p310.

HARRIET D - b 1848 NY d/CONSIDER & MARY (-----) WILCOX of Almond, Allegany Co NY; Ref: 1850 Census Almond NY p74 Dw# 777.

HARRIET/HARRIETT D - b 12 Feb 1849 Springwater, Livingston Co NY d/DAVID H & ADELIA (HOPKINS) WILCOX; m 12 Mar 1867 OSCAR JOHNSON; ch JESSIE, CARL, HARRY, ALBERT, HUBERT, WALTER; Ref: Your Ancestors p1224.

HARRIET E - b 13 Aug 1835 Bergen, Genesee Co NY d/PITMAN & ANNA P (PARISH) WILCOX; m SCHUYLER BUDLONG; Ref: Your Ancestors v3 #1 p282, 1850 Census Bergen NY p46 Dw# 594.

HARRIET E - b 1837 NY; 1860 Res with DANIEL J WILCOX Cherry Creek, Chautauqua Co NY; Ref: 1860 Census Cherry Creek NY p148 Dw# 773.

HARRIET E - b 23 May 1849 Halifax, Windham Co VT d/JABEZ F & MARY ANN (CROSIER) WILCOX; m 02 Jan 1877 ERWIN R CROSIER who d 04 Dec 1877 age 22yr 1mo; m 14 Sep 1877 W H TURNER; Ref: Halifax Wilcox Fam mss.

HARRIET ELIZA - b 26 Nov 1849 Oxford, Chenango Co NY d/NATHANIEL & FANNY H ----- WILCOX; Res Smyrna, Chenango Co NY; Ref: VR of Chenango Co NY p227.

HARRIET ELIZABETH - b 18 Nov 1830 Middlebury, Addison Co VT d/HARVEY & MARY (CURTIS) WILCOX; m 30 Nov 1854 BYRON M DENISON; m 21 Dec 1857 Dr GUILFORD D SANBORN; No ch; Ref: Gen of CT Fam v1 p245.

HARRIET ELIZABETH - b 1840 Westbrook, Middlesex Co CT d/HORACE T & HARRIET D (PIERSON) WILCOX; m 16 Oct 1867 CARROLL E KINGSLEY who was b 28 May 1840 Salem, New London Co CT s/ELIHU & HARRIET S (DOANE) KINGSLEY; Ref: Fam of Early Guilford p1205, John Doane Desc p198.

HARRIET ELLEN - b 21 May 1850 Westminster West, Windham Co VT d/EPHRAIM & HARRIET N (JEWETT) WILCOX; Res Sommerville, Middlesex Co MA; d 05 Nov 1906; Ref: MUH pp758,759.

HARRIET EUNICE - b 21 Jun 1856 New Hartford, Litchfield Co CT d/EDWARD FRANKLIN & MARTHA ANN (HIGLEY) WILCOX; d 21 Jan 1871 age 14y 7m Pine Meadow, Litchfield Co CT; Ref: CT Bible Rec v4 pp456,457.

HARRIET H - b 30 Apr 1814 Thetford, Orange Co VT d/AARON & TENCEY (HORSFORD) WILCOX; Ref: Horsford/Hosford Family p73.

HARRIET J - b 01 Mar 1880 Norwich, Chenango Co NY d/JOHN WILCOX; d Sherburne, Chenango Co NY 23 May 1931 age 51yr 2mo 11da; Buried Sec 32 Lot 80; Ref: Norwich NY Cemetery Assoc Records p324.

HARRIET L - b 06 Sep 1839 Portage Co OH d/ALEXANDER HAMILTON & BETSEY (DIVER) WILCOX of Deerfield, Portage Co OH; m 04 Aug 1867 HENRY CARVER; widowed; Ref: History of Portage Co OH p635, 1850 Census Deerfield OH p186 Dw# 1001, Desc of Wm Wilcoxson p244.

HARRIET/HARRIETT L - b 1845 Lafayette, Onondaga Co NY d/LUTHER & CATHERINE (-----) WILCOX; Ref: Your Ancestors v13 #4 p1643, 1850 Census Lafayette NY p208 Dw# 251.

HARRIET L - b 1846 NY d/STEPHEN & AVAH (-----) WILCOX of Cazenovia, Madison Co NY; Ref: 1850 Census Cazenovia NY p73 Dw# 1736.

HARRIET L - b 1849 CT d/HENRY M & HARRIET N (-----) WILCOX of Preston, New London Co CT; Ref: 1850 Census Preston CT Reel 432 #49 p17.

HARRIET LOUISA - b ca 1842 d/LYMAN & MARIA (BULKELEY) WILCOX; m LEANDER BUNCE; Res New Britain, Hartford Co CT; Ref: MUH p757.

HARRIET LUCINDA - b 20 Aug 1871 d/HENRY FRANKLIN & LUCINDA HARRIET (BROWN) WILCOX; m 02

Apr 1895 RUSSELL F DEWEY; ch MARTHA LOUISE, WILLIAM FARNUM; Ref: Wilcox Excerpts v1 p3, Your Ancestors v3 #1 p1516.

HARRIET LUCY - b 15 Sep 1889 Westerly, Washington Co RI d/GEORGE STEPHEN & NELLIE THERESA (-----) WILCOX; Ref: Arnold v11 p88.

HARRIET/HARRIETT M - b 19 Oct 1832 Wethersfield, Wyoming Co NY d/AMOS & SOPHRONIA (HATFIELD) WILCOX; Ref: 1850 Census Wethersfield NY p86 Dw# 1269, Your Anc v14 #2 p1643.

HARRIET M - b 1839 Tompkins Co NY d/CLARK & SALLY (MAXSON) WILCOX of Groton, Tompkins Co NY; d 1879; Ref: 1850 Census Groton NY p123 Dw# 19, Carol A Cox.

HARRIET M - b 1844 NY d/JOHN & SUSAN (-----) WILCOX of Ellington, Chautauqua Co NY; Ref: 1850 Census Ellington NY p163 Dw# 2255.

HARRIET MARY - b 26 Oct 1852 Rowe, Franklin Co MA d/THOMAS & MARY P (UPTON) WILCOX; single; d 1880; Ref: Halifax VT Wilcox Fam mss.

HARRIET MAY - b 24 Apr 1870 d/HORACE & DERUSHA (HARVEY) CALKINS; d 30 Dec 1923 age 53yr 8mo 6da Gowanda, Erie Co NY bur Pinehill Cem; Ref: Alice Wiatr.

HARRIET NEWEL - b 08 Dec 1817 Killingworth, Middlesex Co CT d/AARON & MABEL (LORD) WILCOX; m AUGUSTUS ELLSWORTH; Res Twinsburg, Summit Co OH; Ref: Lord Gen p289, Wilcox-Meigs p81, Your Ancestors v3 #3 p321, Barbour's VR Killingworth v2 p14.

HARRIET NEWEL - b 22 Oct 1832 d/WILLIAM HENRY & SARAH (COMSTOCK) WILCOX; m 17 Feb 1853 MILLS BROWN; Ref: CT Bible Rec v4 pp 5,6.

HARRIET R - b 20 Jun 1826 Clinton, Middlesex Co CT d/SILAS & ABIGAIL (-----) WILCOX; m 26 Nov 1846 ELISHA S CURTIS of Meriden, New Haven Co CT; Ref: Barbour's VR Clinton v1 pp52,54.

HARRIET R - b 1836 NY d/LYMAN & SALLY M (OSBORN) WILCOX Vernon, Oneida Co NY; Ref: 1850 Census Verona NY p123 Dw# 14, 1860 Census Vernon NY p126, See Lyman.

HARRIET S - b 1835 NY d/AUSTIN G & ELIZA (SPAULDING) WILCOX of Napoli, Cattaraugus Co NY; Ref: 1850 Census Napoli NY p57 Dw# 41.

HARRIET SEFRONIA - b 27 Sep 1842 near Petersburg, Menard Co IL d/ISAAC ALMANZA & MARIETTE (OVIATT) WILCOX; m 09 Oct 1862 Menard Co IL THOMAS HENRY MCLANE; d 26 Dec 1932 Oakridge, Lane Co OR; Ref: Verna Betts.

HARRIET SOPHIA - b 15 May 1817 Sandisfield, Berkshire Co MA d/EBENEZER & MATILDA (HOSMER) WILCOX; Ref: Fiske Card File, Desc of Wm Wilcoxson p245.

HARRIET SUSANNAH - b 01 Jan 1868 d/GARDNER NICHOLS & GENORA EVALINA (COLLINS) WILCOX; d 10 Sep 1868; Ref: Your Ancestors v3 #5 p375.

HARRIET/HARRIETT W - b ca 1825 Smithfield PA d/STEPHEN & POLLY (ALLEN) WILCOX; m NORMAN H WOOD; Ref: Halifax VT Wilcox Fam mss, Wilcox Genealogy p7.

HARRIET/HARRIETT W - b 1840 d/ERASTUS & MARY BELLE (JARRARD) WILCOX; m H M WEST; Ref: Your Ancestors v11 #4 p1377.

HARRINGTON - b 22 Sep 1783 Exeter, Washington Co RI s/JOB & MARY (GATES) WILCOX; m 01 Aug 1802 Exeter RI CHARITY RATHBUN d/PARISH RATHBUN; Res Oxford, Chenango Co NY; ch HARRINGTON, SIMON GATES, JOHN, PARIS, PHILANDER, BENAJAH, CHARLES, CAROLINE, HANNAH; d 1859; Ref: Arnold v5 pt3 pp36,63, Cutter's Western NY v3 p1436.

HARRINGTON - b ca 1805 Exeter, Washington Co RI s/HARRINGTON & CHARITY (RATHBUN) WILCOX; m POLLY DECKER who was b 1805 & d 14 Nov 1889 Smithville, Chenango Co NY; Purchased land in Greene, Chenango Co NY 1831 & 1833; Res Oxford NY; ch NATHAN; d 11 Jun 1877; Ref: Cutter's Western NY v3 p1436, History of Chenango Co NY p304, Ellen Jacobus, From Raft to Railroad pp223,224.

HARRISON - b 1840 s/SAMUEL & HANNAH (-----) WILCOX; Res Earlville, Chenango Co NY; d 1875; Ref: Cemetery Records Chenango Co NY p8.

HARRISON - b 1847 NY s/IRA & MARY (PALMER) WILCOX of Manlius, Onondaga Co & Lincoln, Madison Co NY; m CATHERINE SNYDER who was b 1854 & d 29 Apr 1914 bur Clockville, Madison Co NY d/JOHN

SNYDER; ch MAUDE, JAY; Res Lincoln NY; Ref: Pioneers of Madison Co NY p281, 1850 Census Manlius NY p19 Dw# 275.

HARRISON - b 1848 Arkwright, Chautauqua Co NY s/OLIVER C & MARIA (YALE) WILCOX; Ref: 1850 Census Chautauqua Co NY.

HARROLD C - b Jan 1894 WI s/EDWARD & MARIA (-----) WILCOX; Father b NY; Res Vilas Co WI; Ref: 1900 Soundex.

HARRY - b 1788 CT; m MARY ----- who was b 1794 CT; Res Virgil, Cortland Co NY; ch MARY; Ref: 1850 Census Virgil NY p 397 Dw# 1047.

HARRY - b 1798 CT; m HARRIET ----- who was b 1803 CT; Res Pompey, Onondaga Co NY; ch ANDREW, ROXA, MARCUS, THOMAS, HARRIET, FRANCIS; Ref: 1850 Census Pompey NY p121 Dw# 1891.

HARRY - b 31 May 1803 Newport, Sullivan Co NH s/JESSE & WEALTHY (KELSEY) WILCOX; d young; Ref: Your Ancestors v3 #4 p349.

HARRY - b 1807 Simsbury, Hartford Co CT s/ROBERT & ANNA CLEMENCE (MILLS) WILCOX; m 1844 LUCINDA DODGE who was b 1824 & d 1856; ch JERRY R; Ref: Your Ancestors v13 #2 pp1540,1541.

HARRY - b 14 Feb 1873 s/CHARLES HENRY & FANNY (DISBROW) WILCOX; single; Ref: Desc of Wm Wilcoxson p259.

HARRY - b Aug 1878 NY s/CHARLES R & JANIE L (-----) WILCOX; Ref: 1900 Census Chautauqua Co NY.

HARRY ABBE - b 15 Nov 1876 Porterville, Tulare Co CA s/ORIGEN ABBEY & CLARA JANE (EMERSON) WILCOX; m 24 Jan 1903 JESSIE HANNAH JEFFORD who was b 10 Oct 1883 Mayfield, San Mateo Co CA & d 18 Apr 1955; Res Porterville CA; ch ESTHER MAY, CLARA BERYL, GLADYS MARIE; d 13 Jun 1955; Ref: Jane Smith.

HARRY ADAMS - b 13 Dec 1881 s/FREDERICK THOMAS & GENEVIEVE AMANDA (THURSTON) WILCOX; d 1882; Ref: Your Ancestors v3 #1 p282.

HARRY BEECHER - b 20 Nov 1876 Smithfield Twnshp, Bradford Co PA s/ELLIOT URIAH & TIRZAH ELVIRA (SEYMOUR) WILCOX; m 04 Jan 1900 Wellsburg, Chemung Co NY DELLA BUTTERS who was b 04 Jul 1882

& d 09 Jul 1961 Athens, Bradford Co PA d/SYLVESTER & MARTHA (TRUESDALE) BUTTERS; ch CLAUDE ELLIOT, FRED WILLIAM, HOMER ADELBERT, GILBERT EZRA, HARVEY CHESTER, MARTHA IRENE, NORA ELIZABETH, JOHN FRANCIS, HARRY LEWIS, MYRTLE MAE, ULYSSES GRANT, DELLA LOUISE, ALBERTA MELISSA; d 11 Dec 1961 Athens PA; both bur Union Cem East Smithfield PA; Ref: Wilcox Genealogy pp20,30.

HARRY C - b 1825 NY s/CHAMPLAIN & ELIZABETH (CLARKE) WILCOX of Lebanon, Madison Co NY; m ANNIS ----- who was b 1828 NY; ch LUCY E; Ref: 1850 Census Lebanon NY p118 Dw# 1999, See Champlain.

HARRY CHARLES - b 10 Oct 1888 Abilene, Dickinson Co KS s/FRANK WRIGHT & PRISCILLA (KRIEDER) WILCOX; Single; Ref: Desc of Wm Wilcoxson p141.

HARRY EUGENE - b 07 Apr 1873 s/JOHN FINLEY & EMMA (CLEMENT) WILCOX; m IDA SPRAGUE; Res Minneapolis, Hennepin Co MN; ch MAXINE, JOHN F; d 1954; Ref: Desc of Wm Wilcoxson p127.

HARRY HOLMES - b 19 Nov 1890 Geneva, Ontario Co NY s/WILLIAM & NETTIE (HOLMES) WILCOX; d 23 Apr 1893; Ref: Desc of George Holmes p272.

HARRY JEFFERSON - b 03 Mar 1802 Harpersfield, Delaware Co NY s/JOHN WILCOX; m 21 Dec 1829 ELIZA ANN BROWN who was b Blenheim, Schoharie Co NY 1807 & d 18 Aug 1874; Res Conquest, Cayuga Co NY; ch DELIA, MARY, ROBERT, HENRY, ANN ELIZA, JULIA, MARTHA, JOHN, GEORGE; d after 1879; Ref: History of Cayuga Co NY pp287,288.

HARRY R - b 30 Oct 1898 N B Canada s/JAMES ROBERT & MARGARET A (MATTHEWS) WILCOX; d 07 May 1916 World War I; Ref: Desc of Charles Dyer Wilcox p2.

HARRY S - b 22 Sep 1852 s/WILLIAM & SARAH E (DAY) WILCOX of Carlton, Orleans Co NY; Ref: Your Ancestors v11 #1 p1320.

HARRY THOMAS - b 1887 Alma, Allegany Co NY s/GEORGE S & MARY E (BENTON) WILCOX; m PEARL VERA MAYHUGH who was b 09 Dec 1889 Van Wert, Van Wert Co OH & d 1945 Marion, Grant Co IN d/JOHN E & LUTRICIA MARY (-----) MAYHUGH; Res Marion IN; ch MILDRED PAULINE, HAROLD, GLADYS MARIE, MARY LOUISE; d 1959 Marion IN; both bur IOOF Cem Lot 6 Block 56; Ref: Carol A Cox

HART ARTEMAS - b 09 May 1850 Rowe, Franklin Co MA s/BENJAMIN & ELIZABETH (-----) WILCOX; Ref: Halifax VT Wilcox Fam mss.

HARVEY - b 12 Feb 1796 Chenango Co NY s/FREDERICK WILCOX; Ref: Desc of Wm Wilcoxson p225.

HARVEY - b 05 Jul 1799 Middletown, Middlesex Co CT s/JULIUS & ELIZABETH (BROWN) WILCOX; m 06 Oct 1829 MARY CURTIS who was b 24 Apr 1803 d/CHARLES & AMY (STEVENS) CURTIS of Newburg, Orange Co NY; Res Middlebury, Addison Co VT; ch HARRIET ELIZABETH, HARVEY CURTIS; Ref: Gen of CT Fam v1 p244,245.

HARVEY/HERVEY - of New Hartford, Litchfield Co CT m 02 Jan 1822 Newtown, Fairfield Co CT POLLY SHERMAN; Ref: Barbour's VR Newtown v2 p6.

HARVEY/HERVEY - b 18-- Killingworth, Middlesex Co CT s/SIMEON/ELIHU WILCOX; m 11 Nov 1829 Killingworth CT LYDIA WRIGHT; ch FREDERICK WASHINGTON, CORNELIA, MARY, WILLIAM HENRY, EDWARD, ELIZABETH, LOOMIS, EVELYN, ELLA WHEELER or ELLA L; Ref: Wilcox-Meigs pp85,102, Cutter's New England Families v3 p1077, Barbour's VR Killingworth v3 pp378,381.

HARVEY - b 1817 NY s/ ----- & DINAH (-----) WILCOX; m MARGARET ----- who was b 1823 NY; Res Lafayette, Onondaga Co NY; ch GEORGE, AUGUSTA; Ref: 1850 Census Lafayette NY p216 Dw# 378.

HARVEY - b ca 1818 NY; m SARAH ----- who was b ca 1819 NY; Res Jay, Essex Co NY; ch MARY; Ref: 1850 Census Jay NY p204 Dw# 2914 #2914.

HARVEY - b 30 Mar 1822 s/LOAMINY & HANNAH (PADDOCK) WILCOX; m 01 Oct 1844 HARRIET DEMMOND of Worcester, Worcester Co MA; ch CHARLES FRANCIS, HARVEY EDGAR; d 10 May 1890; Ref: St Johnsville NY Enterprise & News 23 Oct 1952.

HARVEY - b 29 Jul 1824 New Albany, Bradford Co PA s/FREEMAN & CLARINDA (SOUTHWORTH) WILCOX; Moved west to CO; Ref: Your Ancestors v13 #2 p1538.

HARVEY - of Easton, Washington Co NY; m 23 Sep 1849 ANN SOPHIA DURHAM also of Easton; Ref: NYG&BR v199 p168.

HARVEY - b 1853 NY s/HENRY & SARAH (-----) WILCOX of Chautauqua, Chautauqua Co NY; Ref: 1860 Census Chautauqua NY p64 Dw# 478.

HARVEY - b 1854 NY s/JAMES & MARY (-----) WILCOX; Res Ripley, Chautauqua Co NY; Ref: 1870 Census Ripley NY p150.

HARVEY - b 1855 s/DANIEL & ALMA (-----) WILCOX; Ref: Your Ancestors p583.

HARVEY C - b 1824; m ADELINE E ----- who was b 1830; Res Floyd, Oneida Co NY; ch SARAH M; Ref: 1860 Census Floyd NY p376.

HARVEY CURTIS - b 30 Nov 1837 Middlebury, Addison Co VT s/HARVEY & MARY (CURTIS) WILCOX; m 01 Aug 1867 VICTORIA A TAYLOR; ch LAWRENCE C; Ref: Gen of CT Fam v1 p245.

HARVEY EDGAR - b 12 June 1861 s/HARVEY & HARRIET (DEMMOND) WILCOX; Ref: St Johnsville NY Enterprise & News 23 Oct 1952.

HARVEY F - b 1832 NY s/ERASTUS & EUNICE (-----) WILCOX of Palerno, Oswego Co NY; Ref: 1850 Census Palerno NY p32 Dw# 470.

HARVEY G - b 1799 RI; m ZANNIE STRAIGHT; Ref: Nutmegger v7 #3 p430.

HARVEY L - m 29 Dec 1853 Simsbury, Hartford Co CT HELEN CORNISH; Ref: Barbour's VR Simsbury T M5 p282.

HARVEY R - b ca 1810 NY s/AARON & ELIZABETH (-----) WILCOX; Res Laona & Arkwright, Chautauqua Co NY; Ref: Your Ancestors p1438.

HARVEY W - b 16 Jul 1855 Springwater, Livingston Co NY s/EBER & MARILLA (-----) WILCOX; m 1881 CORA COLEGROVE d/THEODORE COLEGROVE; ch PEARL; Ref: Your Ancestors v10 #1 p1200, #2 p1226.

HATTIE - d/ASAPH WILCOX; m ----- BARNES; Res Northville NY; Ref: A Wilcox Book p11.

HATTIE - b 1859 NY d/THEODORE & ELVIRA (-----) WILCOX; Res Kirkland, Oneida Co NY; Ref: 1860 Census Kirkland NY p51.

HATTIE - b 1866 WI d/JOHN & ALVIA (-----) WILCOX who were both b NY; Res Juneau Co WI; Ref: 1880 Soundex WI.

HATTIE A - b 1854 d/CHARLES AUGUSTUS & CYNTHIA A (JOHNSON) WILCOX; m TURNER B WHEELER; Ref: Desc of Wm Wilcoxson p194.

HATTIE AMELIA - b 04 Jul 1860 Smyrna, Chenango Co NY d/WILLIAM STOVER & ANNA MARIA (PARKER) WILCOX; m 27 Sep 1882 GEORGE W SUMNER s/DANIEL & MARY (SMITH) SUMNER; Ref: John Parker Gen p394.

HATTIE EDSON - b 19 Nov 1874 d/NELSON OTIS & FRANCES MARIA (NOBLE) WILCOX; Ref: Your Ancestors v12 #4 p1490.

HATTIE L - b 11 Jun 1856 Troy, Rensselaer Co NY d/WORTHINGTON C & ELLEN L (LEE) WILCOX: Ref: Wilcox-Meigs p106.

HATTIE M - b 1863 IL d/JOHN & KATE (-----) WILCOX; m Saline Co NE AUGUSTUS NORMAN; Ref: Lancaster Co Gen Newsletter v8 #9 p3.

HATTIE MARIA - b 29 Sep 1844 d/WILLET CLARK & ELIZABETH (----) WILCOX; m GEORGE WASHINGTON VICKERY who was b 12 Jul 1842 Pontiac, Kent Co RI s/WILLIAM & CATHARINE (TANNER) VICKERY; Res Coventry, Kent Co RI; ch DORA, MARY ELIZABETH, GEORGE WASHINGTON, HATTIE ESTELLE, FRANK HERBERT, GRACE MAY; Ref: Gen of William Tanner p174.

HATTIE R - d/JOHN A & LUCY A (-----) WILCOX Tiverton, Newport Co RI; d age 6yr 9mo bur Cem #33 Lot 105; Ref: Gen of RI Fam v2 p621.

HATZELL - b 1892 Deep Cove, N B Canada s/JAMES ROBERT & LUCINDA (PLANT) WILCOX; drowned 08 Sep 1901; Ref: Desc of Charles Dyer Wilcox p 6.

HAYDEN - s/MOSES & HULDAH (LORD) WILCOX; Res Twinsburg, Summit Co OH; Ref: Lord Gen p289.

HAZARD - b ca 1740 Kingston/Exeter, Washington Co RI poss s/EDWARD & MERCY (ROBINSON) WILCOX; m EUNICE -----; m SABRA WATSON; Res Cambridge, Washington Co NY 1775; Capt Rev War; Repr from Walloomsac, Albany Co NY [now Rensselaer Co]; Loyalist; ch SARAH, WILLIAM, SABRA, HAZARD; d 03 Feb 1790; Ref: Your Ancestors v12 #1 pp1405,1406, Gen Helper Mar/Apr 1981 p21, Hist of Washington Co

NY p255, Alice Wiatr, Hist of Desc of Edward Wilcox mss pp2,3.

HAZARD - yeoman from Hoosick, Albany Co NY [now Rensselaer Co]; Res Walloomsac Patent; land confiscated 14 Jul 1783; d be 14 Jun 1787 Bennington Co VT; ch HAZARD; Ref: New Loyalist Index, Guardianship Rec Bennington VT Probate Court v1 pp183,294,298, Alice Wiatr.

HAZARD - b 1757-1775; Res Ashford, Windham Co CT; 1 son & 1 dau in 1800; Ref: 1800 Census Windham Co CT p842.

HAZARD - b af 1774 s/THOMAS & RENEW (WEEKS) WILCOX; d be 1814; Res Ashford, Windham Co CT & perhaps Rowe, Franklin Co MA; ch HORACE, ANDREW; Ref: Your Ancestors v3 #7&8 p423; Codicil to THOMAS WILCOX's will, Halifax VT Wilcox Fam mss, Alice Wiatr, Iris Baird.

HAZARD - b 25 Dec 1775 RI s/HAZARD & SABRA (WATSON) WILCOX; m 1797 NANCY MAXSON who was b 06 Aug 1775 Hopkinton RI & d 17 Oct 1863 d/SAMUEL & MARY (DOWNING) MAXSON; m 1819 SARAH SEELY who was b 17 Dec 1780 & d 09 Nov 1856 d/AUGUSTUS & MARY (BRESBEN) SEELY of MO; Res RI, Cambridge, Washington Co NY, AR, & Marion Co MO; ch of 1st wife NANCY, RUHAMA, WILLARD de RUYTER; ch of 2nd wife MARY, SARAH, WILLIAM AUGUSTUS, EUNICE, SABRA, JONATHAN HAZARD, JAMES, JOSEPH, STEPHEN ENOS, CLARISSA JANE, LEMUEL, JOHN HENRY OWEN; Member of the LDS Church; d 16 Feb 1831 Marion Co MO; Ref: Hist of Desc of Edward Wilcox mss pp1-4, Your Ancestors v12 #1 p1405 #2 p1435, Alice Wiatr.

HAZARD - b af 1766 s/HAZARD WILCOX; minor in 1787 when THOMAS JEWET & FREEBORN WATSON were named his guardian in Bennington Co VT; Ref: Guardianship Records Bennington VT v1 pp183,294,298, Alice Wiatr.

HAZARD - b 24 May 1780 s/HOPSON & ELIZABETH (HOLOWAY) WILCOX; m LUCY TISDALE who was b 10 Aug 1782 Exeter, Washington Co RI & d 30 Jul 1811 d/JOSEPH & PHOEBE (CLARKE) WILCOX; m SUSANNAH KNOWLES who was b 13 Jun 1779 & d 13 May 1840; Res Smyrna & Earlville, Chenango Co NY; ch by 1st wife SAMUEL, HAZARD, PHEBE, PATIENCE, RUSSELL; ch by 2nd wife LUCY; d 24 Dec 1838 Will probated 05 Feb 1839 Chenango Co NY Book D 196; Ref: Cem Records of Chenango Co NY p8, Index to Wills of Chenango

Co NY v1, Your Ancestors v3 #1 p278, #6 p397, Desc of James Tisdale pp207,323.

HAZARD - b 1787 CT s/ROBERT & SARAH (WILBUR) WILCOX; m 02 Oct 1825 Lyme, New London Co CT MARY/POLLY WRIGHT who was b 1797 CT & d 14 Dec 1887; ch ASA, PHEBE, DESIAH, HAZARD; d 17 Mar 1874; Ref: VR of Lyme CT pp136,152, Barbour's VR Lyme v2 p185, 1850 Census Lyme CT Reel 432 #49 p394, Your Ancestors v11 #3 p1352 #4 p1377.

HAZARD - b 13 Nov 1790 s/ROBERT HAZARD & SUSANNAH (HOXIE) WILCOX; m DORCAS KENYON who was b 25 Jan 1793 & d 25 Jun 1862; Res Earlville, Chenango Co NY; ch ROBERT H, SUSANNAH, ELIZA ANN, MARY; d 10 Dec 1837; Ref: Cem Records of Chenango Co NY p8, Your Ancestors v3 #2 p298.

HAZARD - b 1790 RI; m BETSEY ----- who was b 1791 RI; Res Georgetown, Madison Co NY; ch WILLIAM, MILO; Ref: 1850 Census Georgetown NY p391 Dw# 268.

HAZARD - b 1807 s/HAZARD & LUCY (TISDALE) WILCOX; m 28 Jan 1830 FLAVILLA PARSONS who was b 29 Jul 1808 & d 25 Dec 1899; Res Smyrna, Chenango Co NY; ch HENRY HOPSON, ORRIN B, MELVIN, NANCY (WILCOX) GREEN, JENNIE (WILCOX) ATKINS, MARY (WILCOX) INGALLS, GEORGE, AMELIA; d 07 Apr 1871 both bur Earlville, Chenango Co NY; Ref: Cutter's Western NY v3 p1439, Your Ancestors v3 #6 p397.

HAZARD - b 06 Feb 1811 Berkshire, Berkshire Co MA s/CALEB & HANNAH (-----) WILCOX; m 16 Oct 1838 Wilmington, Windham Co VT PAMELA BRIDGE; Res Rowe, Franklin Co MA; d 11 Feb 1843 bur Averell Cem Wilmington VT; Ref: Your Ancestors v3 #7&8 p424, Fiske Card File, Alice Wiatr.

HAZARD - b 1821 PA; Res Le Roy, Bradford Co PA 1850; Brother of LEVI; Ref: 1850 Census Bradford Co PA.

HAZARD - b 1827 Orangeville, Wyoming Co NY s/JEFFREY H & DEBORAH (-----) WILCOX; m NANCY ----- who was b 1828 NY; ch FRANK A; Ref: Your Ancestors v4 #5&6 p541, 1850 Census Orangeville NY p38 Dw# 582.

HAZARD - b 15 Feb 1849 s/JOHN HENRY OWEN & MARY (YOUNG) WILCOX; Ref: Your Ancestors v12 #2 p1436.

HAZARD - b 13 Oct 1894 s/JAMES HENRY & HARRIET ANN (DAY) WILCOX; Ref: Your Ancestors v12 #3 p1461.

HAZARD B - of Lyme, New London Co CT; m 14 Oct 1849 ELIZABETH HARVEY of East Haddam, Middlesex Co CT; Ref: Barbour's VR Lyme v3 p204.

HAZARD B - b ca 1801 s/Dr JEREMIAH & SUSANNAH (WILCOX) WILCOX; m 06 Nov 1827 Foster, Providence Co RI MARY ANDREWS d/JEREMIAH ANDREWS;   Ref: Arnold v3 pp31, Your Ancestors v4 #3&4 p520.

HAZARD/HAZZARD H - b 08 Dec 1811 Franklin, New London Co CT s/JOHN CLARK & DORCAS (HARRINGTON) WILCOX; m MARIAH PALMER who was b 1817 VT & d be 1870; m be 1870 ABIGAIL ----- who was b 1816 VT; Res Sherman, Chautauqua Co NY; Purchased land 1836 Township 2 Range 14; ch DENNIS, HANNAH, ELLEN, MALINDA, CLARK, DON; Ref: 1840, 1850 & 1870 Census Chautauqua Co NY, West NY Journal v4 #3 pp130,131, Your Ancestors v14 #2 p1658.

HAZARD R - b 1802; m 17 Mar 1827 Palmyra, Wayne Co NY ELIZABETH GOSS; d 01 Nov 1838; Ref: 10,000 VR of Western NY p250.

HAZARD R - b 02 May 1853 s/ROBERT H & MARY M (FERRIS) WILCOX of Smyrna, Chenango Co NY; m 10 Oct 1876 CORNELIA E POTTER who was b 14 Feb 1851 & d 10 Jul 1909 d/RENSSELAER POTTER of Cazenovia, Madison Co NY; Res Earlville, Chenango Co NY; ch ARZELIA D; d 08 Nov 1884; Ref: Cem Records Chenango Co NY p8, Early Years in Smyrna pp21,22, Your Ancestors v3 #2 p299.

HAZEL - b 28 Apr 1885 Wood Island N B Canada d/MARINER & CORDELIA (CARD) WILCOX; d young; Ref: Desc of Charles Dyer Wilcox p15.

HAZEL - b 02 Feb 1899 N B Canada d/BYRON & CARRIE (BENSON) WILCOX; m HARLEY CRONK; Ref: Desc of Charles Dyer Wilcox p17.

HAZEL ARLETTE - b 18 Dec 1894 Guilford, Windham Co VT s/CHARLES LUMAN & CORA ADELAIDE (CROSIER) WILCOX; m 25 Dec 1915 Fitchburg, Worcester Co MA WILLIAM HORACE DAVIS; Div; m HAROLD ROSS;_Ref: Iris W Baird.

HAZEL SARAH - b 17 May 1896 Smithfield Twnshp, Bradford Co PA d/ELLIOTT URIAH & TIRZAH ELVIRA (SEYMOUR) WILCOX; m 20 Oct 1921 Wellsburg, Chemung

Co NY DELBERT EMERY LEWIS who was b 15 Mar 1899 & d 13 Aug 1961 s/DUDLEY EUGENE & EDIE B (WILDER) LEWIS; 1918 Grad of Mansfield Normal School, Mansfield, Tioga Co PA; Teacher; ch PAULINE E, GERALDINE LOUISE, RONALD EUGENE, GLENORA ANN, DELBERTA HELEN; d 03 Dec 1984 bur Union Cem East Smithfield PA; Ref: Wilcox Genealogy pp20,66.

HEBER/EBER - b 1827 s/ROBERT JOHNSON & LUCY (COLE) WILCOX; m MARILLA ----- who was b 1829 & d 1867; Res Springwater, Livingston Co NY; ch HARVEY W; Ref: Your Ancestors v10 #2 p1226, 1850 Census Springwater NY p235 Dw# 65.

HEBRON - b 1830 NY s/MARTIN & SARAH/SALLY (-----) WILCOX of Dover, Dutchess Co NY; Blacksmith; Ref: 1850 Census Dover NY p328 Dw# 269.

HECTOR LEE - m 1851 CLARISSA NEVINS of Hanover, Chautauqua Co NY who d 22 Apr 1899; ch DELLA A, KITTIE; d 1877; Ref: 19th Cent Death Notices Reported in Fredonia Censor pp595, See Della A.

HELEN/HELLEN - b 1831 NY d/JOSEPH WILCOX of New Hartford, Oneida Co NY; Ref: 1850 Census New Hartford NY p270 Dw# 511.

HELEN - b 1837 Chautauqua Co NY d/OLIVER & MARIA (YALE) WILCOX; d 16 Feb 1872 Laona, Chautauqua Co NY; Ref: Your Ancestors v12 #3 p1463, 19th Cent Death Notices Reported in Fredonia Censor p596.

HELEN - b 14 May 1838 Bergen, Genesee Co NY d/PITMAN & ANNA P (PARRISH) WILCOX; d single; Ref: Your Ancestors v3 #1 p282, 1850 Census Bergen NY p46 Dw# 594, 1860 Census Bergen NY p986 Dw# 407.

HELEN - b ca 1840 d/SAMUEL & SALLY (HUNT) WILCOX of Hobart & Harpersfield, Delaware Co NY; m GANO KENNEDY; Ref: Your Ancestors v4 #7&8 p563 1850 Census Harpersfield NY p175 Dw# 282.

HELEN/HELLEN - b 1841 Twin with ELLEN d/THOMAS R & LOUISA (-----) WILCOX of Belfast, Allegany Co NY; Ref: 1850 Census Belfast NY p266 Dw# 56.

HELEN - d/HIRAM WILCOX; m 13 Mar 1859 ALLEN BENEDICT who was b 19 Apr 1829 s/CYRUS & SUSAN (DOTY) BENEDICT; 4 ch; Ref: Doty Fam Gen p858.

HELEN/HELLEN - b 1849 NY d/DANIEL & ELVIRA E (-----) WILCOX of Varick, Seneca Co NY; Ref: 1850 Census Varick NY p58 Dw# 862.

HELEN - b 1849 NY d/OZIAS WILCOX of Utica, Oneida Co NY; Ref: 1850 Census Utica NY p311 Dw# 25.

HELEN - m 23 Jul 1873 LORRIN H BOTSFORD who was b 27 Mar 1835 s/HUBBARD P & SALLY E (CAMP) BOTSFORD; Ref: CT Bible Rec v6 pp62,63.

HELEN - b 26 Jan 1853 Middlebury, Summit Co OH d/DAVID GILBERT & HANNAH (WHITNEY) WILCOX; m Rev JAMES BROWN; ch DeWITT; Ref: Desc of Wm Wilcoxson p128.

HELEN - b Oct 1855 Minneapolis, Hennepin Co MN d/WILLIAM OZIAS & MARTHA (STERNS) WILCOX; m GEORGE RICKER; ch MAX; d Apr 1908; Ref: Bogue Fam p396.

HELEN - b 16 Jan 1856 d/JOSEPH EDWIN & EUNICE (GREGG) WILCOX of Newport, Sullivan Co NH; Ref: Your Ancestors v3 #6 p400.

HELEN - b 1859 Napoli, Cattaraugus Co NY d/LYSANDER BYRAM & HELEN CHILDS (LEDYARD) WILCOX; Ref: 1860 Census Napoli NY Reel 653 #726 p52, See Lysander Byram.

HELEN - d/CLINTON & BELLE (FULLER) WILCOX of Sandusky, Erie Co NY; m RUSSELL K RAMSEY who was b 27 May 1878 Columbus, Franklin Co OH & d 20 Feb 1920 s/GUSTAVUS & MARGARET A (-----) RAMSEY; 2 ch; Ref: Firelands Pioneers NS v25 p287.

HELEN [ELLA] - b Nov 1871 Plymouth, Marshall Co IN d/CHARLES HENRY & MARY (HARRING/HERRING) WILCOX; m CARLTON D HENDRICKSON of Memphis, Shelby Co TN; Ref: Charlotte Jacob-Hanson.

HELEN - b 19 Oct 1879 Woodstock, Windham Co CT d/LOWELL WILCOX; Ref: Barbour's VR Brown Diary p149.

HELEN - b 04 Mar 1892 Scranton, Lackawanna Co PA d/WILLIAM ALONZO & KATHARINE (JENKINS) WILCOX; Ref: Wilcox-Brown-Medbery p31.

HELEN A - b 1844 NY d/JAMES B & HANNAH H (-----) WILCOX of Alabama, Genesee Co NY; Ref: 1850 Census Alabama NY p320, Dw# 1587.

HELEN CLARISSA - b 19 Jul 1837 Middletown, Middlesex Co CT d/JOSEPH Jr & LUCY (TRYON) WILCOX; Ref: Barbour's VR Middletown v3 p91, See Joseph Jr.

HELEN EDYTHE - b 20 Dec 1877 d/EDMUND CLARK & SARAH ROGERS (DAVIES) WILCOX; m 29 Apr 1897 JOHN H KNOWLES who was b 05 May 1874; ch CAROLINE GREENWOOD, MARION DAVIES; Ref: Wilcox Excerpts v1 p4.

HELEN ELIZABETH - b 13 Apr 1888 d/Dr DEWITT GILBERT & JENNIE (GREEN) WILCOX of Buffalo, Erie Co NY; Ref: Gifford Wilcox, Desc of Wm Wilcoxson p128.

HELEN JOSEPHINE - b 14 Apr 1896 Napoli, Cattaraugus Co NY d/HOSMER H & ELLA S (BURT) WILCOX; Ref: Cutter's Western NY v1 258.

HELEN LECKIE - b 15 Sep 1863 Warrenton, Warren Co N C d/JULIUS & MATTIE JANE (HOLTON) WILCOX; Ref: Gen of CT Fam v1 p245.

HELEN LEORA - b 30 Oct 1872 d/ALBERT HOPKINS & FANNY (PARMENTER) WILCOX of Cohocton, Steuben Co NY; m JAMES C BARBER; Ref: Your Ancestors v10 #2 p1223.

HELEN LOUISE - b 05 Mar 1884 Smithfield Twnshp, Bradford Co PA d/ELLIOTT URIAH & TIRZAH ELVIRA (SEYMOUR) WILCOX; m 04 Mar 1903 Wellsburg, Chemung Co NY JOHN RUTHERFORD COVELL who was b 20 Sep 1876 & d 02 Apr 1950 s/PLATT & EMILY J (DILDINE) COVELL; ch GLEN M, WALTER R; d 30 May 1979 Bradford Co Manor both bur Union Cem East Smithfield PA; Ref: Wilcox Genealogy pp20,57.

HELEN LYDIA - b 06 Jun 1842 Madison, New Haven Co CT d/ZINA EDWIN & LYDIA ANN (HILL) WILCOX; m JUDSON W LEETE; Ref: Fam of Early Guilford p1207.

HELEN M - b 07 Jul 1826 Simsbury, Hartford Co CT d/CHESTER & ELIZABETH (ANDREWS) WILCOX; Ref: Your Ancestors v12 #1 p1408.

HELEN M - b 1835 NY d/----- & CLIMENA (-----) WILCOX of Hamilton, Madison Co NY; Ref: 1850 Census Hamilton NY p102 Dw# 1740.

HELEN M - b 27 Jan 1837 d/DAVID & BETSEY (KELSEY) WILCOX of Newport, Sullivan Co NH; m IRA M BARTON; Ref: Your Ancestors v3 #6 p399.

HELEN/HELLEN M - b 1844 NY d/OLIVER & ELIZA
(-----) WILCOX of Eaton, Madison Co NY; Ref: 1850
Census Eaton NY p350 Dw# 370.

HELEN M - b 1847 NY d/ALFRED & ABIGAIL (-----)
WILCOX of Seneca Falls, Seneca Co NY; Ref: 1850
Census Seneca Falls NY p262 Dw# 1890.

HELEN M - b 29 Dec 1855 Litchfield, Hillsdale
Co MI d/STEWART & HARRIETTE (PORCUPILE) WILCOX; m
18 Feb 1872 Quincy, Branch Co MI; Res Butler MI
WILLIAM TAYLOR s/WILLIAM C & MARY ANN (-----)
TAYLOR; ch BIRDIE HARRIET, CHARLES; Ref: Bogue Fam
p400.

HELEN MARGARET - b 1859 NY; d 1862 Napoli,
Cattaraugus Co NY; Ref: Cem Records.

HELLEN MARIA - b 12 Dec 1817 Coxsackie, Greene
Co NY d/DANIEL B & MARIA (WELLS) WILCOX; Ref: Bpt
Rec Coxsackie NY p105.

HELEN MARIA - b 16 Feb 1840 d/SAMUEL GASKELL &
SALLY (COOK) WILCOX of Mendon, Worcester Co MA;
Ref: Your Ancestors v11 #2 p1346.

HELEN S - b 07 July 1835 Napoli, Cattaraugus Co
NY d/LANSING H & MIRANDA (HOLMES) WILCOX; teacher;
Ref: Cutter's Western NY v1 p257, 1850 Census
Napoli NY p63 Dw# 138, 1860 Census Napoli NY p60.

HELEN SOPHIA - b 21 Jul 1844 Guilford, New
Haven Co CT d/ALMON ORRILL & RUTH DAVIS (KENNEDY)
WILCOX; d unmarried 14 Mar 1865; Ref: Wilcox-Meigs
p91, Fam of Early Guilford p1212.

HELENA REBECCA - b 28 Jun 1846 Madison, New
Haven Co CT d/ALVA ORRIN & RACHEL (DOWD) WILCOX; d
Oct 1896; Ref: Wilcox-Meigs p90, Fam of Early
Guilford p1212

HEMAN - b 10 Sep 1768 Goshen, Litchfield Co CT
s/JOB WILCOX; Res Pittsfield, Otsego Co NY 1850
with DAVID KELSEY WILCOX; Ref: Barbour's VR Goshen
p237, 1850 Census Pittsfield NY p289 Dw# 233.

HEMAN - b 25 Dec 1805 Bergen, Genesee Co NY
s/PITMAN & ELIZABETH (WILCOX) WILCOX; Ref: Fam of
Early Guilford p1202.

HEMAN - b 1810 NY; m ELEANOR -----; Carpenter;
Res Oswego, Oswego Co NY; ch SIMON, FRANCES,

FLORENCE, BYRON, EDWARD, REBECCA; Ref: 1850 Census Oswego NY p153 Dw# 50.

HEMAN - b 1848 NY s/ABEL EDWIN & ELIZABETH (SPENCER) WILCOX of Bergen, Genesee Co NY; Ref: 1860 Census Bergen NY p967 Dw# 248, See Abel Edwin.

HENRIETTA - b 15 Dec 1785 Patterson, Putnam Co NY d/JOHN & MARY (CROSBY) WILCOX; m 29 Sep 1804 ARCHIBALD PENNY who was b 27 Jul 1774 NY & d 01 Oct 1840 s/WILLIAM & SARAH (PARRISH) PENNY; Res Patterson, Putnam Co NY; ch MARY, ALFRED, SARAH, CHARLES W, CHARLOTTE, ADELINE, ELIZA, HIRAM, JAMES K, OLIVER H, CORNELIUS, PHILIP D; d 15 Dec 1854; Ref: Jane Smith, CT Bible Rec v12 p320.

HENRIETTA - m 23 Jan 1831 Berlin, Hartford Co CT JASON BAILEY; Ref: Barbour's VR Berlin v1 p41.

HENRIETTA - b 10 Feb 1812 Sandisfield, Berkshire Co MA d/WILLIAM & LUCINDA (GIBBS) WILCOX; Ref: Sandisfield VR p73, Fiske Card File, See William.

HENRIETTA - b 02 Aug 1814 d/OLIVER & SALLY (STANTON) WILCOX; m 29 Nov 1838 Rev OLIVER W NORTON who was b 09 Dec 1811 s/SERENO & HARRIET (MORSE) NORTON; Res Norwich, Chenango Co NY, IL, WI; ch OLIVER WILLIAM, ELIZABETH L; d 07 Apr 1850; Ref: Your Ancestors v3 #4 p350, NYG&BR April 1978 p94, v118 p57, Wilcox-Meigs p82, Cutter's New England Fam p160, Fam of Early Guilford p915, Marriages in NY Herald p265.

HENRIETTA - b 1833 Sandisfield, Berkshire Co MA d/CHAUNCEY & MARIANNE (POTTER) WILCOX; m SAMUEL ARNOLD Jr; Ref: Your Ancestors v12 #2 p1437.

HENRIETTA - b 1840 NY Twin with HENRY d/JEHIEL & CHLOE (NICHOLS) WILCOX; Res Evans, Erie Co NY; Ref: 1850 Census Evans NY p384 Dw# 174, See Jehiel.

HENRIETTA R - m 05 Jul 1847 N Providence, Providence Co RI CHRISTOPHER A STAFFORD; Ref: Arnold v2 p44.

HENRY - b 1756-1775; m HANNAH MORGAN; Res Voluntown, New London Co CT; 2 sons & 2 daus & HOPE ALMIRA; Ref: 1800 Census Voluntown CT p732, Barbour's VR Voluntown v1 p115.

HENRY - b 1766-1784; Res Batavia, Genesee Co NY; 1 son & 2 daus; Ref: 1810 Census Index Genesee Co NY p95.

HENRY - b ca 1768 RI s/STEPHEN & SARAH (BATES) WILCOX; m EUNICE -----; Ref: Your Ancestors v12 #3 p1461.

HENRY - b 1776-1794; Res Manheim, Herkimer Co NY; 4 sons & 1 dau; Ref: 1820 Census Herkimer Co NY.

HENRY - b 1781-1790; Res Newport, Herkimer Co NY; 3 daus & 2 sons; Ref: 1830 Census Herkimer Co NY p36.

HENRY - b 16 Aug 1781 s/WILLIAM & HANNAH (-----) WILCOX; m POLLY SIBLEY who was b 12 Apr 1783 Sandy Creek, Oswego Co NY & d 06 Aug 1849; Res West Mendon, Monroe Co NY; ch ALMIRA; d 1821; Ref: Your Ancestors v9 #4 p1178.

HENRY - b 01 Mar 1783 Amenia, Dutchess Co NY Twin with SENECA s/AARON & ELIZABETH (BELDEN) WILCOX; Ref: NYG&BR v40 p104.

HENRY - m AMANDA DOTY of Sharon, CT who was b 21 Jan 1791 & d 04 Nov 1820; Ref: Doty Fam Gen p660.

HENRY - b 1784 MA s/RICHARD WILCOX; m ABIGAIL ROLAND; Res Norway, Herkimer Co NY; 7 ch; Ref: Hist of Herkimer Co NY pp215,276.

HENRY - b 22 Jul 1785 Middletown, Middlesex Co CT s/JONATHAN & ELIZABETH (TODD) WILCOX; m 31 Dec 1808 Westbrook, Middlesex Co CT JEANETTE BUSHNELL who was b ca 1791 & d 15 Jun 1830; Res Deep River, Middlesex Co CT; ch WILLIAM TITUS, HENRY TRUMAN, EMILY PATIENCE, JONATHAN SAMUEL, CURTIS NASH, BENJAMIN BUSHNELL, GEORGE FREDERIC; d Jan 1853; Ref: MUH p751, Fam of Early Guilford pp1202-1204, Westbrook 1st Cong Church Rec p197, Your Ancestors v3 #2 p302.

HENRY - b 20 Feb 1787 Killingworth, Middlesex Co CT s/ABEL 2nd & BATHSHEBA (CLARK) WILCOX; Ref: Wilcox-Meigs p80, Your Ancestors v3 #2 p300, Barbour's VR Killingworth v2 p123.

HENRY - b 1791; m PHOEBE ----- who was b 1802 & d 07 Sept 1872 Oberlin, Lorain Co OH; d 22 Dec 1856 bur Oberlin Cem; Ref: OH Cem Rec p409.

HENRY - b 16 Jan 1792 Hillsdale, Columbia Co NY s/NATHANIEL & JOANNA (McGONIGLE/MALLORY) WILCOX; m 19 Feb 1819 SUSANNA MILLER who was b 02 Mar 1800 & d 13 Dec 1887 d/JAMES GARDNER & RUTH (ARNOLD) MILLER; Res Lexington, Greene Co NY & UT; ch RUTH LORANA, MARGARET, JONATHAN FERRIS, CYNTHIA ABIGAIL, JAMES DAVID/DANIEL, JULIA ANNE, WILLIAM HOWARD/ARNOLD, DARVIL/DORWILL MILLER; d 14 Feb 1837 Lexington NY; Ref: Wilcox-Meigs pp83,84,101, 102, Fiske Card File, Your Ancestors v4 #11&12 p612.

HENRY - m 02 Feb 1792 Dartmouth, Bristol Co MA RUBY BARKER; ch ELIZABETH SANFORD, LUCY; Ref: Dartmouth VR pp301-304,546.

HENRY - s/WILLIAM WILCOX of W Mendon, Monroe Co NY; Deserted his wife & ch; Ref: Desc of Wm Wilcoxson p203.

HENRY - b ca 1793; m SALLY ----- who was b 13 Oct 1794 & d 17 Nov 1870 Herkimer Co NY; Ref: NY NSDAR Records v4 p158.

HENRY - b 1795 RI; m WELTHA ----- who was b 1794 CT; Res Smyrna, Chenango Co NY; Ref: Fiske Card File.

HENRY - b 1795; Res Chautauqua Co NY; In poor House 1860; Ref: 1840 Census Chautauqua Co NY, 1860 Census Chautauqua NY.

HENRY - b 22 Apr 1795 Westport, Bristol Co MA s/WILLARD & RUTH (LAWRENCE) WILCOX; m 05 Jan 1821 HANNAH BAILEY who was b 04 Dec 1785; m 30 Sep 1831 ABBY B BOURNE; Res New Bedford, Bristol Co MA; Ref: Westport VR pp102,251, Your Ancestors v14 #1 p1631.

HENRY - b 26 Sep 1797 Bridport, Addison Co VT s/JAMES & EUNICE (VICKERY) WILCOX; m 06/16 Jan 1824 MARY KEZIAH MEACHAM d/Cpt WILLIAM MEACHAM of Port Henry, Essex Co NY; Res Galesburg, Knox Co IL; ch HENRY M, ERASTUS SWIFT, MARY H, WILLIAM H, CLARA A; d 09 Jun 1873; Ref: Wisconsin Fam June 1940 p42, Wilcox-Meigs pp83,101, Your Ancestors v3 #9&10 p450, Texas Society DAR Roster v4 p2287.

HENRY - b ca 1798 Richmond, Washington Co RI or Lee, Berkshire Co MA s/STEPHEN & SARAH (BATES) WILCOX; m EUNICE -----; ch ALFRED, HAMILTON, 2 daus; Ref: Your Ancestors v2 #3 p1462.

HENRY - b 04 Aug 1800 Utica, Oneida Co NY; m 02 Sep 1829 Palmyra, Marion Co MO SARAH PLEASANT PETTUS; d 15 Jul 1864 Van Buren, Crawford Co AR; Lawyer; Ref: NYG&BR v34 p147.

HENRY - d 09 Jul 1853 Herkimer Co NY; Ref: Will Book I p126, Herkimer Co NY.

HENRY - m ca 1825 PAMELA WHITING; Simsbury, Hartford Co CT; Ref: Rev Allen McLean Rec p18.

HENRY - b 1807 NY; m LOUISA ----- who was b 1810 NY; Res Prish, Oswego Co NY; ch EMILY M, ORA L, SELINA, NATHAN I, RUFUS B, LUZINIA, ADELBERT, HOMER; Ref: 1850 Census Parish NY p4 Dw# 50.

HENRY - b 1801-1810; Res Augusta, Oneida Co NY; 3 sons, 2 daus in 1840; Ref: 1840 Census Oneida Co NY p333.

HENRY - bpt 06 Jul 1810 N Stonington, New London Co CT Twin with HANNAH s/STEPHEN & HANNAH (HOLMES) WILCOX; Ref: Your Ancestors v13 #3 p1565, Barbour's VR N Stonington v1 p59.

HENRY - b 1806 NY; m 13 Oct 1827 Windham, Greene Co NY LUCINA P TURNER who was b 1810 NY; Res Milford, Otsego Co NY; ch WILLIAM K; Ref: Marriages Taken From Otsego Co Newspapers v1 p52, 1850 Census Milford NY p117 Dw# 287.

HENRY - m 26 Sep 1830 Preston, New London Co CT BETSEY MORGAN; Ref: Barbour's VR Preston v3 p155.

HENRY - b 24 Feb 1811; d 29 Jun 1853 Tioga Co NY; Ref: Tioga Co NY Cem Records.

HENRY - b 1824 NY; Machinist; Res Lenox, Madison Co NY; Ref: 1850 Census Lenox NY p217 Dw# 809.

HENRY - of Norfolk, Litchfield Co CT m 27 Dec 1831 JENNETTE WHEATON of Washington, Litchfield Co CT; Ref: Barbour's VR Washington v1 p90.

HENRY - m 09 May 1832 Meriden, New Haven Co CT ELIZABETH W SCOVIL; Ref: Barbour's VR Meriden v1 p46.

HENRY - m 22 Dec 1833 Hartford, Hartford Co CT MARY ANN MATHER; Ref: Barbour's VR Hartford v1 p107.

HENRY - of Haddam, Middlesex Co CT m 21 Sep 1834 SALLY H MIX of Wallingford, New Haven Co CT; Ref: Barbour's VR Wallingford v1 p207.

HENRY - b 1814 CT; m BETSEY ----- who was b 1817 CT; Shoemaker; Res Concord, Erie Co NY; ch MARY, HANNAH, ELECTA, ANNA S, AMOS H, SARAH, ALBERT; Ref: 1850 Census Concord NY p54 Dw# 785.

HENRY - b 10 Nov 1815 Schoharie Co NY; m ARTEMISSIA LUCE; Ref: Gen Helper Sep/Oct 1981 p39.

HENRY - b 1818 CT s/JOHN & AMANDA (UPSON) WILCOX; m HANNAH M HOAG who was b 1822 NY & d 1895; Res Maryland & Schenevus, Otsego Co NY Shoemaker; ch STEPHEN; d 1902; Ref; Your Ancestors v4 #1&2 p496 #3&4 p519, 1850 Census Maryland NY p154 Dw# 311.

HENRY - b 1818/22 NY/VT; m SARAH ----- who was b 1822/25 NY; Res Ripley & Chautauqua, Chautauqua Co NY; ch WILLIAM, GEORGE, LYDIA, POLLY, CYRENUS, HARVEY; Ref: 1850 Census Ripley NY p 118 Dw# 249, 1860 Census Chautauqua NY p64 Dw# 478.

HENRY - b 1820 VT; m SUSANNAH -----; Res Adrian, Lenawee Co MI; ch ISAAC; Ref: 1860 Census MI.

HENRY - b 1822 NY; m MARGARET ----- who was b 1823 NY; Res Chautauqua, Chautauqua Co NY; ch ADELAIDE; Ref: 1850 Census Chautauqua NY p273 Dw# 177.

HENRY - b 1823 Sandisfield, Berkshire Co MA s/CHAUNCEY & MARIANNE (POTTER) WILCOX; m HARRIETT AMELIA WEST; d 23 Mar 1888; Ref: Your Ancestors v12 #2 p1437, Desc of Wm Wilcoxson p223.

HENRY - m 19 May 1845 Norwich, New London Co CT HARRIET MARRYOTT; both of Jewett City, New London Co CT; Ref: Barbour's VR Norwich v6 p505.

HENRY - b 1829 NY s/JAMES & NANCY (-----) WILCOX of Pawling, Dutchess Co NY; Ref: 1850 Census Pawling NY p225 Dw# 93.

HENRY - b 30 May 1830 Westfield, Middlesex Co CT s/HEZEKIAH & RAMA (ROBERTS) WILCOX; m SARAH DUNHAM; Ref: Early Fam of Wallingford p333, Your Ancestors v3 #4 p352, Hist of Wallingford p939.

HENRY - b ca 1830; m MARGARET BARTON who was b 10 Jan 1831 & d 12 Sep 1859; Res Mayville, Chautauqua Co NY; Ref: Tree Talks v24 #2 p92.

HENRY - b 1831 s/CALEB & ADELIA (-----) WILCOX; d 04 Aug 1842 Oswego, Oswego Co NY; Ref: Tree Talks v10 #3 p176.

HENRY - b 1831 CT; Res Torrington, Litchfield Co CT; Carriage Maker; Ref: 1850 Census Torrington CT p216 Dw# 37.

HENRY - b 1832 NY; Res with JUSTIN CURTISS fam Mexico, Oswego Co NY; Ref: 1850 Census Mexico NY p91 Dw# 1413.

HENRY - b 1833 s/STEPHEN & POLLY (ALLEN) WILCOX of Smithfield, Bradford Co PA; m TABITHA ALLEN; Civil War Co G 6th Cavalry Inf; Ref: Wilcox Genealogy p7, Halifax VT Wilcox Fam mss.

HENRY - b Jan 1835 Meriden, New Haven Co CT s/HENRY TRUMAN & ELIZABETH W (SCOVILLE) WILCOX; Ref: Fam of Early Guilford p1205.

HENRY - b 1835 NY s/OZIAS WILCOX of Utica, Oneida Co NY; Ref: 1850 Census Utica p311 Dw# 25.

HENRY - b 1837 NY s/THOMAS R & LOUISA (-----) WILCOX of Belfast, Allegany Co NY; Ref: 1850 Census Belfast NY p266 Dw# 56.

HENRY - b 1838 NY s/JONATHAN & SARAH (-----) WILCOX of Sherburne, Chenango Co NY; Ref: 1850 Census Sherburne NY p250 Dw# 1654.

HENRY - b 1839 NY s/WARREN & EMILY (-----) WILCOX of Granby, Oswego Co NY; Ref: 1850 Census Granby NY p17 Dw# 254.

HENRY - b 1840 NY Twin with HENRIETTA s/JEHIEL & CHLOE (NICHOLS) WILCOX; m ca 1860 SARAH BOWERS/POWERS; Res Evans, Erie Co NY; ch GLEN, NELLIE, LOTTIE, BURTON, LESLIE, ARTHUR; Ref: Eden NY Town Hist, 1850 Census Evans NY p384 Dw# 174.

HENRY - b ca 1841 s/MORGAN L & CAROLINE (SATTERLEE) WILCOX; Res Onondaga & Granby, Oswego Co NY; Ref: Your Ancestors v3 #9&10 p447, 1850 Census Granby NY p16 Dw# 243.

HENRY - b 1842 NY s/ALONZO & HARRIET (-----) WILCOX of Pomfret, Chautauqua Co NY; Ref: 1860 Census Pomfret NY p565 Dw# 1844.

HENRY - b 1843 Broome Co NY s/GEORGE S & LOUISA (JONES) WILCOX of Alma, Allegany Co NY; Ref: Carol A Cox.

HENRY - b 1843 NY s/STEPHEN & SUSAN (-----) WILCOX of Pawling, Dutchess Co NY; Ref: 1850 Census Pawling NY p239 Dw# 329.

HENRY - b 1846 s/GARRETT WENDELL & LYDIA (-----) WILCOX of North White Creek, Washington Co NY; Ref: Your Ancestors v13 #3 p1582.

HENRY - b 1847 NY s/LYMAN & JOHANNAH (GUISLER) WILCOX of Sherman, Chautauqua Co NY; Ref: 1850 Census Sherman NY p276 Dw# 68, See Lyman.

HENRY - b 17 Jun 1849 Norwich, Chenango Co NY s/ELI & SOPHIA (-----) WILCOX; Ref: VR of Chenango Co NY p187, 1850 Census Norwich NY p176 Dw# 328.

HENRY - b 1849 NY s/RODMAN & MARY (-----) WILCOX of Ellicott, Chautauqua Co NY; Ref: 1860 Census Ellicott NY p755 Dw# 1514.

HENRY - b 1857 PA s/HEZEKIAH R & POLLY (PARKHURST) WILCOX; Res Le Roy, Bradford Co PA; Ref: 1860 Census Bradford Co PA, See Hezekiah R.

HENRY - b ca 1859 NY s/FRANKLIN & NANCY M (-----) WILCOX; Res Verona, Oneida Co NY; Ref: 1860 Census Verona NY p126 Dw# 509.

HENRY - b 17 Jan 1872 s/STEPHEN FARRINGTON & MARY (BILLINGS) WILCOX; Ref: Your Ancestors v3 #3 p320.

HENRY - b 14 Aug 1878 s/HENRY HOPSON & ELIZABETH (LADD) WILCOX; Ref: Your Ancestors v3 #3 p319.

HENRY - b 03 May 1890 NYC s/WILLIAM GOODENOW & MARY OTIS (GAY) WILCOX; Ref: Cutter's New England Fam p162, Your Ancestors v3 #5 p377.

HENRY - b 08 May 1890 s/JAMES HENRY & HARRIET ANN (DAY) WILCOX; Ref: Your Ancestors v12 #3 p1461.

HENRY - b 31 Jan 1898 Scranton, Lackawanna Co PA Twin with STEPHEN s/WILLIAM ALONZO & KATHARINE (JENKINS) WILCOX; d 23 Apr 1899; Ref: Wilcox-Brown-Medbery p32.

HENRY A - b 1824 Georgia; m 10 Sep 1850 SARAH MARIA LESTER who was b 1825 Plainfield, Windham Co CT; Mechanic Res NH; Ref: Barbour's VR Plainfield v4 p5.

HENRY A - b 24 Dec 1837 Chautauqua Co NY; Res Boon Co IL 1844; m 30 Oct 1861 SUSAN OAKS from ME; Ref: Chautauqua Genealogist v15 #2 p18.

HENRY ALLEN - b 16 Apr 1842 Newport, Sullivan Co NH s/JOSEPH & NANCY (WILMARTH) WILCOX; m 31 Jan 1872 MARIANNE MOORE who was b 10 Sep 1838 Plainfield, Washington Co VT d/JOSEPH & LAURA (NEWTON) MOORE; ch ALVAH, CATHARINE, SARAH, CLARK MOORE; Ref: Gen of NH Fam v3 p1509, Your Ancestors v3 #6 p400.

HENRY B - b 1826 Whitestown, Oneida Co NY s/FRANCIS & SOPHIA (BULKELEY) WILCOX; Ref: Your Ancestors v4 #3&4 p524.

HENRY BEALS - b 01 Feb 1821 Madison, New Haven Co CT s/ABEL & ANNA (FIELD) WILCOX; m 01 Jan 1851 LUCETTA WOODRUFF Hartford, Hartford Co CT who was b 1812 & d 09 Feb 1891 d/DAVID & EUNICE (NORTH) WOODRUFF; ch HENRY CLIFFORD, DWIGHT WOODRUFF, IDA ELLA; d 17 Sep 1895; Civil War; Ref: Wilcox-Meigs pp92,109,110, Fam of Early Guilford pp1213,1215, Col Fam of US v3 p622, Barbour's VR Madison v2 p30,40.

HENRY BENJAMIN - b 08 May 1848 Wethersfield, Wyoming Co NY s/AMOS & SOPHRONIA (HATFIELD) WILCOX; m 04 Mar 1869 Tylerville, Jefferson Co NY LILLIE A KING who was b Livingston Co NY 1853; Res Chenango Co NY; ch DORA BELL, ARTHUR KING, FRED HAMILTON, BENJAMIN FRANKLIN, EARL, WALLIN, IRVING, BESSIE HELEN MEAD (adopted); Ref: Your Ancestors v14 #2 pp1643,1644, 1850 Census Wethersfield NY p86 Dw# 1269.

HENRY BIRDSEY - b 01 Sep 1870 Meriden, New Haven Co CT s/HENRY EDWIN & ESTHER COE (BIRDSEY) WILCOX; m 28 Sep 1896 ELIZABETH PEMBERTON WALLACE; Res Bristol, Hartford Co CT; ch RUTH ELIZABETH; Ref: MUH p764.

HENRY C - b 05 Jul 1826 Simsbury, Hartford Co CT s/CHESTER & ELIZABETH (ANDREWS) WILCOX; d 12 Feb 1896; Ref: Your Ancestors v12 #1 p1408.

HENRY C - Inter Norwich, Chenango Co NY 17 Aug 1897 Sec A; Ref: Norwich NY Cem Assoc Rec p324.

HENRY C - b 23 Jan 1869 Norwich, Chenango Co NY s/JOHN T & LILLIAN (DIBBLE) WILCOX; d Norwich 20 Jul 1919 age 50 yr 5mo 27da; Bur Sec 4 Lot 2; Ref: Norwich NY Cem Assoc Records p324.

HENRY CLAY - b 25/28 Jul 1833 Elyria, Lorain Co OH s/ERASTUS & MARY BELLE (JARRARD) WILCOX; m 04 Dec 1855 MARY BELL JARRARD of Avery, OH who d 18 Sep 1897; Res Oberlin, Lorain Co OH; ch EUPHRASIA, ERASTUS, GARRETT BIRD, NELLIE, SARAH, MARY BELL, CLAYTON, EDNA; d 29 Nov 1903 Milan, Erie Co OH; Ref: Your Ancestors v11 #4 p1377.

HENRY CLAY - b 12 May 1839 Catskill, Greene Co NY s/JUDSON & LAURA (GOODRICH) WILCOX; m 03 Jul 1861 JEANETTE CATLIN d/JOHN CATLIN; Ref: Your Ancestors v4 #7&8 p564, 1850 Census Catskill NY p359 Dw# 322.

HENRY CLIFFORD - b 28 Jul 1852 Madison, New Haven Co CT s/HENRY BEALS & LUCETTA (WOODRUFF) WILCOX; d 27 Feb 1882; Ref: Wilcox-Meigs p109, Fam of Early Guilford p1215, Barbour's VR Madison v2 p40.

HENRY COLE - b 12 Mar 1849 s/EBEN NORTH & MARIE LOUISE (COLE) WILCOX; m HARRIET COBB; ch MARGARET COBB; d 16 May 1874; Ref: Desc of Wm Wilcoxson p260.

HENRY D - b 14 Oct 1821 Chester, Hampden Co MA s/ASA & RELIEF (COLTON) WILCOX; d; Ref: Fiske Card File, Your Ancestors v3 #9&10 p452.

HENRY D - b 27 Aug 1823 Chester, Hampden Co MA s/ASA & RELIEF (COLTON) WILCOX; m MARY W BISHOP who was b 1830; ch MARIAH W, HENRY D; Ref: Fiske Card File, Your Ancestors v3 #9&10 p452.

HENRY D - b 1837 CT; Res Watertown, Litchfield Co CT; Ref: 1850 Census Watertown CT p387 Dw# 111.

HENRY D - b 1838 CT s/RODNEY B & RACHEL (GREEN) WILCOX of Litchfield, Litchfield Co CT; Ref: 1850 Census Litchfield CT p284 Dw# 519, See Rodney B.

HENRY D - b 1848 OH s/ ----- & HENRIETTA (-----) WILCOX of Painesville, Lake Co OH; Ref: 1850 Census Painesville OH Reel 259 p182.

HENRY D - b 1850 s/HENRY D & MARY W (BISHOP) WILCOX; Ref: Your Ancestors v3 #9&10 p452.

HENRY E - b 1838 PA s/NATHAN & SUSAN (-----) WILCOX; Res Le Roy, Bradford Co PA; Ref: 1850 Census Bradford Co PA p68.

HENRY EDWARD - b 15 Jul 1845 Killingworth, Middlesex Co CT s/JOSEPH BENJAMIN & RUTH ELIZABETH (SCRANTON) WILCOX; m MARYETTE O PARKER; Res Jacksonville, Duval Co FL; ch EDWARD, LUCY, RUTH, BLANCHE; Ref: Wilcox-Meigs pp108,122, Fam of Early Guilford p1214.

HENRY EDWIN - b 01 Mar 1844 Middletown, Middlesex Co CT s/SHERMAN & HARRIETT FRIEND (HALL) WILCOX; m 15 Apr 1869 ESTHER COE BIRDSEY who was b 14 Jun 1848; Res Bristol, Hartford Co CT; ch HENRY BIRDSEY, MARION ELIZABETH, LINA DICKENSON; d 1904+; Ref: MUH pp757,764.

HENRY F - b 1839 NY s/ERASTUS & EUNICE (-----) WILCOX of Palerno, Oswego Co NY; Ref: 1850 Census Palerno NY p32 Dw# 470.

HENRY F - b 1851; m MARY C ----- who was b 1854 & d 03 Feb 1877 age 22y 11m 6 da; m LUCY H ----- who was b 1844 & d 1935; d 1926 all bur Tiverton, Newport Co RI Cem Lot 99; Ref: Gen of RI Fam v2 p622.

HENRY F - b 1852 s/WILLIAM & MARY (-----) WILCOX; m 15 Jan 1873 Tiverton, Newport Co RI MARY C MANCHESTER who was b 1845 d/JOHN W & MARY A (-----) MANCHESTER; Ref: Arnold v7 p583.

HENRY FRANKLIN - b 16 Feb 1833 s/AZARIAH CLARK & RACHEL (VAN DEUSEN) WILCOX; m 06 Apr 1859 LUCINDA HARRIET BROWN who was b 21 Feb 1839 & d 17 Jan 1910; ch MARY LOUISA, GEORGE FRANKLIN, MARY ELIZA, HARRIET LUCINDA, JOHN HENRY, EMMA BELL; d 01 Jan 1925; Ref: Wilcox Excerpts v1 pp2,3, Your Ancestors v13 #1 p1516.

HENRY H - b 1807 NY; m MARY A ---- who was b 1820; Res Harmony, Chautauqua Co NY; ch BETSEY, DAVID; Ref: 1850 Census Harmony NY pp251,252 Dw# 183.

HENRY H - b 14 Apr 1814 s/JOHN CLARK & DORCAS (HARRINGTON) WILCOX of Franklin, New London Co CT & Sherman, Chautauqua Co NY; d 05 Jun 1816; Ref: Your Ancestors v14 #2 p1658.

HENRY H - b 20 Nov 1823 Manchester, Ontario Co NY s/EARL & JANE (STEWART) WILCOX; m 22 Jan 1850 MARY E BUTTON who was b Jul 1831 d/WILLIAM & MARY (-----) BUTTON; Res Manchester NY; ch FRANCIS; Ref: Your Ancestors v10 #4 p 1294.

HENRY H - b 01 Jan 1845 Streetsboro, Portage Co OH s/ALANSON & SYLVIA (LAWRENCE) WILCOX; m 10 Sep 1871 AGNES FRENCH d/HENRY & LOUISA (TUCKER) FRENCH; ch MILLARD D, ARTEMAS J, JOHN H; Ref: Hist of Portage Co OH pp898,899, 1850 Census Streetsborough OH p30 Dw# 21.

HENRY H - b 1852; m ALICE E ALMY who was b 1873 & d 1916; Tiverton, Newport Co RI; d 1926 bur Cem #33 Lot 87; Ref: Gen of RI Fam v2 p621.

HENRY HAMILTON - b 24 Oct 1822 Bergen, Genesee Co NY s/AUSTIN & CLARISSA/CHLOE (NETTLETON) WILCOX; m 28 Oct 1845 EUNICE J SMITH who was b 28 Mar 1825 MA d/HENRY SMITH of Northampton, Hampshire Co MA; ch MAY E, LILLIAN E, AUSTIN; Ref: Fam of Early Guilford p1203, Your Ancestors v3 #1 p282.

HENRY HARRISON - b 23 Mar 1858 Waioli, Kauai Hawaii s/ABNER & LUCY ELIZA (HART) WILCOX; m MAY GREEN; Ref: Desc of Abner & Lucy Hart Wilcox p23, Your Ancestor v3 #1 p279.

HENRY HARVEY - b 15 Dec 1831 Surry, Cheshire Co NH s/GEORGE & NANCY PALMYRA (REED) WILCOX; Single; d 05 Apr 1865; Ref: Hist of Surry NH pp381,949.

HENRY HOPSON - b 18 Sep 1803 s/RUSSELL & ELIZABETH (FARRINGTON) WILCOX; m 06 Jan 1840 MARIAN LYLE/LISLE PURDY who was b 10 Jun 1814 & d 10 Mar 1909 d/JAMES & MARIAN (LISLE) PURDIE; Res Earlville, Chenango Co NY; ch JAMES PURDIE, HENRY HOPSON, WILLIAM RUSSELL, STEPHEN FARRINGTON, PRISCILLA; d 02 Nov 1883; Ref: Chenango Co VR, Cem Records Chenango Co p9, Early Years in Smyrna p22, Your Ancestors v3 #2 p299 #3 p319.

HENRY HOPSON - b 16 Jan 1831 Smyrna, Chenango Co NY s/HAZARD & FLAVILLA (PARSONS) WILCOX; m 1861 SOPHIA BURNS of Lewiston, Niagara Co NY; ch

SAMUEL, FRED H, FRANK; d 17 Apr 1910; Ref: Your Ancestors v3 #6 pp397,398.

HENRY HOPSON - b 14 Mar 1843 s/HENRY HOPSON & MARIAN LISLE (PURDIE) WILCOX of Earlville, Chenango Co NY; m 20 Oct 1864 ELIZABETH LADD; ch HENRY, ORTON, MARIAN; d 13 Jun 1920; Ref: Your Ancestors v3 #3 p319.

HENRY HOPSON - b 14 Feb 1883 s/WILLIAM RUSSELL & MARY E (REXFORD) WILCOX; m 1914 BESSIE CONLEY who was b 27 Jan 1884; ch HENRY HOPSON, DOROTHY MAY, MARY E; Ref: Your Ancestors v3 #3 pp319,320.

HENRY HOWARD - b 01 Mar 1867 New York City s/WILLIAM HENRY & ANNE HOLMES (GOODENOW) WILCOX; Ref: Wilcox-Meigs p99.

HENRY J - b 23 Aug 1820 Middlebury, Addison Co VT s/JULIUS & ELIZABETH (BROWN) WILCOX; m 10 Jun 1849 LEVINIA E PRITCHARD who was b 24 Nov 1822 & d 10 Jun 1881 d/HARVEY & EUNICE (DOUGLAS) PRITCHARD; m ELECTA K (WITHERELL) BROWN d/SYLVESTER & ABIGAIL (TURRILL) WITHERELL of Shoreham, Addison Co VT & w/JOHN BANCROFT BROWN; No ch; Tinsmith; Ref: Gen of CT Fam v1 p245, 1850 Census Shoreham VT Reel 920 p145.

HENRY J - m 11 Dec 1839 Middletown, Middlesex Co CT MARY ANN COE; Ref: Barbour's VR Middletown v3 p471.

HENRY J - m MARY ANN ----- who was b 1821 & d 19 Sep 1869 age 48; bur St John's Cem on the Hill Lansingburgh, Rensselaer Co NY; Ref: Burial Ground of Lansingburgh NY p154.

HENRY J - of East Lyme, New London Co CT m 22 May 1851 JANE S GILLETT of Hebron, Tolland Co CT; Ref: Barbour's VR Hebron v4 p52-m.

HENRY J - b 1844 NY s/SAMUEL & EUNICE (-----) WILCOX of Preston, Chenango Co NY; Ref: 1850 Census Preston NY p461 Dw# 2224.

HENRY J - b 1877 Rowe, Franklin Co MA s/HENRY THOMAS & AMELIA M (-----) WILCOX; Ref: Halifax VT Wilcox Fam mss.

HENRY KINSLEY - b 1849 Middletown or Ashland, Orange Co NY s/HORATIO R & SARAH M (KINSLEY) WILCOX; m 1880 FRANCES WHEELER d/GEORGE D WHEELER of Deposit, Delaware/Broome Co NY; Ref: Wilcox-Meigs p121, Hist of Orange Co NY.

HENRY L - b 20 Sep 1794 s/JAMES & EUNICE (VICKERY) WILCOX; m MARY MEACHUM of Port Henry, Essex Co NY; Ref: Desc of Wm Wilcoxson p118.

HENRY L - Purchased lot 55 twnshp 1 range 11 in Chautauqua Co NY from STEPHEN Jr & LUCY (STEWARD) WILCOX 01 Jun 1828; Ref: Chautauqua Co NY Deed v7 p269, See Stephen Jr.

HENRY LUDLOW - b 26 Apr 1848 poss OH s/HORACE FRANKLIN & HENRIETTA FRANCES (SHEPARD) WILCOX; m 06 Sep 1875 MARY SPAULDING ROWLAND St Paul, Ramsey Co MN; d 27 Apr 1876; Ref: Wilcox-Meigs p90.

HENRY LUSK - b 23 Jul 1871 s/ROBERT & ADELIA A (GILLETT) WILCOX; Res Monroe Co NY; d 04 Sep 1871; Ref: Wilcox Excerpts v1 p23.

HENRY M - b 1804 CT; m HARRIET N -----; Res Preston, New London Co CT; ch JANE M, HARRIET L; Ref: 1850 Census Preston CT Reel 432 #49 p17.

HENRY M - m JULIA DENSLOW; moved 1865 from New Hartford, Hartford Co CT to Sandisfield, Berkshire Co MA; Ref: Gazetteer of Berkshire Co MA p335.

HENRY M - s/HENRY & MARY (-----) WILCOX; d 17 Oct 1825 in his 4th yr bur Whitney Cem Port Henry town of Moriah, Essex Co NY; Ref: Branches & Twigs v3 #1 p12.

HENRY M - b 09 Jan 1828 Galesburg, Knox Co IL s/HENRY & MARY K (MEACHAM) WILCOX; d 17 Oct 1828; Ref: Wilcox-Meigs p101.

HENRY M - b 1839 CT s/ABRAHAM & LOIS (-----) WILCOX of New Hartford, Litchfield Co CT; Ref: 1850 Census New Hartford CT p125 Dw# 182.

HENRY MARTIN - b 16 Oct 1829 NY s/LUMAN & ELIZABETH (BLISS) WILCOX; Res Onarga, Iroquois Co IL; Ref: Your Ancestors v2 p254.

HENRY MILLS - b 24 May 1896 IL s/SAMUEL MILLS WILCOX; m 1929 MIDGE PENNOYERS; Res Los Angeles, Los Angeles Co CA; 4 ch; Ref: Your Ancestors v2 p254.

HENRY N - m be 1816 WELTHY ----; Res Griswold, New London Co CT; ch CHESTER PHILLIPS; Ref: Barbour's VR Griswold v1 p31.

HENRY N - b ca 1840 s/AUSTIN SCRANTON & HANNAH (BIDWELL) WILCOX; Res Detroit, Wayne Co MI; Ref: Your Ancestors v3 #1 p281.

HENRY NORTON - b 28 Sep 1832 Colrain, Franklin Co MA s/ABRAHAM & LAURINDA (HARDY) WILCOX; m BORITHA ----- who was b ca 1849; Ref: Halifax VT Wilcox Fam mss, Your Ancestors v4 #9&10 p587.

HENRY P - m 24 Mar 1822 Marietta, Washington Co OH CAROLINE WILLARD; Ref: Washington Co OH Marriages p78.

HENRY PENDLETON - b 28 Dec 1860 Olean, Cattaraugus Co NY s/NATHAN PENDLETON & CELESTINE (BIRGE) WILCOX; m 24 Jul 1886 ROSAMOND AVERY who d 24 Nov 1888 d/MILES AVERY of East Lemon, Wyoming Co PA; Pharmacist; ch ESTHER, ROSAMOND; d 20 Jan 1899; Ref: Wilcox-Brown-Medbery pp24,32.

HENRY PERKINS - b ca New Bedford, Bristol Co MA 1810 s/JOSEPH & ELIZABETH (PERKINS) WILCOX; d in infancy; Ref: Repr Men of Southeastern MA p480.

HENRY PIERSON Dr - b 11 Feb 1792 Killingworth, Middlesex Co CT s/Capt JOSEPH & PHOEBE (MORGAN) WILCOX; m CAROLINE ----- who d 12 Sep 1836 Buffalo, Erie Co NY; m SALLY (MORGAN) STANTON w/George W Stanton; m 07 Mar 1848 Albany, Albany Co NY SARAH M HALL d/George W Stanton Esq; Res Irving, Hanover twnshp, Chautauqua Co NY; ch AARON R, CHARLES H, SUSAN R, JOSEPH M; d 17 May 1870 Wallingford, New Haven Co CT; Ref: Wilcox-Meigs p62, 1840, 1850, 1855 Census Chautauqua Co NY, Barbour's VR Killingworth v2 p132, 19th Cent Marriages Reported in Fredonia Censor p244, 19th Cent Deaths Reported in Fredonia Censor p596, Western NY Journal v10 #3 p129.

HENRY PLATO - b 03 Jun 1870 Cohocton, Steuben Co NY s/ALBERT HOPKINS & FANNY (PARMENTER) WILCOX m JENNIE L ALLEN who was b 15 Feb 1872 d/WILLIAM & CATHARINE or MARY (FOULTS) ALLEN; ch LOUISE, ALLEN ALBERT, LESTER EDWARD; Ref: Your Ancestors v10 #2 p1223.

HENRY PORTER - b ca 1798 s/DAVID & HULDAH (PORTER) WILCOX; Ref: Desc of Wm Wilcoxson p132.

HENRY S - b 22 Feb 1809/10 s/DAVID & PHOEBE (BAILEY) WILCOX; Res CT/Columbia Co NY; d 05 Dec 1810; Ref: Wilcox Excerpts v1 pp2,7, Your Ancestors v13 #1 p1515.

HENRY S - b 1889 Chautauqua Co NY s/GEORGE A & VIOLA (STEWARD) WILCOX; Ref: Your Ancestors v14 #3 p1669.

HENRY SEWARD - b 23 Dec 1860 Albany, Albany Co NY s/GAYLOR SHELDON & MARGARET (WITT) WILCOX; Res Troy, Rensselaer Co NY; Ref: SAR Register NY 1899 p341.

HENRY SILAS - b 16 May 1869 s/NELSON OTIS & FRANCES MARIA (NOBLE) WILCOX; Ref: Your Ancestors v12 #4 p1490.

HENRY THOMAS - b 03 Oct 1840 Rowe, Franklin Co MA s/THOMAS & MARY P (UPTON) WILCOX; m AMELIA M -- --- who was b 1844; ch MADELINE, HENRY J; Ref: Halifax VT Wilcox Fam mss.

HENRY TUCKER - b 05 May 1814 Westport, Bristol Co MA s/BENJAMIN & SARAH (TABER) WILCOX; m 12 Dec 1838 NANCY R WING Dartmouth, Bristol Co MA; Ref: Repr Men of Southeastern MA p1081, Your Ancestors v14 #1 p1631, Dartmouth VR p546.

HENRY TRUMAN - b Feb 1811 Deep River, Middlesex Co CT s/HENRY & JEANNETTE (BUSHNELL) WILCOX; m 09 May 1832 ELIZABETH W SCOVILLE who was b 1810 & d 29 Feb 1880; Druggist; Res Meriden, New Haven Co CT; ch HENRY; d 07 Jan 1885; Ref: Fam of Early Guilford pp1203,1205.

HENRY W - b ca 1785; m 03 Mar 1824 Hartford, Hartford Co CT REBECCA SLOAN; Ref: Fam of Hartford p542, Barbour's VR Hartford v1 p36.

HENRY W - b 1823 NY; m EUNICE J ----- who was b 1825 MA; Res Bergen, Genesee Co NY; ch MARY E, EMERSON H; Ref: 1850 Census Bergen NY p63 Dw# 872.

HENRY W - b 1839 NY s/STEPHEN S & SARAH L (ELMS) WILCOX of Lysander, Onondaga Co NY; Ref: 1850 Census Lysander NY p469 Dw# 135.

HENRY WELLS - b 09 Dec 1870 s/LUCIUS FITCH & ELLEN MARIA (BELDEN) WILCOX of Le Roy Genesee Co NY; m MARY BLOOM; Ref: Your Ancestors v3 #7&8 pp425,426.

HENRY WHITE - b 14 Feb 1826 s/SAMUEL & ABIGAIL (WHITE) WILCOX; m 16 Mar 1863 HANNAH ELIZA WILCOX of Goshen, Litchfield Co CT; Res Whitesboro, Oneida Co NY & Winsted Litchfield Co CT; ch EDWARD H; Ref: MUH pp743,744, Our County & Its People Oneida Co NY p121, Your Ancestors v4 #1&2 p500.

HENRY WILLIAM - b 17 Dec 1850 Panama, Chautauqua Co NY s/GEORGE & SARAH (SPENCER) WILCOX; m 28 Feb 1877 LUCY GLOVER who was b 27 Feb 1860 d/FRANCIS & DEBORAH JANE (MICKLE) GLOVER & who married EUGENE CROSS 1899; ch JENNIE, ROSS GLOVER, MARY MAMIE, EMMA PERMELIA, LEIGH FRANCIS, HENRY WILLIAM; d 25 Oct 1892; Ref: A Wilcox Book pp109,128,129.

HENRY WILLIAM - b 07 Feb 1823 Floyd, Oneida Co NY s/ALBINUS & EUNICE CHACE (ALLEN) WILCOX; m 1850 MARY ELIZA JONES who was b 20 Jan 1831; Res Wauwatosa, Milwaukee Co WI; ch WILLIAM HENRY, JOHN JONES, FRED ALLEN, GEORGE HORNELL, ROBERT JAMES, MARY ELIZABETH; d 1909; Ref: Wills of Oneida Co NY p42, Wilcox-Meigs pp97,117, Col Fam of US v5 p556.

HENRY WILLIAM - b 19 Feb 1869 Guthrie Center, Guthrie Co IA s/LEWIS ALLEN & SABINA McDONALD (HOPKINS) WILCOX; ch EDITH ALMA, ANNA GRACE, HENRY BARTON, JESSIE MAY; Ref: Wilcox-Meigs pp117,131.

HENRY WILLIAM - b 30 Oct 1892 s/HENRY WILLIAM & LUCY (GLOVER) WILCOX; m MARGARET LE BARRON; Ref: A Wilcox Book p129.

HEPZIBAH/HEPSIBA - b 03 Jul 1736 Killingworth, Middlesex Co CT d/STEPHEN & MARY (PIERSON) WILCOX; m 24 Sep 1767 JOHN LEWIS ; d 07 Jun 1816; Ref: Wilcox-Meigs p42, Bogue Fam p395, Cutter's New England Fam p159, Your Ancestors v3 #3 p231, Barbour's VR Killingworth v2 pp74,159.

HEPZIBAH - b 31 Jan 1745 d/DANIEL & SARAH (WHITE) WILCOX; m 22/23 Sep 1763 Wethersfield, Hartford Co CT DAVID BECKLEY who was b 17 Feb 1742 & d 19 Nov 1798 Berlin, Hartford Co CT; ch DAVID, SILAS, CAROLINE, JOSEPH, HEPZIBAH, LUTHER, JOSEPH; d 19 Feb 1821; Ref: ECM v2 p91, MUH p749, Cutter's CT Fam p657, Hist of Berlin p95, Barbour's VR Middletown v1 p102, NEH&GR v160.

HEPZIBAH - b 11 Apr 1782 Killingworth, Middlesex Co CT d/URIAH & HANNAH (WRIGHT) WILCOX; m ca 1808 BENJAMIN KELSEY s/ABSALOM & MERCY (HILL) KELSEY; Res Orwell, Addison Co VT & Churchville,

Monroe Co NY; ch HENRY, SALOME, ELMIRA/MALVINA, ABSALOM, SENECA, ELIHU, BENJAMIN; d 06 Apr 1860 Riga, Monroe Co NY; Ref: Gen of NH Fam v3 p1509, Your Ancestors v3 #5 p378 #6 p399.

HEPZIBAH - b 20 Jul 1788 W Simsbury, Hartford Co CT d/AZARIAH & HEPZIBAH (HUMPHREY) WILCOX; m HENRY HARRINGTON; Ref: Early Settlers of W Simsbury CT p131, Fiske Card File, Wilcox-Meigs p86, Your Ancestors v12 #1 p1407, Barbour's VR Simsbury TM4 p308.

HEPZIBAH - b 1791 Middletown, Middlesex Co CT d/ELIJAH & LOIS (WARNER) WILCOX; d 09 Dec 1792; Ref: Hale Collection.

HEPZIBAH - b 15 Nov 1794 Middletown, Middlesex Co CT d/ELIJAH W & LOIS (WARNER) WILCOX; m ENOCH WILCOX who was b ca 1785 s/ENOCH & CHLOE (-----) WILCOX of Cassadaga, Chautauqua Co NY; ch WALTER W, LEVERETT L; Ref: Your Ancestors v3 #6 p401, Barbour's VR Middletown v2 p108.

HEPZIBAH - b 29 Apr 1796 E Berlin, Hartford Co CT d/JOSIAH & HULDAH (SAVAGE) WILCOX; m 19 Aug 1818 NORRIS GALPIN s/THOMAS GALPIN who was b 22 Mar 1794 & d 03 Mar 1826; ch HENRY NORRIS; m BENJAMIN WILCOX who was b 27 Jun 1782 & d 10 May 1843 s/SAMUEL & PHOEBE (DOWD) WILCOX; d Aug 1853; Ref: MUH p752.

HEPZIBAH - b ca 1811 d/HEZEKIAH & ABIAH (CLARK) WILCOX of Herkimer, Herkimer Co NY; m DANIEL GOLDEN; Res Erie Co NY; Ref: Your Ancestors v3 #6 p402.

HEPZIBAH - bpt 11 May 1818 d/ROBERT & RACHEL (SHERMAN) WILCOX; Res North White Creek, Washington Co NY; Ref: Wilcox Excerpts v1 p22, Your Ancestors v13 #3 p1581.

HERBERT - b 1861 Sandgate, Bennington Co VT s/JOHN AUSTIN & ELMIRA B (ANDREWS) WILCOX; Ref: Desc of Wm Wilcoxson p171.

HERBERT - b 1861 WI s/GEORGE & SUSAN (-----) WILCOX; Father b NY; Res Springlake, Pierce Co WI; Ref: 1880 Soundex Pierce Co WI.

HERBERT - b 1872 KS s/EPHRAIM & EUDORA (-----) WILCOX; Father b NY; Res Otter Creek, Eau Claire Co WI; Ref: 1880 Soundex Eau Claire Co WI.

HERBERT - b 12 Aug 1894 Cassadaga, Chautauqua Co NY s/JAY WARREN & MAY ANGELIA (WILCOX) WILCOX; d 12 Nov 1894 Cassadaga, Chautauqua Co NY whooping cough bur Wrights Corner Villanova, Chautauqua Co NY; Ref: Wilcox Hist mss, Cem Inscr, Death Cert.

HERBERT EUGENE - b 16 Sep 1849 Danbury, Fairfield Co CT s/ORLANDO & SARAH B (BENJAMIN) WILCOX; Single; d 14 Apr 1900; Ref: Desc of Wm Wilcoxson p259.

HERBERT EUGENE - 3 wives; Res Jerome, Yavapai Co AZ in 1895; Ref: SGS Bulletin Jun 1975 p141.

HERBERT H - b 23 Nov 1853 Winfield, Herkimer Co NY s/ELIJAH W & LYDIA M (STRAIGHT) WILCOX; m FLORENCE ORELLA BABCOCK; ch FANNY, FELMER W; Ref: Your Ancestors v3 #6 p402.

HERBERT J - b 28 Dec 1869 s/ANDREW CHESTER & CLARINDA CLINGMAN (RICHART) WILCOX of Harlan, Shelby Co IA; Ref: Your Ancestors v14 #3 p1671.

HERBERT LOVELL - b 10 Oct 1846 s/DAVID & MARY J (DODGE) WILCOX; Ref: Your Ancestors v11 #2 p1346.

HERBERT R - b Jan 1850 NY s/DUDLEY & KEZIAH (TOWNSEND) WILCOX of Litchfield, Herkimer Co NY; Ref: 1850 Census Litchfield NY p133 Dw# 282.

HERBERT SAMUEL - b 31 Aug 1867 s/GEORGE W & JOANNA ELIZABETH (ELLIS) WILCOX of Le Roy, Bradford Co PA; Ref: Your Ancestors v10 #4 p1274.

HERBERT SPENCER - s/FRANK C & SARAH THERESA (SPENCER) WILCOX; m GRACE HOLMAN; Ref: Your Ancestors v3 #7&8 p427.

HERMAN - b 21 Nov 1830 Bloomfield, Ontario Co NY s/EDWIN & CANDACE (GILBERT) WILCOX; Ref: Edward McCarthy.

HERMAN - b 1849 NY s/THOMAS SCUDDER & ELIZABETH (ABBOTT) WILCOX of Varick, Seneca Co NY; Ref: 1850 Census Varick NY p66 Dw# 980, See Thomas Scudder.

HERMAN - b 1857 NY s/ISAAC & SUSAN (-----) WILCOX of Pomfret, Chautauqua Co NY; Ref: 1860 Census Pomfret NY p583 Dw# 1992.

HESTER/ESTHER - b 19 Dec 1673 d/JOHN & ESTHER (CORNWELL) WILCOX of Middletown, Middlesex Co CT; m 10 May 1692 Guilford, New Haven Co CT JOSEPH

HAND who was b 02 Apr 1671 & d ca 1699 s/JOSEPH & JANE (WRIGHT) HAND; ch JANNA, ESTHER, HULDAH; d 15 Mar 1696/8; Ref: Nutmegger v8 #4 p532, Gen of the Hand Fam pp22,23, Fam of Early Guilford p596, Gen of CT Fam v2 p116, Barbour's VR Guilford vA p72.

HESTER - b 28 Feb 1715 Stratford, Fairfield Co CT d/WILLIAM & ESTHER (BRINSMADE) WILCOX; Ref: Wilcox-Meigs p39, Hist of Stratford Fam p1346.

HESTER/HESTHER - b 22 Nov 1723 Middletown, Middlesex Co CT d/SAMUEL & HESTER (BUSHNELL) WILCOX; Ref: Barbour's VR Middletown LR2 p21.

HESTER ANN - b 17 Jan 1833 Pompey, Onondaga Co NY d/GILES & EMILY (PHELPS) WILCOX; m 24 Nov 1851 Lafayette, Onondaga Co NY WILLIAM ROBINSON CLEVELAND; Ref: Your Ancestors v14 #1 p1619, 1850 Census Lafayette NY p215 Dw# 361.

HESTER MALVINA - b 1812 Buffalo, Erie Co NY d/OLIVER & BETSEY (SPRAGUE) WILCOX; m HUMPHREY C PERLEY; d 1881; Ref: Your Ancestors v9 #4 p1177.

HEUSTEN/HUSTIN - b 1783 E Guilford, New Haven Co CT s/EZRA & REBECCA BROWN (MUNGER) WILCOX; m JULIA CRAMPTON who was b 1792 & d 30 May 1876 d/ASHBEL & JULIA (MUNGER) CRAMPTON; ch WILLIAM, REBECCA, HORATIO, HARRIET, JAMES HUSTIN, JULIET, ALFRED, TIMOTHY, JOHN; d 05 Apr 1842; Ref: Wilcox-Meigs pp71,87,88, Fam of Early Guilford pp256,1211-1213.

HETTEAN - m 08 Sep 1826 Killingworth, Middlesex Co CT ALFRED PELTON; Ref: Barbour's VR Killingworth v3 p373.

HEYLER - b 03 Oct 1841 Barkhamsted, Litchfield Co CT s/JEHIEL & RUTH (GAINES) WILCOX; d 29 Nov 1892; Ref: Desc of Wm Wilcoxson p189a.

HEZEKIAH - b 04 1704 Westerly, Washington Co RI s/EDWARD & TAMSEN (STEVENS) WILCOX; Ref: Arnold v5 p144, Hist of Stonington CT p658, NEH&GR v15 p66, Austin p423.

HEZEKIAH - b 25 Jun 1713 Simsbury, Hartford Co CT s/JOSEPH & ABIGAIL (THRALL) WILCOX; d 1789 age 75; Ref: Wilcox-Meigs p32, Nutmegger v10 #2 p213, Early Settlers of W Simsbury p127, Your Ancestors v13 #3 p1567, Desc of Wm Wilcoxson p15.

HEZEKIAH - b 25 Dec 1731 Stonington, New London Co CT s/ELISHA & MARY (MEECH) WILCOX; m 31 Mar 1754 Westerly, Washington Co RI HANNAH PARKER; Res Stonington CT; ch HEZEKIAH, AMEY DANIEL, PELEG, MARTHA, JESSE, ASA, SUSANNAH, ABIGAIL, THOMAS, SYLVESTER, SAMUEL; d 1819; Ref: Hist of Stonington p660, Arnold v5 pt2 p69, p145.

HEZEKIAH - b ca 1731 Stonington, New London Co CT s/DANIEL & MARY (ROBESON) WILCOX; m ABIGAIL -----; Res Orange Co NY; Ref: Your Ancestors v3 #11&12 p470.

HEZEKIAH - b 1744; d Aug 1808 Groton, New London Co CT; Ref: Index of Obits in MA v5 p4913.

HEZEKIAH - b 04 Mar 1744 Middletown, Middlesex Co CT s/JOHN & HANNAH (WILCOX) WILCOX; m 09 Nov 1775 RACHEL BOARDMAN; ch HEZEKIAH; d 11 Sep 1776; Ref: Barbour's VR Middletown v2 pp94,161, Your Ancestors v3 #4 pp351,352, Hale Coll, Early Fam of Wallingford pp331,332, Hist of Wallingford pp937,938.

HEZEKIAH - b 30 Jul 1755 Westerly, Washington Co RI s/HEZEKIAH & HANNAH (PARKER) WILCOX; m MARTHA/PATTY WHITTLESEY; Ref: Arnold v5 p144, Hist of Stonington CT p660, C Douglass Alves Sr.

HEZEKIAH - b ca 1763 W Simsbury, Hartford Co CT s/EZRA & RHODA (HARRIS) WILCOX; Res Whitestown, Oneida Co NY, Fabius, Onondaga Co NY; 3ch; Ref: Early Settlers of W Simsbury p131, Your Ancestors v13 #3 p1568, Desc of Wm Wilcoxson pp25,242.

HEZEKIAH - b be 1765; Res Onondaga Co NY 1810; 4 sons & 7 daus; Ref: 1810 Census Onondaga Co NY.

HEZEKIAH - b Dec 1769 Orange Co NY s/AMOS & MARY (-----) WILCOX; m 19 May 1793 MAHALA WILCOX who was b 1775 d/DANIEL & HANNAH (WILBUR) WILCOX; Res Bradford Co PA; ch HEZEKIAH, DANIEL, HANNAH, ELIZABETH, RICHARD, SAMUEL, MARGARET, JANE, MARY, HEZEKIAH; d Nov 1809; Ref: Your Ancestors v9 #4 p1176, v10 #3 pp1247,1248.

HEZEKIAH - b 11 Oct 1776 Middletown, Middlesex Co CT s/HEZEKIAH & RACHEL (BOARDMAN) WILCOX; d 19 Jan 1792; Ref: Barbour's VR Middletown v2 p161, Hale Coll, Early Fam of Wallingford p332, Your Ancestors v3 #4 p352, Hist of Wallingford p938.

HEZEKIAH - b 28 Mar 1793 Middletown, Middlesex Co CT s/JOSEPH & MIRIAM (BACON) WILCOX; m 30 Nov 1816 RAMA ROBERTS who was b 23 Dec 1792 & d 10 Jan 1869 Middletown, Middlesex Co CT; ch JOSEPH ALSTON, ANN, PHEBE MIRANDA, LAVINIA, HEZEKIAH, HENRY; d 05 Jan 1872; Ref: Barbour's VR Middletown v2 p319, Early Fam of Wallingford p332, Hale Collection, Your Ancestors v3 #4 p352, Hist of Wallingford pp938,939.

HEZEKIAH - b 1793; m HANNAH ----- who was b 1796; Res Groton, New London Co CT; ch MARY, CALVIN, JOHN, SILAS, DANIEL, MARGARET; Ref: 1850 Census Groton CT Reel 432 #49 p346.

HEZEKIAH - b 12 Feb 1794 s/HEZEKIAH & MAHALA (WILCOX) WILCOX; d in infancy; Res Orange Co NY; Ref: Your Ancestors v10 #3 p1248.

HEZEKIAH - b 24 Dec 1809 Orange Co NY s/HEZEKIAH & MAHALA (WILCOX) WILCOX; m 09 Jan 1830 ELIZABETH MOORE who was b 30 Mar 1806; Res Bradford Co PA; ch GEORGE W, SAMUEL W, MARY, E WESTERN, SEVELLON A, RICHARD DORSON; d 22 Mar 1876 Ref: Hist of Bradford Co PA, 1850, 1860 Census Le Roy PA, Your Ancestors v10 #3 p1248 #4 pp1273,1274.

HEZEKIAH - b ca 1815 PA; m 27 Oct 1839 IL DEMEROUS WEST; d 27 Apr 1857 Schuyler Co IL; Ref: Nutmegger v11 #1 p105.

HEZEKIAH - b ca 1818 prob s/HEZEKIAH & HANNAH (-----) WILCOX; m 14 Jul 1839 Groton, New London Co CT PRUDENCE A PACKER who was b 1814 d/----- & MARY (-----) PACKER; ch CHAD; Ref: Barbour's VR v1 p61, 1850 Census Groton CT Reel 432 #49 p346.

HEZEKIAH - b 1822 s/BENJAMIN & SARAH ANN (-----) WILCOX; Ref: Your Ancestors v14 #1 p1618.

HEZEKIAH - b 23 Dec 1827 Westfield, Middlesex Co CT s/HEZEKIAH & RAMA (ROBERTS) WILCOX; d 16 Nov 1833; Ref: Early Fam of Wallingford p333, Your Ancestors v3 #4 p352, Hist of Wallingford p939.

HEZEKIAH - b 12 Oct 1832 Westfield, Middlesex Co CT s/ELISHA BACON & HEPZIBAH (CORNWELL) WILCOX; d 02 May 1860; Ref: Hale Coll, Early Fam of Wallingford p333, Your Ancestors v3 #5 p379, Hist of Wallingford p939.

HEZEKIAH - b 1848 Groton, New London Co CT s/WILLIAM B & MARY (-----) WILCOX; Ref: 1850 Census Groton CT Reel 432 #49 p 346.

HEZEKIAH - m 13 Jan 1874 Westerly, Washington Co RI MARTHA BRYANT; Ref: Arnold v11 p177.

HEZEKIAH - b 1867; d 16 Nov 1873 Middletown, Middlesex Co CT; Ref: Hale Coll.

HEZEKIAH L - s/NATHAN & NANCY (LEWIS) WILCOX; Res Danube, Herkimer Co NY; Ref: Wills of Herkimer Co NY 1839-1840 Book G p182 # 08113.

HEZEKIAH L - b 1807 NY; m NANCY M -----; Res Florence, Oneida Co NY; ch EMILY; Ref: 1850 Census Florence NY p200 Dw# 146.

HEZEKIAH RICHARDSON - b 1828 PA s/ISAAC & ELIZABETH (WILCOX) WILCOX; m ca 1849 POLLY ELIZABETH PARKHURST; Res Preston, New London Co CT & Le Roy, Bradford Co PA; ch NAOMI, HENRY; Ref: Your Ancestors v10 #3 p1248 #4 p1273, 1850,1860 Census Bradford Co PA.

HEZEKIAH WARNER - b 08 Jan 1785 s/ELIJAH Jr & LOIS (WARNER) WILCOX of Middletown, Middlesex Co CT; m 27 Nov 1806 ABIAH CLARK poss d/BENJAMIN & ABIAH (GOODRICH) CLARK; Res Westfield, Middlesex Co CT, Litchfield & Winfield, Herkimer Co NY; ch HOSEA GOODRICH, HEPZIBAH, OLIVE, ELIJAH W; d 31 Aug 1851; Ref: Your Ancestors v3 #6 pp401,402, Fiske Card File, Barbour's VR Middletown v2 p108, Deed Book of Herkimer Co NY v7 p181, v13 p623.

HIEL - b 11 Jan 1731 Killingworth, Middlesex Co CT s/THOMAS & MARTHA (-----) WILCOX; d 28 Jun 1733; Ref: Wilcox-Meigs p44, Barbour's VR Killingworth v2 p160.

HIEL - b 03 May 1734 Killingworth, Middlesex Co CT s/THOMAS & MARTHA (-----) WILCOX; m ca 1758 DEBORAH GILLETTE who d 13 Nov 1812; Res New Concord, Columbia Co NY; ch NATHANIEL, AARON, JESSE, THOMAS, JEHIEL, POLLY (WILCOX) GOTT, JOHN, LOIS/LOUISE (WILCOX) BLINN, JOSEPH; Served in Rev War; d 05 Dec 1822 Canaan, Columbia Co NY; Ref: Wilcox-Meigs pp65,66, Desc of Wm Wilcoxson pp43,58,59, Col Co NY Wills v4 p3, Copy of Will, Barbour's VR Killingworth v2 p160.

HILLENDA - b De Witt, Onondaga Co NY d/ASAHEL & HILLENDA (FOSTER) WILCOX; m PETER LANSING; Ref: Erwin W Fellows.

HIRA - b 29 Apr 1785 Barkhamsted, Litchfield Co CT s/JEHIEL & AZUBA (MOOR) WILCOX; Ref: Barbour's VR Barkhamsted v1 p55, See Jehiel, Desc of Wm Wilcoxson p189a.

HIRAM - b 20 Dec 1790 Halifax, Windham Co VT Twin with WILLIAM s/WILLIAM & RELEAF (-----) WILCOX; Ref: VT VR, Halifax Wilcox Fam mss.

HIRAM - b 1790 s/JOHN & MARY (CROSBY) WILCOX of Litchfield, Herkimer Co & Sardinia, Erie Co NY; d 1850 IL; Ref: Jane Smith.

HIRAM - b ca 1800; m SALLY MARIAH McCHESNEY who was b 1800 & d 28 Jan 1824 d/ROBERT & ELIZA (-----) McCHESNEY; Res Byron, Genesee Co NY; Ref: Tombstone Inscr of Genesee Co p44.

HIRAM - b 1802; m 13 Jul 1837 Granby, Hartford Co CT RHODA GRIFFIN who was b 1814; ch ADELINE; Ref: Barbour's VR Granby v1 pp24,234,235.

HIRAM - b 1802 England; Res Utica, Oneida Co NY; Ref: 1850 Census Utica NY p484 Dw# 1397.

HIRAM - b Jan 1803 VT s/ASHER SMITH & OLIVE (STURDEVANT) WILCOX of Shaftsbury, Bennington Co VT; m JULIA CLARK who was b 22 Feb 1811; d 1854 IN; Ref: Patricia Wetmore.

HIRAM - b 27 Oct 1804 Dartmouth, Bristol Co MA s/WILLIAM & RUTH (DURFEE) WILCOX; m 15 Sep 1824 LUCY STODDARD; m 25 Dec 1828 LUCY BROWN; m LORETTA MARSH; Res Palmyra, Wayne Co NY; Ref: Your Ancestors v10 #3 p1293.

HIRAM - m 15 Oct 1824 Le Roy, Genesee Co NY ----- HUNTLEY; Ref: 10,000 VR in Western NY p250.

HIRAM - m 02 Apr 1827 Plainfield, Otsego Co NY EMILY CHURCH; Ref: Marriages from Newspapers Otsego Co NY v1 p32.

HIRAM - b 1806 NY; ch ANDREW, JOHN, FRANCES, EUNICE, JAMES; Res Little Falls, Herkimer Co NY; Wool sorter; Ref: 1850 Census Little Falls NY p227 Dw# 398.

HIRAM - b 1815 Cortland Co NY s/THOMAS JAMES & LUCY (-----) WILCOX; Parents moved to Dryden, Lapeer Co MI 1837; Ref: Detroit Soc Gen Magazine v54 #2.

HIRAM - b 09 Aug 1816; m SOPHRONIA ----- who was b 02 Feb 1820 & d 03 Nov 1884 Plain Twnship, Franklin Co OH; ch CLINTON; d 18 Mar 1898; Ref: OH Cem Rec p138.

HIRAM - b 1818 NY s/----- & SARAH (-----) WILCOX; m MARY ----- who was b 1826 NY; Res Harford, Cortland Co NY; ch MARY J; Ref: 1850 Census Harford NY p422 Dw# 1421.

HIRAM - b 18/19 Jul 1818 s/EZRA & LAVICIA (HERRICK) WILCOX of East Bloomfield, Ontario Co NY; m 06 Jun 1844 CYNTHIA E LEETE who was b 01 Mar 1818/9 & d 02 Jan 1889 d/JOHN A & SARAH (STOREY) LEETE; Res Victor, Ontario Co NY; ch SARAH LEETE, CHARLES EDWARD, ALICE, MARY; d 20 May 1891 b bur Boughton Hill Cem Victor NY; Ref: Fam of Early Guilford p787, Your Ancestors v10 #2 pp1225,1226, Desc of Wm Wilcoxson p206.

HIRAM - b ca 1822 s/SPRAGUE & ELIZABETH (WILCOX) WILCOX; Res Smyrna, Chenango Co NY; Ref: Your Ancestors v3 #5 p375.

HIRAM - b af 1824 s/CORNISH & EMILY LOUISA (COUCH) WILCOX; d Sandisfield, Berkshire Co MA Dec ---- age 5 years; Ref: Sandisfield VR p109, Fiske Card File, See Cornish.

HIRAM - b 1830 NY s/ISAIAH & LYDIA (-----) WILCOX of Columbus, Chenango Co NY; Ref: 1850 Census Columbus NY p279 Dw# 2126.

HIRAM - b 03 Dec 1831 Barton, Orleans Co VT s/JEHIEL Jr & RUTH (GAINES) WILCOX; Ref: Desc of Wm Wilcoxson p189a.

HIRAM - m ALISON ROSILLA BURROWS who was b 22 Jun 1832 d/EDA & JANE (SEELEY) BURROWS of Moreau, Saratoga Co NY; Res Glen Falls, Warren Co NY; ch ADDA MARIE, CHARLES BURROWS, WALTER, IRENE; Ref: Robert Burrows Desc p862.

HIRAM - b 1839 NY s/LEVI WILCOX of Crown Point, Essex Co NY; Ref: 1850 Census Crown Point NY p360 Dw# 180.

HIRAM - m KATHERINE SLEMMER who was b 1844 & d 1901 bur Woodlawn Cem Schodak, Rensselaer Co NY; Ref: VR Town of Schodak pt 2 p88.

HIRAM - b 1851 NY s/JOSEPH & MELVINA (-----) WILCOX of Gerry, Chautauqua Co NY; Ref: 1860 Census Gerry NY p61 Dw# 65.

HIRAM - b 13 Oct 1893 s/SILAS & ELVIRA JOANNE (LAMBERT) WILCOX; m NELLIE COOK; d 30 Oct 1955 bur St George, N B Canada; Ref: Desc of Charles Dyer Wilcox p2.

HIRAM B - b 1825 NY; Res Hartwick, Otsego Co NY with THOMAS & CLARISSA (ELLSWORTH) WILCOX; Wagonmaker; Ref: 1850 Census Hartwick NY p221 Dw# 276.

HIRAM B - b 1843 NY; Res Greenbush, Rensselaer Co NY; Ref: 1860 Census Greenbush NY p297.

HIRAM K - of Easton, Washington Co NY; m 17 Jul 1850 FRANCES VANDENBURGH at Easton; Ref: NYG&BR v119 p168.

HIRAM K - of Saratoga Co NY enl 19 Nov 1861 77th Rgt Co I; disch 08 Dec 1862; Ref: Hist of Saratoga Co NY p282.

HIRAM LEROY - b 25 Jul 1861 s/ISAIAH CLARK & SALLY (HENRY) WILCOX of Rockdale, Crawford Co PA; d 05 Nov 1862 bur Chapinville Cem Crawford Co PA; Ref: Dennis Davis.

HIRAM M - s/ERASTUS & MARGARET (KING?) WILCOX of Washington, Madison & Ontario Cos NY; m 11 Mar 1830 Dearborn Co IN MARY ANN CURE; Ref: Janet Armbrust.

HIRAM RUE - b 27 Feb 1819 s/DAVID & SARAH (RUE) WILCOX of Manlius, Onondaga Co NY; m 05 May 1840 ELIZA AUSTIN; ch FRANCES, CLARA L; d 18 Mar 1851; Ref: Your Ancestors v3 #11 & 12 p 474, Gifford Wilcox, Desc of Wm Wilcoxson p126.

HIRAM S - b 07 Sep 1807 s/FREEMAN & CLARISSA (SOUTHWORTH) WILCOX; m MARIA VAN ETTEN or MARIA LANGFORD; ch FREEMAN N; Res Albany, Bradford Co PA; Ref: Pioneers of Bradford Co PA p310, Your Ancestors v13 #1 p1513, #2 p1538.

HIRAM SELDEN - b 12 Feb 1819 Madison, New Haven Co CT s/ABEL & ANNA (FIELD) WILCOX; m 17 Apr 1842

Guilford, New Haven Co CT FIDELIA MARILLA DOWD who was b 15 Apr 1824; ch ELLEN ELIZA, SELDEN SYLVESTER, FRANKLIN FIELD; Ref: Wilcox-Meigs pp92,109, Fam of Early Guilford pp1213,1215, Barbour's VR Madison v2 p30, Guilford v2 p353.

HIRAM T - b 08 Oct 1886 s/CHARLES EZRA & MARTHA (TIFFANY) WILCOX; m 27 Aug 1914 HELENE MILLER; ch JOHN C; Ref: Your Ancestors v10 #2 p1226, Desc of Wm Wilcoxson p206.

HIRAM THOMAS - b 1833 Great Valley, Cattaraugus Co NY s/SEYMOUR & SALLY (SARGENT) WILCOX; d 186- Tradition says killed in Civil War; Ref: Dennis Davis, 1850 Census Great Valley NY p149 Dw# 64.

HIRAM WEST - b 08 Feb 1864 Deep Cove, N B Canada s/WILLIAM & JANE (DRISCOLL) WILCOX; m EVA GILPATRICK who was b 23 Sep 1873 & d 30 May 1895; m FLORENCE MAY PYNE who was b 12 Mar 1878 East Boston, Suffolk Co MA & d 23 Sep 1956 d/NAAMAN & JANE (GERMAIN) PYNE; ch ELMER NAAMAN, EDITH ALVA, HELENE JANE; d 12 Apr 1949 bur Castalia, N B Canada; Ref: Desc of Charles Dyer Wilcox pp 11,12.

HODIJAH BAYLIES - b 30 Mar 1832 New Bedford, Bristol Co MA s/BENJAMIN & PATTY (BROWNELL) WILCOX; Ref: Rep Men of Southeastern MA v2 p1081, Your Ancestors v14 #1 p1631.

HOLDER NELSON - b 07 Jul 1813; m 13 Sep 1835 Tiverton, Newport Co RI BETSEY HART who was b 09 Mar 1814 & d 29 Apr 1896 Tiverton RI bur Cem #1; ch HANNAH SEABURY, MARY ALICE, FREDERICK, EDWARD; d 21 Oct 1887; Ref: NEH&GR v67 pp507,508, Arnold v4 pt7 p57, v7 p583, Gen of RI Fam v2 p596.

HOLLIS - b 25 Jul 1810 Surry, Cheshire Co NH Twin with HORACE s/GAYLORD & ORINDA (CARPENTER) WILCOX; m 29 Nov 1832 THANKFUL ROBBINS who was b 25 Apr 1814 & d 22 Jan 1885 70yr 8mo 27da d/JEREMIAH ROBBINS; Res Surry NH; Town clerk & treasurer; ch SARAH LORINDA, GEORGE HORACE, WILLIAM WALLACE, CHARLES ALONZO, EMILY JANE, ALICE LOVISA; d 04 May 1887 76yr 9mo 9da; Ref: Hist of Surry NH pp83,381,946,948, 949.

HOLLIS BRADFORD - b 28 Sep 1881 Surry, Cheshire Co NH s/WILLIAM WALLACE & MARY CATHRINE (MONROE) WILCOX; Res Boston, Suffolk Co MA 1923; Ref: History of Surry NH p950.

HOMER - b 1820 s/LAWRENCE & LAURA (PALMER) WILCOX of Perinton, Monroe Co NY; ch CHESTER E; Ref: Desc of Wm Wilcoxson p162.

HOMER - b ca 1825; m CATHERINE M HUBBARD; Res Sandusky, Erie Co OH; Ref: Nutmegger v9 #1 p106.

HOMER - b ca 1838 s/AUSTIN SCRANTON & HANNAH (BIDWELL) WILCOX; d in infancy; Ref: Your Ancestors v3 #1 p281.

HOMER - b 1843 Hobart & Harpersfield, Delaware Co NY s/SAMUEL & LAURA (TAYLOR) WILCOX; Ref: Your Ancestors v4 #7&8 p563, 1850 Census Harpersfield, NY p175 Dw# 282.

HOMER - b 1847 NY s/HENRY & LOUISA (-----) WILCOX of Parish, Oswego Co NY; Ref: 1850 Census Parish NY p4 Dw# 50.

HOMER - b ca 1880 s/LUTHER H & JEWELL (TRIPP) WILCOX; Res Springwater, Livingston Co NY; Ref: Your Ancestors v10 #2 p1224.

HOMER HELSON - b 15 Oct 1893 Abilene, Dickinson Co KS s/FRANK WRIGHT & PRISCILLA (KRIEDER) WILCOX; Ref: Desc of Wm Wilcoxson p141.

HOMER W - b 1845 NY s/WILLIAM & JANE (-----) WILCOX of Petersburgh, Rensselaer Co NY; Ref: 1850 Census Petersburgh NY p195 Dw# 309.

HOPE ALMIRA - b 05 Feb 1804 Voluntown, New London Co CT d/HENRY & HANNAH (MORGAN) WILCOX; Ref: Barbour's VR Voluntown v1 p115.

HOPSON - b 1739/1740 Exeter, Washington Co RI s/ROBERT & CATHERINE (LILLIBRIDGE) WILCOX; m 10 Dec 1761 Richmond, Washington Co RI ELIZABETH HELWAY/HOLWAY who was b 1745 & d Aug 1818 d/GEORGE HOLWAY; Res Smyrna, Chenango Co NY 1795; Quaker Preacher; ch LILLIBRIDGE/THOMAS L, ROBERT, JOHN, RUSSELL, HAZARD, BETSEY, SUSAN, HANNAH, CATHERINE; d Apr 1822 Earlville/Smyrna, Chenango Co NY Will Probated 28 Apr 1823 Book B 40; Ref: 1774 Census RI, Hist of Chenango Co NY p466, Arnold v5 pt6 p21, Chenango Co Cem p9, Index to Wills of Chenango Co NY v1, Cutters Western NY v3 p1439, Your Ancestor v3 31 p278.

HORACE - b 1776-1795; Res New Hartford, Hartford Co CT; 3 sons; Ref: 1820 Census CT.

HORACE - b 1791-1800; Res Westmoreland, Oneida Co NY; 4 sons & 3 daus; Ref: 1840 Census Oneida Co NY.

HORACE - b 09 Sep 1793 E Berlin, Hartford Co CT s/JOSIAH & HULDAH (SAVAGE) WILCOX; m SOPHIA LOMBARD who was b ca 1796 VT; ch FRANCIS, JULIA, HELEN, EDWARD; Res Apr 1819 Brattleboro, Windham Co VT; Ref: MUH p752, CT Nutmeggers Who Migrated p264, Annals of Brattleboro VT p369.

HORACE - of Stockbridge, Berkshire Co MA m 04 Nov 1824 LOUISANNA STOW New Hartford, Litchfield Co CT; Ref: Barbour's VR New Hartford v3 p11.

HORACE - b ca 1802 CT s/NORMAN & REBECCA (CASE) WILCOX; Res OH; d 18 Apr 1883; Ref: Nutmegger v13 #2 p288.

HORACE - b 10 Jun 1806 Orwell, Addison Co VT s/EBENEZER & THANKFUL (STEVENS) WILCOX; m MARIA HADDOCK; d 10 Nov 1839; Ref: Your Ancestors v3 #2 p301.

HORACE - b ca 1806 CT; Res Lima, Livingston Co NY 1850 with WILLIAM ARNOLD fam; Ref: 1850 Census Lima NY p198 Dw# 194.

HORACE - b 25 Jul 1810 Surry, Cheshire Co NH Twin with HOLLIS s/GAYLORD & ORINDA (CARPENTER) WILCOX; d 10 May 1811; Ref: Hist of Surry NH p946.

HORACE - b 18 Aug 1810 RI; m 11 Mar 1831 Westerly, Washington Co RI HANNAH KENYON who was b 1813 Richmond RI & d 23 Apr 1886; Res Stonington, New London Co CT & Watch Hill, Charlestown, Hopkinton, & Quonochontaug, Washington Co RI; ch SARAH FRANCIS, EUNICE ANN, ISAAC FRANCIS, CHARLES H, CHARLES B, HARRIET A, MARTHA B, HANNAH CAROLINE; d 18 Jul 1895; bur Old Hopkinton Cem Ref: Arnold v5 p2, 1850 Census Stonington CT Reel 432 #48 p281, C Douglass Alves Sr.

HORACE - b 1819 s/FRANCIS & POLLY (WEEKS) WILCOX; m MARTHA MAYNARD; Res Virgil Cortland Co NY; Ref: Your Ancestors v13 #2 p1539, v4 #1 p1617.

HORACE - b 1832 Wyoming Co NY; m MARY H ----- who was b 1837 Montgomery Co NY; ch MARILDA, EVALINA N, MARTHA, EDGAR M; publisher of Wyoming Advertiser 1853/1854; Res 5th Ward Buffalo, Erie

Co NY 1875; Ref: Hist of Wyoming Co NY p244, Alice Wiatr.

HORACE - m AMANDA McCURTY who was b ca 1830 d/THOMAS & CATHERINE (DOTY) McCURTY; Res Woodstock MI; Ref: Doty Fam Gen p560.

HORACE - m PHOEBE LaMUNYON Tiverton, Newport Co RI; m MARY WHITE LaMUNYON 08 Jul 1847 Tiverton RI; Ref: Iowa Surnames v3 p695, Arnold v7 p583.

HORACE - b 1849 OH s/OSCAR & LURA (GILLETTE) WILCOX of Avon, Lorain Co OH; ch EDNA; d 1883; Ref: 1850 Census Lorain Co OH, Carol Wood.

HORACE - b 1858 s/----- & MARGARET (-----) WILCOX; d 14 Apr 1864 age 6; bur Andover, Allegany Co NY; Ref: Yesteryears v2 38 p39.

HORACE - b 17 Dec 1887 s/BOARDMAN HUBBARD & EMMA (OLINGER) WILCOX of Butler Co KS; d 1915; Ref: Desc of Wm Wilcox p131.

HORACE - b 07 Oct 1893 Meriden, New Haven Co CT s/GEORGE HORACE & NETTIE BARKER (CURTIS) WILCOX; Ref: MUH p761.

HORACE ABEL - b 14 Apr 1854 Essex, Middlesex Co CT s/JOHN ELLIOTT & ZYLPHA LUCRETIA (SNOW) WILCOX; m 13 Sep 1876 LAURA AMANDA PARKER who was b 13 Jul 1855 & d 10 Feb 1886; m 04 Jul 1886 HARRIET A POST who was b Jun 1862 & d 29 Jan 1887; Res Essex CT; ch RUSSELL CLIFFORD, REGINALD CONWAY, GEORGE ELLIOTT, GRACE ETHEL; Ref: Wilcox-Meigs pp110,124, Fam of Early Guilford p1215.

HORACE ALEXANDER - b 06 Mar 1807 VT s/JANNA & CANDACE (GOODELL) WILCOX; m SALLY HOWELL; Res Ludlow, Windsor Co VT; Ref: VT VR, Your Ancestors v4 #9&10 p545.

HORACE B - b 1821; m FLAVIA ------ who was b 1823; Res Portland, Middlesex Co CT; ch WILLIAM BARTLETT; Ref: Barbour's VR Portland v1 p267.

HORACE BEACH - b 26 Sep 1862 s/LUCIUS FITCH & ELLEN MARIA (BELDEN) WILCOX; m 14 Dec 1897 LOTTIE MAY WARD; Ref: Your Ancestors v3 #7&8 pp425,426.

HORACE CORNWELL - b 26 Jan 1824 Westfield, Middlesex Co CT s/ELISHA BACON & HEPZIBAH (CORNWELL) WILCOX; m 09 Aug 1848 Middletown CT CHARLOTTE A SMITH d/JABEZ SMITH; m 31 May

1851/1855   ELLEN M PARKER d/EDMUND PARKER; ch by 1st wife ELLA AUGUSTA, GEORGINE, WALTER, ALLYN, GEORGE HORACE, DWIGHT P; ch by 2nd wife HORACE, FLORENCE CORNWELL; Ref: MUH pp760,761, Early Fam of Wallingford p333, Your Ancestors v3 #5 p379, Barbour's VR Middletown v4 p38, Hist of Wallingford p939.

HORACE D - m ELIZABETH A HESSIN who was b 15 Jan 1839 & d 25 Sep 1896; bur Maple Grove Cem Granville, Licking Co OH; Ref: OH Cem Rec p207.

HORACE E - b 1832 Geauga Co OH s/NATHAN BENJAMIN & SAMANTHA (BROOKS) WILCOX; m MARY -----; d Dec 1862? Fort Smith, Sebastain Co AR; Ref: Dan Williams.

HORACE FRANKLIN - b 17 Oct 1810 E Guilford, New Haven Co CT s/ELIJAH & LOIS (FIELD) WILCOX; m 06 Apr 1837 HENRIETTA FRANCES SHEPARD who was b 20 Mar 1810 & d 04 Nov 1890 d/WILLIAM J SHEPARD of NYC; Res OH; ch FRANCES LOUISA, MARY MATILDA, ANNA AMELIA, HENRY LUDLOW; d 27 May 1848; Ref: Wilcox-Meigs pp72,89,90, Saybrook Colony VR p415, Fam of Early Guilford p1210.

HORACE G - b 27 Aug 1870 s/SILAS AMES & HENRIETTA A (FURMAN) WILCOX of Ridgefield Park, Bergen Co NJ; m MAUDE JOHNSON; Ref: Your Ancestors v11 #3 p1272, Judith Schlitt.

HORACE GEORGE - b 16 Jul 1818 Smithfield, Bradford Co PA s/STEPHEN & POLLY (ALLEN) WILCOX; m 31 Dec 1840 Smithfield PA MARY ELIZABETH WARREN who was b 27 Aug 1816 NY & d 23 Jul 1880 Kearney, Buffalo Co NE; Res Athens twnshp, Bradford Co PA & Pine twnshp, Lycoming Co PA went west; Lumberman; ch GEORGE HENRY, WILLIAM B, FRANCIS E, FRANKLIN, ALBERT S, ALICE E, FREEMAN, NORMAN, SUSAN; d 26 Oct 1882 Kearney, NE; Ref: Halifax VT Wilcox Fam mss, Wilcox Genealogy p7.

HORACE H - of Middletown, Middlesex Co CT m 1862? ELVIRA L LANE of Killingworth, Middlesex Co CT; Ref: Barbour's VR Killingworth v3 p410.

HORACE HALL - b 17 May 1827 Middletown, Middlesex Co CT s/GILES & LUCY (CLARK) WILCOX; Ref: Barbour's VR Middletown v3 p32, See Giles.

HORACE HENDERSON - b ca 1820 Adrian, Lenawee Co MI; Ref: Desc of Wm Wilcoxson p335.

HORACE HUBBARD - b 21 Nov 1821 Haddam, Middlesex Co CT s/LYMAN & EMILY (HUBBARD) WILCOX; m OLIVIA RICHARDSON of La Harpe, Hancock Co IL who was b 27 Aug 1820 near Zanesville, Muskingum Co OH & d 26 Oct 1904 Glendora, Los Angeles Co CA; Res Hancock Co IL & Clifford twnshp, Butler Co KS; ch ORPHA, BOARDMAN HUBBARD, LEWIS, ORSOVA, MARY OLIVIA, ARTHUR; d 28 Aug 1808 Clifford KS; Ref: Your Ancestors v4 #1&2 p497, Desc of Wm Wilcoxson p131.

HORACE J - b 1796-1802 CT prob s/HAZARD WILCOX; prob m EDNA -----; m RACHEL ----- who was b 1812 NY; Res Thomastown PA, Leon, Cattaraugus Co NY & Collins, Erie Co NY; ch by 1st wife JOHN G; ch by 2nd wife OLIVER, WILLIAM H, JAMES M, LUCINDA ESTHER, CHARLES D, HARRIET, EDWIN, LYDIA M; Land records show that he inherited land in Whitingham, Windham Co VT from his grandfather THOMAS WILCOX of Rowe, Franklin Co MA; Ref: Alice Wiatr, Iris W Baird.

HORACE MONROE - b 19 Nov 1836 s/ELBRIDGE GERRY & LUCY (SMITH) WILCOX; d 24 Dec 1839; Ref: Your Ancestors v3 #9&10 p452.

HORACE MUNSON - b 08 Oct 1840 s/ELBRIDGE GERRY & LUCY (SMITH) WILCOX; Ref: Your Ancestors v3 #9&10 p452.

HORACE N - b 1818 NY; Res Buffalo, Erie Co NY 1850; Lawyer; Ref: Alice Wiatr.

HORACE NOBLE - b 13 Jul 1852 WI s/ORLANDO B & NANCY ELIZABETH (NOBLE) WILCOX; Ref: Desc of Thomas Noble p463.

HORACE P - b 1819 Cortland Co NY; m MARY ----- who was b 1821 Tompkins Co NY; Hotel keeper Cortlandville, Cortland Co NY; Ref: 1850 Census Cortland NY p345.

HORACE S - b 15 Feb 1817 Chester, Hampden Co MA s/ASA & RELIEF (COLTON) WILCOX; m MARY SMITH; Ref: Fiske Card File, Your Ancestors v3 #9&10 p452.

HORACE TITUS - b 28 Aug 1816 Westbrook, Middlesex Co CT s/AMOS TODD & CYNTHIA (BUSHNELL) WILCOX; m 09 Sep 1839 Saybrook, Middlesex Co CT HARRIET D PIERSON who was b 15 May 1817 & d 05 Apr 1881; ch HARRIET ELIZABETH, EMILY E, ELVIRAH RUSSELL, RICHARD WILLIAM, HORACE; d 03 Jun 1893; Ref: Saybrook Colony VR p127, Fam of Early

Guilford pp1203,1205, Westbrook 1st Cong Church Rec p197, Barbour's VR Saybrook v2 p90.

HORACE W - b 1825/6 Onondaga Co NY; m 12 Jun 1846 Stockton, Chautauqua Co NY ESTHER TOTMAN by Elder Harvey Totman; m 04 Jul 1849 Pomfret, Chautauqua Co NY JULIA TOTMAN who was b 1826; Wagonmaker; Enlisted 16 Sep 1862 Dunkirk, Chautauqua Co NY Co E NY; Killed 03 May 1863 Chancellorsville VA; 5 ch incl MONROE, JUDSON; Ref: Alice Wiatr, 1850, 1855 Census Stockton NY, Adj General Report NY p906, 19th Cent Deaths Reported in Fredonia Censor p596.

HORACE WILDER - b 04 Jan 1876 s/AARON & HELEN M (CLEVELAND) WILCOX; d 13 Mar 1912; Ref: Wilcox-Meigs p118.

HORATIO - b ca 1817 Madison, New Haven Co CT s/HEUSTEN & JULIA (CRAMPTON) WILCOX; m 05 Sep 1844 Saybrook, Middlesex Co CT CAROLINE A CADWELL who was b 1824; ch MARY H, CAROLINE E, ELBERT HORATIO; d 06 Apr 1869; Ref: Saybrook Colony VR p133, Wilcox-Meigs pp87,105, Fam of Early Guilford pp1212,1214, Barbour's VR Saybrook v2 p110, Desc of Wm Wilcoxson p264.

HORATIO - b 1841 NY s/LYSANDER BYRAM & RACHEL (CHILDS) WILCOX of Napoli, Cattaraugus Co NY; Ref: 1850 Census Napoli NY p57 Dw# 43, See Lysander Byram.

HORATIO NELSON - b 07 Jul 1809 Killingworth, Middlesex Co CT s/AARON & MABEL (LORD) WILCOX; Res Twinsburg, Summit Co OH; Ref: Lord Fam Gen p289, Wilcox-Meigs p81, Your Ancestors v3 #3 p321, Barbour's VR Killingworth v2 p14.

HORATIO NELSON - b 11 Sep 1843; d 18 Aug 1890 Tiverton, Newport Co RI; Ref: NEH&GR v67 p508, Gen of RI Fam v2 p596.

HORATIO R - b 25 Sep 1819 Chatham, Columbia Co NY s/OLIVER & CYNTHIA (BEEBE) WILCOX; m 20 Aug 1845 Ashland NY SARAH M KINSLEY who d 1908 d/HENRY KINSLEY; Res Middletown, Orange Co NY; ch HENRY KINSLEY, OLIVIA; d 1909 Middletown NY; Ref: Hist of Orange Co NY, Wilcox-Meigs p121.

HORATIO S - b 31 Jan 1855 s/GEORGE S & CLARA C (WILLIAMS) WILCOX; m 16 Jun 1896 CLARA BROSIUS; Ref: Your Ancestors v9 #3 p1152.

HORTON - b 20 Apr 1828 s/ABNER & SARAH (HORTON) WILCOX; Ref: Desc of Wm Wilcoxson p141.

HORTON - b 16 May 1855 s/ANDREW JACKSON & CAROLINE (MASTIN) WILCOX; Ref: Desc of Wm Wilcoxson p141.

HOSEA - b 10 May 1730 s/JOSEPH & MARY (BUTTOLPH) WILCOX; m 26 Feb 1751 Simsbury, Hartford Co CT HANNAH GRIFFIN who d 24 Jan 1762; m SARAH -----; Res Simsbury, Norfolk, Litchfield Co CT; ch by 1st wife HANNAH, HOSEA, HULDAH, MARY; ch by 2nd wife PHILIP, ELIZABETH, PHILURA, EUNICE, JOSEPH; Ref: Wilcox-Meigs p68, 2nd Boat v7 #1 p28, Nutmegger v10 #2 p213, Barbour's VR Simsbury TM4 p185, Norfolk v1 p3.

HOSEA Jr - b 16 Jul 1754 Simsbury, Hartford Co CT s/HOSEA & HANNAH (GRIFFIN) WILCOX; m 02 Nov 1774 Norfolk, Litchfield Co CT ABIGAIL GILLS who was b 1750 & d 29 Mar 1822; Res OH; ch JOSEPH, MOSES, RHODA, SYLVESTER, DIANTHA, ZYLPHA, FRANCIS, GRIFFIN; Founder of Austinburg, Ashtabula Co OH; Rev War; bur Middlebury Cem Akron, Summit Co OH; Ref: Soldiers bur in OH, DAR, Barbour's VR Norfolk v1 pp3,7,10, Wilcox-Meigs p68.

HOSEA GOODRICH - b 1809 VT s/HEZEKIAH W & ABIAH (CLARK) WILCOX; m ELIZA J ----- who was b 1812 NH; Res Leon, Cattaraugus Co NY; ch JOHNSON, ELMIRA, SARAH, TIMOTHY, FRANCIS; Ref: Your Ancestors v3 #6 p402, 1850 Census Leon NY p 49 Dw# 190.

HOSMER H - b 10 Sep 1847 Napoli, Cattaraugus Co NY s/LANSING H & MIRANDA (HOLMES) WILCOX; m 12 May 1875 ELLA S BURT who was b 17 Sep 1854 & d 19 Feb 1906 d/JAIRUS N & EMMA (BIGELOW) BURT; ch BURT L, ITHA MAY, WALTER J, CARRIE MIRANDA, CHARLES ALVIN, HELEN JOSEPHINE; d 27 Aug 1911 Little Valley, Cattaraugus Co NY; Ref: Cutter's Western NY v1 pp257,258, 1850 Census Napoli NY p63 Dw# 138, 1860 Census Napoli NY p60.

HOWARD - b 1834 s/AARON & ELECTA (-----) WILCOX of Bainbridge, Chenango Co NY; Ref: 1850 Census Chenango Co NY.

HOWARD - b 11 Mar 1835 Catskill, Greene Co NY s/JUDSON & LAURA (GOODRICH) WILCOX; m 12 May 1859 SARAH CLARKE d/ZEBA & MARTHA JANE (BOGARDUS) CLARKE; ch HIRAM; d 11 Feb 1915 Catskill NY; Ref:

Your Ancestors v4 #7&8 p564, 1850 Census Catskill NY p359 Dw# 322.

HOWARD - b 1854 OH s/PELEG & MARGRETT (-----) WILCOX; Res Coe, Isabell Co MI; Parents b NY; Ref: 1860 Census Isabell Co MI, Fiske Card File.

HOWARD DEXTER - b 22 Jun 1881 s/JONATHAN BRENTON SHAW & FANNY ELLEN (IRONS) WILCOX of Cambridge, Middlesex Co MA; m EDITH CLINES d/DOROTHY B CLINES; Ref: Robert Burrows Desc v2 p1482.

HOWARD OSCAR - b 10 Jan 1883 Abilene, Dickinson Co KS s/FRANK WRIGHT & PRISCILLA (KRIEDER) WILCOX; Ref: Desc of Wm Wilcoxson p141.

HOWELL - b 1832 NY s/NATHAN & REBECCA (-----) WILCOX of Minisink, Orange Co NY; Ref: 1850 Census Minisink NY p265 Dw# 337.

HOWLAND - b 20 Jun 1768 Dartmouth, Bristol Co MA s/THOMAS & CATHERINE (HOWLAND) WILCOX; m 11 Mar 1815 Dartmouth MA SUSANNAH ALLEN; ch EDWARD ALLEN; Ref: Dartmouth VR p302,546, Your Ancestors v12 #2 p1452.

HOYT HAMILTON - b 19 Oct 1820 s/ERASTUS & MARTHA/PATTY (HAMILTON) WILCOX of Susquehanna Co PA; Ref: Your Ancestors v3 #11&12 p471.

HUBBARD AVERY - b 29 Mar 1833/4 or May 1837 s/CALVIN PARDEE & HARRIETT (HUBBARD) WILCOX; m ELIZABETH POWERS who was b 03 May 1837 & d 24 Nov 1907; Res Pittsfield & Lagrange, Lorain Co OH; ch EDWARD F, BIRDIE ELIZABETH, AVERY HUBBARD; Ref: Your Ancestors v9 #3 p1153, Desc of Wm Wilcoxson p194.

HUBERT - b Jan 1879 De Witt, Onondaga Co NY s/ORLANDO KING & MARY (WALTER) WILCOX; m RUTH -----; d af 1910; Ref: Erwin W Fellows.

HULDAH - b 21 Jan 1725/6 Middletown, Middlesex Co CT d/JOHN & MARY (WARNER) WILCOX; d 15 Aug 1742; Ref: NEH&GR v14 p138, Nutmegger v4 #3 p330, Barbour's VR Middletown LR2 p21.

HULDAH - b 14 Oct 1739 d/JOSIAH & ELIZABETH (HUBBELL) WILCOX; m JAMES COE Stratford, Fairfield Co CT; Ref: Wilcox-Meigs p57, Hist of Stratford Fam p1348, Cutter's Northern NY v2 p655.

HULDAH - b 16 May 1748 Dartmouth, Bristol Co MA d/JABEZ & HANNAH (HART) WILCOX; Ref: Dartmouth VR p302, Little Compton Fam p771.

HULDAH - b 24 May 1748 Middletown, Middlesex Co CT d/DANIEL & SARAH (WHITE) WILCOX; m JEREMIAH BACON; m 13 Oct 1768 Cromwell, Middlesex Co CT JOSEPH PORTER; Ref: MUH p749, Cutter's CT Fam v2 p65, ECM v2 p92, Hist of Berlin CT p101, Barbour's VR Middletown v1 p102.

HULDAH - d/ELISHA of Middletown, Middlesex Co CT m 09 Nov 1761 Glastonbury, Hartford Co CT JOHN STEVENS of Glastonbury; Ref: Barbour's VR Glastonbury v2 p16.

HULDAH - b 17-- d/GEORGE & ROSE/ANN (-----) WILCOX; m SAMUEL WILSON JACQUES Hopkinton, Washington Co RI; ch MERCY; Ref: RI Roots v8 #1 p12, Nutmegger v6 #3 pp390,391.

HULDAH - b 16 Aug 1751 Goshen, Litchfield Co CT d/GIDEON & MARY (BLANCHARD) WILCOX; Ref: Barbour's VR Goshen v1 p261, See Gideon.

HULDAH - b 14 Apr 1756 Simsbury, Hartford Co CT d/HOSEA & HANNAH (GRIFFIN) WILCOX; Ref: Wilcox-Meigs p68.

HULDA/HULDAH - b 01 Feb 1765 Norwich, New London Co CT d/SAMUEL & LOIS (COGSWELL) WILCOX; Ref: Barbour's VR Norwich v2 p350.

HULDAH - m 01 Feb 1787 ABNER PIERCE who was b 04 Oct 1761 & d 28 Jun 1851 s/LEVI & BATHSHEBA (BABBETT) PIERCE;_Ref: NEH&GR v22 p429.

HULDAH - b 23 Dec 1766 Torrington, Litchfield Co CT d/ASAHEL & MARY (COE) WILCOX; Ref: Desc of Wm Wilcoxson p27, Barbour's VR Torrington v1 p78.

HULDAH - had dau ELIZABETH MOREHOUSE who was b 25 Jan 1788 Torrington, Litchfield Co CT; Ref: Barbour's VR Torrington v1 p78.

HULDAH - m 01 Feb 1789 Conway, Franklin Co MA JOSEPH RICE; Ref: Fiske Card File.

HULDAH - b 13 Jul 1785 d/JAMES & EUNICE (VICKERY) WILCOX; d 30 Sep 1785 Bridport, Addison Co VT; Ref: Your Ancestors v3 #9&10 p449, Wisconsin Fam Jun 1940 p42, Texas Society DAR Roster v4 p2287.

HULDAH - b 11 Oct 1789 E Berlin, Hartford Co CT d/JOSIAH & HULDAH (SAVAGE) WILCOX; m af 1816 REUBEN NORTH; d 11 Sep 1865; Ref: MUH p752.

HULDAH - b 24 Oct 1792 d/JAMES & EUNICE (VICKERY) WILCOX; m 26 Dec 1810 EPHRAIM STONE who d 07 Mar 1841 Bridport VT; d 18 Mar 1841; Ref: Your Ancestors v3 #9&10 p449, Wisconsin Families Jun 1940 pp41-43, Wilcox-Meigs p83, Texas Society DAR Roster v4 p2287, Desc of Wm Wilcox p 118.

HULDAH - b 24 Oct 1795 Middletown, Middlesex Co CT d/LUTHER & HULDAH (PULSIFER) WILCOX; Ref: Barbour's VR Middletown v3 p23, See Luther.

HULDAH - b 19 Dec 1808 Killingworth, Middlesex Co CT d/MOSES & HULDAH (LORD) WILCOX; m LEWIS ALLING; Res Twinsburg, Summit Co OH; Ref: Lord Gen p289, Wilcox-Meigs p81, Your Ancestors v3 #2 p301, Barbour's VR Killingworth v2 p14.

HULDAH - b ca 1810 Bridport, Addison Co VT d/JAMES & MARY (WILCOX) WILCOX; m CALEB INGELSBY; Ref: Wilcox-Meigs p100.

HULDAH - b 12 Apr 1813 Canton, Hartford Co CT d/ALANSON & IRENE (JOHNSON) WILCOX; d be 1820; Ref: Pioneers of Madison Co NY p280.

HULDAH - b 1814 d/THOMAS & LYDIA prob (DALRYMPLE) WILCOX; d 21 Aug 1835 Hinesburg VT; Ref: VT VR, See Thomas.

HULDAH - b 16 Jul 1820 Lenox, Madison Co NY d/ALANSON & IRENE (JOHNSON) WILCOX; m 10 Nov 1841 Clockville, Chenango Co NY B FRANKLIN CHAPMAN; ch ELMER, MATTIE, STEPHEN; Ref:10,000 VR of Central NY, Hist of Chenango Co NY pp734,735, Pioneers of Madison Co NY p280.

HULDAH - b 17 Nov 1824 Westerly, Washington Co RI d/GEORGE S & ANN MARIA (-----) WILCOX; Ref: Arnold v5 p145.

HULDAH - b 30 Apr 1826 Floyd, Oneida Co NY d/ELEAZER CURTIS & CYNTHIA (NOBLE) WILCOX; m 25 Nov 1850 WILLARD F MARVIN; Res Shell Rock, Freeborn Co MN; Ref: A Wilcox Book p20, Gen of Thomas Noble p448.

HULDAH - b 1833; m JAMES HILL 30 Jul 1848 Otselic, Chenango Co NY; Res Lebanon, Madison Co NY; Ref; VR of Chenango Co NY p203.

HULDAH - b 1841 Bridport, Addison Co VT; d 10 Mar 1841; Ref; Your Ancestors v3 #9710 p449, Wisconsin Fam Jun 1940 pp41-43, Wilcox-Meigs p83.

HULDAH ANN - b 20 Jan 1810 d/WEEDEON & MAHALA (-----) WILCOX; d 11 Feb 1834 Avon, Lorain Co OH; Ref: Tombstone Inscr, Carol Wood.

HULDAH ANN - m 03 Nov 1861 HENRY BEECHER BULLARD who was b 09 Apr 1839 s/JOSEPH & OLIVIA P (HILL) BULLARD; ch LOVISA IRENE, ANNIE LAURA, HENRY CLIFFORD, AGNES OLIVIA, FRANKLIN EUGENE, MARY AUGUSTA; Ref: Snow-Estes Ancestry v2 p256.

HULDAH ELIZA - b 10 Oct 1838 Painesville, Lake Co OH d/AARON & ELIZA JANE (MORLEY) WILCOX; Ref: Wilcox-Meigs p98, 1850 Census Painesville OH Reel 259 p181.

HULDAH M - b ca 1805 d/DAVID & HULDAH (PORTER) WILCOX; m 15 Apr 1830 Haddam, Middlesex Co CT LEANDER R BLACKLEY/BLATCHLEY of Killingworth, Middlesex Co CT; Ref: Barbour's VR Haddam v1 p19, Your Ancestors v4 #1&2 p498, Desc of Wm Wilcoxson p132. *probably "Sherman" GEORGE S. WILCOX*

HULDAH S - m 03 Nov 1845 Stonington, New London Co CT JOHN G HULING; Ref: Barbour's VR Stonington v5 p144.

HUMPHREY - b 06 Aug 1780 Westport, Bristol Co MA s/SAMUEL & COMFORT (SEABURY) WILCOX; m 09 Mar 1800 SARAH BOWEN of Tiverton, Newport Co RI who d Fall River, Bristol Co MA d/JOHN J BOWEN; Res Tiverton RI; ch SARAH B & prob HUMPHREY, WILLIAM, SAMUEL, ELLA T; Ref: Westport VR pp102,251, Desc of Robert Waterman v3 p318, Your Ancestors v13 #2 p1554, #3 p1581.

HUMPHREY - prob s/HUMPHREY & SARAH (BOWEN) WILCOX; m 07 Sep 1845 Tiverton, Newport Co RI PRISCILLA BORDEN; ch WILLIAM; Ref: Arnold v4 pt7 p57, Your Ancestors v13 #3 p1581.

HUMPHREY - b 1836 CT s/MASON & LOUISA (BROWN) WILCOX of Stonington, New London Co CT; Ref: 1850 Census Stonington CT Reel 432 #48 p256, See Mason.

HUNTINGTON - m 24 Nov 1851 Clinton, Middlesex Co CT CLARISSA A HALL who was b 01 Jun 1814; Res Brooklyn, Kings Co NY; ch IDA MAY; Ref: Gen of CT Fam v1 p248, Barbour's VR Clinton v1 p26.

HUNTINGTON E - m 23 Aug 1830 Hartford, Hartford Co CT MARTHA ANN EARL; Ref: Barbour's VR Hartford v1 p 80.

HUTCHIN T - b 1818 s/THOMAS & JERUSHA (-----) WILCOX of Waverly, Tioga Co NY; Ref: Your Ancestors v12 #4 p1488.

HYRAM - b 22 Jun 1823 Burlington, Nova Scotia s/CHARLES DYER & ABIGAIL (CARD) WILCOX; d at age of 9; Ref: Desc of Charles Dyer Wilcox p v(2).

--- I ---

IANTHA - b 03 Nov 1799 Westerly, Washington Co RI d/JESSE & MEHITABLE (WILCOX) WILCOX; m MOSES SAWYER; Ref: Hist of Stonington p661, C Douglass Alves Sr.

IDA - b 18 Oct 1848 d/ELIJAH D & ADELIZA (SCOTT) WILCOX; Ref: Your Ancestors v11 #3 p1371.

IDA - b 1848 CT d/ALANSON & CAROLINE (-----) WILCOX of Harwinton, Litchfield Co CT; Ref: 1850 Census Harwinton CT p252 Dw# 239.

IDA - b 1857 McKean Co PA d/ALONZO ISAIAH & LOVISA (HORTON) WILCOX; Ref: Wilcox-Brown-Medbery p22.

IDA - b Homer, Cortland Co NY d/EBER & MARILLA (-----) WILCOX later of Springwater, Livingston Co NY; m GEORGE WILLIS; ch MAY, STARR, FRED, LELAND, GEORGE; Ref: Your Ancestors v10 pp1199,1200.

IDA A - b 1859 NY d/JOHN & MARY E (-----) WILCOX of Mina, Chautauqua Co NY; Ref: 1860 Census Mina NY p336 Dw# 230.

IDA A - b Aug 1877 WI d/CHARLES H & CORNELIA (-----) WILCOX both b NY; Res Vineland, Winnebago Co WI; Ref: 1900 Soundex Winnebago Co WI.

IDA AMANDA - b 19 Apr 1855 WI d/ORLANDO B & NANCY ELIZABETH (NOBLE) WILCOX; Ref: Desc of Thomas Noble p465.

IDA C - b 01 Feb 1845 d/DAVID GILBERT & HANNAH (WHITNEY) WILCOX; m THERON PETERS of MN; Ref: Desc of Wm Wilcoxson p127.

IDA ELLA - b 18 Jan 1861 adopted 14 Nov 1865 d/HENRY BEALS & LUCETTA (WOODRUFF) WILCOX; Ref: Wilcox-Meigs p110.

IDA L - b 11 Feb 1859 Mayville, Chautauqua Co NY d/ALFRED & MARYETT (BARTON) WILCOX; m 30 Jul 1879 GEORGE JOHN CORNELL who was b 08 Feb 1854 Bemus Point, Chautauqua Co NY s/JOHN W & ANN (DURFEE) CORNELL; Res Mayville NY; ch JOHN GEORGE; Ref: Down's Hist of Chautauqua Co NY v2 p127, Cutter's Western NY v1 p91.

IDA M - b 04 Feb 1854 d/WILLIAM RILEY & FREELOVE (AMES) WILCOX; d 1856; Ref: Your Ancestors v11 #3 p1372, Judith Schlitt.

IDA M - b 17 Jul 1858 Windham, Portage Co OH d/ISAAC N & MELISSA S (SCOTT) WILCOX; Ref: Hist of Portage Co OH p924.

IDA M - b 25 Oct 1865 d/ABNER THORP & LYDIA A (CHANDLER) WILCOX of Jackson Co IA; d 21 Jul 1900; Ref: Desc of Wm Wilcoxson p125.

IDA M - m 12 Apr 1875 Norwich, Chenango Co NY GEORGE GRIFFIN; Ref: VR of Chenango Co NY p179.

IDA MAY - b 1862 Sandgate, Bennington Co VT d/JAMES FRANKLIN & MARY ELIZABETH (NICHOLS) WILCOX; d May 1907 Arlington, Bennington Co VT; Ref: Desc of Wm Wilcoxson p172.

IDA MAY - b 09 Nov 1868 Deep Cove, N B Canada d/WILLIAM & JANE (DRISCOLL) WILCOX; d 29 Apr 1882 bur Seal Cove Cem; Ref: Desc of Charles Dyer Wilcox p12.

IDA MUNGER - b 05 Jun 1867 E Bloomfield, Ontario Co NY d/LAWTON H & MARY JANE (PARKER) WILCOX; d 04 Oct 1905; Ref: Edward McCarthy.

IMOGENE - b 25 Mar 1854 Horseheads, Chemung Co NY d/RICHARD & HANNAH (FOOTE) WILCOX; Ref: Foote Fam Gen p271.

IMRI - b 1765 W Simsbury, Hartford Co CT s/WILLIAM & LUCY (CASE) WILCOX; m LUCRETIA HAYES; d 1807 age 42; Ref: Early Settlers of W Simsbury p129, Your Ancestors v10 #4 p1276.

IMRI - b 1798 W Simsbury, Hartford Co CT s/WILLIAM & MERCY (CASE) WILCOX; Single; d 1835 age 37; Ref: Early Settlers of W Simsbury p130.

INA E - b 1878 Perry, Wyoming Co NY d/EDGAR UDAL & EMMA A (PRENTICE) WILCOX; m ----- TARPLEE of Inglewood, Los Angeles Co CA; Ref: Your Ancestors v4 #5&6 p542.

INEZ - b 1835 NY d/WILLIAM & PRISCILLA (-----) WILCOX of Sherburne, Chenango Co NY; Ref: 1850 Census Sherburne NY p243 Dw# 1526.

INEZ/EYENESS - b 1846 Chautauqua Co NY d/ALONZO & HARRIET (-----) WILCOX; m J K P JACKSON; Res Shumla, Chautauqua Co NY; d 21 May 1873; Ref: 19th Cent Death Notices Reported in Fredonia Censor p296, 1860 Census Pomfret NY p565 Dw# 1844.

INEZ - b 08 Jun 1889 d/WELLEN ANDREW & ELIZA B (FOSTER) WILCOX; Single; d 11 Apr 1961 Seal Cove, N B Canada; Ref: Desc of Charles Dyer Wilcox p16.

INEZ A - b 1826 NY Res with DAVID DUBOIS fam of Norway, Herkimer Co NY; Ref: 1850 Census_Norway NY p266 Dw# 138.

IONE - b af 1873; m ----- FLINT; Res Springwater, Livingston Co & Cohocton, Steuben Co NY; Ref: Your Ancestors v10 #2 p1224.

IRA - b 1791-1800; Res Russia, Herkimer Co NY; Purchased land from SAMUEL WILCOX in 1821; 3 sons; Ref: 1830 Census Herkimer Co NY, Land Records BK 14 p313.

IRA - b 22 Aug 1788 Durham, Greene Co NY s/FRANCIS & MEHITABLE (-----) WILCOX; m 22 Sep 1813 RACHEL AUSTIN who was b 22 Sep 1793 Durham NY & d 31 Jul 1817 Oxford, Chenango Co NY; m 16/20 Feb 1819 LUCY WILCOX of Sheffield, Berkshire Co MA who was b Chatham, Columbia Co NY 28 Oct 1793 & d Oxford NY 22 Jan 1873 age 79; moved from Greene Co NY to Oxford NY 1812; ch by 2nd wife CHAUNCEY A, MARY ELIZABETH, ANN AUGUSTA; d Jacksonville, Duval Co FL while vacationing 29 Nov 1852; Will probated 27 Jan 1853 # F-437 Oxford NY; Ref: Hist of Chenango Co NY p265, 10,000 VR of Central NY p265, Index to Wills of Chenango Co NY v2, Annals of Oxford NY pp348,349, Wills of Greene Co NY v1 p39, Your Ancestors v4 #1&2 p499.

IRA - b 24 Sep 1795 Pawlet, Rutland Co VT s/JOHN & CATHERINE (WOODARD) WILCOX; m 01 Jan 1818 MARIA JOHNSON; Ref: Halifax Wilcox Fam mss.

IRA Jr - b ca 1810 s/IRA MOORE & LOIS (MILLER) WILCOX of Swanton twnshp, Fulton Co OH; m MARTHA ------; ch JOSEPH, DOROTHY, NICHOLAS; Res Troy twnshp, Delaware Co OH; Ref: Desc of Wm Wilcoxson p189a

IRA - b 1817 Onondaga Co NY; m MARY PALMER who was b 1817; Res Manlius, Onondaga Co NY, Lincoln, Madison Co NY; ch DAVID & ELISHA, twins, HARRISON, SARAH H, MARIE, SANFORD, DANIEL, RICHARD; Ref: Pioneers of Madison Co NY p281, 1850 Census Manlius NY p19 Dw# 275.

IRA - b 18 Dec 1829 NY s/CLARK & SALLY (MAXSON) WILCOX of McLean & Groton, Tompkins Co NY; d 18 Aug 1832 McLean NY; Ref: Carol A Cox.

IRA - b 1840 NY s/NATHAN & REBECCA (-----) WILCOX of Minisink, Orange Co NY; Ref: 1850 Census Minisink NY p265 Dw# 337.

IRA - b 1848 NY; Res with JAMES & NANCY (-----) WILCOX of Pawling, Dutchess Co NY; Ref: 1850 Census Pawling NY p225 Dw# 93.

IRA - b 21 Apr 1853 Adams, Muskingum Co OH s/JOHN & SARAH A (CRUMBAKER) WILCOX; m 13 Sep 1874 JOSEPHINE SMITH who d 1878 d/FINLEY & ELIZABETH (HAWK) SMITH; m 17 Apr 1883 CHARITY E KNOFF d/JOHN & MARY J (-----) KNOFF; ch by 1st wife NORA E; ch by 2nd wife BERNICE A, ALICE; Ref: Hist of Muskingum Co OH pp606,607.

IRA A - s/NATHAN WILCOX of West Greenwich, Kent Co RI; m 18 Sep 1842 Exeter Washington Co RI SALLY RATHBUN d/SHEFFIELD RATHBUN; Ref: Arnold v5 pt3 p36.

IRA ALLEN - b 07 Feb 1895 Smithfield twnshp, Bradford Co PA s/ELLIOTT URIAH & TIRZAH ELVIRA (SEYMOUR) WILCOX; m 03 Jan 1917 KATHERINE MAY WHEELER who was b 30 Aug 1890 & d 03 May 1940 d/MARSHALL B & FLORENCE (STRATTON) WHEELER; ch IRA ALLEN Jr, IVOR ELLIOTT, SYLVIA NOREEN; d 27 Dec 1924 bur East Smithfield Bradford Co PA; Ref: Wilcox Genealogy pp20,66.

IRA B - b 18 Dec 1829 s/CLARK & SALLY (MAXSON) WILCOX; d 18 Aug 1832 McLean, Tompkins Co NY; Ref: NYG&BR v105 p216.

IRA BIDWELL - b ca 1854 MI s/AUSTIN SCRANTON & HANNAH (BIDWELL) WILCOX; Res Rome Twnshp, Oneida Co NY; Ref: Your Ancestors v3 #1 p281.

IRA MOORE - b 21 Jul 1783 Barkhamsted, Litchfield Co CT s/JEHIEL & AZUBA (MOORE) WILCOX; m LOIS MILLER d/DAVID MILLER; Res Swanton twnshp Fulton Co OH; ch GEORGE E, WILLIAM, IRA Jr; Ref: Desc of Wm Wilcoxson pp189a, 189b.

IRA P - b 04 Apr 1874 s/ABEL J & MABEL A (TENNANT) WILCOX; Ref: Your Ancestors v3 #2 p301.

IRAM - War of 1812 from VT; Ref: VT Roster War of 1812 p455.

IRENE - b 29 Sep 1806 Lowville, Lewis Co NY d/ROSWELL & IRENE (NICHOLSON) WILCOX; m MARTIN CONAN; d 16 Jan 1841; Ref: Cutter's Northern NY v2 p656.

IRENE - b 07 Aug 1827 Lenox, Madison Co NY d/ALANSONCASE & IRENE (JOHNSON) WILCOX; m CHARLES BEECHER JOHNSON; Ref: Pioneers of Madison Co NY p280.

IRENE - b 1846 NY d/ALANSON CASE & CATHERINE (HUYCK) WILCOX of Lenox, Madison Co NY; Ref: 1850 Census Lenox NY p176 Dw# 221, See Alanson Case.

IRENE - b 22 Oct 1876 Teepleville, Crawford Co PA d/JULIUS & MARY (HOTCHKISS) WILCOX; m 02 Dec 1915 Los Angeles, Los Angeles Co CA BERT DOW LORD who was b 10 Sep 1876 & d 21 May 1947 Hot Springs, Garland Co AR s/LOOMIS & ANNA (WHITE) LORD; Ref: A Wilcox Book p119.

IRENE CHARLOTTE - b ca 1865 Smithfield twnshp, Bradford Co PA d/ORIN E & ESTHER A (HARKNESS) WILCOX; m WALTER PHILLIPS; ch LAURA; Ref: Wilcox Genealogy p11.

IRENE JANE - m 02 Jan 1853 Wayne Co IA SANDY B JONES; Ref: Hawkeye Heritage v 14 #1 p19.

IRMAH BELLE - b 13 Aug 1871 Van Buren Co MI d/CALVIN & ROSANNA M (STUYVESANT) WILCOX; m 12 Dec 1900 Alma, Gratiot Co MI LOREY WHITE; d 30 Dec 1953; Ref: George Koppers.

IRVIN - b 1836 OH s/EDWIN & ELIZA (-----) WILCOX of Edinburgh, Portage Co OH; Ref: 1850 Census Edinburgh OH p227 Dw# 1639.

IRVING - Inter 01 Feb 1896 Norwich, Chenango Co NY; Sec A; Ref: Norwich NY Cem Assoc Records p324.

IRVING - b 1839 NY s/JONATHAN & FANNY (-----) WILCOX of Leon, Cattaraugus Co NY; Ref: 1850 Census Leon NY p44 Dw# 115.

IRVING - b 11 Feb 1888 NY s/HENRY BENJAMIN & LILLIE A (KING) WILCOX; Res Orangeville, Wyoming Co NY; Ref: Your Ancestors v14 #2 p1644.

IRVING ADELBERT - b 27 Feb 1849 Arkwright, Chautauqua Co NY s/EDSON IRVING & AMANDA M (SMITH) WILCOX; m 17 Nov 1881 Portland, Chautauqua Co NY EFFIE M FAY who was b ca 1850 & d of lung disease 12 Sep 1897 Canyon City, Fremont Co CO d/O N FAY; m 05 Feb 1902 HELEN C DILL who was b 24 Feb 1869 Mayville, Chautauqua Co NY d/JOHN L & MARGARET (MUCK) DILL; Res Portland NY; ch by 2nd wife FRANCES EDITH, IRVING ADELBERT; Ref: Down's Hist of Chautauqua Co pp262,263; Desc of Wm Wilcoxson p225, Your Ancestors v12 #3 p1463, 19th Cent Marriages Reported in Fredonia Censor p244, 19th Cent Deaths Reported in Fredonia Censor p595, 1860 Census Arkwright NY p589 Dw# 2043.

IRVING D - b 10 Mar 1852 s/WILLIAM RILEY & FREELOVE (AMES) WILCOX; d 1859; Ref: Your Ancestors v11 #3 p1372, Judith Schlitt.

IRWIN P - B 1847 NY s/THURSTON & LYDIA (-----) WILCOX of Portland, Chautauqua Co NY; Ref: 1860 Census Portland NY p244 Dw# 1949.

ISAAC - b ca 1730; m MARY ----- who was b ca 1770 & d 28 Jun 1849 in her 79th yr; Res Tiverton, Newport Co RI; d 1796 Havanna Cuba; Ref: NEH&GR Jan 1963 p22, Gen of RI Fam v2 p598.

ISAAC Jr - b 08 Feb 1737 Stonington, New London Co CT; m DESIRE CRANDALL who was b 28 Jan 1743/4 & d 01 Mar 1810 d/GURDON & MARY (-----) CRANDALL; Res Pawling, Dutchess Co NY & Plains, Luzerne Co PA; ch ISAAC, AMOS, CRANDALL, THANKFUL, DESIRE, LUCY; d 1797; Ref: Your Ancestors v9 #2 p1125, CT Bible Rec v8 pp167,168.

ISAAC - b 08 Feb 1739 Stonington, New London Co CT s/WILLIAM & THANKFUL (ADAMS) WILCOX; d Nov 1797; Ref: Barbour's VR Stonington v3 p203, Desc of Wm Wilcoxson p23.

ISAAC - b ca 1739 Stonington, New London Co CT s/DANIEL & MARY (ROBESON) WILCOX; Res Orange Co NY; Ref: Your Ancestors v3 #11&12 p470.

ISAAC - b ca 1750 Exeter, Washington Co RI s/ABRAHAM & LYDIA (HARRINGTON) WILCOX; m 07 Jan 1773 REBECCA BARBER; m 10 Feb 1803 ALICE BARBER; ch AREHABA, JACOB, REBECCA, JOSEPH, CHARITY, ISAAC, NATHANIEL, JOSIAH; Ref: Your Ancestors v3 #7&8 p561, Arnold v5 pt3 pp36,63,64.

ISAAC - m EUNICE CHASE who was b 1753 d/SETH & SARAH (MILK) CHASE; Ref: Gen of RI Fam v1 p197, Your Ancestors v3 #11&12 p472.

ISAAC - b 08 Jan 1753 s/EZRA & MARY (HUMPHREY) WILCOX of Simsbury, Hartford Co CT; m be 1790 DELIVERANCE TULLER who was b 1751 & d 1805 d/Ens ISAAC & PHOEBE (CASE) TULLER; m MARIA SKINNER; m SALLY -----; Res Pompey, Onondaga Co NY 1801; ch by 1st wife JOSEPH SILAS; ch by 2nd wife FREDERICK, DELIA, CLOE, ISAAC Jr, STARLING, DELILAH; ch by 3rd wife MALINDA, CYNTHIA, BETTY, LOIS/LOUISA; Ref: Early Settlers of W Simsbury CT pp126,131,133, Noble Gen p219, Fiske Card File, Wilcox-Meigs p50, 2nd Boat v5 #3 p135, Your Ancestors v13 #3 p1568 #4 p1597, Desc of Wm Wilcoxson pp25,240.

ISAAC - b 01 Aug 1753 Nine Partners, Dutchess Co NY s/JEFFREY & LUCY (-----) WILCOX; m 1775 Mrs MARTHA (EVANS) BURDICK who was b 1755 w/EPHRAIM BURDICK of Stonington, New London CT, Pawling, Dutchess Co NY, & Easton, Washington Co NY; Res Northeast, Dutchess Co NY; 6 ch incl ELIZABETH, OLIVER; d 1813 Easton NY; Ref: Your Ancestors v4 # 3&4 p520 #5&6 p541.

ISAAC - b 14 Aug 1755 Middletown, Middlesex Co CT s/DANIEL & SARAH (WHITE) WILCOX; Unmarried; d 23 Nov 1775; Rev War; bur Maple Cem Berlin, Hartford Co CT; Ref: MUH p749, Cutter's CT Fam v2 p657, Hist of Berlin CT p89.

ISAAC - b RI; m ELSIE WEAVER who was b RI; Res Chenango Co NY; ch ELSIE & others; Ref: Vorhees Record v1 p15.

ISAAC - b ca 1761 s/ISAAC & DESIRE (CRANDALL) WILCOX; m 1784 NANCY NEWCOMB who was b 26 May 1765 & d 15 Jun 1857 d/THOMAS & BRIDGET (GARDNER) NEWCOMB or SIMON & SARAH (MEAD) NEWCOMB; Res Beekman, Dutchess Co NY, Wyoming, Luzerne Co PA

1794, Ferrisburg, Addison Co VT; ch ELIZABETH, SAMUEL, JANE, NEWCOMB, CORNELIA, MARIA, GILBERT, ISAAC, JAMES, CRANDALL; d 26 Jan 1813 Fishkill, Dutchess Co NY; Ref: Your Ancestors v9 #2 p1125.

ISAAC - b be 1765; m ELCY ----- who d 31 Oct 1828; Res Simsbury, Hartford Co CT, Winchester, Litchfield Co CT, & Pompey, Onondaga Co NY; 2 sons & 4 daus; Ref: 1810 Census Onondaga Co NY, Vorhees Rec v1 p7, Annals of Winchester p216.

ISAAC - b ca 1767 s/AMOS & MARY (-----) WILCOX; m ELIZABETH WILCOX; Res Orange Co NY; ch ISAAC, JACOB, JOSEPH; Ref: Your Ancestors v9 #4 p1176, v10 #2 p1224, Hist of Orange Co NY pp610,661.

ISAAC - b 1771 Simsbury, Hartford Co CT s/ISAAC & DELIVERANCE (TULLER) WILCOX; m MARGARET TOOLEY who was b 1771 CT; Res Lafayette, Onondaga Co NY; ch ARLESIA, ISAAC, LUTHER, CELESTIA; Ref: Your Ancestors v13 #4 p1597, 1850 Census Lafayette NY p208 Dw# 247.

ISAAC - b 30 Nov 1777 Ripton CT s/ELNATHAN & SARAH (WELLS) WILCOX; d 14 Jul 1783; Ref: Stratford Gen p1347, Nutmegger v7 #1 p37.

ISAAC - b 17 May 1779 Berlin, Hartford Co CT s/STEPHEN & MARY (KELSEY) WILCOX; m 26 Dec 1800 LUCY NORTH; m 23 Apr 1822 MARY RANDALL of Washington, Columbia Co OH who was b 18 Oct 1792 & d 01 Mar 1883; 10 ch by 1st wife; 6 ch by 2nd wife; Moved to OH 1809, Res Stowe, Summit Co OH; War of 1812; d 15 Sep 1847; Ref: Hist of Portage Co OH p924, CT Bible Rec v1 pp476-8, v9 pp435-6, v11 pp840,841.

ISAAC - b 22 Feb 1781 Exeter Washington Co RI s/ISAAC & REBECCA (BARBER) WILCOX; m 21 Sep 1806 SYBEL WALTON; Res Exeter RI; ch REBECCA WALTON; Ref: Arnold v5 pt3 pp63,64.

ISAAC - b 1782 NY; m EUNICE SWEET who was b 28 Aug 1781 MA & d 04 Nov 1861 Menard Co IL d/HENRY & PHEBE EUNICE (-----) SWEET; ch ISAAC ALMANZA, ALMIRA, PHOEBE, EUNICE ALMIRA, DRUSILLA; Res Menard Co IL; d 11 Jan 1862 Menard Co IL; both bur Old Concord Cem; Ref: Your Ancestors v12 #3 p1461, #4 pp1487,1488, Verna Betts.

ISAAC - b 1782; brother of PELEG; Moved to Lebanon, Madison Co NY 1804; m EMMA SWIFT who was b 1781; ch ALAMANZA; Ref: Pioneers of Madison Co NY p281.

ISAAC - b 29 Aug 1784 Stratford, Fairfield Co CT s/ELNATHAN & SARAH (WELLS) WILCOX; m 1797; ch JOHN, CHARLES, JERUSHA; Ref: Wilcox-Meigs p97, Stratford Gen p1347.

ISAAC - b 1784 NY; m 2nd FREELOVE MADISON; ch by 1st wife LUCINDA, EMILY, CATHERINE; ch by 2nd wife CALVIN B, EPHRAIM, CELISTA, POLLY, AMASA, MARTHA JANE, MATILDA, MARTIN; d 1857 Auburn PA; Ref: Nutmegger v12 #2 p331, Evangeline A Wilcox.

ISAAC - b 09 Jun 1789 Westerly, Washington Co RI s/PELEG & LUCY (WHITTLESEY) WILCOX; m 17 Jan 1808 EUNICE CLOSSON/CLAWSON; 15 ch incl RICHARD, MARTHA, EUNICE, HORACE, ELISHA, GEORGE; Ref: Arnold v5 p45, C Douglass Alves Sr.

ISAAC - b ca 1790 NY s/ISAAC WILCOX; m 26 Jul 1814 ELIZABETH WILCOX who was b 17 Mar 1798 & d 1858 d/HEZEKIAH & MAHALA (WILCOX) WILCOX; Res Le Roy, Bradford Co PA; ch SAMUEL WHEATON, HEZEKIAH RICHARDSON, CHRISTOPHER, SALLY, JOSEPH; d be 1850; Ref: Your Ancestors v10 #3 p1247, 1850 Census Bradford Co PA p66, Hist of Bradford Co PA p1286.

ISAAC - m 19 Dec 1819 Harpersfield, Delaware Co NY HARRIET DAYTON; d 1838; Letter of Adm issued to MICHAEL DAYTON 06 Oct 1838; Ref: Letters of Administration Delaware Co NY v1 p41, Tree Talks v6 #2 p7.

ISAAC - b 1801-1810; Res Booneville, Oneida Co NY; Ref: 1840 Census Oneida Co NY.

ISAAC - b 17 Aug 1801 s/ISAAC & NANCY (NEWCOMB) WILCOX; m 06 May 1824 SARAH STARK who was b 20 May 1801 & d 27 Jun 1864 d/DANIEL & CHARLOTTE (WORDEN) STARK; Res Dutchess Co NY & Plains, Luzerne Co PA; ch GARDNER L, GEORGE S, JOHN D, MARY, LOVINA M, DANIEL DENNIS, CRANDALL, CARPENTER T; d 19 Apr 1860; Ref: Hist of Luzerne Co PA pp1454-1456, Your Ancestors v9 #2 p1125, #3 p1152.

ISAAC - b 10 Dec 1805 Tiverton, Newport Co RI s/MARY (---) WILCOX; Ref: Arnold v8 p56.

ISAAC - b 1803/1807 NY; m LYDIA ANN ----- who was b 1808 NY; Res Chautauqua, Chautauqua Co NY; ch LEANDER, SAMUEL O, SARAH M; Ref: 1850 Census

Chautauqua NY p279 Dw# 278, 1860 Census Chautauqua NY p58 Dw# 431.

ISAAC - b 1810 NY; m SUSAN ----- who was b 1809 NY; Res Pomfret, Chautauqua Co NY; ch HERMAN; Ref: 1860 Census Pomfret NY p583 Dw# 1992.

ISAAC - b 1819 NY; m CATHERINE ----- who was b 1830 NY; Res Castile, Wyoming Co NY; Ref: 1850 Census Castile NY p161 Dw# 161.

ISAAC - b 1822 s/NEWCOMB & HANNAH (SPRAGUE) WILCOX; Ref: Your Ancestors v9 #3 p1151.

ISAAC - m 08 Oct 1823 Providence, Providence Co RI CLARRISSA R BROWNELL; Ref: Arnold v7 p473.

ISAAC - b ca 1807 Mayville, Chautauqua Co NY s/GILES & LYDIA (FOWLER) WILCOX; m 1825 LYDIA TANNER d/THOMAS & ANNA (WALKER) TANNER; ch LEANDER, SAMUEL, SARAH M; Ref: Your Ancestors v13 #4 p1598.

ISAAC - b 01 Jun 1808 s/CRANDALL & JOANNA (STARK) WILCOX; d 1820 prob Dutchess Co NY; Ref: Your Ancestors v9 #4 p1175.

ISAAC - m 27 Sep 1834 Taunton, Bristol Co MA MARY J WETHERELL; ch MARY E, WILLIAM E; Ref: Taunton VR v2 p522.

ISAAC - b 1809; Res Steuben Co NY; d 24 Nov 1879; Ref: Tree Talks v16 #1.

ISAAC - b 06 Apr 1817 NY s/ISAAC & MARGARET (TOOLY) WILCOX; m NANCY -----; Res Lafayette, Onondaga Co NY; ch SPENCER, MARY, ANN; Ref: Your Ancestors v13 #4 p1597, 1850 Census Lafayette NY p208 Dw# 248.

ISAAC - b 16 Oct 1818 s/LOAMINY & HANNAH (PADDOCK) WILCOX; d 23 Jul 1822 Onondaga Co NY; Ref: St Johnsville NY Enterprise & News 23 Oct 1952.

ISAAC - b 1818; m 10 Nov 1870 Hamburg, Erie Co NY MARY C TAYLOR who was b 1849; Ref: Teacher; Rev Alfred J Wilcox's Marriage Records mss p8.

ISAAC - b 1822 NY; m HESTER ANN ----- who was b 1828 NY; Res Ithaca, Tompkins Co NY; ch JOHN, MARY; Ref: 1850 Census Ithaca NY p227 Dw# 355.

ISAAC - b 1825 PA; m ca 1842 PHILANDA -----;
Res Le Roy, Bradford Co PA; ch WALLACE, EZRA P,
MARY E, AMORA, CHARLOTTE, MARTHA; Ref: 1860 Census
Bradford Co PA p369.

ISAAC - of Boonville, Oneida Co NY m 21 Sep
1853 Fredonia, Chautauqua Co NY Mrs SUSAN ANN
LeBAR of Pomfret, Chautauqua Co NY who was b 18
Sep 1808 & d 02 Sep 1866 Pomfret, Chautauqua Co NY
Cancer; Ref: 19th Cent Marriages Reported in
Fredonia Censor p244, 19th Cent Death Notices
Reported in Fredonia Censor p597.

ISAAC - b 1834 NY s/NATHAN & REBECCA (-----)
WILCOX of Minisink, Orange Co NY; Ref: 1850 Census
Minisink NY p265 Dw# 337.

ISAAC B - b 1834 Harpersfield, Delaware Co NY
s/ALONZO BENJAMIN & HANNAH (SWIFT) WILCOX; Res KS;
Ref: Your Ancestors v4 #7&8 p563, 1850 Census
Harpersfield NY p158 Dw# 28.

ISAAC - b 1836 s/HORACE & HANNAH (-----) WILCOX
of Stonington, New London Co CT; Ref: 1850 Census
Stonington CT Reel 432 #48 p281.

ISAAC - b 1845 s/HENRY & SUSANNAH (-----)
WILCOX; Res Adrian, Lenawee Co MI; Ref: 1860
Census.

ISAAC - b 30 Jan 1871 Plains, Luzerne Co PA
Twin with THOMAS s/DANIEL DENNIS & REBECCA
(STOCKER) WILCOX Luzerne Co PA; d 21 Jul 1871;
Ref: Your Ancestors v9 #4 p1175, Hist of Luzerne
Co PA p1455.

ISAAC Jr - s/ISAAC & DELIVERANCE (TULLER)
WILCOX of W Simsbury, Hartford Co CT m MARY TOOLY;
Ref Early Settlers of W Simsbury CT p133, Fiske
Card File.

ISAAC ALMANZA - b 13 Jun 1816 Madison Co NY
s/ISAAC & EUNICE (SWEET) WILCOX; m 17 Sep 1835
Cleveland, Cuyahoga Co OH MARIETTE OVIATT who was
b 10 Dec 1816 CT & d 05 Aug 1863 Menard Co IL; bur
Old Concord Cem; m 18 Feb 1864 CATHERINE
SHELLABORGER who was b 08 Jun 1834 Allen Co OH &
d 06 Jun 1922 Winterset, Madison Co IA bur Union
Chapel Cem d/JONAS & LYDIA (MORGAN) SHELLABORGER;
ch by 1st wife MILO GEORGE, LEVI; JOHN, HARRIET
SEFRONIA, EMILY E, ANDREW JACKSON; ch by 2nd wife
ULYSSES GRANT, WILLIAM, JOSEPH FRANKLIN, ALMEDA; d
05 May 1880 Winterset, Madison Co IA; both bur

Union Chapel Cem; Ref: Your Ancestors v12 #4 p1488, Verna Betts.

ISAAC FRANCIS - b 03 Jan 1836 Charlestown, Washington Co RI s/HORACE & HANNAH (KENYON) WILCOX; m Sep 1854 SARAH BARBOUR who was b 1838 & d 1888; m 10 May 1890 Westerly, Washington Co RI LAURA ANN GULLY who was b 14 Feb 1865 Cornwall, England & d 27 Jun 1938; ch by 1st wife ELLA E "LOLLIE", AMOS EDWIN; ch by 2nd wife, GEORGE ELLIOT, SADIE ANNIE; d 22 Nov 1910 Groton, New London Co CT; Ref: Arnold v11 p177, C Douglass Alves Sr.

ISAAC H - b 1817 NY; m CAROLINE ----- who was b 1830 CT; Res Dover, Dutchess Co NY; Carpenter; ch JAMES H; Ref: 1850 Census Dover NY p316 Dw# 93.

ISAAC N - b 24 Dec 1833 Cuyahoga Falls, Summit Co OH s/ISAAC & MARY (RANDALL) WILCOX; m 26 May 1857 MELISSA S SCOTT who was b Freedom Twnshp, OH 24 Feb 1836 d/ELIJAH SCOTT; Res Windham, Portage Co OH; ch IDA M, SCOTT S, WESLEY W; Ref: Hist of Portage Co OH p924.

ISAAC T - of Fall River, Bristol Co MA m 21 Jan 1844 MARY ANN W SALISBURY of Newport, Newport Co RI; Ref: Arnold v4 pt1 p14.

ISAAC VAN DEUSEN - b 09/19 Sep 1841 s/AZARIAH CLARK & RACHEL (VAN DEUSEN) WILCOX; d 1863; Ref: Wilcox Excerpts v1 p2, Your Ancestors v13 #1 p1516.

ISABEL - b 09 May 1819 d/THOMAS & ELIZABETH (McCAIN) WILCOX of Hector, Schuyler Co NY; Ref: Your Ancestors v10 #4 p1274.

ISABEL - m 06 May 1870 Tiverton, Newport Co RI GEORGE W GRINNELL; Ref: Arnold v7 p583.

ISABEL D - b 27 May 1845 Newport, Sullivan Co NH d/CALVIN & ISABEL (SILVER) WILCOX; m JUDSON W EWING; Ref: Your Ancestors v3 #4 p350.

ISABELL - b 1857 IL d/JEREMIAH & CATHERINE (SHERWIN) WILCOX; Res Whiteside Co IL & poss Schuyler, Colfax Co NE; Ref: 1860, 1870 Census Whiteside Co IL.

ISABELLA - b 16 June 1762 d/DAVID & ISRAELIA (SALMON) WILCOX; Ref: Stratford Gen p1347.

ISABELLE - b 06 Nov 1887 DePerc, Brown Co WI d/CHESTER GAVIN & SARAH (MILLER) WILCOX; Ref: Your Ancestors v14 #2 p1646.

ISAIAH Elder - b ca 1738 Westerly, Washington Co RI s/STEPHEN & MERCY (RANDALL) WILCOX; m 15 Oct 1761 SARAH LEWIS who was b 1740 & d 02 May 1815 Westerly RI d/JOHN LEWIS; ch ISAIAH, ASA, NATHAN, SARAH, MERCY, STEPHEN, OLIVER, PRUDENCE, MARY LEWIS, ENOCH; d 03 Mar 1795; Ref: Arnold v5 pt2 p69, Westerly & Its Witnesses p301, Wilcox-Brown-Medbery pp8-10, See RIVR, NS v4 p344.

ISAIAH - m 25 Jul 1752 Portsmouth, Newport Co RI ANN EASTES; Ref: Arnold v4 pt1 p47, Fiske Card File.

ISAIAH - b 31 Jan 1763 Westerly, Washington Co RI s/ISAIAH & SARAH (LEWIS) WILCOX; m POLLY PENDLETON d/WILLIAM & JUDITH (-----) PENDLETON; Res Preston, New London Co CT & Danube, Herkimer Co NY; ch POLLY, ISAIAH, WILLIAM PENDLETON, ASA, LYDIA, NANCY, NATHAN PENDLETON; d 13 Jul 1844 Danube NY; Ref: Arnold v5 pp69,145, Hist of Herkimer Co NY p123, Wilcox-Brown-Medbery pp11,12, 1825 Census Herkimer Co NY.

ISAIAH - m 21 Sep 1806 at Exeter, Washington Co RI SYBEL WALTON d/OLIVER WALTON; Ref: Arnold v5 pt3 p36.

ISAIAH - b 30 Nov 1791 Preston, New London Co CT s/ISAIAH & POLLY (PENDLETON) WILCOX; Ref: Arnold v5 p145, Wilcox-Brown-Medbery p11.

ISAIAH - b 1800 RI s/THOMAS & JANE (-----) WILCOX; m LYDIA ----- who was b 1803 NY; Res Columbus, Chenango Co NY; ch HIRAM, AYRSTUD, EMILY, ESTHER, MARY; Ref: Wills of Chenango Co, NYSDAR v22a p157, 1850 Census Columbus NY p279 Dw# 2126.

ISAIAH - b 1804 NY; m POLLY A ----- who was b 1818 NY; Res Columbus, Chenango Co NY; Shoemaker; ch CLARKE, CELESTIA, HANNAH, OSCAR; Ref: 1850 Census Columbus NY p280 Dw# 280.

ISAIAH - b 1805 RI; m ANN ----- who was b 1802 CT; Res Camillus, Onondaga Co NY; ch MARY S, GEORGE W; Ref: 1850 Census Camillus NY p260 Dw# 532.

ISAIAH - Taxed in W Greenwich, Kent Co RI 1830; Ref: RI Roots v6 #2 p42.

ISAIAH - Will probated 11 Aug 1864 Chenango Co NY K-469; Ref: Index to Wills of Chenango Co NY v2.

ISAIAH ALONZO - b 1823 NY s/ASA & CLARISSA (-----) WILCOX of Danube, Herkimer Co NY; Res Santa Clara, Santa Clara Co CA; Ref: Wilcox-Brown-Medbery p11, 1850 Census Danube NY p299 Dw# 180.

ISAIAH CLARK - b 04 May 1834 Great Valley, Cattaraugus Co NY s/SEYMOUR & SALLY (SARGENT) WILCOX; m 1854 SALLY HENRY who was b 05 Feb 1838 Rockdale twnshp, Crawford Co PA & d 31 Jan 1882 Garland Warren Co PA; Res Olean, Cattaraugus Co NY; m MINERVA EVERSON SWARTS a first cousin; ch by 1st wife JOSIAH A, SEYMOUR ISAIAH, HIRAM LEROY, JERUSHA ALMIRA, CARRIE HELENA; Civil War from Jamestown, Chautauqua Co NY; d 22 Sep 1915 Grand Valley Warren Co PA bur Olean NY; Ref: Crawford Co PA Cem Inscr p11, Family Bible, Civil War Records, Dennis Davis, 1850 Census Great Valley NY p149, Dw# 64.

ISAIAH N - b 18-- s/NATHAN & NANCY (LEWIS) WILCOX; Res Herkimer Co NY 1842; Ref: Will of Nathan Wilcox Book G p182.

ISAIAH N - b 1805 NY; m ARMANDA ----- who was b 1807 NY; Res Florence, Oneida Co NY; ch ETHELBERTA, MORRIS, HANNAH E, LESTER H, MARY F; Ref: 1850 Census Florence NY p200 Dw# 144.

ISHMAEL - b ca 1748 N Kingston or Exeter, Washington Co RI s/THOMAS & ABIGAIL (OSBORNE) WILCOX; m 15 Jan 1770 MARY WILCOX who d af 20 Aug 1779; ch ISHMAEL, DELIVERANCE, MARY, ANNE, ABIGAIL, JEREMIAH; Will proved 01 Nov 1779; Ref: Wilcox Excerpts v1 p1, Arnold v5 pt3 p35, Your Ancestors v3 #11&12 p472, See RIGR v2 #2 p97, See RIVR, NS v4 p344.

ISHMAEL - Res S Kingston, Washington Co RI ca 1829; ch SAMUEL C; Ref: Arnold v2 p44.

ISRAEL - b 19 Jun 1656 Middletown, Middlesex Co CT s/JOHN & CATHERINE/KATERN (STOUGHTON) WILCOX; m 28 Mar 1677/8 SARAH SAVAGE who was b 30 Jul 1657 & d 08 Feb 1724 d/JOHN & ELIZABETH (DUBBIN/D'AUBIN) SAVAGE of Middletown CT; ch ISRAEL, JOHN, SAMUEL, THOMAS, SARAH; d 20 Dec 1689; Ref: VR v1 pp 5,33,

MUH p743, Early Fam of Wallingford p330,331, NEH&GR v14 p138, Savage v4 p546, Nutmegger v4 #3 p330, A Wilcox Book pp 16,17,24, Cutter's Western NY v2 pp741,742, Cutter's CT Fam v2 p656, Col Fam of US v5 p554, Hist of Berlin CT p82,83, Hist of Wallingford pp936,937, Torrey's Marriage Rec microfilm.

ISRAEL - b 16 Jan 1679/80 Middletown, Middlesex Co CT s/ISRAEL & SARAH (SAVAGE) WILCOX; m 16 Dec 1717 MARY NORTH who was b 1694 & d 06 Jul 1734; ch RUTH, ISRAEL, GIDEON, NATHANIEL, MARY, CHARLES, JERUSHA; d 06 Jul 1731; Ref: MUH pp743,744, Early Fam of Wallingford p331, NEH&GR v14 p138, Nutmegger v16 #4 p734, Cutter's Western NY v2 p742, Cutter's CT Fam v2 p656, Col Fam of US v5 p554, Barbour's VR Middletown LR2 p11, Hist of Wallingford p937.

ISRAEL - m be 1736 HANNAH -----; Res Middletown, Middlesex Co CT; ch HANNAH; Ref: Barbour's VR Middletown v1 p86.

ISRAEL - b 01 Sep 1720 Middletown, Middlesex Co CT s/ISRAEL & MARY (NORTH) WILCOX; m SYBIL/SEBEL ----- who d 23 Dec 1775; ch AMOS BRONSON; Ref: Nutmegger v4 #3 p330, NEH&GR v14 p138, MUH p744, Barbour's VR Middletown v2 p164.

ISRAEL - m 04 Apr 1749 Cromwell, Middlesex Co CT MARTHA BARNS; ch MARTHA; Res Middletown, Middlesex Co CT; Ref: ECM v2 p88, Barbour's VR Middletown v2 p285.

ISRAEL - m SALLY -----; d May 1813 Clarence, Erie Co NY; Ref: Tree Talks v5 #1 p37.

ISRAEL - m ANNA DOWD who was b 01 Apr 1765 Middletown, Middlesex Co CT d/RICHARD & PHEBE (FOSTER) DOWD; Ref: Fam of Early Guilford p292.

ISRAEL - b 15 Jun 1776 s/SYLVANUS & JUSTINA/CHESTINA (CURTIS) WILCOX; m 21 Apr 1798 ANNE FOWLER; Res West Stockbridge, Berkshire Co MA; ch CLARRISA, BETSEY M, SALLY ELVIRA; d before 18 Jun 1817; Ref: Your Ancestors v9 #4 p1177, Desc of Wm Wilcoxson pp190b,201.

ISRAEL - b 1785 VT; Res Shalersville, Portage Co OH; Ref: 1850 Census Shalersville OH p116 Dw# 150.

ISRAEL - b ca 1800 s/ROSWELL; d be 03 Jun 1834 when will was proved; Ref: Desc of Wm Wilcoxson p222.

ISRAEL BRONSON - b ca 1808 Middletown, Middlesex Co CT s/AMOS BRONSON & SARAH (ROGERS) WILCOX; Res VT; ch FREDERICK WILLIAM; Ref: MUH p744.

ISRAEL S - m 31 Aug 1826 Franklin Co OH SARAH D MESSENGER; Ref: OH Marriages p338.

ISRAELIA - b 14 Nov 1773 White Hills CT d/DAVID & ISRAELIA (SALMON) WILCOX; Ref: Wilcox-Meigs p58.

ISRAHAIH - bpt Jan 1766 Stratford, Fairfield Co CT s/EPHRAIM & RUTH (WHEELER) WILCOX; Ref: Wilcox-Meigs p59, Stratford Gen p1347.

ITHA MAY - b 07 May 1879 Napoli, Cattaraugus Co NY d/HOSMER H & ELLA S (BURT) WILCOX; Ref: Cutter's Western NY v1 p258.

IYLE/TYLER - m 13 Sep 1760 Dartmouth, Bristol Co MA DEBORAH RUSSELL; Ref: Dartmouth VR p546.

--- J ---

J - b 1798 NY; m SARAH -----; Res Wheatland, Monroe Co NY; ch EDGAR, JANE, MARY; Ref: 1850 Census Wheatland NY p240 Dw# 268.

J - b 1807 NY; Res Le Roy, Bradford Co PA 1860; Ref: 1860 Census Bradford Co PA p367.

J A - b ca 1843 Canaan, Columbia Co NY s/Dr SYLVESTER C & EMILY (FOWLER) WILCOX; m CALLIE SMITH 1882 Washington, Tazewell Co IL; Civil War Co A 128th NY Reg Hudson, Columbia Co NY 1862; Res Gilman, Iroquois Co IL, McCook, Red Willow Co NE 1884; Member NE State Legislature 1888; 2 ch E J, Mrs C R Woodruff; d af 1909; Ref: Compendium Western Nebraska Hist p231.

J A - b 1849 NY s/JAMES & ELIZABETH (-----) WILCOX of Seneca Falls, Seneca Co NY; Ref: 1850 Census Seneca Falls NY p293 Dw# 2348.

J B - b 1808; d Augusta, Kennebec Co ME 12 Dec 1886; Ref: VR of Augusta ME v2 p469.

J B - Pastor Presbyterian Church Portage, Wyoming Co NY 1834-1837; Ref: Hist of Wyoming Co NY p202.

J B - of Orangeville, Wyoming Co NY; m 30 Apr 1868 Attica, Wyoming Co NY ROSABELLE WINCHESTER of Attica; Ref: West NY Journal v7 #1 p22.

J B - of Wellsboro, Tioga Co PA; m MARGARET CAMPBELL who was b 04 May 1847; Ref: Hist of Tioga Co PA p730.

J D - b 1810 CT; m CLARASALL ----- who was b 1810 NY; Res Le Roy Genesee Co NY; ch EMILINE; Ref: 1850 Census Le Roy NY p32 Dw# 405.

J E - m MARY LORING FAXON who was b 19 Mar 1836 d/CHARLES & LUCY ANN (STEELE) FAXON of W Hartford, Hartford Co CT; Ref: Col Fam of US v5 p212.

J F - b 04 Jan 1848 Middleburg, Cayuhoga Co OH; Res Minneapolis, Hennepin Co MN 1867; m June 1871 EMMA CLEMENT; ch HARRY, ARCHA, MYRTICE; Ref: Hist of Hennepin Co MN p658.

J H - of Knoxville, Knox Co IL enlisted in army 17 Dec 1863 & mustered out 04 Nov 1865; Ref: Hist of Knox Co IL p371.

J L - m 29 Feb 1852 Lorain Co OH ELIZABETH ROCKWELL; Ref: Marriages Lorain Co OH p119.

J M - b 1827; Res Lewis Co NY & Fredonia, Chautauqua Co NY; d 14 Feb 1873; Ref: 19th Cent Death Notices Reported in Fredonia Censor p596.

J M - b 20 Mar 1844; m MARY A ----- who was b 08 Oct 1848; Civil War Co D 5 Reg O V Inf; Ref: OH Cem Rec p138.

J N - b 1837 NY s/ALFRED & ABIGAIL (-----) WILCOX of Seneca Falls, Seneca Co NY; Ref: 1850 Census Seneca Falls NY p262 Dw# 1890.

J R - settled in Red Wing, Goodhue Co MN 1860; d Dec 1874; Survived by his widow and several ch; Ref: Goodhue County Republican issue dated Dec 31 1874 p4 col 5.

J SPENCER - b 1843 NY s/ABEL & ELIZABETH (-----) WILCOX of Bergen, Genesee Co NY; Ref: 1850 Census Bergen NY p51 Dw# 677.

J W - of Knoxville, Knox Co IL enlisted in 138th Infantry Company E 14 May 1864 & mustered out 14 Oct 1864; Ref: Hist of Knox Co IL p366.

JABEZ - b 21 Mar 1707 Little Compton, Newport Co RI s/JOHN & REBECCA (-----) WILCOX; int to marry 08 Apr 1736 HANNAH HART; m 10 May 1736; Res; Dartmouth, Bristol Co MA; ch MARY, ANSTUS (ANSTRIS), THOMAS, REBEKAH, SARAH, DRUZILLA, HULDAH, EUNICE & LOIS (twins), JABEZ, JOHN, STEPHEN; Ref: Dartmouth VR pp301-304, Arnold v4, pt5 pp71,193, pt7 p57, Little Compton Fam p771, Probate Rec of Bristol Co MA v1 p144.

JABEZ Jr - b 02 Jul 1753 Dartmouth, Bristol Co MA s/JABEZ & HANNAH (HART) WILCOX; Ref: Dartmouth VR p302, See Jabez.

JABEZ - b be 1756; Res Halifax, Windham Co VT 1800; 2 sons & 3 daus; Ref: 1800 Census Windham Co VT p140.

JABEZ - m DORCAS LOUNSBURY who was b 1788 Bethany, New Haven Co CT d/TIMOTHY & HANNAH (FRENCH) LOUNSBURY; Ref: New Haven Fam v5.

JABEZ F - b 30 Oct 1821 Halifax, Windham Co VT s/EMERY & SARAH (FRANKLIN) WILCOX; m 06 Nov 1845 Brattleboro, Windham Co VT MARY ANN CROSIER who was b 14 Sep 1818 Halifax VT & d 23 Apr 1905 Blackinton, Berkshire Co MA d/JAMES & POLLY (STOW) CROSIER; ch CHARLES H, HARRIET E, JULIA F, EUGENE M, NELSON PLIMPTON; d 29 Mar 1880 Whitingham, Windham Co VT; both bur Jacksonville, Windham Co VT; Ref: Halifax Wilcox Fam mss.

JACKSON - b 1831 PA; m JANE ----- who was b 1827 PA; Res Busti, Chautauqua Co NY; ch JANET; Ref: 1850 Census Busti NY p15 Dw# 11.

JACKSON - b 1856 NY s/WILLIAM & MARY (-----) WILCOX of Chautauqua, Chautauqua Co NY; Ref: 1860 Census Chautauqua NY p69 Dw# 521.

JACOB - b 14 Oct 1699 Little Compton, Newport Co RI s/JOHN & REBECCA (-----) WILCOX; Ref: Arnold v4 pt6 p193, Probate Rec of Bristol Co MA v1 p144, Little Comp Fam p771.

JACOB - b Oct 1757 Exeter, Washington Co RI s/ABRAHAM & LYDIA (HARRINGTON) WILCOX; m ca 1777 SARAH BROWN who was b 1757 & d 1829 Mt Holly, Rutland Co VT; bur Packer Cem; ch JACOB, HANNAH,

ISAAC, SPENCER, LYDIA, ABRAHAM, PHEBE; d 1832; Ref: Your Ancestors v4 #7&8 p561, Early Settlers of NY v3 p9, Fiske Card File.

JACOB - b 21 Jun 1758 Middletown, Middlesex Co CT s/DANIEL & SARAH (WHITE) WILCOX; m 07 Jun 1780 Hartford, Hartford Co CT RACHEL PORTER who was b 05 Jul 1758 & d 15 Mar 1847 New Haven, New Haven Co CT at the home of her son NORRIS; ch ALVIN, NORMAN, ORRIN, CYPRIAN, NORRIS, JACOB, ALBERT, BETSEY, LUCETTA; Rev War; d 15 Mar 1841 New Haven CT or 03 Nov 1841 East Berlin; both bur East Berlin; Ref: MUH p749, Cutter's CT Fam v2 p657, Hist of Berlin CT pp93,94, Barbour's VR Middletown v1 p102,v2 p343.

JACOB - b 1784; m SALLY HORTON who was b 1788 & d 1840; Res Mt Holly, Rutland Co VT; 3 sons & 5 daus incl LUCINDA DANIEL PACKER; d 1848; Ref: 1800 Census Mt Holly VT p116, Early Settlers of NY v3 p96, Fiske Card File.

JACOB - b 10 Jan 1790 Exeter, Washington Co RI s/ISAAC & REBECCA (BARBER) WILCOX; m PHILENA KEATING; ch CHARITY, BARNHEART, JOHN, MARY, FANNY JANE; Ref: Your Ancestors p1247, Arnold v5 pt3 p64.

JACOB - b 1802 NY; m MARY E ----- who was b 1801 NY; Res Collins, Erie Co NY; ch WILLIAM, JOHN E, LOIS S, JOSEPH SMITH; Ref: 1850 Census Collins NY p322 Dw# 609.

JACOB - b 1807 NY; m CAROLINE ----- who was b 1821 NY; Res Sherburne, Chenango Co NY; ch OSCAR, MARIA, MARY, HARRIET, LOUISA, DAVID; Ref: 1850 Census Sherburne NY p249 Dw# 1624.

JACOB - b 1814 Lafayette, Onondaga Co NY s/STERLING & PHOEBE (-----) WILCOX; m HARRIET WOOD who was b 1821; Res Lafayette, NY; ch PHOEBE, EFFIE J, LOIS E, FRANKLIN; Ref: Your Ancestors v14 #1 p1620, 1850 Census Lafayette NY p221 Dw# 465.

JACOB - b 1824 NY; Res Hector, Tompkins Co NY; Ref: 1850 Census Hector NY p404 Dw# 671.

JACOB - brother of CHANCEY & MARY/MARIETTA WILCOX; Res Whiteside Co IL 1850; Ref: Mrs Wm Richardson.

JACOB - b 1849 OH s/ALEXANDER HAMILTON & BETSEY (DIVER) WILCOX of Deerfield, Portage Co OH; Ref: 1850 Census Deerfield OH p186 Dw# 1001.

JACOB B - b 15 Feb 1826 s/THOMAS & ELIZABETH (McCAIN) WILCOX of Hector, Schuyler Co NY; Ref: Your Ancestors v10 #4 p1274.

JACOB E - b 1816 NY; m ANN C ----- who was b 1816 NY; Res Worcester, Otsego Co NY;_ch BARNEY F, MARY E; Ref: 1850 Census Worcester NY p182 Dw# 321.

JACOB M - b 1836 NY; brother to SMITH WILCOX; Res Minisink, Orange Co NY; Ref: 1850 Census Minisink NY p265 Dw# 336.

JACOB W - of New Haven m 18 Nov 1852 Bethany, New Haven Co CT CHARLOTTE E HUBBURT of Waterbury, New Haven Co CT; Ref: Barbour's VR Bethany v1 p34.

JAIRUS - b 19 Oct 1751 Cromwell, Middlesex Co CT s/FRANCIS & RACHEL (WILCOX) WILCOX; m MARY ABBEY d/JONATHAN & MARY (prob WESTON) ABBEY of Tolland & Willington, Tolland Co CT; Res Wallingford, New Haven Co CT & Durham, Greene Co NY; ch ANSEL, JAIRUS, FRANCIS, RACHEL, RACHEL & prob IRA, GEORGE, DANIEL B, LYMAN, ELKANAH, SALLY, CHARITY; Ref: Your Ancestors v3 #11&12 pp475,476, Barbour's VR Middletown v1 p127, Wallingford v19 p219, v21 pp213,222.

JAIRUS - b 03 Dec 1783 s/JAIRUS & MARY (ABBEY) WILCOX of Wallingford, New Haven Co CT & Durham, Greene Co NY; Ref: Your Ancestors v3 #11&12 p476, Barbour's VR Wallingford v23 p494.

JAIRUS - b 01 Mar 1802 Middletown, Middlesex Co CT s/BENJAMIN & RACHEL (WILCOX) WILCOX; Ref: Barbour's VR Middletown v3 p88, See Benjamin.

JAIRUS - b 1825 NY s/CLARK & SALLY (MAXSON) WILCOX of McLean & Groton, Tompkins Co NY; d IA; Ref: Carol A Cox.

JAMES - b ca 1732 s/JEFFREY & SARAH (HIMES) WILCOX of N Kingston, Washington Co RI; Ref: Your Ancestors v3 #11&12 p472.

JAMES - m 29 Dec 1768 CT SARAH SCRANTON; Ref: ECM v1 p102.

JAMES - b 1743; m SARAH ----- who was b 1749 & d 26 Mar 1833; d 11 May 1813 Wilmington, Windham Co VT bur Averell Cem Wilmington VT; Ref: Wilmington Cong Ch Rec, Cem Rec, Alice Wiatr.

JAMES - b 16 Mar 1744 Killingworth, Middlesex Co CT s/JONATHAN & EXPERIENCE (WILLIAMS) WILCOX; Ref: Wilcox-Meigs p45, Barbour's VR Killingworth v1 p160, Desc of Wm Wilcoxson pp20,174.

JAMES - b 10 Feb 1751 s/AMOS & JOHANNA (HILLYER) WILCOX of Simsbury, Hartford Co; m 03 Mar 1770 Farmington, Hartford Co CT ELIZABETH BISHOP of Northington CT; ch JAMES; d 27 Dec 1775; Ref: ECM v4 p14, Fiske Card File, Your Ancestors v12 #3 p1464, v13 #3 p1567, Wilcox-Meigs p48.

JAMES - b 23 Jul 1754 Killingworth, Middlesex Co CT s/GILES & LYDIA (WARD) WILCOX; m 09/19 Mar 1777 EUNICE VICKERY/VICERY who was b 16 Apr 1760 & d 10 Aug 1837/1857; Res Bridport, Addison Co VT; ch JAMES, LYDIA, ABNER, HULDAH, ANSON, EUNICE, CLARRISSA, HULDAH, ANSON, HENRY, VICKERY/VILROY; Rev War at Ticonderoga with ETHAN ALLEN; d 4/14 Feb 1839/40; Ref: Your Ancestors v3 #9&10 pp449,450, Wisconsin Fam June 1940 pp41-43, Wilcox-Meigs p83, Hist of Addison Co VT p393, Texas Society DAR Roster v4 p2287, Barbour's VR Killingworth v2 p121, Desc of Wm Wilcoxson p118.

JAMES - b 28 Nov 1755 Middletown, Middlesex Co CT s/JANNA Jr & JEMIMA (WILCOX) WILCOX; Ref: Barbour's VR Middletown v2 p246, See Janna Jr.

JAMES - b 09 Sep 1757 Middletown, Middlesex Co CT s/JONATHAN & DINAH (ORVIS) WILCOX; Ref: Barbour's VR Middletown v2 p11, See Jonathan.

JAMES - b 1756-1775; Res Shoreham, Addison Co VT; 2 sons & 3 daus in 1800; Ref: 1800 Census Addison Co VT p23.

JAMES - b 25 May 1762 Stratford, Fairfield Co CT s/NATHAN & MARY (BEACH) WILCOX; m 1787 MEHETABLE BEARDSLEY; m ANN THOMPSON; Res Ripton CT; ch by 1st wife MABEL; Ref: Wilcox-Meigs pp60,79, Hist of Stratford Fam p1347, Desc of Wm Wilcoxson p37.

JAMES - b ca 1764 s/STEPHEN WILCOX; Res Franklin, Bradford Co PA; Ref: Pioneer Fam of Bradford Co PA p268.

JAMES - d 07 Dec 1775 Simsbury, Hartford Co CT; Ref: Barbour's VR Simsbury TM4 p260.

JAMES - b 12 Feb 1764 Haddam, Middlesex Co CT s/JOHN & ANNA (STEVENS) WILCOX; m 12 Feb 1787 ELIZABETH BRADLEY AUGER who was b 20 Aug 1762 & d 23 Jan 1838 d/ISAAC AUGER ; ch JOHN, POLLY, BETSEY, LYMAN, PRUDENCE; d 1838; Ref: Fiske Card File, Your Ancestors v3 #11&12 p473, v4 #1&2 p497, Barbour's VR Haddam LR7 p226, Desc of Wm Wilcoxson pp122,129,130.

JAMES - b 15 Nov 1764 Middletown , Middlesex Co CT s/FRANCIS & RACHEL (WILCOX) WILCOX; m 10 Nov 1788 JOANNA GIBSON; Ref: Your Ancestors v3 #11 & 12 p475, ECM v2 p96, Barbour's VR Middletown v1 p127.

JAMES - b 1766-1784; Res Dutchess Co NY; 1 son 1810; Ref: 1810 Census NY p221.

JAMES - b ca 1769 s/SMITHIAN & BETHANY (TALLMAN) WILCOX; m 17 Aug 1794 E Greenwich, Kent Co RI LUCY STRANGE ; ch STEPHEN; Ref: Arnold v1 p92, Your Ancestors v3 #11&12 p471.

JAMES - of Longmeadow, Hampden Co MA m 05 May 1796 MARY DAY; Ref: Fiske Card File.

JAMES - b 1771 RI or Dutchess Co NY poss s/CULBERT & RUTH (WHITE) WILCOX; m MARY BROWN who was b 1775 MA & d 24 Apr 1824; m LUCINDA ----- who was b 1788 CT; ch SILAS, RESCUM, ELIJAH, WILLIAM S, GEORGE, JAMES, GILBERT, BASHA, LAUREN; d 1826; Ref: Your Ancestors v10 #3 p1268, v11 #1 p1320.

JAMES - b ca 1773 Madison, New Haven Co CT; m 14 Feb 1799 Whitingham, Windham Co VT SUSANNAH DALRYMPLE; 3 sons 2 daus in 1810 incl JAMES; Ref: VT VR, 1810 Census p401, Nutmegger v7 #1 p111, Green Leaves of Whitingham p196.

JAMES - b 1775/6; m SUSAN ----- who was b 1783 & d 13 Aug 1849; Res Leon, Cattaraugus Co NY; ch prob ELIHU; d 18 Sep 1847; bur Franklin Cem Leon NY; Ref: Alice Wiatr.

JAMES - b 13 Nov 1775 Simsbury, Hartford Co CT s/AMOS & HANNAH (HOSKINS) WILCOX or AMOS & JOANNA (HILLYER) WILCOX; m 28 Jun 1804 HEPZIBAH HUMPHREY d/Cpt AMAZIAH & ELIZABETH (-----) HUMPHREY; ch ----- who d 03 Jun 1805, JAMES; Ref: Wilcox-Meigs pp67,86, Your Ancestors v13 #3 p1567, Barbour's VR

Simsbury TM4 p320, Rec of Marriages at Simsbury CT p5.

JAMES - Bpt 1776; m 14 Feb 1799 Whitingham, Windham Co VT; d 1847 Ellington, Chautauqua Co N; Ref: Alice Wiatr, Dr Clyde Wilcox.

JAMES - d 16 Mar 1812; Ref: Wisconsin Fam June 1940 p42.

JAMES - d Jun 1826 Carlton, Orleans Co NY; ch RESTCOM; Ref: Tree Talks v15 #2 p36.

JAMES - d 12 Nov 1845; Ref: Wisconsin Fam June 1940 p43.

JAMES - b ME; Res Marietta, Washington Co OH 1796/7; m REBECCA CAMPBELL who was from VA; ch GEORGE, CHARLES WILLIAM, JOHN, JESSE, MARY, JAMES & REBECCA twins, EMILY ZEBIDA, SARAH; War of 1812; d age 88; Ref: Hist of Muskingum Co OH p606.

JAMES - b 18 Sep 1778 Killingworth, Middlesex Co CT s/JAMES & EUNICE (VICKERY) WILCOX; m 20 Apr 1801/7 MARY WILCOX; Res Bridport, Addison Co VT; ch EDWIN, EDSON, HULDAH; d 16 Mar 1816; Ref: Your Ancestors v3 #9&10 p449, Wisconsin Fam June 1940 p41, Wilcox-Meigs p99, Texas Society DAR Roster v4 p2287, Desc of Wm Wilcoxson p118.

JAMES - b 1779 NY; m NANCY ----- who was b 1790; Res Pawling, Dutchess Co NY; ch ALANSON, LORENZO, WARREN, HENRY, WASHINGTON S; Ref: 1850 Census Pawling NY p225 Dw# 93.

JAMES - b ca 1780 s/JEHIEL & ABIGAIL (CRAMPTON) WILCOX; Res Sunderland, Bennington Co VT; Ref: Desc of Wm Wilcoxson p28.

JAMES - b 1781-1790; Res Little Falls, Herkimer Co NY 1840; 1 son & 2 daus; Ref: 1840 Census Herkimer Co NY p41.

JAMES - b 14 Mar 1793 Foster, Providence Co RI s/STEPHEN & PHEBE (HAMMOND) WILCOX; Ref: Arnold v3 p42, Your Ancestors v4 #1&2 p495.

JAMES - b ca 1796 s/GIDEON & ANNA (HANFORD) WILCOX; m CATHERINE BARRY; Ref: Desc of Wm Wilcoxson p 36.

JAMES - b 1797; Res Cassadaga, Chautauqua Co NY; boatman; drowned 02 Sep 1852 in an attempt to rescue others; Ref: 19th Cent Death Notices Reported in Fredonia Censor p596.

JAMES - b 1799 s/ISAAC & NANCY (NEWCOMB) WILCOX; Ref: Your Ancestors v9 #2 p1125.

JAMES - b 1799 VT s/JAMES & SUSANNAH (DALRYMPLE) WILCOX; m wife #3 MELINDA E DURFEE who was b 1818 NY; owned Lot 50 valued at $35 in Leon, Cattaraugus Co NY 1833; ch MARTIN V, JAMES M, SABRINA, JOSEPH; Ref: Hist of Cattaraugus Co NY p486, West NY Journal v2 #1 p44, 1850 Census Leon NY p49 Dw# 191, Nutmegger v7 #1 p111.

JAMES - b 10 Apr 1804 Halifax, Windham Co VT s/JOSEPH & PRUDENCE (DALRYMPLE) WILCOX; Ref: Bible Rec, Halifax Wilcox Fam mss, Samuel Gorton Desc p586.

JAMES - b 28 Jun 1805 s/DANIEL & ESTHER (MERRITT) WILCOX; d 05 Oct 1858; Ref: CT Bible Rec v11 p551.

JAMES Jr - b 15 Apr 1807 Simsbury, Hartford Co CT s/JAMES & HEPZIBAH (HUMPHREY) WILCOX; m 15 Oct 1829 LUCINDA TULLER who d 05 Oct 1858; Ref: Rev Allen McLean Rec p20, Your Ancestors v11 #3 p1353, v13 #3 p1567, Barbour's VR Simsbury TM4 pp320,517, Wilcox-Meigs p86.

JAMES - m 19 Jun 1817 MAHALA ROE d/CHARLES ROE; Res Hagerstown, Wayne Co IN; no issue; Ref: Fiske Card File.

JAMES - b 1807 England; m JANE ----- who was b 1806 England; Res Granger, Allegany Co NY; ch JOHN, MARY, JAMES, ELIZABETH, JOSEPH, THOMAS; Ref: 1850 Census Granger NY p9 Dw# 157.

JAMES - b 1801-1810; Res Little Falls Herkimer Co NY; 1 son & 2 daus; Ref; 1840 Census Herkimer Co NY p41.

JAMES - b ca 1810 Bridport, Addison Co VT s/ABNER WILCOX; d 1867; Ref: Wilcox-Meigs p100.

JAMES - b 22/23 May 1813 Berkshire, Berkshire Co MA s/CALEB & HANNAH (-----) WILCOX; m ca 1835 SARAH ANN ----- ; Res Rowe, Franklin Co MA; d 06 Dec 1867; Ref: Your Ancestors v3 #7&8 p424, Fiske Card File, Halifax VT Wilcox Fam mss.

JAMES - b 1814 Marion Co MO s/HAZARD & SARAH (SEELEY) WILCOX; d in infancy; Ref: Your Ancestors v12 #2 p1435.

JAMES - b 1814 colored; d 21 Feb 1848 age 34 New Haven, New Haven Co CT; Ref: Barbour's VR New Haven v5 p175.

JAMES - b ca 1815 s/ROSWELL & BERNICE (PEARSALL) WILCOX; Res Livingston Co NY; Ref: NYG&BR v107 p71.

JAMES - from Groveland, Livingston Co NY; m DELIA TRAVIS; moved to Firelands Area OH 1831; Res Fulton Co OH; Ref: Firelands Pioneer v3 3rd Series p70.

JAMES - b ca 1817 s/ROWLAND & ELIZABETH (VANETTA) WILCOX; Res Albany, Bradford Co PA; Ref: Pioneers of Bradford Co PA p309.

JAMES - b 1817 s/ERASTUS & MARTHA (HAMILTON) WILCOX; Res Conesus, Livingston Co NY; d 06 Oct 1832; Ref: Hist of Conesus NY p175.

JAMES - b 1819 NY; m ELIZABETH ----- who was b 1819 PA; Res Seneca Falls, Seneca Co NY; Painter; ch C R, ELIZABETH, J A; Ref: 1850 Census Seneca Falls NY p293 Dw# 2348.

JAMES - b 09 Sep 1819 s/SAMUEL & CLARISSA LOVE (MONTAYNE) WILCOX; m 1844 SARAH DAVENPORT; Ref: Your Ancestors v9 #2 p1126.

JAMES - b 1822 NY; m be 1852 MARY ----- who was b 1816 NY; Res Ripley, Chautauqua Co NY; ch JEREMIAH, HARVEY, JAMES; Ref: 1870 Census Ripley NY p150.

JAMES - b 20 Mar 1823 s/SADOCE & DEBORAH (PEASE) WILCOX; m LAURA E FOX; 2 dau; Ref: Desc of Wm Wilcoxson p218, CT Bible Rec v18 pp520,521.

JAMES - b 1825; d 17 Dec 1847 Newport, Newport Co RI; Ref: Arnold v8 p493.

JAMES - m 05 May 1846 New Haven, New Haven Co CT SARAH ANN CANN; colored; Ref: Barbour's VR New Haven v5 p160

JAMES - m 05 Nov 1850 New Haven, New Haven Co CT ELIZABETH A ROBBINS; colored; Ref: Barbour's VR New Haven v6 p147.

JAMES - b 1832 Sandisfield, Berkshire Co MA s/CHAUNCEY & MARIANNE (POTTER) WILCOX; m JANE MOODY; Ref: Your Ancestors v12 #2 p1437.

JAMES - b 1834 NY; s/REUBEN & ORRY (-----) WILCOX of McDonough, Chenango Co NY; Ref: 1850 Census Chenango Co NY, Your Ancestors v4 #11&12 p610.

JAMES - b 1836 England s/JAMES & JANE (-----) WILCOX of Granger, Allegany Co NY; Ref: 1850 Census Granger NY p9 Dw# 157.

JAMES - b 1839 NY s/SAMUEL & DEBORAH (SMITH) WILCOX of Concord, Erie Co NY; Ref: 1850 Census Concord NY p52 Dw# 758, See Samuel.

JAMES - b 1840 NY s/JOHN & MARY ANN (-----) WILCOX of Parish, Oswego Co NY; Ref: 1850 Census Parish, NY p5 Dw# 67.

JAMES - b 1841 New Haven, New Haven Co CT colored; d 28 Mar 1846; Ref: Barbour's VR New Haven v5 p159.

JAMES - b 1844 New Haven, New Haven Co CT colored; d 06 Jun 1846; Barbour's VR New Haven v5 p160.

JAMES - b 1844/5 OH s/LEANDER & JANE (MOE) WILCOX of Avon, Lorain Co OH; Ref: 1850 Census Lorain Co OH, Carol Wood.

JAMES - b 1846 Meriden, New Haven Co CT s/BENJAMIN BUSHNELL & ELIZA ANN (BRAINARD) WILCOX; Ref: Fam of Early Guilford p1206.

JAMES - b 1846 NY Twin with LYDIA s/CHENEY & AMITY (-----) WILCOX of Onondaga, Onondaga Co NY; Ref: 1850 Census Onondaga NY p324 Dw# 1492.

JAMES - b 1847 NY s/DARIUS & LUCE (-----) WILCOX of Truxton, Cortland Co NY; Ref: 1850 Census Truxton NY p152 Dw# 376.

JAMES - b 1849 OH s/REUBEN & HANNAH A (-----) WILCOX of Hiram, Portage Co OH; Ref: 1850 Census Hiram OH p3 Dw# 34.

JAMES - b 1849 Twin with MEHITABLE s/ELNATHAN & JULIA (DENISON) WILCOX of Stonington, New London Co CT ; Ref: 1850 Census Stonington CT Reel 432 #48 p256.

JAMES - b 1849 OH s/Rev MARTIN & MARTHA (-----) WILCOX of Madison, Lake Co OH; Ref: 1850 Census Madison OH Reel 259 p134.

JAMES - b 1849 NY s/HIRAM WILCOX of Little Falls, Herkimer Co NY; Ref: 1850 Census Little Falls NY p227 Dw# 398.

JAMES - b 1851 NY s/OZIAL Jr & SYLVIA (STEVENS) WILCOX of Georgetown twnshp, Madison Co NY; Ref: Desc of Wm Wilcoxson p169.

JAMES - b Apr 1857 s/ANDREW JACKSON & CAROLINE (MASTIN) WILCOX; Ref: Desc of Wm Wilcoxson p141.

JAMES - b 1858 NY s/JAMES & MARY (-----) WILCOX; Res Ripley, Chautauqua Co NY; Ref: 1870 Census Ripley NY p150.

JAMES - b Sep 1859 NY s/FRANCIS S & SALLY (-----) WILCOX of Busti, Chautauqua Co NY; Ref: 1860 Census Busti NY p46 Dw# 357.

JAMES - b 1870 WI s/JOHN & ALVIA (-----) WILCOX; Parents b NY; Res Juneau Co WI; Ref: 1880 Soundex WI.

JAMES - b 10 Mar 1877 CT s/EDWARD AUGUSTUS & EMMA A (BAILEY) WILCOX; m 26 Oct 1904 Westbrook, Middlesex Co CT SARAH E THOMPSON; Res East Haven, New Haven Co CT; no ch; Ref: Your Ancestors v2 p257.

JAMES - b 21 Oct 1881 s/JAMES HENRY & HARRIET ANN (DAY) WILCOX; Ref: Your Ancestors v12 #3 p1461.

JAMES A - Enrolled in Co B 16th Inf NY Volunteers St Lawrence Co NY 15 May 1861; Ref: Hist of St Lawrence Co NY p484.

JAMES A - b 1878 WI s/GEORGE & EMMA C (------) WILCOX; Father b NY; Res Eagle, Richland Co WI; Ref: 1880 Soundex Richland Co WI.

JAMES ALBION - b 30 Jan 1886 s/REUBEN CLIFTON & SARAH JANE (WILCOX) WILCOX; Single; d 16 Mar 1969 bur Black's Harbour, N B Canada; Ref: Desc of Charles Dyer Wilcox p1.

JAMES ANDREWS - b 23 Sep 1828 Columbus, Franklin Co OH s/PHINEAS BACON & SARAH D (ANDREWS) WILCOX; Educated at Yale ca 1851 Lawyer; m 1863

LUCY SULLIVANT who d 1915 d/JOSEPH SULLIVANT; Ref: OH Cem Rec p244.

JAMES AUGUSTUS - b 06 Aug 1857 Danbury, Fairfield Co CT s/ORLANDO & SARAH B (BENJAMIN) WILCOX; m LILLIAN COWEN d/WILLIAM COWEN; ch JULIA, NELLIE; d 12 Feb 1892; Ref: Desc of Wm Wilcoxson p259.

JAMES B - b 1796 CT; m HANNAH H ---- who was b 1807 MA; Res Alabama, Genesee Co NY; Druggist; ch JOHN A I, HARRIET A, WILLIAM H, HELEN A, FLORA M; Ref: 1850 Census Alabama NY p320 Dw# 1587.

JAMES B - b 1821; m SUSAN E ----- who was b 1830; Res Plainfield, Windham Co CT; ch EDWARD B; Ref: Barbour's VR Plainfield v4 p31.

JAMES B - s/HARLOW G & MARY J (McEWEN) WILCOX; Res NY, IL, Sedalia, Pettis Co MO; Ref: Desc of Wm Wilcoxson p225.

JAMES B - b 20 Mar 1856 Portage Co OH s/ALEXANDER HAMILTON & ADALINE (BARRACK) WILCOX; m 02 Jul 1882 SUSANNA SHIVELY of Deerfield, Portage Co OH; Ref: Hist of Portage Co OH p636, Desc of Wm Wilcoxson p244.

JAMES C - b 07 Jul 1818 Orangeville, Wyoming Co NY s/JEFFREY H & DEBORAH (----) WILCOX; m 01 Feb 1842 ORPHA JANE SPINK who was b 01 Mar 1823 Shaftsbury, Bennington Co VT d/WHITMAN SPINK; ch MARY MIRANDA, THOMAS B, CORDELIA D, EMMA J, CLARA E, EDWARD J; Ref: Your Ancestors v4 #5&6 p542, 1850 Census Orangeville NY p35 Dw# 548.

JAMES C - b be 1823 Livingston Co NY; Res Greece, Monroe Co NY; Ref: Hist of Monroe Co NY p316.

JAMES DAVID - b 17 Jan 1827 Lexington, Greene Co NY s/HENRY & SUSANNAH (MILLER) WILCOX; m 25 Nov 1854 UT ANNA MARIA ROBINSON d/JOSEPH L ROBINSON; m 15 Feb 1862 Mrs JUDITH (OVIATT) KNAPP; ch of 1st wife JAMES HENRY, JOSEPH DORVIL, EBENEZER ORLANDO, JULIA MARIA, LUCY A, OLIVER LEROY, ANNABELLE, MARGARET RUTH, DAVID EUGENE, WILLIAM ARNOLD, GEORGE WALLAS, MARY HELEN, ORSON CHARLES; 10 ch by 2nd wife; Ref: Pioneers & Prominent Men of Utah p1245, Your Ancestors v4 #11&12 p612, Desc of Wm Wilcoxson p144.

JAMES E - b Nov 1818 Bridport, Addison Co VT s/ABNER & GLORIANNA (ELDRIDGE) WILCOX; d 1867 Hawaiian Islands; Ref: Your Ancestors v3 #9&10 p450, Desc of Wm Wilcoxson p118.

JAMES E - b 03 Jan 1869 s/WILLIAM ALBERT & ELLA ALMEDA (SMITH) WILCOX; m CATHERINE -----; ch NORMAN, JAMES, AUDREY; bur Rangeley, Franklin Co ME; Ref: Desc of Charles Dyer Wilcox p4.

JAMES F - m LOUISA S ----- Be 1843; Res Taunton, Bristol Co MA; ch FRANK JAMES, MARIA LOUISA; Ref: Taunton MA VR v1 p 455.

JAMES FRANKLIN - b 01 Jun 1830 Sandgate, Bennington Co VT s/OZIAL & NANCY (PAINE) WILCOX; m MARY ELIZABETH NICHOLS who was b 01 Jun 1829 & d 06 Feb 1915; ch EMILENE, ELIZA, NANCY ANN, WILLIE OZIAL, IDA MAY, CLARA B; Civil War; d 26 May 1899 bur Arlington Cem Arlington, Bennington Co VT; Ref: Desc of Wm Wilcoxson p171.

JAMES G - b 1831 NY s/BENJAMIN & SOPHIA (-----) WILCOX of Palmyra, Portage Co OH; Ref: 1850 Census Palmyra Co OH p208 Dw# 1334.

JAMES H - m 18-- POLLY M ----- who was b 1829 & d 12 Sep 1852; Res Chenango Co NY; Ref: Tree Talks v10 #3.

JAMES H - b 12 May 1831 s/WILLARD De RUYTER & SYBIL (GODFREY) WILCOX of De Ruyter, Madison Co NY & Homer, Cortland Co NY; m SARAH J HANER d/CHARLES & SARAH (SLITER) HANER; Res Washtenaw Co MI 1836; ch ALBERT, LOUIS; d 1890 Ypsilanti, Washtenaw Co MI; Ref: Your Ancestors v12 #2 p1436, 1850 Census De Ruyter NY p292 Dw# 299.

JAMES H - b 1846 NY s/DANIEL & ELVIRA E (-----) WILCOX of Varick, Seneca Co NY; Ref: 1850 Census Varick NY p58 Dw# 862.

JAMES H - b Jun 1850 NY s/ISAAC H & CAROLINE (-----) WILCOX of Dover, Dutchess Co NY; Ref: 1850 Census Dover NY p316 Dw# 93.

JAMES HARVEY - b 1829 Geauga Co OH s/NATHAN BENJAMIN & SAMANTHA (BROOKS) WILCOX; Mexican War; d af 1890 CA; Ref: Dan Williams.

JAMES HENRY - b 07 Oct 1855 s/JAMES DAVID & ANNA MARIA (ROBINSON) WILCOX; Ref: Wilcox-Meigs p120, Desc of Wm Wilcoxson p144.

JAMES HENRY - b 10 Nov 1855 s/JAMES HENRY OWEN & MARY (YOUNG) WILCOX; m HARRIET ANN DAY who was b 27 Dec 1864 & d 29 Sep 1900; ch JAMES, HARRIET, EPHRAIM, GEORGE, HENRY, EDGAR, HAZARD, QUINTON, PERL & RUBY twins, ANNA; d 25 Nov 1939; Ref: Your Ancestors v12 #2 p1436 #3 p1461.

JAMES HORATIO - b 29 Sep 1864 Brooklyn NY s/JAMES & FANNY (GRAVES) WILCOX; Ref: Wilcox-Meigs p105, Desc of Wm Wilcoxson p264.

JAMES HEUSTEN - b 27 Dec 1823 E Guilford, New Haven Co CT s/HEUSTEN & JULIA (CRAMPTON) WILCOX; m 11 Feb 1851 CLARISSA H GRISWOLD of Clinton, Middlesex Co CT who was b 30 Jan 1828 & d 24 Feb 1858 d/EDWARD GRISWOLD; m FANNY GRAVES who d 13 Feb 1873; m LUCINA H POWERS 30 Nov 1876; Res Madison, New Haven Co CT, Brooklyn NY; ch by 1st wife NELLIE H, EDWARD G, FANNIE A; ch by 2nd wife ALBERT GRAVES, JAMES HORATIO, ARTHUR HERBERT; d 19 Mar 1895; Ref: Wilcox-Meigs pp87,105, Barbour's VR Madison v2 p140, Desc of Wm Wilcoxson p264, Fam of Early Guilford pp 1212-1214.

JAMES JEWETT - b 03 Aug 1830 Madison, New Haven Co CT s/AUGUSTUS BENJAMIN & CLARISSA (JEWETT) WILCOX; Ref: Fam of Early Guilford p1204, Barbour's VR Madison v1 p137.

JAMES K HAMILTON - b 14 Oct 1842 NY s/ALBERT OLIVER & ANNE ELIZABETH (HAMILTON) WILCOX; d 23 Nov 1898; Ref: Wilcox-Meigs p99.

JAMES L - m 17 Sep 1855 Marshall, Calhoun Co MI HELEN ARMSTRONG; Res Shoreham, Addison Co VT & Marshall MI; Ref: Nutmegger Jun 1987.

JAMES LESTER - b ca 1825 s/WILLIAM B & IRENA (LARKIN) WILCOX of Putnam, Windham Co CT; m 12/13 Oct 1844 Thompson, Windham Co CT RUBY WILBUR; both of Sturbridge, Worcester Co MA; Ref: Your Ancestors v4 #11&12 p609, Sturbridge VR p290, Barbour's VR Thompson v2 p73.

JAMES M - m 04 Sep 1813 PA ELIZA ORN; Ref: Daily Advertiser Philadelphia p16.

JAMES M - b 1801 NY; m RUTH ----- who was b 1805 NY; purchased Lot 17 Twnshp 4 Range 14 in Chautauqua Co NY 1827; Blacksmith; Res Westfield, Chautauqua Co NY; ch ADELINE A, SARAH P, ELLEN E; Ref: Deed Book Chautauqua Co NY v5 p558, 1850 Census Westfield NY p143 Dw# 280.

JAMES M - s/ERASTUS & MARGARET (KING?) WILCOX of Washington, Madison & Ontario Cos NY; m MARY A -----; Ref: Janet Armbrust.

JAMES M - b 1821 Exeter, Washington Co RI; m 01 Oct 1845 Pomfret, Windham Co CT SUSAN E WILLIAMS who was b 1830; Res Plainfield, Windham Co CT; Tailor; ch EDWARD B; Ref; Barbour's VR Plainfield v4 p31, Pomfret v3 p73.

JAMES M - b 1839 Cattaraugus Co NY s/HORACE J & RACHEL (-----) WILCOX; Res Collins, Erie Co NY; d 10 Feb 1908 age 69 yr bur Pine Hill Cem Gowanda, Erie Co NY Sec C Lot 23; Ref: Alice Wiatr.

JAMES M - b 1849 NY s/JAMES & MELINDA E (DURFEE) WILCOX of Leon, Cattaraugus Co NY; Ref: 1850 Census Leon NY p49 Dw# 191, See James.

JAMES M - b 1861 s/----- & MARGARET (-----) WILCOX; d 06 Oct 1867 age 6yr 10 da; bur Andover, Allegany Co NY; Ref: Yesteryears v2 #8 p39.

JAMES M - b 1870 NY s/JAMES & MARTHA (BLANDBURY) WILCOX; d 02 Feb 1914 age 44 Gowanda, Erie Co NY bur Pine Hill Cem Sec C Lot 23; Ref: Burials in Pine Hill Cem, Alice Wiatr.

JAMES M - b 1892 NY s/PORTER B & MARY MAY (FROST) WILCOX; m LOUISE CLARK; Res Arkwright, Chautauqua Co NY; ch GORDON, GEORGE, MARGUERITE, DORIS; Ref: Wilcox Hist mss, 1910 Census Arkwright NY.

JAMES MADISON - b 04 Jul 1810 s/ABNER & SARAH (HORTON) WILCOX; Ref: Desc of Wm Wilcoxson p141.

JAMES MARTIN - b 05 Feb 1843 Rowe, Franklin Co MA s/BENJAMIN & ELIZABETH (-----) WILCOX; Ref: Halifax VT Wilcox Fam mss.

JAMES NELSON - b 20 Dec 1814 NY s/STEPHEN & PHOEBE (ROGERS) WILCOX; Ref: LDS Fam Group Sheet.

JAMES PHILIP - b 02 Oct 1852 Plymouth England; m ALICE THOMAS Apr 1885; Res Chicago, Cook Co IL 1867; ch PHILIP ALLEN; Ref: Narragansett Reg p293.

JAMES PICKWICK - b 02 Jun 1829 Holt, Wiltshire England; m 1855 ERURUA DURRAN; Res Chicago IL 1855; ch MARIAN, ALRUA, ALICE, MAY; Ref: Narragansett Reg p293.

JAMES PURDIE/PURDY - b 06 Nov 1840 s/HENRY HOPSON & MARRION LYLE (PURDY) WILCOX; m 02 Oct 1862 SABRINA STANBRO who was b 13 Jun 1842 & d 22 Oct 1894/6; m MARTHA A/M POWERS who was b 22 Dec 1844 & d 19 Sep 1910; ch HARRIETT, HADWIN P; d 07 Apr 1910 Earlville, Chenango Co NY; Ref: Chenango Co NY Cem Records p9, Your Ancestors v3 #3 p319.

JAMES ROBERT - b 18 Jul 1848 Trescott, Washington Co ME s/CHARLES DYER & PRUDENCE (PARKER) WILCOX; m LUCINDA PLANT who was b 1866 & d 11 May 1959 d/BENJAMIN & NANCY (LAWSON) PLANT; ch PHILIP LEWIS, ARNOLD, EVA, VICTORIA, HATZELL; d 07 Jan 1926 bur Deep Cove Cem, N B Canada; Ref: Desc of Charles Dyer Wilcox p6.

JAMES ROBERT - b 15 Oct 1868 Outer Wood Island, N B Canada s/ALFRED ANANIAS & CHARLOTTE ANN (HOLLAND) WILCOX; m MARGARET A MATTHEWS who was b 19 Jan 1873 & d 04 Apr 1933; ch HARRY R, FANNIE, LEVI W, GEORGE O; bur St George N B Canada; Ref: Desc of Charles Dyer Wilcox p2.

JAMES RUSSELL - s/JOHN & RACHEL F (POST) WILCOX; Res Medina, Medina Co OH; Ref: Desc of Wm Wilcoxson p130.

JAMES SMITH - b 1777 Philadelphia, Philadelphia Co PA s/JOHN WILCOX; Res New London, New London Co CT, PA, CA; d 23 Feb 1838; Ref: Desc of Wm Wilcoxson p335, Daily Advertiser, Philadelphia PA.

JAMES VAN DYKE - b 19 Aug 1853 s/HENRY COLE & MARIE LOUISE (COLE) WILCOX; d 10 Oct 1930; Ref: Desc of Wm Wilcoxson p260.

JAMES W - b 1851; m NELLIE -----; Res Hanover, Chautauqua Co NY; ch BESSIE, 2 other dau; Ref: 1910 Census Hanover NY.

JANE - b 04 Jan 1706 Middletown, Middlesex Co CT d/EPHRAIM & SILENCE (HAND) WILCOX; m 03 Nov 1727 JOHN CLARK Jr; Ref: Nutmegger v4 #3 p330, v13 #3 p389, Your Ancestors v4 #3&4 pp524,525, NEH&GR v14 p138, Barbour's VR Middletown LR1 pp1,32.

JANE - of W Greenwich, Kent Co RI; m 17 Jun 1756 JONATHAN SPRAGUE of Whitingham, Windham Co VT; Ref: Alice Wiatr.

JANE/TAMER - b 14 Feb 1747 Killingworth, Middlesex Co CT d/ABEL & MARTHA (STEVENS) WILCOX;

m 10 Jan 1776 JOHN RUTTY; Ref: Wilcox-Meigs p41, Your Ancestors v3 #1 p280.

JANE prob Mrs - b 1766 RI; Res Columbus, Chenango Co NY with BENJAMIN & POLLY (-----) ROWE; d af 19 Sep 1850; Ref: 1850 Census Columbus NY p279 Dw# 2124.

JANE - b ca 1785/1788 d/AARON & ELIZABETH (BELDEN) WILCOX of Amenia, Dutches Co NY; m BENJAMIN KNICKERBOCKER; Ref: NYG&BR v40 p104, Desc of Wm Wilcoxson p162.

JANE - b Aug 1794 d/ISAAC & NANCY (NEWCOMB) WILCOX; Ref: Your Ancestors v9 #2 p1125.

JANE - m 01 Mar 1818 Dartmouth, Bristol Co MA DANIEL PEASE; Ref: Dartmouth VR p546.

JANE - b 18 Nov 1806 NY/PA d/HEZEKIAH & MAHALA (WILCOX) WILCOX; m RUSSELL LINDLEY; Res Bradford Co PA; Ref: Your Ancestors v10 #3 p1248.

JANE - b ca 1822 Otis, Berkshire Co MA d/CHAUNCEY & MARIANNE (POTTER) WILCOX; m 27 Mar 1845 AMOS SMITH; Ref: Your Ancestors v12 #2 p1437, Desc of Wm Wilcoxson p222.

JANE - m 02 Oct 1839 E Hartford, Hartford Co CT CHARLES GRIMMAN of Philadelphia PA; Ref: Barbour's VR E Hartford v1 p130.

JANE - of Canton, Hartford Co CT; m 16 Mar 1843 Canton CT DRYDEN BARBER; Moved to Firelands District (Huron & Erie Co) OH 1849; Res Traer IA; Ref: Firelands Pioneer v3 3rd Series p70, Barbour's VR Canton v1 p18.

JANE - m 24 Sep 1845 Hartford, Hartford Co CT EDWIN P BROWN of New Hampshire; Ref: Barbour's VR Hartford v1 p207.

JANE - d Dec 1850 Columbus, Chenango Co NY; Ref: VR of Chenango Co NY p33.

JANE - of Albany, Albany Co NY m 14 Feb 1847 Suffield, Hartford Co CT JOHN J FOWLER of Suffield CT; Ref: Barbour's VR Suffield NB1 p405.

JANE - b 1830 NY d/WILLIAM & LUTICIA (-----) WILCOX of Milford, Otsego Co NY; Ref: 1850 Census Milford NY p113 Dw# 227.

JANE - b 1832 NY d/EMERY & MARTHA (-----) WILCOX of Newport, Herkimer Co NY; Ref: 1850 Census Newport NY p173 Dw# 289.

JANE - b 1834 CT d/EBENEZER & CAROLINE (COTTRELL) WILCOX of Stonington, New London Co CT; Ref: 1850 Census Stonington CT Reel 432 #48 p255.

JANE - b 1836 NY d/RANSOM WILCOX of Pawling, Dutchess Co NY; Ref: 1850 Census Pawling p228 Dw# 145.

JANE - b 02 Oct 1836 d/JEFFREY & ANNE (STILLMAN) or (MASON) WILCOX; Ref: Gen of CT Fam v2 p537, Your Ancestors v13 #1 p1515.

JANE - b 1836 NY d/ERASTUS & LOUISA (-----) WILCOX of Tully, Onondaga Co NY; Ref: 1850 Census Tully NY p162 Dw# 167.

JANE - d/Dr Wilcox of E Bloomfield, Ontario Co NY m 18 Jun 1846 Houston, Harris Co TX LEWIS B HARRIS; Ref: 10,000 VR of Central NY p109.

JANE - b 1839 NY d/J & SARAH (-----) WILCOX of Wheatland, Monroe Co NY; Ref: 1850 Census Wheatland NY p240 Dw# 268.

JANE/JENNIE - b ca 1838 Bridport, Addison Co CT d/ABNER & BETSEY (WINES) WILCOX; d ca 1861; Ref: Wilcox-Meigs p100, Your Ancestors v3 #9&10 p450..

JANE - b 1839 NY d/ROBERT & NINA (-----) WILCOX of Oswego, Oswego Co NY; Ref: 1850 Census Oswego NY p233 Dw# 292.

JANE - b 1839 NY d/THOMAS R & LOUISA (-----) WILCOX of Belfast, Allegany Co NY; Ref: 1850 Census Belfast NY p266 Dw# 56.

JANE - b 1841 England d/WILLIAM & RACHEL (-----) WILCOX of Beekman, Dutchess Co NY; Ref: 1850 Census Beekman NY p274 Dw# 171.

JANE - b ca 1845 d/JOHN F & LUCRETIA (GORDON) WILCOX of Grand Isle, Grand Isle Co VT; m WARREN HALL; Ref: Cutter's Northern NY v1 p172.

JANE - Will probated 28 Sep 1861 Chenango Co NY I-259; Ref: Index to Wills of Chenango Co NY.

JANE - b 1850 Sandgate, Bennington Co VT d/JOHN AUSTIN & ELMIRA B (ANDREWS) WILCOX; Ref: Desc of Wm Wilcoxson p170.

JANE - b 1854 NY d/LYSANDER BYRAM & HELEN CHILDS (LEDYARD) WILCOX of Napoli, Cattaraugus Co NY; Ref: 1860 Census Napoli NY Reel 653 #726 p52, See Lysander Byram.

JANE A - m 1863 ORA WINSOR a widower Whitestown, Vernon Co WI; d 1875; Ref: Hist of Vernon Co WI p758.

JANE A - b 07 Oct 1850 Norwich, New London Co CT d/WILLIAM & NANCY (-----) WILCOX; Ref: Barbour's VR Norwich v7/8 p100.

JANE AGNES - b 21 July 1895 Boston, Suffolk Co MA d/WILLIAM DRISCOLL & JULIA AGNES (GANEY) WILCOX; m ELMER JUSTASON; ch CARROLL ELMER, VERA, LOIS, MARION; d 20 Mar 1963 bur Pennfield, N B Canada; Ref: Desc of Charles Dyer Wilcox p11.

JANE E - m 10 Dec 1846 Southington, Hartford Co CT ASAHEL R THOMPSON of Manchester, Hartford Co CT; Ref: Barbour's VR Southington v1 p121.

JANE E - b 1836 NY d/WILLARD De RUYTER & SYBIL (GODFREY) WILCOX of De Ruyter, Madison Co NY & Homer, Cortland Co NY; Ref: Your Ancestors v12 #2 p1436, 1850 Census De Ruyter NY p292 Dw# 299.

JANE E - b 1838 NY d/ABEL & ELIZABETH (-----) WILCOX of Bergen, Genesee Co NY; Ref: 1850 Census Bergen NY p51 Dw# 677.

JANE ELIZA - of Batavia, Genesee Co NY m 20 Aug 1824 East Bloomfield Ontario Co NY HENRY TISDALE merchant of Pembroke, Genesee Co NY who was b 1795 Frankfort, Herkimer Co NY & d 19 Jan 1851 Jackson, Jackson Co MI s/BENJAMIN & NANCY (SAUNDERS) TISDALE; ch LUCIEN WILCOX, NANCY J, CHARLES HENRY, HOBART, BENJAMIN FOLLETT, EMMA ELIZABETH, MARIA ELIZABETH; Removed to 338 4th Ave NYC NY after 1851; Ref: 10,000 VR Western NY p229, Desc of James Tisdale pp210,328,329.

JANE ELIZABETH - b 16 Jun 1816 Danbury, Fairfield Co CT d/AUGUSTUS & FANNY (BENEDICT) WILCOX; m 26 Mar 1835 PHILANDER BETTS Sr who was b 17 Aug 1812 Danbury CT & d 10 Nov 1894 Farmington, Franklin Co Me; 9 ch incl PHILANDER 3rd; d 09 Jul 1884 Brooklyn, Kings Co NY; bur Wooster Cem

Danbury CT; Ref: Parmelee Fam p240, Barbour's VR Danbury v3 p84, Desc of Wm Wilcoxson p259.

JANE F - b 1817/1828 Tompkins Co NY d/CLARK & SALLY (MAXSON) WILCOX of Groton, Tompkins Co NY; m ----- VIELE; Ref: 1850 Census Groton NY p123 Dw# 19, Carol A Cox.

JANE F - b 1836 NY d/BENONI & CATHERINE (WILCOX) WILCOX of Pawling, Dutchess Co NY; Ref: 1850 Census Pawling NY p225 Dw# 94.

JANE HULDAH - b 21 May 1826 Cherry Creek, Chautauqua Co NY d/THOMAS WARD & HULDAH PRUDENCE (McMANUS) WILCOX; m 25 Nov 1847 Fredonia, Chautauqua Co NY REVILLO N TANNER who was b 07 May 1820 & d 07 Jul 1898; ch ARABELLA J, BENTON, NETTIE, ORVIN, unnamed baby; d 19 Dec 1902 Cherry Creek NY; Ref: Wilcox Hist mss p2, Tombstone Inscr, 19th Cent Marriages Reported in Fredonia Censor p119.

JANE JEMIMA - b 28 Nov 1822 d/LUMON & ZIBAH (HOWARD) WILCOX; m 01 Oct 1848 at Westminster, Windham Co VT DAVID CROWELL GORHAM who was b 09 Mar 1818; ch SUSAN JANE, CLARA ELLA, HENRY CROWELL, EDWIN EDGAR; Ref: MUH pp755,760.

JANE M - b 1847 CT d/HENRY M & HARRIET N (-----) WILCOX of Preston, New London Co CT; Ref: 1850 Census Preston CT Reel 432 #49 p17.

JANE MARIA - b 01 Feb 1885 d/SILAS & ELVIRA JOANNE (LAMBERT) WILCOX; m MOODY DOTTEN; d 30 Oct 1966 bur St George, N B Canada; Ref: Desc of Charles Dyer Wilcox p2.

JANE MINDWELL - b 16 May 1850 Milford, Oakland Co MI d/LEVI SHELDON & ISABELLA (LAMBIE) WILCOX; m ALBERT FIFIELD who was b 28 Apr 1843; ch LUCY, LEONARD; Ref: Your Ancestors v14 #2 p1646, #3 p1671.

JANE P - b 06 Oct 1827 Lenox, Madison Co NY d/ALANSON & IRENE (JOHNSON) WILCOX; Ref: Pioneers of Madison Co NY p281.

JANE POLAND - b 1838 OH d/BENJAMIN & SOPHIA (-----) WILCOX of Palmyra, Portage Co OH; Ref: 1850 Census Palmyra OH p208 Dw# 1334.

JANNA - b 20 Sep 1701 Chatham/Middletown, Middlesex Co CT s/EPHRAIM & SILENCE (HAND) WILCOX;

m 29 Apr 1725 RACHEL BOARDMAN who was b 16 Nov 1706 Wethersfield, Hartford Co CT d/SAMUEL & MEHITABLE (CADWELL) BOARDMAN; Res Westminster, Windham Co VT; ch SILENCE, JANNA, MEHITABLE, RACHEL, WAITSTILL, EPHRAIM, MARY, JOHN, AARON & MOSES twins, ESTHER; Ref: Barbour's VR Chatham v1 p114, Middletown LR1 p22, MUH pp744,747, Nutmegger v4 #3 p330, v13 #3 p385, Your Ancestors v4 #3&4 p524, NEH&GR v14 p138.

JANNA - b 25 Jul 1728 Middletown, Middlesex Co CT s/JANNA & RACHEL (BOARDMAN) WILCOX; m 14 Nov 1751 JEMIMA WILCOX who was b 01 Jul 1723 d/JOHN & MARY (BARNES) WILCOX; Res Middletown CT; Ref: MUH p747, Nutmegger v4 #3 p330, Your Ancestors v4 #3&4 p524, Barbour's VR Middletown TR1 p22, v2 p246.

JANNA - b 30 Jan 1780 Westminster, Windham Co VT s/EPHRAIM & DIADEMA (FRENCH) WILCOX; m 1801 CANDACE GOODELL who was b 1783 & d 03 Aug 1850 d/EDWARD & DORCAS (SHEPARD) GOODELL; Res Ludlow, Windsor Co VT; ch HORACE ALEXANDER, LUCENA, OLIVE ALMIREA, WELTHY ANN, JANNA GOODELL; Ref: Goodell mss from VT State Library, MUH p750, Your Ancestors v4 #5&6 p545, Texas Society DAR Roster v4 p2287.

JANNA - m ca 1800 RUTHANNA ----- who was b 30 Jun 1773 & d 31 Aug 1861; Res Cavendish, Windsor Co VT; Ref: VT State Library.

JANNA - b 06 Aug 1803 Westminster, Windham Co VT s/LUMON & ZIBAH (HOWARD) WILCOX; d 31 May 1868; Ref: MUH p755.

JANNA GOODELL - b ca 1810 VT s/JANNA & CANDACE (GOODELL) WILCOX Ludlow, Windsor Co VT; Ref: Your Ancestors v4 #5&6 p545.

JARED - b 1756-1775; Res Pawlet, Rutland Co VT; 2 sons & 6 dau in 1800; Ref: 1800 Census Rutland Co VT p119.

JARED - b 1770 s/NATHAN & TABITHA (PROSSER) WILCOX; m BRIDGET STANTON; Res Stonington, New London Co CT; ch JARED, STANTON, WILLIAM, BRIDGET, CHRISTIANA, CODDINGTON, SARAH, SUSAN; Ref: Hist of Stonington CT p661, Barbour's VR Stonington v4 p107.

JARED - b 1776-1795; Res New Hartford, Hartford Co CT; ch 1 son & 1 dau 1820; Ref: 1820 Census CT.

JARED - b 28 Dec 1788 Stonington, New London Co CT s/JARED & BRIDGET (STANTON) WILCOX; Ref: Barbour's VR Stonington v4 p107.

JARED - b 10 Jun 1790 Killingworth, Middlesex Co CT s/ELIJAH & MARY (FRENCH) WILCOX; m IRENE/IRENA BARTLETT who was b 27 May 1795 d/REUBEN & SUSANNA (KELSEY) BARTLETT; Res Madison, New Haven Co CT, Bergen, Genesee Co NY; ch ZINA EDWIN, ADELINE MELISSA, ELIZA JENNETTE, ANN AMELIA; Ref: Wilcox-Meigs p80, Fam of Early Guilford pp41,1206,1207, Gen of CT Fam v1 p108, Barbour's VR Killingworth v2 p14, Madison v2 p32, 1850 Census Bergen NY p51 Dw# 676.

JARED - of NY m 16 Apr 1845 MARY ELIZABETH ASHBEY of Groton, New London Co CT; Ref: Barbour's VR Groton v1 p68.

JARED B - s/JARED & NANCY (WELLS) WILCOX; mentioned in 1853 will of BENEDICT WELLS of Clarkstown, Rockland Co NY; Ref: Rockland Co NY Wills v1-4 p42.

JARED J - s/JARED & ANN (----AY) WILCOX d 1844 age 2yr 11mo 5da; Bur Oak Hill Cem Nyack, Rockland Co NY; Ref: Gravestone Inscr Rockland Co NY p40.

JARED O - b 15 Apr 1818 Clinton, Middlesex Co CT s/SILAS & ABIGAIL (-----) WILCOX; Ref: Barbour's VR Clinton v1 p52.

JARVIS - b 1800 NY; m SARAH ----- who was b 1805 NY; Res Pomfret & Stockton Chautauqua Co NY; ch ENOCH, LUCIUS C, SAMANTHA, FRANCES; d be 1860; Ref: Gen Helper Mar/Apr 1987, Mrs Dorothy Willis, 1850 Census Pomfret NY p209 Dw# 352, 1860 Census Stockton NY p281 Dw# 2271.

JASON - b 22 Jan 1759 Killingworth, Middlesex Co CT s/ELIJAH & SARAH (WILCOX) WILCOX; Ref: Barbour's VR Killingworth v2 p103.

JASON - b 28 Dec 1780 Killingworth, Middlesex Co CT s/ELIJAH Jr & MARY (FRENCH) WILCOX; m LUCY FESSENDEN who was b 1774 CT; Res Bergen, Genesee Co NY; ch EUNICE, MARY, SALLY, ELIJAH; d af 1860; Ref: Wilcox-Meigs p80, Fam of Early Guilford pp1206,1207, Barbour's VR Killingworth v2 p14, 1850 Census Bergen NY p58 Dw# 778, 1860 Census Bergen NY p272 Dw# 295.

JASON - of Schuylerville, Saratoga Co NY m Lakeville, Livingston Co NY 01 Jan 1849 MARY COON of Lakeville NY; Ref: NYG&BR v119 p168.

JASON - b 11 Nov 1844 Middletown, Middlesex Co CT s/JEDEDIAH & MARY ANN (-----) WILCOX; Ref: Barbour's VR Middletown v4 p8.

JASPER - b 1847 Painesville, Lake Co OH s/ORLANDO BLISS & LYDIA (ALLEN) WILCOX; d young af 1850; Ref: Bogue Fam p398, 1850 Census Painesville OH Reel 259 p197.

JASPER LEVI - b 15 Aug 1831 VT/NH s/ASA & SYBIL (BLISS) WILCOX; Res Perry, Lake Co OH; d 27 Aug 1846; Ref: Bogue Fam p397, Your Ancestors v3 #5 p378.

JAY - b 1846 NY s/ASA & HARRIET (STEVENS) WILCOX of Hamilton & Georgetown, Madison Co NY; Ref: Desc of Wm Wilcoxson p169, 1850 Census Georgetown NY p388 Dw# 210.

JAY - b 1879 Lincoln, Madison Co NY s/HARRISON & CATHERINE (SNYDER) WILCOX; m EDITH BURGDORF; Ref: Pioneers of Madison Co NY p281.

JAY EUGENE - b 04 Jan 1851 IL or WI; m 2nd KATE IDA LOVELL who was b 12 Feb 1862/3 River Falls, Pierce Co WI & d Mar 1946 Estacada, Clackamas Co OR; ch LYNN FRANCIS, MINA MAUDE; d Eckman ND; Ref: FGS Seattle Gen Soc.

JAY P - b 1838 NY s/ERASMUS D & SARAH (-----) WILCOX of Vernon, Oneida Co NY; Ref: 1850 Census Vernon NY p97 Dw# 379.

JAY WARREN - b 28 May 1868 Buffalo, Erie Co NY s/HARLOW MARTIN & MARILLA (JAY) WILCOX; m 06 Sep 1890 MAY ANGELIA WILCOX who was b 29 Jan 1874 Villanova, Chautauqua Co NY & d 25 Jan 1945 d/ALFRED JAMES & MARY ANGELIA (BABCOCK) WILCOX; Res Silver Creek, Chautauqua Co NY; ch ALICE HAZEL, HERBERT, HARLOW MERLE, MARTELLA ANGELIA, DEXTER WARREN, LARRY MERLE, HULDAH MAY; d 17 Dec 1936 Silver Creek NY; Ref: Marriage cert, Obits, birth cert, personal knowledge, death cert, Wilcox Hist mss, May A Wilcox's family record.

JEANETTE - d/BENJAMIN & ELIZABETH (OTIS) WILCOX of Jefferson Co NY & Portage Co OH; m ALANSON PLUM; Ref: Hist of Portage Co OH p898, See Benjamin.

JEANETTE - b ca 1814 Killingworth, Middlesex Co CT d/SIMEON WILCOX; m OLIVER DOWD; Ref: Wilcox-Meigs p85.

JEANETTE - b 22 May 1822 d/ABNER & SARAH (HORTON) WILCOX; Ref: Desc of Wm Wilcoxson p141.

JEANETTE - m 01 Jul 1858 Wayne Co IA JAMES A KOONS; Ref: Hawkeye Heritage v14 #1 p22.

JEANETTE - b ca 1890 d/JOHN & CARRIE (COLE) WILCOX of Adrian, Lenawee Co MI; Ref: Your Ancestor p1319.

JEDEDIAH - b 29 Jan 1723/4 Simsbury, Hartford Co CT s/WILLIAM Jr & THANKFUL (ADAMS) WILCOX; d 1727/8; Ref: Nutmegger v10 #2 p214, Your Ancestors v10 #4 p1275, Desc of Wm Wilcoxson p23.

JEDEDIAH - b 1763 s/AMOS & HANNAH (HOSKINS) WILCOX; m SARAH CASE who was b 1764 & d 1830 d/ZACHEUS & ABIGAIL (BARBER) CASE Simsbury, Hartford Co CT; Res Canton, Hartford Co CT; ch THOMAS; d 1818 age 53; Ref: Goodwin's Gen Notes p280, Wilcox-Meigs pp67,85, The Munson Record p344, Early Settlers of W Simsbury p129, Desc of Wm Wilcoxson p209.

JEDEDIAH - m ANNA ----- who was b 1788 & d 08 Mar 1841 Middletown, Middlesex Co CT; bur Highland Cem; Ref: Hale Collection.

JEDEDIAH - b 01 Jun 1778 Middletown, Middlesex Co CT s/JOHN Jr & EUNICE (NORTON) WILCOX; d 10 Oct 1787; Ref: Your Ancestors v3 #4 p351, Early Fam of Wallingford p332, Barbour's VR Middletown v2 p143, Hist of Wallingford p938.

JEDEDIAH - b 07 Feb 1788 Middletown, Middlesex Co CT s/JOSEPH & MARIAM (BACON) WILCOX; m MARY ANN WILCOX who was b 1805 & d 09 Mar 1858 d/SETH; ch JASON, ANNA MARIA, PHINEAS B; d 28 Feb 1858 bur Highland Cem Middletown CT; Ref: Hale Coll, Nutmegger v4 #1 p133, Early Fam of Wallingford p332, Your Ancestors v3 #4 p352, Barbour's VR Middletown v2 p319, v3 p504, v4 p8, Hist of Wallingford p938.

JEDEDIAH - m 09 Jun 1814 Middletown, Middlesex Co CT ANNA YALE; Ref: Barbour's VR Middletown v3 p247.

JEDEDIAH - b 24 Mar 1797 Exeter, Washington Co RI s/ASA & ELEANOR (LAWTON) WILCOX; Ref: Your Ancestors v4 #11&12 p610.

JEDEDIAH - b 04 Mar 1827 Westfield, Middlesex Co CT s/ELISHA BACON & HEPZIBAH (CORNWELL) WILCOX; Ref: Early Fam of Wallingford p333, Your Ancestors v3 35 p379, Hist of Wallingford p939.

JEDEDIAH 2nd - of Middletown, Middlesex Co CT m 06 Sep 1848 CLARISSA HOVEY of Berlin, Hartford Co, CT; Ref: Barbour's VR Berlin v1 p125.

JEDEDIAH A - b 28 Oct 1821 Dartmouth, Bristol Co MA; Ref: Dartmouth VR p302.

JEDUTHAN - b 18 Nov 1768 Middletown, Middlesex Co CT s/JOHN & EUNICE (NORTON) WILCOX; m May 1793 SALLY FISK; Res Hanover Grafton Co NH; ch LEONARD, ERASTUS; Ref: Your Ancestors v3 #4 p351, Early Fam of Wallingford p331, Barbour's VR Middletown v2 p143, Hist of Wallingford p937.

JEDUTHAN - d 07 Aug 1838; Ref: Deaths from NY Herald p551.

JEFFERSON - b 29 May 1835 Madison, New Haven Co CT s/JOHN ROMEO & ELIZABETH (CRAMPTON) WILCOX; Unmarried; Civil War; d 14 May 1862; Ref: Fam of Early Guilford p1204, Barbour's VR Madison v2 p31.

JEFFERSON MONROE - b 01 Dec 1826 Floyd, Oneida Co NY s/OZIAS & SUSAN (MOULTON) WILCOX; m 13 Sep 1848 at Turin, Lewis Co NY MARY HARVEY HUMASON who was b 13 Jul 1828 & d 25 Jul 1895 Lincoln, Lancaster Co NE d/LEONARD HUBBARD & MARY (SYKES) HUMASON; Res Fredonia, Chautauqua Co NY & Lincoln, NE; ch OLIN JEFFERSON, STEPHEN MOULTON, LEONARD HAMLINE, MARY SUSAN; d 14 Feb 1873 Fredonia NY; Ref: Col Fam of US v5 p552, 19th Cent Death Notices Reported in Fredonia Censor p596.

JEFFERY - b ca 1690 N Kingston, Washington Co RI s/THOMAS & MARTHA (HAZARD) WILCOX; m 24 Apr 1726 N Kingston RI SARAH HIMES/HYAMS; ch THOMAS, ABRAHAM, MARY, JAMES, JEREMIAH, JEFFREY, DORCAS, STEPHEN, DANIEL; d 1759; Ref: Arnold v5 p51, Hist of Stonington p659, Austin p423, Your Ancestors v3 #11&12 p472, Barbour's VR Stonington v3 p39, See RIGR v2 #2 p94.

JEFFEREY/JEFFREY - b 29 Sep 1698 s/ROBERT & AMEY (-----) WILCOX; m 13 Aug 1726 MARY -----; Ref: Col Fam of US v3 p226.

JEFFERY/JEFFREY - b ca 1736 s/JEFFERY & SARAH (HIMES) WILCOX; Ref: Your Ancestors v3 #11&12 p472.

JEFFERY - b 28 Dec 1786 Dartmouth, Bristol Co MA s/WILLIAM & MERIBAH (TUCKER) WILCOX; m HENRIETTA MOSHIER; no ch; d 28 Feb 1853 Ledyard, Cayuga Co NY; Ref: Dartmouth VR p302, Wilcox Excerpts v1 p22, Your Ancestors v13 #3 p1582.

JEFFERY/JEFFRY - b 22 May 1796 Simsbury, Hartford Co CT s/ROGER & ELIZABETH (CASE) WILCOX; m 25 Nov 1822 New Hartford, Litchfield Co CT ANNE MASON who was b 20 Feb 1797 Simsbury CT; ch CHLOE, LUCY, MARIETTE, JANE; Ref: Wilcox-Meigs p85, Your Ancestors v12 #4 p1490, v13 #1 p1515, Barbour's VR Simsbury TM4 p302, New Hartford v3 p8, NEH&GR v17 p217.

JEFFERY/JEFFREY - m 01 Nov 1822 ANNE STILLMAN d/SAMUEL NOYES & ELIZABETH ANN (-----) STILLMAN; ch CHLOE, LUCY, MARIETTE, JANE; Ref: Gen of CT Fam v2 p537.

JEFFERY/JEFFREY H - b 11 Oct 1783 Exeter, Washington Co RI s/JEFFERY & SARAH (-----) WILCOX; m 1827 Exeter, Washington Co RI DEBORAH JAMES who was b 15 Apr 1784 d/JOSEPH & SARAH (SISSON) JAMES; Res Warsaw, Wyoming Co NY 1816 & Orangeville, Wyoming Co NY 1818; ch ALFRED SISSON, JAMES C, HAZARD; d 03 May 1870 Orangeville NY; Ref: Arnold v5 pt3 p64, Hist of Wyoming Co NY p236, Your Ancestors v4 #5&6 p541, v13 #3 p1581, 1850 Census Orangeville NY p35 Dw# 544, Gen of RI Fam v1 p594.

JEFFEREY H - b 15 Nov 1857 Orangeville, Wyoming Co NY s/ALFRED SISSON & ALMENA COLE (WEAVER) WILCOX; m CARRIE WOLF; Ref: Your Ancestors v4 #5&6 p542.

JEHIEL/HIEL - b 25 Jan 1731/2 Killingworth, Middlesex Co CT s/THOMAS & MARTHA (-----) WILCOX; d 1733; Ref: Your Ancestors v4 #11&12 p611, See Hiel.

JEHIEL/HIEL - b 12 Jun 1731 E Guilford, New Haven Co CT s/JOSEPH & HANNAH (GOODALE) WILCOX; m 1759 ABIGAIL CRAMPTON who was b 04 Jun 1737 & d 24 Dec 1796 d/JAMES & MARY (COE) CRAMPTON of E

Guilford CT; ch NATHAN, JEHIEL, SAMUEL, ABIGAIL, MOLLY, ROSWELL, ELIZABETH, ABEL, JAMES; d 07 Apr 1786; Ref: Wilcox-Meigs pp33,53,54, Cutter's CT Fam p1769, Fam of Early Guilford pp250,1208,1210, Barbour's VR Guilford v2 p81, Desc of Wm Wilcoxson pp15,28.

JEHIEL - b 03 May 1734 Killingworth, Middlesex Co CT; m ca 1758 DEBORAH GILLETT who was b 25 Sep 1734 & d 13 Jan 1812 d/JOSEPH & DEBORAH (CHAPPELL) GILLETT; Res Nine Partners, Dover Plains, Dutchess Co NY, & Canaan, Columbia Co NY; ch NATHANIEL, AARON, DEBORAH, THOMAS, MARY/POLLY, JESSE, JEHIEL, JOHN, JOSEPH, LOIS; d 05 Dec 1822; Ref: Copy of Will, Your Ancestors v4 #11&12 pp611,612, Wilcox-Meigs pp44,65,66.

JEHIEL - b 31 Mar 1748 Hebron, Tolland Co CT Twin with JERUSHA s/EBENEZER & ELIZABETH (DEWEY) WILCOX; m 18 Apr 1771 LYDIA MACK; Res Surry, Cheshire Co NH; ch JEHIEL, LYDIA, MARY, EBENEZER, ELIZABETH, AZUBA, EZRA, OLIVER, ELIHU; Ref: ECM v3 p93, Wilcox-Meigs pp50,69, Hebron Church Records, Barbour's VR Hebron v2 pp48,123,260,261,361, Desc of Wm Wilcoxson p25.

JEHIEL - b 1756-1775; Res Clarendon, Rutland Co VT; 1 son & 1 dau in 1800; Ref: 1800 Census Rutland Co VT p109.

JEHIEL - b 17 Mar 1761 Simsbury, Hartford Co CT s/EPHRAIM WILCOX; m Apr 1779 Barkhamsted, Litchfield Co CT AZUBAH MOORE d/SAUNDERS MOORE of Granby Hartford Co CT; m CLARRISSA ----- who was b 1788 & d 1818; Res Barkhamsted, Litchfield Co CT 1808 & Marlborough, Delaware Co OH; ch JEHIEL, IRA MOORE, HIRA, AZUBA, EZRA; In Rev War; d 17 Sep 1848 bur Old Norton Cem; Ref: Early Settlers of W Simsbury CT p135, Fiske Card File, Barbour's VR Barkhamsted v1 p55, Desc of Wm Wilcoxson p189a, Rev War Soldiers bur in OH.

JEHIEL - b 1762 E Guilford, New Haven Co CT s/JEHIEL & ABIGAIL (CRAMPTON) WILCOX; m 26 Mar 1798 RACHEL (-----) BISHOP who was b 17 Aug 1773 & d 22 Apr 1799, w/EZRA BISHOP; m THANKFUL LEWIS who was b 1772 & d 20 Feb 1856; 2 sons; d 04 Dec 1835; Ref: Wilcox-Meigs p54, Fam of Early Guilford pp1210-1212, Desc of Wm Wilcoxson p28.

JEHIEL - b 10 Nov 1771 Hebron, Tolland Co CT s/JEHIEL & LYDIA (MACK) WILCOX; Res Hancock

Addison Co VT; d 30 Mar 1849; Ref: Wilcox-Meigs p69, Barbour's VR Hebron v2 p259.

JEHIEL - b 1774 Killingworth, Middlesex Co CT s/JEHIEL & DEBORAH (GILLETT) WILCOX; Res Dutchess Co NY; Ref: Desc of Wm Wilcoxson p59, Your Ancestors v4 #11&12 p612.

JEHIEL - b 04 Oct 1775 prob Conway, Franklin Co MA s/JOHN & MARY (-----) WILCOX; m ROXANY -----; Res Colrain, Franklin Co MA & Salem, Washington Co NY; Ref: Halifax VT Wilcox Fam mss.

JEHIEL - b 10 Jul 1781 Barkhamsted, Litchfield Co CT s/JEHIEL & AZUBAH (MOOR) WILCOX; m RUTH GAINES d/who was b ca 1781 W Simsbury, Hartford Co CT d/MOSES & LUCY (BARBER) GAINES; ch HIRAM, ALICE, JEHIEL 3rd, ANSTRESS, EVALENE, HEYLER, CHAUNCEY; Ref: Barbour's VR Barkhamsted v1 p55, Desc of Wm Wilcox p189a, Early Settlers of W Simsbury p70.

JEHIEL - War of 1812; Res Hunter, Greene Co NY; Ref: Index of Awards NY p135.

JEHIEL - 1825 Purchased Lot 51 Twnshp 1 Range 14 in Chautauqua Co NY from Willink & Co; Ref: Chautauqua Co Deed Book v5 p216.

JEHIEL - b 02 Jul 1797 Dutchess Co NY s/AARON & ELIZABETH (BELDEN) WILCOX; m 1823 CHLOE NICHOLS who was b 1807 VT; Shoemaker; Res Evans, Erie Co NY 1824; War of 1812; ch CHLOE, GEORGE, MARY, CYRUS, CHARLES, ALANSON, ALMYRA, BELDEN, HENRY & HENRIETTA twins, SARAH, ALBERT/ADLEBERT, ELLEN; d 1884; Ref: 1850 Census Evans NY p384 Dw# 174, Obit, NYG&BR v40 p104.

JEHIEL - b 26 Sep 1802 Lexington, Greene Co NY s/NATHANIEL & JOANNA (McGONIGLE/MALLORY) WILCOX; m SARAH STREETER; Ref: Wilcox-Meigs p84, Your Ancestors v4 #11&12 p612.

JEHIEL 3rd - b 23 Mar 1835 s/JEHIEL Jr & RUTH (GAINES) WILCOX; d young; Ref: Desc of Wm Wilcoxson p189a.

JEMIMA - b 30 Oct 1699 Guilford, New Haven Co CT d/OBADIAH & SILENCE (MANSFIELD) WILCOX; m 24 Feb 1726 Wallingford, New Haven Co CT JOHN MERRIMAN; Res Southington, Hartford Co CT; ch JOHN, THANKFUL, SILAS, EBER; d 11 Oct 1764; Ref: Wilcox-Meigs p26, Desc of Wm Wilcoxson p9, Fam of

Early Guilford p1208, Barbour's VR Wallingford v5 p510, Hist of Surry NH p944.

JEMIMAH - b 21 Jul 1705 Stonington, New London Co CT d/WILLIAM & DOROTHY GILBERT (PALMER) WILCOX; m 07 Jul 1728 OWEN CARTEY/CARTEE; m 13 Dec 1743 NATHANIEL CRANDALL who was b 28 Feb 1718 s/EBER & PATIENCE (LAMPHERE) CRANDALL; ch of 2nd husband JARED, PAUL; Ref: Hist of Stonington CT p659, Arnold v2 p50, v3 p40, Austin p423, Elder John Crandall Desc p15, Your Ancestors v3 #1 p290, Barbour's VR Stonington v2 p50, v3 p40.

JEMIMA - b 11 Jul 1723 Middletown, Middlesex Co CT d/JOHN & MARY (WARNER) WILCOX; m 14 Nov 1751 JANNA WILCOX Jr who was b 25 Jul 1728 s/JANNA & RACHEL (BOARDMAN) WILCOX; Ref: MUH pp746,747, Nutmegger v4 #3 p330, NYG&BR v14, p138, Barbour's VR Middletown LR2 pp21,246.

JEMIMAH - b 24 Feb 1745 Killingworth, Middlesex Co CT d/DANIEL & HANNAH (BUELL) WILCOX; m SAMUEL STANNARD; Ref: Barbour's VR Killingworth v2 p157, Wilcox-Meigs p45, Desc of Wm Wilcoxson p20.

JEMIMA - m 01 Jul 1762 Middletown, Middlesex Co CT JONATHAN EDWARDS; Ref: Barbour's VR Middletown v1 p57.

JEMIMAH - b 15 Jul 1768 Westminster West, Windham Co VT d/EPHRAIM & DIADEMA (FRENCH) WILCOX; d 25 Sep 1774 Westminster VT; Ref: VT VR, MUH p750, Your Ancestors v4 #5&6 p545, Texas Society DAR Roster v4 p2287.

JEMIMA - b 17 Apr 1777 Westminster West, Windham Co VT d/EPHRAIM & DIADEMA (FRENCH) WILCOX; Ref: Your Ancestors v4 #5&6 p545, MUH p750, Texas Society DAR Roster v4 p2287.

JEMIMAH - b 08 Mar 1793 RI/NY d/SHEFFIELD & EUNICE (ROSS) WILCOX; m 02 Mar 1814 CORNELIUS COOLBAUGH who was b 13 Jan 1793 & d 20 Aug 1860 s/MOSES & HANNAH (SCHOONMAKER) COOLBAUGH; Res Wysox. Bradford Co PA; ch DANIEL M, RANSOM, EUNICE; d 03/13 Jan 1822 Wysox PA; Ref: Pioneer Fam of Bradford Co PA p309, Your Ancestors v12 #4 p1488, v13 #2 pp1538,1539.

JEMIMAH - b 01 May 1822 Floyd, Oneida Co NY d/ELEAZER CURTIS & CYNTHIA (NOBLE) WILCOX; m 1842 WILLIAM PENTECOST; Res Forest Grove, Washington Co OR; d 10 Nov 1876 Walla Walla, Washington

Territory; Ref: A Wilcox Book p20, Gen of Thomas Noble p448.

JENNETTE - b ca 1814 Simsbury, Hartford Co CT d/BENAJAH HUMPHREY & EUNICE (FANCHER) WILCOX; Ref: Wilcox-Meigs p103.

JENNETTE - b 1822 d/ABNER & SALLY (HORTON) WILCOX of Livonia, Livingston Co NY; m AUGUSTINE W HOVEY; Ref: Your Ancestors v4 #9&10 p586.

JENNETTE D - of Killingworth, Middlesex Co CT m 1845? Clinton, Middlesex Co CT OLIVER GATES DOWD of Madison, New Haven Co CT s/HUBBARD & TEMPERANCE (KELSEY) DOWD; no ch; Ref: Fam of Early Guilford p311, Barbour's VR Clinton v1 p76.

JENNET E - of Canaan, Litchfield Co CT; m 26 Nov 1829 JOHN G RUSSELL of Great Barrington, Berkshire Co MA; Ref: Barbour's VR Canaan vA p87.

JENNIE - b 18-- d/CHARLES & BEULAH (RANDOLPH) WILCOX; d age 18 MI; Ref: Wilcox Excerpts v1 p6.

JENNIE - d/FREDERICK DUNBAR & JULIA (LOVENGUTH) WILCOX of Camden, Oneida Co NY; m WILLIAM GARLICK; Ref: Your Ancestors v14 #3 p1672.

JENNIE - b 20 Oct 1877 Villanova, Chautauqua Co NY d/ALFRED JAMES & MARY ANGELIA (BABCOCK) WILCOX; m be 1897 DELL KESTER; ch ALLEN; d 1911 Fredonia, Chautauqua Co NY; Ref: Wilcox Hist mss, Alice Wilcox's Birthday Book.

JENNIE - b 4 Aug 1879 d/HENRY WILLIAM & LUCY (GLOVER) WILCOX; d 17 Apr 1881; Ref: A Wilcox Book p129.

JENNIE - b 1883; d 1908 Napoli, Cattaraugus Co NY; bur Napoli Corners Cem; Ref: Cem Records copied by Anna Waite.

JENNIE A - b 17 Aug 1840 d/HAZARD & FLAVILLA (PARSONS) WILCOX of Smyrna, Chenango Co NY; m 14 Dec 1877 IRVING D ATKINS; Ref: Cutter's Western NY v3 p1439, Your Ancestors v3 #6 p397.

JENNIE L - b 17 Jul 1860 d/AUSTIN WILCOX; Ref: CT Bible Rec v15 p254.

JENNIE LOUISE - b 04 May 1872 Madison, New Haven Co CT d/MANFRED AUGUSTUS & JENNIE LODEMA (SNOW) WILCOX; Ref: Fam of Early Guilford p1216.

JENNIE M - b 1836 NY d/LOUISA (-----) WILCOX; m JOSEPH S AVERY; Res Kirkland, Oneida Co NY; Ref: 1860 Census Kirkland NY p5.

JENNY - b 02 Nov 1802 Halifax, Windham Co VT d/WILLIAM & RELIEF (-----) WILCOX; Ref: Fiske Card File, Halifax Wilcox Fam mss.

JEPTHA - b ca 1785 W Simsbury, Hartford Co CT s/ AMOS Jr & ANNA (CASE) WILCOX; Ref: Early Settlers of W Simsbury p134.

JERAULD O - b ca 1800 s/DANIEL & MARY (ARNOLD) WILCOX; m 31 Aug 1820 Cumberland, Providence Co RI AMELIA DARLING who was b 09 Apr 1805 & d 27 Feb 1849 d/ELIJAH DARLING; Res Bellingham, Norfolk Co MA; m 02 Sep 1849 Blackstone, Worcester Co MA PHEBE J WILKINSON; ch by 1st wife JERAULD, FENNER, ELIJAH D, OLIVER B, SUSAN A, SAMUEL; Ref: Arnold v3 p69, v15 p442, v17 p231, Your Ancestors v11 #3 p1371.

JERAULD - s/JERAULD O & AMELIA (DARLING) WILCOX of Bellingham, Norfolk Co MA; m CECELIA ANN (THAYER) CHILSON; Ref; Your Ancestors v11 #3 p1371.

JEREMIAH - b ca 1660 Westerly, Washington Co RI prob s/DANIEL WILCOX; m 1685 MARY MALLETT d/THOMAS & MARY (WOOD) MALLETT; ch ELISHA; Ref: Your Ancestors v14 #2 p1657.

JEREMIAH - b 1680 Westerly, Washington Co RI s/STEPHEN & HANNAH (HAZARD) WILCOX; Ref: Hist of Stonington CT pp658,659, Wilcox-Brown-Medbery p6, Col Fam in US v3 p225.

JEREMIAH - b 24 Sep 1683 Dartmouth, Bristol Co MA s/SAMUEL & MARY (WOOD) WILCOX; d in infancy; Ref: Dartmouth VR p302, Austin p423, Wilcox Excerpts v1 p21, Your Ancestors v12 #4 p1504.

JEREMIAH - b 24 Sep 1683 Portsmouth, Newport Co RI s/SAMUEL & ESTHER (COOK) WILCOX; m ca 1708 MARY SMITH; int to marry 11 Feb 1738 JUDITH BRIGGS who was b 27 May 1710 Little Compton, Newport Co RI d/WILLIAM & ELIZABETH (FOBES) BRIGGS; ch by 1st wife MARY, SARAH; ch by 2nd wife SAMUEL, WILLIAM, BENJAMIN; d 1751; Ref: Austin p423, Wilcox Excerpts v1 pp21,22, Repr Men of Southeastern MA p1081, Arnold v4 pt5 p71, Your Ancestors v13 #1 p1529.

JEREMIAH - b ca 1710 South Kingston, Washington Co RI s/JEREMIAH & MARY (MALLETT) WILCOX; m MARY HAZARD d/JEFFREY & MARY (-----) HAZARD; ch ARNOLD; Ref: Your Ancestors v14 #2 p1657.

JEREMIAH - b 14 Aug 1711 Little Compton, Newport Co RI s/JOHN WILCOX; Ref: Arnold v4 pt6 p193.

JEREMIAH - b 20 Sep 1715 Middletown, Middlesex Co CT s/SAMUEL & ESTHER (BUSHNELL) WILCOX; m 29 Apr 1736 MARY STOWE who was b 30 Nov 1717; ch JEREMIAH, ESTHER, WILLIAM, MARY, REBECCA, GRACE, ELI, LEMUEL, LUCY, MARTHA; d 08 Dec 1760 Middletown CT; Ref: Your Ancestors v3 #4 p351, #5 p380, Nutmegger v 4 #3 p330, v15 #1 p26, NEH&GR v14 p138, Early CT Probate Records v2 p253, Barbour's VR Middletown v1 p95, LR2 p21.

JEREMIAH - b 11 Feb 1716 Killingworth, Middlesex Co CT s/SAMUEL & RUTH (WESTCOTT) WILCOX; m REBECCA -----; ch EUNICE; Ref: Wilcox-Meigs pp30,43, Desc of Wm Wilcoxson pp12,43, Your Ancestors v3 #7&8 p426, Barbour's VR Killingworth v2 p147.

JEREMIAH - b 16 Oct 1725 S Kingston, Washington Co RI s/ROBERT & SARAH (WILCOX) WILCOX; ch ROBERT, JEREMIAH, STEPHEN; Ref: Your Ancestors v11 #3 p1351, RI Freeman p40.

JEREMIAH - b 01 June 1729 Tiverton, Newport Co RI s/JOSIAH & PATIENCE BORDEN (CHASE) WILCOX; Ref: Repr Men of Southeastern MA p480, See Josiah.

JEREMIAH - b ca 1734 s/JEFFREY & SARAH (HIMES) WILCOX of N Kingston, Washington Co RI; m 09 Nov 1755 Exeter, Washington Co RI MARY MOREY d/JOSEPH MOREY; Res Richmond Washington Co RI; ch JEREMIAH, DIANA, RUTH; Ref: Arnold v5 pt3 p35, Your Ancestors v3 #11&12 p472, v4 #3&4 p520.

JEREMIAH - Res Scituate, Providence Co RI in 1774; 1 son & 1 dau; Ref: 1774 Census RI.

JEREMIAH - b 10 Nov 1744 Middletown, Middlesex Co CT s/JEREMIAH & MARY (STOWE) WILCOX; m 07 Dec 1780 Middletown CT RUTH DUDLEY who was b 1752 & d 1836; ch RUTH, MARY, JEREMIAH, ASAHEL, THOMAS, LORINDA, JESSE, MABEL; d 1830; Ref: Mrs Wm Richardson, Barbour's VR Middletown v1 p95, v2 pp152,259.

JEREMIAH - b 27 Feb 1752 Clove/Union Vale, Dutchess Co NY; Rev War; Res Lancaster, Coos Co NH & Warrensburg, Warren Co NY; ch SALLY, ELIZABETH/BETSY, ALFRED STUART, MARY/POLLY V, REBECCA BRAIDEN, PHILIP BRIDGES; d af 1837; Ref: NH VR, Iris W Baird.

JEREMIAH Dr - b 15 Jan 1761 s/SEDOTIA & MARY (HUMPHREY) WILCOX of Simsbury, Hartford Co CT; Grad Jefferson College PA; m AMELIA -----; Res Simsbury & Hartland, Hartford Co CT & OH; ch AMELIA, AURORA AMARET, JEREMIAH CULLEN; Ref: Your Ancestors v11 #4 p1379, Barbour's VR Simsbury TM4 p301.

JEREMIAH - b 23 Aug 1763 Westport, Bristol Co MA s/SAMUEL & COMFORT (SEABURY) WILCOX; d 21 Jul 1772; Ref: Westport MA VR pp102,293, Your Ancestors v13 #2 p1554.

JEREMIAH - b 05 Aug 1767 Little Compton, Newport Co RI s/JEREMIAH & SARAH (BAILEY) WILCOX; Ref: Arnold v4 pt6 p193.

JEREMIAH D - b ca 1770 Richmond, Washington Co RI s/JEREMIAH & MARY (MOREY) WILCOX m 09 Feb 1793 W Greenwich, Kent Co RI SUSANNAH WILCOX d/THOMAS & ELIZABETH (JAQUES) WILCOX; Res Foster, Providence Co RI; ch DINAH, NAOMI, LUCY, RHODA, HAZARD B, NATHAN R, NELSON J, ESTHER B, HAZARD H, NELSON J; Ref: Arnold v3 p31, Your Ancestors v4 #3&4 p520, See RIGR v7 #3 p219.

JEREMIAH - b 06 Sep 1770 Dartmouth, Bristol Co MA s/BENJAMIN & PATIENCE (TUCKER) WILCOX; m 29 Jan 1809 Westport, Bristol Co MA RUTH ALLEN who was b 1787 & d 06 Feb 1844 d/THOMAS ALLEN; Res Westport, Bristol Co MA & Genoa, Cayuga Co NY; no ch; d 09 Oct 1853; Ref: Westport VR p251, Dartmouth VR p302, Repr Men of Southeastern MA p1081, Your Ancestors v13 #4 p1610.

JEREMIAH - b 1771 s/EDWARD D & RUTH (-----) WILCOX; d 01 Apr 1773; Bur Boland District Burying Grounds Amenia, Dutchess Co NY; Ref: Amenia Burying Grounds p74.

JEREMIAH - b be 1775; Res Martinsburg, Lewis Co NY 1820; 1 son & 1 dau; Ref: 1820 Census Lewis Co NY p20.

JEREMIAH - b 29 May 1785 s/JEREMIAH & RUTH (DUDLEY) WILCOX; m HANNAH HOUGHTAILING; d 1844; Ref: Mrs. Wm Richardson.

JEREMIAH - b 19 Nov 1785 Killingworth, Middlesex Co CT s/NATHAN 3rd & RACHEL (BENNET) WILCOX; Ref: Wilcox-Meigs p79, Barbour's VR Killingworth v2 p83.

JEREMIAH - b 1794 s/ROBERT & SARAH (WILBUR) WILCOX of Lyme, New London Co CT; m LYDIA ----- who d 23 May 1892; no ch; Ref: Your Ancestors v11 #3 p1352.

JEREMIAH - m 1815 MELINDA ABBE; Res Sardinia, Erie Co NY; Ref: Fiske Card File.

JEREMIAH - m be 1816 RI HULDAH -----; ch ROBERT; Ref: Arnold v9 p293.

JEREMIAH - b 1807 Westport, Bristol Co MA s/BENJAMIN & SARAH (TABOR) WILCOX; d 09 Jul 1871; Ref: Your Ancestors v14 #1 p1631.

JEREMIAH - m 01 Jun 1827 Westport, Bristol Co MA THANKFUL BRIGHTMAN; Ref: Westport VR p251.

JEREMIAH - m 02 Mar 1834 Saybrook, Middlesex Co CT JERUSHA SHIPMAN; ch JOSEPH AUGUSTUS, JOSEPH SHIPMAN; Ref: Saybrook Colony VR p119, Barbour's VR Saybrook v2 p62.

JEREMIAH - of Lebanon, New London Co CT; m 06 Sep 1840 Colchester, New London Co CT SUSANNAH D WILLIAMS; Ref: Barbour's VR Colchester v2 p158.

JEREMIAH - b 1821; Carriage maker; d 07 Sep 1849 age 28 Granby, Hartford Co CT; Ref: Barbour's VR Granby v1 p254/5.

JEREMIAH - b 1823 NY; m BELINDA ----- who was b 1834; Res Sardinia, Erie Co NY; Ref: 1850 Census Sardinia NY p116 Dw# 1723.

JEREMIAH - b 04 May 1825 Cherry Creek, Chautauqua Co NY s/ELIPHALET & NANCY (KENT) WILCOX; m ca 1843 CATHERINE SHERWIN who was b 1825 & d 16 Dec 1884; Res Sterling, Whiteside Co IL & Schuyler, Colfax Co NE; ch EFFIE, WILLIAM, CHARLES J, FRANK, NANCY ISABELL, PERRY; d Mar 1910 Peabody, Marion Co KS bur Schuyler NE; Ref: Census Rec, Tombstone Inscr, Will of Eliphalet Wilcox, Mona Watkins, Dave Arasmith.

JEREMIAH - b 1827 CT Prob s/ABRAHAM WILCOX; Res New Hartford, Litchfield Co CT; Wagonmaker; Ref: 1850 Census New Hartford CT p125 Dw# 182.

JEREMIAH - b 1846 s/WILLIAM & AVINA (BARKER) WILCOX; d 1874; Ref: Jane Smith.

JEREMIAH - b 19 Jul 1851; d 19 Sep 1855 age 4yr 2mo Sterling, Windham Co CT; Ref: Barbour's VR Sterling v2 p63.

JEREMIAH - b 1853 NY s/JAMES & MARY (-----) WILCOX of Ripley, Chautauqua Co NY; Ref: 1870 Census Ripley NY Fam #3 p150.

JEREMIAH ALONZO - b 15 Sep 1862 Porterville, Tulare Co CA s/ABEL MORTON & BETSY (SAUNDERS) WILCOX; m MAGGIE BOLAND; ch FRANK A; d 15 Feb 1898; Ref: Jane Smith.

JEREMIAH C - b 1833; m 25 Apr 1866 PERLIA J/RESLIA SAUNDERS Omaha, Douglas Co NE; ch SHERMAN, CHAUNCY, LENNA, SAMUEL, PEARL, MARY H; d 1908 NE; Ref: Mrs Wm Richardson, Early NE Records p64, Nebr & Midwest Gen Rec v12 #3 & 4 p34.

JEREMIAH CULLEN Dr - b 06 Dec 1790 Hartland, Hartford Co CT s/Dr JEREMIAH & AMELIA (-----) WILCOX; m 1816 LORENA BUSHNELL who d 1831; m 1839 Mrs JULIA (WILDER) PITTEE who was b 19 Sep 1814 Johnstown, Fulton Co NY; Res Richfield, Summit Co OH; ch by 1st wife, JEREMIAH B of Deer Lodge, Powell Co MT, Mrs GEN STURGES of Louisville, Jefferson Co KY; ch by 2nd wife, AMELIA, HENRY C, CULLEN, FRANK A, STELLA H; d 26 Jan 1873; Ref: Hist of Summit Co OH p1013, Some Nutmeggers who Migrated p264, Your Ancestors v11 #4 p1379.

JEREMIAH N - See RIGR v7 #3 p219.

JEREMIAH W - b 1807 Stonington, New London Co CT; m 11 Dec 1831 Groton, New London Co CT SABRINA A BROWN who was b 1815; Res RI & Stonington CT; ch ALICE JANE, JULIA EMMA, E B; Ref: Elder John Crandall p291, 1850 Census Stonington CT Reel 432 #48 p256, Barbour's VR Groton v1 p39, Stonington v5 p79.

JERMAINE W - b 1840 ch/OZIAS & SUSAN (MOULTON) WILCOX; Res NY; Ref: Colonial Fam of US p554.

JEROME - b 1824 NY prob s/CHARLES & LOUISA (-----) WILCOX; m SUSAN -----; Res New Hartford,

Oneida Co NY; ch WILLIAM MASON; Ref: 1850 Census New Hartford NY p284 Dw# 682.

JEROME - b 1847 NY s/ANSON & BETSEY (-----) WILCOX of Pomfret, Chautauqua Co NY; Ref: 1860 Census Pomfret NY p533 Dw# 1576.

JEROME B - b 02 Apr 1888 Adrian, Lenawee Co MI s/CHARLES G & JEANETTE (MARVIN) WILCOX; Ref: Your Ancestor p1319.

JEROME BAILEY - b 01 Mar 1844 Cambridge, Middlesex Co MA s/SILAS & LAURA ANN (PATTEN) WILCOX; Ref: VR Cambridge MA v1 p763.

JEROME BONAPART - b 04 Sep 1819 NY s/STEPHEN & PHOEBE (ROGERS) WILCOX; m 04 Sep 1849 SUSAN M SHEPHERD New Hartford, Oneida Co NY; m CLARENO -----; Ref: LDS Fam Group Sheet, 10,000 VR of Central NY p264.

JEROME EVERETT - b 25 Sep 1856 Essex, Middlesex Co CT s/JOHN ELLIOTT & ZYLPHA LUCRETIA (SNOW) WILCOX; m 26 Nov 1884 LAURA MARTILLA BURNHAM who was b 20 Jul 1857 & d 19 Mar 1885; m 03 Mar 1886 HATTIE F DIBBLE of Westbrook, Middlesex Co CT who was b 28 Jul 1866; ch of 2nd wife LOUISA GILBERT; Ref: Wilcox-Meigs pp110,124, Fam of Early Guilford p1215.

JERRY - b 1805 s/ROBERT & ANNA CLEMENCE (MILLS) WILCOX of Becket, Berkshire Co MA; Ref: Your Ancestors v13 #2 p1540.

JERRY - m 25 Jan 1832 Granby, Hartford Co CT FLORA WILCOX; Ref: Barbour's VR Granby v1 p10.

JERRY/JERORY - m 10 Apr 1833 Simsbury, Hartford Co CT MARY CASE; Ref: Barbour's VR Simsbury TM4 p472.

JERRY R - b 1847 s/HARRY & LUCINDA (DODGE) WILCOX; m 1870 ELLA WAY who was b 1851; Res Dodgeville, OH; ch CARRIE; Ref: Your Ancestors v13 #2 p1541.

JERUSHA - b 07 May 1734 Middletown, Middlesex Co CT d/ISRAEL & MARY (NORTH) WILCOX; d 17 Apr 1748; Ref: NEH&GR v14 p138, Barbour's VR Middletown LR2 p11.

JERUSHA - b 31 Mar 1748 Hebron, Tolland Co CT Twin with JEHIEL d/EBENEZER & ELIZABETH (DEWEY)

WILCOX; Ref: Barbour's VR Hebron v1 p48, Wilcox-Meigs p50.

JERUSHA - b 28 May 1755 Killingworth, Middlesex Co CT d/NATHANIEL & MINDWELL (WILCOX) WILCOX; m 10 Mar 1783/5 JOSIAH GRAVES; Ref: Wilcox-Meigs p44, Barbour's VR Killingworth v2 p148, Desc of Wm Wilcoxson p20.

JERUSHA - b 13 Feb 1767 d/ELIAB & JERUSHA (SPENCER) WILCOX of Dover, Dutchess Co NY; d 1775; Ref: Your Ancestors v4 #3&4 p522.

JERUSHA - b 22 Mar 1769 Lee, Berkshire Co MA d/PETER & JERUSHA (-----) WILCOX; m 07 Jan 1790 WILLIAM FREEMAN s/ELISHA FREEMAN; Res Lee, Berkshire Co MA 1799; Ref: Fiske Card File, Desc of Wm Wilcoxson p59, Janet Armbrust.

JERUSHA - b 21 Aug 1770 Kent, Litchfield Co CT d/JOHN & SARAH (STURDEVANT) WILCOX; Ref: Barbour's VR Kent v1 p209, See John.

JERUSHA - b 12 Apr 1771 Westminster, Windham Co VT d/EPHRAIM & DIADEMA (FRENCH) WILCOX; Ref: Your Ancestors v4 #5&6 p545.

JERUSHA - b 14 Nov 1773 White Hills CT d/DAVID & ISRAELIA (SALMON) WILCOX; Ref: Wilcox-Meigs p58, Hist of Stratford Fam p1347.

JERUSHA - bpt 02 May 1773 Amenia, Dutchess Co NY; Ref: Fiske Card File.

JERUSHA - d/REUBEN & CHLOE (SACKETT) WILCOX of Amenia, Dutchess Co NY; m JAMES SACKETT; Ref: Your Ancestors v4 #3&4 p522.

JERUSHA - b 01 Aug 1774 Sandisfield, Berkshire Co MA d/ABEL & SUSANNAH (HALL) WILCOX; d 03 Apr 1795 [drowned]; Ref: Sandisfield MA VR p108, Fiske Card File, Desc of Wm Wilcoxson p243.

JERUSHA - b 27 Jul 1777 d/JOHN & MARY (-----) WILCOX of Conway, Franklin Co MA; bpt 16 Jul 1789; Ref: Halifax VT Wilcox Fam mss.

JERUSHA - b 1785 Harpersfield, Delaware Co NY d/SAMUEL & SALLY (HUNT) WILCOX; m TOLMAN HAMILTON; ch HOSEA, HARRY, HOMER, HYMEN, HARRIET, HANNAH, HELEN; d 1859; Ref: Your Ancestors v4 #5&6 p543.

JERUSHA - b Nov 1791 d/JOEL & SARAH (BOOTH) WILCOX Stratford, Fairfield Co CT; Ref: Wilcox-Meigs p78, Hist of Stratford Fam p1347, Desc of Wm Wilcoxson p36.

JERUSHA - b Jul 1803/1806 d/RETURN, & ABIGAIL (WILLARD) WILCOX; m Aug 1827 Madison, New Haven Co CT SAMUEL KELSEY DOWD who was b 1803 & d 14 Sep 1874 s/HUBBARD & TEMPERANCE (KELSEY) DOWD; Res Madison CT; ch ELIZABETH, ELLEN MARIA; d 03 Jun 1841; Ref: Wilcox-Meigs p73, Fam of Early Guilford p311, Fam of Early Guilford p1211, Barbour's VR Madison v1 p13.

JERUSHA - b 1806 d/ELISHA & HANNAH (-----) WILCOX; d 26 Jun 1827 Leyden, Lewis Co NY; Ref: Tree Talks v7 #1 p36.

JERUSHA - b 1830 Granby, Hartford Co CT; m 18 Dec 1851 EDWIN WILCOX, merchant who was b 1823; Ref: Barbour's VR Granby v1 p134.

JERUSHA - b ca 1835 d/SIMON GATES & HANNAH (LOOMIS) WILCOX; Res Smithville NY; d be 1910; Ref: Cutter's Gen of Western NY v3 p1436.

JERUSHA ALMIRA - b 29 Feb 1864 d/ISAIAH CLARK & SALLY (HENRY) WILCOX of Rockdale, Crawford Co PA; m 10 Sep 1880 Rockdale Twnshp PA WILLIAM WRIGHT PIERCE who d 1937; ch ARDELIA, FRANK H, CLARE VICTOR; d 09 Aug 1941 Sanford, Warren Co PA bur Sanford Cem; Ref: Dennis Davis.

JESSE - b 04 Oct 1744 Killingworth, Middlesex Co CT s/STEPHEN & MARY (PIERSON) WILCOX; m 11 Jun 1767 THANKFUL STEVENS who was b 30 Dec 1746 Killingworth CT & d 16 Aug 1827 d/EBENEZER STEVENS; Res Newport, Sullivan Co NH ca 1767; ch MARY, MIRIAM, NATHANIEL, JESSE, NATHAN, MARY/POLLY, STEPHEN, OLIVER, THANKFUL, MARIAN, GRACE, ABIGAIL/NABBY, UNNAMED CHILD; d 12 Mar 1823 Newport NH; Ref: Barbour's VR Killingworth v2 p159, Wilcox-Meigs pp42,63, Bogue Fam p395, Cutter's New England Fam pp159,160, Nebr & Midwest Gen Rec v8 #1 pp22,23, Your Ancestors v3 #3 p321 #4 p349.

JESSE - b 16 Jul 1757 Goshen, Litchfield Co CT s/NATHANIEL 2nd & ABIGAIL (HURLBUTT) WILCOX; Ref: Barbour's VR Goshen v1 p273, See Nathaniel.

JESSE - b ca 1762 s/JOSIAH & ELIZABETH (CURTIS) WILCOX; m 28 Nov 1782 RHODA CEVERRUS/CEVELRUS; Res

E Berlin, Hartford Co CT; Ref: A Wilcox Book p18, Col Fam of US v5 p555.

JESSE - m 02 May 1782 New Marlboro, Berkshire Co MA LOUISA LEE; Ref: Fiske Card File.

JESSE - m 16 Dec 1788 Farmington, Hartford Co CT RHODA ANDRUSS; Ref: ECM v4 p17, Fiske Card File.

JESSE - a widower of Northington CT; m 05 Feb 1794 COMFORT (-----) PECK a widow of Bristol, Hartford Co CT; Ref: Fiske Card File.

JESSE Capt - b 29 Dec 1762 Westerly, Washington Co RI s/HEZEKIAH & HANNAH (PARKER) WILCOX; m 09 Dec 1784 ANNE/NANCY PENDLETON who was b 04 Jun 1762 & d 02 Sep 1796 Stonington, New London Co CT d/PELEG & ANN (PARK) PENDLETON; m 06 May 1798 MEHITABLE WILCOX who was b 1774 & d 1868 d/EBENEZER & IANTHA (MASON) WILCOX; ch by 1st wife SUSANNAH, NANCY, JESSE Jr, ABIGAIL, PHINEAS, LODOWICK; ch by 2nd wife IANTHA, EBENEZER, ELISHA, MASON, ELNATHAN F, SILAS, ELIAS; d 05 Jul 1828 at sea with his son, JESSE Jr; Ref: Arnold v2 pp69,145, v5 pt1 p69, Hist of Stonington p660, Barbour's VR Stonington v4 p122 v5 p18, Early NE Pendletons p140, 1850 Census Stonington CT Reel 432 #48 p256, C Douglass Alves Sr.

JESSE - b 1764 or 1773 CT s/HIEL & DEBORAH (GILLETT) WILCOX; Res Dover Plains, Dutchess Co NY & Canaan, Columbia Co NY; d New Concord, Columbia Co NY; Ref: Desc of Wm Wilcoxson p59, Wilcox-Meigs p65, Your Ancestors v4 #11&12 p612.

JESSE - b 27 Apr 1769 Middletown, Middlesex Co CT s/JONATHAN & RACHEL (LEWIS) WILCOX; Ref: Barbour's VR Middletown v2 p181, See Jonathan.

JESSE - b 14 Sep 1771 Killingworth, Middlesex Co CT or Newport, Sullivan Co NH s/JESSE & THANKFUL (STEVENS) WILCOX; m 15 Mar 1798 WEALTHY KELSEY d/ABSALOM & MERCY (HILL) KELSEY; ch ELIZA, HARRY, CALVIN, ALBERT, JESSE; d 27 Feb 1811; Ref: Wilcox Meigs p63, Your Ancestors v3 #4 p349, Nebr & Midwest Gen Rec v8 #1 p23.

JESSE - b 08 Jun 1774 Killingworth, Middlesex Co CT s/ADAM & ESTHER (POST) WILCOX; m CYNTHIA ----- who was b 1777 & d 1858; Res Carthage Jefferson Co NY; ch NANCY, LEWIS J, ANNA M, AMBROSE, MARY EMMA; d 1867; Ref: Early Settlers of

NY p339, Hist of Lewis Co NY p148, Barbour's VR Killingworth v2 p106.

JESSE Jr - b Nov 1788 Stonington, New London Co CT s/JESSE & ANN/NANCY (PENDLETON) WILCOX; m 10 Feb 1810 SALLY ARDEN; m 27 Dec 1822 REBECCA MINOR who was b 02 Jul 1790 & d 17 May 1858 d/WILLIAM & ABIGAIL (HALEY) MINER; d 05 Jul 1828 with his father at sea; Ref: Hist of Stonington p660, Barbour's VR Stonington v4 p122, The Lyon's Whelp p260, C Douglass Alves Sr, Thomas Minor Desc p89.

JESSE - b 22 Mar 1793 Middletown, Middlesex Co CT s/JEREMIAH & RUTH (DUDLEY) WILCOX; m NANCY ANN TIFANY; ch LAFAYETTE; Ref: Barbour's VR Middletown v2 p159.

JESSE - b ca 1800; m 22 Sep 1825 Lebanon, New London Co CT LUCY SPAFFORD; Ref: Barbour's VR Lebanon v1 p115.

JESSE - b 05 Nov 1809 Newport, Sullivan Co NH s/JESSE & WEALTHY (KELSEY) WILCOX; d 11 Feb 1875 Cincinnati, Hamilton Co OH; Ref: Your Ancestors v3 #4 p349.

JESSE - b 06 Nov 1849 Newport, Sullivan Co NH s/CALVIN & ISABEL (SILVER) WILCOX; Ref: Your Ancestors v3 #4 p350.

JESSE M - s/ROBERT H & MARY M (FERRIS) WILCOX of Smyrna, Chenango Co NY; m CLARA HOLLEY d/HENRY HOLLEY; ch BURT H who d at two months; Ref: Early Years in Smyrna p22, Your Ancestors v3 #2 p298.

JESSIE - b 1871 Chautauqua Co NY d/HARLOW MARTIN & MARILLA (JAY) WILCOX; d 1876; Ref: Wilcox Hist mss.

JESSIE AMELIA - b 07 Dec 1857 Kalamazoo, Kalamazoo Co MI d/FREDERICK WILLIAM & MARGARET (BOGARDUS) WILCOX; Ref: Your Ancestors v2 p257.

JESSIE CATHERINE - b 24 Jul 1898 Fayetteville, Onondaga Co NY; m ----- FELLOWS; Ref: Erwin W Fellows.

JESSIE KELSEY - b 02 Oct 1861 Passaic, Passaic Co NJ d/CHARLES MORRISON & MARY ELIZABETH (KELSEY) WILCOX; m 20 Oct 1887 WILLIAM A AYCRIGG of Stamford, Fairfield Co CT; Ref: Wilcox-Meigs p113, Fam of Early Guilford p1216.

JESSIE LOUISA - b 04 May 1872 Madison, New Haven Co CT d/MANFRED AUGUSTUS & JEANETTE LODENA (SNOW) WILCOX; Ref: Wilcox-Meigs p111.

JESSIE O - b 1867 WI d/FRANKLIN & LOUISA (-----) WILCOX; Res Juneau Co WI; Ref: 1880 Soundex WI.

JIRAH/JIRETH - Called TYLER & JERRY; b 18 Oct 1737 Dartmouth, Bristol Co MA s/STEPHEN & MARY (RICKETSON) WILCOX; m 16/17 Oct 1760 DEBORAH RUSSELL; m BATHSHEBA LAPHAM who was b 24 Apr 1743 d/THOMAS & ABIGAIL (WILBUR) LAPHAM of Gloucester, Providence Co RI; Res Burrillville, Smithfield, & Gloucester, Providence Co RI & Uxbridge, Worcester Co MA; ch ELIZABETH, WILLARD, WILLIAM, AUGUSTUS, JIRAH, WILBUR, MARY PHEBE BATHSHEBA, ASENETH; d 21 Jan 1807; Ref: Am Gen v19 #1 p30, Your Ancestors v10 #3 p1268, v11 #4 p1397, Dartmouth VR p302.

JIRAH - Res Gloucester, Providence Co RI 1774; 4 sons & 2 daus; Ref: 1774 RI Census.

JIRAH - b ca 1790; m 1815 SARAH HORTON Chester, Morris Co NJ; Res Washington Co NE; Ref: 2nd Boat v4 #1 p7.

JOAN - d/ELISHA & ABIGAIL (RANNEY) WILCOX of Chester, Hampden Co MA; m CALEB BLISS; Ref; Your Ancestors v3 #9&10 p451.

JOANNA/JOHANNAH - b 8 Jul 1667 Stratford, Fairfield Co CT d/TIMOTHY & JOHANNAH (BIRDSEYE) WILCOX; m JOSEPH FAIRCHILD s/THOMAS FAIRCHILD Jr; ch TIMOTHY, JEREMIAH, JOSEPH, NATHAN, SARAH; d 15 Aug 1813; Ref: Desc of Wm Wilcoxson pp28,36, Wilcox-Meigs p23.

JOANNA - b 21 Aug 1737 Windsor, Hartford Co CT d/AMOS & JOANNA (HILLYER) WILCOX; d 09 Sep 1737; Ref: Wilcox-Meigs p48.

JOANNA - b 26 May 1740 Windsor, Hartford Co CT d/AMOS & JOANNA (HILLYER) WILCOX; m JOB CASE who d 06 Oct 1798 s/JOHN & ABIGAIL (HUMPHREY) CASE; Res Simsbury, Hartford Co CT; ch JOB, JOANNA, VIOLET, ARIEL, LUCY, ASENATH, LUKE, BETSEY, FREDERICK, GROVE, FRIEND; d 17 Dec 1812; Ref: Goodwin's Gen Notes p279, Wilcox-Meigs p48, Your Ancestors v12 #3 p1464, v13 #3 p1567.

JOANNA - b 11 Feb 1741/2 Stratford, Fairfield Co CT d/TIMOTHY & ABIGAIL (PLATT) WILCOX; Ref: Wilcox-Meigs p39, Hist of Stratford Fam p1347.

JOANNA - m be 1821 Sparta, Livingston Co NY ROBERT McCARTNEY; Ref: Nutmegger v8 #4 p582.

JOANNA - b 07 Sep 1809 d/CALEB & HANNAH (-----) WILCOX; m 1835 LEVI GIFFORD; Res Berkshire, Berkshire Co MA and perhaps Rowe, Franklin Co MA; d 29 Jan 1891; Ref: Your Ancestors v3 #7&8 p424, Fiske Card File.

JOANNA - m 13 Oct 1832 Providence, Providence Co RI GEORGE G CHAMPLAIN; Ref: Arnold v17 p179.

JOANNA - d/SAMUEL WILCOX; m ----- LEWIS; Res Chautauqua Co NY; Ref: Fenton Library Jamestown NY.

JOANNA ELDREDGE - d/LEONARD WILCOX; m 12 Aug 1823 Providence, Providence Co RI MARTIN SEAMANS/SIMMONS; Ref: Arnold v7 p512, v16 p586.

JOB - b ca 1732 Exeter, Washington Co RI s/THOMAS & ANNE (HYAMS) WILCOX; m 09 Dec 1756 Richmond, Washington Co RI PATIENCE JAMES who was b ca 1738 d/BENJAMIN & PATIENCE (COTTRELL) JAMES; Res Exeter RI; ch THOMAS; Ref: Arnold v5 pt6 p21, Gen of RI Fam v1 p588, See RIGR v2 #2 p96.

JOB - b 07 Apr 1734 Portsmouth, Newport Co RI s/JOSEPH & SARAH (-----) WILCOX; Int to m 10 Jul 1761 Dartmouth, Bristol Co MA ELIZABETH MERIHEU; m LUCY -----; Res Freetown, Bristol Co MA, Wallingford, Rutland Co VT, Stanford, Dutchess Co NY; ch JOB, REBECCA, DEBORAH; d ca 1803/4; Ref: Dartmouth VR p547, VR of Freetown MA, Arnold v4 pt1 p104, Your Ancestors v12 #3 p1477 #4 pp1503,1504.

JOB - m 26 Oct 1757 Goshen, Litchfield Co CT LOIS WATSON; ch JOB, EUNICE, HEMAN; Ref: Barbour's VR Goshen v1 p225,236,237.

JOB - b 14 Feb 1743 Exeter, Washington Co RI s/ABRAHAM & LYDIA (HARRINGTON) WILCOX; m 07 Feb 1771 MARY GATES who was b 11 Jul 1754 Preston, New London Co CT & d 22 Oct 1832 d/ASA GATES or ROBERT & MARY (CLARK) GATES; ch all b Exeter RI ASA, NATHAN, ESTHER, SIMON GATES, EUNICE, JOB, HARRINGTON, MARY, PRUDENCE, GATES, HANNAH, THURSTON; Rev War; d 01 Nov 1808 Oxford, Chenango

Co NY Will probated 26 Jan 1809 Chenango Co NY A-103; bur Wilcox Cem north of Smithville, Chenango Co NY; Ref: Your Ancestors v4 # 7&8 p561, #11&12 pp609,610, 1774 Census RI, Arnold v5 pt3 pp35,63,203, v1 p199, Index to Wills of Chenango Co NY v1, Cutter's Western NY v3 p1436.

JOB - b 1758 Exeter, Washington Co RI s/EDWARD & ESTHER (----) WILCOX; m BRIDGET CLARKE who was b 15 Mar 1767 & d 26 Jan 1837 McLean, Tompkins Co NY; ch CLARK; Ref: Your Ancestors v12 #1 p1405, Nutmegger v6 #3 pp394,395.

JOB - b ca 1762 s/JOB & ELIZABETH (MERIHEU) WILCOX of Freetown, Bristol Co MA; m HANNAH CHASE who was b be 1762 Freetown MA d/CHARLES & ABIGAIL (STRANGE) CHASE; Ref: Gen of RI Fam v1 p155, Your Ancestors v12 #4 p1504, NEH&GR v19 p326.

JOB - m 28 Jul 1779 Dartmouth, Bristol Co MA SUSANNAH BABCOCK; Ref: Dartmouth VR p547.

JOB - m 30 Nov 1779 Richmond, Washington Co RI FREELOVE TENNANT; Ref: Arnold v5 pt6 p21.

JOB - b 30 Oct 1764 Goshen, Litchfield Co CT s/JOB & LOIS (WATSON) WILCOX; Ref: Barbour's VR Goshen v1 p236.

JOB - b 12 Mar 1782 Exeter, Washington Co RI s/JOB & MARY (GATES) WILCOX; m RUTH TERRY; m ELIZABETH PHELPS/PHILLIPS; Res Oxford, Chenango Co NY; d Aug 1849 Will probated 15 Nov 1849 Chenango Co NY F-118; Ref: Cutter's Western NY v3 p1436, VR of Chenango Co NY p228, Arnold v5 pt3 pp35,63, Barber's Index to Wills of Chenango Co v1, Your Ancestors v4 #11&12 p610.

JOB - m 30 Oct 1800 Freetown, Bristol Co MA HANNAH WHITWELL (widow); Ref: VR of Freetown MA.

JOB - b 26 Apr 1807 Chenango Co NY s/SIMON GATES & ANNA (CARTWRIGHT) WILCOX; m ASENATH WHITE who was b 1808 & d 31 Mar 1878; Res Tioga Co PA 1833; ch CHARLES C, SIMON, EDWIN & EDWARD twins, GALUSHA B, GEORGE, CAROLINE; d 31 May 1874 Delmar, Tioga Co PA; Ref: Ellen Jacobus, Hist of Tioga Co PA pp730,731.

JOB - b 25 Feb 1817 Burlington, Nova Scotia s/CHARLES DYER & ABIGAIL (CARD) WILCOX; m MARIA GREEN who was b 06 Oct 1820 & d 21 May 1899; ch ELVIRA, JULIA ANNE, MARINER, LEAMAN, BYRON,

EVELYN, WELLEN ANDREW; d Grand Manan Island, Canada 29 May 1875; both bur Hardwood Cove Cem Wood Island, Canada; Ref: Desc of Charles Dyer Wilcox pp v(2), 14-16.

JOEL - b 19 Oct 1746 Hebron, Tolland Co CT s/EBENEZER Jr & ELIZABETH (DEWEY) WILCOX; m Sandisfield, Berkshire Co MA LYDIA ----- who d 13 Sep 1807; ch MARTHA, LYDIA, JOEL, Deacon EBENEZER, WILLIAM JOHN, SAMUEL [Called Deacon Samuel]; d 13 Mar 1830; both bur Beach Plain Cem Otis, Berkshire Co MA; Ref: Barbour's VR Hebron v1 p45, Desc of Wm Wilcoxson p245.

JOEL - b 05 Dec 1753 Killingworth, Middlesex Co CT s/NATHANIEL & MINDWELL (WILCOX) WILCOX; single; d 1776; Ref: Wilcox-Meigs p44, Barbour's VR Killingworth v2 p148, Desc of Wm Wilcoxson p20.

JOEL - b 1755; m CATHERINE ----- who was b 1862 & d 22 Sep 1819 Wells, Rutland Co VT; d 24 Aug 1827; both bur Wells VT Cem, East Side; Ref: Hist of Wells VT p143.

JOEL - b 24 Aug 1762 Killingworth, Middlesex Co CT s/NATHAN & THANKFUL (STONE) WILCOX; m 22 Oct 1786 ELIZABETH HAND COAN d/EVAN COAN; ch RUTH, ELIZABETH, NANCY; Ref: Wilcox-Meigs pp61,79,80, Barbour's VR Killingworth v2 p93.

JOEL - b 15 Jan 1765 Stratford, Fairfield Co CT s/WILLIAM & HANNAH (PEAT) WILCOX; m 19 Jan 1789 SARAH BOOTH d/ABIJAH & RUTH (LEAVENWORTH) BOOTH; ch JERUSHA, NANCY, SARAH, THEODOSIA, SUSAN, URANIA, ANSON, JULIA, JOEL, ALDEN; Methodist Minister; Ref: Wilcox-Meigs p78, Hist of Stratford Fam p1347, Desc of Wm Wilcoxson p36.

JOEL - b 26 Jul 1765 W Simsbury, Hartford Co CT Twin of ELIZABETH/BETSY s/AMOS & HANNAH (HOSKINS) WILCOX; d 1826 age 61; Ref: Wilcox-Meigs p67, 2nd Boat Mar 1987, Early Settlers of W Simsbury pp 133,134, Fiske Card File, Your Ancestors v12 #4 p1489.

JOEL - b 05 Aug 1777 Sandisfield, Berkshire Co MA s/JOEL & LYDIA (-----) WILCOX; Ref: Sandisfield MA VR p72, Fiske Card File, Desc of Wm Wilcoxson p245.

JOEL - m 03 Nov 1801 Sharon, Litchfield Co CT CATHERINE RANDALL/RANDOLPH; Res Chestertown CT; ch AARON; Ref: 2nd Boat v6 #3 p141, Fiske Card File.

JOEL - b 1803 Sandgate, Bennington Co VT s/OZIAL & NANCY (PAINE) WILCOX; m BETSEY SPRAGUE who was b 1806 NY; Res Georgetown, Madison Co NY; ch JOHN, AMELIA, CHARLES, LEROY; Ref: Desc of Wm Wilcoxson p169, 1850 Census Georgetown NY p388 Dw# 211.

JOEL - b 1806 s/JOEL & SARAH (BOOTH) WILCOX; m PHOEBE ----- who was b 1808; ch HANFORD I, SARAH A; Ref: Desc of Wm Wilcoxson p36.

JOEL - b 08 Oct 1811 Halifax, Windham Co VT s/NATHANIEL & BETSEY (BOLSTER) WILCOX; m 19 Jan 1835 Guilford, Windham Co VT LUCINDA M WEATHERHEAD who was b 18 Oct 1815 & d 29 May 1882 d/IRA & TABITHA (-----) WEATHERHEAD; d 14 Mar 1869 bur Guilford Center Cem; Ref: Green Leaves of Whitingham p225, VT VR, Halifax Wilcox Fam mss.

JOEL - b 20 Oct 1814; m 14 Jun 1855 Hebron, Tolland Co CT ANN ELIZABETH STRONG who was b 07 Aug 1827 d/GEORGE & ANNA (BUELL) STRONG; d 11 Apr 1891; Ref: CT Bible Rec v11 pp752-754.

JOEL - m 14 Jun 1838 Hebron, Tolland Co CT LUCY BURNHAM; Ref: Barbour's VR Hebron v4 p35-m

JOEL JAIRUS - b 15 Jul 1814 s/SAMUEL & ELIZABETH (-----) WILCOX of Sandisfield, Berkshire Co MA; Sandisfield VR p73, Fiske Card File, Desc of Wm Wilcoxson p245.

JOEL S - b 01 Oct 1809 Lebanon, New London Co CT or Vesper, Onondaga Co NY s/JONATHAN & CELIA/SYBIL (SMITH) WILCOX; m 29 Dec 1833 JANE SHIELDS who was b 06 Jan 1811 Truxton, Cortland Co NY d/JAMES & LUCRETIA (GILMORE) SHIELDS; Res Milwaukee, Milwaukee Co WI 17 Jul 1835; ch LOUISE JANE; d 21 Sep 1873; Ref: Your Ancestors v4 #7&8 p 566, v4 #9&10 p587, Memoirs of Milwaukee Co WI v1 p189.

JOHANNA - b 08 Jul 1667 Stratford, Fairfield Co CT d/TIMOTHY & JOHANNA (BIRDSEYE) WILCOX; m JOSEPH FAIRCHILD s/ THOMAS FAIRCHILD JR; Ref: Hist of Stratford Fam p1346.

JOHANNAH - b 11 Feb 1741; m DAVID WELLS who was b 28 Mar 1738 & d 29 May 1790; ch DAVID; d 02 Mar 1800; Ref: Col Fam of US v7 p335.

JOHANNAH - b 11 Apr 1774 Killingworth, Middlesex Co CT d/SIMEON & LUCRETIA (KELSEY)

WILCOX; m 12 Dec 1798 JAMES DAVIS; Ref: Wilcox-Meigs p67, Barbour's VR Killingworth v2 p88.

JOHANNA - b ca 1785 Williamstown, Berkshire Co MA; m 1804 JOHN D DEMING; m THEOPHILUS SWEET; d be 1837 Sangamon Co IL; Ref: Nutmegger v5 #1 p80.

JOHANNA - b ca 1800 d/GILES & LYDIA (FOWLER) WILCOX; Res Mayville, Chautauqua Co NY; Ref: Your Ancestors v13 #4 p1598.

JOHN - b England; Original proprietor of Hartford CT 1639; m ca 1615 England MARY ----- who d 1668/71 in Hartford, Hartford Co CT; ch JOHN, MARY; d 01 Oct 1651; Ref: Hist of Berlin pp80,81, Savage v4 p546, Early Fam of Wallingford p330, Torrey's Marriage Rec microfilm.

JOHN - b England s/JOHN & MARY (-----) WILCOX; m 17 Sep 1646 Hartford, Hartford Co CT SARAH WADSWORTH who was b 1626 & d ca 1648 d/WILLIAM & ELIZABETH (STONE) WADSWORTH; m 18 Jan 1649 CATHERINE/RETORN STOUGHTON d/THOMAS STOUGHTON of Windsor, Hartford Co CT; m ca 1660 MARY ----- who d be 7 Sep 1671 w/----- LONG & w/----- FARNSWORTH; m 1671 ESTHER CORNWALL who was b 1650 & d 02 May 1733 d/WILLIAM & MARY (-----) CORNWALL; She later m JOHN STOW; ch by 1st wife SARAH; ch by 2nd wife JOHN, THOMAS, MARY, ISRAEL, SAMUEL; ch by 4th wife EPHRAIM, ESTHER, MERCY/MARY; d 24 May 1676 Middletown, Middlesex Co CT; Ref: Hinman p264, MUH pp742,743, Early Fam of Wallingford p330, Gen of CT Fam v1 p485, Hist of Berlin CT pp 81-83, Barbour's VR Hartford vD pp22,24, Middletown LR1 p48, NEH&GR v13 p141, Hist of Wallingford p936, Torrey's Marriage Rec microfilm.

JOHN - b 1633 England s/WILLIAM & MARGARET (-----) WILCOXSON; m by 1657 Stratford, Fairfield Co CT JOHANNAH TITHERTON d/DANIEL TITHERTON; m 19 Mar 1663 Stratford CT ELIZABETH (BOURNE) WELLES who d 08 Oct 1668 w/JOHN WELLES; ch JOHN, WILLIAM, PATIENCE, HANNAH, ELIZABETH, MARY; d Nov 1690; Ref: Wilcox-Meigs pp21,22, American Marriages p447, Nutmegger v13 #4 p639, Desc of Wm Wilcoxson p27, Bogue Fam p393, Cutter's Northern NY v2 p654, Hist of Stratford Fam p1346, Torrey's Marriage Rec microfilm, Hist of Surry NH p943.

JOHN - b 29 Oct 1650 Hartford, Hartford Co CT s/JOHN Jr & CATHERINE (STOUGHTON) WILCOX; d 24 May 1676 Middletown, Middlesex Co CT; Ref: MUH p743,

NEH&GR v12 p197, Cutter's Western NY v2 p741, Col Fam of US v5 p554, Hist of Wallingford p936.

JOHN - b Mar 1657 Stratford, Fairfield Co CT s/JOHN & JOHANNAH (TITHERTON) WILCOX; m Jun 1707 ELIZABETH TOMLINSON who was b 11 Aug 1684; m 19 Mar 1713 SARAH CURTIS who "died soon"; m 13 Jan 1714 DEBORAH H BRINSMADE who was b 1692 & d 1758; ch by 1st wife JOSIAH, TIMOTHY, ch by 3rd wife ELIZABETH, HANNAH, DAVID, REBECCA, JOHN, RUTH, SAMUEL, EPHRAIM, DEBORAH; d 12 Sep 1748; Ref: Wilcox-Meigs pp37,38, Nutmegger v7 #1 p37, Hist of Stratford Fam p1346, Cutter's Northern NY v2 pp654,655.

JOHN - b 1657; m 14 Mar 1683 Concord, Middlesex Co MA ELIZABETH (JONES) BUEL w/JOSEPH BUEL; Ref: Torrey's Marriage Rec microfilm.

JOHN - b 1670 s/DANIEL & ELIZABETH (COOKE) WILCOX of Tiverton, Newport Co RI; m 1698 Little Compton, Newport Co RI REBECCA -----; [Some sources say Rebecca Mosher but date of marriage given is 1729 & this John died 1726]; Res Little Compton, Newport Co RI; ch JACOB, DANIEL, ELIZABETH, JOHN, JABEZ, BARJONA, THOMAS, REBECCA, TABITHA; Will dated 16 Nov 1725 Prob 21 Mar 1726/7; Ref: Your Ancestors v10 #2 p1244, Arnold v4 pt5 p71,193, pt7 p56, Wilcox Excerpts v1 p21, Probate Rec of Bristol Co v1 p144, Mayflower Soc Application of Earley Vernon Wilcox.

JOHN Lt - b 1675 Killingworth, Middlesex Co CT s/JOSEPH & ANN (SHEATHER) WILCOX; m 1703 HANNAH SHAILOR who was b 25 Nov 1681 & d 08 Nov 1751 bur Old Southwest Cem Killingworth CT; ch JOHN, ABIJAH, ELIZABETH, MARGARET, MINDWELL, ABRAHAM, EBENEZER, SILAS, HANNAH, AMOS; d 09 Feb 1733/4; Ref: Wilcox-Meigs p31, Desc of Wm Wilcoxson pp12,13,28,36, Bogue Fam p395, Savage v4 p547, Nutmegger v10 #2 p229, Barbour's VR Killingworth v1 p73, v2 p185.

JOHN - b 05 Jul 1682/9 Middletown, Middlesex Co CT s/ISRAEL & SARAH (SAVAGE) WILCOX; m 12 Apr 1710 MARY WARNER who d 23 Apr 1735; ch MARY, JOHN, JOSEPH, SARAH, EBENEZER, ESTHER, JEMIMA, HULDAH, MOSES, OZIAS; Ref: MUH pp743,746, Early Fam of Wallingford p331, NEH&GR v14 p138, Nutmegger v4 #3 p331, Cutter's Western NY v2 p742, Col Fam of US v5 p554, Barbour's VR Middletown LR1 p33, LR2 p21, Hist of Wallingford p937.

JOHN - b 09 Nov 1692 Guilford, New Haven Co CT s/OBADIAH & SILENCE (MANSFIELD) WILCOX; m 11 Jan 1716/18/19 DEBORAH PARMELEE who was b 11 Aug 1700 Guilford CT & d 10 Jan 1792 d/JOHN & MARY (MASON) PARMELEE; ch OBADIAH, SARAH, JOHN, EZRA, MARY, ASAHEL; d 20 Apr 1753/56 or 01 May 1753; both bur Madison, New Haven Co CT; Ref: Wilcox-Meigs p33, Desc of Wm Wilcoxson pp8,15, Parmelee Fam p239, Barbour's VR Guilford v2 p20,33, Hist of Surry NH p944.

JOHN - b 10 Apr 1698 Simsbury, Hartford Co CT s/SAMUEL & MINDWELL (GRIFFEN) WILCOX; Ref: Nutmegger v10 #2 p214, Desc of Wm Wilcoxson p14.

JOHN - b 01 Jan 1704/5 Killingworth, Middlesex Co CT s/JOHN & HANNAH (SHAILOR) WILCOX; d young; Ref: Desc of Wm Wilcoxson pp13,36, Bogue Fam p395, Barbour's VR Killingworth v2 p185.

JOHN Jr - d 27 Mar 1732 Killingworth, Middlesex Co CT; Ref: Barbour's VR Killingworth v1 p79.

JOHN - b 22 Sep 1704 Little Compton, Newport Co RI s/JOHN & REBECCA (-----) WILCOX; int to marry 28 Dec 1728 m 20 Jan 1729 REBECCA MOSHER d/NICHOLAS & ELIZABETH (-----) MOSHER; Res Tiverton, Newport Co RI; Ref: Arnold v4 pt5 p193, pt7 p56, Little Compton Fam p771.

JOHN - m 28 Dec 1728 Little Compton, Newport Co RI PHEBE CORNELL; Ref: Arnold v4 pt7 p56.

JOHN - b ca 1710 Westerly, Washington Co RI s/STEPHEN & ELIZABETH (CRANDALL) WILCOX; Ref: Hist of Stonington p659, Austin p423, Wilcox Genealogy p5.

JOHN - b 1710 s/WILLIAM & ELIZABETH (WILSON) WILCOX of Simsbury, Hartford Co CT; Not mentioned in fathers will 1732; Ref: Your Ancestors v10 #4 p1275, Desc of Wm Wilcoxson p14.

JOHN Deacon - m 02 May 1738 Middletown, Middlesex Co CT BETHIA JESSEUPS of Long Island; ch ELIZABETH JESUP; d 12 May 1751 Middletown CT; Ref: Barbour's VR Middletown v1 p45.

JOHN - b 08 Aug 1711 Middletown, Middlesex Co CT s/EPHRAIM & SILENCE (HAND) WILCOX; m 06 Jul 1738 HANNAH WILCOX who was b 1718 & d 13 Nov 1807 d/SAMUEL & HANNAH (SAGE) WILCOX; ch JOHN, SAMUEL, HEZEKIAH, JOSEPH, HANNAH, GILES, SIMEON, SUBMIT,

COMFORT, SARAH; d 21 Oct 1795; Ref: Hale Collection, Barbour's VR v2 pp29,94, MUH pp744,747, Your Ancestors v3 #4 p351 v4 #3&4 pp524,538, Cutter's Western NY p90, Nutmegger v4 #1 p138, Early Fam of Wallingford p331, NEH&GR v14 p138, Hist of Wallingford p937.

JOHN - m 17 Jan 1739/40 Guilford, New Haven Co CT MARTHA COE who was b 21 Mar 1712 d/ROBERT & BARBARA (PARMELEE) COE; ch BARBARA, JOHN, BENJAMIN, ESTHER, REBECCA, SARAH, MARTHA/MATILDA; d 21 Oct 1791 Bristol, Hartford Co CT; Ref: Wilcox-Meigs pp46,47, Nutmegger v4 #3 p407, Your Ancestors v4 #3&4 p524 v4 #9&10 p587, SGS Bulletin Jun 1971 p200, Barbour's VR Guilford v2 pp42,57,75,78.

JOHN - b 01 Aug 1712 Middletown, Middlesex Co CT s/SAMUEL & HESTER/ESTHER (BUSHNELL) WILCOX; Ref: Your Ancestors v3 #4 p351, Barbour's VR Middletown LR2 p21, NEH&GR v14 p138.

JOHN - b 13 Feb 1712/13 Middletown, Middlesex Co CT s/JOHN & MARY (WARNER) WILCOX; d 15 Apr 1713; Ref: Barbour's VR Middletown LR2 p21, See John.

JOHN - b 1720+ Dartmouth, Bristol Co MA s/STEPHEN & JUDITH (BARNARD) WILCOX; Ref: Austin p423.

JOHN - b 10 Nov 1721 Stratford, Fairfield Co CT s/JOHN & DEBORAH (BRINSMADE) WILCOX; m SARAH ----- who was b 1732 & d 1792; ch AMY, JOHN; d 1795; Ref: Wilcox-Meigs pp37,59, Hist of Stratford Fam p1346.

JOHN - b 07 Sep 1725 Portsmouth, Newport Co RI s/JOSEPH & SARAH (-----) WILCOX; m 30 Nov 1746 Portsmouth RI MARY COOK who was b 1730 & d 19 Mar 1807; 4 sons in 1744 incl JOHN, COOK, DANIEL; d 21 May 1787; both bur Brownell-Wilcox Cem; Ref: Arnold v4 pt1 pp47,104, 1774 Census of RI, Gen of RI Fam v2 p584, Your Ancestors v12 #3 p1477.

JOHN - b 17 Aug 1727 Guilford, New Haven Co CT s/JOHN & DEBORAH (PARMELEE) WILCOX; m 1753/4 GRACE NORTH GRISWOLD who was b 02 Apr 1734 & d 13 May 1823 d/DANIEL & JERUSHA (STEVENS) GRISWOLD; Res Clinton, Middlesex Co CT; Served in French & Indian War; ch SAMUEL, SARAH, SAMUEL, JOEL, GRACE, JOHN, PAMELIA, POLLY, LYDIA, BEULAH, EDWARD, ABIGAIL, ELIZABETH; d 16 Jun 1794; Ref: Wilcox-

Meigs pp51,52, Desc of Wm Wilcoxson pp26,27, Parmelee Fam p239, Barbour's VR Guilford v2 p18.

JOHN - b 04 Apr 1732 Killingworth, Middlesex Co CT s/WILLIAM & RUTH (BLANCHARD) WILCOX; m 27 Aug 1759 Haddam, Middlesex Co CT ANNA STEVENS who was b 1733 & d 1821; ch EBENEZER, JOHN Jr, JAMES, WILLIAM, ANNE/ANNA, DAVID LEVI, AMY, DINAH; Will proved 29 Aug 1808 Haddam CT; Ref: Fiske Card File, Your Ancestors v3 #11 & 12 p473, Gifford Wilcox, Desc of Wm Wilcoxson pp43,122, Barbour's VR Killingworth v2 p158, Haddam LR7 p226.

JOHN - b 16 Jul 1734 Stonington, New London Co CT s/WILLIAM & ELIZABETH (BROWN) WILCOX; Ref: Hist of Stonington p660, Barbour's VR Stonington v2 p48.

JOHN - b 21 Aug 1736 Killingworth, Middlesex Co CT s/ELISHA & MARY (BEACH) WILCOX; Ref: Wilcox-Meigs p41, Your Ancestors v3 #3 p321, Barbour's VR Killingworth v2 p162.

JOHN - b 16 Sep 1736 Killingworth, Middlesex Co CT s/NATHANIEL & MINDWELL (WILCOX) WILCOX; Ref: Wilcox-Meigs p44, Barbour's VR Killingworth v2 p148.

JOHN - bpt 15 Nov 1738 Little Compton, Newport Co RI s/EPHRAIM & MARY (-----) WILCOX; Res Tiverton, Newport Co RI; Ref: Arnold v8 p34.

JOHN - b 15 Jan 1740 Middletown, Middlesex Co CT s/JOHN & HANNAH (WILCOX) WILCOX; m 16 Oct 1766 Cromwell CT EUNICE NORTON of Kensington, Hartford Co CT who was b 1739 & d 13 Oct 1804 Middletown, Middlesex Co CT d/JEDEDIAH & ACHSAH (-----) NORTON; ch SETH, JEDUTHAN, JOHN, EUNICE, JEDEDIAH; d 25 Apr 1823; Ref: ECM v2 p92, Your Ancestors v3 #4 p351, Early Fam of Wallingford pp331,332, Barbour's VR Middletown v2 p143, Hist of Wallingford pp937,938.

JOHN - m 22 Oct 1757 at Dartmouth, Bristol Co MA JONE BRIGHTMAN; Res Little Compton, Newport Co RI; Ref: Dartmouth VR p547.

JOHN - m 30 Sep 1759 Exeter, Washington Co RI SARAH RATHBUN d/OBADIAH RATHBUN; Res S Kingston, Washington Co RI; Ref: Arnold v5 pt3 p35.

JOHN - s/EZRA & MARY (HUMPHREY) WILCOX of Simsbury, Hartford Co CT; Res Whitestown, Oneida Co NY 1791; Ref: Noble Gen p219, Fiske Card File.

JOHN Jr - m 25 Mar 1762 Goshen, Litchfield Co CT MARY NERVEL; Ref: Barbour's VR Goshen v1 p225.

JOHN - b 09 Jul 1741 Exeter, Washington Co RI s/ABRAHAM & LYDIA (HARRINGTON) WILCOX; m 31 Jan 1762 MARY BARBER d/DANIEL & ELIZABETH (TEFFTT) BARBER; Res Norwich, Chenango Co CT; ch THOMAS, THURSTON, LEBBENS, LYDIA, DANIEL, MARY, DELIVERANCE, LARKIN, JOHN, SUSANNA; Will proved 12 Dec 1785; Ref: Your Ancestors v4 #7&8 p561, 1774 RI Census, Nutmegger v2 #1 p65, Wilcox Excerpts v1 p1, Arnold v5 pt3 p63.

JOHN - b 10 Oct 1742 Middletown, Middlesex Co CT s/JANNA & RACHEL (BOARDMAN) WILCOX; Ref: Barbour's VR LR1 p22, Your Ancestors v4 #3&4 p524.

JOHN - b 1742 Guilford, New Haven Co CT s/JOHN & MARTHA (COE) WILCOX; Ref: Wilcox-Meigs p47.

JOHN - b 14 Sep 1745 Killingworth, Middlesex Co CT s/NATHANIEL & MINDWELL (WILCOX) WILCOX; m 15 Dec 1778 MARY KELSEY who was b 1749 & d 26 Oct 1836; Ref: Wilcox-Meigs p44, Desc of Wm Wilcoxson p59, MUH p749, Barbour's VR Killingworth v2 p148.

JOHN - b 07 Mar 1746 Portsmouth, Newport Co RI s/JOHN & MARY (COOK) WILCOX; m be 1765 SUSANNA/JANE SHERMAN; ch THOMAS, ANNIE [4 sons & 3 daus in 1774]; Ref: Arnold v4 pt1 p105, 1774 Census RI, Your Ancestors v12 #3 p1478.

JOHN - m 23 Nov 1769 Kent, Litchfield Co CT SARAH STURTEVANT; ch JERUSHA; Ref: Barbour's VR Kent v1 p209, See Jerusha.

JOHN - b 24 Nov 1748 Stratford, Fairfield Co CT s/JOSIAH & ELIZABETH (HUBBELL) WILCOX; Ref: Wilcox-Meigs p58, Hist of Stratford Fam p1348, Cutter's Northern NY v2 p655.

JOHN - b 18 Oct 1752 Hebron, Tolland Co CT s/OBADIAH & SARAH (TALCOTT) WILCOX; Res Gilsum & Surry, Cheshire Co NH; d 18 Jan 1798; Ref: Desc of Wm Wilcoxson p26, Wilcox-Meigs p50, Barbour's VR Hebron v2 p254, Hist of Surry NH p380, p945.

JOHN - s/EDWARD & ELEANOR (RATHBONE) WILCOX; m POLLY PACKER; Res Stonington, New London Co CT; Ref: Hist of Stonington CT p661.

JOHN - b 01 Oct 1753 Harwinton, Litchfield Co CT s/DAVID & MARY (HUTCHINSON) WILCOX; Ref: Desc of Abner & Lucy Hart Wilcox pp19,20, Barbour's VR Harwinton LR1 p26.

JOHN - b 02 Apr 1754 Middletown, Middlesex Co CT s/MOSES & DESIRE (RANNEY) WILCOX; Ref: Barbour's VR Middletown v2 p292, See Moses.

JOHN - b 03 Sep 1754 Dartmouth, Bristol Co MA s/JABEZ & HANNAH (HART) WILCOX; Ref: Dartmouth VR p302, Little Compton Fam p771, See John.

JOHN - m MARY ----- who d 04 Mar 1825; Res Conway, Franklin Co MA; ch JOHN, DAVID, NATHANIEL, OZIEL, JEHIEL, ZELINDA, MARGARET, JERUSHA, MINDWELL; d 16 Dec 1824; Ref: Halifax VT Wilcox Fam mss.

JOHN - b 1755 Richmond, Washington Co RI s/WILLIAM & ELIZABETH (BAKER) WILCOX; m CATHERINE WOODARD who was b 1762 & d 22 Aug 1819 Wells, Rutland Co VT; Res Halifax, Windham Co & Wells VT; ch JOHN, LUCY, AMOS, BETSEY, POLLY, WEALTHY, IRA, ARTEMUS, PHEBE, CEPHA, EMILY; d 31 Aug 1827; Ref: Vermont--Once No Man's Land p107, Halifax Wilcox Fam mss, Samuel Gorton Desc v2 p586.

JOHN - b 1755-1774; Res Litchfield, Herkimer Co NY; 3 daus under 10 in 1800; Ref: 1800 Census Herkimer Co NY p568.

JOHN - b 1755-1774; Res Litchfield, Herkimer Co NY; 5 sons, 2 daus in; Ref: 1800 Census p539, 1810 Census p439.

JOHN - b be 1756; Res Fairfield, Herkimer Co NY; Ref: 1800 Census Herkimer Co NY p576.

JOHN - b be 1756; Res Pawlet, Rutland Co VT; 4 sons & 4 daus; Ref: 1800 Census Rutland Co VT p119.

JOHN - b ca 1757 Richmond, Washington Co RI s/EDWARD & ESTHER (-----) WILCOX; m MARY CROSBY who was b ca 1757 & d ca 1832 d/ISAAC & MERCY (FOSTER) CROSBY; Res Stonington, New London Co CT, Litchfield, Herkimer Co NY 1787, Sardinia, Erie Co NY 1813; ch JOHN, CHARLOTTE MERCY, JEREMIAH,

HIRAM, OLIVER, MARY, ROSWELL, POLLY, CHARLES; d ca 1823; Ref: Your Ancestors v12 #1 p1405, Jane Smith.

JOHN - b ca 1760 Simsbury, Hartford Co CT s/EZRA & RHODA (HARRIS) WILCOX; m EUNICE FOWLER who was b 1760 d/SAMUEL & NAOMI (NOBLE) FOWLER; [Noble Gen says John was b Southwick, Hampden Co MA & Res Westfield, Hampden Co MA]; m AMELIA EDGECOMB; Res Whitestown & Clinton, Oneida Co NY 1788, Lafayette & Pompey, Onondaga Co NY 1789; ch of 2nd wife GILES, STERLING, AMY, EMILY A, CLARISSA B, CORRELL, JOSEPH, JOHN Jr; Ref: Your Ancestors v13 #3 p1568, #4 p1598, v14 #1 p1619, Gen of CT Fam v1 p627, Desc of Wm Wilcoxson p242.

JOHN - s/JOHN deceased m 20 Dec 1778 Little Compton, Newport Co RI MEREBAH TALLMAN; Ref: Arnold v4 pt7 p57

JOHN - b ca 1760 W Simsbury, Hartford Co CT s/EZRA & MARY (HUMPHREY) WILCOX; Res Whitestown, Oneida Co NY 1791; Ref: Early Settlers of W Simsbury p131.

JOHN - b 1760 Killingworth, Middlesex Co CT; Rev War 7th CT Line 27 Aug to 13 Dec 1780; Ref: SAR Register NY 1899 p577.

JOHN - b 12 Nov 1760 Westerly, Washington Co RI s/VALENTINE & ABIGAIL (KENECOME) WILCOX; Ref: Arnold v5 p144, See RIGR v1 p29.

JOHN Capt - b 15 Dec 1760 Clinton, Middlesex Co CT s/JOHN & GRACE NORTH (GRISWOLD) WILCOX; m 17 Jun 1780/1 Saybrook, Middlesex Co CT MARGARET KELSEY who was b 01 Aug 1760 & d ca 1790 d/SILAS & LYDIA (WELLMAN) KELSEY; m 28 May 1804 SARAH HUNTINGTON who d 29 Sep 1830; ch of 1st wife SAMUEL, EBEN, POLLY, WILLIAM, AUGUSTUS, CHARLES, SILAS, BETSEY, ORLANDO, JOHN, ch of 2nd wife ELIPHALET, HUNTINGTON, two others; d 08 Jul 1812 Clinton CT; Ref: Probate of will, Wilcox-Meigs pp 52,70,71, Your Ancestors v2 p255, Nutmegger v3 #2 p167, Desc of Wm Wilcoxson p26, Parmelee Fam p239, Barbour's VR Clinton v2 p94, Hurd Diary.

JOHN - m 30 Nov 1780 RUTH PENFIELD who was b Chatham, Middlesex Co CT 30 Oct 1758 d/JOHN & RUTH (STOCKING) PENFIELD; ch LUCY; Ref: Gen of CT Fam v3 p87, Barbour's VR Chatham v1 p118.

JOHN Jr - b 23 Jan 1762 Haddam, Middlesex Co CT s/JOHN & ANNA (STEVENS) WILCOX; m 26/28 Feb 1784 LOIS AUGER who was b 18 Feb 1758 & d 29 Apr 1851 ISAAC & EUNICE (TYLER/TULLER) AUGER/AUGUR; Res Glen & Charleston, Montgomery Co NY; ch EBENEZER, ELIZABETH, DAVID, ANNA, PRUDENCE, LOIS, MARY; d 10 Nov 1848; Ref: Fiske Card File, Your Ancestors v3 #11 & 12 p473, Gifford Wilcox, Barbour's VR Haddam LR7 p226, Desc of Wm Wilcoxson pp122,123.

JOHN - b 14 Jun 1764 Middletown, Middlesex Co CT s/EPHRAIM & DIADEMA (FRENCH) WILCOX; 2 daus; d 01 Sep 1839; Ref: Barbour's VR Middletown v2 p207, MUH p750, Your Ancestors v4 #5&6 p545, 1790 Census, Texas Society DAR Roster v4 p2287.

JOHN - b be 1765; Res Canaan, Columbia Co NY 1810; 3 sons & 4 daus; Ref: 1810 Census Columbia Co NY.

JOHN - b be 1765; Res Pompey, Onondaga Co NY 1810; 5 sons & 5 daus; Ref: 1810 Census Onondaga Co NY p26.

JOHN - b 07 Feb 1765 Dover, Dutchess Co NY s/ELIAB & JERUSHA (SPENCER) WILCOX; m SARAH JUDSON who d Jan 1850 age 85; Res Harpersfield, Delaware Co NY 1781; Res Conquest Cayuga Co NY 1840; ch HARRY JEFFERSON, JUDSON; d 1841; Ref: Desc of Wm Wilcoxson p58, Hist of Cayuga Co NY p287, Your Ancestor v4 #3&4 p522 #7&8 p563.

JOHN - b ca 1766 Stonington, New London Co CT s/NATHAN & TABITHA (PROSSER) WILCOX; Ref: Hist of Stonington CT p661.

JOHN - m JOANNA ----- who d 22 Nov 1809 Tiverton, Newport Co RI; d be 1809; Ref: Gen of RI Fam v2 p649.

JOHN - b 1767 s/JOHN & SARAH (-----) WILCOX; m MARY ----- who was b 1769 & d 1839; Deacon of church Monroe, Orange Co NY; d 1824; Ref: Wilcox-Meigs p59, Hist of Stratford Fam p1347.

JOHN - b 30 Oct 1769 Westerly, Washington Co RI s/DAVID & TABITHA (-----) WILCOX; Ref: Arnold v5 p144.

JOHN - b 1770; d 12 Dec 1802 Salisbury, Hartford Co CT; Ref: Hale Collection VR v1 p119.

JOHN - b 21 Apr 1771 Sandisfield, Berkshire Co MA s/EBENEZER & MARY (EDDY) WILCOX; Ref: Sandisfield MA VR p89, Fiske Card File.

JOHN - b 13 Sep 1771 Middletown, Middlesex Co CT s/JOHN & EUNICE (NORTON) WILCOX; m 1795 SYBIL GUILD who was b 1778 & d 24 Nov 1842; Purchased land in Herkimer Co NY 1817; Res W Winfield, Herkimer Co NY; ch EUNICE, RUTH, CLARISSA, HARRIETT, NEWTON, MILTON JOHN; d 12 Nov 1848; Ref: Early Fam of Wallingford CT p331, Land & Cem Records of Herkimer Co NY v11 pp359,360,361, NYSDAR Records v15 p4, Your Ancestors v3 #4 p352, v4 #9&10 p588, Barbour's VR Middletown v2 p143, Hist of Wallingford p937.

JOHN - m ca 1790 RI MEREBAH ----- who d age 94 Monmouth NY; Res Little Compton, Newport Co RI; ch ELEANOR, WASHINGTON, DELIVERANCE; Ref: Arnold v8 p56.

JOHN - b 03 Dec 1771 W Greenwich, Kent Co RI s/THOMAS & ELIZABETH (-----) WILCOX; Ref: Arnold v1 pt3 p103.

JOHN - b 22/24 Apr 1774 s/HOPSON & ELIZABETH (HELWAY) WILCOX; m SUSANNAH NICHOLS who was b 25 Jan 1784 & d 25 May 1848 Earlville, Chenango Co NY; ch OLIVE, BETSEY, SUSANNAH, ELIZABETH, JOHN, GARDNER NICHOLS, ROBERT HAZARD, HANNAH; d 09 Mar 1815 Earlville NY; d 09 Mar 1815, Will prob 22 Jun 1815 #A-215; Ref: Chenango Co Cem Records p9, Barber's Index of Wills Chenango Co v1, Early Days in Smyrna pp21,24,25, Your Ancestors v3 #1 p276, #4 p348.

JOHN - b 1777 RI; m SARAH ----- who was b 1787 MA; Res McDonough, Chenango Co NY; ch WILLIAM, MINA, SETH, JOHN; Ref: 1850 Census Chenango Co NY.

JOHN - d 08 Oct 1797 PA; Ref: Daily Advertiser Philadelphia p511.

JOHN - b 05 Apr 1777 Middletown, Middlesex Co CT s/JONATHAN & ELIZABETH (TODD) WILCOX; m ELECTA GOODRICH; ch WILLIAM HENRY; Ref: MUH p754, Fam of Early Guilford pp1202,1203, Your Ancestors v3 #2 p302.

JOHN - b 13 Oct 1777 Woodbury, Litchfield Co CT s/STEPHEN & DEMARIS (-----) WILCOX; Res Manchester, Bennington Co VT; Ref: Nutmegger v8 #2 p284, Barbour's VR Woodbury v1 p75.

JOHN - s/JOHN & MARY (-----) WILCOX of Conway, Franklin Co MA; m be 1824 PHEBE -----; Ref: Halifax VT Wilcox Fam mss.

JOHN - b 04 Jan 1778, bpt 02 May 1779 Amenia, Dutchess Co NY s/JEHIEL & DEBORAH (GILLETT) WILCOX; m 1802 BETSEY CADY who d 1857; Res Ancram, Columbia Co NY ch WEALTHY (WILCOX) HUBBARD, ANNA (WILCOX) FORD, EDGAR M, EMMA (WILCOX) BATTERSHELL, ALBERT, SYLVESTER C, VALENTINE J, SIDNEY S; d 06 May 1850 Will probated 23 Sep 1850 Columbia Co NY; Ref: Columbia Co Wills v8 p36, Wilcox-Meigs p66, Desc of Wm Wilcoxson p59, Fiske Card File, Your Ancestors v4 #11&12 p612.

JOHN - m 23 Apr 1809 ELIZABETH DOANE who was b 27 Jul 1787 & d 19 Aug 1821 d/SETH & MERCY (PARKER) DOANE of Middle Haddam, Middlesex Co CT; Ref: John Doane Desc p109.

JOHN - b 23 Feb 1781 s/JOHN & CATHERINE (WOODWARD) WILCOX; m SOPHIA BEARDSLEY; Res Pawlet, Rutland Co VT; Ref: Halifax Wilcox Fam mss.

JOHN - b 05 Apr 1781; m ANNIE ----- who was b 1787 & d 24 Aug 1829 Tiverton, Newport Co RI; d 23 Sep 1868; both bur Cem #1 Tiverton; Ref: Gen of RI Fam v2 p596.

JOHN - b 11 Apr 1781 Surry, Cheshire Co NH s/OBADIAH & HANNAH (MERRIAM) WILCOX; Ref: Hist of Surry NH p946.

JOHN - b ca 1785; m SOPHIA ----- who was b 1789 & d 04 Feb 1824; Res Warsaw, Wyoming Co NY; purchased land in Orangeville, Wyoming Co NY 1805; Ref: Tree Talks v12, Hist of Wyoming Co NY p227.

JOHN - s/NOAH WILCOX; m 29 Jun 1806 E Greenwich, Kent Co RI MARTHA FOSTER d/WILLIAM FOSTER; Ref: Arnold v1 p92, Your Ancestors v3 #11&12 p472.

JOHN - m ca 1815 RI ANNA -----; ch EDWARD; Ref: Arnold v7 p583.

JOHN - m Smithville Co NY 16 Aug or Nov 1825 CAROLINE HILL; Ref: 10,000 VR of Central NY p265.

JOHN - s/BENJAMIN & PATIENCE (TUCKER) WILCOX m 09 Feb 1812 RI HANNAH LISCOMB who was b 09 Feb 1812 & d 17 Dec 1851 Newport, Newport Co RI d/JOHN

& ABIGAIL (-----) LISCOMB; Ref: Arnold v8 pp356,493, Your Ancestors v13 #4 p1610.

JOHN - s/JOHN & MARY (CROSBY) WILCOX of Sardinia, Erie Co NY; m MELINDA PALMER; d 1874 IL; Ref: Jane Smith.

JOHN Major - b 24 Jan 1786 s/ABRAHAM & ANNA (TILLINGHAST) HOXIE WILCOX; m 01 Sep 1805 Exeter, Washington Co RI MARY BARBER who was b 19 Jul 1785 Exeter RI & d 03 Oct 1886 d/REYNOLDS & ALCEA (DAWLEY) BARBER; Res Preston & Norwich, New London Co CT; ch ANN, WILLIAM BISSELL, ESTHER, ABRAHAM, ALCEA, ASHER B, JOHN, JAMES, EMILY H; d 22 Apr 1856 bur Rixton Cem; Ref: Cem Records of New London Co CT v2 p48, Arnold v5 pt3 p36, Your Ancestors v4 #7&8 p562, Esther Palmer Clark.

JOHN - b 27 Apr 1787 Foster Providence Co RI s/STEPHEN & PHEBE (HAMMON) WILCOX; m be 1828 AMANDA UPSON who was b 1794 & d 1844; Res Middletown, Middlesex Co CT, MD & Schenevus, Otsego Co NY; ch HENRY, ALBERT, JOHN D, STEPHEN S, dau; d 1870; Ref: Arnold v3 p42, Your Ancestors v4 #1&2 pp495,496.

JOHN - b 1788 CT; m SALLY ----- who was b 1790 CT; Res Rome, Oneida Co NY; ch WILLIAM; Ref: 1860 Census Rome NY p198.

JOHN - b 1788 CT; Shoemaker; Res Maryland, Otsego Co NY with ELMIRA WILCOX who was b 1807 NY She could be dau or wife; Ref: 1850 Census Maryland NY p156 Dw# 336.

JOHN - b 1788 RI; m ELIZABETH ----- who was b 1787 RI; Res Sangerfield, Oneida Co NY; ch CLARINDA, ADALINE, FRANKLIN; Ref: 1850 Census Sangerfield NY p54 Dw# 413.

JOHN - b 1789 s/JAMES & ELIZABETH (AUGER) BRADLEY WILCOX; m Mar 1816 Saybrook, Middlesex Co CT RACHEL FLORILLA POST who d 01 Feb 1858; ch JOHN LEANDER, JAMES RUSSELL, WILLIAM LYMAN, ELIZABETH SARAH, NOAH POST, RACHEL FLORILLA; d 04/14 Jun 1865; Ref: Saybrook Colony VR p513, Your Ancestors v4 #1&2 p497, Desc of Wm Wilcox p130.

JOHN - b 15 Jan 1789 s/URIAH & HANNAH (WRIGHT or BARTLETT) WILCOX; m LYDIA P SAWYER d/JOSEPH SAWYER; Res Newport, Sullivan Co NH; d 09 Nov 1872; Ref: Gen of NH Fam v3 p1509, Your Ancestors v3 #5 p378.

JOHN - b 28 Jun 1793 Halifax, Windham Co VT s/WILLIAM & RELIEF (-----) WILCOX; Ref: VR of VT, Halifax Wilcox Fam mss.

JOHN - of Roxbury, Washington Co VT; War of 1812; Ref: VT Roster War of 1812 p455.

JOHN - m 26 Dec 1822 Chatham, Middlesex Co CT LAURA SHEPARD; Ref: Barbour's VR Chatham v1 p282.

JOHN - b 28 Apr 1794 Chatham, Middlesex Co CT s/DAVID & POLLY (CHAPPELL) WILCOX; m 14 Dec 1826 ABIGAIL W WRIGHT who was b 25 May 1801 Pittsford, Rutland Co VT & d 28 Mar 1861 d/Rev NATHAN D & ABIGAIL (WOODRUFF) WRIGHT; Res Milford, Otsego Co NY; ch MENZO, MARIA, SOPHRONIA; d 24 Jun/Jul 1856; Ref: Westcott Hist p388, Your Ancestors v4 #7&8 p565, 1850 Census Milford NY p119 Dw# 324.

JOHN - s/NATHAN & SYLVIA (HOPKINS) WILCOX; Res Bloomfield, Ontario Co NY & Oakland Co MI; Ref: Desc of Wm Wilcoxson p204.

JOHN - b 02 Dec 1795 Canaan, Litchfield Co CT; d 25 Nov 1860; Ref: CT Bible Rec v7 p656.

JOHN - b 1797 NY; m BELINDA ----- who was b 1820 NY; Res Yorkshire, Cattaraugus Co NY; ch PHILANDER, ALPHEUS, WILLIAM, BETSEY; Ref: 1850 Census Yorkshire NY p458, Dw# 1205.

JOHN - b 03 Jan 1798 Killingworth, Middlesex Co CT s/JOHN & MARGARET (KELSEY) WILCOX; Res Clinton, Middlesex Co CT; m ----- who was b ca 1809 & d 24 Jan 1874; ch CHARLES EDWARD, FRANCES HENRIETTA; d 29 Dec 1864; Ref: Your Ancestors v2 p255, Wilcox-Meigs p71, Barbour's VR Clinton Hurd Diary, v1 p42.

JOHN - b 19 Apr 1799 Halifax, Windham Co VT s/BENJAMIN & THANKFUL (WORDEN) WILCOX; m SOPHRONIA SHEPARDSON; d 09 Nov 1862 age 63; Ref: Your Ancestors v3 #9&10 p447, Halifax Wilcox Fam mss.

JOHN - b 28 Jul 1800 Amity, Orange Co NY s/JOSEPH & MARGARET (SCINONSON) WILCOX; m 1823 HANNAH HOWELL d/ROGER HOWELL; Res Warwick, Orange Co NY; ch LEWIS, JOSEPH, WILLIAM H, J WICKHAM, MARGARET, MARY, SARAH, HARRIET, PRUDENCE, EUNICE AMELIA; Ref: Hist of Orange Co NY p610.

JOHN Jr - b 1800 s/JOHN & AMELIA (EDGECOMB) WILCOX of Pompey, Onondaga Co NY; m HANNAH -----; ch AMELIA, JOHN B; Ref: Desc of Wm Wilcoxson p242.

JOHN - b 1800 VT; m LUCY ----- who was b 1801 VT; Res Concord, Erie Co NY; Ref: 1850 Census Concord NY p56 Dw# 823.

JOHN - b 1800 CT; m AMY ----- who was b 1800 NY; Res Mina, Chautauqua Co NY; ch ASA, EDWIN, LYMAN; Ref: 1850 Census Mina NY p298 NY Dw# 75.

JOHN - b 1800 NY; m ANN C ----- who was b 1800; Res Rushford, Allegany Co NY; ch FANNY D, MARY E; Ref: 1850 Census Rushford NY p349 Dw# 66.

JOHN - b 1802 NY; m FIDELIA -----; Res Lafayette, Onondaga Co NY; ch NELSON B, ELLEN A, ADELINE, WILLIAM H Ref: 1850 Census Lafayette NY p216 Dw# 374.

JOHN - b 1803 NY; m EMELINE ----- who was b 1820 NY; Res Amenia, Dutchess Co NY; ch JONATHAN, SARAH E; Ref: 1850 Census Amenia NY p339 Dw# 398.

JOHN - s/THOMAS & LYDIA (DIBBLE) WILCOX settled in Warren Co PA ca 1820; Ref: Fiske Card File.

JOHN - s/MARK & MARY (-----) WILCOX; d 16 Jul 1826 Concord PA; Ref: Daily Advertiser Philadelphia PA p154.

JOHN - b 10 Jan 1805 s/EPHRAIM JOHN & MARY (WHEELER) WILCOX; d 30 Mar 1870; Ref: Wilcox-Meigs p78.

JOHN - b 1805 NY; Res Jamestown, Chautauqua Co NY; ch prob AMOS P with whom he lived; Ref: 1860 Census Jamestown NY p725 Dw# 1302.

JOHN - b 1806 NY; m ELIZA ----- who was b 1812 NY; Blacksmith; Res Westfield, Chautauqua Co NY; ch LUCY, FRANCIS, MARYETTE; Ref: 1850 Census Westfield NY p143 Dw# 288.

JOHN 3rd - b 26 Apr 1808 Montgomery Co NY s/EBENEZER & JAEL (HANCHETT) WILCOX; m in Canada MARY MARIAH CASWELL who was b 04 Feb 1814; Res Jackson Co IA; ch SARAH ANN, BENJAMIN HUDSON, WARREN DAVIS, MARY S, LEONARD CLINE, LEONARD C, COLUMBUS EATON, EBENEZER FERDINAND; d 25 Jan 1899 Jackson Co IA; Ref: Desc of Wm Wilcoxson p123.

JOHN - b 18 Jul 1808 Lexington, Greene Co NY s/NATHANIEL & JOANNA (McGONIGLE/MALLORY) WILCOX; m MARIA REYNOLDS; d 22 Feb 1876 Meredith, Delaware Co NY; Ref: Wilcox-Meigs p84, Deaths Taken From Delhi Gazette Delaware Co NY v3 p39, Your Ancestors v4 #11&12 p612.

JOHN - b 1808 NY; m HANNAH *Wallace?* ----- who was b 1810; Res Jewett, Greene Co NY; ch WALLACE, CHARLES, EDWIN, HARRIET; Ref: 1850 Census Jewett NY p327 Dw# 117.

JOHN - b 1808 NY s/LARKIN WILCOX; m MARY ANN ----- who was b 1811 NY; Res Parish, Oswego Co NY; ch JAMES, ORLANDA, CATHERINE, PATTY E; Ref: 1850 Census Parish NY p5 Dw# 67.

JOHN - m 07 Mar 1827 Saybrook, Hartford Co CT ADELAIDE ROSSITER; both were from Killingworth, Middlesex Co CT; ch poss ADELAIDE AUGUSTA; Ref: VR of CT v9 p118, Barbour's VR Saybrook v1 p63, Clinton v1 p42.

JOHN - b 1810; m be 1848 MARY ----- who was b 1812; Res Voluntown, New London Co CT; ch ERASMUS S; Ref: Barbour's VR Voluntown v3 p22.

JOHN - b 1812 Adams Twnshp, Muskingum Co OH s/JAMES & REBECCA (CAMPBELL) WILCOX; m Sep 1852 SARAH A CRUMBAKER who was b 21 Mar 1820 d/JOHN & CATHERINE (KALOR) CRUMBAKER of Louden Co VA; ch IRA, ALICE, JAMES M, JOHN W; Ref: Hist of Muskingum Co OH p606.

JOHN - b 28 Feb 1812 Chenango Co NY s/JOHN & SUSANNAH (NICHOLS) WILCOX; m 03 Jul 1843 SARAH H BROOKS who was b 23 Aug 1826 & d 08 Oct 1870 d/ANSON & SALLY (BROWN) BROOKS of Madison, Madison Co NY; Res Earlville, Chenango Co NY; ch ALICE D, FLORENCE DIETTE, AVALINE/ADALINE, ETTA JULIETTE, WALTER GARDNER; d 30 Jan 1898; Ref: Cem Rec Chenango Co NY p9, Early Years in Smyrna p24, VR of Chenango Co p250, Your Ancestors v3 # p348, #5 p375

JOHN - m 28 Oct 1835 Middletown, Middlesex Co CT CYNTHIA P HALL both of Wallingford, New Haven Co CT; Ref: Barbour's VR Middletown v3 p415.

JOHN - b 21 Mar 1814 Killingworth, Middlesex Co CT s/NATHANIEL & FANNY (MANN) WILCOX; Ref: Wilcox-Meigs p84, Barbour's VR Killingworth v2 p103.

JOHN - m be 1840 JANE ALLEN who was b 01 May 1817 Freeport, Cumberland Co ME & d 1901 at Concord, Merrimack Co NH; ch WILLIAM, ROZETTA, ALFONSO ALLEN, GEORGE, JOHN, EVELINE; Ref: Gen of NH Fam v3 p1510.

JOHN - m SARAH SPOONER 14 Dec 1811 New Bedford, Bristol Co MA; Ref: New Bedford VR p585.

JOHN - b ca 1814 s/GEORGE & MARY (-----) WILCOX; m EMELINE -----; m CHARLOTTE -----; Res Walworth, Wayne Co NY & Lenawee Co MI; ch PHILETUS, PHILANDER, CHARLES G, AMOS; d 12 Mar 1897 MI; Ref: Your Ancestors v11 #1 p1319.

JOHN - b 1816 RI s/EDWARD & ANNA (-----) WILCOX; m ELIZA A ----- who was b 1813 RI; Res Sangerfield, Oneida Co NY; Ref: 1850 Census Sangerfield NY p51 Dw# 351.

JOHN - b 1816 NY; Res Sardinia, Erie Co NY; Ref: 1850 Census Sardinia NY p101 Dw# 1479.

JOHN - b 1816; m ROSE L ----- who was b 1816 NY; Res Rome, Oneida Co NY; ch SUSAN L, LEROY; Ref: 1860 Census Rome NY p198.

JOHN - b 1818; d 23 Jun 1890 age 72 Hamburg, Erie Co NY; Ref: West NY Journal v14 #3 p129.

JOHN - b 1818 NY; m HANNAH ----- who was b 1820 NY; Res Freedom, Cattaraugus Co NY; ch CHARLOTTE L, ADELINE T, ROBERT; Ref: 1850 Census Freedom NY p439, Dw# 931.

JOHN - s/Major JOHN & MARY (BARBER) WILCOX of Norwich, New London Co CT; m ABBY REYNOLDS; m Mrs ANN ADAMS; ch by 1st wife WILLIAM, ESTHER, HENRY ALBERT; Ref: Esther Palmer Clark.

JOHN - b 1819 NY; Res Jamestown, Chautauqua Co NY; Hatter; Ref: 1860 Census Jamestown NY p701.

JOHN - b ca 1820; m J----- ----- who was b 1824 & d 16 Dec 1884; Res Shell Creek, Colfax Co NE; Ref: Schuyler Sun Newspaper Colfax Co NE Dec 18 1884.

JOHN - of W Greenwich, Kent Co RI; m 08 Jun 1851 ABBY GORDON of Voluntown, New London Co CT; Ref: Barbour's VR Voluntown v2 p139.

JOHN - b ca 1820; m ----- ----- who d 14 Feb 1879 age 55 Woodstock, Windham Co CT; Ref: Barbour's VR Woodstock Brown Diary p148.

JOHN - b 1820 NY; m SUSAN ----- who was b 1819 NY; Res Ellington, Chautauqua Co NY; ch HARRIET M, WILLIE A; Ref: 1850 Census Ellington NY p163 Dw# 2255.

JOHN - m 15 Jun 1854 Lorain Co OH HANNAH SEELEY; Ref: Marriages Lorain Co OH p119.

JOHN - b 1821 NY; m ELIZABETH -----; Res Pompey, Onondaga Co NY; Ref: 1850 Census Pompey NY p110 Dw# 1713.

JOHN - b 1825 NY; m ca 1854 ALVIA ----- who was b 1836; Res Juneau Co WI; ch ETTA, HATTIE, JAMES, ADDA; Ref: 1880 Soundex WI.

JOHN - b 1825 s/JOHN & SARAH (-----) WILCOX of McDonough, Chenango Co NY; Ref: 1850 Census Mc Donough NY Dw# 1791.

JOHN - b 1825 NY s/ERASTUS & LOUISA (-----) WILCOX of Tully, Onondaga Co NY; Ref: 1850 Census Tully NY p162 Dw# 167.

JOHN - b 1826 CT; m CHLOE ---- who was b 1825 CT; Res Torrington, Litchfield Co CT; Ref: 1850 Census Torrington CT p221 Dw# 135.

JOHN - of Providence, Providence Co RI m 18 Aug 1844 SARAH ANN BROWN of Johnston, Providence Co RI; Ref: Arnold v2 pt1 p200 v7 p583.

JOHN - m 16 Oct 1845 Dover, Dutchess Co NY EMELINE FAIRCHILD; Ref: Marriage Notices from Dutchess Co Newspapers p315.

JOHN - s/STEPHEN WILCOX m 02 Feb 1846 Warwick, Kent Co RI Mrs ROBEY BATES; Res W Greenwich Kent Co RI; Ref: Arnold v1 p134.

JOHN - b 1826 Cortland Co NY; m 1856 ESTHER NEWELL; Res De Ruyter, Madison Co NY; 4 ch; Ref: Hist of Chenango Co NY [appendix], 1850 Census De Ruyter NY p278 Dw# 64.

JOHN - b 1826 s/WEEDEON & MAHALA (-----) WILCOX of Avon, Lorain Co OH; Ref: 1850 Census Lorain Co OH, See Weedeon, Carol Wood.

JOHN - m 05 Feb 1846 Maryland, Otsego Co NY ALMIRA SALISBURY; Ref: Marriages from Otsego Co Newspapers v2 p50.

JOHN - s/THOMAS & JANE (-----) WILCOX; d af 1847 Columbus, Chenango Co NY; Ref: NSDAR Records of NY v22a p157.

JOHN - b 1827 NY m LOUISA -----; Res Kirkland, Oneida Co NY; ch ALICE, ANNA, ADA; Ref: 1860 Census Kirkland NY p35 Dw# 244.

JOHN - b 1827 NY s/CONSIDER & MARY (-----) WILCOX of Almond, Allegany Co NY; Ref: 1850 Census Almond NY p74 Dw# 777.

JOHN - b 20 Mar 1830 s/O G & E (-----) WILCOX; Res Oswego, Oswego Co NY; d 07 May 1846; Ref: Tree Talks v10 #3 p176.

JOHN - b 1830 s/MORRIS & PHEBE (BROWN) WILCOX of Whitestown, Oneida Co NY; Ref: Your Ancestors v4 #3&4 p523.

JOHN - b 1830 CT s/HEZEKIAH & HANNAH (-----) WILCOX of Groton, New London Co CT; Ref: 1850 Census Groton CT Reel M432 #49 p346.

JOHN - b 01 Aug 1830; m MARY E ------ who was b 1837 NY; Res Mina & Findley Lake, Chautauqua Co NY; ch BERTUS, IDA A; d 28 Jan 1885 bur Findley Lake Cem; Ref: Alice Wiatr, 1860 Census Mina NY p336 Dw# 230.

JOHN - b 03 Sep 1830 Middletown, Middlesex Co CT s/JOSEPH Jr & MARIA (TRYON) WILCOX; Ref: Barbour's VR Middletown v3 p91, See Joseph Jr.

JOHN - b 1831 s/ELIHU & HANNAH (-----) WILCOX; d Jun 1833 Wilmington, Windham Co VT bur Averell Cem; Ref: Alice Wiatr.

JOHN - b 1831 NY; Res Columbus, Chenango Co NY; Ref: 1850 Census Columbus NY p273 Dw# 2013.

JOHN - b 1831 NY s/BENJAMIN & ESTHER (-----) WILCOX of Verona, Oneida Co NY; Ref: Your Ancestors v4 #1&2 p498, 1850 Census Verona NY p173 Dw# 743.

JOHN - b 1832 Tompkins Co NY; Res Lansing, Tompkins Co NY; Blacksmith; Ref: 1850 Census Lansing NY p176 Dw# 853.

JOHN - b 1832 NY; Res Ithaca, Tompkins Co NY; Ref: 1850 Census Ithaca NY p234 Dw# 449.

JOHN - b 1832 Canada; Res Clarkson, Monroe Co NY; Ref: 1850 Census Clarkson NY p147 Dw# 133.

JOHN - b 1832 England s/JAMES & JANE (-----) WILCOX; Res Granger, Allegany Co NY; Ref: 1850 Census Granger NY p9 Dw# 157.

JOHN - b 10 Jan 1833 E Guilford, New Haven Co CT s/HEUSTEN & JULIA (CRAMPTON) WILCOX; m 02 May 1870 ADELLA SIGNOVIA DIBBLE who was b 26 Mar 1838 & d 13 Mar 1871 d/GEORGE & BETSEY W (UNDERHILL) DIBBLE of Westbrook, Middlesex Co CT; m 15 Jul 1874 EMILY A DUDLEY who was b 1834 d/LINUS DUDLEY of Killingworth, Middlesex Co CT; ch by 1st wife JULIA ADELLA; Res Madison, New Haven Co CT; Postmaster; d 15 Sep 1895; Ref: Wilcox-Meigs pp88,106, Fam of Early Guilford pp1213,1214, Desc of Wm Wilcoxson p264, CT Bible Rec v6 pp190-192.

JOHN - b 1834 Cortland Co NY s/ASHER & ROZELLA (BEMENT) WILCOX of Cortlandville, Cortland Co NY; Ref: 1850 Census Cortland NY p343 Dw# 188.

JOHN - b 1835 NY s/----- & SUSAN (-----) WILCOX of Greenwich, Washington Co NY; Ref: 1850 Census Greenwich NY p232 Dw# 499.

JOHN - b 1836 NY s/JOEL & BETSEY (SPRAGUE) WILCOX of Georgetown, Madison Co NY; Ref: 1850 Census Georgetown NY p388 Dw# 211, See Joel.

JOHN - b 1838 NY Twin with EUNICE s/STEPHEN D & ALMINA (-----) WILCOX of Manlius, Onondaga Co NY; Ref: 1850 Census Manlius NY p18 Dw# 268.

JOHN - b 16 Nov 1840 Menard Co IL s/ISAAC ALMANZA & MARIETTE (OVIATT) WILCOX; m 03 Sep 1863 Menard Co IL MARY CATHRINE/KATE HAROM/HARMS; d 13 Sep 1912 Oxford, Harlan Co NE; Ref: Verna Betts.

JOHN - b 24 Jun 1841 Ashtabula, Ashtabula Co OH s/ASA & HARRIET (-----) WILCOX; m ca 1866 SARAH JANE ROBINS; Res Sandwich, De Kalb Co IL; ch MINNIE, SARAH, CHARLES, HARRIET, ALLIE; d 04 Apr 1904; Ref: Wilcox Excerpts v1 p13.

JOHN - b 1843/4 OH s/SENECA & SAMANTHA (WILSON) WILCOX of Deerfield, Portage Co OH; Ref: 1850 Census Deerfield OH p188 Dw# 1039, See Seneca.

JOHN - b 12 Jan 1844 NY; d 22 Jul 1869 bur Mayville, Chautauqua Co NY; Ref: Tree Talks v24 #2 p92.

JOHN - b 1845 NY s/WILLIAM & ANN (-----) WILCOX of Stockbridge, Madison Co NY; Ref: 1850 Census Stockbridge NY p152 Dw# 223.

JOHN - b 1849 NY s/ISAAC & HESTER ANN (-----) WILCOX of Ithaca, Tompkins Co NY; Ref: 1850 Census Ithaca NY p227 Dw# 355.

JOHN - b ca 1850 s/CHARLES DYER & PRUDENCE (PARKER) WILCOX; m 01 Mar 1869 CLARINDA STANHOPE; ch LEVI, ALFRED, FLORA, ALFRED, CORA, ADDIE ADELAIDE, LEWIS WESLEY, ALFRETTA, GROVER, ALICE, AMANDA; d 10 Sep 1917 bur Lubec, Washington Co ME; Ref: Desc of Charles Dyer Wilcox pp6,7.

JOHN - d of consumption bur 01 Jul 1863 Riverside Cem Onondaga Co NY; Ref: Vorhees Record v1 p96.

JOHN - b 1854 Bergen, Genesee Co NY s/CHARLES S & DIANNA (-----) WILCOX; Ref: 1860 Census Bergen NY p969 Dw# 270.

JOHN - b 08 Feb 1865 Milford, Otsego Co NY s/MENZO & PERMELIA (WENTWORTH) WILCOX; m 24 Apr 1889 New Lisbon, Otsego Co NY NORA C POTTER who was b 1860 & d 1904 d/CHAUNCEY POTTER; m LEONA BELLE (WESTCOTT) MANCHESTER who was b 21 Jul 1870 & d 25 Aug 1934 w/EUGENE MANCHESTER & d/ORVILLE D WESTCOTT; d 22 Feb 1915; Ref: Your Ancestors v4 #7&8 p566, Westcott Hist p388.

JOHN - b 11 Aug 1867 NY s/CHARLES G & JEANETTE (MARVIN) WILCOX; m ca 1895 MI CARRIE COLE; Res Adrian, Lenawee Co MI; ch PHILANDER, JEANETTE; Ref: Your Ancestors v11 #1 p1319.

JOHN - b 28 Jan 1888 s/JOHN D & AUGUSTA (STARK) WILCOX; Res Luzerne Co PA; d 27 Mar 1888; Ref: Your Ancestors v9 #4 p1175, Hist of Luzerne Co PA p1455.

JOHN - b 29 Mar 1888 s/CHARLES HENRY & FANNY I (DISBROW) WILCOX; d young; Ref: Desc of Wm Wilcoxson p259.

JOHN - s/AVERY HUBBARD & AUGUSTA (STEVENSON) WILCOX; ch BRUCE, KEITH, CALVIN; Ref: Desc of Wm Wilcoxson p195.

JOHN A - b 1814; Res E Greenwich, Kent Co RI; d 17 Mar 1893; Ref: Arnold v11 p455.

JOHN A Capt - b 1815 CT; m 13 Aug 1837 Stonington, New London Co CT REBECCA C TAYLOR who was b 1818 CT; Coaster; Ref: 1850 Census Stonington CT Reel 432 #48 p284, Barbour's VR Stonington v5 p50.

JOHN A - b 1821; m LUCY A ----- who was b 1828 & d 1905 Tiverton, Newport Co RI; ch HATTIE R; d 1901; both bur Lot 105 Cem #3 Tiverton; Ref: Gen of RI Fam v2 p621.

JOHN A - b 1831 NY s/BENJAMIN & SOPHIA (-----) WILCOX of Palmyra, Portage Co OH; Teacher; Ref: 1850 Census Palmyra OH p208 Dw# 1334.

JOHN A - b 1843 NY s/AMON R & OLIVE (-----) WILCOX of Van Buren, Onondaga Co NY; Ref: 1850 Census Van Buren NY p453 Dw# 544.

JOHN A Dr - b 23 Apr 1847 CT s/ABRAM & REBECCA A (SHELDON) WILCOX of Griswold, New London Co CT; m SARAH A WELLS d/AMOS WELLS; Ref: 1850 Census Griswold CT Reel 432 #49 p3, Your Ancestors v4 #7&8 p562.

JOHN A I - b 1836 NY s/JAMES B & HANNAH H (-----) WILCOX of Alabama, Genesee Co NY; Ref: 1850 Census Alabama NY p320 Dw# 1587.

JOHN ABBE - b 08 Dec 1816 Springville, Erie Co NY s/JEREMIAH & MELINDA (ABBEY) WILCOX; m 13 Jan 1840 FANNY OSBURN MANTER who was b Mohawk Valley & d Erie Co NY be 1850; m ?03 Aug 1851 HANNAH T GUINN who was b 14 Apr 1820 Hamburg, Erie Co NY & d 27 Jul 1896; Res Taylor Falls, Chisago Co MN; ch of 1st wife ORIGEN ABBE; ch of 2nd wife SOPHIA L, MINNIE C, JOHN ALBERT; d 11 Jul 1863 Taylor Falls MN; Ref: Jane Smith.

JOHN ALBERT - b 20 Jan 1861 s/JOHN ABBE & HANNAH T (GUINN) WILCOX of Taylors Falls, Chisago Co MN; Ref: Jane Smith.

JOHN ALFRED - b 28 Mar 1872 Porterville, Tulare Co CA s/ORIGEN ABBEY & CLARA JANE (EMERSON) WILCOX; m ca 1947 JANETTE (MARSHALL) TAYLOR who was b 1896 Buffalo, Wright Co MN & d 22 Jan 1962 Porterville, CA; no ch; d 20 Apr 1966 bur Hillcrest Cem Porterville, CA; Ref: Jane Smith.

JOHN ALFRED - s/JOHN D & FANNIE (MARTIN) WILCOX; m 1908 Berkeley, Alameda Co CA BERTINE WOLLENBERG; ch JOHN MARTIN, ROBERT E; d Oct 1948 Longview, Cowlitz Co WA; Ref: Desc of Wm Wilcoxson p199.

JOHN ALEXANDER - b 07 Oct 1874 Jackson Co IA s/EBENEZER FERDINAND & ELIZABETH (MacCRACKEN) WILCOX; m EFFIE WINONA -----; ch GALEN E; d 20 Sep 1948; Ref: Desc of Wm Wilcoxson p124.

JOHN ANDREW - b 04 Dec 1824 Surry, Cheshire Co NH s/ASA & NANCY (HARVEY) REED WILCOX; m 09 Dec 1856 GEORGIANNA PHILLIPS of Fitchburg, Worcester Co MA; no ch; d Vineland, Cumberland Co NJ; Ref: Hist of Surry NH p947.

JOHN ANTHONY - b 12 Apr 1816 RI; m 04 Feb 1838 MARY EMILY BARBER who was b 10 Nov 1810; Res WI; Ref: Nutmegger v4 #2 p289.

JOHN AUGUSTINE HAND - b 07 Jun 1833 Middletown, Middlesex Co CT s/JONATHAN SAMUEL & CHLOE (HAND) WILCOX; d 20 Sep 1854; Ref: Fam of Early Guilford p1204, Barbour's VR Middletown v2 p31.

JOHN AUSTIN - b 1824 VT s/OZIAL & NANCY (PAINE) WILCOX of Sandgate, Bennington Co VT; m ELMIRA B ANDREWS; ch ZILPHA, RHODA, JANE, EDGAR, ALBERT, FLORA, HERBERT, JOHN AUSTIN Jr, CORA, BELLE, JAMES FRANKLIN; Ref: Desc of Wm Wilcoxson p170.

JOHN AUSTIN Jr - b 1864 Sandgate, Bennington Co VT s/JOHN AUSTIN & ELMIRA B (ANDREWS) WILCOX; Ref: Desc of Wm Wilcoxson p171.

JOHN B - b 02 Jun 1820 NY s/THOMAS & ELIZABETH (McCAIN) WILCOX; Res Hector, Tompkins Co NY; m af 1850 LORINDA ----- who was b 1834 & d 14 Nov 1903; d 02 Oct 1890 Bur Union Cem Hector, Schuyler Co NY; Ref: Cem Between the Lakes v2 p370, Your Ancestors v10 #4 p1274, 1850 Census Hector NY p367 Dw# 128.

JOHN B - b 1827 NY; m 07 Feb 1849 Utica, Oneida Co NY LOUISA DELAND who was b 1831 NY; Res Augusta, Oneida Co NY; ch ALICE, ANNA, ADA; Ref: 10,000 VR of Central NY p264, 1860 Census Oneida Co NY p35.

JOHN B - b 1832 Tompkins Co NY s/CLARK & SALLY (MAXSON) WILCOX of Groton, Tompkins Co NY; d 1900

IN; Ref: 1850 Census Groton NY p123 Dw# 19, Carol A Cox.

JOHN B - b 1855 s/BENJAMIN & DELIA (-----) WILCOX; Res Tiverton, Newport Co RI; d 05 Nov 1868 at sea; Ref: NEH&GR v67 p507, Gen of RI Fam v2 p596.

JOHN BRIGHTMAN - b 02 Feb 1799 Westport, Bristol Co MA s/DANIEL & EUNICE (ALLEN) WILCOX; Ref: Westport, VR p102, Your Ancestors v4 #7&8 p561.

JOHN C - m 28 Oct 1821 Mansfield, Tolland Co CT ELIZABETH BARROWS; Ref: Barbour's VR Mansfield vD p297.

JOHN C - b 1814 NY; m 31 Aug 1841 Whitingham, Windham Co VT SUSAN M ALLEN; Res Bradford Co PA; ch CHARLOTTE, CHARLES, PERMAN S, MARTHA, LERVINA, ARNETT, FRANK; Ref: 1850 Census Bradford Co PA p66, Hudson NY News.

JOHN C - b 1833 Rocky Hill, Hartford Co CT; m 05 Apr 1854 Wethersfield, Hartford Co CT JULIA A WELLS who was b 1833 Wethersfield CT; Artist Res Bristol, Hartford Co CT; Ref: Barbour's VR Wethersfield v5 p1936/7.

JOHN CARLOS - b 13 Mar 1858 s/JOHN HENRY OWEN & MARY (YOUNG) WILCOX; Ref: Your Ancestors v12 #2 p1436.

JOHN CHARLES - b 15 Jul 1868 MI s/DAVID BAILEY & ANN ELIZABETH (OVENSHIRE) WILCOX; m BESSIE FRANCES TAFT who d 1908 d/WILLIAM & ANN (-----) TAFT; ch DAVID TAFT; Ref: Wilcox Excerpts v1 pp5,6.

JOHN CLARK - b 15 Oct 1775 Stonington, New London Co CT s/ARNOLD & SUSANNAH (CHAMPLIN) WILCOX; m 1798 DORCAS HARRINGTON who was b 1780 & d af 1850 d/EBENEZER & MARY (MOREY) HARRINGTON; Res Franklin, New London Co CT, Sherman, Chautauqua Co NY; Purchased land in Chautauqua Co 1836 Township 2 Range 14 Lot 56 as did JOHN C Jr; ch HANNAH, JOHN CLARK, MARY, CHARLES WINTHROP, SALLY, NANCY, HAZZARD H, HENRY H, LYMAN, HARRIETT; d 15 Aug 1837 Sherman NY; Ref: Your Ancestors v13 #2 p1658, Barbour's VR Franklin v1 p89, 1840 Census Chautauqua Co NY, 1850 Census Sherman NY p277, West NY Journal v4 #3 pp130,131, Alice Wiatr.

JOHN CLARK - purchased land in Herkimer Co NY 1810; Ref: Herkimer Co NY Deed Book 5 p255.

JOHN CLARK - b 13 Dec 1800 Franklin, New London Co CT s/JOHN CLARK & DORCAS (HARRINGTON) WILCOX; Res Sherman, Chautauqua Co NY; ch JOHN SPENCER, LYMAN ASA, EUNICE; d 1894; Ref: Your Ancestors v14 #2 p1658, Barbour's VR Franklin v1 p89.

JOHN CLARK - b 21 Apr 1836 s/AZARIAH CLARK & RACHEL (VAN DEUSEN) WILCOX; Prob res NY; d 22 Jul 1854; Ref: Wilcox Excerpts v1 p2, Your Ancestors v13 #1 p1516.

JOHN CLINTON - b 30 Jul 1878 s/EDWIN IVES & MARY ELLEN (MOFFAT) WILCOX of Montour, Tama Co IA; m ANNA -----; Ref: Your Ancestors v14 #3 p1672.

JOHN CRANSTON - b 19 Jul 1825 Little Compton, Newport, Co RI s/CRANSTON & ELIZABETH/BETSEY (COOKE) WILCOX; Ref: Arnold v4 pt6 p193 (See Cranston).

JOHN D - b 1820-1825 Guilford, Windham Co VT s/EMERY & SARAH (FRANKLIN) WILCOX; Ref: Halifax Wilcox Fam mss.

JOHN D - b 28 May 1828 Plains, Luzerne Co PA s/ISAAC & SARAH (STARK) WILCOX; m [prob 2nd wife] 03 Jul 1884 AUGUSTA C STARK d/WILLIAM & MARY (HEAD) STARK natives of Tompkins Co NY; Res Luzerne Co PA; ch MARY LOUISE, JOHN, ADELAIDE; Ref: Your Ancestors v9 #3 p1152 #4 p1175, Hist of Luzerne Co PA p1455.

JOHN D - b 02 Sep 1830 s/JOHN & AMANDA (UPSON) WILCOX; m Wataga, Knox Co IL JULIA A HOAG who was b Otsego Co NY d/JAMES & LOUISA (LEE) HOAG; ch LEWIS, JENNIE, BRUCE, ADDIE, ELLIE M, FRANK, MARY, ESTELLA, RALPH, CHARLES H; Ref: Your Ancestors v4 #1&2 p496.

JOHN D - s/Dr RALPH WILCOX Jr; m FANNIE MARTIN d/EDWARD MARTIN of San Francisco, San Francisco Co CA; ch JOHN ALFRED; Ref: Desc of Wm Wilcoxson p199.

JOHN D - b 1848 NY s/THURSTON & SARAH (-----) WILCOX of Greenwich, Washington Co NY; Ref: 1850 Census Greenwich NY p230 Dw# 463.

JOHN DEMPSTER - b 09 Apr 1863 s/GEORGE & JOANNA ELIZABETH (ELLIS) WILCOX of Le Roy, Bradford Co PA; Ref: Your Ancestors v10 #4 p1274.

JOHN DENNIS - b 04 Sep 1825 Preston, Chenango Co NY s/SIMON GATES & PHOEBE (CARTWRIGHT) WILCOX; Res Tioga Co PA 1840; m 24 Feb 1844 ORRILLA DIMMICK who was b 1826 & d 17 May 1868; m SARAH M WILSON d/JOHN WILSON 13 May 1869; ch by 1st wife MARY L, PHOEBE C, MARIA A, ELAM E, CLARENCE A, SIMON G, ORLANDO R, EDWIN H, SANFORD D; ch by 2nd wife LILLIAN M, SARAH E, WILLIAM D; d af 1897; Ref: Hist of Tioga Co PA p732, Paul R Mead.

JOHN E - b 1846 NY; Father b in VT; m LIBBIE -----; Res Livonia, Wayne Co MI; ch CARRIE, GRANT, GEORGE, MAY; Ref: Detroit Gen Mag v48 #3 p107.

JOHN E - b 1846 NY s/JACOB & MARY E (-----) WILCOX of Collins, Erie Co NY; Ref: 1850 Census Collins NY p322 Dw# 609.

JOHN ELLIOTT - b 29 Jun 1825 Madison, New Haven Co CT s/ABEL & ANNA (FIELD) WILCOX; m 30 Jul 1848 Madison CT ZYLPHA LUCRETIA SNOW of Killingworth, Middlesex Co CT who d 07 Nov 1874 d/WILLIAM SNOW; Res Madison, New Haven Co, Centerbrook & Ivoryton, Middlesex Co CT; ch ANNA FIELD, HORACE ABEL, JEROME EVERETT, ETTA MARILLA, ALFRED AUGUSTUS, FREDERICK WILSON, BERTHA LOUISA; d 13 Dec 1886; Ref: Wilcox-Meigs pp92,110,111, Fam of Early Guilford pp1213,1215, Barbour's VR Madison v2 pp30,118.

JOHN F - b 1776 CT; Res 1850 Litchfield, Litchfield Co CT with son RODNEY B & RACHEL (GREEN) WILCOX; Ref: 1850 Census Litchfield CT p284 Dw# 519.

JOHN F - b 1825; m MARY F -----; Res Saybrook, Middlesex Co CT; 1 son; Ref: Saybrook Colony VR p186.

JOHN F - s/E & M A (-----) WILCOX; m MARTHA GOODWIN; Res Wayne Co IA; Ref: Hawkeye Heritage v14 #1 p21.

JOHN FAXON - b 31 Mar 1834 Whitingham, Windham Co VT s/ANDREW & SALLY (PARSONS) WILCOX; m 18 Mar 1858 HARRIET PIKE; d 13 Sep 1914 Flint, Genesee Co MI; Ref: Iris W Baird.

JOHN FELIX - b 16 Oct 1880 s/WALLACE ALONZO & FRANCES M (TERPENING) WILCOX; m FLORENCE KIECHLE; ch JOHN Jr; Ref: Desc of Wm Wilcoxson p127.

JOHN FINLEY - b 04 Jan/Jun 1847 Middlebury [now Akron], Summit Co OH s/DAVID GILBERT & HANNAH (WHITNEY) WILCOX; m 13/14 Jun 1871 EMMA CLEMENT who was b 22 Dec 1853 & d 15 Apr 1928; Res Minneapolis, Hennepin Co MN; ch HARRY EUGENE, ARCHA E, MYRTICE, RALPH DeWITT, BEATRICE; d 18 Apr 1918; Ref: Gifford Wilcox, Desc of Wm Wilcoxson pp127,128.

JOHN FISH - b 30 July 1812 Grand Isle, Grand Isle Co VT s/DANIEL & EUNICE (BARNES) WILCOX; m LUCRETIA GORDON who was b 06 June 1813 Grand Isle VT d/WILLARD & CLARA (ARMSTRONG) GORDON; ch EUNICE, DARIUS, WILLARD GORDON, JANE, CHARLES; d 1862; Ref: Cutter's Northern NY v1 p172.

JOHN FLAVEL - b 25 Nov 1775 Cornwall, Litchfield Co CT s/SAMUEL & PHEBE (-----) WILCOX m JOHANNA -----; War of 1812; d 1860 OH; Ref: CT Nutmeggers Who Migrated p264, Barbour's VR Cornwall LR3 p10.

JOHN FRANKLIN - b 22 Sep 1831 NY s/WILLIAM & HARRIET (CALKINS) WILCOX; Res Varysburg, Wyoming Co NY; Ref: Your Ancestors v14 #2 p1644.

JOHN G - b be 1775; Res Goshen, Litchfield Co CT; 5 sons & 3 daughters; Ref: 1820 Census.

JOHN G - b 11 Aug 1817 Thomastown PA s/HORACE & EDNA? (-----) WILCOX; m 22 Feb 1852 Rockdale Twnshp Crawford Co PA ROXA A COWDRY who was b 23 Dec 1829 Collins, Erie Co NY & d 17 May 1912 d/JOHN & CHRISTINA (PETERS) COWDRY; Res Collins & Gowanda, Erie Co NY; ch JOHN HENRY, ELIZABETH, JULIA ELLEN, THEODORE, DE FOREST, ALICE, ORRIN, DAVID ALBERT, BURT; d 15 Nov 1906 age 89 bur Pine Hill Cem Gowanda NY N half Lot 70 Sec C; Ref: Alice Wiatr.

JOHN G - b 1823 s/BENJAMIN & SARAH ANN (-----) WILCOX; m ANGELINA SCHNELL; Ref: Your Ancestors v14 #1 p1618.

JOHN G - b 17 Nov 1833 Charlestown, Washington Co RI s/JOSEPH & HULDAH (SHERMAN) WILCOX; Ref: Arnold v5 pt5 p28, See Joseph.

JOHN G - b 1847 NY s/WILLIAM & JANE (-----) WILCOX of Petersburgh, Rensselaer Co NY; Ref: 1850 Census Petersburgh NY p195 Dw# 309.

JOHN G - b 05 June 1874 Harford, Cortland Co NY s/THERON GATES & EMMA (McPHERSON) WILCOX; m 25 Dec 1907 MARY DECKER d/WILLIAM & ANNA (WILCOX) DECKER; Ref: Cutter's Western NY v3 p1437.

JOHN GOULD - b 28 Jun 1817 Middletown, Middlesex Co CT s/BENJAMIN & RACHEL (WILCOX) WILCOX; Ref: Barbour's VR Middletown v3 p88

JOHN H - b 1800; d 02 May 1857 Clinton, Middlesex Co CT; Ref: Barbour's VR Clinton Hurd Diary.

JOHN H - b 1811-1820; Res Western, Oneida Co NY; 3 sons & 2 daughters in 1840; Ref: 1840 Census Oneida Co p148.

JOHN H - of Norwich, New London Co CT m 19 Apr? 1847? Griswold, New London Co CT MARY C TEFFT; Res Lisbon, New London Co CT; ch ANNA A; Ref: Barbour's VR Griswold v1 p270, Lisbon v2 p5.

JOHN H - s/ROBERT WILCOX; m 15 Feb 1849 Providence, Providence Co RI CORDELLA V BROWNELL d/ABBY BROWNELL ; Ref: Arnold v2 pt1 p200.

JOHN H - m 28 Feb 1854 Butternuts, Otsego Co NY DELIA CLINTON; Ref: Marriages from Otsego Co Newspapers v3 p6.

JOHN H - of Woodstock, Windham Co CT; Civil War Co G 18th Regt; d 19 Jul 1864 Spickers Gap VA; Surviving ch RUTH, CHARLES, JOHN; Ref: Barbour's VR Woodstock v3 p430.

JOHN H - b 1832 NY s/STEPHEN & RACHEL (-----) WILCOX of Butternuts, Otsego Co NY; Ref: 1850 Census Butternuts NY p218 Dw# 317.

JOHN H - b 1834 Clinton, Middlesex Co CT; m 19 Nov 1856 Saybrook, Middlesex Co CT MARY F JONES; Ref: Saybrook Colony VR p194.

JOHN H - b 1841 Norway, Herkimer Co NY s/JOHN P & ANNA (-----) WILCOX; d 27 Apr 1848 bur Norway Cem; Ref: Tombstone Inscr.

JOHN H - b 1847 NY s/WILMAN & BETSEY (-----) WILCOX of Ripley, Chautauqua Co NY; Ref: 1850 Census Ripley NY p115 Dw# 138.

JOHN H - b 28 Feb 1871 Wyoming, Stark Co IL s/WILLIAM H & ELIZA P (KELLOGG) WILCOX; Ref: Wilcox-Meigs p120.

JOHN HASKINS - b 10 Feb 1886 New Bedford, Bristol Co MA s/BENJAMIN & CHARLOTTE W (HASKINS) WILCOX; Ref: Repr Men of Southeastern MA v2 p1082, Your Ancestors v14 #1 p1632.

JOHN HAZARD - b ca 1836 s/WILLIAM B & IRENE (LARKIN) WILCOX of Putnam, Windham Co CT; m LUCY A (STETSON) PERRIN; Ref: Your Ancestors v4 #11&12 p609.

JOHN HENRY - b 1827 s/JACOB Jr & CATHARINE (SHELLMAN) WILCOX of Savannah, Chatham Co GA; Organist of Boston, Suffolk Co MA; d 1875; Ref: Hist of Berlin CT p94.

JOHN HENRY - b May 18 1855 PA s/JOHN G & ROXY (COWDRY) WILCOX; Single; d 05 Nov 1937 bur Pine Hill Cem Gowanda, Erie Co NY; Ref: Alice Wiatr.

JOHN HENRY - b 26 Aug 1875 s/HENRY FRANKLIN & LUCINDA HARRIET (BROWN) WILCOX; m 30 Nov 1899 Alford, Berkshire Co MA JENNIE E BUCKLEY/BUCKBEE; ch BERTHA F, CHARLES H, HAROLD J, FRANK A, RAYMOND E; Ref: Wilcox Excerpts v1 pp2,3, Your Ancestors v13 #1 p1516.

JOHN HENRY OWEN - b 14 Feb 1824 Benton, Salina Co AR s/HAZARD & SARAH (SEELEY) WILCOX; m 14 Aug 1848 MARY YOUNG; ch HAZARD, ELIZABETH, SABRA, JAMES HENRY, JOHN CARLOS, MARY MEHITABEL, CLARISSA JANE, SABRA ELLEN, HANNAH, MARTHA ANN, JUSTUS AZEL; d 21 Nov 1909; Ref: Hist of Edward Wilcox mss p4, Your Ancestors v12 #2 pp1435,1436.

JOHN HENRY SERRAGE - b 07 Aug 1850 Portland, Cumberland Co ME s/JOHN & JANE (ALLEN) WILCOX; m 25 Nov 1883 Concord, Merrimack Co NH EMMA C INGALLS who was b 06 Aug 1850 d/LEAVITT & LYDIA (-----) INGALLS; Res Boston, Suffolk Co MA & Concord, Merrimack Co NH; ch FRANCES E, EDITH C, JOHN W, EMMA E; Ref: Gen of NH Fam v3 p1510.

JOHN HOPSON - b 08 Sep 1800 Killingworth, Middlesex Co CT s/ASA & DEBORAH HOPSON (BRAINARD) WILCOX; m 26 Sep 1822 Saybrook, Middlesex Co CT

ANN CHAPMAN who was b 20 Apr 1795 & d 23 Nov 1886 d/JEDEDIAH CHAPMAN; Res Clinton, Middlesex Co CT; ch ASA CHAPMAN, CHARLES AUGUSTUS, SAMUEL SHERRILL, JOHN HOPSON, DEBORAH JANE, WILLIAM WATSON, SARAH AUGUSTA, ALPHEAS WESLEY; d 02 May 1857; Ref: Wilcox-Meigs pp82,98, Your Ancestors v3 #3 p322, # 4 p349, Chapman Gen p133, Saybrook Colony VR p81, VR of CT v9 p108, Westbrook 1st Cong Ch Rec p197, Barbour's VR Saybrook v1 p31, Killingworth v2 p98, Clinton v1 p42.

JOHN HOPSON - b 07 Jun 1829 Clinton, Middlesex Co CT s/JOHN HOPSON & ANN (CHAPMAN) WILCOX; Ref: Your Ancestors v3 #4 p349, Chapman Gen p133.

JOHN HOTCHKISS - b 11 May 1875 Teepleville, Crawford Co PA s/JULIUS MARVIN & MARY (HOTCHKISS) WILCOX; Single; d June 1923; Ref: A Wilcox Book p119.

JOHN HUBBARD - b 1845 NY s/JUDSON & LAURA (GOODRICH) WILCOX of Catskill, Greene Co NY; Ref: 1850 Census Catskill NY p359 Dw# 322, See Judson.

JOHN J - b 1845 s/WILLIAM S & SARAH E (DAY) WILCOX of Carlton, Orleans Co NY; Ref: Your Ancestors v11 #1 p1320.

JOHN JONES - b 05 Apr 1854 Wauwatosa, Milwaukee Co WI s/HENRY WILLIAM & MARY ELIZA (JONES) WILCOX; d 05 May 1879; Ref: Wilcox-Meigs p117.

JOHN K - b ca 1852 Johnston, Providence Co RI s/SAMUEL & ADELIA (-----) WILCOX; m 02 May 1875 Providence RI ELIZA A WATERMAN who was b ca 1857 d/EDMUND SHELDON & ELIZA (FENNER) WATERMAN; Ref: Desc of Robert Waterman v3 p323.

JOHN K - Will probated 1857 Niagara Co NY File W-5; Ref: West NY Journal v6 #3 p131.

JOHN KING - b 10 Nov 1815 Cazenovia, Madison Co NY s/ERASTUS & MARGARET (KING?) WILCOX; m 13 Sep 1843 Dearborn Co IN MEHITABLE SELINA KELSEY who was b 03 Aug 1813 Whiting, Addison Co VT & d 1888 Humboldt, Allen Co KS d/JOHN & SUSAN (TAYLOR) KELSEY; Res Cincinnati, Hamilton Co OH, Lawrenceburg, Dearborn Co IN, Indianapolis, Marion Co IN, Humboldt KS; Baptist or Presbyterian, Printer/Boatman; Civil War; ch ERASTUS, ALLEN, MARY, JOHN KING Jr, FRANCES MALVINA; d 08 Sep 1888 Humbolt KS; Ref: Janet Armbrust.

JOHN KING Jr - b 23 Feb 1852 Aurora, Dearborn Co IN s/JOHN KING & MEHITABLE SELINA (KELSEY) WILCOX; d Wichita, Sedgewick Co KS; Ref: Janet Armbrust.

JOHN L - m 08 Mar 1839 Killingworth, Middlesex Co CT EMILY E WELLMAN; Ref: Barbour's VR Killingworth v3 p398.

JOHN L - of Killingworth, Middlesex Co CT m 29 Jul 1846 HARRIETT PARKER of Wallingford, New Haven Co CT; Ref: Barbour's VR Wallingford v1 p255.

JOHN L - b 22 Feb 1837; m ESTA ----- who was b 1837 & d 23 Sep 1868 age 31; d 14 Feb 1870 age 33y 8d; both bur Plain Twnshp Cem Franklin Co OH; Ref: OH Cem Rec p138.

JOHN L - b 1858 s/LEMUEL T & MARY A (HOLMES) WILCOX; Res Preston, New London Co CT; d 13 May 1860; Ref: Cem Rec of New London Co CT v2 p4.

JOHN L - b 20 Jul 1862 Smithfield twnshp, Bradford Co PA s/ORIN E & ESTHER (HARKNESS) WILCOX; m 14 Sep 1887 ETTA RAYNOR who was b 22 Jul 1852 d/WILLIAM H & SARAH E (BROWN) RAYNOR; Res Bentley Creek, Bradford Co PA; merchant, postmaster; member Disciple Church East Smithfield PA; ch EARL; Ref: Wilcox Genealogy pp11,12.

JOHN L - b Aug 1878 NY s/MAINE & LYDIA A (PRICE) WILCOX; m CARRIE REMINGTON; m ROSE HUBBARD; Res Dayton, Cattaraugus Co NY; ch CHARLES, GRACE LORE, MAUDE, BLOSSOM, MILLARD, EVELYN, JOHN A; Ref: Wilcox Hist mss, 1900 Census, Lois Barris.

JOHN LARKIN - b ca 1781; m PATTY ----- who was b 11 Feb 1781 & d 20 Jul 1848 bur Salt Springs Cem De Witt, Onondaga Co NY; d af 1865 Central NY; Ref: Eleanor Matthews.

JOHN LEANDER - b ca 1812 s/JOHN & RACHEL (POST) WILCOX; Res Medina, Medina Co OH; Ref: Desc of Wm Wilcoxson p130.

JOHN LEONARD - b 24 Nov 1878 Janesville, Rock Co WI; m 01 Jan 1900 MABEL BARRET LEWIS who was b 24 Aug 1879 Whitewater, Walworth Co WI d/FRANKLIN FILMORE & VICTORINE (ROCKWELL) LEWIS; ch JOHN FRANKLIN, ANNETTE LEWIS, FRANKLIN CLINTON; d Mar 1938 bur Oak Hill Cem Janesville WI; Ref: Desc of Robert Burrows v2 p1236.

JOHN LYMAN - b 31 Aug 1845 Dartmouth, Bristol Co MA s/HENRY T & NANCY R (WING) WILCOX; Ref: Dartmouth VR p302, See Henry T.

JOHN M - moved from Bristol, Ontario Co NY to Oakland Co MI 1832; Ref: Yesteryears v23 #92 p81.

JOHN M - s/CHARLES & JULIA ANN (MERRILL) WILCOX; m AMANDA GRANT d/WILLIAM & CHRISTINE (McINTOSH) GRANT; ch CHARLES G, JOHN T, GEORGE W; Ref: Your Ancestors v9 #2 p1128.

JOHN M - m 10 Sep 1842 Oxford, Chenango Co NY MARY HOLMES; Res Norwich NY; ch GEORGE W; Ref: VR Chenango Co NY p185, 10,000 VR of Central NY p264.

JOHN M - m 18 Nov 1851 ANNA MARIE VAIL; Ref: Marriages in NY Herald p131.

JOHN M - b 12 Mar 1832 Sodus, Wayne Co NY s/DURFEE & SAMANTHA (WELLS) WILCOX; m 07 Nov 1861 ELLEN BABCOCK; Ref: Your Ancestors v10 #4 p1294.

JOHN MAXSON Dr - b 07 Apr 1891 Buffalo, Erie Co NY s/Dr DEWITT GILBERT & JENNIE (GREEN) WILCOX; m 29 Jun 1918 Burlington, Middlesex Co MA FREDA LORRAINE WALKER who was b 02 Feb 1895 Burlington MA d/FRED FREELAND & BERTHA (WOOD) WALKER; Res Kennebunkport, York Co ME; ch DEWITT GIFFORD, DAVID WALKER; d 26 Aug 1972 Hanover, Grafton Co NH; Ref: Gifford Wilcox, Desc of Wm Wilcoxson p128.

JOHN MURRAY - b 10Jul 1893 Guilford, Windham Co VT s/CHARLES LUMAN & CORA ADELAIDE (CROSIER) WILCOX; m 04 Jun 1930 Richmond VA HAZEL AUGUSTA McALWEE; World War I; member Orcutt Baptist Church; d 31 Dec 1978 Hampton VA; bur Greenlawn Cem; Ref: Iris W Baird.

JOHN P - b 1815/6; m ANNA -----; Res Norway & Ohio, Herkimer Co NY; ch JOHN H, SARAH A, ANDREW M, MARGARET E, CALVIN H, CHARLES J, DAVID H, SARAH; d 1881; Ref: 1850 Census Ohio NY p280 Dw# 141, Tombstone Inscr.

JOHN P - b 1817 NY; m LUCY ----- who was b 1822 NY; Res Tully, Onondaga Co NY; Ref: 1850 Census Tully NY p153 Dw# 16.

JOHN PAUL - b 30 Mar 1812 NY/PA s/CRANDALL & JOANNA (STARK) WILCOX; m MARY STARK; Res Dutchess

Co NY & Luzerne Co PA; Ref: Gen of Aaron Stark Fam p43, Your Ancestors v9 #4 p1175.

JOHN PETTIT - b 02 Aug 1816 s/DAVID & SARAH (RUE) WILCOX of Manlius, Onondaga Co NY; m Dec 1839 ANN SMITH; d 27 Mar 1881; Ref: Your Ancestors v3 #11 & 12 p474, Gifford Wilcox, Desc of Wm Wilcoxson p126.

JOHN QUINCY - m MAYMIE -----; Res McPherson Co NE Jun 1892 & North Platte, Lincoln Co NE 1906; ch JOHN QUINCY;Ref: Obit of John Quincy Jr, Nebraska Ancestree v15 #2 p60.

JOHN REYNOLDS - b ca 1855 s/CHARLES WILLIAM & CATHERINE (SHERMAN) WILCOX; m 30 Nov 1878 IDA MAY ADAMS who was b 03 Nov 1859 d/JOHN FANNING & ANNE E (OATLEY) ADAMS of S Kingston RI; Res Kingston, Washington Co RI; ch JESSE, CHARLES; Ref: Nutmegger v17 #4 p704.

JOHN ROMEO - b 28 May 1803 Guilford, New Haven Co CT s/CURTISS & WEALTHY (HILL) WILCOX; m ORPAH DOWD who was b 29 Aug 1798 & d 22 Dec 1827 d/WILLIAM & REBECCA (GRAVES) DOWD; m 13 Apr 1829 ELIZABETH CRAMPTON who d 18 Nov 1877 d/JONATHAN & CHLOE (MUNGER) CRAMPTON; Res NY; ch by 1st wife CURTIS, JEFFERSON, CAROLINE ELIZABETH HANNAH; ch by 2nd wife ELIZABETH HANNAH, JOHN ROMEO; d 13 Jul 1875; Ref: Fam of Early Guilford pp 256,300,1203,1204, Barbour's VR Guilford v2 p31, Madison v1 p68, v2 p31.

JOHN ROMEO - b 27 Mar 1840 Madison, New Haven Co CT s/JOHN ROMEO & ELIZABETH (CRAMPTON) WILCOX; d 11 Oct 1841; Ref: Barbour's VR Madison v1 p31.

JOHN S - b 1766-1785; Res Litchfield, Herkimer Co NY; 3 sons in 1810; Ref: 1810 Census.

JOHN S - b 1812 NY; m ELIZA M ----- who was b 1816 NY; Res Preston, Chenango Co NY; ch EDGAR C, CHARLES, NANCY E; Ref: 1850 Census Preston NY p462 Dw# 2239.

JOHN S Capt - b ca 1820; m 22 Nov 1838 Harmony, Chautauqua Co NY POLLY CARPENTER; purchased lot 48 Twnshp 2, Range 12 in Chautauqua Co NY 1851; Ref: Index to Deed Book v55 p354, West NY Journal v XII #4 p174, 10,000 VR of Western NY p2, 19th Cent Marriages Reported in Fredonia Censor p244.

JOHN S - of Torrington, Litchfield Co CT m 1849 CHLOE S STRICKLAND of Warren, Litchfield Co CT; Ref: Barbour's VR Torrington v1 p135.

JOHN SHULER Col - b 18 Mar 1833 Fultonville, Montgomery Co NY s/ELIJAH & SALLY (SHULER) WILCOX; m 03 Sep 1856 IL LOIS AMELIA CONGER d/UZZIAH CONGER of Galesburg, Warren Co IL; Civil War; Postmaster Elgin, Kane Co IL; ch MARIE W, DWIGHT CONGER, MARGUERITE & others; d 1926; Ref: Your Ancestors v9 #2 pp1127,1128, Desc of Wm Wilcoxson p192.

JOHN S - b 1849 OH s/BENJAMIN & SARAH (-----) WILCOX of Ravenna, Portage Co OH; Ref: 1850 Census Ravenna OH p25 Dw# 141.

JOHN SAWYER - b 12 Jun 1815 Surry, Cheshire Co NH s/JOHN TALCOTT & SALLY (SAWYER) WILCOX; Went to TX & was killed by Mexicans ca 1860; Tinsmith; Ref: Hist of Surry NH p948.

JOHN SELDEN - b 24 Dec 1833 Madison, Lake Co OH s/RICHARD SELDEN & ELIZABETH (BOYNTON) WILCOX; m 29 Apr 1858 SARAH ELIZABETH HUBBARD d/MOSES B HUBBARD; ch SARAH ELIZABETH; Ref: Wilcox-Meigs pp89,106,107, 1850 Census Madison OH Reel 259 p116.

JOHN ST CLAIR - b 29 Nov 1893 s/MARINER & CORDELIA (CARD) WILCOX; m ALICE GREENLAW; d World War I in Egypt; Ref: Desc of Charles Dyer Wilcox p17.

JOHN T - m 03 Nov 1834 Lorain Co OH SARAPLA LACY; Ref: Marriages Lorain Co OH p119.

JOHN T - b 07 Jan 1834 Middletown, Middlesex Co CT s/NATHAN & POLLY (IVES) WILCOX; Ref: Barbour's VR Middletown v4 p30, See Nathan.

JOHN T - b ca 1850; m LILLIAN DIBBLE who was b 05 Oct 1851 Holmesville, Chenango Co NY d/IRA & HENRIETTA (HOLMES) DIBBLE & d Norwich, Chenango Co NY 22 Apr 1928 age 76yr 6mo 17da; bur Sec A Lot 437; ch JOHN T, LILLIAN, HENRY C; Inter 30 Jan 1906 Ira Dibble Lot; Ref: Norwich NY Cem Assoc Records pp 324,325.

JOHN T - b 31 Oct 1852 s/NOAH & MARY (SHERMAN) WILCOX; d 07 May 1924; Ref: Your Ancestors v4 #1&2 p495

JOHN T - b 13 Feb 1889 Norwich, Chenango Co NY s/JOHN T & LILLIAN (DIBBLE) WILCOX; d Norwich 31 Aug 1937 age 48yr 5mo 18da; bur Sec 32 Lot 80 N half; Ref: Norwich Cem Assoc Records p324.

JOHN TALCOTT - b 31 Mar 1786 Surry, Cheshire Co NH s/ASA & DINAH (LOVELAND) WILCOX; m 04 Feb 1812 SALLY SAWYER d/SAMUEL SAWYER; Res Lansingburg, Rensselaer Co NY & perhaps in PA; in Plating business with JOHN BLISH; ch ANN JANE, JOHN SAWYER; Ref: Hist of Surry NH pp946,948.

JOHN THOMPSON - b 13 Apr 1806 Westerly, Washington Co RI s/BENJAMIN & NANCY (THOMPSON) WILCOX; d 04 May 1836; Ref: Arnold v4 p106, v5 p145, v11 p144.

JOHN W - b 25 Sep 1818 Lorain Co OH s/EPHRAIM A & SARAH (WOLVERTON) WILCOX; Ref: Desc of Wm Wilcoxson p200.

JOHN W - b 1826; m 28 Dec 1847 Ira, Cayuga Co NY AMANDA M SIMONS who was b 1826; Ref: Tree Talks v3 #2 p10.

JOHN W - b 09 Dec 1878 Concord, Merrimack Co NH s/JOHN HENRY & EMMA C (INGALLS) WILCOX; Res Pittsburgh PA; Ref: Gen of NH Fam v3 p1510.

JOHN WARREN - of Oneida Co NY m 15 Jun 1841 POLINA ALZINA WEEKES who was b 05 Apr 1818 Smyrna, Chenango Co NY & d 04 Nov 1878 Hempstead Nassau Co NY d/DAVID JEWETT & ELIZABETH (MARSH) WEEKES; ch CHARLES FRANKLIN, JOSEPHINE ELIZABETH, MYRON LA ROY, MARY ALICE, MYRTILLA MAY, FREDERICK WEEKS, ELLA POLINA; Ref: Geo Weekes Gen p155.

JOHN WHITNEY - b 01 Jun 1892 Minneapolis, Hennepin Co MN s/FRANK EUGENE & DAISIE (ROSE) WILCOX; m LOUISE LENNERTZ; Res Hollywood, Los Angeles Co CA; ch JOHN WHITNEY; Ref: Desc of Wm Wilcoxson p129.

JOHN WILLIAM - b 28 Jun 1782 Sandisfield, Berkshire Co MA s/JOEL & LYDIA (-----) WILCOX; Ref: Sandisfield MA VR p72, Fiske Card File.

JOHNSON - b 1821 NY; m ELIZABETH -----; Tailor; Res Chester, Orange Co NY; ch WILLIAM A; Ref: 1850 Census Chester NY p163 Dw# 1508.

JOHNSON - b 1832 NY s/HOSEA GOODRICH & ELIZA J (-----) WILCOX of Leon, Cattaraugus Co NY; Ref: 1850 Census Leon NY p49 Dw# 190.

JONAH - b 12 Oct 1752 Goshen, Litchfield Co CT s/NATHANIEL 2nd & ABIGAIL (HURLBUTT) WILCOX; Ref: Barbour's VR Goshen v1 p271, See Nathaniel 2nd.

JONAH - m ANNE ----- who d 1771 Farmington, Hartford Co CT; Ref: Nutmegger v18 #4 p631.

JONAS JESSE - b 18 Feb 1847 s/LEWIS JESSE & CYNTHIA (BAILEY) WILCOX; m 21 May 1873 HARRIET ELIZABETH STEARNS d/ISAAC KELSEY & EMILY FIDELIA (TECHINOR) STEARNS; ch WILLIAM HARVEY, MARY BELLE; Ref: Geo Weekes Gen p258.

JONATHAN - b 22 Sep 1705 Killingworth, Middlesex Co CT s/NATHANIEL & HANNAH (LANE) WILCOX; m 30 Jun 1732 EXPERIENCE WILLIAMS who was b 1712 & d 09 Jun 1790 Killingworth CT d/THOMAS & EXPERIENCE (HAYDEN) WILLIAMS; ch ELIHU, ELISHA, JONATHAN, EXPERIENCE, SIMEON, ELIZABETH, JAMES, SYBIL, LYDIA, JONATHAN; d 18 Dec 1761; Ref: Wilcox-Meigs p45, Desc of Wm Wilcoxson pp12,20,36, Nutmegger v10 #2 p228, Barbour's VR Killingworth v2 pp60,160,191, Your Ancestors v4 #11&12 p611.

JONATHAN - s/JOHN WILCOX of Haddam Middlesex Co CT; Res Manlius, Onondaga Co NY; Sold land in 1810 in Haddam, CT to brother JAMES of Killingworth, Middlesex Co CT; Ref: Fiske Card File.

JONATHAN - b 08 Mar 1736 Killingworth, Middlesex Co CT s/JONATHAN & EXPERIENCE (WILLIAMS) WILCOX; d young; Ref: Wilcox-Meigs p45, Barbour's VR Killingworth v2 p160, Desc of Wm Wilcoxson p20.

JONATHAN - b 14 Apr 1737 Hebron, Tolland Co CT s/DANIEL; Ref: Barbour's VR Hebron v1 p33.

JONATHAN - b 24 Jan 1722/3 Middletown, Middlesex Co CT s/THOMAS & ANNA (NORTH) WILCOX; m 15 Nov 1743 DINAH ORVIS of Farmington, Hartford Co CT who d 11 Feb 1761; m May 1762 RACHEL LEWIS; Res VT; ch by 1st wife RUTH, CHRISTIANA, EZEKIEL, THOMAS, OLIVER, GERSHOM, JAMES; ch by 2nd wife OLIVER, ASA, JESSE; Ref: NEH&GR v14 p138, MUH p747, Nutmegger v4 #3 p331, Barbour's VR Middletown v1 p80, v2 pp10,11,181.

JONATHAN - b 19 Sep 1753 Killingworth, Middlesex Co CT; m ELIZABETH DUDLEY 16 Apr 1778 Madison New Haven Co CT; Ref: ECM v1 p102.

JONATHAN - m be 1774 SARAH -----; Res Sharon, Litchfield Co CT; ch ELIZABETH & MERCY twins; Ref: Barbour's VR Sharon LR7 p308.

JONATHAN - b 13 Jul 1753 Guilford, New Haven Co CT s/THOMAS & FREELOVE (BRADLEY) WILCOX; m 1774 ELIZABETH TODD who was b 10 Feb 1754/1764 & d 29 Sep 1833 d/TIMOTHY TODD; ch CURTIS, JOHN, AMOS TODD, ELIZABETH TODD, HENRY, MATILDA, SARAH, JONATHAN SAMUEL, AUGUSTUS BENJAMIN; d 19 Oct 1818; Served in Rev War; Ref: MUH pp750,754, Fam of Early Guilford pp 1175,1201,1202, Gen of CT Fam v3 p490, Your Ancestors v3 #2 p302, Barbour's VR Guilford v1 p99.

JONATHAN - b 19 Sep 1753 Killingworth, Middlesex Co CT s/JONATHAN & EXPERIENCE (WILLIAMS) WILCOX; m ELIZABETH DUDLEY; d 17 Sep 1819; Ref: Wilcox-Meigs p45, Barbour's VR Killingworth v2 p160, Desc of Wm Wilcoxson pp20,174.

JONATHAN - m BETTEY -----; Res Wilmington, Windham Co VT; ch CHARLES; Ref: Fiske Card File.

JONATHAN - b 1756-1775; Res Whitingham, Windham Co VT; 1 son & 2 daughters in 1800; Ref: 1800 Census Windham Co VT p154.

JONATHAN - b 1756-1775; Res Westminster, Windham Co VT; 2 sons & 5 daughters in 1800; Ref: 1800 Census Windham Co VT.

JONATHAN - b ca 1770 s/ABRAHAM WILCOX & MARY (CARD) WILCOX; m 01 Jan 1792 Exeter, Washington Co RI PHEBE RATHBUN who was b 12 Jul 1776 & d 23 Nov 1798 d/NATHAN & ROBIE (HOPKINS) RATHBUN; m 03 Apr 1800 ANNA PARKER; ch by 1st wife POLLY L, THOMAS; Ref: Arnold v5 pt3 p36, Your Ancestors v4 #7&8 p562, #11&12 p609.

JONATHAN - b 07 Jul 1772 Westerly, Washington Co RI s/DAVID & CONTENT (LEWIS) WILCOX; Ref: Arnold v5 p145.

JONATHAN - b af 1775 s/DAVID & SARAH (HOWLAND) WILCOX; m SALLY WILCOX; Res New Braintree, Worcester Co MA; Ref: Your Ancestors v11 #4 p1398.

JONATHAN - b 06 Aug 1779 Lebanon, New London Co CT s/DANIEL & ALICE (MARSH) WILCOX; m 22 Jan 1807 CELIA/SYBIL SMITH; ch JOEL S; Ref: Your Ancestors v4 #7&8 p566, Desc of Wm Wilcoxson p174.

JONATHAN - m CIBBIL -----; Res Truxton, Cortland Co NY; d 06 Mar 1811; Ref: Residents of Cortland Co NY 1800-1810.

JONATHAN - m 10 Jan 1796 New Braintree, Worcester Co MA SIBAL SWAN; Ref: Fiske Card File.

JONATHAN - Res South Wick, Hampden Co MA 1790; Ref: Fiske Card File.

JONATHAN - b 1784 Killingworth, Middlesex Co CT s/SIMEON & PHOEBE (KELSEY) WILCOX; d 17 Sep 1849; Ref: Wilcox-Meigs p67.

JONATHAN - b 1784 RI; Res Norwich, Chenango Co NY; d 12 Sep 1869 bur Stover Cem; Ref: VR of Chenango Co NY p143.

JONATHAN - b 13 Dec 1789; m LOUISA SCUDDER who was b 01 Oct 1792 & d 04 Sep 1860; ch THOMAS SCUDDER; d 25 May 1848 bur Kendaia, Seneca Co NY; Ref: Cem Between the Lakes v3 p778.

JONATHAN - b ca 1790 RI; m SARAH ----- who was b 1800 MA; Res Sherburne, Chenango Co NY; ch EMILY, HENRY; d 12 Sep 1869 bur Smyrna Cem; Ref: Your Ancestors v4 #11&12 p609, 1850 Census Sherburne NY p250 Dw# 1654.

JONATHAN - b 1816 VT; m FANNY ----- who was b 1819 Monroe Co NY; Res Leon, Cattaraugus Co NY; ch IRVING, BAILEY, PATTY, MARIUS, FANNY D; Ref: 1850 Census Leon p44 Dw# 115, 1865 Census Leon NY #18.

JONATHAN - b 1821 NY; m JULIA ----- who was b 1819 NY; Res Sherburne, Chenango Co NY; ch EDWIN, MARION; Ref: 1850 Census Sherburne NY p246 Dw# 1571.

JONATHAN - b 1824 NY; m JANE A ----- who was b 1825 NY; Res Stamford, Delaware Co NY; ch MARY J; Ref: 1850 Census Stamford NY p194 Dw# 531.

JONATHAN - b 1826 NY; Res with JOHN DOUBLEDAY fam Fabius, Onondaga Co NY; Ref: 1850 Census Fabius NY p146 Dw# 369.

JONATHAN - b 1847 NY s/JOHN & EMELINE (-----) WILCOX of Amenia, Dutchess Co NY; Ref: 1850 Census Amenia NY p339 Dw# 398.

JONATHAN A - b 1802 MA; m ABBA ----- who was b 1815 CT; Res New Hartford, Litchfield Co CT; Teamster; ch MARY; Ref: 1850 Census New Hartford CT p125 Dw# 183.

JONATHAN A - b May 1850 s/ELIHU & PHILOMILA (-----) WILCOX of Leon, Cattaraugus Co NY; d 1853 bur Franklin Cem Leon NY; Ref: Alice Wiatr, 1850 Census Leon p44 Dw# 118.

JONATHAN BRENTON SHAW - m 22 Jan 1872 FANNY ELLEN IRONS who was b 25 Oct 1853 d/DEXTER & MARY ANN (CRUMB) IRONS; Res Cambridge, Middlesex Co MA; ch FANNY ESTHER, NELLIE CASE, HOWARD DEXTER; Ref: Desc of Robert Burrows v2 p1482.

JONATHAN FERRIS - b 27 Sep 1823 s/HENRY & SUSANNA (MILLER) WILCOX of Hillsdale, Columbia Co NY; m IDA A RICE; d 30 Sep 1875; Ref: Wilcox-Meigs p102, Your Ancestors v4 #11&12 p612.

JONATHAN HAZARD - b 16 Jan 1812 Marion Co Mo s/HAZARD & SARAH (SEELEY) WILCOX; d 1821; Ref: Your Ancestors v12 #2 p1435.

JONATHAN JUDD - b ca 1820 s/CURTISS & RUTH (JUDD) WILCOX; Ref: Fam of Early Guilford p1203.

JONATHAN SAMUEL - b 01 Nov 1791 Middletown, Middlesex Co CT s/JONATHAN & ELIZABETH (TODD) WILCOX; m 1815 CHLOE HAND who was b 06 Nov 1791 Guilford, New Haven Co CT & d 21 Sep 1875 d/DANIEL & ARTEMISIA (MEIGS) HAND; ch WILLIAM WALLACE, ELIZA MARIA, JONATHAN SAMUEL, JONATHAN SAMUEL, CATHERINE ARTEMESIA, DANIEL HAND, GEORGE AUGUSTUS, JOHN AUGUSTUS HAND; d 10 Feb 1875 Madison, New Haven Co CT; Ref: MUH p754, Gen of the Hand Family p28, Fam of Early Guilford pp 600,1202,1204, Your Ancestors v3 #2 p302, Barbour's VR Middletown v2 p31, Madison v2 p31.

JONATHAN SAMUEL - b 1813/1815 Deep River, Middlesex Co CT s/HENRY & JEANNETTE (BUSHNELL) WILCOX; m 19 Oct 1834 Saybrook, Middlesex Co CT DOLLY ANN SOUTHWORTH; ch ELLEN, EMILY, MARY JANE, MYRTA; Ref: Fam of Early Guilford pp1204,1205, Saybrook Colony VR pp120,156, Barbour's VR Saybrook v2 p66.

JONATHAN SAMUEL - b 28 Feb 1820 Madison, New Haven Co CT s/JONATHAN SAMUEL & CHLOE (HAND) WILCOX; d 14 Dec 1820; Ref: Fam of Early Guilford p1204, Barbour's VR Madison v2 p31.

JONATHAN SAMUEL - b 21 Nov 1821 Madison, New Haven Co CT s/JONATHAN SAMUEL & CHLOE (HAND) WILCOX; m SARAH JANE ANSLEY of Augusta, Richmond Co GA; Res CT; ch WILLIAM WALLACE, GEORGE ANSLEY, KATHERINE JESSIE, SARAH JANE, JOHN SAMUEL; d 01 Sep 1869; Ref: MUH pp 754,755, Fam of Early Guilford p1204, Your Ancestors v3 #2 p302.

JONES - b 18-- s/GEORGE HENRY & LUCY (JONES) WILCOX; m JULIA -----; Res MI; Ref: Wilcox Excerpts v1 p6.

JORDAN H - b 1830 s/WHITMAN & LUCINDA (PARKER) WILCOX of Norwich, Chenango Co NY; Doctor; Ref: 1850 Census Norwich NY p179 Dw# 565, See Whitman.

JOSEPH - b ca 1636 Concord/Watertown, Middlesex Co MA s/WILLIAM & MARGARET (-----) WILCOX; m 1658/9 Stratford, Fairfield Co CT ANNA SHEATHER d/JOHN & ELIZABETH (WELLMAN) SHEATHER; Res Killingworth, Middlesex Co CT; ch JOSEPH, THOMAS, SAMUEL, HANNAH, NATHANIEL, WILLIAM, MARGARET, JOHN; d 09 Feb 1703 Killingworth CT; Ref: Wilcox-Meigs p 22,23, Desc of Wm Wilcoxson p27, Bogue Fam p393, Savage v4 p547, Desc of Abner & Lucy Hart Wilcox p18, Gen of NH Fam v3 p1508, Hist of Stratford Fam p1346, Cutter's Northern NY v2 p656, Cutter's New England Fam v1 p159, Torrey's Marriage Rec microfilm, Hist of Surry NH p943.

JOSEPH - b 19 Oct 1659 Stratford, Fairfield Co CT s/JOSEPH & ANN (SHEATHER) WILCOX; m 14 Feb 1693 HANNAH KELSEY who d 02 Feb 172- d/JOHN/JOSEPH & PHOEBE/HANNAH (DISBOROUGH) KELSEY; m 22 Mar 1732 ELIZABETH ARNELL ; ch HANNAH, JOSEPH, DAVID, ABEL, ELISHA, STEPHEN, LYDIA; d 29 Sep 1747 Killingworth, Middlesex Co CT; Ref: Wilcox-Meigs pp29,30, Desc of Wm Wilcoxson p27, Desc of Abner & Lucy Hart Wilcox pp18,19; Bogue Fam p394, Savage v4 p547, Hist of Stratford Fam p1346, Cutter's Northern NY v2 656, Cutter's New England Fam v1 p159, Torrey's Marriage Rec microfilm.

JOSEPH - m HANNAH ALLIN who was b 26 Jul 1659 d/JOHN & ELLEN (BRADLEY) ALLIN; Ref: Gen of CT Fam v1 p312.

JOSEPH - b ca 1674 Simsbury, Hartford Co CT s/SAMUEL & HANNAH (RICE) WILCOX; m 29 Apr 1703 Windsor, Hartford Co CT ABIGAIL THRALL who d 10 Jul 1725 d/TIMOTHY THRALL; ch JOSEPH, ABIGAIL, SARAH, HEZEKIAH, ABIGAIL, NATHANIEL & MERCY/MARY twins, EZRA, ROGER; d 04 Dec 1770 age 96; Ref: Wilcox-Meigs p32, Desc of Wm Wilcoxson pp6,14,15,28, Early Settlers of W Simsbury p127, Your Ancestors v13 #3 p1567.

JOSEPH - m 25 Jan 1687 Philadelphia, Philadelphia Co PA ANN POWELL; Ref: Am Marriages p447.

JOSEPH - b 28 Oct 1687 Portsmouth, Newport Co RI s/DANIEL & HANNAH (COOK) WILCOX; m SARAH -----; ch SUSANNAH, JOSEPH, HANNAH, RUTH, JOHN, JOSIAH/JOSIAS, MARY, DANIEL, JOB; Ref: Arnold v4 pt1 p104, Am Gen v19 #1 p28, Austin p423, Your Ancestors v10 #3 p1267, v12 #3 p1477.

JOSEPH - b 1694 s/OBADIAH & SILENCE (MANSFIELD) WILCOX; m 1722 HANNAH GOODALE of Long Island NY; Res E Guilford & Madison, New Haven Co CT; ch TIMOTHY, JOSEPH, ELIZABETH, JEHIEL, HANNAH; d 15 Jul 1770; Ref: Wilcox-Meigs p33, Nutmegger v3 #4 p406, Desc of Wm Wilcoxson pp8,15, Cutter's CT Fam v4 p1769, Fam of Early Guilford p1208, Barbour's VR Guilford v2 p20,81, Hist of Surry NH p944.

JOSEPH Lt - b 17 Jan 1695 Killingworth, Middlesex Co CT s/JOSEPH & HANNAH (KELSEY) WILCOX; m 13 Aug 1724 REBECCA HURD who was b 1695 & d 03 May 1774 Killingworth CT; ch ELIZA, REBECCA, JOSEPH, NATHAN, HANNAH, ADAM, ELIJAH, ABIGAIL, SARAH, LUCY, ABIGAIL, JOSEPH; d 29 Sep 1747 Killingworth; Ref: Nutmegger v10 #2 p231, v11 #3 p389, Wilcox-Meigs p40, Desc of Abner & Lucy Hart Wilcox p19, Bogue Fam p394, Cutter's Northern NY v2 p656, Barbour's VR Killingworth v1 p80,v2 pp188,189,193, Desc of Wm Wilcoxson p65.

JOSEPH - m SARAH ----- who was b 1700 & d 31 Aug 1775 Killingworth, Middlesex Co CT bur Union Cem; Ref: Nutmegger v10 #2 p232.

JOSEPH - b 03 Jul 1701 Simsbury, Hartford Co CT s/SAMUEL & MINDWELL (GRIFFIN) WILCOX; m 28 Feb 1723 ELIZABETH HOLCOMB who d 23 Aug 1727 d/JONATHAN HOLCOMB; ch ELIZABETH; Ref: Wilcox-Meigs pp33,48, Nutmegger v10 #2 p214.

JOSEPH 2nd - b 09 Feb 1705 Simsbury, Hartford Co CT s/JOSEPH & ABIGAIL (THRALL) WILCOX; m 31 Jul 1729 MARY BUTTOLPH who d 1735; m 27 Oct 1735 ELIZABETH HUMPHREY d/SAMUEL & LYDIA (NORTH) HUMPHREY; ch HOSEA, ELIZABETH, MARY, LURANNA, JOSEPH, DAVID, MINDWELL; d 15 Jan 1759; Ref: Wilcox-Meigs pp32,49, Early Settlers of W Simsbury p127, Your Ancestors v13 #3 p1567, Barbour's VR Simsbury TM3 p218, Desc of Wm Wilcoxson p15.

JOSEPH - m 22 Mar 1732 Killingworth, Middlesex Co CT ELIZABETH ARNELL; Ref: Nutmegger v11 #3 p390. Barbour's VR Killingworth v1 p191.

JOSEPH - b 14 Aug 1714 Middletown, Middlesex Co CT s/JOHN & MARY (BARNES) WILCOX; d 11 Feb 1736/7; Ref: Nutmegger v4 #3 p331, NEH&GR v14 p138, Barbour's VR Middletown LR2 p21.

JOSEPH - b 14 Dec 1718 Portsmouth, Newport Co RI s/JOSEPH & SARAH (-----) WILCOX; Ref: Arnold v4 pt1 p104.

JOSEPH - b 19 Sep 1721 Stratford, Fairfield Co CT s/WILLIAM & ESTHER (BRINSMADE) WILCOX; Ref: Wilcox-Meigs p39, Hist of Stratford Fam p1346.

JOSEPH - of Portsmouth, Newport Co RI m 19 Apr 1747 AMIE COGGESHALL of Middletown, Newport Co RI ch SARAH; Ref: Arnold v4 pt1 p47.

JOSEPH Jr - b 27 May 1726 E Guilford, New Haven Co CT s/JOSEPH & HANNAH (GOODALE) WILCOX; m 17 Sep 1754 SARAH MUNGER who was b 10 Feb 1729 & d 08 Sep 1782 d/JAMES & SUSANNAH (PEYER) MUNGER or JONATHAN & SARAH (GRAVES) MUNGER; m 1784 PRUDENCE DUDLEY who was b 31 May 1741 & d 14/15 Apr 1804 d/SAMUEL & JANE (TALMAN) DUDLEY; ch by 1st wife MABEL, ABEL, JOSEPH, SARAH; d 02 Apr 1808 bur Hamonasset Cem Guilford CT; Ref: Wilcox-Meigs pp37,53, Cutter's CT Fam v4 p1769, Fam of Early Guilford pp 338,1208-1210, Gen of CT Fam v2 pp576,577, Barbour's VR Guilford v2 pp20,70, Desc of Wm Wilcoxson pp15,28.

JOSEPH - b 11 Sep 1728 Killingworth, Middlesex Co CT s/JOSEPH & REBECCA (HURD) WILCOX; d 15 Jun 1747; Ref: Wilcox-Meigs p40, Barbour's VR Killingworth v1 p189.

JOSEPH - b 27 Aug 1730 Westerly, Washington Co RI s/EDWARD & DINAH (BARBER) WILCOX; m 28 Jul 1748 MARY BURDICK; m ELIZABETH CRUMB; ch DESIRE, AMEY,

551

PRUDENCE, EDWARD, JOSEPH, OLIVER; d 08 May 1804; Ref: Arnold v5 p144, pt5 p16, 2nd Boat v7 #1 p22.

JOSEPH - s/JOSEPH & MARY (BUTTOLPH) WILCOX m 01 Jan 1761 Simsbury, Hartford Co CT SARAH POST; ch JOSEPH, CALEB, SETH, SARAH; Ref: Wilcox-Meigs p68.

JOSEPH - b 1738; d 27 Jan 1808 Litchfield, Litchfield Co CT bur Cem #52; Ref: Hale Collection, Rev Soldiers of Litchfield p124.

JOSEPH - b 06 Jun 1738 s/JOSEPH & ELIZABETH (HUMPHREY) WILCOX of Simsbury, Hartford Co CT; Ref: Your Ancestors v13 #3 p1567.

JOSEPH - b 13 Sep 1742 Killingworth, Middlesex Co CT s/JOSEPH WILCOX; Ref: Barbour's VR v1 p190.

JOSEPH - b ca 1746 s/NATHANIEL & RACHEL (MOSES) WILCOX of W Simsbury, Hartford Co CT; d prisoner in 1776; Ref: Early Settlers of W Simsbury CT p128.

JOSEPH - b 29 Mar 1746 Middletown, Middlesex Co CT s/JOHN & HANNAH (WILCOX) WILCOX; m 30 Nov 1785 MIRIAM BACON who was b 07 Feb 1762 & d 19 Mar 1825 Middletown CT d/JOSIAH & SYBIL (-----) BACON; ch SARAH, JEDEDIAH, SUBMIT, JOSEPH, HEZEKIAH, ELISHA BACON, LAVINIA, MARIA/MIRIAM; d 31 Jan 1832; Ref: MUH pp747,751, Your Ancestors v3 #4 pp351,352, Nutmegger v4 #1 p133, Early Fam of Wallingford pp331,332, Barbour's VR Middletown v2 p94,319, Hale Coll, Hist of Wallingford pp937,938.

JOSEPH - b 18 Sep 1747 Killingworth, Middlesex Co CT s/JOSEPH & REBECCA (HURD) WILCOX; Ref: Barbour's VR Killingworth v2 p189.

JOSEPH - b 23 Jan 1755 Killingworth, Middlesex Co CT Twin with LYDIA s/STEPHEN & MARY (PIERSON) WILCOX; m 30 Jan 1785 PHEBE MORGAN who was b 26 Nov 1765 Killingworth CT & d 19 Apr 1835 Irving, Hanover twnshp, Chautauqua Co NY d/THEOPHILUS & PHEBE (MERRILL) MORGAN; Res Marietta, Washington Co OH ca 1810; Rev Army disch 01 Jan 1783; Ens 1777, 2nd Lt 1778, 1st Lt 1780, Cpt 1781, Adj Gen 1781; ch REBECCA, SUSANNA, JOSEPH MORGAN, HENRY PIERSON; d 17 Jan 1817 Marietta OH; Ref: Your Ancestors v3 #7&8 p425, Wilcox-Meigs p62, Arnold v14 p423, Barbour's VR Killingworth v2 pp38,132,159, 1855 Census Hanover NY, Alice Wiatr.

JOSEPH - b 27 Aug 1756 Middletown, Middlesex Co CT s/MOSES & DESIAH (RANNEY) WILCOX; m 1785 LUCY STOCKING; m MARY COOPER; d 26 Mar 1836; Ref: Nutmegger v11 #3 p449, Barbour's VR Middletown v2 p292.

JOSEPH - m 04 Mar 1776 Killingworth, Middlesex Co CT GRACE WILCOX who was b 11 Jul 1755 Killingworth CT d/GILES & SARAH (-----) WILCOX; ch HANNAH, JOSEPH, PHILINDA, SILAS, ADA, AMELIA, MARTHA, ELIAS, ABIGAIL, BELA/BELER, GRACE, BELA/BELE; Ref: Barbour's VR Killingworth v2 pp39, 124,149, Wilcox-Meigs p64.

JOSEPH - b 1758 Killingworth, Middlesex Co CT; d 18 Feb 1819 Cayuga Co NY; Ref: Tree Talks v8 #1 p21.

JOSEPH - b 18 Jul 1758 Exeter, Washington Co RI; m NANNY PLACE; Res Hinesburg, Windham Co VT; ch OLIVER, JOHN, THOMAS, POLLY, NANCY; d 1835; Ref: Your Ancestors v3 #3 p318.

JOSEPH - b 19 Apr 1760 RI s/WILLIAM & ELIZABETH (HATHAWAY) WILCOX; m 22 Mar 1793 PRUDENCE DALRYMPLE who was b 23 Mar 1773 Northbridge, Worcester Co MA & d Halifax Windham Co VT 17 Jul 1856 d/WILLIAM & MARY (STRAIGHT) DALRYMPLE; Res Halifax VT; ch JOSEPH, TYLER, LOVISA, MARY, SAMUEL, JAMES, LEWIS, ELIZABETH, ANNA; d 29 Nov 1829; Ref: 1800 Census Windham Co VT p140, 1850 Census Halifax VT p131, VT VR, Bible Rec, Halifax Wilcox Fam mss, Samuel Gorton Desc v2 p586.

JOSEPH - b 1761 CT; d Dec 1849 Jefferson Co NY; Ref: Tree Talks v5 #1 p14.

JOSEPH - b 1762 CT; d 1850 NY; Ref: Tree Talks v5 #1.

JOSEPH - b 20 Jan 1762 Simsbury, Hartford Co CT s/JOSEPH & SARAH (POST) WILCOX; Ref: Wilcox-Meigs p68.

JOSEPH - b 1763 E Guilford, New Haven Co CT s/JOSEPH & SARAH (MUNGER) WILCOX m 1783 OLIVE DOUD/DOWD who was b 03 Jan 1757 & d 09 Nov 1835 d/ABRAHAM & MARY (BISHOP) DOWD; ch PRUDENCE, OLIVE, ANNA, ABEL, ZENAS, ROXANNA; d 02 Nov 1826; Ref: Wilcox-Meigs p73,74, Cutter's CT Fam v4 p1769, Fam of Early Guilford pp1209,1211, Desc of Wm Wilcoxson p28.

JOSEPH Jr - m Dec 1784 Barkhamsted, Litchfield Co CT HANNAH BANNING; ch CHLOE; Ref: Barbour's VR Barkhamsted v1 p56, Fiske Card File.

JOSEPH - b 1769 CT; Res Canaan, Litchfield Co CT with RUSSELL H WILCOX; Ref: 1850 Census Canaan CT p46 Dw# 665.

JOSEPH - b 04 Aug 1772 Middletown, Middlesex Co CT s/DANIEL & MERCY (GIBSON) WILCOX; d 25 Feb 1773; Ref: Hist of Berlin CT p89, Barbour's VR Middletown v2 p150.

JOSEPH - m be 1799 HULDAH SHERMAN; Res Charleston, Washington Co RI; ch GEORGE S, MARY, REBECCA, EDWARD, HANNAH, REBECCA, NANCY, CHARLIE W, JOSEPH D, ELIZA A, SUSAN F, JOHN G, NATHAN, BENJAMIN F; Ref: Arnold v5 pt5 p28, See George S.

JOSEPH - b 06 Sep 1774 Exeter, Washington Co RI s/ISAAC & REBECCA (BARBER) WILCOX; m MARY PULLMAN d/NATHANIEL PULLMAN 07 Jan 1796; Ref: Arnold v5 pt3 pp36,63.

JOSEPH - b be 1790; m MABEL -----; Sold land in Herkimer Co NY 1811 & 1817; Ref: Herkimer Co Deed Index pp824,826, Deed Book v5 p461, v10 pp597,599.

JOSEPH - b ca 1775 s/AMOS & MARY (-----) WILCOX; m ca 1799 MARGARET SIMONSON; m NANCY STAGG; Res Orange Co NY; ch by 1st wife JOHN, WILLIAM, MARY, SUSAN, SALLIE, HARRIET; ch by 2nd wife CHARLES, DAVID, PHOEBE; d 1863; Ref: Your Ancestors v9 #4 p1176, Hist of Orange Co NY p610.

JOSEPH - had negro twins CESAR & PRIMA b 15 Dec 1777 Killingworth; Ref: Barbour's VR Killingworth v2 p132.

JOSEPH - b 05 Sep 1778 Killingworth, Middlesex Co CT s/JOSEPH & GRACE (WILCOX) WILCOX; Ref: Wilcox-Meigs p64, Barbour's VR Killingworth v2 p149.

JOSEPH - of Fairfax, Franklin Co VT; Served in War of 1812; Ref: VT Roster War of 1812 p455.

JOSEPH - b 01 Jul 1780 Norfolk, Litchfield Co CT s/HOSEA & SARAH (-----) WILCOX; Ref: Barbour's VR Norfolk v1 p3.

JOSEPH - b 1780 s/HIEL & DEBORAH (GILLETT) WILCOX Killingworth, Middlesex Co CT; Res Dutchess

Co NY; Ref: Desc of Wm Wilcoxson p59, Your Ancestors v4 #11&12 p612.

JOSEPH - b 18 Dec 1782 Tiverton, Newport Co RI s/THOMAS & KEZIAH (BENNETT) WILCOX; m 21 Nov 1807 New Bedford, Bristol Co MA REBECCA PERKINS d/HENRY PERKINS; m ELIZABETH PERKINS who was b 04 Apr 1782 & d 03 Nov 1881 Dartmouth, Bristol Co MA d/HENRY PERKINS; ch by 1st wife JOSEPH, HENRY; ch by 2nd wife HENRY PERKINS, THOMAS, REBECCA; d 13 Oct 1868; Ref: New Bedford MA VR p521,522,596, Repr Men of Southeastern MA v1 p480.

JOSEPH - b 14 Jun 1784 Barkhamsted, Litchfield Co CT s/ABEL & EXPERIENCE (RAMSDELL) WILCOX; Ref: Barbour's VR Barkhamsted v2 p310.

JOSEPH - b 1784 NY; Res New Hartford, Oneida Co NY; ch LOUISA, HELLEN; Ref: 1850 Census New Hartford p270 Dw# 511.

JOSEPH - m ?01 Dec 1785 GRACE STOCKING who was b 08 May 1763 d/BENJAMIN & PHOEBE (-----) STOCKING; Res Prob Chatham, Middlesex Co CT; Ref: Gen of CT Fam v3 p452.

JOSEPH - b 1785 NY; Res Tully, Onondaga Co NY; ch MINERVA, ADELINE; Ref: 1850 Census Tully NY p162 Dw# 168.

JOSEPH - b ca 1790 s/BENJAMIN & BATHSHEBA (-----) of Verona, Oneida Co NY; m EUNICE DOUGLAS; ch JULIA; Ref: Your Ancestors v4 #3&4 p521.

JOSEPH Jr - b 21 Oct 1791 Middletown, Middlesex Co CT s/JOSEPH & MIRIAM (BACON) WILCOX; m 06 Oct 1818 MARIA TRYON who was b 1795 & d 18 Oct 1830 Middletown, Middlesex Co CT bur Washington St Cem; m LUCY TRYON who was b 1800 & d 30 Jan 1840 Middletown, Middlesex Co CT; ch by 1st wife EMILY MARIA, JOSEPH DWIGHT, LUCY TRYON, MARY, JOHN; ch by 2nd wife CORNELIUS, CHARLES CORNELIUS, HELEN CLARISSA; d 02 Jan 1858; Ref: Hale Coll, Early Fam of Wallingford p332, Your Ancestors v3 #4 p352, Barbour's VR Middletown v2 p319, v3 p91, Hist of Wallingford p938.

JOSEPH - b 1791; Moved from Orange Co NY to Luzerne Co PA 1833; Res Canton, Bradford Co PA; 8 daus & 3 sons incl WILLIAM S; d af 1880; Ref: Hist of Luzerne Co PA p1455.

JOSEPH - b 08 Sep 1793 s/JOSEPH & PRUDENCE
(DALRYMPLE) WILCOX; m MARGARET PEARCE; Ref: Samuel
Gorton Desc v2 p586.

JOSEPH - b 1795; d 31 Jan 1831 Middletown,
Middlesex Co CT bur Highland Cem; Ref: Hale Coll.

JOSEPH - b 28 Feb 1798 Hamilton, Madison Co NY
s/FREDERICK & EUNICE (-----) WILCOX; m MELISSA
ABBOTT d/WILLARD ABBOTT; Res Palerno, Oswego Co
NY; ch NANCY, ROSINA, LAVINIA, JOSEPH YATES; d 10
May 1869; Ref: Your Ancestors v12 #3 p1464, 1850
Census Palerno NY p28 Dw# 389.

JOSEPH - b 26 May 1798 Lexington, Greene Co NY
s/NATHANIEL & ANNA/JOANNA (McGONIGLE/MALLORY)
WILCOX; d 1851; Ref: Hist of Orange Co NY, Wilcox-
Meigs p84, Your Ancestors v4 311&12 p612.

JOSEPH - b 11 Feb 1799 Newport, Sullivan Co NH
s/URIAH & HANNAH (WRIGHT) WILCOX; m 10 Jan 1826
NANCY WILMARTH d/DANIEL & NANCY (MONROE) WILMARTH;
ch JOSEPH EDWIN, DANIEL WILMARTH, GEORGE MUNROE,
HENRY ALLEN; d 23 Feb 1882; Ref: Gen of NH Fam v3
p1509, Your Ancestors v3 #5 p378, #6 p400.

JOSEPH - b 18-- s/SAMUEL & AMANDA (SAVAGE)
WILCOX; Res Charlotte, Chautauqua Co NY; Ref:
Dilly's Hist of Chautauqua Co NY pp245,246.

JOSEPH - m SARAH ANN ----- who was b 1809 & d
08 Sep 1881 Little Compton, Newport Co RI; bur
Wilbor-Gifford Cem; Ref: Gen of RI Fam v2 p461.

JOSEPH - s/ABEL & CHLOE (-----) WILCOX; m be
1825; Res New Hartford, Oneida Co NY; ch
ELIZABETH; Ref: Barber's Abstract of Wills p21,
10,000 VR of Central NY p216.

JOSEPH - m 11 Jan 1838 Palmyra, Wayne Co NY
ELIZA BARROWS; Ref: 10,000 VR of Western NY p250.

JOSEPH - s/MARK & MARY (-----) WILCOX; d 14 Jan
1815 PA; Ref: Daily Advertiser Philadelphia p275.

JOSEPH - b 1800 Simsbury, Hartford Co CT s/JOHN
& AMELIA (EDGECOMB) WILCOX; m 30 Mar 1825 ESTHER C
LUM of Monroe, Fairfield Co CT; Res Newtown,
Fairfield Co CT; Ref: Your Ancestors v13 #4 p1598,
Barbour's VR Monroe v1 p53.

JOSEPH - b 13 Sep 1800 s/THOMAS & ELIZABETH
(McCAIN) WILCOX of Hector, Schuyler Co NY; m 1823

FRANCES MARIE LAIN; Ref: Your Ancestors v10 #4 p1274.

JOSEPH 2nd - m 20 Jan 1814 Charlestown, Washington Co RI MARIAH BLIVEN; Ref: Arnold v5 pt5 p16.

JOSEPH - b 1801; m ELECTA ----- who was b 1813 & d 31 May 1863; d 04 Nov 1860 both bur Kirkersville Cem, Licking Co OH; Ref: OH Cem Rec p284.

JOSEPH J N - b 1808 CT; Res Litchfield, Litchfield Co CT (in jail); Sailor; Ref: 1850 Census Litchfield CT p255 Dw# 42.

JOSEPH - b 1814 Marion Co MO s/HAZARD & SARAH (SEELEY) WILCOX; d in infancy; Ref: Your Ancestors v12 #2 p1435.

JOSEPH - b 1816 CT; m ca 1845 JANE C ----- who was b NY 1827; Res Preston, New London Co CT; ch GEORGE G; Ref: 1850 Preston CT Census p21.

JOSEPH - m be 1840 LUCY -----; ch ADALINE b Middletown, Middlesex Co CT; Ref: Barbour's VR Middletown v3 p91.

JOSEPH - b 1818; d 14 Apr 1887 Middletown, Middlesex Co CT bur Highland Cem; Ref: Hale Coll.

JOSEPH - b 1825 NY; m JANE -----; Res Clarksville, Allegany Co NY; Ref: 1850 Census Clarksville NY p137 Dw# 94.

JOSEPH - b 1825 NY; Res with JOSEPH COTMAN fam Ellicottville, Cattaraugus Co NY 1850; Ref: 1850 Census Ellicottville NY p237 Dw# 120.

JOSEPH - b 1825 NY; m MELVINA -----; Res Gerry, Chautauqua Co NY; ch HIRAM, EUGENE; Ref: 1860 Census Gerry NY p61 Dw# 65.

JOSEPH - b 1825 NY; Res Perry, Lake Co OH; Carpenter; Ref: 1850 Census Perry OH Reel 259 p240.

JOSEPH - b ca 1830 s/ISAAC & ELIZABETH (WILCOX) WILCOX; m HANNAH McMULLEN HOAGLAND; Ref: Your Ancestors v10 #3 pp1247,1248.

JOSEPH - b ca 1830 NY; m LUCY KINGSLEY; Ref: Nutmegger v9 #2 p302.

JOSEPH - b 1834 s/GEORGE S & ELIZA (-----) WILCOX of Stonington, New London Co CT; Ref: 1850 Census Stonington CT Reel 432 #48 p236.

JOSEPH - m be 1844 RHODA -----; Res Tiverton, Newport Co RI; ch WILLIAM A; Ref: Arnold v7 p583.

JOSEPH - m 04 Jul 1847 Jasper, Steuben Co NY JANE WEBSTER; Res Troupsburg, Steuben Co NY; Ref: 10,000 VR of Western NY p250, Marriages & Deaths from Steuben Co Newspapers p41.

JOSEPH - b 1841 NY s/CHENEY & AMITY (-----) WILCOX of Onondaga, Onondaga Co NY; Ref: 1850 Census Onondaga NY p324 Dw# 1492.

JOSEPH - b 1842 NY s/BENJAMIN & HARRIET (-----) WILCOX of Lincklaen, Chenango Co NY; Ref: 1850 Census Chenango Co NY.

JOSEPH - b 1842 NY s/JAMES & JANE (-----) WILCOX of Granger, Allegany Co NY; Ref: 1850 Census Granger NY p9 Dw# 157.

JOSEPH - b 20 Jul 1843 Portage Co OH s/ALEXANDER HAMILTON & BETSEY (DIVER) WILCOX of Deerfield, Portage Co OH; d 16 May 1865; Ref: Hist of Portage Co OH p635, 1850 Census Deerfield OH p186 Dw# 1001, Desc of Wm Wilcoxson p244.

JOSEPH - b 18 Nov 1852 Jackson Co IA s/ABNER THORP & LYDIA A (CHANDLER) WILCOX; School teacher Baldwin, Jackson Co IA; d 1935; Ref: Desc of Wm Wilcoxson p125.

JOSEPH ALSTON - b 15 Oct 1817 Westfield, Middlesex Co CT s/HEZEKIAH & RAMA (ROBERTS) WILCOX; m 19 Dec 1839 LUCY ANN BACON who was b 1819 & d 23 Apr 1872 Middletown, Middlesex Co CT; Ref: Early Fam of Wallingford CT p332. Your Ancestors v3 #4 p352, Hale Coll, Barbour's VR Middletown v3 p463, Hist of Wallingford p938.

JOSEPH AUGUSTUS - b 03 Jan 1836 Saybrook, Middlesex Co CT s/JEREMIAH & JERUSHA (SHIPMAN) WILCOX; Ref: Saybrook Colony VR p557.

JOSEPH B - b 1817; m ELISA -----; Res Saybrook, Middlesex Co CT; son b in 1855; Ref: Saybrook Colony VR p180.

JOSEPH B - m 05 Sep 1853 Vernon Co WI JANE L WILLARD; married by Rev IRA WILCOX; Ref: Hist of Vernon Co WI p161.

JOSEPH B - m 28 Dec 1841 M HOLLY; Ref: Nebr & Midwest Gen Rec v15 #1 p11.

JOSEPH BENJAMIN - b 19 Sep 1815 Madison, New Haven Co CT s/ABEL & ANNA (FIELD) WILCOX; m 01 Jan 1838 RUTH ELIZABETH SCRANTON who was b 01 Jan or 20 Aug 1818 & d 22 Apr 1863 d/COMFORT OLDS & RUTH (EVARTS) SCRANTON of Madison, New Haven Co CT; m 31 Jul 1865 BETSY BUEL FIELD; ch MARY ELIZABETH, CORNELIA EVALINA, HENRY EDWARD, ALBERT EUGENE; d Apr 1895; Ref: Wilcox-Meigs pp92,108,109, Fam of Early Guilford pp 1049,1213,1214, Barbour's VR Madison v1 p75, v2 p30.

JOSEPH BENJAMIN - Int to marry 08 Apr 1837 Cambridge, Middlesex Co MA SARAH SIMES WESTON of Reading, Middlesex Co MA who was b 22 Apr 1812 & d 21 Feb 1841 d/JOHN Jr & POLLY (-----) WESTON ch SARAH ADELINE; m 03 Oct 1841 SARAH SCRIBNER of Newton, Middlesex Co MA; Ref: VR Cambridge MA v2 p422, VR Reading MA pp 249,251,478,584.

JOSEPH BROOKS - m 10 Apr 1871 Westerly, Washington Co RI MARGARET MERRETT; Res Stonington, New London Co CT; Ref: Arnold v11 p47.

JOSEPH BUSHNELL - bpt 16 Sep 1821 Westbrook, Middlesex Co CT s/AMOS T & CYNTHIA (BUSHNELL) WILCOX; m 20/30 Sep 1835 MARY STEVEN WATROUS of Killingworth, Middlesex Co CT; Both joined Westbrook Cong Church 05 Feb 1837 & dismissed Sep 1849; Res Saybrook, Middlesex Co CT, Fair Haven, New Haven Co CT; ch CYNTHIA JENNETTE, ALFRED, CHARLES, MARY, JOSEPH; d 14 Jun 1853; Ref: Fam of Early Guilford pp1203,1205, Westbrook Cong Ch Rec p198, Barbour's VR Killingworth v3 p389.

JOSEPH C - b 1833 Chenango Co NY s/HAMILTON & SOPHIA (-----) WILCOX; Res Norwich & Smyrna, Chenango Co NY; Ref: Your Ancestors v12 #4 p1487, 1850 Census Norwich NY p186 Dw# 686.

JOSEPH COOK - b 21 Nov 1779 Portsmouth, Newport Co RI s/COOK & SARAH (ESLECK) WILCOX; Ref: Arnold v4 pt1 p105.

JOSEPH D - b 12 Feb 1829 Charlestown, Washington Co RI s/JOSEPH & HULDAH (SHERMAN) WILCOX; Ref: Arnold v5 pt5 p28, See Joseph.

JOSEPH DORVIL - b 1857 UT s/JAMES DAVID & ANNA MARIA (ROBINSON) WILCOX; died young; Ref: Desc of Wm Wilcoxson p144.

JOSEPH DUNBAR - b 17 Oct 1877 s/ANDREW CHESTER & CLARINDA CLINGMAN (RICHART) WILCOX of Harlan, Shelby Co IA; Ref: Your Ancestors v14 #3 p1671.

JOSEPH DWIGHT - b 12 Dec 1823 Middletown, Middlesex Co CT s/JOSEPH & MARIA (TRYON) WILCOX; Ref: Barbour's VR v3 p9, See Joseph.

JOSEPH E - of Middletown, Middlesex Co CT m 30 Oct 1847 ANN I TRYON of Glastonbury, Hartford Co CT; ch COURINE A; Ref: Barbour's VR Glastonbury v3 p200, Middletown v4 pp114,115.

JOSEPH EDWIN - b 16 Sep 1826 Newport, Sullivan Co NH s/JOSEPH & NANCY (WILMARTH) WILCOX; m EUNICE GREGG d/Dr JAMES GREGG; ch SARAH A, HELEN, GEORGE M, NANCY M, PRISCILLA G, CHARLES E, DANIEL W, GRACE L; Ref: Gen of Fam of NH v3 p1509, Your Ancestors v3 #6 p400.

JOSEPH F - b 14 Jul 1834 Westerly, Washington Co RI s/GEORGE S & ELIZABETH (-----) WILCOX; Ref: Arnold v5 p145.

JOSEPH F - m 12 Oct 1844 Sturbridge, Worcester Co MA LYDIA ANN WILBUR; Ref: Sturbridge VR p290.

JOSEPH F - of Westville, New Haven Co CT; m 02 Mar 1845 New Haven, New Haven Co CT MARIA R WHITNEY of Whitneyville, New Haven Co CT; Ref: Barbour's VR New Haven v6 p70.

JOSEPH F - b 1844 NY s/ERASTUS & EUNICE (-----) WILCOX of Palerno, Oswego Co NY; Ref: 1850 Census Palerno NY p32 Dw# 470.

JOSEPH FRANKLIN - b 14 Feb 1870 Winterset, Madison Co IA s/ISAAC ALMANZA & CATHERINE A (SHELLABORGER) WILCOX; m ca 1894 MYRTLE MAY HAXTON; m LIZZIE MAY IRWIN; d 16 Oct 1954 Winterset IA; Ref: Verna Betts.

JOSEPH H - b 1809 NY; m MARY ANN ----- who was b 1814 NY; Res Tully, Onondaga Co NY; ch WILLIAM H, CALVIN, CHARLES, ROSETTA; Ref: 1850 Census Tully NY p218 Dw# 472.

JOSEPH H - b 1820 NY; Res Little Falls, Herkimer Co NY with JOSEPH K CHAPMAN family;

Stonecutter; Ref: 1850 Census Little Falls NY p229 Dw# 428.

JOSEPH H - b 1843 Taunton, Bristol Co MA; Enl in Service 15 Sep 1862; Ref: Taunton MA VR v1.

JOSEPH L - b 14 Jan 1828 s/ASA & SYBIL (BLISS) WILCOX; m 18 Dec 1862 Perry, Lake Co OH MARY S IVES d/HORATIO GATES & SARAH (PERRY) IVES; Res Geneva, Ashtabula Co OH; ch PERRY EMMET, HALLETT M, MINNIE A, CARRIE, ZELLA, BLISS O; d 22 Nov 1912; Ref: Bogue Fam pp398,399, Your Ancestors v3 #5 p378.

JOSEPH L - b Apr 1894 WI s/GEORGE W & EMMA C (-----) WILCOX; Father b in NY; Ref: 1900 Soundex Richland Co WI.

JOSEPH M - d 15 Feb 1814 PA; Ref: Daily Advertiser Philadelphia PA p250.

JOSEPH M - b 1837 Hanover, Chautauqua Co NY s/HENRY PIERSON & SARAH (MORGAN) WILCOX; Ref: Alice Wiatr, See Henry Pierson.

JOSEPH MONROE - d 04 Apr 1857 Westerly, Washington Co RI; Ref: Arnold v11 p127.

JOSEPH MORGAN - b 15 Mar 1790 Killingworth, Middlesex Co CT s/Capt JOSEPH & PHOEBE (MORGAN) WILCOX; Parents moved to Marietta, Washington Co OH 1810; Ref: Wilcox-Meigs p62, Your Ancestors v3 #7&8 p425, Barbour's VR Killingworth v2 p132.

JOSEPH PERKINS - b 05 Jun 1862 s/EDWIN D & MARIA C (PERKINS) WILCOX of Crown Point, Essex Co NY; Ref: Your Ancestors v3 #9&10 p450, Desc of Wm Wilcoxson p118.

JOSEPH R - b 1842 NY s/ASA & HARRIET (STEVENS) WILCOX of Hamilton & Georgetown, Madison Co NY; Ref: Desc of Wm Wilcoxson p169, 1850 Census Georgetown NY p388 Dw# 210.

JOSEPH RUGGLES - b 1819 VT s/OZIAL & NANCY (PAINE) WILCOX of Sandgate, Bennington Co VT; Res Worthington, Nobles Co MN; 13 ch incl RALPH, MARTHA, ABBIE, JAMES, HERBERT, AUSTIN; Ref: Desc of Wm Wilcoxson pp169,170.

JOSEPH RUSSELL - b 16 Jan 1774 Berlin, Hartford Co CT s/JOSIAH & ELIZABETH (TREAT) WILCOX; m 02 Dec 1795 LENA FOSTER; m 02 Jan 1849 BETTY

(HASKELL) SMITH who was b 1779 d/JOHN HASKELL & w/WILLIAM SMITH; ch by 1st wife CHAUNCEY, ALSA; d 25 Jan 1852; Ref: MUH pp752,756, Barbour's VR Ridgefield v1 p242, Middletown v2 p221, v4 p126/7.

JOSEPH SAMUEL - b 05 Feb 1828 Killingworth, Middlesex Co CT s/BELA & AMANDA (GRUMBY) WILCOX; Ref: Wilcox-Meigs p83, Barbour's VR Killingworth v2 p92.

JOSEPH SHIPMAN - b 1844 s/JEREMIAH & JERUSHA (SHIPMAN) WILCOX Saybrook, Middlesex Co CT; Ref: Saybrook Colony VR p559.

JOSEPH SMITH - b 1850 Collins, Erie Co NY s/JACOB & MARY E (-----) WILCOX; Ref: 1850 Census Collins NY p322 Dw# 609.

JOSEPH 3RD - m 09 Aug 1798 Clinton, Middlesex Co CT MABEL CARTER; Ref: ECM v6 p63, Fiske Card File.

JOSEPH THORP - b 20 May 1877 Eau Claire, Eau Claire Co WI s/NELSON CHAPMAN & ANGELINE (TEWKESBURY) WILCOX; m 12 June 1902 MINNIE McDONOUGH d/DENNIS McDONOUGH; ch PETRONILLA, MARGARET; Ref: Hist of Eau Claire Co WI p900.

JOSEPH U - m be 1846 MARIA A GARDNER; Res Taunton, Bristol Co MA; ch LIZZIE HANNAH; Ref: Arnold v8 p293.

JOSEPH YATES - b 11 Nov 1832 Hamilton, Madison Co NY s/JOSEPH & MELISSA (ABBOTT) WILCOX of Palerno, Oswego Co NY; m GRACE ADAMS; ch MARY, JOSEPH, ABBOTT YATES; Ref: Your Ancestors v12 #3 p1464, 1850 Census Palerno NY p28 Dw# 389.

JOSEPHINE - b 30 Aug 1830 d/MARTIN & MEHITABLE (WELLS) WILCOX; Res RI/NY; Ref: NYG&BR v107 p193.

JOSEPHINE - b 02 Apr 1842 Horseheads, Chemung Co NY d/RICHARD & HANNAH (FOOTE) WILCOX; m 03 Jul 1865 LEMAN C PALMER s/LEWIS & REBECCA (WEST) PALMER; Res Centerville PA; ch ROY M; Ref: Foote Fam Gen p271.

JOSEPHINE - b 28 Apr 1842 d/DAVID HENRY & ADELIA (HOPKINS) WILCOX of Cohocton, Steuben Co NY; m STILLMAN FISHER; Ref: Your Ancestors v10 #1 p1200.

JOSEPHINE - b 1848 NY d/BENJAMIN & HARRIET (-----) WILCOX of Lincklaen, Chenango Co NY; Ref: 1850 Census Chenango Co NY.

JOSEPHINE - of Portland, Chautauqua Co NY m ca 1872/3 G W E ENSWORTH of New Hartford, Oneida Co NY; Ref: 19th Cent Marriages Reported in Fredonia Censor p119.

JOSEPHINE - b 04 Jul 1849 Norwich, Chenango Co NY d/WILLIAM & ALTA ZERA (-----) WILCOX; Ref: VR of Chenango Co NY p186.

JOSEPHINE - b 1868 WI d/GEORGE & SUSAN (-----) WILCOX; Father b in NY; Res Springlake, Pierce Co WI; Ref: 1880 Soundex Pierce Co WI.

JOSEPHINE A - b 1849 NY d/WILMAN & BETSEY (-----) WILCOX of Ripley, Chautauqua Co NY; Ref: 1850 Census Ripley NY p115 Dw# 138.

JOSEPHINE A - b 1853 NY d/AMOS P & JANE A (MEAD) WILCOX of Busti, Chautauqua Co NY; m 30 Dec 1874 Busti NY Methodist Episcopal Church FRANK W ROOT who was b 1850; Ref: 1860 Census Busti NY p47 Dw# 363, Chautauqua Genealogist v15 #3 p33.

JOSEPHINE ELIZABETH - b 31 Jul 1843 d/JOHN WARREN & POLINA ALZINA (WEEKS) WILCOX of Oneida Co NY; m 01 Jan 1862 DANIEL B BALL; Res Brooklyn NY; Ref: Gen of George Weekes p155.

JOSEPHINE F - b 02 Feb 1846 Middletown, Middlesex Co CT d/GUSTAVUS VASA & LUCY (LEE) WILCOX; Ref: Wilcox-Meigs p89.

JOSHUA - s/EDWARD & ELEANOR (RATHBONE) WILCOX; m JANE ASHCRAFT; Res Stonington, New London Co CT; Ref: Hist of Stonington p661.

JOSHUA - b 13 Aug 1781 Halifax, Windham Co VT s/STEPHEN & ELINOR (EWING) WILCOX; m Halifax VT 19 Jan 1804 EUNICE W McCLURE who later m ----- STAFFORD & d 09 Feb 1862 age 82; 4 sons & 3 daus in 1820; d 09 Nov 1839 age 58; Ref: 1810 Census Windham Co VT p289, VT VR, 1820 Census p149, Halifax Wilcox Fam mss, Fiske Card File.

JOSHUA - b 28 Jun 1782 N Stonington, New London Co CT s/FRANCIS & MARTHA (WORDEN) WILCOX; d Af 1850; Ref: Barbour's VR N Stonington v1 p36, 1850 Census N Stonington CT Reel 432 #48 p309, Your Ancestors v13 #2 p1539.

JOSHUA - b 25 Feb 1792 Killingworth, Middlesex
Co CT s/URIAH & HANNAH (WRIGHT/BARTLETT) WILCOX; m
ABIGAIL KELSEY who was b 1796 & d 24 Feb 1844
d/JOEL & JEMIMA (BUELL) KELSEY; m RACHEL ----- who
was b 1796; Res Newport, Sullivan Co NH; ch
ROXANNA, OSCAR, URIAH M, CORNELIA, JANE; d 08 Oct
1848 Greece, Monroe Co NY; Ref: Gen of NH Fam v3
p1509, Your Ancestors v3 #5 p378, #6 p399.

JOSIAH - b 22 Sep 1701 Tiverton, Newport Co RI
s/EDWARD & SARAH (MANCHESTER) WILCOX; m ca 1718
PATIENCE BORDEN CHASE who was b 16 Apr 1699
d/BENJAMIN & AMY (BORDEN) CHASE; m 2nd MARY LAWTON
11 Mar 1745 Portsmouth, Newport Co RI; Res
Tiverton, Newport Co RI; ch THOMAS, EDWARD,
GIDEON, BENJAMIN, DANIEL, JEREMIAH, WILLIAM,
SARAH, BARDEN; d 01 Mar 1772; Ref: Fiske Card
File, Little Comp Fam p771, Repr Men of
Southeastern MA v1 p480, Cutter's New England Fam
v4 p2016, Gen of RI Fam v1 p676.

JOSIAH - b 1705 Stratford, Fairfield Co CT
s/JOHN & ELIZABETH (TOMLINSON) WILCOX; m 18 Jun
1735 ELIZABETH HUBBELL who was b 15 Mar 1713/4
d/JOSIAH & MARTHA (-----) HUBBELL; ch RUTH,
ELIZABETH, HULDAH, MARTHA, ELISHA, ABIAH, DAVID,
JOHN, GIDEON, ANN, EZRA, JOSIAH, GRACE; Ref:
Wilcox-Meigs pp37,57,58, Cutter's Northern NY v2
p655.

JOSIAH - b 04 Apr 1706 Killingworth, Middlesex
Co CT s/SAMUEL & RUTH (WESTCOTT) WILCOX; m 03 Mar
1731 KEZIAH KELSEY who was b 08 Mar 1704; Res
Dutchess Co NY; ch ELIAB, ANNA, ROSSEL/ROSWELL,
JOSIAH, KEZIAH, ABNER, ELIZABETH; Ref: Barbour's
VR Killingworth v1 p120, v2 pp120,157, Wilcox-
Meigs pp30,43, Nutmegger v8 #4 p503, v11 #2 p209,
Desc of Wm Wilcoxson p43, Your Ancestors v3 #7&8
p426, v4 #3&4 p521.

JOSIAH/JOSEPH - m 16 May 1742/3 Middletown,
Middlesex Co CT ANNA/ANNE BUTLER who was b 07 Feb
1722 d/GERSHOM & MARY (DEMING) BUTLER; no
children; Ref: Barbour's VR Middletown v1 p130,
Wisconsin Fam Dec 1940 p142.

JOSIAH - of Tiverton m 11 Mar 1744/45
Portsmouth, Newport Co RI MARY (-----) LAWTON
w/Thomas Lawton; Ref: Arnold v4 pt1 p47.

JOSIAH - b 28 Jun 1717 Middletown, Middlesex Co
CT s/SAMUEL & HANNAH (SAGE) WILCOX; m 01 Jan
1750/1 Farmington, Hartford Co CT ELIZABETH

CURTISS (one source gave ELIZABETH NOTT); ch JOSIAH, EZRA, ELEAZER CURTIS, ANNE/ANNA, MARY ANN, HANNAH, SALOME, LOUISA/LOVISA, JESSE; d 1788; Ref: Barbour's VR Farmington v7 pp35,540, LR8 p9, Middletown v2 p29, A Wilcox Book p17, NEH&GR v14 p138, Nutmegger v4 #3 p331, Early CT Probate Records v2, Cutter's Western NY v2 p742, Col Fam of US v5 p555.

JOSIAH/JOSEPH - b 31 Aug 1727 Portsmouth, Newport Co RI s/JOSEPH & SARAH (-----) WILCOX; m ANN ESTES 25 Jul 1752; m 16 OCT 1760 Smithfield, Providence Co RI CASHABA LAPHAM; m be 1768 SARAH -----; Res Middletown & Portsmouth, Newport Co RI; ch by 1st wife ROBERT, SARAH, HANNAH, SUSANNAH, MARTHA; ch by 3rd wife SAMUEL WILBUR, RODMAN, ANNE, JOSIAH; Ref: Arnold v2 105, v3 pt6 p80, v4 pt3 p42, v7 p39, Your Ancestors v12 #4 p1503.

JOSIAH - b 14 May 1739 Killingworth, Middlesex Co CT s/JOSIAH & KEZIAH (KELSEY) WILCOX; m ANNA -----; Res Amenia, Dutchess Co NY 1758; ch ELISHA, ROSWELL, poss AMOS & GEORGE 6 daus; d 18 Jan 1832 Amenia, NY; bur Spencer's Corner near Millerton, Dutchess Co NY; Ref: Barbour's VR Killingworth v2 p157, Desc of Wm Wilcoxson pp43,58, Wilcox-Meigs p43, Your Ancestors v4 #3&4 p521 #9&10 p585.

JOSIAH - b 18 Aug 1745 s/JOSIAH & ELIZABETH (HUBBELL) WILCOX; Ref: Stratford Fam p1348, Cutter's Northern NY v2 p655.

JOSIAH - b 31 Mar 1750 Middletown, Middlesex Co CT s/DANIEL & SARAH (WHITE) WILCOX; m 23 Sep 1773 ELIZABETH TREAT who d 13 May 1775; m 20 Mar 1777 HULDAH SAVAGE who was b 25 May 1755 & d 22 Jan 1816 d/JOHN SAVAGE; m NAOMI KIRBY who d 1837; ch by 1st wife JOSEPH RUSSELL, ELIZABETH, ch by 2nd wife OLIVE, LEMUEL, LYMAN, LYMAN, LYNDA, HULDAH, HORACE, HEPZIBAH, SAMUEL; d 03 Sep 1835 Berlin CT; Fifer in Rev Army; Ref: MUH pp749,752, ECM v2 p94, Barbour's VR Middletown v1 p102, v2 p221, Cutter's CT Fam v2 p657, Hist of Berlin CT p99.

JOSIAH - b 10 Apr 1752 Farmington, Hartford Co CT s/JOSIAH & ELIZABETH (CURTIS) WILCOX; m 1782 ROSANNA WOODFORD; d 27 Jun 1832; Ref: A Wilcox Book p18, Col Fam of US v5 p555, Barbour's VR Farmington LR8 p9.

JOSIAH - b 15 Sep 1753 Killingworth, Middlesex Co CT s/SILAS & SARAH (STEVENS) WILCOX; m 08 Apr 1779 Conway, Franklin Co MA Mrs JEMIMA KELSEY; ch

ORRIN, EUNICE, AMBROSE, EBBA; d Brecksville OH; Ref: Barbour's VR Killingworth v2 p124, Bogue Fam p395, Wilcox-Meigs p47.

JOSIAH - b 18 Aug 1754 Stratford, Fairfield Co CT s/JOSIAH & ELIZABETH (HUBBELL) WILCOX; Ref: Wilcox-Meigs p58.

JOSIAH - b ca 1760 brother of BIRDEN; m widow ANNA WALSWORTH; ch JAMES, ANNA; Rev War; d 1836 Batavia, Genesee Co NY; Ref: Fiske Card File.

JOSIAH - b 22 Aug 1770 Killingworth, Middlesex Co CT s/ELNATHAN & THANKFUL (BENNET) WILCOX; Ref: Wilcox-Meigs p65, Barbour's VR Killingworth v2 p81, Your Ancestors v4 #1&2 p498.

JOSIAH - b 1772 CT; m ELEANOR ----- who was b 1788; Res Caneadea, Allegany Co NY; ch ABBY SHOOP, MARY M; Ref: 1850 Census Caneadea NY p195 Dw# 202.

JOSIAH - b 23 Jun 1774 Middletown, Newport Co RI s/JOSIAH & SARAH (-----) WILCOX; m 19 Aug 1795 HANNAH BEEBE; ch SARAH, prob JOSIAH; Ref: Arnold v4 pt3 pp20, Your Ancestors v12 #4 p1503, French's Hist of Westchester Co NY p469.

JOSIAH - b 10 Jul 1774 s/ELIAB & JERUSHA (SPENCER) WILCOX of Dover, Dutchess Co NY; d 1813 unmarried; Ref: Your Ancestors v4 #3&4 p522.

JOSIAH/JOSEPH - m ca 1799 Charlestown, Washington Co RI HULDAH SHERMAN; ch GEORGE S, MARY, REBECCA, EDWARD, HANNAH, REBECCA, NANCY; Ref: Arnold v5 pt5 p28.

JOSIAH - b 16 Dec 1778; m HANNAH BULLISS d/GERMAN/JARMOND BULLISS of Manchester, Bennington Co VT; Res Dutchess Co NY; Ref: DAR Mag v87 p1288, Fiske Card File.

JOSIAH - b 1781; d 05 Jan 1826 Falmouth, Barnstable Co MA; Ref: Falmouth VR p262.

JOSIAH - s/GIDEON & PHEBE (DAVENPORT) of Tiverton, Newport Co RI; m 02 Nov 1800 HANNAH SEABURY d/CONSTANT & SUSANNAH (-----) SEABURY of Little Compton, Newport Co RI; Ref: Arnold v4 pt5 p72, See Gideon, See RIGR v7 #3 p242.

JOSIAH - b 05 Jun 1785 Exeter, Washington Co RI s/ISAAC & REBECCA (BARBER) WILCOX; Ref: Arnold v5 pt3 p63.

JOSIAH - b 1802; poss s/AARON & IRANA (BARNARD) WILCOX; Res Hamilton, Madison Co NY; Ref: Your Ancestors v12 #2 p1438.

JOSIAH 2nd - b 09 May 1804 Middletown, Middlesex Co CT s/JOSIAH & prob HANNAH (BEEBE) WILCOX; m 24 Aug 1828 Berlin, Hartford Co CT CELESTIA WILCOX who was b 11 Sep 1806 & d 28 Mar 1873 Riversville, Fairfield Co CT; ch JOSIAH NORTH; d 13 Jun 1883 Riversville, CT; Ref: Barbour's VR Berlin v1 p32, French's Hist of Westchester Co NY p469.

JOSIAH - b 1811 CT; m ELIZA ----- who was b 1811 NY; ch EVALINA A; Res Cortlandville, Cortland Co NY; Ref: 1850 Census Cortlandville NY p353 Dw# 443.

JOSIAH - b 1811 Orwell, Addison Co VT s/EBENEZER & THANKFUL (STEVENS) WILCOX; m MARY ROOT who was b 1813 VT; Res Orwell VT; ch MARY, HARLAN, JOSIAH; Ref: 1850 Census Orwell VT Reel 920 p41, Your Ancestors v3 #2 p301.

JOSIAH - b 1817 CT; m FRANCES ----- who was b 1825 NY; Res Rome, Oneida Co NY; ch FRANCES A; Ref: 1860 Census Rome NY p204.

JOSIAH - m 2nd be 1835 POLLY ANN LOTTRIDGE; Res Columbus, Chenango Co NY; ch ANN C; Ref: Fiske Card File.

JOSIAH - b 01 Jan 1820 s/ O G & E (-----) WILCOX; Res Oswego, Oswego Co NY; d 06 Feb 1832; Ref: Tree Talks v10 #3 p176.

JOSIAH - b 1848 VT s/JOSIAH & MARY (-----) WILCOX of Orwell, Addison Co VT; Ref: 1850 Census Orwell VT Reel 920 p41.

JOSIAH A - b 04 Aug 1855 s/ISAIAH CLARK & SALLY (HENRY) WILCOX of Rockdale, Crawford Co PA; m IDA -----; Res Warren Co PA; Ref: Dennis Davis.

JOSIAH NORTH - b 06 Nov 1847 Riversville, Fairfield Co CT s/JOSIAH & CELESTIA (WILCOX) WILCOX; m HENRIETTA LYON who was b 09 Ap 1853 d/WILLIAM PENN & PHOEBE ELIZABETH (SHERWOOD) LYON; Res Port Chester, Westchester Co NY; ch ARTHUR RUSSELL; Ref: French's Hist of Westchester Co p469.

JOSIAH TRYON - b 26 Jul 1819 Middletown, Middlesex Co CT s/JOSEPH & MARIA (TRYON) WILCOX; m 09 Dec 1850 Middletown CT HELEN M WATSON who was b 1830 d/ARNOLD WATSON; Res NYC NY; Ref: Barbour's VR Middletown v3 p91, v4 pp178,202,203.

JOSIAS - b 31 Aug 1737 Portsmouth, Newport Co RI s/JOSEPH & SARAH (-----) WILCOX; Ref: Arnold v4 pt1 p104.

JOSIAS - b 06 Jan 1759 Little Compton, Newport Co RI s/JEREMIAH & SARAH (BAILEY) WILCOX; Ref: Arnold v4 pt6 p193.

JOSIAS CARD - b 19 Jul 1766 Portsmouth, Newport Co RI s/JANE (CARD); Ref: Arnold v4 pt1 p105.

JOTHAM - b 16 Sep 1841; m LUCY PRATT who was b 01 Oct 1846 & d Mar 1931; Res Covert, Seneca Co NY; ch MARY ELLEN; d 24 Aug 1905 bur Pratt Fam Vault Covert NY Cem; Ref: Cem Between The Lakes v2 p310.

JUDAH - m 26 Jan 1777 Dartmouth, Bristol Co MA RICHARD AKIN; Ref: Dartmouth VR p547.

JUDE D - b 1837 NY s/ALBERT & DIADAMA (-----) WILCOX of Georgetown, Madison Co NY; Ref: 1850 Census Georgetown NY p386 Dw# 192.

JUDITH - b 16-- d/DANIEL & ELIZABETH (COOKE) WILCOX; Res Little Compton, Newport Co RI; Ref: Wilcox Excerpts v1 p21.

JUDITH - b 22 Jul 1765 Westport, Bristol Co MA d/SAMUEL & COMFORT (SEABURY) WILCOX; m 09 Dec 1787 GARNER BRIGHTMAN s/HENRY BRIGHTMAN; Ref: Westport VR pp102,252, Your Ancestors v13 #2 p1554.

JUDITH - b 12 Jan 1797 Benson, Rutland Co VT d/MARTIN & JUDITH (CARTER) WILCOX; Ref: VT VR, See Martin.

JUDSON - b 25 Dec 1795 Harpersfield, Delaware Co NY s/JOHN & SARAH (JUDSON) WILCOX; m 28 Aug 1825 LAURA GOODRICH who was b 13 Jul 1804 & d Jan 1900 d/JARED & SARAH (KEELER) GOODRICH; War of 1812 from Catskill, Greene Co NY; ch FRANCES D, GEORGE, MARY GOODRICH, HOWARD, HENRY CLAY, SARAH AUGUSTA, JOHN HUBBARD, EDWARD KEELER; d 07 Jun 1879; Ref: Index of Awards NY p538, Your Ancestors v4 #7&8 pp563,564, 1850 Census Catskill NY p359 Dw# 322.

JUDSON - b 18 Mar 1808 Barkhamsted, Litchfield Co CT s/DANIEL & ESTHER (MERRITT) WILCOX; m 18 Apr 1831 RUTH TULLER who d 19 Dec 1860; m 09 Oct 1861 NANCY S CHAPMAN d/JULIUS & NANCY (DAVIS) CHAPMAN of Southampton, Hampshire Co MA; Res Simsbury, Hartford Co CT, IL, OH; ch ELLA RUTH; d 06 Jun 1879 Simsbury CT; Ref: Rev Allen McLean Rec p20, Your Ancestors v11 #3 p1353, Barbour's VR Simsbury TM4 p521, CT Bible Rec v11 p551.

JULIA - b Jefferson Co NY d/BENJAMIN WILCOX; m JAMES W CLARK; Moved to Portage Co OH 1832; Ref: Hist of Portage Co OH p898.

JULIA - b 03 Nov 1797 Goshen, Litchfield Co CT; d 25 Oct 1818; Ref: CT Bible Rec v7 p656.

JULIA - b 17 Feb 1807 Sandisfield, Berkshire Co MA d/WILLIAM & LUCINDA (GIBBS) WILCOX; m 15 Nov 1827 Portage Co OH RILEY HALLECK; ch GIBBS, LOUISA, WILLIAM, LUCY ANN, MARION, JOEL, BETSEY, ERWIN, HARRIET, ELIJAH, BENJAMIN; Ref: Sandisfield VR p73, Hist of Portage Co OH p635, Desc of Wm Wilcoxson p244.

JULIA - b 05 Aug 1807 Haddam, Middlesex Co CT d/LEVI & MARY (SPENCER) WILCOX; Ref: Desc of Wm Wilcoxson p 133.

JULIA - b 1808 CT d/----- & REBECCA (-----) WILCOX who was b 1762 CT; m ALANSON B BALDWIN who was b 1792 MA; Res Charleston, Portage Co OH; ch LORIN, ELMIRA, ANSLIE; Ref: 1850 Census Charleston OH p154 Dw# 508.

JULIA - of Avon, Hartford Co CT; m 04 Sep 1831 SAMUEL CLYDE of Rome, Oneida Co NY; Ref: Barbour's VR Avon LR1 p565.

JULIA - of New Haven, New Haven Co CT; m 29 Aug 1833 GEORGE CLINTON TALLMAN of NY; Ref: Barbour's VR New Haven v4 p142.

JULIA - of Stratford, Fairfield Co CT; m 27 Nov 1833 NORTON NICHOLS of Trumbull, Fairfield Co CT; Ref: Barbour's VR Stratford vA p43.

JULIA - b 11 Sep 1816; m JOHN LOCKWOOD; d 16 Nov 1878 age 62y 2m 5d; bur Maple Grove Cem Granville, Licking Co OH; Ref: OH Cem Rec p206.

JULIA - b 13 Oct 1822 Rush, Monroe Co NY d/ELIAS & NANCY (SCOVIL) WILCOX; d 10 Dec 1877 Romeo, MI; Ref: Mrs Jonathan R Hix.

JULIA - b 07 Jan 1826 Westfield, Middlesex Co CT d/ELISHA BACON & HEPZIBAH (CORNWELL) WILCOX; m Middletown, Middlesex Co CT 02 Sep 1846 HARTLEY M BOWERS of Berlin, Hartford Co CT; Ref: Early Fam of Wallingford p333, Your Ancestors v3 #5 p379, Barbour's VR Middletown v3 p553, Hist of Wallingford p939.

JULIA - b 1826 d/JOSEPH & EUNICE (DOUGLAS) WILCOX of Verona, Oneida Co NY; m ALMON D PETTS s/LOUIS & THANKFUL (-----) PETTS; Ref: Your Ancestors v4 #3&4 p521.

JULIA - b 1828 d/ELISHA & ZERVIAH (ANDREWS) WILCOX of Chautauqua Co NY & Boone Co IL; Ref: Your Ancestors v12 #1 p1407.

JULIA - b 1836 NY; Res Pawling, Dutchess Co NY; Ref: 1850 Census Pawling NY p234 Dw# 245.

JULIA - b 1838 d/JEREMIAH W & SABRINA A (BROWN) WILCOX of Stonington, New London Co CT; Ref: 1850 Census Stonington CT Reel 432 #48 p256.

JULIA - b 1844 NY d/----- & SUSAN (-----) WILCOX of Greenwich, Washington Co NY; Ref: 1850 Census Greenwich NY p232 Dw# 499.

JULIA - b 1845 NY d/OZIAL Jr & SYLVIA (STEVENS) WILCOX; Res Georgetown twnshp, Madison Co NY; Ref: Desc of Wm Wilcoxson p169.

JULIA - b 1845 d/Rev SAMUEL CURTIS & ANNA (-----) WILCOX; Res Owego, Tioga Co NY; d 1845; bur Presbyterian Churchyard Owego NY Ref: Tioga County Cemeteries.

JULIA - b 1849 NY d/GILBERT & ANNA (-----) WILCOX of Concord, Erie Co NY; Ref: 1850 Census Concord NY p52 Dw# 759.

JULIA - b Jul 1850 Deep Cove, N B Canada d/WILLIAM & JANE (DRISCOLL) WILCOX; Single; d 22 Nov 1871 bur Seal Cove Cem; Ref: Desc of Charles Dyer Wilcox p9.

JULIA Mrs - m 25 Jun 1874 Fredonia, Chautauqua Co NY SEWELL S CLARK; Ref: 19th Cent Marriages Reported in Fredonia Censor p119.

JULIA - b 1852 Genesee Co NY d/RUSSELL & MARIAH (BURBEE) WILCOX; m WARD DELUDE; Ref: Your Ancestors v14 #3 p1669, See Russell.

JULIA - b 24 Apr 1886 d/JAMES AUGUSTUS & LILLIAN (COWEN) WILCOX of Danbury, Fairfield Co CT; m 17 Jun 1908 Bridgeport, Fairfield Co CT HARRY J WARDE of NYC; 4 ch; Ref: Desc of Wm Wilcoxson p259.

JULIA A - b 23 Nov 1806 Cortlandville, Cortland Co NY d/EBEN & RHODA (MERRILL) WILCOX; m JOHN PEET s/GIDEON PEET; Ref: Fiske Card File.

JULIA A - m 18 May 1836 Middletown, Middlesex Co CT EDWIN BURR of Haddam, Middlesex Co CT; Ref: Barbour's VR Middletown v3 p421.

JULIA A - b 25 Nov 1822 d/EZRA AARON & SARAH (DAVIS) WILCOX; m HENRY FROST; Res Somerset, Niagara Co NY; Ref: Col Fam of US v5 p555.

JULIA A - b 1825 Canton, Hartford Co CT; m 04 Jul 1849 ELI S CASE who was b 1819 Barkhamsted, Litchfield Co CT; Ref: Barbour's VR Barkhamsted v1 p230, Canton v1 p33.

JULIA A - b 1827 N Providence, Providence Co RI d/ROBERT & DEBORAH (COOKE) WILCOX; m 08 Nov 1848 Pawtucket, Providence Co RI EDWIN JERAULD who was b 1827 s/HENRY & LOUISA (-----) JERAULD; Ref: Arnold v9 p367, See Robert.

JULIA A - b 17 Feb 1838 Portage Co OH d/ALEXANDER HAMILTON & BETSEY (DIVER) WILCOX of Deerfield, Portage Co OH; m 24 Nov 1858 WILLIAM B WILSON of Palmyra, Portage Co OH; d 05 Apr 1872; Ref: Hist of Portage Co OH p635, 1850 Census Deerfield OH p186 Dw# 1001, Desc of Wm Wilcoxson p244.

JULIA A - d Apr 1842 Sturbridge, Worcester Co MA; Ref: Sturbridge VR p39.

JULIA A - b 1845 NY d/OZIAL Jr & SYLVIA (STEVENS) WILCOX of Georgetown, Madison Co NY; Ref: 1850 Census Georgetown NY p387 Dw# 208, See Ozial Jr.

JULIA ADELLA - b 13 Mar 1871 Madison, New Haven Co CT d/JOHN & ADELLA S (DIBBLE) WILCOX; Ref: Wilcox-Meigs p106, Fam of Early Guilford p1214, Desc of Wm Wilcoxson p264.

JULIA ALTHEA - b 26 Jan 1853 d/AUSTIN WILCOX; Ref: CT Bible Rec v15 p254.

JULIANNE - b ca 1817 Douglas, Worcester Co MA d/AUGUSTUS & LYDIA (YEATS) WILCOX; m 19 May 1837 ABEL ROBBINS; Ref: Your Ancestors v11 #4 p1397.

JULIA ANN - b 04 Jul 1809 Middletown, Middlesex Co CT d/BENJAMIN & RACHEL (WILCOX) WILCOX; Ref: Barbour's VR Middletown v3 p88.

JULIA ANN - d/SILVESTER WILCOX m 20 Dec 1829 EDMUND ROMNEY Albany, Albany Co NY; Ref: 10,000 VR of Eastern NY p66.

JULIA ANN - b 1813 d/LYMAN & LINA (DICKENSON) WILCOX; m 19 Aug 1830 LEVI R BARNES of Southington, Hartford Co CT; Res E Berlin & New Britain, Hartford Co CT; d 16 May 1864; Ref: MUH p757, Barbour's VR Berlin v1 p40.

JULIA ANN - b 13 Jul 1817 Haddam, Middlesex Co CT d/LYMAN & EMILY (HUBBARD) WILCOX; Ref: Desc of Wm Wilcox p130.

JULIA ANN - b 1820 d/SAMUEL & ABIGAIL (WHITE) WILCOX of Whitestown, Oneida Co NY; d 19 Mar 1859; Ref: Your Ancestors v4 #1&2 p500.

JULIA ANN - m 16 Apr 1850 New London, New London Co CT ELIAS DAVIS; both of Stonington, New London Co CT; Ref: Barbour's VR New London v4 p153.

JULIA ANN - d/AMOS & ELIZABETH (POLLOCK) WILCOX; m MORRIS CRAYTOR; Ref: Desc of Wm Wilcoxson p243.

JULIA ANN - m ca 1865 JOHN D FLINT; Res Germantown, Columbia Co NY; ch ALLIE M; Ref: Settlers of Germantown NY v1 p94.

JULIA ANN - b 03 Sep 1845 d/HERMAN & SUSAN (-----) WILCOX; m 25 Jul 1861 Readsboro, Bennington Co VT WARNER PARSONS who was b 08 Feb 1841 Williamstown, Berkshire Co MA s/ORRIN & FLORINDA (SMITH) PARSONS; ch WILLIAM WARNER, ELLEN, RUTH EVELINE, FREDERICK EUGENE, RUFUS GRANT; d 21 May 1920 Erving, Franklin Co MA; Ref: Parsons Fam Gen pp189,190.

JULIA ANNA TRUMBULL - b 28 Oct 1824 Detroit, Wayne Co MI d/CHARLES & ALMIRA (ROOD) WILCOX; m 07

May 1844 DAVID ANTHONY McNAIR who was b 19 Aug 1809 & d 15 Jun 1895; d 15 Aug 1878; Ref: Wilcox-Meigs p87.

JULIA ANNE - b 31 Dec 1830 d/HENRY & SUSANNA (MILLER) WILCOX of Hillsdale, Columbia Co NY; m FRANCIS FISHERDICK; d 03 Oct 1886; Ref: Wilcox-Meigs p102, Your Ancestors v4 #11&12 p612.

JULIA ANNE - b 1844 Wood Island, N B Canada d/JOB & MARIA (GREEN) WILCOX; m EDWARD JOY who was b North Lubec, Washington Co ME & d 03 Oct 1889; ch NELLIE, ERNEST; m ISAAC URQUHART who d 09 June 1927; d 27 July 1933 bur Wood Island Cem; Ref: Desc of Charles Dyer Wilcox p14.

JULIA E - b 07 Jun 1851 Twin with MARY E d/AARON & ELIZA JANE (MORLEY) WILCOX of Painesville, Lake Co OH; Ref: Your Ancestors v3 #2 p301.

JULIA E - b 1828 Buffalo, Erie Co NY; m 11 May 1848 Norwalk, Fairfield Co CT WILLIAM O BEARD who was b 1813 Trumbull, Fairfield Co CT; Ref: Barbour's VR Norwalk v1 p47.

JULIA E M - b 11 Jan 1827 d/WILLARD & HANNAH (GASKELL) WILCOX of Mendon, Worcester Co MA; m 1844 IRA COOK who was b 1822 s/CLARK & ABIGAIL (-----) COOK; Ref: Your Ancestors v11 #2 p1345.

JULIA ELIZA - b 01 Sep 1838 Berlin, Hartford Co CT d/SAMUEL CURTIS & ELIZA ANN (PARSONS) WILCOX; d 28 Dec 1852 or 02 Apr 1852; Ref: MUH p763, Cutter's CT Fam v2 p658.

JULIA ELLEN - b 10 Feb 1857 Gowanda, Erie Co NY d/JOHN G & ROXY (COWDRY) WILCOX; m 16 May 1876 Gowanda NY GEORGE B SCHRAGEL who was b 14 Aug 1847 Buffalo, Erie Co NY & d 04 Mar 1929; ch ERNEST; d 27 Apr 1931 Buffalo NY; Ref: Alice Wiatr.

JULIA EMMA - b 10 Apr 1837 Stonington, New London Co CT d/JEREMIAH W & SABRINA A (BROWN) WILCOX; Ref: Barbour's VR Stonington v5 p79.

JULIA F - m 27 Nov 1839 Middletown, Middlesex Co CT ISAAC J HOUGH; Ref: Barbour's VR Middletown v3 p463.

JULIA F - b 02 Feb 1854 Halifax, Windham Co VT d/JABEZ & MARY ANN (CROSIER) WILCOX; d 08 Mar 1860; Ref: Halifax Wilcox Fam mss.

JULIA FINETTE - b 29 Nov 1843 Litchfield, Herkimer Co NY d/RODNEY & EMILY (DAVIS) WILCOX; d 08 Feb 1844; Ref: DAR Record Book v15 p4, Your Ancestors v13 #4 p1595.

JULIA H - b 01 Jan 1849; m 05 May 1869 DENISON PALMER; ch ALBERT, EUGENE, LULA, FREDDIE M, ANNA MAY; Ref: Denison Gen p505.

JULIA LOUISE - b 25 Aug 1888 d/MOSES HAVENS & ESTELLA FISH (MAYO) WILCOX; m ALBERT RATHBUN; ch HERBERT, CATH,(sic) NANCY; Ref: Desc of Robert Burrows p120, Denison Gen p505.

JULIA M - m 06 Jan 1853 Meriden, New Haven Co CT HENRY A MOFFIT; Ref: Barbour's VR Meriden v1 p118.

JULIA M - b 1844 d/MARK & HANNAH (-----) WILCOX of Belvidere, Boone Co IL; Ref: Your Ancestors v10 #1 p1202.

JULIA MARIA - b 14 Mar 1861 d/JAMES DAVID & ANNA MARIA (ROBINSON) WILCOX; m WALTER W STEED; Ref: Wilcox-Meigs p120, Desc of Wm Wilcoxson p144.

JULIA MARIE - b 25 Nov 1806 d/NATHAN & MARY (CHENEVARD) WILCOX; Ref: Your Ancestors v3 #9&10 p451.

JULIA MYRA - b 31 Dec 1863 d/EBEN NORTH & MARIE LOUISE (COLE) WILCOX; d af 1938; Ref: Desc of Wm Wilcoxson p260.

JULIA W - b 1821 NY d/MORRIS & PHOEBE (BROWN) WILCOX; Res Whitestown, Oneida Co NY; Ref: 1860 Census Whitestown NY p64, Your Ancestors v4 #3&4 p523.

JULIAN PARSONS - b 03 Apr 1884 s/ORLANDO BOLIVAR & JULIA ELIZABETH (McREYNOLDS) WILCOX; Ref: Wilcox-Meigs p104.

JULIET - b 27 Jun 1826 E Guilford, New Haven Co CT d/HEUSTEN & JULIA (CRAMPTON) WILCOX; m 06 Nov 1847 THOMAS SUMNER FIELD who was b 1824 & d 28 Feb 1884 s/JEDEDIAH & REBECCA (BRADLEY) FIELD; ch FREDERIC W, FRANK SAMUEL, GEORGE CLEVELAND; Ref: Wilcox-Meigs pp87,88, Fam of Early Guilford pp 440,1213, Desc of Wm Wilcoxson p264.

JULIET E - b 1829 Bridport VT d/ABNER & BETSEY (WINES) WILCOX; m 02/11 May 1849 Dr GRIDLEY L

PERKINS; d 1898; Ref: Wilcox-Meigs p100, Your Ancestors v3 #9&10 p450, Desc of Wm Wilcoxson p118.

JULIET ELIZABETH - b 20 Apr 1844 Painesville, Lake Co OH d/AARON & ELIZA JANE (MORLEY) WILCOX; m 16 Oct 1872 CHARLES E DOOLITTLE of Hamilton, Hancock Co IL; Ref: Wilcox-Meigs p98, 1850 Census Painesville OH Reel 259 p181.

JULIETTE - b ca 1794 d/GIDEON & ANNA (HANFORD) WILCOX; Ref: Desc of Wm Wilcoxson p36.

JULIETTE - b 30 Apr 1808 Winchester, Litchfield Co CT d/DANIEL & MEHITABLE (WRIGHT) WILCOX; Res Great Barrington, Berkshire Co MA; Ref: Annals of Winchester CT p329,330, Barbour's VR Winchester v2 p107.

JULIETTE - b 1828 NY d/FRANCIS CLARK & LAURA (-----) WILCOX of Franklin, Delaware Co NY; Ref: 1850 Census Franklin NY p43 Dw# 226.

JULIETTE - b 10 Sep 1835 Middletown, Middlesex Co CT d/NATHAN & POLLY (-----) WILCOX; Ref: Barbour's VR Middletown v4 p30.

JULIETTE - m 16 Nov 1847 Madison, New Haven Co CT THOMAS S FIELD; Ref: Barbour's VR Madison v2 p119.

JULIETTE - b 14 Mar 1854 d/JOHN & SARA H (BROOKS) WILCOX; m CARLOS L SHEPARD; Ref: Your Ancestors v3 #5 p375.

JULIUS - b May 1769 E Guilford, New Haven Co CT s/EZRA & ESTHER (MEIGS) WILCOX; m 21 Sep 1797 ELIZABETH BROWN who was b 29 Apr 1778 CT & d 03 Dec 1855 d/HUGH & OLIVE (SAGE) BROWN; Res Middlebury, Addison Co VT; ch HARVEY, MARY, GILES SAGE, GEORGE, ELIZABETH BROWN, GILES SAGE, MARY OLIVE, JULIUS, HENRY J; d be 1850; Ref: Desc of Wm Wilcoxson p27, Fam of Early Guilford pp 154, 1209,1210, Gen of CT Fam v1 pp244,245, 1850 Census Middlebury VT Reel 920 p148.

JULIUS - b 1810 s/EZRA & LAVICIA (HERRICK) WILCOX of East Bloomfield, Ontario Co NY; m SOPHIA ----- who was b 1811 Canada; Res Springwater, Livingston Co NY; ch GEORGE H; Ref: Your Ancestors v10 #2 p1225, Desc of Wm Wilcoxson p205.

JULIUS - b 13 Mar or 26 Apr 1812 Granville, Hampden Co MA s/ELEAZER CURTIS & CYNTHIA (NOBLE) WILCOX; m NAOMI CARRIER 01 Mar 1837; d Af 1876 Glenwood, Schuyler Co MO; Ref: A Wilcox Book p19, Desc of Thomas Noble p447.

JULIUS - b 14 Mar 1817 Middlebury, Addison Co VT s/JULIUS & ELIZABETH (BROWN) WILCOX; m 16 Oct 1845 SARAH ANN NICHOLS who was b 09 Dec 1820 & d 14 May 1856 d/Rev NOAH & MARY ANN (-----) NICHOLS; m ca 1858 MATTIE JANE HOLTON d/ASA & ORRA (-----) HOLTON; Res Warrenton, Warren Co N C; ch by 1st wife CORA ELLEN, ELLA GRAVES, JULIUS HARVEY, NELSON GRAVES, NELSON GRAVES; ch by 2nd wife MARY KATE, MAURICE HOLTON, FRANK EVARTS, HELEN LECKIE, MATTIE JULIUS; d 29 Jun 1865; Ref: Gen of CT Fam v1 p245.

JULIUS - m 07 Jul 1819 Kinderhook, Columbia Co NY MARIA GOES/HOES who was b 06 Jan 1793 d/JOHN L & MARYTJE (VAN ALAN) GOES; Ref: NYG&BR v82 p148.

JULIUS Hon - d 30 May 1850; Ref: Deaths from NY Herald p551.

JULIUS - b 1837 VT s/AMON & EMALINE (MacDONALD) WILCOX of Middlebury, Addison Co VT; Ref: 1850 Census Middlebury VT Reel 920 p149, See Amon.

JULIUS - m be 1867 HANNAH LEACH; Res Bakersfield, Franklin Co VT; ch LAURA E; Ref: Branches & Twigs v13 #3 p99.

JULIUS ABNER - b 02 Oct 1879 Crown Point, Essex Co NY s/EDWIN D & ALICE (MINER) WILCOX; Ref: Wilcox-Meigs p119, Your Ancestors v3 #9&10 p450, Desc of Wm Wilcoxson p118.

JULIUS AUGUSTUS/AUGUSTINE - b 20 Aug 1825 Bridport, Addison Co VT s/ABNER & BETSEY (WINES) WILCOX; Ref: Wilcox-Meigs p100, 1850 Census Bridport VT Reel 920 p8, Your Ancestors v3 #9&10 p450, Desc of Wm Wilcoxson p118.

JULIUS E - b 1843 MI; m MARY -----; Father b VT & Mother b NY; Res Livonia, Wayne Co MI; ch JENNIE, HARRY; Ref: Detroit Gen Mag v48 #3 p107.

JULIUS HARVEY - b 02 Jun 1852 s/JULIUS & SARAH ANN (NICHOLS) WILCOX; Single; Ref: Gen of CT Fam v1 p245.

JULIUS MARVIN - b 12 Nov 1842 Panama, Chautauqua Co NY s/GEORGE & SARAH (SPENCER) WILCOX; m 07 May 1871 Townville, PA MARY ELIZABETH HOTCHKISS who was b 13 May 1843 Clarks Corners PA & d 09 Jan 1891 d/JOHN & SUSAN (HATHAWAY) HOTCHKISS; Res Harmony, Chautauqua Co NY, Rockdale, Crawford Co PA; ch GEORGE, JOHN HOTCHKISS, IRENE, SARA SUSAN; d 07 Apr 1917; Ref: A Wilcox Book pp 109,117,118, 1850 Census Harmony NY p267 Dw# 621.

JUSTUS - b 10 Dec 1749 Middletown, Middlesex Co CT s/ELIJAH & ABIGAIL (CHURCHILL) WILCOX; m MARY WHITMORE of Cornwall, Litchfield Co CT; ch FRANCIS W, ABIGAIL, JUSTUS, WHITMORE; Ref: Your Ancestors v3 #6 p401, Barbour's VR Middletown v1 p18.

JUSTUS - b 1800 s/JUSTUS & MARY (WHITMORE) WILCOX of Cornwall, Litchfield Co CT; d 10 Mar 1801; Ref: Your Ancestors v3 #6 p401.

JUSTUS - b 1811 Southington, Hartford Co CT s/FRANCIS W & PAULINA (ANDREWS) WILCOX; d 1814; Ref: Your Ancestors v3 #7&8 p427.

JUSTUS AZEL - b 01 Aug 1874 s/JOHN HENRY OWEN & MARY (YOUNG) WILCOX; Ref: Your Ancestors v12 #2 p1436.

JUSTUS DENSLOW - b 27 Mar 1800 s/STERLING & SOPHIA (DENSLOW) WILCOX; m 1825 EMELINE HAYES who was b 21 Aug 1805 & d 07 Apr 1881 d/ALPHEUS & BETSEY (HIGLEY) HAYES; Res Canton, Hartford Co CT; ch LUCIAN SUMNER, CHARLES HAYES, THAMES ANDREW, MASON GOOD, ELIZABETH EMELINE, CLEVELAND JUSTUS; d 27 Mar 1871 West Granby, Hartford Co CT; Ref: NYG&BR v78 p179, Your Ancestors v11 #3 p1354.

--- K ---

KATE - b Mar 1850 NY d/GEORGE & ELIZABETH (-----) WILCOX of Pomfret, Chautauqua Co NY; Ref: 1860 Census Pomfret NY p533 Dw# 1576.

KATE - m 14 Dec 1870 Fredonia, Chautauqua Co NY THOMAS A BARBER; Ref: 19th Cent Marriages Reported in Fredonia Censor p119.

KATE ELIZABETH - b 07 Mar 1858 NYC NY d/VINCENT MEIGS & CATHERINE MILLICENT (WEBB) WILCOX; d 07 Oct 1858; Ref: Wilcox-Meigs p112, Cutter's CT Fam v4 p1769, Fam of Early Guilford p1216.

KATE L - b 1850 d/WILLIAM S & SARAH E (DAY) WILCOX of Carlton, Orleans Co NY; Ref: Your Ancestors v11 #1 p1320.

KATE MARIA - d 20 Jul 1854; Ref: Deaths from NY Herald p551.

KATHERINE/CATHERINE - b 25 Feb 1717 Dartmouth, Bristol Co MA d/DANIEL & SARAH (-----) WILCOX; m OLIVER BRIGGS; Ref: Dartmouth VR p302, Your Ancestors v10 #3 p1267.

KATHERINE - b 17 Sep 1741 Dartmouth, Bristol Co MA d/STEPHEN & MARY (RICKETSON) WILCOX; m 28 Mar 1765 THOMAS CORNELL; Ref: Your Ancestors v10 #3 p1268.

KATHERINE - d/OTHANIEL & NANCY (TILLINGHAST) WILCOX of Exeter, Washington Co RI; m 18-- JOHN VALETTE; no ch; Ref: Westcott Hist p108.

KATHERINE ADELE - b 17 Dec 1886 Rockdale, Crawford Co PA d/GEORGE NELSON & CLARISSA ADELE (HOTCHKISS) WILCOX; m ROBERT A WILSON; Ref: A Wilcox Book p133.

KATHERINE GOODENOW - b 03 May 1871 NYC NY d/WILLIAM HENRY & ANNE HOLMES (GOODENOW) WILCOX; d 04 Aug 1871; Ref: Wilcox-Meigs p99.

KATHERINE MAYO - b 04 Dec 1884 d/MOSES H & ESTELLA FISH (MAYO) WILCOX; Ref: Desc of Robert Burrows p120.

KATHLEEN - b 13 Jun 1877 Wood Island, N B Canada d/ABEL & HANNAH (GREEN) WILCOX; m WILLIAM GUPTILL who was b 04 Mar 1883 Moose River, Somerset ME & d 23 Apr 1934; ch ROSWELL, RONALD, WILMINA, MILDRED, MERLE, FLORENCE VIRGINIA, REGINA EULALIA; d 11 Oct 1956 both bur Wood Island N B Canada; Ref: Desc of Charles Dyer Wilcox p27.

KATIE - b ca 1877 Chautauqua Co NY d/MAINE & LYDIA A (PRICE) WILCOX; m GEORGE CLARK; d 3 months after marriage; Ref: Wilcox Hist mss.

KATIE BELLE - b 11 Jul 1868 Smyrna, Chenango Co NY d/WILLIAM STOVER & ANNA MARIA (PARKER) WILCOX; m 29 Jun 1892 HORACE D COVELL of Pomfret Landing, Windham Co CT; Ref: John Parker Gen p395.

KENNETH - b 08 Nov 1889 s/Dr DeWITT GILBERT & JENNIE (GREEN) WILCOX; d 23 Jul 1890; Ref: Desc of Wm Wilcoxson p128.

KEZIAH - b 03 Jun 1742 Killingworth, Middlesex Co CT d/JOSIAH & KEZIAH (KELSEY) WILCOX; Res Dutchess Co NY; Ref: Desc of Wm Wilcoxson p43, Your Ancestors v4 #3&4 p521, Barbour's VR Killingworth v2 p157.

KEZIAH - b ca 1770 Dutchess Co NY; m EPHRAIM HAMBLIN; m Dr JOHN D BULL; Ref: Nutmegger v11 #2 p235.

KEZIAH/KESIAH - b 1849 PA d/ALFRED & KEZIAH (CALHOUN) WILCOX; m 17 Sep 1871 BENJAMIN KNEE of Lancaster Co NE who was b 1842 IN s/JOHN & REBECCA (-----) KNEE; Ref: Nebr & Midwest Gen Rec v17 #2 p35.

KEZZIE - b 1862 prob d/ELIHU & PHILOMILA (-----) WILCOX of Leon, Cattaraugus Co NY; m ----- CARNAHAN; d 1886 bur Franklin Cem Leon NY; Ref: Alice Wiatr.

KITTY - b 1865 prob d/ELIHU & PHILMILA (-----) WILCOX of Leon, Cattaraugus Co NY; d 1867 bur Franklin Cem Leon NY; Ref: Alice Wiatr.

KITTY CORNELIA - b 1864 d/GILBERT ANSON LIVINGSTON & HARRIETT SABRINA (-----) WILCOX; m 18 Jun 1885 Dr LYMAN GUY BARTON; ch LYMAN GUY, PHILIP BENNING, NORMA KEEFE; Ref: Your Ancestors v9 #3 p1151.

--- L ---

L D - m 13 Nov 1841 DEXTER CHAPIN; Ref: Marriages from NY Herald p265.

L ADLINE - b 21 Aug 1876; related to JOSEPH NELSON WILCOX; d 25 Nov 1936, bur Graham Co AZ; Ref: Arizona Death Rec v1 p1391.

LACEFILLIAS - b 1847 NY ch/CALVIN & ELIZA (-----) WILCOX of Black Brook, Clinton Co NY; Ref: 1850 Census, Florence Arnhart.

LAFAYETTE - b ca 1825 s/JESSE & NANCY ANN (TIFANY) WILCOX; Res CT; Ref: Mrs Wm Richardson.

LAFAYETTE - b 1846 OH s/LEANDER & JANE (MOE) WILCOX of Avon, Lorain Co OH; Ref: 1850 Census Lorain Co OH, Carol Wood.

LAFAYETTE T - b 04 Apr 1866; m ANNA YOHE who was b 1876 & d 1946; d 27 Sep 1935 Preston, New London Co CT; Ref: Cem Records of New London Co CT v2 p40.

LAMIRA PRUDENCE - b 03 May 1817 Sandisfield, Berkshire Co MA d/JOEL & ROXEY (-----) WILCOX; Ref: Sandisfield MA VR p73, Fiske Card File.

LAMONT - b 1801-1810; Res Augusta, Oneida Co NY; 2 sons & 2 daus in 1840; Ref: 1840 Census Oneida Co NY.

LANDFORD - b 1845 NY ch/CALVIN & ELIZA (-----) WILCOX of Black Brook, Clinton Co NY; Ref: 1850 Census, Florence Arnhart.

LANNA C - b Jan 1889 WI d/GEORGE W & EMMA C (-----) WILCOX; Father b NY; Res Eagle, Richland Co WI; Ref: 1900 Soundex Richland Co WI.

LANSING H - b 07 Jan 1809 NY s/WILLIAM & LORAINE/LURANAH (GREEN) WILCOX; m 15 Sep 1830 MIRANDA HOLMES who was b 17 June 1808 NY & d 15 June 1867; purchased Lot 21 Napoli, Cattaraugus Co NY; ch MARY S, ALVIN H, CHARLES P, HELEN S, ELIZA L, LUCY E, ZELOTIS, HOSMER H; d 27 Mar 1894 Napoli NY; Ref: Cem Inscr Napoli NY, Cutter's Western NY v1 p257, Hist of Cattaraugus Co NY p478, 1860 Census Napoli NY Reel 653 #726 p60, 1850 Census Napoli NY p63 Dw# 138.

LANSING A - b 1829 WI; Res Fenner, Madison Co NY with CYRENUS WILCOX; Ref: 1850 Census Fenner NY p116 Dw# 1685.

LARA ORANDA - b 04 May 1821 NY d/JEREMIAH & MELINDA (ABBEY) WILCOX of Springville, Erie Co NY; d 26 Mar 1839 Ashford, Cattaraugus Co NY bur Springville; Ref: Jane Smith.

LARKIN - b ca 1764 Exeter, Washington Co RI s/ABRAHAM & LYDIA (HARRINGTON) WILCOX; d ca 1780; Ref: Your Ancestors v4 #7&8 p561.

LARKIN - 1781 RI; ch JOHN & prob SUSAN; Res Parish, Oswego Co NY; Ref: 1850 Census Parish NY p4 Dw# 50.

LARKIN - b 1790-1800; Res Ellery, Chautauqua Co NY in 1840; Ref: 1840 Census Chautauqua Co NY p80.

LARRY - m LAURA -----; Res Monroe Co NY; 8 ch; d 03 May 1845; Ref: Tree Talks v12 #1 p38.

LAURA - b 25 May 1797 Alford, Berkshire Co MA d/RUFUS & SARAH (ADAMS) WILCOX; m FRANCIS HERRICK of Wellington, Middlesex Co MA; Ref: Your Ancestors v9 #3 p1154, Desc of Wm Wilcoxson p200.

LAURA - of Canton, Hartford Co CT; m 30 Nov 1825 New Hartford, Litchfield Co CT ----- BEARDSLEY of Sandisfield, Berkshire Co MA; Ref: Barbour's VR New Hartford v3 p12.

LAURA - m 15 Feb 1815 Twinsburg, Summit Co OH HARVEY MURRAY s/JESSE & RACHEL (NORTON) MURRAY; Ref: Fam of Early Guilford p853.

LAURA - b 06 Aug 1813 Thetford, Orange Co VT d/DAVID & LUCINDA (HORSFORD) WILCOX; Ref: Horsford/Hosford Family p72.

LAURA - 2nd m 07 Jan 1806 at Cheshire, Berkshire Co MA JOHN HALL of Lanesboro, Berkshire Co MA; Ref: Fiske Card File.

LAURA - b 29 Oct 1818 Lenox, Madison Co NY Twin with ALANSON CASE d/ALANSON CASE & IRENE (JOHNSON) WILCOX;; Ref: Pioneers of Madison Co NY p280.

LAURA - b 11 Aug 1820 d/ABNER & SARAH (HORTON) WILCOX; Ref: Desc of Wm Wilcoxson p141.

LAURA - b 1836 Geauga Co OH d/NATHAN BENJAMIN & SAMANTHA (BROOKS) WILCOX; m FRANK HARTMAN 1855 AR; Ref: Dan Williams.

LAURA - m FRANK G SLOANE of Sandusky, Erie Co OH who was b 06 Sep 1857 s/RUSH R & SARAH E (MORRISON) SLOANE; ch ESTHER MORRISON; Ref: Firelands Pioneer NS v25 p296.

LAURA - b 1838 NY d/WILLIAM & ELIZABETH (-----) WILCOX of Kinderhook, Columbia Co NY; Ref: 1850 Census Kinderhook NY p366 Dw# 311.

LAURA - b 1839 Clockville, Madison Co NY d/SALMON & HANNAH (BUYEA) WILCOX; Ref: Pioneers of Madison Co NY p281.

LAURA - b 1878 Clockville, Madison Co NY d/ELISHA & ELIZABETH (HALL) WILCOX; Ref: Pioneers of Madison Co NY p281.

LAURA A - b 06 Oct 1841 d/JOHN WILCOX; m ----- FLETCHER; m 27 Feb 1870 CHARLES FOWLER s/ORREN STARR & ABIGAIL (CRAMPTON) FOWLER of Madison, New Haven Co CT; ch KATIE ELVIRA; Ref: Fam of Early Guilford p494.

LAURA A - of N Canton, Hartford Co CT m 23 Sep 1849 CHARLES G THOMPSON of New Hartford, Litchfield Co CT; Ref: Barbour's VR Canton v1 p34.

LAURA A - b 04 Oct 1849 d/CHARLES AUGUSTUS & CYNTHIA A (JOHNSON) WILCOX of Lagrange, Lorain Co OH; d in infancy; Ref: Desc of Wm Wilcoxson p194.

LAURA ADELAIDE - b 1866 Deep Cove, N B Canada d/WILLIAM & JANE (DRISCOLL) WILCOX; m LESTER KENT s/OLIVER & MARY (DAKIN) KENT; ch ASHTON WILLIAM; d Apr 1895 bur Seal Cove N B; Ref: Desc of Charles Dyer Wilcox p12.

LAURA ALMENA - b 24 Sep 1860 Orangeville, Wyoming Co NY d/ALFRED SISSON & ALMENA COLE (WEAVER) WILCOX; m BENONI CARPENTER; Ref: Your Ancestors v4 #5&6 p542.

LAURA ANN - b 29 Dec 1847 Smyrna, Chenango Co NY d/WILLIAM STOVER & ANNA MARIA (PARKER) WILCOX; m 22 May 1870 N Norwich, Chenango Co NY EDWIN G BROWN s/SYLVESTER G & REBECCA (MARTIN) BROWN; Res Woodhull, Steuben Co NY; ch LYNN D, EVA MARIA, BERTHA; Ref: John Parker Gen p394.

LAURA DIMON - b 1841 RI; d 18 Nov 1856 Bristol, Bristol Co RI; Ref: Arnold v8 p220.

LAURA E - b 18 Aug 1851 d/CHARLES AUGUSTUS & CYNTHIA A (JOHNSON) WILCOX of Lagrange, Lorain Co OH; m NELSON U BARNUM; Ref: Desc of Wm Wilcoxson p194.

LAURA E - m 20 Nov 1870 RI EDWARD P HART; Ref: Arnold v7 p583.

LAURA E - b 1867 Bakersfield, Franklin Co VT d/JULIUS & HANNAH (LEACH) WILCOX; m 03 Apr 1883 ALFREDAH E GOING who was b 1858 Dixon, Lee Co IL s/GEORGE W & MARIAH J (CASE) GOING; Res Brownington, Orleans Co VT; farmer; Ref: Branches & Twigs v13 #3 p99.

LAURA JANE - b 1852 Canada; m 1868 IA JOHN WESLEY NIMS; d 1911; Ref: Iowa Surnames v3 p695.

LAURA LOUISA - d/SAMUEL WILCOX of Newport, Newport Co RI; m May 1829 NY BENJAMIN A MUMFORD; Ref: Arnold v16 p587.

LAURA PARSONS - b 17 Mar 1837 E Berlin, Hartford Co CT d/SAMUEL CURTIS & ELIZA ANNE (PARSONS) WILCOX; d 28 Dec 1866; Ref: MUH p763, Cutter's CT Fam v2 p658.

LAURA ROSE - b 30 Jun 1899 Lytton, Sac Co IA d/CHARLES TRUMAN & IZELL EMMA (LEE) WILCOX; m 1920 DAVID MAITLAND CHRISTIE; Ref: Jean Klooster.

LAURETTA - b 1829 NY d/----- & POLLY (-----) WILCOX; Res Milford, Otsego Co NY with brother MONROE WILCOX; Ref: 1850 Census Milford NY p115.

LAVINA - b ca 1782 d/SYLVANUS & CHESTINA (CURTIS) WILCOX of Nine Partners, Dutchess Co NY & Alford, Berkshire Co MA; Ref: Desc of Wm Wilcoxson p190b.

LAVINA - b 09 Jan 1787 Halifax, Windham Co VT d/STEPHEN & ELINOR (EWING) WILCOX; Ref: VT VR, Halifax Wilcox Fam mss.

LAVINA - m be 1798 ENOS PECK; Res Pompey, Onondaga Co NY; ch CHLOE; Ref: Desc of Robert Waterman v1 p489.

LAVINA - b 1808 d/THOMAS LILLIBRIDGE & ANNA (HOXIE) WILCOX; m ----- RICHER; Ref: Your Ancestors v3 #4 p347.

LAVINA - b 1846 d/LEWIS & NANCY (-----) WILCOX of Johnsonburg, Wyoming Co NY; Ref: Your Ancestors v14 #3 p1670, 1850 Census Java NY p53 Dw# 803.

LAVINA ARMINA - b 23 Jun 1842 Orangeville, Wyoming Co NY d/ALFRED SISSON & ALMENA COLE (WEAVER) WILCOX; m JONATHAN SPINK; Ref: Your Ancestors v4 #5&6 p542.

LAVINIA/LOVINIA - b 19 Jul 1758 E Guilford, New Haven Co CT d/EZRA & ESTHER (MEIGS) WILCOX; m BELA DUDLEY; Ref: Wilcox-Meigs p52, Desc of Wm Wilcoxson p27, Fam of Early Guilford p1209.

LAVINIA - b 31 Jan 1797 Middletown, Middlesex Co CT d/JOSEPH & MIRIAM (BACON) WILCOX; d 24 Sep 1843; Ref: Early Fam of Wallingford p332, Your Ancestors v3 #4 p352, Barbour's VR Middletown v2 p319, Hist of Wallingford p938.

LAVINIA - m 05 Oct 1813 Middletown, Middlesex Co CT EBENEZER BACON 2nd; Ref: Barbour's VR Middletown v3 p11.

LAVINIA - b ca 1800 NY d/GEORGE & MARY (-----) WILCOX of Sodus, Wayne Co NY; Ref: Your Ancestors v11 #1 p1319.

LAVINIA - b 03 Jun 1801 d/GEORGE & SUSANNAH (HUMPHREY) WILCOX; m 18 Mar 1824 LYMAN COUCH; Ref: Desc of Wm Wilcoxson p223.

LAVINIA - b 29 Jul 1825 Westfield, Middlesex Co CT d/HEZEKIAH & RAMA (ROBERTS) WILCOX; m 19 Nov 1845 WILLIAM F HALL of Meriden, New Haven Co CT; Ref: Early Fam of Wallingford p333, Your Ancestors v3 #4 p352, Barbour's VR Middletown v3 p541, Hist of Wallingford p939.

LAVINIA - d/JOSEPH & MELISSA (ABBOTT) WILCOX of Madison Co NY; m ARASPA PADDOCK; Ref: Your Ancestors v12 #3 1464.

LAVINIA - of Stratford, Fairfield Co CT; m HERBERT/HENRY SMITH who was b 26 Aug 1842 s/LAZARUS NORTHRUP & ADELINE (SMITH) SMITH; ch LILLIAN AMELIA, EUGENE, HOWARD; Ref: Fam of Early Milford CT p665.

LAWRENCE - b ca 1792 Amenia, Dutchess Co NY s/AARON & ELIZABETH (BELDEN) WILCOX of NY; m LAURA PALMER; Res Perinton, Monroe Co NY; ch CATHERINE, HOMER, MILTON, ELIZABETH, LOUISA, LAWSON, MORTIMER; Ref: NYG&BR v40 p104, Desc of Wm Wilcoxson p162.

LAWRENCE - b 1828 OH s/WILLIAM & LUCINDA (GIBBS) WILCOX; m CLARISSA -----; Res Deerfield, Portage Co OH; ch URSALA; Ref: 1850 Census Deerfield OH p195.

LAWRENCE A - b 1840 NY s/CONSIDER & MARY (-----) WILCOX of Almond, Allegany Co NY; Ref: 1850 Census Almond NY p74 Dw# 777.

LAWSON - b 1833 s/LAWRENCE & LAURA (PALMER) WILCOX of Perinton, Monroe Co NY; Ref: Desc of Wm Wilcoxson p162.

LAWSON LIONEL - b 06 May 1897 Prob Wood, Island, N B Canada s/CASWELL LEWIS & NELLIE (SCHOFIELD) WILCOX; m HILDA WILCOX who was b 03 Mar 1905 & d 29 Mar 1956; m ALFRETTA INGALS who d

13 Jan 1974; ch by 1st wife KEITH, BRENTON CLAIR, HAZEN FREDERICK; d 16 Jun 1976 bur Wesleyan Cem; Ref: Desc of Charles Dyer Wilcox p26.

LAWTON - b 27 Jan 1799 Exeter, Washington Co RI s/ASA & ELEANOR (LAWTON) WILCOX; Ref: Your Ancestors v4 #11&12 p610.

LAWTON H "LOT" - b 13 Sep 1833 s/EDWIN & CANDACE (GILBERT) WILCOX; m 21 Feb 1860 E Bloomfield, Ontario Co NY MARY JANE PARKER who was b 18 Jul 1842 & d 22/28 Feb 1919/20 Holcomb, Ontario Co NY d/AARON COLLINS & BARBARA ANN (CATOR) PARKER; ch EMMA, GEORGE COLLINS, CHARLES GILBERT, IDA MUNGER, WILLIE LAWTON, EDNA MARY, ZADIE HELENA; d 20 Mar 1901; Ref: Edward McCarthy, Keator Fam Gen p116.

LEAH - b 03 Mar 1745 Killingworth, Middlesex Co CT d/ABEL & MARTHA (STEVENS) WILCOX; m 18 Dec 1771/7 Haddam, Middlesex Co CT EDMUND PORTER/PARKER; Ref: Wilcox-Meigs p41, Your Ancestors v3 #1 p280, Barbour's VR Killingworth v2 p158, Haddam LR9 p549.

LEAMAN - b 1850 prob Wood Island. N B Canada s/JOB & MARIA (GREEN) WILCOX; m 21 Nov 1873 EMMA JOY who d 13 Apr 1905 d/EDWARD JOY; d 03 Oct 1889 bur Hardwood Cove Cem; Ref: Desc of Charles Dyer Wilcox p15.

LEANDER - b 1814 NY; m 28 Feb 1841 Lorain Co OH JANE MOE who was b 1823 OH d/ISAAC & CLARISSA (-----) MOE; Res Avon, Lorain Co OH until 1861; ch JAMES, LAFAYETTE, ROSETTA; Ref: 1850,1860 Census Lorain Co OH, Carol Wood, Marriages Lorain Co OH p120.

LEANDER - b 1831/33 NY s/ISAAC & LYDIA (TANNER) WILCOX of Chautauqua, Chautauqua Co NY; m af 1860 AMANDA ----- ; Res Mayville, Chautauqua Co NY; Attended college 1860; Ref: Your Ancestors v13 #4 p1598, 1850 Census Mayville NY p279 Dw# 278, 1860 Census Mayville NY p58 Dw# 431.

LEANDER - b 1849 CT s/ELIAS & HANNAH (DENISON) WILCOX of Stonington, New London Co CT; Ref: 1850 Census Stonington Co CT Reel 432 #48 p255, See Elias.

LEANDER H - b 1840 NY s/DUDLEY & KEZIAH (TOWNSEND) WILCOX of Litchfield, Herkimer Co NY; Ref: 1850 Census Litchfield NY p133 Dw# 282.

LEANDER NOBLE - b 22 Jun 1854 s/WILLIAM GOOL/GOOD & HARRIET (CLARK) WILCOX of Waupaca, Waupaca Co WI; m 19 Mar 1883 EMMA FAULKS; Ref: Your Ancestors v3 #11 & 12 p474.

LEANDER P - b 1821 NY; m ESTHER ----- who was b 1826 NY; Res Vernon, Oneida Co NY; ch CELIA L, GEORGIANA; Ref: 1850 Census Vernon NY p84 Dw# 165.

LEBBENS - b 22 Aug 1763 Exeter, Washington Co RI s/ABRAHAM & MARY (CARD) WILCOX m 27 Jan 1793 ELIZABETH BATES d/JOHN BATES; Ref: Your Ancestors v4 #7&8 p561, Arnold v5 pt3 pp36,63, See Abraham.

LEICESTER - s/ROSWELL WILCOX d 1805 en route to OH; Ref: Desc of Wm Wilcoxson p222.

LEIGH FRANCIS - b 01 Jan 1891 s/HENRY WILLIAM & LUCY (GLOVER) WILCOX; m BLANCHE LORD; Ref: A Wilcox Book p129.

LELAND CASWELL - b 27 Feb 1896 Wood Island, N B Canada s/CASWELL LEWIS & NELLIE (SCHOFIELD) WILCOX; m CLARA JANE SCHOFIELD; ch ALTA CLAIRE, HOLLIS EVERETT, ESTHER MAY, NELLIE LURANA, A MANSON BAKER, LESTER HILYARD, WALTER CLEVELAND, WILLIS EUGENE, DONALD, KATHLEEN MAYBELLE, LYDIA VAUGHAN, ELLA RAMONA; Ref: Desc of Charles Dyer Wilcox pp 25,26.

LELOTE - b 1845 d/LANSING H & MIRANDA (HOLMES) WILCOX; d 1852 Napoli, Cattaraugus Co NY; Ref: Cem Inscr, See Lansing H.

LEMIRA - b 22 Dec 1834 Thetford, Orange Co VT d/DAVID & LUCINDA (HORSFORD) WILCOX; Ref: Horsford/Hosford Fam in Am p72.

LEMUEL - b 30 May 1720 Dartmouth, Bristol Co MA s/DANIEL & SARAH (-----) WILCOX; d 19 Jan 1727; Ref: Dartmouth VR p302, Your Ancestors v10 #3 p1267.

LEMUEL - b 1758; d Apr 1839 Ballston, Saratoga Co NY bur Briggs Cem; Rev War CT Line; Ref: DAR Mag Nov 1977 p923, CT Nutmeggers Who Migrated p264, Hist of Saratoga Co NY pp91,120,231.

LEMUEL - b 26 Mar 1759 Middletown, Middlesex Co CT s/JEREMIAH & MARY (STOWE) WILCOX; Ref: Barbour's VR Middletown v1 p95.

LEMUEL - b 28 Feb 1780 Middletown, Middlesex Co CT s/JOSIAH & HULDAH (SAVAGE) WILCOX; m 1801 RHODA NORTH who was b 20 Jul 1779 Berlin, Hartford Co CT & d 03 May 1835 Hinkley OH; ch ADELIA; d 24 Nov 1864 E Berlin CT; Ref: MUH p756, Nutmegger v16 #4 p735, Barbour's VR Middletown, Middlesex Co CT v2 p221.

LEMUEL - of Ballston, Saratoga Co NY mortgaged land in Warren, Herkimer Co NY 1808; Ref: Herkimer Co Mortgage Book A p246.

LEMUEL - b 01 Oct 1821 White Co IL s/HAZARD & SARAH (SEELEY) WILCOX; d in infancy; Ref: Your Ancestors v12 #2 p1435.

LEMUEL - b 1826; m 28 Nov 1847 West Turin, Lewis Co NY KATE SHELL who was b 1828; Ref: Tree Talks v4 #4 p11.

LEMUEL - b 1832 NY s/SAMUEL & DEBORAH (SMITH) WILCOX of Concord, Erie Co NY; Ref: 1850 Census Concord NY p52 Dw# 758.

LEMUEL - b 03 Jan 1860 Sharon MN s/CALVIN & SHARON JANE (RANDALL) WILCOX; m 03 Nov 1881 CYNTHIA BEATRICE PARRISH; d 18 Jul 1920 Boise, Ada Co ID; Ref: SGS Ancestral Lineage 2nd Book p100.

LEMUEL R - b 1829 s/GILES & EMILY (PHELPS) WILCOX; Ref: Your Ancestors v14 #1 p1619.

LEMUEL T - b ca 1819; m MARY A HOLMES who was b 1818/19 & d 28 Sep 1905; Res Preston, New London Co CT; ch WATY A, JOHN L; d 14 May 1891; Ref: Cem Records of New London Co CT v2 p4, See RIGR v2 p4.

LEMUEL T - b 1822 RI s/POTTER S & LYDIA (-----) WILCOX of Griswold, New London Co CT; Ref: 1850 Census Griswold CT Reel 432 #49 p31.

LENG - b 1870 prob Clockville, Madison Co NY s/ELISHA & ELIZABETH (HALL) WILCOX; Ref: Pioneers of Madison Co NY p281.

LEONAR C - b 11 Aug 1848 Jackson Co IA s/JOHN 3rd & MARY MARIAH (CASWELL) WILCOX; Ref: Desc of Wm Wilcoxson p123.

LEONARD - b 17--; Res Providence, Providence Co RI; ch JOANNA ELDREDGE, CAROLINE HILL, SARAH; Ref: Arnold v16 p586.

LEONARD - b 29 Jan 1799 Hanover, Grafton Co NH s/JEDUTHAN & SALLY (FISK) WILCOX; Ref: Your Ancestors v3 #4 p351.

LEONARD "LESTER" - b ca 1812 NY; m ca 1837 ELVIRA/ALVIRA ----- who was b ca 1817 NY; Res Plymouth, Marshall Co IN; ch WILLARD, ALICE, CHARLES HENRY, GEORGE W, MARY JANE, EVA M, ANGELINE (LINA); d 20 Nov 1862 Plymouth IN; Ref: 1840-1860 Census, Charlotte Jacob-Hanson.

LEONARD - b 1831 CT; Res Stonington, New London Co CT; m 21 Sep 1856 Stonington CT MARTHA CRANDALL; Ref: 1850 Census Stonington CT Reel 432 #48 p247, Barbour's VR Stonington v6 p26.

LEONARD Hon - d 24 Jun 1850; Ref: Deaths from NY Herald p551.

LEONARD - b 1838 NY s/LYSANDER BYRAM & RACHEL (CHILDS) WILCOX of Napoli, Cattaraugus Co NY; Ref: 1850 Census Napoli NY p57 Dw# 43.

LEONARD - b ca 1879 s/CLINTON H WILCOX who was b NY; Res Rock Co WI; Ref: 1880 Soundex WI.

LEONARD CLINE - b 04 Jan 1846 Jackson Co IA s/JOHN 3rd & MARY MARIAH (CASWELL) WILCOX; d in infancy; Ref: Desc of Wm Wilcoxson p123.

LEONARD CLINE - b 08 Nov 1850 Jackson Co IA s/ABNER THORP & LYDIA A (CHANDLER) WILCOX; d 1853; Ref: Desc of Wm Wilcoxson p125.

LEONARD DUDLEY - b 06 June 1876 Deep Cove, N B Canada s/WILLIAM & JANE (DRISCOLL) WILCOX; Single; d 15 Oct 1948 bur Seal Grove N B; Ref: Desc of Charles Dyer Wilcox p12.

LEONARD HAMLINE - b 22 Jun 1855 NY s/JEFFERSON MONROE & MARY HARVEY (HUMASON) WILCOX; Unmarried; Res Los Angeles, Los Angeles Co CA; Ref: Colonial Fam of US v5 p552.

LEONARD OVIT - b 29 Jun 1877 Otoe Co NE s/ANDREW JACKSON & CARRIE HELEN (SARNES) WILCOX; m 07 Jan 1899 Ottawa Co Indian Terr [OK] BERTHA MAY ALBRO; m Mrs BURLY WYAT; m Mrs ELIZABETH KNIGHT; m Mrs BLANCH (MENDEL) HOGGSETT; d 16 Jul 1935 Payette, Payette Co ID; bur Mt View Cem Pueblo, Pueblo Co CO; Ref: Verna Betts.

LEONARD W - b Feb 1896 WI s/GEORGE W & EMMA C (-----) WILCOX; Father b NY; Res Eagle, Richland Co WI; Ref: 1900 Soundex Richland Co WI.

LEORA - b 1852 NY d/LYSANDER BYRAM & HELEN CHILDS (LEDYARD) WILCOX of Napoli, Cattaraugus Co NY; Ref: 1860 Census Napoli NY Reel 653 #726 p52, See Lysander Byram.

LEROY - b 1823 NY; Res Columbus, Chenango Co NY; Ref: 1850 Census Columbus p267 Dw# 1920.

LEROY - b 1836 NY s/MORGAN L & CAROLINE (SATTERLEE) WILCOX; Res Onondaga Co & Granby, Oswego Co NY; Ref: Your Ancestors v3 #9&10 p447, 1850 Census Granby NY p16 Dw# 243.

LEROY - b 1836 s/JOHN & ROSE L (-----) WILCOX; Res Rome, Oneida Co NY; Ref: 1860 Census Rome NY p198.

LEROY - b 1846 NY s/JOEL & BETSEY (SPRAGUE) WILCOX of Georgetown, Madison Co NY; Ref: 1850 Census Georgetown NY p388 Dw# 211, See Joel.

LEROY NOBLE - b 07 Jun 1846 Rockdale, Crawford Co PA s/GEORGE & SARAH (SPENCER) WILCOX; d 15 Aug 1860; Ref: A Wilcox Book p109.

LEROY SETH - b 10 Apr 1881 s/ANDREW CHESTER & CLARINDA CLINGMAN (RICHART) WILCOX of Harlan, Shelby Co IA; Ref: Your Ancestors v14 #3 p1671.

LERVINA - b 1842 PA d/JOHN C & SUSAN (-----) WILCOX; Res Le Roy, Bradford Co PA; Ref: 1850 Census Bradford Co PA p66.

LESLIE - s/HENRY & SARAH (BOWERS/POWERS) WILCOX; Res Eden, Erie Co NY; Ref: Information from Town Historian.

LESLIE - b 30 May 1897 Ipswich, Edmunds Co SD s/GEORGE WASHINGTON & EVA (SMITH) WILCOX; Ref: Erwin W Fellows.

LESLIE EUGENE - b 20 Aug 1887 Minneapolis, Hennepin Co MN s/FRANK EUGENE & DAISIE (ROSE) WILCOX; m ISABELLE GAULKE; no ch; Res Los Angeles, CA; Ref: Desc of Wm Wilcoxson p128.

LESTER - b 03 Mar 1810 Sandisfield, Berkshire Co MA s/GEORGE & SUSANNAH (HUMPHREY) WILCOX; Res

Schoharie Co NY; Ref: Your Ancestors v12 #1 p1408, Desc of Wm Wilcoxson p223.

LESTER AMI - b 11 Mar 1872 Twin with ANDREW C s/ANDREW CHESTER & CLARINDA CLINGMAN (RICHART) WILCOX of Harlan, Shelby Co IA; m LYDIA VIOLA GEHERS; Ref: Your Ancestors v14 #3 p1671.

LESTER H - b 1839 NY s/ISAIAH & ARMANDA (-----) WILCOX of Florence, Oneida Co NY; Ref: 1850 Census Florence NY p200 Dw# 144.

LESTER RICHARD - b 28 Apr 1879 Guilford, New Haven Co CT s/RICHARD CHRISTOPHER & LUCY C (PAGE) WILCOX; Ref: Fam of Early Guilford p1214.

LEVERETTE - b 1824 s/WILLIAM & MERCY (-----) WILCOX; Res Clockville, Madison Co NY; Ref: Pioneers of Madison Co NY p281.

LEVERITT - b 1825 CT; m REBECCA ----- who was b 1832 PA; Res Middleburg PA 1850; Ref: Nutmegger v17 #2 p204.

LEVI - b 11 Dec 1771 or 16 Sep 1772 s/JOHN & ANNA (STEVENS) WILCOX of Haddam, Middlesex Co CT; m 03 May 1795 MARY SPENCER who was b 26 Sep 1776 Haddam CT & d 04 Oct 1850; Res West Springfield, Hampden Co MA & Genesee Co NY; ch MELINDA, LEVI, ALFRED, MARY, SAMUEL, JULIA, MARTIN, HARRIETT B, EDWARD, ELIAS, MORTON, ALLEN; Ref: Fiske Card File, Your Ancestors v3 #11 & 12 p473, Desc of Wm Wilcoxson p132.

LEVI Dr - b 1773 CT s/DAVID WILCOX; m ABIGAIL THOMPSON who was b 1790 & d 1876 age 86; Res Ticonderoga, Essex Co NY; ch HAMILTON, LEVI, FORTIS M, ROLLIN T, PHILO S, LUCRETIA, MARIA, WILLIAM KIRBY; d 15 Sep 1837; Ref: Cutter's Northern NY v2 p655, 1850 Census Ticonderoga NY p360 Dw# 180.

LEVI - b 1775-1784; Res Benson, Rutland Co VT; Ref: 1800 Census Rutland Co VT p104.

LEVI - b 18 Jun 1797 Haddam, Middlesex Co CT s/LEVI & MARY (SPENCER) WILCOX; m 04 Jan 1829 NANCY ROGERS; Ref: Desc of Wm Wilcoxson p132.

LEVI - m MARTHA ALLEN d/JEDIDIAH ALLEN 06 Nov 1808 Westport, Bristol Co MA; Ref: Westport VR p252.

LEVI - m 12 Dec 1818 Wilton, Fairfield Co CT ESTHER/HITTA HYATT; moved to Milan, Erie Co OH 1825; ch ESTHER ANTOINETTE; Ref: Firelands Pioneer Jun 1867 p90, Arnold v15 p443, Gen of the Whittlesey Fam p290.

LEVI - m MARY FOX; ch EMMA G, GILBERT H; Ref: Desc of Wm Wilcoxson p240.

LEVI - b 1812 NY s/Dr LEVI & ABIGAIL (THOMPSON) WILCOX; ch PHILO, HIRAM; Cabinet maker Res Crown Point, Essex Co NY; Ref: 1850 Census Crown Point NY p360 Dw# #180, See Dr Levi.

LEVI - b 29 Oct 1839 Menard Co IL s/ISAAC ALMANZA & MARIETTE (OVIATT) WILCOX; m 23 Sep 1858 near Concord IL TURZA ANN WELDON; d 27 Jun 1917 Burr, Otoe Co NE bur Wilcox Cem; Ref: Verna Betts.

LEVI - b ca 1843 s/CHARLES DYER & PRUDENCE (PARKER) WILCOX; d ca 1864; Ref: Desc of Charles Dyer Wilcox p6.

LEVI - b 1871 s/JOHN & CLARINDA (STANHOPE) WILCOX; Ref: Dec of Charles Dyer Wilcox p7.

LEVI C - b 1822 NY; m MARY -----; Res Le Roy, Bradford Co PA; ch NATHAN; Ref: 1850 Census Bradford Co PA p66.

LEVI C - b 1826 PA; m ABBEY -----; Res Le Roy, Bradford Co PA; ch B L, THEODORE L, BETSEY M, GERTRUDE E; Ref: 1860 Census Bradford Co PA.

LEVI L - b 25 Sep 1824 s/RICHARD & ELIZABETH (LEWIS) WILCOX of Canton, Bradford Co PA; Ref: Your Ancestors v10 #4 p1273.

LEVI L - b 1837 RI s/WHITMORE & LYDIA/LAURA A (-----) WILCOX of Georgetown, Madison Co NY; d 1863; Ref: Your Ancestors v3 #6 p401, 1850 Census Georgetown NY p378 Dw# 32.

LEVI P - b 1830 RI; m 1849 ELIZA CURTIS who was b in Ireland; moved to WI 1845 then MI & back to Randall, Kenosha Co WI 1863; 7 ch 4 boys 3 girls; Ref: Hist of Racine & Kenosha Co WI p737.

LEVI SHELDON - b 03 Dec 1819 Pompey, Onondaga Co NY s/CHESTER & AURALIA (SPERRY) WILCOX; m 1846 ISABEL LAMBIE who was b Lenoxshire, Scotland d/JOHN & JEAN (ALLEN) LAMBIE & d Camden, Oneida Co NY; ch CHESTER GAVIN, JOHN LAMBIE, JANE MINDWELL,

LILLIAN; d Sep 1896 DePerc, Brown Co WI; Ref: Your Ancestors v14 #2 pp1645,1646.

LEVI SHELDON - b 04 Oct 1873 s/CHESTER GAVIN & SARAH (MILLER) WILCOX of DePerc, Brown Co WI; m 02 Feb 1898 ANNIE ELIZABETH WORKMAN d/W & MARGARET (MILLER) WORKMAN; ch WORKMAN MILLER, ISABELLE, JOHN GAVIN, MARGARET MILLER; Ref: Your Ancestors v14 #2 p1646, #3 p1671.

LEWIS - b 17 Nov 1780 Westerly, Washington Co RI s/ISAIAH & SARAH (LEWIS) WILCOX; d in the south; Ref: Wilcox-Brown-Medbery p10, See RIGR v1 p30.

LEWIS - b 10 Apr 1806 Halifax, Windham Co VT s/JOSEPH & PRUDENCE (DALRYMPLE) WILCOX; Ref: VT VR, 1850 Census Halifax VT p131, Bible Rec, Halifax Wilcox Fam mss, Samuel Gorton Desc v2 p586.

LEWIS - b 1815 NY s/BENJAMIN & SARAH ANN (-----) WILCOX; m NANCY who was b 1820 NY; Res Johnsonburg & Java, Wyoming Co NY & MI; ch ALBERT, CHARLES, WILLIAM, VICTOR, ADELBERT, EMMA, ROSE, RUDD, CARRIE, LAVINA, LUCY A, FIDELIA, MAY, ETTA; Ref: Your Ancestors v14 #1 p1618, #3 p1670, 1850 Census Java NY p53 Dw# 803.

LEWIS - of Hartford, Hartford Co CT m 05 Sep 1832 CAROLINE BROOKS of Burlington, Hartford Co CT; Ref: Barbour's VR Burlington v7 p29.

LEWIS - b 1821 NY; m MARY A ----- ca 1847; Res Le Roy, Bradford Co PA; ch ANNA R; Ref: 1850 Census Bradford Co PA p65.

LEWIS - b 27 Jun 1822 Cherry Creek, Chautauqua Co NY s/THOMAS WARD & HULDAH PRUDENCE (McMANUS) WILCOX; d 1826; Ref: Wilcox Hist mss.

LEWIS - b 1823; m SUSAN VANCOURT who was b 1829 & d 1912; Res Orange Co NY; d 1899; Ref: Graveyards of Orange Co NY v1 p43.

LEWIS - m MARIA ----- 18--; Res McLean, Tompkins Co NY; ch MARY ANN; Ref: NYG&BR v4 p216.

LEWIS - b 1832 France; Res with DANIEL ROBINSON fam Oswego, Oswego Co NY; Ref: 1850 Census Oswego NY p230 Dw# 242.

LEWIS - b 1834 NY s/ALFRED & ABIGAIL (-----) WILCOX of Seneca Falls, Seneca Co NY; Ref: 1850 Census Seneca Falls NY p262 Dw# 1890.

LEWIS - b 27 Dec 1834 s/WILLIAM W WILCOX; m HELEN M ----- who was b 17 Apr 1846 & d 13 Feb 1897 Chester, Orange Co NY; d 28 Feb 1885 Orange Co NY; Ref: Graveyards of Orange Co NY v1 p43.

LEWIS - b 27 Jun 1842 Colesville, Broome Co NY s/DAVID & SARAH/SALLY (CRITTENDEN) WILCOX; m 10 Jun 1868 Toledo, Tama Co IA RACHEL ANN GLENN who was b 05 Jun 1850 Holloway, Belmont Co OH d/WILLIAM & ESTHER (OLIVER) GLENN; ch MENZO J, DAVID L, ELETTIE, ROBERT SCOTT, LULU EVALINA, MARIETTE, CORA, BESSE BELLE, GRACE RACHEL; d 28 Jun 1910 Tama, Tama Co IA; bur Oak Hill Cem; Ref: Marjorie Stoner Elmore.

LEWIS - m 23 Oct 1853 LYDIA AUGUSTA DERTHICK who was b 06 Dec 1823 Warren, Herkimer Co NY & d 01 Oct 1854 Canandaigua, Ontario Co NY d/DUDLEY OTIS & ANN (BIRCH) DERTHICK; Ref: Derthick/Derrick Gen p428.

LEWIS - b 1842 NY s/CHARLES W & EMILY (-----) WILCOX of Ripley, Chautauqua Co NY; Ref: 1850 Census Ripley NY p119 Dw# 259.

LEWIS - b 1843 NY; Res Chautauqua, Chautauqua Co NY with ELIJAH MOORE fam; Ref: 1860 Census Chautauqua NY p58 Dw# 428.

LEWIS - b 1842/3 NY s/DAVID & SARAH/SALLY (CRITTENDEN) WILCOX of Greene, Chenango Co NY; Ref: 1850 Census Chenango Co NY, From Raft to Railroad p294, Marjorie S Elmore.

LEWIS - b 1846 NY s/GEORGE & SARAH (SPENCER) WILCOX of Harmony, Chautauqua Co NY; Ref: 1850 Census Harmony NY p267 Dw# 621.

LEWIS - b 1849 Halifax, Windham Co VT s/TYLER & TEMPERANCE (FIFE) WILCOX; Ref: 1850 Census Halifax VT p131, Halifax Wilcox Fam mss.

LEWIS - b 19 Nov 1851 s/HORACE HUBBARD & OLIVIA (RICHARDSON) WILCOX of Hancock Co IL & Butler Co KS; d 12 Mar 1867; Ref: Desc of Wm Wilcoxson p131.

LEWIS ALLEN - b 17 Oct 1827 Floyd, Oneida Co NY s/ALBINUS & EUNICE CHACE (ALLEN) WILCOX; m be 1852 MARGARET ----- who was b 1832; m af 1860 SABINA

McDONALD HOPKINS who was b 30 Mar 1832 d/ANDREW HOPKINS; Res Floyd & Rome Oneida Co NY, Guthrie Center, Guthrie Co IA; ch by 1st wife CECELIA; ch by 2nd wife ORA, ANNAMS, ALBINUS, CLARA L, ANDREW HOPKINS, HENRY WILLIAM, MYRTLE, CHARLES G, ELSA GRACE; d 05 Feb 1902 IA; Ref: Wilcox-Meigs pp97,117,118, Col Fam of US v5 p556, 1860 Census Rome NY p6 Dw# 41.

LEWIS B - m 31 Dec 1858 Narragansett, Washington Co RI SARAH J BATES; Res Seekonk, Bristol Co MA; Ref: Arnold v10 p351.

LEWIS B B - b 12 Sep 1852 Seekonk, Bristol Co MA s/LEWIS D & LYDIA S (JUSTIN) WILCOX; Ref: Arnold v8 p507.

LEWIS C - b 1828 NY; m MARIAN ----- who was b 1830 NY; Res Buffalo, Erie Co NY with ELZADE GREEN fam; Ref: 1850 Census Buffalo NY p143 Dw# 724.

LEWIS CORNELIUS - b 06 Feb 1872 Guilford, New Haven Co CT s/RICHARD CHRISTOPHER & LUCY CAROLINE (PAGE) WILCOX; Ref: Fam of Early Guilford p1213, Wilcox-Meigs p108.

LEWIS D - s/GEORGE & SUSAN (-----) WILCOX; m 11 Feb 1850 LYDIA S JUSTIN d/GEORGE & RUTH (-----) JUSTIN; All of Seekonk, Bristol Co MA; ch LEWIS B B; Ref: Arnold v2 pt1 p200 v9 p244.

LEWIS D - m 02 Feb 1854 Providence, Providence Co RI SUSAN S BROWNING; Ref: Arnold v7 p583.

LEWIS E - b 1831 Chenango Co NY; m ELVINA/ELIZA -----; Res Gerry, Chautauqua Co NY; ch CELESTUS; Ref: 1855 Census Gerry NY, 1860 Census Gerry NY p81, 1873/4 Business Directory of Chautauqua Co NY p214.

LEWIS EDWARD - b 12 Mar 1849 New Haven, New Haven Co CT s/SAMUEL AUGUSTUS & RUTH (ELLIOTT) WILCOX; Ref: Wilcox-Meigs pp90,91, Fam of Early Guilford p 1212.

LEWIS F - b 1878 Utica, Oneida Co NY s/ARTHUR LEE & LUCINDA MARY (GUSTIN) WILCOX; m RUTH -----; m FLORA -----; Res San Diego, San Diego Co CA; ch LEWIS F Jr; Ref: Judith K Schlitt.

LEWIS FRANKLIN - b 1849 CT; Ref: Nutmegger v9 #1 p106.

LEWIS JESSE - b 1818 s/JESSE & CYNTHIA (BAILEY) WILCOX; m 22 Sep 1842 ANNA MARIA WEEKES/WICKES who was b 14 Aug 1816 Reading, Schuyler Co NY d/JONAS & SARAH (BETTS) WEEKES; ch JONAS JESSE, CHAUNCEY WICKES, ANNA LOUISE; d 1900 Carthage, Jefferson Co NY; Ref: Early Settlers of NY p339, Geo Weekes Gen p258.

LEWIS LAFOREST - b 02 Dec 1836 Surry, Cheshire Co NH s/GEORGE & NANCY PALMYRA (REED) WILCOX; d 03 Aug 1837; Ref: Hist of Surry NH pp382,949.

LEWIS LUMAN - b 25 May 1889 Guilford, Windham Co VT s/CHARLES LUMAN & CORA ADELAIDE (CROSIER) WILCOX; d 01 Oct 1906 pulmonary phtisis following whooping cough; Ref: Iris W Baird.

LEWIS S - b 1874 WI s/CHESTER W & SARAH D (-----) WILCOX; Father b NY; Res Brown Co WI; Ref: 1880 Soundex WI.

LEWIS STERLING - m ca 1865 JANETTE BAILEY who was b 15 May 1845 & d 12 Jun 1913; Res Crandon, Forest Co WI; Ref: Nutmegger v4 #1 p110.

LEWIS T - b ca 1852 MI s/AUSTIN SCRANTON & HANNAH (BIDWELL) WILCOX; d in infancy; Ref: Your Ancestors v3 #1 p281.

LEWIS WESLEY - b 03 Nov 1885 s/JOHN & CLARINDA (STANHOPE) WILCOX; m ADELAIDE SHEPHERD who was b 12 Dec 1886 & d 15 Nov 1974; ch HILDA, RALPH, ESTHER, ASHLEY, RUTH, NORMA, CLINE, PRESTON; d 08 Nov 1972; Ref: Desc of Charles Dyer Wilcox p7.

LIBBIE M - b 1862 MI; bur 27 Oct 1891 Baldwinsville, Onondaga Co NY Lot 27 Riverview Cem; Ref: Vorhees Records v1 p125.

LIDA - b ca 1840 d/MARTIN & SARAH (-----) WILCOX of Dover, Dutchess Co NY; m DAVID KELLY; Ref: Your Ancestors v4 #9&10 p585.

LILIAN DENISON - b 09 Jul 1893 Stonington, New London Co CT d/DENISON ELMER & PHOEBE (DENISON) WILCOX; d 20 Mar 1983 Stonington CT; Ref: C Douglass Alves Sr.

LILLIA MAUDE - b 03 Aug 1898 Waterbury, New Haven Co CT d/ARTHUR RAY & JULIA CAROLINE (SAVAGE) WILCOX; m 16 Jun 1925 NYC NY MAX BERNARD KAMPF; Res Utica, Oneida Co NY; ch JUDITH EVELYN; d 06 Jun 1982; Ref: Judith K Schlitt.

LILLIAN MAY - b 26 Apr 1880 Hampton, Rush Co KS d/ANDREW JACKSON & CARRIE HELEN (SARNES) WILCOX; d 30 Oct 1897 Cowskin Prairie, AR; Ref: Verna Betts.

LILIS - b 1760 d/CUTHBERT & RUTH (WHITE) WILCOX; m Oct 1774 Tiverton, Newport Co RI PELEG SANFORD who was b 23 Oct 1751 Tiverton RI & d 13 May 1789 s/WILLIAM SANFORD; Res Dartmouth Bristol Co MA & Tiverton, Newport Co RI; ch MARY, SAMUEL, RESTCOME, STEPHEN; d 13 Mar/May 1834; Ref: Am Gen v19 #1 p31, Your Ancestors v10 #3 p1268, Sanford Gen p26, Arnold v4 pt7 p57.

LILLIAN - b 22 Sep 1864 d/LEVI SHELDON & ISABELLA (LAMBIE) WILCOX of DePerc, Brown Co WI; Ref: Your Ancestors v14 #2 p1646.

LILLIAN - b 28 Jul 1879 Norwich, Chenango Co NY d/JOHN T & LILLIAN (DIBBLE) WILCOX; d 10 Feb 1920 age 40yr 6mo 12da; Bur Sec 4 Lot 2; Ref: Norwich NY Cem Assoc Records p325.

LILLIAN AGNES - b 25 Jul 1861 d/DANIEL WILMARTH & MARTHA ANN (CHAPIN) WILCOX of Boston, Suffolk Co MA; Ref: Your Ancestors v3 #6 p400.

LILLIAN M - b ca 1870 Tioga Co PA d/JOHN D & SARAH M (WILSON) WILCOX; m JOHN DORTT of Shippen twnshp Tioga Co PA; Ref: Hist of Tioga Co PA p732.

LILLIBRIDGE [THOMAS] - b 01 Jan 1773 prob Exeter, Washington Co RI s/HOPSON & ELIZABETH (HELWAY/HOLLOWAY) WILCOX; m ANNA HOXIE who was b 4 Jul 1781 & d 01 Sep 1858; ch THOMAS L, SUSANNAH, SAMUEL H, RUSSELL, LAVINA, ANNA, ORVILLE; d 01 Sep 1853 Earlville, Chenango Co NY Will probated 14 Feb 1854 Chenango Co NY G-17; Ref: Cem of Chenango Co NY p9, Barber's Index to Wills of Chenango Co v2, Cutter's Western NY v3 p1439, Early Years in Smyrna p22, Your Ancestors v3 #4 p347, See RIGR v1 p153, v2 #2 p100.

LILY - b 19 May 1876 Waters MI; m 02 May 1892 JOHN BATCHELOR; Ref: LDS Record of Edith Smith.

LINA - b ca 1774; d 11 Sep 1847 age 73 Middletown, Middlesex Co CT; Ref: Barbour's VR Middletown v4 pp72,73.

LINA DICKENSON - b 05 Feb 1875 Middletown, Middlesex Co CT d/HENRY EDWIN & ESTHER COE (BIRDSEY) WILCOX; m 30 Oct 1899 CHARLES WEBSTER

LEE; Res New Britain, Hartford Co CT; Ref: MUH p764.

LINCOLN N - b Dec 1869 NY s/ASAHEL FOSTER & CELIA (ALLEN) WILCOX; Res De Witt, Onondaga Co NY; Ref: Erwin W Fellows.

LINNIE M - b 07 Oct 1880 d/MARINER & CORDELIA (CARD) WILCOX; m FRANK GRIFFIN who was b 13 Oct 1878 s/JAMES & ELLA (GLIDDEN) GRIFFIN; ch GLADYS B, NORDICA G, LEAMON M, ALTHEA B, CORDELIA E, SHERMAN R, RHODA W, ORA M, HELENA L; d 30 Nov 1948 bur Wood Island Cem, N B Canada; Ref: Desc of Charles Dyer Wilcox p15.

LINUS - b 12 Mar 1799 s/ELIJAH W Jr & LOIS (WARNER) WILCOX of Middletown, Middlesex Co CT; Ref: Your Ancestors v3 #6 p401, Barbour's VR Middletown v2 p108.

LINUS - b 1799 VT; m 03 May 1834 Berlin, Worcester Co MA THANKFUL COFRAN who was b 1809 NH; Res Orwell, Addison Co VT; ch CARLOS, ROLLIN, CORNELIA; Ref: Berlin MA VR p284, 1850 Census Orwell VT Reel 920 p44.

LINUS - m 13 Feb 1825 Bristol, Hartford Co CT EMELINE HART; Ref: Barbour's VR Bristol v1 p26.

LINUS - b 1833 s/WHITMORE & LYDIA/LAURA A (-----) WILCOX of Georgetown, Madison Co NY; Ref: Your Ancestors v3 #6 p401, 1850 Census Georgetown NY p378 Dw# 32.

LINUS LYMAN - b 06 Jul 1819 Haddam, Middlesex Co CT s/LYMAN & EMILY (HUBBARD) WILCOX; m 13 Apr 1839 ABIGAIL BURR who d 1857 d/STEPHEN & CYNTHIA (HUBBARD) BURR; m 05 Oct 1858 FANNY M BUELL who was b 24 Oct 1828 Killingworth, Middlesex Co CT; Res Durham, Hancock Co IL; ch by 1st wife DANIEL WEBSTER, CYNTHIA E, EDWARD A, ELLSWORTH, ch by 2nd wife FLETCHER E, COLLINS HENLEY, FRED; Ref: Your Ancestors v4 #1&2 p497, Desc of Wm Wilcoxson p130, Barbour's VR Middletown v3 p457, Killingworth v3 p415.

LIZZIE EDITH - 10 Oct 1865 d/WALTER R & JULIA P (-----) WILCOX of Fredonia, Chautauqua Co NY; d 10 Jun 1870 of paralysis; Ref: 19th Cent Death Notices Reported in Fredonia Censor p596.

LIZZIE HANNAH - b 22 Jan 1847 Taunton, Bristol Co MA d/JOSEPH U & MARIA A (GARDNER) WILCOX; Res

Seekonk, Bristol Co MA; d 28 Sep 1895; Ref: Arnold v9 p293.

LIZZIE M - b 09 Mar 1882 Cherry Creek, Chautauqua Co NY d/GEORGE O & ALYRA L (HARTLEY) WILCOX; m 28 Feb 1909 S C BENTLEY; Res Sisterville, Tyler Co WV; Ref: Hist of Cherry Creek NY p154.

LLOYD W - b 1895 s/GALVIN & LURA JANE (WALKER) WILCOX; Ref: Your Ancestors v9 #2 p1126.

LOAMINY - b CT; m 14 Apr 1812 HANNAH PADDOCK who was b 29 Apr 1786 & d 22 July 1866; Res Onondaga Co NY; ch CAROLINE, EDMUND, ISAAC, HARVEY, CORDELIA; Ref: St Johnsville NY Newspaper 23 Oct 1952.

LODEMA - ch/THOMAS & LYDIA (DIBBLE) WILCOX who settled in Warren Co PA ca 1820; Ref: Fiske Card File.

LODEMA - b 1826 NY; Res with SYLVANUS COLLINS fam Fabius, Onondaga Co NY; Ref: 1850 Census Fabius NY p129 Dw# 80.

LODOWICK - b 18 Sep 1794 Westerly, Washington Co RI s/JESSE & NANCY (PENDLETON) WILCOX; m FANNY COTTRELL; ch NELSON; Ref: Hist of Stonington p660, Denison Gen p461, C Douglass Alves Sr.

LODOWICK P - d 05 Apr 1833; Ref: CT Bible Rec v13 p109.

LODOWICK P - b 1823 CT; m SARAH A DAVIS of Preston who was b 1823 CT; Res Stonington, New London Co CT; ch CHARLES, EUNICE, SARAH, NANCY, FANNY F; Ref: 1850 Census Stonington CT Reel 432 #48 p 257, Barbour's VR Preston v4 p80.

LOIS - b 03 May 1708 Killingworth, Middlesex Co CT d/SAMUEL & RUTH (WESTCOTT) WILCOX; m 18 May 1732 EBENEZER HULL; ch MARY, NATHAN; Ref: Wilcox-Meigs p30, Your Ancestors v3 #7&8 p426, Desc of Wm Wilcoxson p12, Barbour's VR Killingworth v2 p191.

LOIS - b 14 Jun 1738 Middletown, Middlesex Co CT d/DANIEL & SARAH (WHITE) WILCOX; m 14 Sep 1756 Cromwell, Middlesex Co CT SOLOMON SAGE Jr who was b 18 Aug 1737 & d 28 Aug 1805 s/DAVID & BATHSHEBA (JUDD) SAGE; ch GRACE, SOLOMON, HOSEA, CALVIN & MABEL twins, OLIVER & MINDWELL twins, LOIS, JOSEPH, ISAAC, LUTHER; d 18 Aug 1805; Ref: ECM v2 p91, MUH p748, Cutter's CT Fam v2 p657, Gen of CT Fam v3 p279, Hist of Berlin CT p93 , Barbour's VR Middletown v1 p102 v2 p5.

LOIS - b 20 Jan 1740 Killingworth, Middlesex Co CT d/DANIEL & HANNAH (BUELL) WILCOX; m SELAH MURRAY; Ref: Barbour's VR Killingworth v2 p157, Wilcox-Meigs p45, Desc of Wm Wilcoxson p20.

LOIS - d/WILLIAM & RUTH (BLANCHARD) WILCOX m 22 May 1760 Saybrook, Middlesex Co CT EDMUND SHIPMAN; Ref: ECM v1 p89, Desc of Wm Wilcoxson p43, Saybrook Colony VR p562, Your Ancestors v3 #11&12 p473.

LOIS - b 20 Mar 1750 Dartmouth, Bristol Co MA d/JABEZ & HANNAH (HART) WILCOX; Ref: Dartmouth VR p302, See Jabez.

LOIS - b 04 Aug 1760 Goshen, Litchfield Co CT d/JOB WILCOX; Ref: Barbour's VR Goshen v1 p224.

LOIS - b 10 Jul 1769 Middletown, Middlesex Co CT d/NATHAN & LOIS (SAGE) WILCOX; Ref: Barbour's VR Middletown v2 p223, See Nathan.

LOIS - b 05 Feb 1773 RI/NY d/SHEFFIELD & EUNICE (ROSS) WILCOX; m 11 Nov 1790 TIMOTHY ALDEN of Otis, Berkshire Co MA who was b 22 Feb 1770 & d 29 Sep 1859; Res Monroe, Bradford Co PA; ch ADONIJAH, SOPHRONIA, PHILINDA, LOUISA, PARMELIA, SYLVESTER & SEVELLON twins; d 10 Jan 1851; Ref: Pioneer Fam of Bradford Co PA p309, Your Ancestors v12 #4 p1488, v13 #2 p1538.

LOIS - m 10 Jan 1788 Lenox, Berkshire Co MA STEPHEN LEONARD; Both of Lee, Berkshire Co MA; Ref: ECM v3 p141, Fiske Card File.

LOIS - b ca 1777; d 12 Aug 1847 age 70 Middletown, Middlesex Co CT; Ref: Barbour's VR Middletown v4 pp74,75.

LOIS - b ca 1780; m 15 Oct 1801 Whitingham, Windham Co VT JOHN BRATTON; Ref: VT VR.

LOIS/LOUISE - b 1781 d/HIEL & DEBORAH (GILLETT) WILCOX; m ELISHA BLINN; Res Dutchess Co NY; Ref: Desc of Wm Wilcoxson p59, Wilcox-Meigs p66, Will of Jehiel Wilcox, Your Ancestors v4 #11&12 p612.

LOIS - m 05 Apr 1803 Norfolk, Litchfield Co CT JOSEPH FERRY Jr; Ref: Barbour's VR Norfolk v1 p13a.

LOIS - b 25 May 1787 Peru, Berkshire Co MA d/SAMUEL & LOIS (COGSWELL) WILCOX; d 25 Oct 1797; Ref: Peru MA VR p52.

LOIS - b Dec 1789 Middletown, Middlesex Co CT d/EIJAH W Jr & LOIS (WARNER) WILCOX; m ----- WARD; Res prob Corry, Erie Co PA; Ref: Your Ancestors v3 #6 p401, Barbour's VR Middletown v2 p108.

LOIS - b 1792 d/BENJAMIN & PHILENA (ROWE) WILCOX of Bristol, Hartford Co CT; m 1812 HORACE ADAMS who was b 1787 & d 1878; ch PERRY ADAMS; d 1877 Triangle, Broome Co NY; Ref: Your Ancestors v4 #9&10 p588.

LOIS - b 1797 d/FRANCIS & MARTHA (WORDEN) WILCOX; m 1812 SELAH HUBBARD; ch ASHER; d 1874; Ref: Your Ancestors v13 #2 p1539, #4 p1595.

LOIS - b 05 Apr 1798 d/JOHN & LOIS (AUGER) WILCOX of Charleston, Montgomery Co NY; d single 29 Jun 1814; Ref: Your Ancestors v3 #11 & 12 p473, Desc of Wm Wilcoxson p122.

LOIS - b 30 Apr 1810 Harwinton, Litchfield Co CT d/AARON & LOIS (PHELPS) WILCOX; m 12 May 1834 MARKHAM SCOTT of Plymouth, Litchfield Co CT; Ref: Your Ancestors v3 #1 p279, Barbour's VR Harwinton LM p54.

LOIS - b 03/13 Jan 1829 d/ORRIN & HANNAH (HAMLIN) WILCOX of East Bloomfield, Ontario Co NY; m JOHN GATES; Res prob Romeo, Macomb Co MI; Ref: Your Ancestors v10 #3 p1249, Desc of Wm Wilcoxson p208.

LOIS - b 1846 NY d/WARREN & EMILY (-----) WILCOX of Granby, Oswego Co NY; Ref: 1850 Census Granby NY p17 Dw# 254.

LOIS - d/FREDERICK DUNBAR & JULIA (LOVENGUTH) WILCOX of Camden, Oneida Co NY; d age 16; Ref: Your Ancestors v14 #3 p1672.

LOIS - b 14 Feb 1892 Cortland, Cortland Co NY d/LYNN DEE & MAY (NEWELL) WILCOX; m REUBEN McBRIDE; m ARMAND R HALL; Ref: Your Ancestors v3 #6 p397.

LOIS ANN - b 26 Feb 1813 NY d/DAVID & SARAH (RUE) WILCOX; m ALVIN STREET/SMITH; 1 son; Ref: Your Ancestors v3 #11 & 12 p473, Desc of Wm Wilcoxson p126.

LOIS ANN - b 06 Feb 1821 d/AMOS & ELIZABETH (POLLOCK) WILCOX; m GEORGE CORY; d 24 Apr 1919; Ref: Desc of Wm Wilcoxson p243.

LOIS ANN - b 1833 NY d/ERASMUS D & SARAH (-----) WILCOX of Vernon, Oneida Co NY; Ref: 1850 Census Vernon NY p97 Dw# 379.

LOIS ANN - b 15 May 1850/60 MI d/FELIX AUGUR & ELIZABETH (LITTLE) WILCOX; m ELI A BEAL; ch BEULAH W, DELAND P, LOWELL; d 28 Oct 1920; Ref: Your Ancestors v3 #11 & 12 p 474, Desc of Wm Wilcoxson p127.

LOIS C - b 1813 Manlius, Onondaga Co NY d/ASAHEL & HILLENDA (FOSTER) WILCOX; m 1839 JOSEPH BENNETT; Res IL; ch LOIS; Ref: DAR Lineage v162 p68, Erwin W Fellows.

LOIS E - b 1848 Lafayette, Onondaga Co NY d/JACOB & HARRIET (WOOD) WILCOX; Ref: Your Ancestors v14 #1 p1620, 1850 Census Lafayette NY p221 Dw# 465.

LOIS JANE - b 13 Mar 1882 Manchester, Bennington Co VT d/EDGAR & ELLEN (BENTLEY) WILCOX; Single; Bur in Ira Allen Cem Sunderland, Bennington Co VT; Ref: Desc of Wm Wilcoxson p170.

LOIS JANETTA - b 1855 d/WHITMAN & WEALTHY (-----) WILCOX; Res Tioga Co NY; d 12 Sep 1861; Ref: Tioga Co Cem Records.

LOIS S - b 1848 NY d/JACOB & MARY E (----) WILCOX of Collins, Erie Co NY; Ref: 1850 Census Collins NY p322 Dw# 609.

LOLA - m 06 Nov 1895 Fredonia, Chautauqua Co NY WILLIS BARTLETT; both of Laona, Chautauqua Co NY; Ref: 19th Cent Marriages Reported in Fredonia Censor p119.

LOLA MILDRED - b 26 Oct 1885 Sharon MN d/LEMUEL & CYNTHIA BEATRICE (PARRISH) WILCOX; m 22 May 1912 Jasper Co MO JAMES WILLIAM CARTER who was b 19 Dec 1884 Creston, Union Co IA s/LOUIS ALVIN & MARTHA ANN (LUCAS) CARTER; Res Boise, Ada Co ID; ch MARTHA BEATRICE; Ref: SGS Ancestral Lineage p99.

LONSON - b 21 Aug 1802 s/DAVID & PHOEBE (BAILEY) WILCOX; Res NY & Jackson, Jackson Co MI; d 15 Sep 1883; Ref: Wilcox Excerpts v1 p2, Your Ancestors v13 #1 p1515.

LONSON - b ca 1840 MI s/GEORGE HENRY & MARY M (YOUNGLOVE) WILCOX; Res Portland, Multnomah Co OR; ch HAROLD, ELIZABETH; Ref: Wilcox Excerpts v1 pp5,6.

LORA - b Mar 1875 Perry, Wyoming Co NY d/EDGAR UDAL & EMMA A (PRENTICE) WILCOX; Ref: Your Ancestors v4 #5&6 p542.

LORAN/LOREN - b ca 1820/21 Madison Co NY s/DANIEL & poss OLIVE (-----) WILCOX; m MARY A ----- who was b 1825 NY/England; Res Brookfield, Madison Co NY; ch EMILY M, MARY, ANN, MYRON; Ref: 1850 Census Brookfield NY p57 Dw# 970, Judith Schlitt, Your Ancestors v4 #9&10 p583, See Lorin.

LORAN - b 1826; d 09 Mar 1886 age 60 Oxford, Chenango Co NY; Ref: Annals of Oxford NY p564.

LORANA A - b 1836 NY d/ALFRED & ABIGAIL (-----) WILCOX of Seneca Falls, Seneca Co NY; Ref: 1850 Census Seneca Falls NY p262 Dw# 1890.

LORANCA I - b 1830 NY d/ASA & CLARISSA (-----) WILCOX of Danube, Herkimer Co NY; Ref: 1850 Census Danube NY p299 Dw# 180.

LOREN C - b 1851 NY s/THURSTON & LYDIA (-----) WILCOX of Portland, Chautauqua Co NY; Ref: 1860 Census Portland NY p244 Dw# 1908.

LORENA BRUCE - b ca 1885 d/GEORGE SAMUEL & MARGARET E (BARNUM) WILCOX; m WALTER GRAY; Ref: Your Ancestors v12 #2 p1437.

LORENZO - b 16 Apr 1801 s/MARTIN & GERUSHA/JERUSHA (DEWEY) WILCOX of Saratoga & Albany Co NY; d 26 Jan 1820; Ref: Detroit Mag v6 p71, Fiske Card File.

LORENZO - b 1813 NY s/JAMES & NANCY (-----) WILCOX of Pawling, Dutchess Co NY; Ref: 1850 Census Pawling NY p225 Dw# 98.

LORENZO - b 1817 Bridport, Addison Co VT s/ABNER & GLORIANNA (ELDRIDGE) WILCOX; d 03 Jun

1840; Ref: Your Ancestors v3 #9&10 p450, Desc of Wm Wilcoxson p118.

LORENZO - b ca 1820; m ABIGAIL ----- who was b 1820 & d 30 Mar 1848; Res Oneida Co NY; Ref: Tree Talks v2 #2 p2.

LORETTA - b 1798 CT; Res with JAMES WILCOX fam Seneca Falls, Seneca Co NY; Ref: 1850 Census Seneca Falls NY p293 Dw# 2348.

LORIN - m 26 Apr 1827 Plainfield, Otsego Co NY FANNY STILLMAN; Ref: Marriages from Otsego Co Newspapers v1 p33.

LORIN - b 1820 NY prob s/DANIEL WILCOX; m MARY A ----- who was b 1825 NY; ch EMILY; Ref: Your Ancestors v4 #9&10 p583.

LORIN - b 1846 VT s/OTIS & ABIGAIL (-----) WILCOX of Hancock, Addison Co VT; Ref: 1850 Census Hancock VT Reel 920 p64.

LORINDA - b 27 Mar 1791 Middletown, Middlesex Co CT d/JEREMIAH & RUTH (DUDLEY) WILCOX; m SAM CRANDALL; 6 ch; Ref: Mrs. Wm Richardson, Barbour's VR Middletown v2 p159.

LORING P - b 08 Jun 1830 Naples, Ontario Co NY s/NEWCOMB & MIRANDA (STEARNS) WILCOX; m BELINDA LAMPORT; Ref: Fiske Card File.

LORITA - b 17 Nov 1803 d/MARTIN & GERUSHA (DEWEY) WILCOX of Saratoga & Albany Co NY; d 02 May 1890; Ref: Detroit Mag v6 p71, Fiske Card File.

LOTTA ESTELLE - b 16 Feb 1877 Marysville, Union Co OH d/WILLIAM FRANKLIN & VIOLA EVELYN (KELLOGG) WILCOX; Ref: Wilcox-Meigs p107.

LOTTA M - b Jan 1871/1873 MO d/DAVID & LUCY (LA DOW) WILCOX of Tama, Tama Co IA; Ref: Marjorie Stoner Elmore.

LOTTIE - b 18-- NY d/HENRY & SARAH (BOWERS/POWERS) WILCOX; Res Eden, Erie Co NY; Ref: Eden Town Historian.

LOUELLA - b af 1865 d/CYRUS & MARTHA A (HALL) WILCOX; m F J WHITCOMB; Ref: Your Ancestors v3 #9&10 p447.

✓ LOUIS - b 1842 Simsbury, Hartford Co CT s/WATSON & CORDELIA (ENO) WILCOX; d 23 Oct 1853; Ref: Rev Allen McLean Rec p16.

LOUISA/LOVISA - b ca 1760 d/JOSIAH & ELIZABETH (CURTIS) WILCOX; m 20 Jun 1779 ASA THOMPSON; Res E Berlin, Hartford Co CT & poss NY; Ref: A Wilcox Book p18, Colonial Fam of US p555.

LOUISA/LOIZA - m 20 Jul 1834 Killingworth, Middlesex Co CT WILLIAM R GLADWIN; Ref: Barbour's VR Killingworth v3 p384.

LOUISA - b 24 Sep 1806 Killingworth, Middlesex Co CT d/AARON & MABEL (LORD) WILCOX; d 1834 unmarried; Ref: Wilcox-Meigs p81, Your Ancestors v3 #3 p321, Barbour's VR Killingworth v2 p14.

LOUISA - of Quinnabog, Stonington, New London Co CT m 25 Oct 1849 JOSEPH STETSON; Ref: Barbour's VR Stonington v5 p250.

LOUISA - m ANTHONY HATHAWAY who was b ca 1810 s/MICHAEL & HANNAH (DAVIS) HATHAWAY; Ref: NEH&GR v20 p302.

LOUISA - b 1821 NY d/JOSEPH WILCOX of New Hartford, Oneida Co NY; Ref: 1850 Census New Hartford p270 Dw# 511.

LOUISA - b 1823 NY d/FRANCIS CLARK & LAURA (-----) WILCOX of Franklin, Delaware Co NY; Ref: 1850 Census Franklin NY p43 Dw# 226.

LOUISA - b 1827 NY d/ROBERT & NINA (-----) WILCOX of Oswego, Oswego Co NY; Ref: 1850 Census Oswego NY p233 Dw# 292.

LOUISA - d/THOMAS & LYDIA (DIBBLE) WILCOX who settled in Warren Co PA ca 1820; Ref: Fiske Card File.

LOUISA - b 1830 d/LAWRENCE & LAURA (PALMER) WILCOX of Perinton, Monroe Co NY; Ref: Desc of Wm Wilcoxson p162.

LOUISA - b 1831 NY; Res with JOSEPH B RICE fam Ellery, Chautauqua Co NY; Ref: 1860 Census Ellery NY p353 Dw# 2857.

LOUISA - b 1835 NY d/CHARLES & BARBARA (WILKS) WILCOX of Sardinia, Erie Co NY & MN; Ref: 1850 Census Sardinia NY p117 Dw# 1733, See Charles.

LOUISA - b 1836 d/MORGAN L & MARY (-----) WILCOX of Victor, Ontario Co NY; Ref: Your Ancestors v10 #2 p1225.

LOUISA - of Palmyra, Wayne Co NY m 12 Apr 1831 GAYLORD TAYLOR of Manchester Ontario Co NY; Ref: 10,000 VR Western NY p223.

LOUISA - m BERTRAM OSCAR ESTES who was b Mar 1834 s/SILAS & PHEBE (CRONKHITE) ESTES of Oaksville, Otsego Co NY; Ref: Snow-Estes Ancestry v2 p38.

LOUISA - b 1843 Meriden, New Haven Co CT d/BENJAMIN BUSHNELL & ELIZA ANN (BRAINARD) WILCOX; Ref: Fam of Early Guilford p1206.

LOUISA - b 1844 Clockville, Madison Co NY d/SALMON & HANNAH (BUYEA) WILCOX; Ref: Pioneers of Madison Co NY p281.

LOUISA - b 1844 NY d/MILO & HARRIET (-----) WILCOX of Ellington, Chautauqua Co NY; Ref: 1850 Census Ellington NY p159 Dw# 2193 1860 Census Ellington NY p119 Dw# 525.

LOUISA - b 1845 NY d/JACOB & CAROLINE (-----) WILCOX of Sherburne, Chenango Co NY; Ref: 1850 Census Sherburne NY p249 Dw# 1624.

LOUISA - b ca 1846 d/AUSTIN SCRANTON & HANNAH (BIDWELL) WILCOX; m WILLIAM S KNAPP of Topeka, Shawnee Co KS; Ref: Your Ancestors v3 #1 p281.

LOUISA - b 1846 NY d/DAVID KELSEY & MARY (-----) WILCOX of Pittsfield, Otsego Co NY; Ref: 1850 Census Pittsfield NY p289 Dw# 233.

LOUISA - b 1849 d/SAMUEL & HANNAH (KNOWLES) WILCOX; d 1889 unmarried; Ref: Your Ancestors v3 #2 p299.

LOUISA - m 21 Nov 1867 Stratford, Fairfield Co CT CURTISS THOMPSON s/GEORGE & LUCY ANN (-----) THOMPSON; Ref: Barbour's VR Stratford LR 5 p144.

LOUISA Mrs - widow d 27 Apr 1868 Clinton, Middlesex Co CT; Ref: Clinton VR Hurd Diary.

LOUISA A - m 05 Jan 1858 Pawtucket, Providence Co RI SIMON E THORNTON; Res Providence RI; Ref: Arnold v9 p367.

LOUISA A - b 1829/30 d/CHESTER & AURALIA (DUNBAR) WOODS WILCOX of Camden, Oneida Co NY; m Rev JOEL HOWD; Ref: Your Ancestors v14 #2 p1645, 1850 Census Camden NY p231 Dw# 145.

LOUISA C - b 1830 NY d/STEPHEN & RACHEL (-----) WILCOX of Butternuts, Otsego Co NY; Ref: 1850 Census Butternuts NY p218 Dw# 317.

LOUISA C - b 1853 PA d/O S & J C (-----) WILCOX; Res Le Roy, Bradford Co PA; Ref: 1860 Census Bradford Co PA p26.

LOUISA D - of Middletown, Middlesex Co CT m 10 Nov 1841 H DEXTER CHAPIN of Springfield, Hampden Co MA; Ref: Barbour's VR Middletown v3 p484.

LOUISA DORT - b 22 Sep 1819 Surry, Cheshire Co NH d/ASA & LUCINDA (BEMIS) PHILLIPS WILCOX; d 01 Jul 1838; Ref: Hist of Surry NH p947.

LOUISA FIELD - b 01 Aug 1807 d/ELIJAH & LOIS (FIELD) WILCOX; m JARED CHIDSEY of North Branford, New Haven Co CT; Ref: Wilcox-Meigs p72, Fam of Early Guilford p1210.

LOUISA M - b 27 Sep 1829 d/DURFEE & SAMANTHA (WELLS) WILCOX; Res Sodus, Wayne Co NY; d 27 Aug 1847; Ref: Your Ancestors v10 #4 p1294.

LOUISA M - m 23 Jan 1862 Wayne Co IA WILLIAM BRANDAN; Ref: Hawkeye Heritage v14 #1 p24.

LOUISA M - Inter 26 Nov 1900 Norwich, Chenango Co NY Sec B Lot 115; Ref: Norwich Cem Assoc Records p324.

LOUISA MARIA - b ca 1810 d/CURTISS & WEALTHY (HILL) WILCOX; m 01 Feb 1831 Madison, New Haven Co CT GEORGE DOWD who was b 06 Feb 1807 & d 25 Mar 1883 s/WILLIAM & REBECCA (GRAVES) DOWD; Ref: Fam of Early Guilford pp300,1203, Barbour's VR Madison v1 p16.

LOUISA MARIA - b 11 Dec 1824 NY d/STEPHEN & PHOEBE (ROGERS) WILCOX; m ELISHA WILLIAM RODGERS; Ref: LDS Fam Group Sheet.

LOUISA MATILDA - b 06 Apr 1842 Reading, Middlesex Co MA d/AMAZIAH S & MARRET (-----) WILCOX; Ref: Reading VR p251.

LOUISA RIDER - b 25 Jan 1826 NY d/ROBERT G & KEZIAH (RIDER) WILCOX; m PHILIP SCHUYLER GREEN 1852; d 11 Dec 1905 IA; Ref: New England, NY Ancestors p445, Myrtle Prohaska.

LOUISE - m 02 Jan 1780 Cromwell, Middlesex Co CT AMOS SAVAGE; Ref: ECM v2 p95.

LOUISE - b ca 1865 d/CHARLES DYER & MARY DUNN (CORBETT) WILCOX; m FRANK WILSON who d 12 Apr 1958; ch MARIETTA; d 01 Apr 1884; Ref: Desc of Charles Dyer Wilcox p5.

LOUISE - b 23 Sep 1885 Plains, Luzerne Co PA d/JOHN D & AUGUSTA C (STARK) WILCOX; d 07 Aug 1886; Ref: Hist of Luzerne Co PA p1455.

LOUISE CHILD - b 1848 d/LYSANDER BYRAM & RACHEL (CHILD) WILCOX; d 1862 Napoli, Cattaraugus Co NY; Ref: Napoli Cem Inscr, 1850 Census Napoli NY p57 Dw# 43, See Lysander Byram.

LOUISE M - m 10 Oct 1893 Fredonia, Chautauqua Co NY VACIL D BOZOVSKY of Ann Arbor, Washtenaw Co MI; Res Dunkirk, Chautauqua Co NY; ch ELIZABETH K, LOUISE B; Ref: 19th Cent Marriages Rep in Fredonia Censor p119, Lois Barris.

LOVINA - b 19 Jul 1758 Guilford, New Haven Co CT d/EZRA & ESTHER (MEIGS) WILCOX; Ref: Barbour's VR Guilford v2 p100, See Ezra.

LOVINA - b 03 Jun 1801 Sandisfield, Berkshire Co MA d/GEORGE & SUSANNAH (HUMPHREY) WILCOX; Ref: Your Ancestors v12 #1 p1408.

LOVINA - b ca 1804 d/BENJAMIN & ELIZABETH (RECORD) WILCOX; m JOSHUA HOLMES; Ref: Your Ancestors v14 #1 p1618.

LOVINA ARMINA - b 1842 d/ALFRED SISSON & ALMENA COLE (WEAVER) WILCOX of Orangeville, Wyoming Co NY; m 22 Nov 1860 JONATHAN O SPINK; Ref: Hist of Wyoming Co NY p235, 1850 Census Orangeville NY p35 Dw# 544, See Alfred Sisson.

LOVINA FIDELIA - b 15 Jun 1822 d/ASA & SYBIL (BLISS) WILCOX; unmarried; d 03 Jun 1845 Perry, Lake Co OH; Ref: Bogue Fam p397, Your Ancestors v3 #5 p378.

LOVINA M - b 28 Aug 1832 d/ISAAC & SARAH (STARK) WILCOX of Plains, Luzerne Co PA; m Rev

WILLIAM W LOOMIS; d 12 Nov 1903; Ref: Your Ancestors v9 #3 p1152.

LOVINA SYBIL - b 12 Dec 1815 d/ASA & SYBIL (BLISS) WILCOX; d 27 Feb 1817 Perry, Lake Co OH; Ref: Bogue Fam p397.

LOVISA/LOUISA - b 1767 W Simsbury, Hartford Co CT d/WILLIAM & LUCY (CASE) WILCOX; m DUDLEY MILLS who was b 1766 s/BENJAMIN & HANNAH (HUMPHREY) MILLS; Ref: Early Settlers of W Simsbury pp97, Your Ancestors v10 #4 p1276.

LOVISA - b 15 Mar 1779 Cornwall, Litchfield Co CT d/ZADOCK & LOIS (-----) WILCOX; Res with brother REUBEN WILCOX; d af 1850; Ref: Barbour's VR Cornwall v3 p26, 1850 Census Cornwall CT p4 Dw# 62.

LOVISA - b 23 Mar 1797 Halifax, Windham Co VT d/JOSEPH & PRUDENCE (DALRYMPLE) WILCOX; m 07 Dec 1817 JARED W PEARCE; Ref: Halifax Wilcox Fam mss, Samuel Gorton Desc v2 p586.

LOWELL HOLBROOK - b 25 Feb 1846 s/WILLIAM B & IRENE (LARKIN) WILCOX of Putnam, Windham Co CT; m 07 Jun 1870 HELEN R GIFFORD who d 24 Oct 1879 age 30; m Sep 1880 ALICE HOWARD; Res Woodstock, Windham Co CT, Union, Tolland Co CT 1879, VT 07 Jun 1880; ch HELLEN; Ref: Your Ancestors v4 #11&12 p609, Barbour's VR Woodstock, Brown Diary pp130,146,148-151.

LOWELL JOHN - b 20 Jul 1885 Griswold, New London Co CT s/WILLIAM BISSELL & CLARA MABEL (KENYON) WILCOX; m ALMEDA CAPRON; Ref: Your Ancestors v4 #9&10 p584.

LOYAL - b 1800 W Simsbury, Hartford Co CT s/WILLIAM & MERCY (CASE) WILCOX; m ALMIRA REED; Res Clockville, Madison Co NY; Ref: Pioneers of Madison Co NY p281, Early Settlers of W Simsbury CT p130.

LUANY - b ca 1830 d/SIMON GATES & HANNAH (LOOMIS) WILCOX; m JACOB RORAPAUGH; Res Smithville, NY; Ref: Cutter's Western NY v3 p1436.

LUCENA - b 08 Jul 1809 VT d/JANNA & CANDACE (GOODELL) WILCOX; m 01 Nov 1836 Ludlow, Windsor Co VT CHARLES BISHOP; ch ORLANDO; Ref: Bible Records VT State Library.

LUCIA - b 15 Oct 1738 Killingworth, Middlesex Co CT d/DANIEL & HANNAH (BUELL) WILCOX; m 09 Aug 1784 WILLIS BUELL; Ref: Wilcox-Meigs pp44.

LUCIA/LUSHA - b 22 Mar 1764 Killingworth, Middlesex Co CT d/BENJAMIN & ELIZABETH (WHITTLESEY) WILCOX; Ref: Wilcox-Meigs p66, Barbour's VR Killingworth v2 p122.

LUCIA - b 14 Oct 1806 d/ALLYN & CHLOE (WOODFORD) WILCOX; m Jan 1832 ----- PRAH; m 16 Nov 1834 ----- -----; Ref: CT Bible Rec v15 pp253,254.

LUCIA - m 27 Sep 1837 Cornwall, Litchfield Co CT ALMOND T JANES/JONES; Ref: Barbour's VR Cornwall v3 p52.

LUCIAN - m 08 Dec 1862 Lorain Co OH ZILPHA RUGG; Ref: Marriages Lorain Co OH p119.

LUCINDA - b 24 Dec 1774 Suffield, Hartford Co CT d/DAVID & RUTH (SMITH) WILCOX; Ref: Barbour's VR Suffield NB1 p112.

LUCINDA - b 08 Jan 1780 Gilsum, Cheshire Co NH d/OBADIAH & SARAH (TALCOTT) WILCOX; d 07 May 1800 Surry, Cheshire Co NH; Ref: Desc of Wm Wilcoxson p26, Hist of Surry NH pp380,945.

LUCINDA - b 17 Feb 1792 Halifax, Windham Co VT d/BENJAMIN & THANKFUL (WORDEN) WILCOX; m ----- STANCLIFF; d 30 May 1841 age 49; Ref: Your Ancestors v3 #9&10 p447, Halifax Wilcox Fam mss.

LUCINDA - b ca 1801 d/GILES & LYDIA (FOWLER) WILCOX; Ref: Your Ancestors v13 #4 p1598.

LUCINDA - b ca 1801 d/ISAAC WILCOX; m CHRISTOPHER VAN DUSEN; Ref: Evangeline A Wilcox.

LUCINDA - b 17 Jul 1807 Mt Holly, Rutland Co VT d/JACOB & SALLY (HORTON) WILCOX; Ref: VT VR.

LUCINDA - b 1808 NY d/SAMUEL WILCOX; m PETER ECKER; Res Chautauqua Co NY; ch WILLIAM, ALVIN, LOIS, BETSY, ANNICE, LAFAYETTE, CHARLES, DAVID, SYLVESTER, DELLA, RHODA; Ref: Fenton Library Jamestown, Chautauqua Co NY, 1850 Census Chautauqua Co NY p142.

LUCINDA - b 15 Apr 1808 N Stonington, New London Co CT d/LYMAN & ELIZA A (WHEELER) WILCOX of VT & Homer, Cortland Co NY; m 07 Jan 1838 N

Stonington CT GEORGE W EDWARDS; Ref: Your Ancestors v13 #3 p1565, Barbour's VR N Stonington v1 pp36,166.

LUCINDA - b 01 Apr 1811 Portsmouth, Newport Co RI d/WILLARD & HANNAH (GASKELL) WILCOX; m CORNELIUS METCALF; Ref: Arnold v2 p167, Your Ancestors v11 #2 p1345.

LUCINDA - b 12 Sep 1811 Thetford, Orange Co VT d/DAVID & LUCINDA (HORSFORD) WILCOX; Ref: Horsford-Hosford Fam in America p72.

LUCINDA - b ca 1822 VT; m ca 1840 JOHN A SMITH; Res NY; Ref: Nutmegger v8 #4 p610.

LUCINDA - b 08 Feb 1824 Deerfield, Portage Co OH d/WILLIAM & LUCINDA (GIBBS) WILCOX; m 26 Nov 1846 JOSEPH DIVER; ch EDWIN, ELLA, GERTIE, JOHN, WALLACE, JULIA, MINNIE, EUGENE; d 04 Mar 1877; Ref: Hist of Portage Co OH p635, Desc of Wm Wilcoxson p245.

LUCINDA - b 22 Aug 1824 d/AMOS & ELIZABETH (POLLOCK) WILCOX; Ref: Desc of Wm Wilcoxson p244.

LUCINDA - b 1830 Twin with CHRISTIANA d/SIMEON & EUNICE (-----) WILCOX of Independence, Allegany Co NY; Ref: 1850 Census Independence NY p159 Dw# 5.

LUCINDA - b 12 Sep 1831 d/RICHARD & ELIZABETH (LEWIS) WILCOX of Canton, Bradford Co PA; Ref: Your Ancestors v10 #4 p1273.

LUCINDA - b ca 1832 Sodus, Wayne Co NY d/GEORGE & MARY (-----) WILCOX; m ASA C WAINWRIGHT; Ref: Your Ancestors v11 #1 p1319.

LUCINDA - b 02 Oct 1834 Ripley, Chautauqua Co NY d/THOMAS & ELIZABETH (-----) WILCOX; m 22 Feb 1859 IA JOHN HEMPSTEAD; ch SYLVIA ELIZABETH, RUTH; d Sep 1931 Cedar Falls, Black Hawk Co IA; Ref: Obit, 1850 Census Ripley NY p114 Dw# 184.

LUCINDA - b 1836 NY d/CHENEY & AMITY (-----) WILCOX of Onondaga, Onondaga Co NY; Ref: 1850 Census Onondaga NY p324 Dw# 1492.

LUCINDA - b 1839 OH d/SENECA & SAMANTHA (WILSON) WILCOX of Deerfield, Portage Co OH; Ref: 1850 Census Deerfield OH p188 Dw# 1039, See Seneca.

LUCINDA - d 22 Mar 1867; Relative of THOMAS WARD WILCOX of Cherry Creek, Chautauqua Co NY; Ref: Huldah (McManus) Wilcox's Diary.

LUCINDA - b 1837 Chautauqua Co NY d/ELIPHALET & NANCY (KENT) WILCOX; m SILAS ECKER; Res Redwing, Goodhue Co MN; ch OZRO, ADDA, REUBEN, BYRON, TILDEN; d af 1877; Ref: Fenton Library, 1855, 1860 Census, Hist of Goodhue Co MN.

LUCINDA - b Dec 1873 Sherburne, Chenango Co NY; d 20 Aug 1874; Ref: VR of Chenango Co NY p301.

LUCINDA ESTHER - b 1843 Cattaraugus Co NY d/HORACE J & RACHEL (-----) WILCOX; Res Collins, Erie Co NY; Ref: 1850 Census Collins NY #581,1855 Census Collins NY #28.

LUCINDA JANE - m 17 Jun 1810 Batavia, Genesee Co NY PHILANDER KELLOGG s/ELISHA & ELIZABETH/BETSY (DERRICK) KELLOGG; ch JANE; Ref: Derthicks & Derrick Gen p451.

LUCIUS - b 1776-1794; Res Conway, Franklin Co MA; 1 son & 4 daus in 1820; Ref: 1820 Census Franklin Co MA p8.

LUCIUS - b 27 May 1814 Weatogue, Hartford Co CT s/DANIEL & ESTHER (MERRITT) WILCOX; m FRANCES A CRAWFORD d/ANDREW JACKSON CRAWFORD of Demopolis, Marengo Co AL; Res Canandaigua, Ontario Co NY & Demopolis AL; ch MERRITT CRAWFORD; d 28 Aug 1885; Ref: Your Ancestors v11 #3 p1353, CT Bible Rec v11 p551.

LUCIUS - b 1811 Cornwall, Litchfield Co CT prob s/REUBEN & OLLIE (-----) WILCOX; m 24 Jul 1834 Canaan, Middlesex Co CT BELINDA S DEMING who was b 1814 CT; Blacksmith; ch HARRIET, MARY, GEORGE, EMMA; Ref: Barbour's VR Canaan vA p93, 1850 Census Cornwall CT p4 Dw# 61.

LUCIUS - b 1823 NY; Res with LYDIA NETTLETON fam Le Roy, Genesee Co NY; Ref: 1850 Census Le Roy NY p38 Dw# 496.

LUCIUS - b 09 Sep 1834 Bergen, Genesee Co NY s/PITMAN & ANNA P (PARRISH) WILCOX; m MELISSA KINGMAN; Ref: Your Ancestors v3 #1 p282, 1850 Census Bergen NY p46 Dw# 594.

LUCIUS - of Stockton, Chautauqua Co NY m 04 Jul 1851 Fredonia, Chautauqua Co NY NANCY S SHERLEAND;

Ref: 19th Cent Marriages Reported in Fredonia Censor p244.

LUCIUS - b 1847 s/LUCIUS B & MABEL (-----) WILCOX; Ref: Desc of Wm Wilcoxson p36.

LUCIUS B - b 17 Aug 1811/12 Stratford, Fairfield Co CT s/EPHRAIM JOHN & MARY (WHEELER) WILCOX; m MABEL -----; ch CHARLES, LUCIUS; Ref: Wilcox-Meigs p78, Desc of Wm Wilcoxson p36.

LUCIUS C - s/JARVIS WILCOX; Res Chautauqua Co NY & Angelo WI; ch STELLA, MORRIS, MORTIMER, LUCIUS M, WALTER; Ref: Mrs Dorothy Willis.

LUCIUS FITCH - b 11 Aug 1823 s/STEPHEN PIERSON & ELECTA MARETTA (NETTLETON) WILCOX of Le Roy, Genesee Co NY; m 21 Jun 1853 ELLEN MARIA BELDEN; ch STEPHEN JARED, CLARENCE EUGENE, GEORGE ABEL, MARK STUART, HORACE BEACH, EDITH MAY, HENRY WELLS, CORAL GUY; Ref: Your Ancestors v3 #7&8 pp425,426.

LUCRETIA - b 28 Mar 1767 Killingworth, Middlesex Co CT d/SIMEON & LUCRETIA (KELSEY) WILCOX; Ref: Wilcox-Meigs p67, Barbour's VR Killingworth v2 p72.

LUCRETIA - m Sep 1793 Norfolk, Litchfield Co CT EBENEZER COWLES; Ref: ECM v1 p68.

LUCRETIA - m ISAAC NOBLE LANSING who was b 08 Nov 1796 Hoosick, Rensselaer Co NY s/JACOB & HEPZIBAH (NOBLE) LANSING; Res Palermo, Oswego Co NY; Ref: Desc of Thomas Noble p410.

LUCRETIA - b 25 Apr 1803 d/FREDERICK & EUNICE (-----) WILCOX of Chenango Co NY; m ISAAC M LANSING who was b 1798 NY; Res Palerno, Oswego Co NY; ch JOSEPH L, WILLIAM O; Ref: Desc of Wm Wilcoxson p225, 1850 Census Palermo NY p28 Dw# 387.

LUCRETIA - d/ELIHU WILCOX of Killingworth, Middlesex Co CT; m 07 Dec 1834 WYLLIS DUDLEY who was b 1809 & d 07 Jun 1873 s/NATHANIEL & HANNAH (DOWD) DUDLEY; ch MARY GEHENNA, SYLVIA ROXANNA, DARIUS NEWTON, SEVILIAN BENEJAH, HARRIET ISABELLA; d Sep 1889; Ref: Fam of Early Guilford p324.

LUCRETIA - m 17 Apr 1836 Dartmouth, Bristol Co MA JOHN SAWYER; Res New Bedford, Bristol Co MA; Ref: Dartmouth VR p547.

LUCRETIA - m 14 Oct 1840 Middletown, Middlesex Co CT HENRY W CHITTENDEN; Ref: Barbour's VR Middletown v3 p470.

LUCRETIA - b 1828 NY d/Dr LEVI & ABIGAIL (THOMPSON) WILCOX of Ticonderoga, Essex Co NY; Res Crown Point, Essex Co 1850 with her brother LEVI; Ref: 1850 Census Ticonderoga NY p360 Dw# 180.

LUCRETIA - m 22 May 1842 Stonington, New London Co CT WILLIAM F REYNOLDS: Ref: Barbour's VR Stonington v2 p157.

LUCY - b 13 Oct 1738 Killingworth, Middlesex Co CT d/DANIEL & HANNAH (BUELL) WILCOX; m JOSEPH CARTER; Ref: Desc of Wm Wilcoxson p20, Barbour's VR Killingworth v2 p157.

LUCY - b 01 Feb 1741 Killingworth, Middlesex Co CT d/JOSEPH & REBECCA (HURD) WILCOX; m 31 Dec 1767 SAMUEL HULL; Ref: Wilcox-Meigs p40, Barbour's VR Killingworth v2 p189.

LUCY - b ca 1745 Simsbury, Hartford Co CT d/AMOSSr & JOANNAH (HILLYER) WILCOX; m 18 Nov 1762 ARIEL LAWRENCE who was b 21 Jun 1743 Killingly, Windham Co CT s/SAMUEL & PATIENCE (BIGELOW) LAWRENCE; Res Norfolk, Litchfield Co CT; Ref: Your Ancestors v12 #3 p1464, CT Bible Rec v7 pp339,340.

LUCY - b 30 Apr 1747 Middletown, Middlesex Co CT d/JEREMIAH & MARY (STOWE) WILCOX; m 27 Dec 1770 JESSE ROBERTS; Ref: Barbour's VR Middletown v1 p95, v2 p346.

LUCY - b 25 Mar 1750 Stonington, New London Co CT d/WILLIAM & THANKFUL (-----) WILCOX; m 19 Feb 1778 BENJAMIN PECKHAM; Ref: Barbour's VR Stonington v3 p203, v4 p4.

LUCY - b 04 Sep 1752 E Guilford, New Haven Co CT d/TIMOTHY & EUNICE (PIERSON) WILCOX; Ref: Desc of Wm Wilcoxson p27, Wilcox-Meigs p53, Fam of Early Guilford p1209.

LUCY Mrs - m 01 Apr 1778 N Stonington, New London Co CT JOSHUA SMITH; Res Groton CT; Ref: ECM v1 p62, Barbour's VR Stonington v3 p252.

LUCY - m 26 Nov 1778 Durham, Middlesex Co CT EBENEZER SQUIRE; Ref: Barbour's VR Durham TR p406.

LUCY - b 1754 W Simsbury, Hartford Co CT d/WILLIAM & LUCY (CASE) WILCOX; m MOSES CASE ca 1770; ch LUCY, ROXANNA, MOSES, MARTHA; d 1779; Ref: Goodwin's Gen Notes p298, Early Settlers of W Simsbury p129, Your Ancestors v10 #4 p1276, Desc of Wm Wilcoxson p209.

LUCY - b 12 Mar 1754 Hebron, Tolland Co CT d/OBADIAH & SARAH (TALCOTT) WILCOX; m DANIEL BLISH who was b 16 Sep 1752 & d 05 Dec 1817 Gilsum, Cheshire Co NH; d 20 Dec 1843; Ref: Wilcox-Meigs p50, Desc of Wm Wilcoxson p26, Barbour's VR Hebron v2 p254, Hist of Surry NH p945.

LUCY - b 10/12 Nov 1754 Simsbury, Hartford Co CT d/EZRA & MARY (HUMPHREY) WILCOX; m JOHN NEARING who was b 12 Apr 1752 & d 22 Apr 1826; Res Lafayette, Onondaga Co NY; ch JOHN Jr, ALSON; d 24 Aug 1828; Ref: Noble Gen p219, Fiske Card File, Wilcox-Meigs p50, Early Settlers of W Simsbury p131, Your Ancestors v13 #3 p1568, #4 p1597, Desc of Wm Wilcoxson p25.

LUCY - b 27 Jul 1756 d/EPHRAIM & RUTH (WHEELER) WILCOX; Res Stratford, Fairfield Co CT; d 09 Jun 1784; Ref: Nutmegger v7 #1 p37, Wilcox-Meigs p59, Stratford Fam p1347.

LUCY - b 1759; d Dec 1848 Wethersfield, Hartford Co CT; Ref: Barbour's VR Wethersfield v4 pp1914,1915.

LUCY - b 25 Feb 1759 Westerly, Washington Co RI d/DAVID & TABITHA (-----) WILCOX; m 22 May 1779 SAMUEL BABCOCK; Ref: Arnold v5 pt2 pp69,144.

LUCY - b 22 Aug 1774 Middletown, Middlesex Co CT d/OZIAS & MABLE (GOULD) WILCOX; m ROBERT JOHNSON; mentioned in will of brother OZIAS WILCOX New Hartford, Oneida Co NY probated 26 Feb 1839; d be 1839; Ref: Barbour's VR Middletown v2 p322, Wills of Oneida Co NY v3 p42.

LUCY - m ca 1782 WILLARD GREEN; Res Bradford Co PA; Ref: Nutmegger v19 #1 p91.

LUCY - b ca 1779 d/ISAAC & DESIRE (CRANDALL) WILCOX; m ----- GREEN; Ref: Your Ancestors v9 #2 p1125.

LUCY - b 27 Apr 1780 Newport, Sullivan Co NH d/PHINEAS & CHLOE (DUDLEY) WILCOX; m MOSES NOYES; Ref; Your Ancestors v3 #5 p377.

LUCY - b 31 Aug 1781 Chatham, Middlesex Co CT d/JOHN & RUTH (PENFIELD) WILCOX; d 08 Jan 1802; Ref: Gen of CT Fam v3 p87, Barbour's VR Chatham v1 p18.

LUCY - b 19 Jan 1783 Pawlet, Rutland Co VT d/JOHN & CATHERINE (WOODARD) WILCOX; m 24 Jan 1802 NAHUM WYMAN; Ref: Halifax Wilcox Fam mss.

LUCY - d/EZRA & PHOEBE (WOODRUFF) WILCOX m 09 Sep 1798 Cromwell, Middlesex Co CT ROBERT JOHNSON; Res Floyd Oneida Co NY; Ref: ECM v2 p98, Abstract of Wills p42.

LUCY - b 08 Dec 1787 Halifax, Windham Co VT d/BENJAMIN & THANKFUL (WORDEN) WILCOX; d 06 May 1851 age 64; Ref: Your Ancestors v3 #9&10 p447, Halifax Wilcox Fam mss.

LUCY - b 10 Apr 1790 d/REUBEN & HANNAH (JOHNSON) WILCOX of Whitestown, Oneida Co NY; m 14 Oct 1810 ETHAN CLARKE s/HENRY & CATHERINE (PENDLETON) CLARKE; ch LUCY; d 30 Aug 1812 Brookfield, Madison Co NY; Ref: Your Ancestors v4 #1&2 p500 #3&4 p523.

LUCY - b 25 Nov 1790 Ripton CT d/ELNATHAN & SARAH (WELLS) WILCOX; Ref: Stratford Gen p1347.

LUCY - b 1796 d/JEREMIAH & SUSANNAH (WILCOX) WILCOX; m 04 Dec 1814 Foster, Providence Co RI WALTER/WATERMAN HERRINGTON s/JENCKES HERRINGTON; Ref: Arnold v3 p31, Your Ancestors v4 #3&4 p520.

LUCY - d/ASAHEL & LUCY (CRITTENDEN) WILCOX of Portland, Middlesex Co CT; m 09 Mar 1820 ASAHEL PENFIELD who was b 1797 & d Auburn, Shawnee Co KS; 8 ch; d 1863 Auburn KS; Ref: Gen of CT Fam v3 p88, Your Ancestors v4 #7&8 p565.

LUCY - b 17 Oct 1799 Goshen, Litchfield Co CT; Ref: CT Bible Rec v7 p656.

LUCY - of Middletown, Middlesex Co CT; m 02 May 1826 BENJAMIN R CRANE of Springfield, Hampden Co MA; Ref: Barbour's VR Middletown v3 p227.

LUCY - b ca 1802 Smyrna, Chenango Co NY d/ROBERT HAZARD & SUSANNAH (HOXIE) WILCOX; m ASA HARRINGTON; Ref; Your Ancestors v3 #2 p298.

LUCY - b 05 Mar 1805 Lowville, Lewis Co NY d/ROSWELL & IRENE (NICHOLSON) WILCOX; Ref: Cutter's Northern NY v2 p656.

LUCY - b 05 Jun 1808 Westerly, Washington Co RI d/PARKER & POLLY (CLOSSEN) WILCOX; Ref: Arnold v5 pt4 p145, See Parker.

LUCY - m HARRISON FOOTE who was b 23 Jun 1807 s/THADDEUS & POLLY (FORWARD) FOOTE; Res Southwick & Westfield, Hampden Co MA; ch WILLIAM HARRISON, JOHN HENRY, ELLEN ANNETTE, SARAH HOLMES, MARGARET WILCOX; Ref: Foote Fam Gen pp171,304.

LUCY/LUCE - b 09 Apr 1811 Dartmouth, Bristol Co MA d/HENRY & RUBY (BARKER) WILCOX; Ref: Dartmouth VR p303.

LUCY - m 15 Nov 1831 Dartmouth, Bristol Co MA THOMAS WEEKS; Ref: Dartmouth VR p547.

LUCY - b 1813 NY d/ELISHA & ELIZABETH (WILCOX) SHIPPEN WILCOX; Res Dover, Dutchess Co NY; Ref: 1850 Census Dover NY p311 Dw# 4, See Elisha.

LUCY - d/BENJAMIN & SUSANNAH (-----) WILCOX d 02 Dec 1821 Rowe, Franklin Co MA; Ref: Fiske Card File.

LUCY - b 1821; m 06 Oct 1847 Lyme, Jefferson Co NY JOSEPH BARADOUGH; Ref: Tree Talks v24 #1 p41.

LUCY - of Voluntown, New London Co CT m 08 Nov 1846 Griswold, New London Co CT JAMES R SUMM of New Berlin, Chenango Co NY; Ref: Barbour's VR Griswold v1 p161.

LUCY - b 12 Aug 1826 d/JEFFREY & ANNE (STILLMAN) WILCOX; Ref: Gen of CT Fam v2 p537.

LUCY - b 1830 NY d/----- & ELIZABETH (-----) WILCOX; m ca 1848 CHARLES F NEAR; Res Worcester, Otsego Co NY; ch LANE; Ref: 1850 Census Worcester NY p182 Dw# 321.

LUCY - b 1834 NY d/JOHN & ELIZA (-----) WILCOX of Westfield, Chautauqua Co NY; Ref: 1850 Census Westfield NY p143 Dw# 288.

LUCY - b 1835 NY; Res Preston, Chenango Co NY; Ref: 1850 Census Preston p473 Dw# 2380.

LUCY - b 1841 CT d/RUDOLF O & EMELINE (-----) WILCOX of Goshen, Litchfield Co CT; Ref: 1850 Census Goshen CT p102 Dw# 213.

LUCY - b 1843 England d/WILLIAM & RACHEL (-----) WILCOX of Beekman, Dutchess Co CT; Ref: 1850 Census Beekman NY p274 Dw# 171.

LUCY - b 1845 NY d/FRANCIS S & SALLY (-----) WILCOX of Busti, Chautauqua Co NY; Ref: 1860 Census Busti NY p46 Dw# 357.

LUCY - b 1846 Broome Co NY d/GEORGE S & LOUISA (JONES) WILCOX of Alma Allegany Co NY; Ref: Carol A Cox.

LUCY - b 1846 NY d/GEORGE & ABIGAIL (-----) WILCOX of Harmony, Chautauqua Co NY; Ref: 1850 Census Harmony NY p251 Dw# 373.

LUCY - b 1847 NY d/----- & CATHERINE (-----) WILCOX; Res Cicero, Onondaga Co NY; Ref: 1860 Census Cicero NY.

LUCY - b 1849 Belvidere, Boone Co IL d/ELISHA C & ESTHER (-----) WILCOX; Ref: Your Ancestors v12 #1 p1408.

LUCY (Mrs) - d 23 Mar 1835 Sandisfield, Berkshire Co MA; Ref: Fiske Card File.

LUCY A - b 23 Oct 1822 d/DANIEL & ESTHER (MERRITT) WILCOX of Weatogue, Hartford Co CT; m 24 Nov 1834 Simsbury, Hartford Co CT DECIUS LATIMER; Ref: Rev Allen McLean Rec p20, Your Ancestors v11 #3 p1353, Barbour's VR Simsbury TM5 p231.

LUCY A - b 14 Jun 1823 Middletown, Middlesex Co CT d/GUSTAVUS VASA & LUCY (LEE) WILCOX; m STEPHEN C JOHNSON of Tyringham, Berkshire Co MA; Ref: Wilcox-Meigs p88.

LUCY A - of Salisbury, Litchfield Co CT; m 30 Dec 1850 Middletown, Middlesex Co CT HENRY THOMPSON of Denmark; Ref: Barbour's VR Middletown v4 p179.

LUCY A - b 1833 d/ASAHEL & HILLENDA (FOSTER) WILCOX; m SIMEON RICE; Res Manlius, Onondaga Co NY; Ref: Erwin W Fellows, 1850 Census Manlius NY p41 Dw# 613.

LUCY A - b 1842 NY d/THURSTON & SARAH (-----) WILCOX of Greenwich, Washington Co NY; Ref: 1850 Census Greenwich NY p230 Dw# 463.

LUCY A - b 1848 d/LEWIS & NANCY (-----) WILCOX of Johnsonburg & Java, Wyoming Co NY; m TIMOTHY GLADDEN; Ref: Your Ancestors v14 #3 p1670, 1850 Census Java NY p53 Dw# 803.

LUCY ANN - b 12 May 1814 Middletown, Middlesex Co CT d/GILES & LUCY (CLARK) WILCOX; m 16 Apr 1835 WILLIAM FREDERICK BOARDMAN who was b 29 May 1813 & d 17 Jun 1847 s/NATHAN BOARDMAN; ch ARTHUR; d 21 Oct 1843; Ref: MUH pp751,756, Your Ancestors v3 #5 p380, Barbour's VR Middletown v3 pp32,407.

LUCY ANN - b 1819 CT d/----- & BETSY (-----) WILCOX; Res Griswold, New London Co CT; Ref: 1850 Census Griswold CT Reel 432 #49 p34.

LUCY ANN - b 1822 Middletown, Middlesex Co CT; m 03 Oct 1847 STEPHEN C JOHNSON who was b 1817 W Stockbridge, Berkshire Co MA; Res Lee, Berkshire Co MA; Ref: Barbour's VR Middletown v4 pp64,65.

LUCY ANN - b 02 Mar 1827 Middletown, Middlesex Co CT d/ANSEL & BETSEY L (STOCKING) WILCOX; Ref: Barbour's VR Middletown v3 p31.

LUCY ANN - b Sturbridge, Worcester Co MA; Res Thompson, Windham Co CT; d 05 Aug 1848; Ref: Barbour's VR v3 p20.

LUCY ANN - of Middletown, Middlesex Co CT m 18 Oct 1846 SALMON H DUNHAM of Berlin, Hartford Co CT; Ref: Barbour's VR Middletown v4 p39.

LUCY ANN - b 1834 NY d/ERASTUS & LOUISA (-----) WILCOX of Tully, Onondaga Co NY; Ref: 1850 Census Tully NY p162 Dw# 167.

LUCY ARBELLA - b 22 Sep 1863 d/JAMES DAVID & ANNA MARIA (ROBINSON) WILCOX; d 30 Sep 1864; Ref: Wilcox-Meigs p120, Desc of Wm Wilcoxson p144.

LUCY AURELIA - b 23 Oct 1811 d/DANIEL & ESTHER (MERRITT) WILCOX; d 25 Oct 1876; Ref: CT Bible Rec v11 p551.

LUCY B - b 09 Dec 1816 d/SAMUEL & ABIGAIL (WHITE) WILCOX of Whitestown, Oneida Co NY; d 1896 Whitesboro NY; Ref: Your Ancestors v4 #1&2 p500.

LUCY B - b ca 1823 d/WILLIAM & ESTHER S (COLE) WILCOX of Portland, Chautauqua Co NY; m 01 Jun 1857 Arkwright, Chautauqua Co NY JAMES BARCLAY of Albion, Erie Co PA; Res Laona, Chautauqua Co NY & Brooklyn NY; d 1895 Ref: 19th Cent Marriages Reported in Fredonia Censor p119, 19th Cent Death Notices Reported in Fredonia Censor p 33, Your Ancestors v12 #3 p1463.

LUCY C - b 1825 Portland, Middlesex Co CT; m 21 Jan 1850 Portland CT HENRY F FISH who was b 1815; Res Waterbury, New Haven Co CT; Ref: Barbour's VR Portland v1 p273.

LUCY C - b 1846 NY d/ERASTUS & EUNICE (-----) WILCOX of Palerno, Oswego Co NY; Ref: 1850 Census Palerno NY p32 Dw# 470.

LUCY E - m 13 Oct 1819 Providence, Providence Co RI MATTHEW C RONNINGS; Res Beverly, Essex Co MA; Ref: Arnold v7 p512 v15 p441, v17 p566.

LUCY E - b 1841 NY d/LANSING H & MIRANDA (HOLMES) WILCOX of Napoli, Cattaraugus Co NY; Ref: 1850 Census Napoli NY p63 Dw# 138.

LUCY E - b 1849 NY d/HARRY C & ANNIS ----- WILCOX of Lebanon, Madison Co NY; Ref: 1850 Census Lebanon NY p118 Dw# 1999.

LUCY EMILY - b 08 Oct 1854; m 13 Apr 1871 NATHAN STRICKLAND; ch LUELLA, LOUISE; Ref: Denison Gen p505.

LUCY L - m 20 Sep 1828 Norwich, New London Co CT CHARLES C DALEY; Ref: Barbour's VR v5 p181.

LUCY LATHROP - b 31 Dec 1811 Norwich, New London Co CT d/De LAFAYETTE & EUNICE (MANNING) WILCOX; Ref: Barbour's VR Norwich v4 p227, See De Lafayette.

LUCY LOUISE - b 23 Mar 1807 d/ISAAC WILCOX; Ref: CT Bible Rec v11 p840.

LUCY M - m 02 Sep 1851 Hartford, Hartford Co CT SAMUEL F JONES Jr; Ref: Barbour's VR v1 p311.

LUCY MARIA - b 15 Jun 1820 Westfield, Middlesex Co CT d/ELISHA BACON & HEPZIBAH (CORNWELL) WILCOX; m 05 Aug 1845 GEORGE MILLER of Meriden, New Haven Co CT; Ref: Early Fam of Wallingford p333, Your

Ancestors v3 #5 p379, Barbour's VR Middletown v3 p536, Hist of Wallingford p939.

LUCY MARIA - b 08 Jun 1830 Madison, New Haven Co CT d/ZENAS/ZEUS & LOVISA (MEIGS) WILCOX; m 11 Feb 1855 DR WALTER SEWARD MUNGER of Watertown, Litchfield Co CT who d 15 Jun 1918; d 11 Feb 1906; Ref: Wilcox Meigs p93, Cutter's CT Fam v4 p1769, Fam of Early Guilford p1213, Barbour's VR Madison v2 p30.

LUCY MATILDA - b 06 Mar 1834 d/JEREMIAH & MELINDA (ABBEY) WILCOX of Springville, Erie Co NY; Res PA; m ALDEN KELLOGG; m ERASTUS WRIGHT; m LUMAN ROUP; ch by 1st husband CARLOS W, LUCY MARIE; ch by 2nd husband ERASTUS G, LURA E, LINDA MATILDA; Ref: Jane Smith.

LUCY MILLER - b 12 Feb 1796 Killingworth, Middlesex Co CT d/NATHAN & RACHEL (BENNET) WILCOX; Ref: Wilcox-Meigs p79, Barbour's VR Killingworth v2 p83.

LUCY TRYON - d 19 Jun 1826 Middletown, Middlesex Co CT d/JOSEPH Jr & MARIA (TRYON) WILCOX; Ref: Barbour's VR Middletown v3 p91.

LUCYETTE - b 1830 d/SYLVESTER & CAROLINE (BISSELL) WILCOX; m 19 Nov 1850 Colesville, Broome Co NY CHARLES PEASE of Speedsville, Tompkins Co NY who was b 1829 Tioga Co NY; d 1851; Ref: Marjorie Stoner Elmore.

LUELLA - b 08 Jan 1892 Farmington, Davis Co UT d/JAMES HENRY WILCOX; m 31 Jan 1917 ALBERT BRANDLEY; ch MARY W, REINARD WILCOX, PATRICIA, MONA; Ref: Desc of Wm Wilcoxson p148.

LUELLA AUGUSTA - b 06 Apr 1852 d/RANSLER & ANN JANE (SMITH) WILCOX; Ref: CT Bible Rec v4 p5.

LUELLY - b May 1860 NY d/RAMSLER & MARY (-----) WILCOX of Ellicott, Chautauqua Co NY; Ref: 1860 Census Ellicott NY p753 Dw# 1503.

LUKE - b 25 Apr 1812; m CAROLINE ----- who was b 1821 & d 12 Oct 1850 age 28; d 07 Jan 1870; both bur Maple Grove Cem Granville, Licking Co OH; Ref: OH Cem Rec p207.

LULA M - b 1873 IA d/ADELIA (-----) WILCOX who was b in NY; Res Lowell, Dodge Co WI; Ref: 1880 Soundex Dodge Co WI.

LULU EVALINA - b 28 Jul 1875 Tama, Tama Co IA d/LEWIS & RACHEL ANN (GLENN) WILCOX; m 23 Jun 1903 ELBA W LYKE; d 05 Feb 1904 Eagle Grove, Wright Co IA; Ref: Marjorie Stoner Elmore.

LUMAN - b 24 Sep 1782 Middletown, Middlesex Co CT s/EPHRAIM & DIADAMA (FRENCH) WILCOX; m 26 May 1803 ZIBA HOWARD who was b 04 Dec 1781; ch JANNA, CLARISSA, ANCIL, MARY, EPHRAIM, ADLINE DIADAMA, RHODA, JEMIMA; d 17 Apr 1847 Westminster, West Windham Co VT; Ref: MUH pp750,755, Your Ancestors v4 #5&6 p545, Texas Society DAR Roster v4 p2287.

LUMAN - b 01 Feb 1789 Barkhamsted, Litchfield Co CT s/JOSEPH & HANNAH(-----) WILCOX; Ref: Barbour's VR Barkhamsted v1 p56.

LUMAN Rev - b ca 1796 NH; m ELIZABETH C BLISS who was b Longmeadow CT (sic) [MA] & d 1876/7 Ford Co IL; Congregational minister; ch LUMAN B; Ref: Hist of Ford Co IL v2 p564-567.

LUMAN B - b Apr 1840 Loraine Twnshp, Jefferson Co NY s/ Rev LUMAN & ELIZABETH C (BLISS) WILCOX; m IDA B NORTON who was b 19 Aug 1846 Genesee Co NY d/HERMAN & LAURA (BROWN) NORTON; Res Ford Co IL; ch ERNEST NORTON, ALICE, LLOYD, ELIZABETH C; Ref: Your Ancestors v2 p255, Hist of Ford Co IL v2 pp564-567.

LUMAN C - b 1840 s/ANDREW & SALLY (PARSON) WILCOX of Whitingham, Windham Co VT; d 29 Dec 1862; Ref: Iris W Baird.

LUMAN H/LYMAN - Res Greene, Chenango Co NY 1820 3 sons & 4 dau; Ref: From Raft to Railroad p237.

LUNA - b ca 1850 s/LUTHER H & JEWELL (TRIPP) WILCOX; Res Springwater, Livingston Co NY; Ref: Your Ancestors v10 #3 p 1224.

LUNA F - b 1819; m JAMES GENOA ALMY who was b 1820 & d 1899; Res Interlaken, Seneca Co NY; d 1917; bur Lakeview Cem; Ref: Cem of Between the Lakes Country v2 p281.

LURA - b 1790 d/ROBERT & ANNA CLEMENCE (MILLS) WILCOX; m DRAYTON JONES; Ref: Your Ancestors v13 #2 p1540.

LURA - b ca 1800 d/STEPHEN & SABRA (PALMER) WILCOX of Busti, Chautauqua Co NY; m EDWARD AKIN;

Ref: Young's Hist of Chautauqua Co NY p241, Edson's Hist of Chautauqua Co p808.

LURANA - b 17 Oct 1829 Tiverton, Newport Co RI d/PARDON WILCOX; Ref: Arnold v8 p514.

LURINDA - b 23 Aug 1780 Wallingford, New Haven Co CT d/JAIRUS & MARY (ABBEY) WILCOX; Ref: Barbour's VR Wallingford v22 p408.

LURMAN C - b 1840 prob Whitingham, Windham Co VT s/ANDREW & SALLY (PARSONS) WILCOX; d 29 Dec 1862; Ref: Iris W Baird.

LUTHER - b 15 Dec 1764 Torrington, Litchfield Co CT s/ASAHEL & MARY (COE) WILCOX; Ref: Desc of Wm Wilcoxson p27, Barbour's VR Torrington v1 p107.

LUTHER - b 14 Apr 1771 Middletown, Middlesex Co CT s/NATHAN & LOIS (SAGE) WILCOX; m 01 Oct 1794 HULDAH PULSIFER/PILSIFER of Glastonbury, Hartford Co CT; ch HULDAH, ELECTY, NATHAN, FANNY, BETSEY; Res Middletown, Middlesex Co CT; Ref Barbour's VR Middletown v2 p223, v3 p23, Rocky Hill v1 p65.

LUTHER - b 28 Jan 1780 Portland, Middlesex Co CT s/AARON & SARAH (BELL) WILCOX; m LUCY BURT; Ref: Your Ancestors v4 #7&8 p565.

LUTHER - b 26 Apr 1781 Killingworth, Middlesex Co CT s/NATHAN 3rd & RACHEL (BENNET) WILCOX; Ref: Wilcox-Meigs p79, Barbour's VR Killingworth v2 p83.

LUTHER - m HARRIET FINCH d/CALEB FINCH of Galesburg, Knox Co IL; Ref: Hist of Knox Co IL p629.

LUTHER - b 1815 s/ISAAC & MARGARET (TOOLY) WILCOX of Lafayette, Onondaga Co NY; m CATHERINE ----- who was b 1825 NY; Res Lafayette NY; ch CAROLINE, HARRIETT L, MARGARETT ANN; Ref: Your Ancestors v13 #4 p1597, 1850 Census Lafayette NY p208 Dw# 251.

LUTHER - b 1828 VT; Res Bridport, Addison Co VT; Ref: 1850 Census Bridport VT Reel 920 p6.

LUTHER - b 1839 NY s/BENONI & CATHERINE (WILCOX) WILCOX of Pawling, Dutchess Co NY; Ref: 1850 Census Pawling NY p225 Dw# 94.

LUTHER D - s/SYLVESTER & CAROLINE (BISSELL) WILCOX; Ref: Marjorie Stoner Elmore.

LUTHER H - b 18 Feb 1847 Springwater, Livingston Co NY s/DAVID H & ADELIA (HOPKINS) WILCOX; m 19 Apr 1875 JEWELL TRIPP; ch CHARLES, LUNA, HOMER, NELLIE; Ref: Your Ancestors v10 #1 p1200 #2 p1224.

LUTHER M - m 28 Jun 1848 Wallingford, New Haven Co CT SARAH H DUDLEY; both of Middletown, Middlesex Co CT; Ref: Barbour's VR Wallingford v1 p255.

LUTHER P - b ca 1830 Brooklyn NY s/VILROY & HANNAH (PRATT) WILCOX; ch EDWIN; Ref: Wilcox-Meigs p120.

LUTHER P - b Plains, Luzerne Co PA s/SAMUEL & ELEANOR (KILMER) WILCOX; Ref: Hist of Luzerne Co PA p1456.

LUTHER T - b 02 Oct 1832 s/PETER C & MARY (YOUKER) WILCOX of Oswego NY & Decatur, Van Buren Co MI; m Dec 1859 REBECCA N CALDWELL; d 07 Apr 1904; Ref: George Koppers.

LUZINIA - b 1843 NY s/HENRY & LOUISA (-----) WILCOX of Parish, Oswego Co NY; Ref: 1850 Census Parish NY p4 Dw# 50.

LYDIA - b ca 1675 d/DANIEL & ELIZABETH (COOKE) WILCOX; m 26 May 1702 Portsmouth, Newport Co RI THOMAS SHEARMAN who was b 08 Aug 1658 s/PELEG & ELIZABETH (LAWTON) SHEARMAN; m 08 Dec 1720 THOMAS POTTER; ch by 1st husband JOSHUA/JOSIAH, RUTH, DANIEL, BENJAMIN; Res Dartmouth, Bristol Co MA & S Kingston, Washington Co RI; d be 1727; Ref: Am Gen v19 #1 p28, Your Ancestors v10 #3 p1244, Wilcox Excerpts v1 p21, Arnold v4 pt1 p47, Little Compton Fam p770, Talcott's Gen Notes p688, NEH&GR v24 p71.

LYDIA - b 14 Oct 1678 E Guilford, New Haven Co CT d/OBADIAH & LYDIA (ALLING) WILCOX; d 4 Nov 1678; Ref: Wilcox-Meigs p26, Desc of Wm Wilcoxson p8, Hist of Surry NH p944.

LYDIA - b ca 1704 d/SAMUEL & ----- (GRIFFIN) WILCOX of Simsbury, Hartford Co CT; m SAMUEL HAYS of Windsor CT; Ref: Wilcox-Meigs p31.

LYDIA - b 28 Jul 1713 Killingworth, Middlesex Co CT d/JOSEPH & HANNAH (KELSEY) WILCOX; m 01 Jan 1734/5 SAMUEL BUELL; Ref: Bogue Fam p394, Wilcox Meigs p30, Desc of Abner & Lucy Hart Wilcox p19, Barbour's VR Killingworth v2 p145.

LYDIA - b 12 Apr 1716 Hebron, Tolland Co CT d/EBENEZER & MARTHA (GAYLORD) WILCOX; m 12 Oct 1743 OBADIAH WILCOX of Guilford, New Haven Co CT who was b 15 Apr 1717 & d 26 Aug 1771 s/JOHN & DEBORAH (PARMELEE) WILCOX; Res Gilsum, Cheshire Co NH; ch LYDIA, OBADIAH, ELEAZER, DEBORAH; d 16 Jan 1796; Ref: Wilcox-Meigs pp32,50,51; Barbour's VR Hebron v1 p77, Guilford v2 p58, Desc of Wm Wilcoxson p15.

LYDIA - b 06 Apr 1725/6 Westerly, Washington Co RI d/EDWARD & DINAH (BARBER) WILCOX; Ref: Arnold v5 pt4 p144.

LYDIA - b 07 Sep 1734 Killingworth, Middlesex Co CT Twin with MARY d/STEPHEN & MARY (PIERSON) WILCOX; m 1756 SAMUEL/STEPHEN HURD; ch SAMUEL, STEPHEN, REBECCA, ASA, HEPSIBAH, LYDIA, POLLY, ELNATHAN; Ref: Bogue Fam p395, Cutter's New England Fam v1 p159, Your Ancestors v3 #3 pp321,322, Barbour's VR Killingworth v2 p159.

LYDIA - m 17 Dec 1761 GIDEON KIRTLAND; Res Saybrook, Middlesex Co CT; ch GIDEON, LYDIA, SARAH, RUTH, PHILIP; Ref: VR of CT v9 p59, Barbour's VR Saybrook v3 p213, NEH&GR v14 p244.

LYDIA - b 04 Mar 1735/6/7 Simsbury, Hartford Co CT d/AZARIAH & MARY (FAXTON) WILCOX; Ref: Wilcox-Meigs p49, Your Ancestors v11 #4 p1380, Desc of Wm Wilcoxson p23, Barbour's VR Simsbury TM3 p240, TM4 p249.

LYDIA - m 05 Oct 1748 Westfield, Hampden Co MA JEHIEL MESSINGER; Ref: Nutmegger v13 #1 p86.

LYDIA - b 10 May 1745 prob Guilford, New Haven Co CT d/OBADIAH & LYDIA (WILCOX) WILCOX; m 1767 ICHABOD SMITH; Res Surry, Cheshire Co NH; d 12 Apr 1830; Ref: Desc of Wm Wilcoxson p26, Wilcox-Meigs p51, Fam of Early Guilford p1209, Hist of Surry NH p946.

LYDIA - m 06 Jul 1768 RI DANIEL BROWN; Ref: Arnold v7 p372.

LYDIA - b 07 Nov 1751 Guilford, New Haven Co CT d/JONATHAN & EXPERIENCE (WILLIAMS) WILCOX; m 27 Feb 1773 JOB DOWD; Ref: Wilcox-Meigs p45, Barbour's VR Guilford v2 p160.

LYDIA - b 09 Jan 1756 Middletown, Middlesex Co CT d/ELIJAH & ABIGAIL (CHURCHILL) WILCOX; Ref: Barbour's VR Middletown v1 p28.

LYDIA - b 1757 Middletown, Middlesex Co CT; d Mar 1829 Ashford, Windham Co CT; Ref: Bowman's CT VR.

LYDIA - b 11 Mar 1764 Exeter, Washington Co RI d/JOHN & MARY (BARBER) WILCOX; Res Norwich, New London Co CT; Ref: Your Ancestors v4 #7&8 p561, Arnold v5 pt3 p63.

LYDIA - b 11 Oct 1766 d/JEFFREY & LUCY (-----) WILCOX; Ref: Your Ancestors v4 #3&4 p520.

LYDIA - b 11 Oct 1766 d/ABRAHAM & MARTHA (WILCOX) WILCOX m 23 Feb 1786 Foster, Providence Co RI JOHN PLACE; ch SAMUEL, JOB, HAZARD, ABRAHAM; d 29 Jul 1849; Ref: Arnold v3 31, Your Ancestors v4 #1&2 p495, #3&4 p519.

LYDIA - b 19 Feb 1767 Westport, Bristol Co MA d/SAMUEL & COMFORT (SEABURY) WILCOX; m 11 Dec 1788 ELLIS BRIGHTMAN s/HENRY BRIGHTMAN; Ref: Westport VR pp102,252, Your Ancestors v13 #2 p1554.

LYDIA - b 28 Jul 1767 Newport, Newport Co RI d/SAMUEL & ELIZABETH (GODDARD) WILCOX; d 07 Sep 1770; Ref: Arnold v7 p82, See Samuel.

LYDIA - b ca 1768 d/JOHN & GRACE NORTH (GRISWOLD) WILCOX; m MARCUS MERRIAM; Res Clinton, Middlesex Co CT; Ref: Desc of Wm Wilcoxson p26, Wilcox-Meigs p52.

LYDIA - b ca 1768 d/ABRAHAM & LYDIA (HARRINGTON) WILCOX; m JOHN LILLIBRIDGE who was b 19 Feb 1763 & d 07 Apr 1835 s/EDWARD & PATIENCE (TEFFT) LILLIBRIDGE of Richmond, Washington Co RI; Res Exeter Washington Co RI; ch LYDIA; Ref: Your Ancestors v4 #7&8 p561, Gen of RI Fam v1 p654.

LYDIA - b 13 Dec 1770 Goshen, Litchfield Co CT d/ELIJAH & SILENCE (-----) WILCOX; m 16 Jan 1789 JOHN NOBLE who was b 25 Oct 1762 Hebron, Tolland Co CT & d 29 Apr 1842 Orwell VT s/Capt JAMES NOBLE; Res Orwell, Addison Co VT; ch AURELIA,

LYDIA, JOHN, LUCRETIA, HIRAM JEFFERSON, JOHN DWIGHT; d 01 Jan 1807; Ref: Iowa Surnames v3 p695, Desc of Thomas Noble p659.

LYDIA - b 28 Aug 1772 Killingworth, Middlesex Co CT d/SIMEON & LUCRETIA (KELSEY) WILCOX; Ref: Wilcox-Meigs p67, Barbour's VR Killingworth v2 p88.

LYDIA - b 01 Jan 1773 Hebron, Tolland Co CT d/JEHIEL & LYDIA (MACK) WILCOX; Ref: Wilcox-Meigs p69, Barbour's VR Hebron v2 p259.

LYDIA - b 18 Sep 1773 d/SAMUEL & ELIZABETH (GODDARD) WILCOX; Ref: Your Ancestors v11 #3 p1372.

LYDIA - b 15 Jan/22 Nov 1775 Gilsum, Cheshire Co NH d/OBADIAH & SARAH (TALCOTT) WILCOX; m BENJAMIN PORTER; m 1821 HENRY SCOVILLE; d 24 Dec 1869 Surry NH; Ref: Desc of Wm Wilcoxson p26, Hist of Surry NH p945.

LYDIA - b 26 Jul 1775 Sandisfield, Berkshire Co MA d/JOEL & LYDIA (-----) WILCOX; Ref: Sandisfield MA VR p72, Fiske Card File, Desc of Wm Wilcoxson p245.

LYDIA - b 23 Nov 1779 d/STEPHEN Jr & SARAH (HULL) WILCOX; Ref: Your Ancestors v3 #3 p322, Barbour's VR Killingworth v2 p116.

LYDIA - b 23 Aug 1780 Bridport, Addison Co VT d/JAMES & EUNICE (VICKERY) WILCOX; m 27 Sep 1797 BENJAMIN MOORE; Ref: Your Ancestors v3 #9&10 p449, Texas Society DAR Roster v4 p2287, Desc of Wm Wilcoxson p118.

LYDIA - b 21 Mar 1782 Chicopee, Hampden Co MA; m 21 Mar 1799 Suffield Hartford Co CT SAMUEL WARNER Jr who was b 04 Jun 1780 Suffield CT & d 05 Jun 1816; Ref: Nutmegger v13 #2 p239, v17 #4 p607, Barbour's Vr Suffield NB1 p311.

LYDIA - b 19 Sep 1791 Killingworth, Middlesex Co CT Twin with RACHEL d/NATHAN & RACHEL (BENNETT) WILCOX; Ref: Wilcox-Meigs p79, Barbour's VR Killingworth v2 p83.

LYDIA - b 1797 NY; d Apr 1850 Grove, Allegany Co NY; Ref: Tree Talks v6 #1 p10.

LYDIA - b 10 Oct 1799 Danube, Herkimer Co NY d/ISAIAH & POLLY (PENDLETON) WILCOX; Ref: Wilcox-Brown-Medbery p11.

LYDIA - b 14 Mar 1804 Cumberland, Providence Co RI d/STEPHEN & SUSANNA (TILLSON) WILCOX; Ref: Arnold's VR v3 p134 #2 p173, Your Ancestors v11 #2 p1345.

LYDIA - d/ERASTUS & MARGARET (KING?) WILCOX of Washington, Madison, Ontario Cos NY; m 05 Oct 1828 Dearborn Co IN JOSEPH NORRIS; Ref: Janet Armbrust.

LYDIA - b 16 Aug 1806 Ashford, Windham Co CT d/WEEKS & SALLY (HUTCHINSON) WILCOX; Ref: Your Ancestors v3 #9&10 p448, Wilcox Genealogy p7.

LYDIA - b 01 Jan 1815 Lowville, Lewis Co NY d/ROSWELL & IRENE (NICHOLSON) WILCOX; m CHARLES PUTTEREL of Fulton, Oswego Co NY; d 1866; Ref: Cutter's Northern NY v2 p656, Desc of Wm Wilcoxson p65.

LYDIA - m 10 Jan 1844 Brandon, Franklin Co NY WILLIAM H HOYT; Ref: Tree Talks v4 #3 p2.

LYDIA - m 04 Feb 1846 E Greenwich, Kent Co RI JESSE CARR; Ref: Arnold v1 p92.

LYDIA - b 1829 NY d/BENJAMIN & ESTHER (-----) WILCOX of Verona, Oneida Co NY; Ref: Your Ancestors v4 #1&2 p498, 1850 Census Verona NY p173 Dw# 743.

LYDIA - b 22 Mar 1844 d/DAVIS YEATS & HANNAH (YOUNG) WILCOX; Ref: Your Ancestors v11 #4 p1397.

LYDIA - d/STERLING & NANCY (BUSH) WILCOX of Hastings, Barry Co MI; m ISAAC VAN VOORHEES; Ref: Your Ancestors v14 #2 p1645.

LYDIA - b 1845 NY d/HENRY & SARAH (-----) WILCOX of Ripley & Chautauqua, Chautauqua Co NY; Ref: 1850 Census Ripley NY p118 Dw# 249, 1860 Census Chautauqua NY p64 Dw# 478.

LYDIA - b 1846 NY Twin with JAMES d/CHENEY & AMITY (-----) WILCOX of Onondaga, Onondaga Co NY; Ref: 1850 Census Onondaga NY p324 Dw# 1492.

LYDIA F - b 1849 CT d/ABRAM & REBECCA A (-----) WILCOX of Griswold, New London Co CT; Ref: 1850 Census Griswold CT Reel 432 #49 p23.

LYDIA G - b ca 1800 d/AARON & ELIZABETH (-----) WILCOX NY; Res Madison & Chautauqua Co NY; Ref: Your Ancestors v12 #2 p1438.

LYDIA HART - b 08 Jul 1824 Middletown, Middlesex Co CT d/ALSA & EMILY (TREAT) WILCOX; m 11 Jun 1844 ALBERT BACON who d 01 Mar 1907 s/EBENEZER & LAVINIA (WILCOX) BACON; d at Middletown CT 22 Jul 1893; Ref: MUH p756, Barbour's VR Middletown v3 p518.

LYDIA J - b 1847 Cherry, Creek Chautauqua Co NY d/ERASTUS B & ROXY (BUGBEE) WILCOX; m af 1870 ROLLIN/ROLAND ALDRICH who d 1934; Res Chautauqua Co NY; ch ADDIE, ABBIE, MANLEY; d 1930; Ref: Wilcox Hist mss, 1850 Census Cherry Creek NY p136 Dw# 1842, 1860 Census Villanova NY p545 Dw# 1496, 1870 Census Chautauqua Co NY p187.

LYDIA M - b 1856 NY d/HORACE J & RACHEL (-----) WILCOX of Collins, Erie Co NY; Ref: Alice Wiatr.

LYDIA PLACE - b 14 Jun 1808 Foster, Providence Co RI d/STEPHEN & SUSANNAH (LEWIS) WILCOX; Ref: Arnold v3 p42, Your Ancestors v4 #1&2 p496.

LYMAN - b 20 Aug 1782 Middletown, Middlesex Co CT s/JOSIAH & HULDAH (SAVAGE) WILCOX; d 05 Sep 1782; Ref: MUH p752, Barbour's VR Middletown v2 p221.

LYMAN 2nd - b 19 Dec 1783 s/JOSIAH & HULDAH (SAVAGE) WILCOX; m LINA DICKENSON who was b 1787 & d 1858; Res Berlin, Hartford Co CT; ch JULIA ANN, LYMAN, SHERMAN; d 1828; Ref: MUH p757, Barbour's VR Middletown v2 p221.

LYMAN - b 25 Sep 1784 N Stonington, New London Co CT s/FRANCIS & MARTHA (WORDEN) WILCOX; m ca 1806 ELIZA/ELIZABETH A WHEELER who was b 1788 RI; Res CT & Homer, Cortland Co NY 1814; ch LUCINDA, ELIZA ANN, AMOS N, NELSON F, CONTENT, LYMAN, GEORGE W; Ref: Your Ancestors v13 #2 p1539, #3 p1565, 1850 Census Stonington CT Reel 432 #48 p309, Barbour's VR Stonington v1 p36.

LYMAN - s/FRANCIS & MEHITABLE (-----) WILCOX of Durham, Greene Co NY; Ref: Your Ancestors v3 #11&12 p476, Wills of Green Co NY v1 p39.

LYMAN - b 24 Jun 1785 Woodstock, Windham Co CT; Ref: Barbour's VR Woodstock Brown Diary p35.

LYMAN - b 1791 s/NATHAN & SYLVIA (HOPKINS) WILCOX of E Bloomfield, Ontario Co NY; m HOPIE GREEN d/JAMES & HOPESTILL (-----) GREEN; Res Bristol, Ontario Co NY; m SALOME ----- who was b 1804; Ref: Your Ancestors v10 #1 p1201, Desc of Wm Wilcoxson p204.

LYMAN - b 13 Jan 1795 Haddam, Middlesex Co CT s/JAMES & ELIZABETH BRADLEY (AUGER) WILCOX; m 30 Nov 1815 EMILY HUBBARD who was b 26 Sep 1797 & d 03/12 Jun 1868; Res Hancock Co IL; ch JULIA ANN, LINUS LYMAN, HORACE HUBBARD, ELECTA ELIZABETH, EMILY NERRITS, CLARISSA, FANNY CALISTA, WILBUR FISK; d 20 Aug 1874 Hancock IL Ref: Your Ancestors v4 #1&2 p497, Desc of Wm Wilcox pp130-132.

LYMAN - b 04 Jun 1795 Exeter, Washington Co RI s/ASA & ELEANOR (LAWTON) WILCOX; d 1796; Ref: Your Ancestors v4 #11&12 p610.

LYMAN - b 11 May 1798 or 17 Jul 1800 Richmond, Washington Co RI s/BENJAMIN & ELIZABETH (RECORDS) WILCOX; m 1823 HANNAH LILLIBRIDGE d/CHAMPLIN & HANNAH (WILCOX) LILLIBRIDGE ch ROSANNA, HARRIET, DELOS; d 09 Feb 1868; Ref: Your Ancestors v14 #1 p1618, #2 p1643.

LYMAN - b 1799 MA s/JAIRUS & MARY (ABBEY) WILCOX; m MARY ----- who was b 1798; ch HARRIETT, ELIAS, ALMIRA, ELIZABETH, LYMAN; Ref: Your Ancestors v4 #1&2 p499.

LYMAN - b ca 1802 RI s/THOMAS JAMES & LUCY (-----) WILCOX; Res Cortland Co NY, Parents moved to Lapeer Co MI; Ref: Detroit Soc Gen Research Mag v54 # 2.

LYMAN - of Granby, Hartford Co CT m 13 Jan 1830 Simsbury, Hartford Co CT ANNA TULLER; Ref: Rev Allen McLean Rec p20, Barbour's VR Simsbury TM4 p518.

LYMAN - of Preston, Chenango Co NY; m EUNICE ----- who was b 1800 & d 17 June 1820 or 08 Jun 1821; Ref: 10,000 VR Central NY p265.

LYMAN - b 1812 NY; m ca 1835 SALLY M OSBORNE who was b 1809 CT; Res Verona & Vernon, Oneida Co NY; ch HARRIET R, WILLIAM C; Mentioned in will of WAKEMAN OSBORNE Verona, Oneida Co NY probated 08 Nov 1841; also mentioned in will of CATHARINE KENNEDY of Vernon, Oneida Co NY probated 08 Nov

1841; Ref: 1840 Census Verona NY p123 Dw# 14, 1860 Census Vernon NY, Oneida Co Wills v4 p24.

LYMAN - b 1814 s/LYMAN & ELIZA A (WHEELER) WILCOX; m ANGELINE -----; Res Stonington, New London Co CT & Homer, Cortland Co NY; Ref: Your Ancestors v13 #3 p1565.

LYMAN - b 03 Jun 1816 Franklin, New London Co CT s/JOHN CLARK & DORCAS (HARRINGTON) WILCOX; m JOHANNAH GUISLER who was b 1816 Saxony; Res MI, TX & Sherman, Chautauqua Co NY; ch CAROLINE, FRANCIS, ELIZA, HENRY, MARY, PERRY; d af 1870; Ref: 1850 Census Sherman NY p276 Dw# 68, 1870 Census Sherman NY, Your Ancestors v14 #2 p1658.

LYMAN - b 14 Aug 1818 Halifax, Windham Co VT s/JOSEPH & MARGARET (PEARCE) WILCOX; Ref: Halifax Wilcox Fam mss.

LYMAN - b 1819 CT s/LYMAN & LINA (DICKENSON) WILCOX; m 26 Sep 1843 MARIA BULKLEY; Res Berlin, Hartford Co CT; ch LYMAN, ROBERT, HARRIET LOUISA; d 10 Mar 1855; Ref: MUH p757, Barbour's VR Berlin v1 p74.

LYMAN - b 01 June 1824 Lowville, Lewis Co NY s/ROSWELL & IRENE (NICHOLSON) WILCOX; m 10/20 Feb 1849 MARTHA B WEAVER; ch ELLA LOUISA; Ref: Cutter's Northern NY v2 p656, Desc of Wm Wilcoxson p65.

LYMAN - b 14 Jan 1825 Warsaw, Wyoming Co NY; m 06 Oct 1853 Delavan, Walworth Co WI ELIZABETH COTTON; ch HENRIETTA; d 03 Nov 1905 Delavan WI; Ref: Edna L Weaver.

LYMAN - s/LYMAN & MARIA (BULKELY) WILCOX; m ca 1840 E Berlin, Hartford Co CT ADDIE SPERRY; Ref: MUH p757.

LYMAN - b 1838 NY s/JOHN & AMY (-----) WILCOX of Mina, Chautauqua Co NY; Ref: 1850 Census Mina NY p298 Dw# 75.

LYMAN - s/LYMAN & MARY (-----) WILCOX; d 1844; Ref: Your Ancestors v4 #1&2 p499.

LYMAN - b 1840/43 NY s/OZIAL Jr & SYLVIA (STEVENS) WILCOX; Res Georgetown twnshp, Madison Co NY; Ref: Desc of Wm Wilcoxson p169, 1850 Census Georgetown NY p387 Dw# 208.

LYMAN G Sr - Moved from Rome, Oneida Co NY to Oakland Co MI 1824; Ref: Yesteryears v23 #92 p81.

LYMAN S - b 1828 NY; m ASENETH ----- who was b 1826 NY; ch WALTER; Res Wirt, Allegany Co NY; Ref: 1850 Census Wirt NY p149 Dw# 158.

LYMAN W - b Jan 1893 NY s/PORTER B & MARY MAY (FROST) WILCOX; m 08 Oct 1916 Cassadaga, Chautauqua Co NY MABEL J BRIGGS of Sinclairville, Chautauqua Co NY; Res Arkwright, Chautauqua Co NY; ch LYMAN; Ref: Wilcox Hist mss, 1910 Census Arkwright NY, Lois Barris.

LYNDA - b 31 Oct 1786 d/JOSIAH & HULDAH (SAVAGE) WILCOX; m 1811 REUBEN NORTH who was b 1787 & d 04 Apr 1853; d 18 Mar 1816; Ref: MUH p752.

LYNN DEE - b 12 Feb 1865 s/GARDNER NICHOLS & GENORA EVALINA (COLLINS) WILCOX; m 23 Dec 1885 MAY NEWELL who was b 01 Jun 1865; Res 90 Ft Madison St Cortland, Cortland Co NY; ch LOIS, CHARLOTTE FLORENCE, GENORA, NEWELL LYNN; Ref; Your Ancestors v3 #5 p375, #6 p397.

LYNN FRANCIS - b 25 Oct 1888 Gilby, Dakota Terr s/JAY EUGENE & KATE IDA (LOVELL) WILCOX; Res Portland, Multnomah Co OR; m 05 Feb 1913 Sask CANADA LUCY M HARRIOTT who was b Havelock IA d/JESSE HARRIOTT; ch ROBERTA BLANCHE (adpt), JESSE HARRIOTT (adpt), HARRIET MARCEE (natural); Ref: Anne Ritchie FGS.

LYSANDER - b 02 Aug 1799 s/MARTIN & GERUSHA (DEWEY) WILCOX of Saratoga Co & Albany Co NY; d 08 Apr 1800; Ref: Detroit Mag v6 p71, Fiske Card File.

LYSANDER - b 1835 NY s/SAMUEL & DEBORAH (SMITH) WILCOX of Concord, Erie Co NY; Ref: 1850 Census Concord NY p52 Dw# 758, See Samuel.

LYSANDER BYRAM - b 1810 Stamford, Fairfield Co CT prob s/WILLIAM J & LURANAH (GREEN) WILCOX; m RACHEL (CHILDS) LEDYARD who was b 1816 & d 1859; m MATILDA SHELDON who was b 1826 & d 1897; ch by 1st wife LEONARD, SOPHIA, HORATIO, WILLIAM, LEORA/LOUISA, JANE, HELEN; d 1903 Napoli, Cattaraugus Co NY; Ref: Cem Inscr Napoli Corners, Hist of Cattaraugus Co NY p478, 1850 Census Napoli NY p57 Dw# 43, 1860 Census Napoli NY Reel 653 #726 p52.

LYSTER - b 1846 OH s/SYLVESTER & HARRIET (-----) WILCOX of Hiram, Portage Co OH; Ref: 1850 Census Hiram OH p3 Dw# 37.

--- M ---

M A - b 1842; m CARRIE L who was b 1845 & d 1904; bur Maple Grove Cem Granville, Licking Co OH; Ref: OH Cem Rec p206.

M ANNIE - b 20 Oct 1857 d/BENJAMIN & DELIA (-----) WILCOX: d 04 Nov 1882 Tiverton, Newport Co RI; Ref: NEH&GR v67 p507, Gen of RI Fam v2 p596.

M B - b 1820 NY; Res Ravenna, Portage Co OH; Lawyer; Ref: 1850 Census Ravenna OH p124.

M I - b 1772 CT; Res Seneca Falls, Seneca Co NY; Painter; ch ALFRED with whom he lived;_Ref: 1850 Census Seneca Falls NY p262 Dw# 1890.

M LAVINA - b 12 Jan 1843 Clinton, Middlesex Co CT d/DANIEL & LAVINA (-----) WILCOX; m 29 Oct 1859 ALBERT H WOODRUFF; Ref: CT Bible Rec v8 pp302,303.

M R - b 1837 Monroe Co NY; Postmaster Fairport, Monroe Co NY; Ref: Hist of Monroe Co NY p318.

MABEL - b 14 Apr 1747 Killingworth, Middlesex Co CT d/NATHANIEL & MINDWELL (WILCOX) WILCOX; Ref: Wilcox Meigs p44, Desc of Wm Wilcoxson p20, Barbour's VR Killingworth v2 p148.

MABEL - b 06 Dec 1752 Killingworth, Middlesex Co CT d/STEPHEN & MARY (PIERSON) WILCOX; m 07 Apr 1768 NATHAN GRAVES; Ref: Wilcox-Meigs p42, Bogue Fam p395, Cutter's New England Fam v1 p159, Your Ancestors v3 #3 p321, Barbour's VR Killingworth v2 p159.

MABEL - b ca 1754; m 15 Feb 1779 Cromwell, Middlesex Co CT WILLIAM BULKLEY; Ref: ECM v2 p94.

MABEL - b 25 May 1755 East Guilford, New Haven Co CT d/JOSEPH Jr & SARAH (MUNGER) WILCOX; m CHRISTOPHER FOSTER who was b 26 Aug 1753 s/CHRISTOPHER & HANNAH (TURNER) FOSTER; Ref: Wilcox-Meigs p53, Cutter's CT Fam v4 p1769, Fam of Early Guilford pp452,1209, Desc of Wm Wilcoxson p28, Barbour's VR Guilford v2 p100.

MABEL - b 01 Feb 1756 Middletown, Middlesex Co
CT d/OZIAS & MABEL (GOULD) WILCOX; d 26 Sep 1774;
Ref: Barbour's VR Middletown v2 p322, Hale Coll.

MABEL - bpt Dec 1788 Ripton CT d/JAMES &
MEHETABLE (BEARDSLEY) WILCOX; Ref: Wilcox-Meigs
p79, Stratford Gen p1347.

MABEL - b 02 Sep 1795 d/JEREMIAH & RUTH
(DUDLEY) WILCOX of Middletown, Middlesex Co CT;
Ref: Mrs Wm Richardson, Barbour's VR Middletown v2
p159.

MABEL - b 31 Oct 1815 Killingworth, Middlesex
Co CT d/AARON & MABEL (LORD) WILCOX; Res
Twinsburg, Summit Co OH; d 08 Jul 1835; Ref: Gen
of Lord Fam p289, Wilcox Meigs p81, Your Ancestors
v3 #3 p321, Barbour's VR Killingworth v2 p14.

MABEL - m ----- ROBBINS; Mentioned in brother
OZIAS WILCOX'S will probated New Hartford, Oneida
Co NY 26 Feb 1838; Ref: Wills of Oneida Co NY v3
p42.

MABEL - b 1874 NY d/GEORGE S & MARY E (BENTON)
WILCOX of Alma, Allegany Co NY; Ref: Carol A Cox.

MABEL - b 12 Jul 1882 Butler Co KS d/BOARDMAN
HUBBARD & EMMA (OLINGER) WILCOX; Ref: Desc of Wm
Wilcoxson p131.

MABEL E - b 13 Feb 1871 Lycoming Co PA d/GEORGE
HENRY & ORRILLA ELIZABETH (ROOT) WILCOX; m 21 Mar
1891 AUGUST CHARLES ROSENTHALB who was b 05 Jun
1866 & d 04 May 1952; d 16 Nov 1967; Ref: Halifax
VT Wilcox Fam mss.

MABEL MARIAH - b 18 Sep 1798 Killingworth,
Middlesex Co CT d/NATHAN2nd & ELIZABETH (ELIOT)
WILCOX; Ref: Wilcox-Meigs p65, Barbour's VR
Killingworth v2 p97.

MABEL RUTH - b 24 May 1822 IL d/FREDERICK
WILLIAM & MARY ELIZABETH (MEAGHER) WILCOX; m LEWIS
MOODEY WORLEY; Res Aurora, Kane Co IL; ch ELVA
NEVIN, GRACE ELIZABETH; Ref: MUH p745.

MADELINE - b 1871 Rowe, Franklin Co MA d/HENRY
THOMAS & AMELIA M (-----) WILCOX; Ref: Halifax VT
Wilcox Fam mss.

MADISON - b 1830; m ELIZABETH ----- who was b 1847 & d 1925; d 1908 Frenchville, Oneida Co NY; Ref: Tree Talks v14.

MAGGIE - b ca 1880 d/RUSH WRIGHT & JENNIE (PORTER) WILCOX; m ----- MILLER; Res Chautauqua Co NY; Ref: Wilcox Hist mss.

MAGGIE R - m 02 Aug 1882 Greene Co IA GEORGE J MARTIN; Ref: Hawkeye Heritage v15 #3 p134.

MAHALA - b ca 1775 d/DANIEL & HANNAH (WILBUR) WILCOX; m 19 MAY 1793 HEZEKIAH WILCOX who was b Dec 1769 s/AMOS & MARY (-----) WILCOX; Res Bradford Co PA; ch HEZEKIAH, DANIEL, HANNAH, ELIZABETH, RICHARD, SAMUEL, MARGARET, JANE, MARY, HEZEKIAH; Ref: Your Ancestors v10 #3 pp1247,1248.

MAHALA - b 09 Aug 1837 d/RICHARD & ELIZABETH (LEWIS) WILCOX of Canton, Bradford Co PA; Ref: Your Ancestors v10 #4 p1273.

MAHALA C - b ca 1829 Chautauqua Co NY d/WILLIAM & ESTHER S (COLE) WILCOX; d 1831; Ref: Your Ancestors v12 #3 p1463.

MAIN W - b Apr 1853 Chautauqua Co NY s/DANIEL T & POLLY M (COX) WILCOX; m 17 Jul 1876 Villanova, Chautauqua Co NY LYDIA A PRICE of Cherry Creek, Chautauqua Co NY who was b Sep 1851 NY; Res Ellington, Chautauqua Co NY; ch KATIE, JOHN L; Ref: Wilcox Hist mss, 1860 Census Ellington NY p109 Dw# 442, 1910 Census, 19th Cent Marriages Reported in Fredonia Censor p244.

MALINA - b 1805 d/ENOCH & NANCY (WOODRUFF) WILCOX of East Bloomfield, Ontario Co NY; Ref: Your Ancestors v10 #1 p1202.

MALINDA - b 1820 NY d/EBEN & RACHEL (-----) WILCOX of Cortlandville, Cortland Co NY & WI; Ref: Your Ancestors v9 #4 p1178.

MALINDA - b 20 Feb 1854 Deep Cove, N B Canada d/WILLIAM & JANE (DRISCOLL) WILCOX; m CLEVELAND RUSSELL s/SOLOMON & JENETT (GREEN) RUSSELL; ch IDA MAY, JENNIE, MABURY OLEE; d 23 Oct 1953 bur Seal Cove N B Canada; Ref: Desc of Charles Dyer Wilcox p10.

MALINDA CAROLINE - b 09 Jan 1882 N B Canada d/SILAS & ELVIRA JOANNE (LAMBERT); m HERBERT

PARKS; d & bur Blue Lake, Humboldt Co CA; Ref: Desc of Charles Dyer Wilcox p2.

MALISSA - b 21 Jun 1781 RI d/DANIEL & OLIVE (-----) WILCOX; Ref: Arnold v2 p96.

MALISTA - m 10 Jun 1821 Barkhamsted, Litchfield Co CT MATTHEW MOSES; Ref: Barbour's VR Barkhamsted v1 p186.

MALVILLE I - b 1843 NY s/DUDLEY & KEZIAH (TOWNSEND) WILCOX of Litchfield, Herkimer Co NY; Ref: 1850 Census Litchfield NY p133 Dw# 282.

MALVINA - b ca 1820 Galesburgh, Knox Co IL d/ANSON & MILLY (RUSSELL) WILCOX; Ref: Wilcox Meigs p100.

MAMIE FLOELLA - b 26 May 1884 N B Canada d/REUBEN CLIFTON & SARAH JANE (WILCOX) WILCOX; m CALVIN BENSON who was b 1883 & d 17 Dec 1963; ch ELEANOR E, GEORGE WALTON, ELSIE G, ETHEAL, EMILY E, EMERSON W, ELDEN G, ELLA M, ETHELWYN E, EULAH E, EVERETTE C, GEORGIA M; d 12 Jun 1966; Bur Wesleyan Cem; Ref: Desc of Charles Dyer Wilcox pp19,20.

MAMIE JESSIE - b 12 Jul 1869 CA d/ORIGEN ABBEY & CLARA JANE (EMERSON) WILCOX; m 21 Mar 1891 JAMES AJAX PUTNAM who was b 29 Jan 1864 Covington PA & d 20 Jan 1944 nephew of PORTER PUTNAM after whom Porterville is named; Res Porterville, Tulare Co CA; ch ROYAL FREDRICK, JAMES ALBERT, EMORY ORIGIN, MARVIN EMERSON; d 28 Nov 1958 bur Home of Peace Cem Porterville CA; Ref: Jane Smith.

MANFRED AUGUSTUS - b 15 May 1830 E Guilford, New Haven Co CT s/ABEL & ANNA (FIELD) WILCOX; m 27 Jun 1852 Saybrook, Middlesex Co CT NANCY SOPHRONIA SMITH of Westbrook, Middlesex Co CT who d 04 Apr 1857; m 16 Oct 1864 JEANETTE LODENA SNOW of Clinton Middlesex Co CT; ch of 1st wife NANCY SMITH, ch of 2nd wife BLANCHE EDITH, EDWARD ARTHUR, JESSIE LOUISA, WALTER AUGUSTUS; d Jan 1906; Ref: Saybrook Colony VR p335, Wilcox-Meigs pp92,111, Fam of Early Guilford p1213, Barbour's VR Westbrook v1 p12, Madison v2 p30.

MANLEY - b 1825 Cortland Co NY s/FRANCIS & POLLY (WEEKS) WILCOX; m CATHARINE WELCH who was b 1830 Cortland Co NY; Ref: Your Ancestors v13 #2 p1539, v14 #1 p1617, 1850 Census Cortland NY p343.

MANLY - b 1848 NY s/WILLIAM & MARY (-----) WILCOX of Chautauqua, Chautauqua Co NY; Ref: 1860 Census Chautauqua NY p69 Dw# 521.

MANLY M - m 14 Feb 1836 Madison, New Haven Co CT MABEL NORTON who was b 29 Oct 1812 d/DANIEL & LOIS (HILL) NORTON; Ref: Fam of Early Guilford p905, Barbour's VR Madison v1 p22.

MARA - b 1851 d/EZRA STILES & MARTHA (PETTIT) WILCOX of Clockville, Madison Co NY & IA; Ref: Pioneers of Madison Co NY p281.

MARCELLUS - b 03 Dec 1829 Lowville, Lewis Co NY s/ROSWELL & IRENE (NICHOLSON) WILCOX; m MARY J WILCOX d/ELISHA J WILCOX Jr; ch MINNIE; Ref: Cutter's Northern NY v2 p657, Desc of Wm Wilcoxson p65.

MARCENAH B - int to marry 22 Apr 1864 ANGENETTE F BLISS both of Taunton, Bristol Co MA; Ref: VR Freetown MA.

MARCUS - b 1834 NY s/HARRY & HARRIET (-----) WILCOX of Pompey, Onondaga Co NY; Ref: 1850 Census Pompey NY p121 Dw# 1891.

MARCUS - m 23 Sep 1869 Smith's Mills, Chautauqua Co NY SARAH A WHITE both of Leon, Cattaraugus Co NY; Ref: 19th Cent Marriages Reported in Fredonia Censor p244.

MARCUS A - b 1855 NY s/ANDREW J & ESTHER T (-----) WILCOX of Ellicott, Chautauqua Co NY; Ref: 1850 Census Ellicott NY p753 Dw# 1502.

MARCUS B - b 24 Jun 1821 Arkwright, Chautauqua Co NY s/WILLIAM & ESTHER S (COLE) WILCOX; Res Pinckney, Livingston Co MI; MI State Senator & Atty; d 08 Sep 1868 Columbus, Franklin Co OH; Ref: Down's Hist of Chautauqua Co p262, Your Ancestors v12 #3 p1463, Desc of Wm Wilcoxson p223, 19th Cent Deaths Reported in Fredonia Censor p596.

MARCUS CALVIN - b 30 Nov 1817/18 s/WILLIAM & GULIELMA (ESTES) WILCOX; m 19 Apr 1846 ELIZA A KNOWLTON d/METIAH & POLLY (-----) KNOWLTON; Res Blackstone, Worcester Co MA; Ref: Snow-Estes Ancestry v2 p18, Your Ancestors v11 #2 p1345.

MARCUS D - b 1805 NY; m 18 Oct 1832 Onondaga, Onondaga Co NY JULIA A HUMPHREY who was b 1805 NY; Res Elba Genesee Co NY; Ref: 10,000 VR of

Central NY p264, 1850 Census Elba NY p354 Dw# 2078.

MARCUS W Dr - b 14 Jun 1832 Honeoye Falls, Monroe Co NY; m ANGELINE C HALL; m LYDIA MARTIN 1881; Moved to Clay Co NE 1872; Ref: Nebraska Ancestree v13 #2 p64.

MARGARET - b 09 Jan 1671 Killingworth, Middlesex Co CT d/JOSEPH & ANN (SHEATHER) WILCOX; m JOSEPH GRAVES; d 09 Feb 1763 Guilford, New Haven Co CT; Ref: Wilcox-Meigs p23, Desc of Wm Wilcoxson pp28,36, Bogue Fam p394, Desc of Abner & Lucy Hart Wilcox p18, Cutter's Northern NY v2 p656, Cutter's New England Fam v1 p159.

MARGARET - b ca 1676 Simsbury, Hartford Co CT d/SAMUEL & HANNAH (RICE) WILCOX; d 1714; ch BENONI VIETS who inherited her estate; Ref: Wilcox-Meigs p25, Desc of Wm Wilcoxson pp6,28.

MARGARET - b 20 Apr 1712 Killingworth, Middlesex Co CT d/JOHN & HANNAH (SHAILOR) WILCOX; m 10 May 1737 HIEL KELSEY; ch died young; d 1752; Ref: Wilcox-Meigs p31, Nutmegger v11 #2 p208, #3 p390, Bogue Fam p395, Desc of Wm Wilcoxson p13, Barbour's VR Killingworth v2 pp145,185.

MARGARET - m 29 Sep 1808 Exeter, Washington Co RI STEPHEN RICHMOND; Ref: Arnold v5 pt3 p35.

MARGARET - m 03 Jan 1811 Suffield, Hartford Co CT JUSTUS RISING who was b 19 Nov 1783 & d 09 Aug 1834 s/ABEL & DESIRE (MASON) RISING; ch SILENCE; Ref: VR of CT v7 p154, Gen of CT Fam v3 p215, Barbour's VR Suffield LB 1 p308.

MARGARET - b 22 Mar 1799 Lexington, Greene Co NY d/NATHANIEL & JOANNA (McGONIGLE/MALLORY) WILCOX; m JESSE HEATON; d 21 Sep 1880; Ref: Wilcox-Meigs p84, Your Ancestors v4 #11&12 p612.

MARGARET - b 18 Jan 1804 NY/PA d/HEZEKIAH & MAHALA (WILCOX) WILCOX; m MYRON GRIFFIN; Res Bradford Co PA; Ref: Your Ancestors v10 #3 p1248.

MARGARET - m 28 Aug 1825 Hartford, Hartford Co CT ANNOR HAMILTON; Ref: Barbour's VR Hartford v1 p44.

MARGARET - b 12 Mar 1815 d/THOMAS & ELIZABETH (McCAIN) WILCOX of Hector, Schuyler Co NY; d 12 Jun 1816; Ref: Your Ancestors v10 #4 p1274.

MARGARET - b 05 May/Jul 1822 Hillsdale, Columbia Co NH d/HENRY & SUSANNA (MILLER) WILCOX; d 24 Sep 1862; m CHARLES E BALLOU; Ref: Wilcox-Meigs p101, Your Ancestors v4 #11&12 p612.

MARGARET - d/ERASTUS & MARGARET (KING?) WILCOX of Washington, Madison, Ontario Cos NY; m 24 Jan 1828 Dearborn Co IN RICHARD NORRIS; Ref: Janet Armbrust.

MARGARET - b 17 Mar 1832 d/DAVID & BETSEY (KELSEY) WILCOX of Newport, Sullivan Co NH; m ABNER MORRILL of Lowell, Middlesex Co MA; Ref: Your Ancestors v3 #6 p399.

MARGARET - b 1837 Clockville, Madison Co NY d/SALMON & HANNAH (BUYEA) WILCOX; d 17 Sep 1862; Ref: Pioneers of Madison Co NY p281.

MARGARET - b 1840 CT d/HEZEKIAH & HANNAH (-----) WILCOX of Groton, New London Co CT; Ref: 1850 Census Groton CT Reel 432 #49 p346.

MARGARET - b 1847 Smyrna, Chenango Co NY d/SAMUEL & HANNAH (KNOWLES) WILCOX; m DELOS KENYON; no ch; d 1903; Ref: Your Ancestors v3 #2 p299.

MARGARET - b Aug 1850 d/CHARLES & MARGARET (-----) WILCOX of Andover, Allegany Co NY; Ref: 1850 Census Andover NY p127 Dw# 185.

MARGARET - b 21 Aug 1884 Akron, Summit Co OH d/Dr DEWITT GILBERT & JENNIE (GREEN) WILCOX; m 15 Feb 1913 JOHN MAY COLONY; d 14 Feb 1975; Ref: Gifford Wilcox, Desc of Wm Wilcoxson p128.

MARGARET - b 20 Jan 1893 IL d/SAMUEL MILLS WILCOX; m 1916 JAMES V RICHARDS; Res Pekin, Tazewell Co IL; 4 ch; Ref: Your Ancestors v2 p254.

MARGARET - b 1896 d/ARTHUR R WILCOX; m RALPH L HACKER; ch MARGARET, PATRICIA A; Ref: Desc of Wm Wilcoxson p 196.

MARGARET ANN - b 1848 Lafayette, Onondaga Co NY d/LUTHER & CATHERINE (-----) WILCOX; Ref: Your Ancestors v13 #4 p1597, 1850 Census Lafayette NY p208 Dw# 251.

MARGARET B - b 1800 CT; Perhaps a sister who Res with HEZEKIAH & HANNAH (-----) WILCOX of

Groton, New London Co CT; Ref: 1850 Census Groton CT Reel 432 #49 p346.

MARGARET BRUCE - b 1889 d/GEORGE SAMUEL & MARGARET E (BARNUM) WILCOX; d 1890; Ref: Your Ancestors v12 #2 p1437.

MARGARET COBB - b 26 Oct 1874 d/HENRY COLE & HARRIET (COBB) WILCOX; m VINCENT L PRICE; 4 ch; Ref: Desc of Wm Wilcoxson p240.

MARGARET De WITT - m 22 Oct 1852 BRADDOCK E STRONG; Ref: Marriages from NY Herald p265.

MARGARET J - b af 1825 d/SAMUEL & HANNAH (BAILEY) WILCOX; m PETER L MELLICK; Res Huntington, Luzerne Co PA; Ref: Your Ancestors v9 #4 p1176, Hist of Luzerne Co PA p1456.

MARGARET J - b 06 Apr 1892 Detroit, Wayne Co MI d/ELON FARNSWORTH & BLANCHE (-----) WILCOX; d 10 Apr 1894; Ref: Wilcox-Meigs p122.

MARGARET JANE - b 1872 Deep Cove, N B Canada d/WILLIAM & JANE (DRISCOLL) WILCOX; Single; d 08 Feb 1896 bur Seal Cove N B Canada; Ref: Desc of Charles Dyer Wilcox p12.

MARGARET K - m 29 Jan 1849 Danbury, Fairfield Co CT MORRIS C HULL; Ref: Barbour's VR Danbury v3 p160.

MARGARET KELSEY - b 15 Dec 1830 d/AUGUSTUS & FANNY (BENEDICT) WILCOX; m be 1858 MAURICE CHAPMAN HULL; no ch; d Feb 1898 NYC NY; Ref: Desc of Wm Wilcoxson p259.

MARGARET POWERS - b 1856; d 1858; Napoli, Cattaraugus Co NY; Ref: Tombstone Incsriptions.

MARGARET RUTH - b 30 Sep 1869 d/JAMES DAVID & ANNA MARIA (ROBINSON) WILCOX; Ref: Wilcox-Meigs p121, Desc of Wm Wilcoxson p144.

MARGARET S - m 17 Apr 1856 Hartwick, Otsego Co NY JAMES STERNBERGER MD; Ref: Marriages from Otsego Co NY Newspapers p26.

MARGARETTA - b 07 Aug 1827 d/RICHARD & ELIZABETH (LEWIS) WILCOX of Canton, Bradford Co PA; Ref: Your Ancestors v10 #4 p1273.

MARGERY - b 04 Aug 1720 Middletown, Middlesex Co CT d/FRANCIS & ABIGAIL (GRAVES) WILCOX; Ref: Nutmegger v4 #3 p331, NEH&GR v14 p138, Barbour's VR Middletown LR2 p24.

MARGERY - m 05/15 Feb 1740 Cromwell, Middlesex Co CT ELISHA STOCKING; ch ZEBULON, THEODOSIA, SUBMIT, RACHEL, JOHN, ELISHA, ELISHA, WILLIAM; d 29 Jun 1757; Ref: ECM v2 p82, Gen of CT Fam v3 p454.

MARGRALL - m 23 Feb 1862 Wayne Co IA JAMES R DAVIS; Ref: Hawkeye Heritage v14 #1 p24.

MARGUERITE - d/JOHN SHULER & LOIS A (CONGER) WILCOX of Elgin, Kane Co IL; Ref: Desc of Wm Wilcoxson p192.

MARIA - b 20 Apr 1798 d/ISAAC & NANCY (NEWCOMB) WILCOX; m ISAAC THOMPSON; Ref: Your Ancestors v9 #2 p1125.

MARIA - b 15 May 1801 Winchester, Litchfield Co CT d/DANIEL & MEHITABLE (-----) WILCOX; Ref: Barbour's VR Winchester v2 p107.

MARIA - b 19 May 1801 Orwell, Addison Co VT d/NATHAN & LUCY (HURD) WILCOX; Ref: Your Ancestors v3 #4 p350.

MARIA/MIRIAM - b 19 Mar 1801/2 d/JOSEPH & MIRIAM (BACON) WILCOX of Wallingford, New Haven Co CT; d Mar 1847; Ref: Early Fam of Wallingford p332, Your Ancestors v3 #4 p352, Hist of Wallingford p938.

MARIA - m 30 Mar 1828 Providence, Providence Co RI JOHN POTTS; Ref: Arnold v7 p473.

MARIA - m 22 Apr 1830 Hebron, Tolland Co CT BENJAMIN BLISS Jr; Ref: Barbour's VR Hebron v4 p21-M.

MARIA - b ca 1802 d/WILLIAM & GULIELMA (ESTES) WILCOX of RI; unmarried; Ref: Snow-Estes Ancestry v2 p18.

MARIA - b ca 1803 d/THOMAS WILCOX; m ROBERT SUTTON; Res Bradford Co PA; Ref: Pioneers of Bradford Co PA p309.

MARIA - b 1805; d 1892 Carthage, Jefferson Co NY; Ref: Early Settlers of NY p339.

MARIA - m 01 May 1837 Berlin, Hartford Co CT ABIJAH HURLBURT; Ref: Barbour's VR Berlin v1 p67.

MARIA/MAMAH - b 18 Jul 1818 Harwinton, Litchfield Co CT d/AARON & LOIS (PHELPS) WILCOX; m 21 Apr 1840 JOHN J WELTON; Ref: Desc of Abner & Lucy Hart Wilcox p21, Your Ancestors v3 #1 p279, Barbour's VR Harwinton vM p41.

MARIA - b 1819 NY d/WILLIAM & ELIZABETH (-----) WILCOX of Kinderhook, Columbia Co NY; Ref: 1850 Census Kinderhook NY p366 Dw# 311.

MARIA - m 20 Oct 1841 Middletown, Middlesex Co CT JOHN HASKELL; Ref: Barbour's VR Middletown v3 p484.

MARIA - of Moreau, Saratoga Co NY m 11 Feb 1846 GEORGE RYON of Wilton Saratoga Co NY; Ref: NYG&BR v119 p93.

MARIA - b 1820 Sandisfield, Berkshire Co MA d/CHAUNCEY & MARIANNE (POTTER) WILCOX; d 11 Mar 1844; Ref: Your Ancestors v12 #2 p1437, Desc of Wm Wilcox p222.

MARIA - m 08 Jan 1846 Westerly, Washington Co RI SAMUEL B HOXSIE; Res Charlestown, Washington Co RI; Ref: Arnold v5 pt5 p16 v11 p47.

MARIA - b 1824 NY d/Dr LEVI & ABIGAIL (THOMPSON) WILCOX of Ticonderoga, Essex Co NY; Res Crown Point, Essex Co NY with her brother LEVI 1850; Ref: 1850 Census Crown Point NY p360 Dw# 180.

MARIA - b 1828 Cherry Creek, Chautauqua Co NY d/ELIPHALET & NANCY (KENT) WILCOX; m ca 1848 OSCAR F BROWN who was b 1828 NY & d ca 1890 prob Schuyler, Colfax Co NE; ch JOHN; d af 1900 prob Schuyler NE; Ref: 1850 Census Cherry Creek NY; Will of Eliphalet Wilcox; Land Records in Colfax Co NE Book Z p72, 1900 Census Schuyler NE, *The Schuyler Sun* 30 Aug 1883 issue.

MARIA - b 1828 NY; Res Harpersfield, Delaware Co NY; Ref: 1850 Census Harpersfield p170 Dw# 203.

MARIA - b 1831 NY d/JACOB & CAROLINE (-----) WILCOX of Sherburne, Chenango Co NY; Ref: 1850 Census Sherburne p249 Dw# 1624.

MARIA - b 20 Dec 1832 Chatham, Middlesex Co CT d/JOHN & ABIGAIL (WRIGHT) WILCOX of Milford, Otsego Co NY; d 14 Nov 1855; Ref: Your Ancestors v4 #7&8 p565, 1850 Census Milford NY p119 Dw# 324.

MARIA - b 1834 Norway, Herkimer Co NY d/PELEG Jr & LUCINDA (-----) WILCOX; Res with WILLIAM H HURLBUTT fam 1850; Ref: Herkimer Co Letter of Adm, 1850 Census Norway NY p265 Dw# 131.

MARIA - b 26 Feb 1834 Lenox, Madison Co NY d/ALANSON & IRENE (JOHNSON) WILCOX; m WILLIAM V BOSWORTH; Ref: Pioneers of Madison Co NY p281.

MARIA - b 1834 NY d/EMERY & MARTHA (-----) WILCOX of Newport, Herkimer Co NY; Ref: 1850 Census Newport NY p173 Dw# 289.

✓ **MARIA** - b 1835 NY d/JOHN & ABIGAIL W (WRIGHT) WILCOX of Milford, Otsego Co NY; Ref: 1850 Census Milford NY p119 Dw# 324.

MARIA - b 1835 Dayton, Cattaraugus Co NY d/ALANSON & ALMIRA H (-----) WILCOX; m 06 Jan 1856 Forestville, Chautauqua Co NY DAVID BARTLETT of Collins, Erie Co NY; Ref: Your Ancestors v13 #4 p1609, 19th Cent Marriages Reported in Fredonia Censor p119.

MARIA - m 05 Dec 1841 Foster, Providence Co RI JEREMIAH BENNETT Jr; Ref: Arnold v3 p31.

MARIA - b 1836 NY d/CHARLES & LOUISA (-----) of New Hartford, Oneida Co NY; Ref: 1850 Census New Hartford NY p284 Dw# 681.

MARIA - b 1838 NY d/ROBERT & NINA (-----) WILCOX of Oswego, Oswego Co NY; Ref: 1850 Census Oswego NY p233 Dw# 292.

MARIA - b 1839 NY d/WELCOME & HARRIET (-----) WILCOX of Wethersfield, Wyoming Co NY; Ref: 1850 Census Wethersfield NY p92 Dw# 1378.

MARIA - b 1842 NY d/A W & HARRIET (-----) WILCOX of Arkwright, Chautauqua Co NY; Ref: 1850 Census Arkwright NY p127 Dw# 1764.

MARIA - b 1847 Genesee Co NY d/RUSSELL & MARIAH (BIRBEE) WILCOX; Ref: Your Ancestors v14 #3 p1669, See Russell.

MARIA CAROLINE - b 12 Sep 1810 Thetford, Orange Co VT d/AARON & TENCY (HORSFORD) WILCOX; Ref: Horsford Hosford Fam p73.

MARIA FIDELIA - b 19 Feb/Dec 1838 Shelburne Falls, Franklin Co MA d/ABRAHAM & LAURINDA (HARDY) WILCOX; Ref: Halifax VT Wilcox Fam mss, Your Ancestors v4 #9&10 p587.

MARIA H - b 1786; d 19 Dec 1869 age 83; Ref: CT Bible Rec v11 p376.

MARIA JANE - b 01 Jul 1837 E Bloomfield, Ontario Co NY d/EDWIN & CANDACE (GILBERT) WILCOX; m 01 Jan 1859 E Bloomfield NY BYRON DAVIS PARMELE; d 16 Dec 1904 Le Roy, Genesee Co NY; Ref: Edward McCarthy.

MARIA L - d/WILLIAM WILCOX m 14 Jan/Feb 1849 Milford, Otsego Co NY JOHN DWIGHT CHAFFEE who was b 16 Feb 1828 Adams, Berkshire Co MA & d Apr 1884 ✓ s/EBENEZER & PHILA (FARNUM) CHAFFEE; Res Hartwick & Gilbertsville, Otsego Co NY; ch HENRY T, SARAH C, ALICE C, WINNIE J; Ref: Chaffee Gen pp203,364, Marriages from Otsego Co Newspapers p76.

MARIA LANSIN - b 21 Feb 1839 Lagrange, Lorain Co OH d/CALVIN PARDEE & HARRIET (HUBBARD) WILCOX; m WILLIAM L GOTT; ch HATTIE PHEBE, LUCY A, CALVIN H, BESSIE EDITH; Ref: Desc of Wm Wilcoxson p195.

MARIA LOUISA - b 1833 NY d/THOMAS S & ANN (-----) WILCOX of Davenport, Delaware Co NY; Ref: 1850 Census Davenport NY p129 Dw# 26.

MARIA LOUIS - b 05 Feb 1844 Taunton, Bristol Co MA d/JAMES F & LOUISA S (-----) WILCOX; Ref: Taunton MA VR v1.

MARIA M - m 07 Jul 1828 Middletown, Middlesex Co CT EDWARD NORTH of Berlin, Hartford Co CT; Ref: Barbour's VR Middletown v3 p309.

MARIA MIRIAM - b 19 March 1801 Middletown, Middlesex Co CT d/JOSEPH & MIRIAM (BACON) WILCOX; Ref: Barbour's VR Middletown v2 p319.

MARIA P - b 1834 Lenox, Madison Co NY_d/ALANSON CASE & IRENE (JOHNSON) WILCOX; Ref: 1850 Census Lenox NY p175 Dw# 216, See Alanson Case.

MARIA R - d/Capt THOMAS WILCOX; m Feb 1820 Newport, Newport Co RI BENJAMIN H WILBOUR; ch

SARAH T; Ref: Arnold v16 p586, Gen of RI Fam v2 p550.

MARIAH - b 1812 W Simsbury, Hartford Co CT d/WILLIAM & ANNA (EDGERTON) WILCOX; m MARVIN CASE; Ref: Early Settlers of W Simsbury p130.

MARIAH - b 10 Jun 1813 d/EBENEZER & JAEL (HANCHETT) WILCOX of CANADA & Jackson Co IA; m LEONARD CLINE of Aylmer Canada; d 1895; Ref: Desc of Wm Wilcoxson p124.

MARIAH - m 10 May 1848 Granby, Hartford Co CT CHESTER CASE of Barkhamsted, Litchfield Co CT; Ref: Barbour's VR Granby v1 p55.

MARIAH - b 1841 NY d/OZIAS WILCOX of Utica, Oneida Co NY; Ref: 1850 Census Utica NY p311 Dw# 25.

MARIAH L - b af 1827 d/CALVIN P & HARRIETT (HUBBARD) WILCOX of Lagrange, Lorain Co OH; m WILLIAM I GOTT; Ref: Your Ancestors v9 #3 p1153.

MARIAH L - b 1847 d/HENRY D & MARY W (BISHOP) WILCOX; Ref: Your Ancestors v3 #9&10 p452.

MARIAN - b 24 Jan 1784 Killingworth, Middlesex Co CT d/JESSE & THANKFUL (STEVENS) WILCOX; Ref: Wilcox-Meigs p63.

MARIAN/MARION - b 1849 NY d/JONATHAN & JULIA (-----) WILCOX of Sherburne, Chenango Co NY; Ref: 1850 Census Sherburne NY p246 Dw# 171.

MARIAN - b 10 Dec 1874 d/HENRY HOPSON & ELIZABETH (LADD) WILCOX; Ref: Your Ancestors v3 #3 p319.

MARIE - b 1853 NY d/IRA & MARY (PALMER) WILCOX of Manlius, Onondaga Co & Lincoln, Madison Co NY; Ref: Pioneers of Madison Co NY p281, See Ira.

MARIE - b 29 May 1898 MI d/FRED & MARY (OSWALD) WILCOX; m 1922 San Antonio, Bexar Co TX ROY MALTAGERGER; Ref: Wilcox Excerpts v1 p6.

MARIE - b 23 Dec 1899 Warsaw, Wyoming Co NY d/FRED HAMILTON & FLORENCE (RELYEA) WILCOX; Ref: Your Ancestors v14 #2 p1644.

MARIE LOUISE - b 24 Jul 1853 d/ORLANDO BOLIVAR & MARIE LOUISE (FARNSWORTH) WILCOX; m STEPHEN C

MILLS; Res Camp Verdi, Yavapai Co AZ; Ref: Wilcox-Meigs p104, 1880 Census Camp Verdi AZ Reel 37 p459.

MARIE LOUISE - b 01 May 1862 d/EBEN NORTH & MARIE LOUISE (COLE) WILCOX; m 26 Apr 1900 JOHN G LAWRENCE; no ch; Ref: Desc of Wm Wilcoxson p260.

MARIE W - d/JOHN SHULER & LOIS AMELIA (CONGER) WILCOX of Elgin, Kane Co IL; m 16 Mar 1892 ROBERT F FITZ/FITTS of Elgin IL; Res Reading, Middlesex Co MA; Ref: Your Ancestors v9 #2 p1128, Desc of Wm Wilcoxson p192.

MARIEL - b 1830; Listed in Census with DAVID & SALLY (CRITTENDEN) WILCOX Fam of Greene, Chenango Co NY; Ref: 1850 Census Greene NY, See David.

MARIENA B - b 08 Jun 1845 Dartmouth Bristol Co MA; s/CHARLES & JUDITH ANN (-----) WILCOX; Ref: Dartmouth VR p303.

MARIETTA - b 23 Nov 1805 d/ELIJAH & LOIS (FIELD) WILCOX; m Jun 1829 EDWARD MORRISON MEIGS who d 01 Aug 1869 Madison, New Haven Co CT; ch RICHARD S, EDWARD E, ELLEN E; d 03/30 Apr 1850; Ref: Wilcox-Meigs p72, Fam of Early Guilford pp 822,1210, Barbour's VR Madison v1 p50.

MARIETTA - d/JESSE m ----- WEST; m ----- HARRIS; m ----- CLIFTON; d Feb 1890 Keya Paha Co NE; Res Whiteside Co IL, IA, & NE; Ref: Mrs Wm Richardson.

MARIETTA - b 1838 NY d/CHENEY & AMITY (-----) WILCOX of Onondaga, Onondaga Co NY; Ref: 1850 Census Onondaga NY p324 Dw# 1492.

MARIETTA - b 12 Sep 1843 d/ELBRIDGE & LUCY (SMITH) WILCOX; Ref: Your Ancestors v3 #9&10 p452.

MARIETTA - b 24 May 1897 d/ULYSSES D & EDNA (CHENEY) WILCOX; d 28 Mar 1975; Ref: Desc of Charles Dyer Wilcox p6.

MARIETTA A - b 1850 NY; Res with LOIS BARTON Chautauqua, Chautauqua Co NY 1860; Ref: 1860 Census Chautauqua NY p14 Dw# 91.

MARIETTA P - b 1835 d/WILLIAM & ESTHER S (COLE) WILCOX of Portland, Chautauqua Co NY; d 27 Jan 1878 Arkwright, Chautauqua Co NY of consumption; Ref: Your Ancestors v12 #3 p1463, 19th Cent Deaths

Reported in Fredonia Censor p596, 1850 Census Arkwright NY p111 Dw# 1473.

MARIETTE - b ca 1801 d/SETH & HANNAH (WILCOX) WILCOX; m JAIRUS WILCOX s/BENJAMIN & RACHEL (WILCOX) WILCOX; Ref: Your Ancestors v3 #9&10 p451.

MARIETTE - b 01 Sep 1830 d/JEFFREY & ANNE (STILLMAN/MASON) WILCOX; Ref: Gen of CT Fam v2 p537, Your Ancestors v13 #1 p1515.

MARIETTE - b 21 Mar 1878 Tama, Tama Co IA d/LEWIS & RACHEL ANN (GLENN) WILCOX; d 13 Nov 1932 Tama, Tama Co IA; Ref: Marjorie Stoner Elmore.

MARILDA - d/JOHN & SOPHIA (-----) WILCOX of Warsaw, Wyoming Co NY; m 05 Oct 1849 SANFORD ARMSTRONG of Perry, Wyoming Co NY; Ref: Hist of Wyoming Co p247.

MARILDA - b 1857 Erie Co NY d/HORACE & MARY H (-----) WILCOX; Ref: 1875 Census Buffalo NY, Alice Wiatr.

MARINDA - m 10 Sep 1832 Hartford, Hartford Co CT WILLIAM E BATES; Ref: Barbour's VR Hartford v1 p97.

MARINDA - b 1832 NY d/NATHAN & MERCY L (-----) WILCOX of Petersburgh, Rensselaer Co NY; Ref: 1850 Census Petersburgh NY p195 Dw# 310.

MARINER - b 07 Aug 1847 Wood Island, N B Canada s/JOB & MARIA (GREEN) WILCOX; m CORDELIA CARD who was b 1850 & d 09 Feb 1914 d/JOHN BENJAMIN & MARY (WILCOX) CARD; ch BYRON A, MARY M, LINNIE, EDNA, HAZEL, JOHN; d 18 June 1908 bur Wood Island Cem; Ref: Desc of Charles Dyer Wilcox pp14,15.

MARION - b ca 1876 s/DANIEL HAND & FRANCES LOUISA (ANSLEY) WILCOX; m ELEANOR SANCHEZ; Ref: Your Ancestors v3 #2 p303.

MARION ELIZABETH - b 02 Nov 1842 d/EDWIN & FANNY (EGGLESTON) WILCOX; Ref: Your Ancestors v3 #9&10 p452.

MARION ELIZABETH - b 25 Dec 1871 Middlefield, Middlesex Co CT d/HENRY EDWIN & ESTHER COE (BIRDSEY) WILCOX; m 18 Jun 1896 WILLIAM MONROE NEWTON; Res S Royalton, Windsor Co VT; ch DEAN WILLIAM, ELIZABETH MARION; Ref: MUH p764.

MARION NEWELL - b 22 Apr 1869 s/DANIEL WILMARTH & MARTHA ANN (CHAPIN) WILCOX of Boston, Suffolk Co MA; Ref: Your Ancestors v3 #6 p400.

MARIUS - b 1850 Cattaraugus Co NY s/JONATHAN & FANNY (-----) WILCOX of Leon, Cattaraugus Co NY; Ref: Alice Wiatr.

MARJORIE ANN - b 01 Dec 1899 Wood Island, N B Canada d/CASWELL LEWIS & NELLIE (SCHOFIELD) WILCOX; m CHARLES RAMSDELL; ch JASPER, ETTA, LEORA, ROBERTA, LOIS, GLENDON; d 24 Nov 1965 Lubec, Washington Co ME; Ref: Desc of Charles Dyer Wilcox p26.

MARJORIE BREWSTER - b 10 Nov 1886 d/STEPHEN MOULTON & MARY STEWART (SHEARMAN) WILCOX; Ref: Col Fam of US v5 p552.

MARK - m MARY -----; Res Concord PA; ch JAMES, ELLEN (WILCOX) JENKINS, JOHN, JOSEPH; d 18 Feb 1827; Ref: Daily Advertiser Philadelphia PA p206.

MARK - m ------ who d 1840 Milford, New Haven Co CT; m 15 Apr 1849 MARY EMILINE LAMBERT d/JOHN & ESTHER (-----) LAMBERT Ref: Barbour's VR Milford vBP p84, v1 p52.

MARK - d 1855; Ref: CT Bible Rec v6 p64.

MARK - b 1800 s/NATHAN & SYLVIA (HOPKINS) WILCOX of East Bloomfield, Ontario Co NY; m HANNAH -----; Res Belvidere, Boone Co IL, Tuscola Co MI; ch REBECCA, SELAH, GEORGE, CAROLINE, BYRON, JULIA M; d 1864/5; Ref: Your Ancestors v10 #1 pp1201,1202.

MARK STUART - b 08 Sep 1860 s/LUCIUS FITCH & ELLEN MARIA (BELDEN) WILCOX of Le Roy, Genesee Co NY; m MARGARET PRESTON; Ref: Your Ancestors v3 #7&8 pp425,426.

MARSENA - d 10 Mar 1854 age 2__Woodstock, Windham Co CT; Ref: Barbour's VR Woodstock v3 p31a.

MARSHALL - b 01 Aug 1842; Served 4 yr Civil War Co A 31st Reg; d 08 Sep 1865/1875; bur Maple Grove Cem Granville, Licking Co OH; Ref: OH Cem Rec pp181,206.

MARTHA - b 30 Oct 1704 Simsbury, Hartford Co CT d/WILLIAM & ELIZABETH (WILSON) WILCOX; d 21/31 May

1724; Ref: Wilcox-Meigs p32, Nutmegger v10 #2 p214, Your Ancestors v10 #4 p1275, Desc of Wm Wilcoxson p17.

MARTHA - b 03 Jun 1710 Hebron, Tolland Co CT d/EBENEZER & MARTHA (GAYLORD) WILCOX; m 12 Mar 1734/5 Deacon EBENEZER DEWEY who was b 24 Jan 1711/12 Lebanon, New London Co CT & d 24 Nov 1791 Royalton, Windsor Co VT s/EBENEZER & EXPERIENCE (-----) DEWEY; ch EBENEZER, TIMOTHY; d 24 Jan 1744/5; Ref: Barbour's VR Windsor v2 p112, Hebron v1 pp20,40,77, Wilcox-Meigs p32, NYG&BR v6 p69, Hist of Sullivan NH p935, Desc of Wm Wilcoxson p15, Hist of Surry NH p944.

MARTHA - b 21 Apr 1718 Middletown, Middlesex Co CT d/THOMAS & ANNA (NORTH) WILCOX; Ref: NEH&GR v14 p138, MUH p747, Barbour's VR Middletown LR2 p10.

MARTHA - b 26 Jan 1729/30 Simsbury, Hartford Co CT d/WILLIAM & THANKFUL (ADAMS) WILCOX; Ref: Nutmegger v10 #2 p214, Wilcox-Meigs p48, Your Ancestors v10 #4 p1275, Desc of Wm Wilcoxson p23.

MARTHA - b 30 Sep 1729 Killingworth, Middlesex Co CT d/ABEL & MARTHA (STEVENS) WILCOX; m 07 Feb 1754 ISAAC KELSEY Jr who was b 22 Feb 1732/3 & d 07 Nov 1781 s/ISAAC & JANE (CRANE) KELSEY; ch ISAAC, RACHEL, LUCY, REUBEN, AZUBAH, ABEL, TAMAR, MABEL; d 1804; Ref: Wilcox-Meigs p41, Your Ancestor v3 #1 p280, Barbour's VR Killingworth v1 p189, v2 p120.

MARTHA - b 30 Mar 1737 Hebron, Tolland Co CT Twin with ELIZABETH d/EBENEZER Jr& ELIZABETH (DEWEY) WILCOX; m 11 May 1757 Hebron, Tolland Co CT AMOS HALL; Ref: Wilcox-Meigs p50, Desc of Wm Wilcoxson p25, Barbour's VR Hebron v1 p23, v2 p42.

MARTHA - m 19 Oct 1738 Cromwell, Middlesex Co CT ANDREW WARNER; Ref: ECM v2 p87, Barbour's VR Middletown v1 p111.

MARTHA - m 08 Dec 1748 Durham, Middlesex Co CT JOSEPH HICKOX; Ref: Nutmegger v4 #4 p496, Barbour's VR Durham TR p376.

MARTHA - b ca 1731 d/STEPHEN & MARY (THOMAS) WILCOX; m 11 Apr 1750 Dartmouth, Bristol Co MA JOB GIFFORD; Ref: Dartmouth VR p547, Demaris Hickey, See Stephen.

MARTHA - b 26 Aug 1741 Ripton CT d/JOSIAH & ELIZABETH (HUBBELL) WILCOX; m ----- BEACH; Ref: Wilcox-Meigs p58, Stratford Gen p1348, Cutter's Northern NY v2 p655.

MARTHA - b 24 Jan 1744 Exeter, Washington Co RI d/ABRAHAM & LYDIA (HARRINGTON) WILCOX; m ABRAHAM WILCOX; Ref: Your Ancestors v4 #7&8 p561.

MARTHA - b 29 Aug 1749 Middletown, Middlesex Co CT d/JEREMIAH & MARY (STOWE) WILCOX; Ref: Barbour's VR Middletown v1 p95.

MARTHA - b 13 Jan 1750/1 Middletown, Middlesex Co CT d/ISRAEL & MARTHA (BARNS) WILCOX; d 23 Jan 1750/1; Ref: Barbour's VR Middletown v2 p285.

MARTHA - b 1752 d/ROBERT & CATHERINE (LILLIBRIDGE) WILCOX of Exeter & Richmond, Washington Co RI; Ref: Your Ancestors v3 #1 p277.

MARTHA - b 30 Oct 1754 Guilford, New Haven Co CT d/JOHN & MARTHA (COE) WILCOX; Ref: Wilcox-Meigs p47, Fam of Early Guilford p1209, Barbour's VR Guilford v2 p95.

MARTHA - b 13 Sep 1756 Middletown, Middlesex Co CT Twin with MARY d/ISRAEL & MARTHA (BARNS) WILCOX; Ref: Barbour's VR Middletown v2 p285.

MARTHA - b 23 Nov 1757 Hebron, Tolland Co CT d/OBADIAH & SARAH (TALCOTT) WILCOX; Ref: Barbour's VR Hebron v2 p257.

MARTHA - b 05 Nov 1760 Westerly, Washington Co RI d/HEZEKIAH & HANNAH (PARKER) WILCOX; m 27 Oct 1782 TRISTAM DICKENS who was b 09 Mar 1761; Ref: Arnold v5 pp2,69,144, Gen of RI Fam v1 p428, C Douglass Alves Sr.

MARTHA - b 25 Nov 1761 Hebron, Tolland Co CT d/OBADIAH & SARAH (TALCOTT) WILCOX; m BENJAMIN ISHAM s/TIMOTHY & REBECCA (FULLER) ISHAM; m ELIAS BUNDY; Res Gilsum, Cheshire Co NH; Ref: Desc of Wm Wilcoxson p26, Hebron VR v2 p257, Barbour Index, Wilcox-Meigs p50, Hist of Sullivan NH p1044, Hist of Surry NH p945.

MARTHA - b 06 Jan 1762 Killingworth, Middlesex Co CT d/ELIJAH & SARAH (WILCOX) WILCOX; Ref: Barbour's VR Killingworth v1 p103.

MARTHA - b 21 Mar 1762 Killingworth, Middlesex Co CT d/ELNATHAN & THANKFUL (BENNET) WILCOX; Ref: Wilcox-Meigs p65, Your Ancestors v4 #1&2 p498, Barbour's VR Killingworth v1 p81.

MARTHA - b 06 Jun 1762 d/ELIJAH & SARAH (WILCOX) WILCOX m 04 Sep 1783 JOHN SPENCER; Res Killingworth, Middlesex Co CT Ref: Wilcox-Meigs p61.

MARTHA - b 22 Aug 1762 Killingworth, Middlesex Co CT d/BENJAMIN & ELIZABETH (WHITTLESEY) WILCOX; Ref: Wilcox-Meigs p66, Barbour's VR Killingworth v2 p122.

MARTHA - b 05 Feb 1763 Portsmouth, Newport Co RI d/JOSIAH & ANN (ESTES) WILCOX; Ref: Arnold v4 pt1 p105, See Josiah, Your Ancestors v12 #4 p1503.

MARTHA - m 08 May 1791 Simsbury, Hartford Co CT THOMAS THOMPSON; Ref: Rec of Marriages at Simsbury CT p3.

MARTHA - b 15 Jan 1774 Sandisfield, Berkshire Co MA d/JOEL & LYDIA (-----) WILCOX; Ref: Sandisfield VR, Fiske Card File, Desc of Wm Wilcoxson p245.

MARTHA - m 17 Mar 1793 Hopkinton, Washington Co RI DANIEL BURDICK; d 1815 Stonington, New London Co CT; Ref: Arnold v5 p28, Nutmegger v13 #2 p273.

MARTHA - b 1775 d/NATHAN & TABITHA (PROSSER) WILCOX; m SAMUEL STANTON; Res Stonington, New London Co CT; Ref: Hist of Stonington p661.

MARTHA - b 04 May 1777 Winchester, Litchfield Co CT d/ELISHA & MARY (CLARK) WILCOX; Ref: Annals of Winchester p125.

MARTHA - bpt 23 Dec 1777 Tiverton Baptist Church, Tiverton, Newport Co RI; Ref: Arnold v8 p514.

MARTHA - b 30 Mar 1787 Hebron, Tolland Co CT d/EBENEZER WILCOX Jr; Ref; Barbour's VR Hebron v1 p23.

MARTHA - b 12 May 1788 Killingworth, Middlesex Co CT d/JOSEPH & GRACE (WILCOX) WILCOX; Ref: Wilcox-Meigs p64, Barbour's VR Killingworth v2 p149.

MARTHA - See RIGR v3 #4 p302.

MARTHA - b 1793 Killingworth, Middlesex Co CT d/SIMEON WILCOX; m PETER SEWARD who was b 28 Feb 1788 & d 17 Feb 1872 s/JOB & LOIS (FARNHAM) SEWARD; ch ACHSAH, DANIEL, SABRA; d 21 Jul 1839; Ref: Fam of Early Guilford p1081.

MARTHA - b ca 1812 RI d/ISAAC & EUNICE (CLAWSON/CLOSSON) WILCOX; m PERRY BABCOCK; bur River Bend Cem Westerly, Washington Co RI; Ref: C Douglass Alves Sr.

MARTHA - m 02 Dec 1852 Wayne Co IA PHILO PRESTON PRATHER; Ref: Hawkeye Heritage v14 #1 p19.

MARTHA - b 1830 NY d/OZIAS WILCOX of Utica, Oneida Co NY; Ref: 1850 Census Utica NY p311 Dw# 25.

MARTHA - b 1832 NY d/NEWEL & MARTHA (-----) WILCOX of Granby, Oswego Co NY; Ref: 1850 Census Granby NY p9 Dw# 125.

MARTHA - m 29 Nov 1873 Westerly, Washington Co RI MARK CLANCEY; Res Stonington, New London Co CT; Ref: Arnold v11 p47.

MARTHA - m 17 Sep 1850 Auburn, Cayuga Co NY CLINTON SISSON; Ref: 10,000 VR of Central NY p218.

MARTHA - b 1839 CT d/RUDOLF O & EMELINE (-----) WILCOX of Goshen, Litchfield Co CT; Ref: 1850 Census Goshen CT p102 Dw# 213.

MARTHA - b 1841 NY d/GEORGE S & LOUISA (JONES) WILCOX of Broome Co & Alma, Allegany Co NY; Ref: Carol A Cox.

MARTHA - b 1843 Halifax, Windham Co VT d/SAMUEL & MARTHA G (----) WILCOX; Ref: 1850 Census Halifax VT p131, Halifax Wilcox Fam mss.

MARTHA - b 1843 NY d/SAMUEL & MARY (COREY) WILCOX of Chautauqua, Chautauqua Co NY; Ref: 1850 Census Chautauqua NY p272 Dw# 169, See Samuel.

MARTHA - b 1844 Canada; m 1870 IA JAMES FRANKLIN VAN EMBURGH; d 1916; Ref: Iowa Surnames v3 p695.

MARTHA - b 1846 PA d/JOHN C & SUSAN (-----) WILCOX; Res Le Roy, Bradford Co PA; Ref: 1850 Census Bradford Co PA p66.

MARTHA - b 1847 OH d/MARTIN & MARTHA (-----) WILCOX of Madison, Lake Co OH; Ref: 1850 Census Madison OH Reel 259 p134.

MARTHA - b 1856 PA d/ISAAC & PHILANDA (-----) WILCOX; Res Le Roy, Bradford Co PA; Ref: 1860 Census Bradford Co PA p369.

MARTHA - b 19 Jan 1861 CA d/SARDIS DENSLOW & SARAH GREY (BOND) WILCOX; m H S TEMPLETON; ch SARDIS W, LOUISE, HERMA, CARLOS; Ref: Jane Smith.

MARTHA - b 1868 Erie Co NY d/HORACE & MARY H (-----) WILCOX; Ref: Alice Wiatr.

MARTHA A - b ca 1843 Chautauqua, Chautauqua Co NY d/SAMUEL 2nd & MARY (-----) WILCOX; d 02 Jul 1852; Ref: 19th Cent Death Notices Reported in Fredonia Censor p596.

MARTHA A - m 01 Jan 1846 Westerly, Washington Co RI NATHANIEL J L CHASE; Ref: Arnold v5 p2.

MARTHA ALAMEDA - b 22 Nov 1829 Thetford, Orange Co VT d/AARON & TENCEY (HORSFORD) WILCOX; Ref: Horsford/Hosford Fam p73.

MARTHA AMY - b Nov 1841 Watertown, Jefferson Co NY d/PETER C & MARY (YOUKER) WILCOX; m 19 Dec 1859 WILLIAM CALDWELL; Ref: George Koppers.

MARTHA ANN - b 22 Feb 1846 Madison, New Haven Co CT d/ZINA EDWIN & LYDIA ANN (HILL) WILCOX; m CHARLES PECK; Ref: Fam of Early Guilford p1207.

MARTHA ANN - b 23 Jul 1871 d/JOHN HENRY OWEN & MARY (YOUNG) WILCOX; Ref: Your Ancestors v12 #2 p1436.

MARTHA B - b 13 Jul 1850 Watch Hill, Washington Co RI d/HORACE & HANNAH (KENYON) WILCOX; d 15 Aug 1926; Ref: C Douglass Alves Sr.

MARTHA CHAPIN - b 05 Jun 1871 d/DANIEL WILMARTH & MARTHA ANN (CHAPIN) WILCOX of Boston, Suffolk Co MA; Ref: Your Ancestors v3 #6 p400.

MARTHA E - b 27 Jul 1826 Bloomfield, Ontario Co NY d/EDWIN & CANDACE (GILBERT) WILCOX; d 07 Apr 1844 E Bloomfield NY; Ref: Edward McCarthy.

MARTHA E - b 1845 CT d/DANIEL & HARRIET (-----) WILCOX of New London, New London Co CT; Ref: 1850 Census New London CT Reel 432 #49 p166.

MARTHA ELVIRA/ELVIA - b 06 Feb 1831 d/ORRIN & HANNAH (HAMLIN) WILCOX of East Bloomfield, Ontario Co NY; m EDWARD BROOKS; m M E FLETCHER; d 14 Feb 1920 Ref: Your Ancestors v10 #3 p1249; Ref: Desc of Wm Wilcoxson p208.

MARTHA JANE - b 1824 PA d/ISAAC & FREELOVE (MADISON) WILCOX; Ref: Evangeline A Wilcox.

MARTHA M - b 04 Jan 1835 d/ELBRIDGE GERRY & LUCY (SMITH) WILCOX; m PAUL C TOWNE; Ref: Your Ancestors v3 #9&10 p452.

MARTHA MUNRO - b 1819 d/JOHN WILCOX; d 04 Nov 1820 Bristol, Bristol Co RI; Ref: Arnold v6 pt1 p173.

MARTHA N - m 10 Feb 1875 Angola, Erie Co NY JOHN J SHEAR of Evans, Erie Co NY; Ref; 19th Cent Marriages Reported in Fredonia Censor p119.

MARTIN - m 02 Mar 1758 RUTH IVES who d 04 Jul 1760; ch RUTH; Killed by lightening 06 June 1767 Goshen, Litchfield Co CT; JAMES ROYCE was also killed; Ref: NH Gazette 1767, Barbour's VR Goshen v1 pp262,269,272.

MARTIN - b 09 Jun 1759 Hebron, Tolland Co CT; m 12 Mar 1787 JERUSHA DEWEY who was b 30 Apr 1766 Hebron CT & d 18 May 1818; Res Half Moon, Saratoga Co NY 1790 & 1793 Albany Co NY; ch RODOLPHUS D, CLARINDA, ROMULUS B, ZARENA, REMUS, LYSANDER, LORENZO, LORITA L, AMANDA N; d 06 Jan 1813; Ref: Desc of Wm Bradford p351, Detroit Mag v6 p71, Fiske Card File.

MARTIN - b Feb or 27 Apr 1767 Goshen, Litchfield Co CT s/ELIJAH WILCOX; d 06 Jun 1767; Ref: Barbour's VR Goshen v1 p236.

MARTIN - b 1767; m 29 Oct 1795 JUDITH CARTER who was b 1776 & d 05 Feb 1834; Res Benson, Rutland Co VT; ch SILENCE, HARRIET, JUDITH; d 21 May 1848; Ref: VT VR, 1800 Census VT p104.

MARTIN - b 11 May 1792 RI; m MATILDA M STILLMAN who was b Feb 1797; m 14 Jun 1822 MEHITABLE WELLS who was b 20 Feb 1799 & d 17 Aug 1878; Res RI; ch ALBERTUS, MATILDA M, EMERGENE, SARAH P, JOSEPHINE, FANOZINA; d 19 Jan 1856; Ref: NYG&BR v107 p193.

MARTIN - b 07 Dec 1798; m 1818 POLLY ----- who was b 1797 & d 14/24 Feb 1872 age 75; d 15 Apr 1891; Ref: CT Bible Rec v15 pp253-255.

MARTIN - b 09 Nov 1809 W Springfield, Hampden Co MA s/LEVI & MARY (SPENCER) WILCOX; Res Genesee Co NY; d 1871; Ref: Desc of Wm Wilcoxson p133, 1850 Census Bergen NY p61 Dw# 543.

MARTIN Rev - b 03 Mar 1811 Killingworth, Middlesex Co CT s/AARON & MABEL (LORD) WILCOX; m MARTHA ----- who was b 1822 OH; Clergyman; Res Twinsburg, Summit Co OH & Madison, Lake Co OH; ch MARY, MARTHA, JAMES; d 27 Sep 1851; Ref: 1850 Census Madison OH Reel 259 p134, Lord Fam Gen p289, Wilcox-Meigs p81, Your Ancestors v3 #3 p321, Barbour's VR Killingworth v2 p14.

MARTIN - b 1811; m CHARLOTTE ----- who was b 05 Sep 1813 & d 03 Jun 1872 bur Cheshire, Delaware Co OH; Ref: OH Cem Records p223.

MARTIN - b 1805 NY s/ELISHA & BETSEY (WILCOX) SHIPPEN WILCOX; m SARAH/SALLY ----- who was b 1812 NY; Res Dover, Dutchess Co NY; ch HEBRON, CARY, OSCAR, MARY E, GEORGE A BENJAMIN, HERBERT, LIDA; Ref: 1850 Census Dover NY p328 Dw# 269, Your Ancestors v4 #9&10 p585.

MARTIN - b ca 1816 prob Smithfield, Bradford Co PA s/STEPHEN & POLLY (ALLEN) WILCOX; d age 23; Ref: Halifax VT Wilcox Fam mss.

MARTIN - b 1816 Herkimer Co NY; Res Delaware Co OH; Ref: Carol Wood.

MARTIN - m 19 Aug 1842 Lorain Co OH MARTHA A WILLIAMS; Ref: Marriages Lorain Co OH p119.

MARTIN - b 1827 CT; m ANTOINETTE ----- who was b 1831 CT; Res New Hartford, Litchfield Co CT; Ref: 1850 Census New Hartford CT p115 Dw# 59.

MARTIN - b 1830 PA s/ISAAC & FREELOVE (MADISON) WILCOX; Ref: Evangeline A Wilcox.

MARTIN H - b 14 Oct 1844 Cherry Creek, Chautauqua Co NY s/ERASTUS B & ROXY (BUGBEE) WILCOX; m 24 Oct 1877 ANNA E BROWN who was b 1848 & d 16 Sep 1906 Cherry Creek NY d/HORACE & LYDIA A (MEYERS) BROWN; Res Villanova, Chautauqua Co NY; ch WARREN FERDE, GERRY H, WILLIAM B, ALLEN M, SHIRLEY J; Funeral 25 May 1919 Villanova, NY; Ref: Wilcox Hist mss, 1850 Census Cherry Creek NY p136 Dw# 1842, 1860 Census Villanova NY p545 Dw# 1496, 1870 Census Chautauqua Co NY p187, 1910 Census, Down's Hist of Chautauqua Co NY p507, Highland Memorial Cem Records, Lois Barris.

MARTIN H - b 17 May 1851 Springwater, Livingston Co NY s/DAVID H & ADELIA (HOPKINS) WILCOX; m 17 Sep 1873 PHEBE ROOT; Res Steuben Co NY; ch EDITH, IONE, GUY, ARCHIE D; d 26 Jan 1916 Cohocton, Steuben Co NY; Ref: Your Ancestors v10 #1 p1200 #2 p1224.

MARTIN H - Res Hadley, Saratoga Co NY; Town Clerk 1868 & Justice of the Peace 1875; Ref: Hist of Saratoga Co NY p416.

MARTIN L - poss b Richland, Oswego Co NY s/ROMULUS B & POLLY ANN (THOMPSON) WILCOX; Res Monroe Co WI; Civil War Private Company H 16th Infantry of WI; d 28 Aug 1864 Rome, Floyd Co GA; Ref: Hist of Monroe Co WI p146, Hist of Chippewa Valley WI p473.

MARTIN V - b 1840 NY s/JAMES & MELINDA (DURFEE) WILCOX of Leon, Cattaraugus Co NY; Enlisted in Co K 64th NY Reg 29 Sep 1861; Discharged 15 Oct 1864; Ref: Hist of Cattaraugus Co NY p150, 1850 Census Leon NY p49 Dw# 191, See James.

MARVEL Mrs - d 20 Mar 1850 Ref: Deaths from NY Herald p551.

MARVIN - b ca 1806 s/EZRA P & LAVICIA (HERRICK) WILCOX of E Bloomfield, Ontario Co NY; Res near Marshall, Calhoun Co MI; ch MARY (WILCOX) MORLEY; Ref: Desc of Wm Wilcoxson p205.

MARVIN - b 1836 NY s/----- & CHLOE (-----) WILCOX of Columbus, Chenango Co NY; Ref: 1850 Census Columbus NY p274 Dw# 2028.

MARVIN W - b 1869 WI s/FRANKLIN & LOUISA (-----) WILCOX; Father b OH, Mother b NY; Res Lemonwien, Juneau Co WI; Ref: 1880 Soundex Juneau Co WI.

MARY - b 13 Nov 1654 Middletown, Middlesex Co CT d/JOHN & CATHERINE (STOUGHTON) WILCOX; d be 1676; Ref: Nutmegger v4 #3 p331, Early Fam of Wallingford p330, Cutter's CT Fam v2 656, Col Fam of US v5 p554, Barbour's VR Middletown LR1 p5, Hist of Wallingford p936.

MARY - b 16--; m EBER SHERMAN who was b Dec 1634 s/PHILIP & SARAH (-----) SHERMAN; Ref: RI Roots Mar 1984 p2.

MARY - 16--; m THOMAS KIMBERLY; m 09 Jul 1673 ELIASAPH PRESTON; Res Stratford, Fairfield Co & Wallingford, New Haven Co CT; ch MARY; d 25 Apr 1674; Ref: Early Fam of Wallingford CT p280.

MARY - b 25 Feb 1662 Dartmouth, Bristol Co MA d/DANIEL & ELIZABETH (COOKE) WILCOX; m 1686 JOHN EARLE who d 1728 s/RALPH & DORCAS (SPRAGUE) EARLE; ch JOHN, DANIEL, BENJAMIN, MARY, REBECCA, ELIZABETH; d Apr/May 1735; Ref: Am Gen v19 #1 p27, Your Ancestors v10 #3 p1244, Austin p423, Wilcox Excerpts v1 p21, Little Compton Fam p770, Bristol Co MA Probate Rec v1 p24.

MARY - b Apr 01/04 1668 Stratford, Fairfield Co CT d/JOHN & ELIZABETH (BOURNE) WELLES WILCOX; Ref: Wilcox-Meigs p22, Desc of Wm Wilcoxson p27, Stratford Gen p1346.

MARY - b 24 Mar 1676 Middletown, Middlesex Co CT d/JOHN & ESTHER (CORNWALL) WILCOX; m 10 Jul 1695 Middletown CT BENJAMIN HAND of Guilford, New Haven Co CT who was b 08 Feb 1672/3 & d Aug 1744 s/JOSEPH & JANE (WRIGHT) HAND; ch NATHANIEL, JOHN, MARY, SUBMIT, EBENEZER, BENJAMIN, MARY; d 24 Oct 1749; Ref: Nutmegger v4 #3 p331, v8 #4 p532, Gen of the Hand Fam pp22,23, Early Fam of Wallingford p330, A Wilcox Book p16, Cutter's Western NY v2 p741, Col Fam of US v5 p554, Barbour's VR Middletown LR1 p48, Chatham v1 p114, Guilford vA p95, Hist of Wallingford p936.

MARY - b 11 Dec 1676 E Guilford, New Haven Co CT d/OBADIAH & LYDIA (ALLING) WILCOX; m 15 Sep 1694 THOMAS MUNSON who was b 12 Mar 1671 & d 28 Sep 1746 Cheshire, New Haven Co CT s/SAMUEL & MARTHA (BRADLEY) MUNSON; ch LYDIA, THOMAS, MARY, OBADIAH, HANNAH, JOANNA, RACHEL, EUNICE, THANKFUL, EBENEZER; d 18 Nov 1755; Ref: Wilcox-Meigs p26, Desc of Wm Wilcoxson p8, Munson Rec v1 p65, Fam of Early Guilford p1208, Barbour's VR New Haven v1 p137, Hist of Surry NH p944.

MARY - b ca 1680 Westerly, Washington Co RI d/EDWARD & MARY (HAZARD) WILCOX; m 1716 JOSEPH LEWIS; Ref: Austin p423, Col Fam of US v3 p226, Hist of Stonington p658.

MARY - b 25 Feb 1682 Portsmouth, Newport Co RI d/DANIEL & HANNAH (COOK) WILCOX; m DAVID LAKE who was b 02 Jun 1679 & d 04 Aug 1767 Portsmouth RI; 10 ch; Ref: Am Gen v19 #1 p28, Austin p423, Your Ancestors v10 #3 p1267.

MARY - b 14 Feb 1688 Dartmouth, Bristol Co MA d/SAMUEL & MARY (WOOD) or ESTHER (COOK) WILCOX; m THOMAS BROOKS; Ref: Dartmouth VR p393, Wilcox Excerpts v1 p21, Rep Men of Southeastern MA p1081, Your Ancestors v12 #4 p1504.

MARY - b 10 Dec 1705/8 Middletown, Middlesex Co CT d/EPHRAIM & SILENCE (HAND) WILCOX; m JOHN WARNER; Ref: MUH p744, Nutmegger v4 #3 p331, NEH&GR v14 p 138, Your Ancestors v4 #3&4 p524, Barbour's VR Middletown LR1 p1.

MARY - m 21 Sep 1732 Middletown, Middlesex Co CT DANIEL CLARK; Ref: Nutmegger v13 #3 p389, Barbour's VR Middletown v1 p70.

MARY - b 10 Feb 1709 Dartmouth, Bristol Co MA d/JEREMIAH & MARY (SMITH) WILCOX; m 01 Apr 1731 Dartmouth MA HUMPHREY SMITH who d 04 Nov 1777 s/DELIVERANCE & MARY (TRIPP) SMITH; ch SARAH, HENRY, HUMPHREY, ABIGAIL, DANIEL; d 14 Nov 1757; Ref: Dartmouth VR pp303,547, Wilcox Excerpts v1 p22, Your Ancestors v13 #1 pp1529,1530.

MARY - b 01 Dec 1709 Stonington, New London Co CT d/WILLIAM & DOROTHY GILBERT (PALMER) WILCOX; m BRIAN PENDLETON; Ref: Barbour's VR Stonington v2 p50, Hist of Stonington CT p659, Austin p423, Early NE Pendletons pp120,121.

MARY - b 25 Jan 1710/11 Middletown, Middlesex Co CT d/JOHN & MARY (BARNES) WILCOX; Ref: Nutmegger v4 #3 p331, NEH&GR v14 p138, Barbour's VR Middletown LR2 p21.

MARY - b 17 Dec 1712 Dartmouth, Bristol Co MA d/DANIEL & SARAH (-----) WILCOX; m 25 Jun 1730 ISAAC SMITH who was b 1699 & d 1768 s/GERSHOM & REBECCA (-----) SMITH; ch JOHN, GEARS, DANIEL, LEMUEL; Ref: Am Gen v19 #1 p28, Dartmouth VR pp546,547, Bristol Co Probate Rec v2 p172, Your Ancestors v10 #3 p1267, v12 #3 p1477.

MARY - b ca 1712/3 poss d/SAMUEL & RUTH (WESTCOTT) of Killingworth, Middlesex Co CT; m OBADIAH KELSEY brother of KEZIAH & BENJAMIN KELSEY; Ref: Your Ancestors v3 #7&8 p426.

MARY - b 1713 d/WILLIAM & ELIZABETH (WILSON) WILCOX of Simsbury, Hartford Co CT; Ref: Pioneers of Madison Co CT p281.

MARY - b Nov 1716 Stratford, Fairfield Co CT d/WILLIAM & ESTHER (BRINSMADE) WILCOX; Ref: Wilcox-Meigs p39, Stratford Gen p1346.

MARY - b 04 Oct 1717 Westerly, Washington Co RI d/EDWARD & DINAH (BARBER) WILCOX; Ref Arnold v5 p144.

MARY - b 14 May 1718 d/ROBERT & AMEY (-----) WILCOX; m 06 Jun 1739 EBENEZER DRUCE; Ref: Col Fam of US v3 p226.

MARY - b 1719; m 1731 SAMUEL HUMPHREY III; Res CT; d 1756; Ref: NE & NY Ancestors v3 #9&10 p445.

MARY - m 15 Jan 1735/6 Middletown, Middlesex Co CT JOHN WARNER; Ref: Barbour's VR Middletown v1 p86.

MARY - m 06 Sep 1744 Farmington, Hartford Co CT DAVID ANDRUSS; Ref: Nutmegger v6 #1 p18, v7 #1 p30, Barbour's VR Farmington LR7 p35.

MARY - b 01 Sep 1725 Middletown, Middlesex Co CT d/ISRAEL & MARY (NORTH) WILCOX; Ref: Nutmegger v4 #3 p331, NEH&GR v14 p138, Barbour's VR Middletown LR2 p11.

MARY - b ca 1726 E Greenwich, Kent Co RI d/STEPHEN & ALICE (BROWNELL) WILCOX; m ----- CASPER/GASPER; Ref: Halifax VT Wilcox Fam mss, Samuel Gorton Desc p585, Wilcox Genealogy p6.

MARY - b 04 Jun 1727 S Kingston, Washington Co RI d/ROBERT & SARAH (WILCOX) WILCOX; Ref: Your Ancestors v11 #3 p1351, Arnold v5 pt2 p59.

MARY - b 21 Jan 1729 Stonington, New London Co CT d/STEPHEN & SUSANNAH (PENDLETON) WILCOX; Ref: Hist of Stonington p660, Barbour's VR Stonington v2 p63.

MARY - b 27 May 1729 W Greenwich, Kent Co RI d/THOMAS WILCOX; Ref: Arnold v1 pt3 p103, See RIGR v2 #2 p122.

MARY - b ca 1730 d/JEFFREY & SARAH (HIMES) WILCOX of N Kingston, Washington Co RI; m JEREMIAH WILCOX; Ref: Your Ancestors v3 #11&12 p472.

MARY - b 13 May 1730 Portsmouth, Newport Co RI d/JOSEPH & SARAH (-----) WILCOX; Ref: Arnold v4 pt1 p104, Your Ancestors v12 #3 p1477.

MARY - m 06 Sep 1750 Tiverton, Newport Co RI JOHN HORSWELL; Ref: Arnold v4 pt7 p57.

MARY - m 24 Dec 1753 Exeter, Washington Co RI JAMES TANNER; Ref: Arnold v5 pt3 p35.

MARY - b 01 Dec 1731 Guilford, New Haven Co CT d/JOHN & DEBORAH (PARMELEE) WILCOX; m 06 Nov 1752 Killingworth, Middlesex Co CT ENOS FRENCH who was b 09 Dec 1735 E Guilford s/THOMAS & SARAH (GRAVES) FRENCH; ch MARY, SENE, EBENEZER, DEBORAH, SARAH, ENOS, THOMAS; d 28 Sep 1777; Ref: Nutmegger v3 #3 p294, v17 #2 p294, Wilcox-Meigs p33, Fam of Early Guilford pp499,1208, Gen of CT Fam v1 p641, Desc of Wm Wilcoxson p15, Barbour's VR Guilford v2 p57.

MARY - b 04 Feb 1732/3 Killingworth, Middlesex Co CT d/SAMUEL & MARY (STEVENS) WILCOX; m 15 Nov 1753 ABRAHAM HURD; 10 ch; Ref: Wilcox-Meigs p42, Barbour's VR Killingworth v2 pp117,185, Desc of Wm Wilcoxson p43.

MARY - b 02 Sep 1733/4 d/AZARIAH & MARY (FAXTON) WILCOX; m DANIEL MOSES who was b 1732 & d 08 Sep 1776 s/CALEB MOSES; m JOSEPH MALLISON; Res North Canton Hartford Co CT; ch DANIEL, ZEBINA, ROGER, LOIS, HANNAH, CHARLOTTE, SYBIL, MARY; d 1816; Ref: Your Ancestors v11 #4 p1380, v12 #2 p1438, Wilcox-Meigs p49, Desc of Wm Wilcoxson p23, Barbour's VR Simsbury TM3 p240, TM4 p249.

MARY - b 03 Nov 1733 Simsbury, Hartford Co CT d/JOSEPH & MARY (BUTTOLPH) WILCOX; Ref: Wilcox-Meigs p49.

MARY - b 07 Sep 1734 Killingworth, Middlesex Co CT Twin with LYDIA d/STEPHEN & MARY (PIERSON) WILCOX; m 14 Jul 1751 JAMES WARD who was b 08 Feb 1729 s/IRA & LYDIA (PARMELEE) WARD; ch TEMPERANCE; d 09 Feb 1753 or 18 Jun 1805; Ref: Andrew Ward Fam p84; Bogue Fam p395, Wilcox-Meigs p42, Fam of

Early Guilford pp1190,1191, Your Ancestors v3 #3 p321, Cutter's New England Fam v1 p159, Barbour's VR Killingworth v2 pp120,159.

MARY - b ca 1735 d/STEPHEN & MARY (THOMAS) WILCOX of Dartmouth, Bristol Co MA; int to m 03 Nov 1759 WILLIAM AKIN; Ref: Dartmouth VR p547, Demaris Hickey.

MARY - bpt 21 Mar 1735 Little Compton, Newport Co RI d/WILLIAM & PRISCILLA (PEABODY) WILCOX; Ref: Arnold v8 p34, See William, See RIGR v3 34 p348.

MARY - b ca 1736 Little Compton, Newport Co RI d/JEREMIAH & MARY (-----) WILCOX; d 14 Nov 1752; Ref: Repr Men of Southeastern MA p1081.

MARY (JAYCOCKS) Mrs - b 1736; w/----- Wilcox m 17 Jan 1750; McGREGOR VAN AVERY who was b 27 Apr 1723 & d 25 Sep 1786; Res Arents NY & Niagara, Ontario Canada; Loyalist; Ref: New Loyalist Index.

MARY - b 27 Jan 1736/7 Middletown, Middlesex Co CT d/JEREMIAH & MARY (STOWE) WILCOX m ELISHA TREAT 29 May 1766 Cromwell, Middlesex Co CT; Ref: ECM v2 p92, Your Ancestors v3 #5 p380, Barbour's VR Middletown v1 p95.

MARY - b 23 Jul 1737 Dartmouth, Bristol Co MA d/JABEZ & HANNAH (HART) WILCOX; Ref: Dartmouth VR p303, Little Compton Fam p771.

MARY - m 04 Feb 1755 N Stonington, New London Co CT THOMAS LARRISON; Ref: ECM v1 p57.

MARY - b 22 Jun 1740 Middletown, Middlesex Co CT d/JANNA & RACHEL (BOARDMAN) WILCOX; m 10 Dec 1759 JOHN FRENCH of Guilford, New Haven Co CT & Westminster NH who was b 02 Jun/Jul 1735 Dummerston, Windham Co VT s/THOMAS & SARAH (GRAVES) FRENCH; ch JOHN, MARY; d 19 Apr 1791 Westminster NH; Ref: Your Ancestors v4 #3&4 p524, Fam of Early Guilford p499, Gen of CT Fam v1 p642, Barbour's VR Middletown TR1 p22, Guilford v2 p72.

MARY - b 01 Oct 1740 Hebron, Tolland Co CT d/DAVID & MARY (HUTCHINSON) WILCOX; Ref: Barbour's VR Hebron v1 p33, Desc of Abner & Lucy Hart Wilcox pp19,20.

MARY - b 19 Mar 1743 Hebron, Tolland Co CT d/EBENEZER Jr & ELIZABETH (DEWEY) WILCOX; Res

Surry, Cheshire Co NH; Ref: Barbour's VR Hebron v1 p36, Wilcox-Meigs p50, Desc of Wm Wilcoxson p25.

MARY - b ca 1743 d/STEPHEN & ALICE (-----) WILCOX; m ----- GOSPER; Ref: Your Ancestors v3 #7&8 p423.

MARY - Convict from Middlesex England transported to America Mar 1760 on ship *Friendship*; Ref: Eng Convicts in America v1 p289.

MARY - m 02 Sep 1761 PA SIMON GUERT; Ref: Marriages in PA p263.

MARY - of Westfield, Middlesex Co CT; m 04 Dec 1764 as his 3rd wife MEDAD PUMROY Jr; Ref: Barbour's VR Suffield Private Rec.

MARY - of Hebron, Tolland Co CT; m 18 Dec 1766 Bolton, Tolland Co CT DAVID WEBSTER; Ref: Bolton VR p19, Barbour's VR Bolton v1 p212.

MARY - m 15 Jan 1770 Exeter, Washington Co RI ISHMEAL WILCOX; Ref: Arnold v5 pt3 p35.

MARY - m Jun 1771 Tiverton, Newport Co RI WILLIAM ALMY; Ref: Arnold v4 pt7 p57.

MARY - m 08 Apr 1779 Dartmouth, Bristol Co MA THEOPHILAS WHITE; Ref: Dartmouth VR p547.

MARY - b 27 Jul 1748 Simsbury, Hartford Co CT Twin with RACHEL d/EZRA & MARY (HUMPHREY) WILCOX; d 02 Sep 1755; Ref: Wilcox-Meigs p49, Noble Gen p219, Fiske Card File, Early Settlers of W Simsbury p131, Your Ancestors v13 #3 p1567.

MARY - b 1753 d/ROBERT & MARTHA (POTTER) WILCOX of Exeter & Richmond, Washington Co RI; Ref: Your Ancestor v3 #1 p277.

MARY Mrs - m 14 Dec 1771 Simsbury, Hartford Co CT Capt NATHANIEL HOLCOMB; Ref: Barbour's VR Simsbury TM4 p221.

MARY - b 06 Jan 1754 Dartmouth, Bristol Co MA d/STEPHEN & MARY (RICKETSON) WILCOX; m 20 May/Jul 1772 STEPHEN PECKHAM Jr; 4 ch; Ref: Dartmouth VR p303, Am Gen v19 #1 p30; Your Ancestors v10 #3 p1268.

MARY - m 09 Jan 1782 CHISTOPHER WHITING who was b 1758 & d 06 Jul 1812 age 54 s/BENJAMIN & ESTHER

(MARCUM) WHITING; Res Winchester, Litchfield Co CT; ch LORRAIN, RILEY, CLARA, LUMAN, ESTHER MIRIAM, NORMAN; Ref: Annals of Winchester CT p137, Barbour's VR Winchester v1 p10.

MARY - b 13 Sep 1756 Middletown, Middlesex Co CT Twin with MARTHA d/ISRAEL & MARTHA (BARNS) WILCOX; Ref: Barbour's VR Middletown LR2 p285.

MARY - b 04 Mar 1757 Lebanon, New London Co CT d/EPHRAIM & ABIGAIL (BASCOM) WILCOX; Ref: Your Ancestors v4 #5&6 p566, Barbour's VR Lebanon v1 p347.

MARY - b 04 Nov 1758 Goshen, Litchfield Co CT d/GIDEON & MARY (BLANCHARD) WILCOX; Ref: Barbour's VR Goshen v1 p262.

MARY - b ca 1758 W Simsbury, Hartford Co CT d/WILLIAM & LUCY (CASE) WILCOX; m ELIPHALET CURTIS Jr who was b 1758 & d 1816 age 58 s/ELIPHALET & MARGARET (DYER) CURTIS; Ref: Early Settlers of W Simsbury CT pp32,129, Your Ancestors v10 #4 p1276.

MARY - b 22 Dec 1759 W Greenwich, Kent Co RI d/THOMAS & ELIZABETH (-----) WILCOX; Ref: Arnold v1 pt3 p103.

MARY - b 31 Jan 1760 Killingworth, Middlesex Co CT d/ABEL 2nd & MARY (HULL) WILCOX; m 05 Nov 1789 SAMUEL PRATT; Ref: Wilcox-Meigs p62, Your Ancestors v3 #1 p280, Barbour's VR Killingworth v2 pp42,133.

MARY - b 18 Mar 1760 Middletown, Middlesex Co CT d/MOSES & DESIRE (RANNEY) WILCOX; d 04 Oct 1762; Ref: Barbour's VR Middletown v2 p292.

MARY - b 04 Apr 1760 White Hills CT d/DAVID & ISRAELIA (SALMON) WILCOX; Ref: Wilcox-Meigs p58, Stratford Gen p1347.

MARY - b 04 May 1760 Simsbury, Hartford Co CT d/HOSEA & HANNAH (GRIFFIN) WILCOX; Ref: Wilcox-Meigs p68.

MARY - m 15 Nov 1784 Winchester, Litchfield CT JOSHUA BENEDICT s/TIMOTHY BENEDICT; ch ANNA, Res Montreal Canada; Ref: Annals of Winchester CT p72, Barbour's VR Winchester v1 p38.

MARY - d/BENJAMIN & ESTER (SHEFFIELD) WILCOX of Richmond Washington Co RI & Newport, Nova Scotia

Canada; m JOHN ARMSTRONG; Ref: Desc of Charles Dyer Wilcox p v, Samuel Gorton Desc v2 p587.

MARY - b 21 Jan 1761 Jamestown, Washington Co RI d/DANIEL & LYDIA (------) WILCOX; Ref: Arnold v5 pt5 p30.

MARY - m 08 Feb 1781 Middletown, Middlesex Co CT AMOS TREAT; Ref: Barbour's VR Middletown v2 p273.

MARY - b 04 Apr 1762 Newport, Newport Co RI d/SAMUEL & ELIZABETH (GODDARD) WILCOX; m 04 Oct 1815 WILLIAM MITCHELL s/RICHARD & MARY (-----) MITCHELL; Ref: Arnold v7 pp39,82,163, Your Ancestors v11 #3 p1372.

MARY - b 23 Jun 1762 Westport, Bristol Co MA d/SAMUEL & COMFORT (SEABURY) WILCOX; Ref: Westport VR p102, Your Ancestors v13 #2 p1554.

MARY - b 24 Oct 1762 Middletown, Middlesex Co CT d/ELIJAH & MARY (BUSHNELL) WILCOX; d 07 Dec 1762; Ref: Barbour's VR Middletown v2 p28, See Elijah.

MARY - b 29 Sep 1764 Goshen, Litchfield Co CT d/JOHN Jr; Ref: Barbour's VR Goshen v1 p237.

MARY - b 22 Nov 1764 Middletown, Middlesex Co CT d/ELIJAH & MARY (BUSHNELL) WILCOX; Ref: Barbour's VR Middletown v2 p28.

MARY - b 1765; m BENJAMIN GRANNIS who was b 1757 & d 19 May 1832 age 75 North Haven, New Haven Co CT s/ENOS & THANKFUL (BROCKETT) GRANNIS; ch BENJAMIN, BENJAMIN, HORACE, GEORGE BENJAMIN, CHARLES B, JOHN WILSON, HENRY E; d 19 Jun 1849 at Brooklyn NY; bur Old Graveyard North Haven CT; Ref: Fam of Ancient New Haven v1 p683.

MARY - b 26 Feb 1768 Killingworth, Middlesex Co CT d/JESSE & THANKFUL (STEVENS) WILCOX; d 09 Mar 1768 12days old; Ref: Wilcox-Meigs p63, Nebr & Midwest Gen Rec v8 #1 p22,23, Your Ancestors v3 #4 p349.

MARY/POLLY - b 1768 Killingworth, Middlesex Co CT d/HIEL & DEBORAH (GILLETT) WILCOX; m 01 Mar 1787 NY STORY/HISTORY GOTT who was b 30 Nov 1765 Colchester, New London Co CT & d 05 Jun 1841; Res Spencertown, Columbia Co NY; ch POLLY, STORY, GUY, SUSAN, ALVIN, LOISAH, HARVEY, SARAH, HARRY D,

LUCRETIA, ALMIRA, ANNA, JOHN, JOSEPH; Ref: Wilcox-Meigs p66, Desc of Wm Wilcoxson p59, Pension Rec of Story Gott, Will of Hiel Wilcox, Your Ancestors v4 #11&12 p612.

MARY - b 07 May 1769 Torrington, Litchfield Co CT d/ASAHEL & MARY (COE) WILCOX; Ref: Barbour's VR Torrington v1 p107.

MARY - b 04 Jun 1771 Exeter, Washington Co RI d/JOHN & MARY (BARBER) WILCOX; Ref: Your Ancestors v4 #7&8 p561, Arnold v5 pt3 p63.

MARY - m 01 Dec 1811 Exeter, Washington Co RI GEORGE GARDNER CHAMPLIN who was b 19 Jul 1754 & d 30 Sep 1821 s/JEFFERY CHAMPLIN; Ref: Arnold v5 pt3 p36, RI Roots v8 #1 p16.

MARY - b 1771; m JAMES BATES; d 1828 NY; Ref: 2nd Boat v5 #4 p166.

MARY - b 03/05 Jan 1772 Stratford, Fairfield Co CT d/NATHAN & MARY (BEACH) WILCOX; m BREWSTER DAYTON; Ref: Wilcox-Meigs p60, Stratford Gen p1347, Desc of Wm Wilcoxson p37.

MARY - b 16 Feb 1772 Dartmouth, Bristol Co MA d/TYLER & DEBORAH (RUSSELL) WILCOX; Ref: Dartmouth VR p303, See Tyler.

MARY - b 11 Mar 1772 Middletown, Middlesex Co CT d/STEPHEN & MARY (KELSEY) WILCOX; m SAMUEL HART; Ref: Hist of Berlin Co CT p100, Barbour's VR Middletown v2 p202.

MARY - b 03 Jun 1773 Burrillville, Providence Co RI d/JIRAH & BATHSHEBA (LAPHAM) WILCOX; Ref: Your Ancestors v11 #4 p1397.

MARY - b 04 Apr 1774 N Stonington, New London Co CT d/DANIEL & HANNAH (WILBUR) WILCOX; Ref: Barbour's VR N Stonington v2 p96, Will of Daniel Wilcox 1803, See Daniel.

MARY - b 02 Nov 1774 Hebron, Tolland Co CT d/JEHIEL & LYDIA (MACK) WILCOX; Ref: Wilcox Meigs p69, Barbour's VR Hebron v2 p260.

MARY - b 14 Mar 1776 Newport, Sullivan Co NH d/JESSE & THANKFUL (STEVENS) WILCOX; m be 1798 NATHANIEL FISHER; m JOSEPH KIMBALL; ch by 1st husband NATHANIEL WILCOX; Ref: Hist of Chester NH p113, Wilcox-Meigs p63, Nebr & Midwest Gen Rec v8 #1 pp22,23, Your Ancestors v3 #4 p349.

MARY - b 08 Jan 1777 Westerly, Washington Co RI d/ISAIAH & SARAH (LEWIS) WILCOX; Ref: Arnold v5 p145.

MARY - b 25 May 1777 Simsbury, Hartford Co CT d/AMOS & HANNAH (HOSKINS) WILCOX; m 10 Nov 1789 GABRIEL CORNISH; Ref: Wilcox-Meigs p67.

MARY - m 31 Dec 1789 Westerly, Washington Co RI ARNOLD BLIVEN; Ref: Arnold v5 pt2 p69.

MARY - m 16 Feb 1792 Exeter, Washington Co RI JOHN PERKINS; Ref: Arnold v5 pt3 p36.

MARY - b 04 Apr 1774 d/DANIEL & ANNA (ROGERS) WILCOX; m 17 Mar 1794 Cumberland, Providence Co RI WILLIAM BALLOU; Ref: Arnold v3 p69, Your Ancestors v11 #1 p1320.

MARY - b 07 May 1778 Portsmouth, Newport Co RI d/COOK & SARAH (ESLECK) WILCOX; Ref: Arnold v4 pt1 p105, See Cook.

MARY - b 13 Oct 1778 Surry, Cheshire Co NH d/OBADIAH & HANNAH (MERRIAM) WILCOX; Ref: Hist of Surry NH p946.

MARY - b 25 Oct 1778; m 29 Sep 1799 SHEPARD COTTRELL who was b 11 Sep 1773 & d 07 Apr 1847; d 23 Aug 1860; Ref: CT Bible Rec v13 pp108,109.

MARY - d/ALEXANDER WILCOX; m 18 Oct 1804 PA C J INGERSOLL; Ref: Daily Advertiser Philadelphia p116.

MARY - m 22 May 1794 Portsmouth, Newport Co RI THOMAS CORY Jr; Ref: Arnold v4 pt1 p48.

MARY - m 06 Sep 1797 Portsmouth, Newport Co RI JOB FISH; Ref: Arnold v4 pt1 p48.

MARY - m 01 Sep 1808 Stockbridge, Berkshire Co MA NATHANIEL RICE; Ref: Fiske Card File.

MARY - d/JOHN WILCOX; m 14 Mar 1805 PA WILLIAM BALN; Ref: Philadelphia Daily Advertiser p127.

MARY - b ca 1780 d/ROBERT & CATHERINE (TRIPP) WILCOX; m 30 Mar 1809 N. Kingston, Washington Co RI 2nd wife/WILLIAM GREENE who was b 13 Feb 1769 &

d 30 Mar 1848 s/ABRAHAM & PATIENCE (ARNOLD) GREENE; ch ROBERT WILCOX; d Nov 1809; Ref: Your Ancestors v3 #1 p277, Arnold v5 p51.

MARY - b 1780 Stonington, New London Co CT d/ELISHA & MOLLY (GATES) WILCOX; m 1805 ISAIAH W FISH s/JAMES FISH; Res Groton, New London Co CT & Brooklyn, Cuyahoga Co OH; ch MARY, JAMES, ELISHA, SALLY, ISAIAH W; Ref: Your Ancestors v3 #5 p376.

MARY - b 1781 d/EZRA Jr & ROSANNA (CASE) WILCOX; Ref: Noble Gen p219, Fiske Card File, Early Settlers of W Simsbury CT p132, Your Ancestors v13 #3 p1568.

MARY - b 11 May 1783 Middletown, Middlesex Co CT d/JEREMIAH & RUTH (DUDLEY) WILCOX; Res CT & OH; d 1837; Ref: Mrs. Wm Richardson, Barbour's VR Middletown v2 p159.

MARY - b 22 Aug 1785 Exeter, Washington Co RI d/JOB & MARY (GATES) WILCOX; m 1802 Hopkinton, Washington Co RI CLARK LEWIS; Res Oxford, Chenango Co NY; ch EUNICE, SUSAN, FRANCES, CAROLINE, LOUISA, ELIZABETH, SARAH, JANE; d 21 Nov 1855; Ref: Arnold v5 pt3 pp35,63, Cutter's Western NY v3 p1436, Hist of Chenango Co NY p261, Your Ancestors v4 #11&12 p610.

MARY - b 03 Dec 1785 Killingworth, Middlesex Co CT d/EBENEZER & MARY (NETTLETON) WILCOX; Ref: Wilcox-Meigs p66, Desc of Wm Wilcoxson p59, Barbour's VR Killingworth v2 p81.

MARY - b 1787 E Guilford, New Haven Co CT d/BENJAMIN BRADLEY & MARY (TODD) WILCOX; m SYLVESTER WALKLEY; d Nov 1812; Ref: Fam of Early Guilford p1202.

MARY - d/SYLVESTER & AMY (RICHMOND) WILCOX m GEORGE G CHAMPLAIN 01 Dec 1811 Exeter, Washington Co RI; Ref: Arnold v5 pt3 p36, RI Roots v8 #1 p16.

MARY - b 02 Oct 1791 Halifax, Windham Co VT d/STEPHEN & ELINOR (EWING) WILCOX; Ref: VT VR, Halifax Wilcox Fam mss.

MARY - b 1791 d/DAVID WILCOX; m 20 Mar/Dec 1815 Palmyra, Wayne Co NY ALVA HENDEE; d 16 Feb/May 1842 age 52; Ref: 10,000 VR of Western NY p108.

MARY - b 1791 CT; Res Whitestown, Oneida Co NY; Ref: 1850 Census Whitestown p65 Whitestown Asylum.

MARY - b 1793 d/ROBERT & SARAH (WILBUR) WILCOX of Lyme, New London Co CT; m AARON BROWN; Ref: Your Ancestors v11 #3 p1352.

MARY - b 1796 Litchfield, Herkimer Co NY d/JOHN & MARY (CROSBY) WILCOX; m STEPHEN TOWNSEND; d 1850 Litchfield NY; Ref: Jane Smith.

MARY - b 28 Apr 1798 Westport, Bristol Co MA d/SAMUEL & MATILDA (BRIGHTMAN) WILCOX; Ref: Westport VR p102, Your Ancestors v13 #2 p1554.

MARY - b 27 May 1798 Dover, Dutchess Co NY d/REUBEN & CHLOE (SACKETT) WILCOX; m 19 Nov 1818 JONSON NASH REYNOLDS who was b 13 Mar 1793 s/JAMES & ESTHER (NASH) REYNOLDS; ch MARY, HARRIETT, EMMA, CAROLINE, ALMIRA, ANN E, ESTHER D & JAMES JOHNSON twins; Ref: Your Ancestors v4 #3&4 p522.

MARY - b 18 Jul 1799 Halifax, Windham Co VT d/JOSEPH & PRUDENCE (DALRYMPLE) WILCOX; m 18/20 Jul 1817 LUTHER EDWARDS who was b 15 Sep 1793 Guilford, Windham Co VT & d 1863 Hampton s/BENJAMIN or BENAJAH & MOLLY (STOWELL) EDWARDS; ch ELIZA, BETSEY FIDELIA, LUTHER DANA; d 1850 Rock Island, Rock Island Co IL; Ref: Halifax Wilcox Fam mss, Samuel Gorton Desc v2 p586.

MARY - b 21 Jan 1800 d/JOHN Jr & LOIS (AUGUR) WILCOX; m 21 Feb 1827 ASA SMITH; d 20 Aug 1840; Ref: Desc of Wm Wilcoxson p123.

MARY - b 03 Jun 1800 Dartmouth, Bristol Co MA d/WILLIAM & RUTH (DURFEE) WILCOX; d 24 Sep 1843; Ref: Your Ancestors v10 #4 p1293.

MARY - m 23 Apr 1825 Ridgefield, Huron Co OH DANIEL CLARY who was b 1799 Herkimer Co NY Res OH 1817 & d 29 Apr 1863; ch HOMER C, GEORGE W; Ref: Firelands Pioneers NS 1864 p32, v10 p133.

MARY - m Sep 1828 Providence, Providence Co RI CALEB W MILLER; Ref: Arnold v20 p473.

MARY - b 13 Jul 1801 Middletown, Middlesex Co CT d/JULIUS & ELIZABETH (BROWN) WILCOX; d 19 Aug 1801; Ref: Gen of CT Fam v1 p245.

MARY - b 11 Aug 1801 Charlestown, Washington Co RI d/JOSEPH & HULDAH (SHERMAN) WILCOX; m DANIEL BABCOCK s/ELISHA & RUTH (GREEN) BABCOCK; ch DANIEL S, JOHN S, HULDAH, MATILDA; Ref: Your Ancestors v3 #5 p376, Arnold v5 pt5 p28.

MARY - b 21 Jan 1802 d/JOHN & LOIS (AUGER) WILCOX of Charleston, Montgomery Co NY; Ref: Your Ancestors v3 #11 & 12 p473.

MARY - b 16 Oct 1802 Ernestown, Canada d/HAZARD & SARAH (SEELEY) WILCOX; m JOHN LOWRY; Ref: Your Ancestors v12 #2 p1435.

MARY - b 24 Dec 1802 Franklin, New London Co CT d/JOHN & DORCAS (-----) WILCOX; Ref: Barbour's VR Franklin v1 p89.

MARY - b 22 Jun 1803 Killingworth, Middlesex Co CT d/NATHAN & ELIZABETH (ELIOT) WILCOX; Ref: Wilcox-Meigs p65, Barbour's VR Killingworth v2 p97.

MARY - m 08 Apr 1825 Killingworth, Middlesex Co CT JAMES ADAMS; Ref: Barbour's VR Killingworth v1 p107.

MARY - b 29 Dec 1804 d/JOHN CLARK & DORCAS (HARRINGTON) WILCOX of Franklin, New London Co CT; m DAVID Y STANTON; ch HERRINGTON, CHARLES, SPENCER WILCOX, MARY, AMY, HANNAH; Ref: Your Ancestors v14 #2 p1658.

MARY - m 05 Jul 1827 Voluntown, New London Co CT VARMUS SWEET; Ref: Barbour's VR Voluntown v2 p81.

MARY - b 29 Jun 1806 Killingworth, Middlesex Co CT d/ABNER & PHILINDA (WILCOX) WILCOX; Ref: Wilcox-Meigs p80, Barbour's VR Killingworth v2 p88.

MARY - b 1806 Killingworth, Middlesex Co CT; d 08 May 1839 Carthage, Jefferson Co NY; Ref: Early Settlers of NY p339.

MARY - b 23 May 1807 Chester, Hampden Co MA d/ASA & RELIEF (COLTON) WILCOX; d 24 Mar 1811; Ref: Fiske Card File, Your Ancestors v3 #9&10 p452.

MARY - b 17 Jul 1807 Stratford, Fairfield Co CT d/EPHRAIM JOHN & MARY (WHEELER) WILCOX; Ref: Wilcox-Meigs p78,94, Desc of Wm Wilcoxson p36.

MARY - b 29 Jan 1808 d/HEZEKIAH & MAHALA (WILCOX) WILCOX Bradford Co PA; m HIRAM HOLCOMB who was b 05 Jan 1806 & d 1895; Res Le Roy,

Bradford Co PA; Ref: Your Ancestors v10 #3 p1248, #4 p1273.

MARY - of Canton, Hartford Co CT; m DEXTER BACON; Res Firelands Area [Fulton & Erie Co] OH 1849; Res Wakeman, Huron Co OH; Ref: Firelands Pioneers v3 3rd Series p70.

MARY - m 25 Sep 1829 Griswold, New London Co CT VINE A STARR; Ref: Barbour's VR Griswold v1 p238.

MARY - b 1809 Pembroke, Plymouth Co MA d/ISRAEL WILCOX; m AARON GORHAM; Res Genesee Co NY, Ontario Canada; ch STEVEN, ARAM, CHARLES, AURETTA, CHRISTINE, HARRIET, JASPER, EMILY, NELSON, JOHN JAMES, LAURENA; Ref: Tree Talks v24 #1 p19, Nutmegger v12 #3 p518, v16 #4 p633.

MARY - m 03 Aug 1831 Southington, Hartford Co CT RUSSELL TREADWAY of Middletown, Middlesex Co CT; Ref: Barbour's VR Southington v1 p43.

MARY - d/Dr. ----- WILCOX; m 04 Jul 1833 E Bloomfield, Ontario Co NY E B BIRDSALL; Ref: 10,000 VR of Central NY p22.

MARY - m 22 Sep 1833 Simsbury, Hartford Co CT HENRY TULLER; Ref: Barbour's VR Simsbury TM4 p473.

MARY - m 27 Oct 1833 Stratford, Fairfield Co CT WILSON H FAIRCHILD; Ref: Barbour's VR Stratford vA p42.

MARY - m 12 Oct 1835 Avon, Hartford Co CT HENRY WATERS; both of Goshen, Litchfield Co CT; Ref: Barbour's VR Avon LR1 p570.

MARY - m 28 Nov 1839 Providence, Providence Co RI RUFUS SMITH; both from Seekonk, Bristol Co MA; Ref: Arnold v2 pt1 pp172,200.

MARY - b 04 Mar 1811 d/ALLYN & CHLOE (WOODFORD) WILCOX; Ref: CT Bible Rec v15 pp253,254.

MARY - b 26 Jun 1811 Windham. Windham Co CT d/ERASTUS & MARY ANN (RIPLEY) WILCOX; Ref: Barbour's VR Windham v3 p54, Desc of Wm Bradford p351.

MARY - d/WILLIAM J & LURANAH (GREEN) WILCOX; Res Napoli, Cattaraugus Co NY; d 1844; Ref: Hist of Cattaraugus Co NY p478.

MARY - b 26 Feb 1812 Westminster, Windham Co VT d/LUMON & ZIBAH (HOWARD) WILCOX; d 27 Jul 1862; Ref: MUH p755.

MARY - b 1813 d/BENJAMIN & SARAH ANN (-----) WILCOX; m LEONARD GRIFFIN who was b 1805 & d 16 Mar 1889 Orangeville, Wyoming Co NY; ch SARAH, LUCRETIA, SOPHIA, DEMETRIA, ELIZABETH, GEORGE, CHARLES; d 01 Dec 1889; Ref: Your Ancestors v14 #1 p1618, #3 p1670.

MARY - d/JULIUS & ELIZABETH (BROWN) WILCOX of VT; m ----- GRAVES; Ref: Fam of Early Guilford p1210.

MARY - b 1811/1815 NY d/JASON & LUCY (FESSENDEN) WILCOX of Bergen, Genesee Co NY; Ref: 1850 Census Bergen NY p58 Dw# 778, See Jason, 1860 Census Bergen NY p272 Dw# 295.

MARY - b 25 Sep 1816; Ref: CT Bible Rec v7 p656.

MARY - b 11 Apr 1817 Pawling, Dutchess Co NY d/ELISHA & BETSEY (WILCOX) SHIPPEN WILCOX; Ref: Your Ancestors v4 #9&10 p585.

MARY - b 03 Aug 1817 Bloomfield, Ontario Co NY d/EDWIN & CANDACE (GILBERT) WILCOX; m BENNET MUNGER; Ref: Edward McCarthy.

MARY - b 30 Jan 1819 Burlington, Nova Scotia Canada d/CHARLES DYER & ABIGAIL (CARD) WILCOX; m JOHN BENJAMIN CARD who was b 13 Jun 1817 & d 03 Nov 1902 s/BENJAMIN & LYDIA (HARVIE) CARD; ch EMILY, CORDELIA, STANLEY, LELAND, RUBY M; d 17 Jul 1914 bur Cogmagun Cem Nova Scotia; Ref: Desc of Charles Dyer Wilcox p v(2),17.

MARY - b 25 Jan 1826 d/JACOB & PHILENA (KEATING) WILCOX; m SAMUEL BROWN; Res Bradford Co PA; ch JACOB, POLLY, MARY ANN, MARGARET, AUSTIN, VINCENT, FRANKIE, MASON, EVA JANE, ELLA, ALVA; Ref: Your Ancestors v10 #3 p1247.

MARY - b 1826 CT d/HEZEKIAH & HANNAH (-----) WILCOX of Groton, New London Co CT; Ref: 1850 Census New London Co CT Reel M432 #49 p346.

MARY - b 1826 NY d/HARRY & MARY (-----) WILCOX of Virgil, Cortland Co NY; Ref: 1850 Census Virgil NY p397 Dw# 1047.

MARY - b 1826 d/NATHAN & MARIA (-----) WILCOX; d Herkimer Co NY 12 Aug 1838; Ref: DAR Records Book v4 p158.

MARY - m 28 Aug 1844 S Kingston, Washington Co RI GIDEON SUNDERLAND; Ref: Arnold v8 p507.

MARY - d/SAMUEL & MARY (COREY) WILCOX; d 06 Nov 1864; bur Hunt Cem Chautauqua Co NY; Ref: Cem Inscr p12.

MARY - b 1828 Surry, Cheshire Co NH d/Capt ASA Jr & NANCY (HARVEY) REED WILCOX; d 01 Jul 1838; Ref: Hist of Surry NH p381.

MARY - b 19 Jan 1829 Middletown, Middlesex Co CT d/JOSEPH Jr & MARIA (TRYON) WILCOX; Ref: Barbour's VR Middletown v3 p91.

MARY - b 1829 VT; Res with FRANCIS CRANE fam Buffalo, Erie Co NY; Ref: 1850 Census Buffalo NY p73.

MARY - b 1829 NY; Res with DANIEL ROBINSON fam Oswego, Oswego Co NY; Ref: 1850 Census Oswego NY p230 Dw# 242.

MARY - b 1829 NY d/CHARLES & LOUISA (-----) WILCOX of New Hartford, Oneida Co NY; Ref: 1850 Census New Hartford p284 Dw# 681.

MARY - b 06 Jul 1830 d/ISAAC & SARAH (STARK) WILCOX of Plains, Luzerne Co PA; d 26 Jan 1834; Ref: Your Ancestors v9 #3 p1152.

MARY - b 1831 NY d/----- & CHLOE (-----) WILCOX of Columbus, Chenango Co NY; Ref: 1850 Census Columbus NY p274 Dw# 2028.

MARY - b 1831 CT; Res Torrington, Litchfield Co CT with JOHN WILCOX fam; Ref: 1850 Census Torrington CT p221 Dw# 135.

MARY - b ca 1832 Evans, Erie Co NY d/JEHIEL & CHLOE (NICHOLS) WILCOX; Ref: Eden NY Town Historian.

MARY - b 1832 CT d/HENRY & BETSEY (-----) WILCOX of Concord, Erie Co NY; Ref: 1850 Census Concord NY p54 Dw# 785.

MARY - b 1832 Smyrna, Chenango Co NY d/HAZZARD & DORCAS (KENYON) WILCOX; Ref: Your Ancestors v3 #2 p298.

MARY - b 1832 NY d/ROBERT & NINA (-----) WILCOX of Oswego, Oswego Co NY; Ref: 1850 Census Oswego NY p233 Dw# 292.

MARY - b 1833 NY d/----- & SUSAN (-----) WILCOX of Greenwich, Washington Co NY; Ref: 1850 Census Greenwich NY p232 Dw# 499.

MARY - b 1833 NY; Res Davenport, Delaware Co NY; Ref: 1850 Census Davenport NY p138 Dw# 154.

MARY - b 1833 MA; Res New Hartford, Litchfield Co CT; Ref: 1850 Census New Hartford p120 Dw# 119.

MARY - b 1834 England d/JAMES & JANE (-----) WILCOX of Granger, Allegany Co NY; Ref: 1850 Census Granger NY p9 Dw# 157.

MARY - b 1834 d/STERLING OWENS & HARRIETT (HAYES) WILCOX; m 1864 JAMES N LEWIS; d 1912; Ref: Your Ancestors v11 #3 p1354.

MARY - b 23 Mar 1836 Le Roy, Bradford Co PA d/HEZEKIAH & ELIZABETH (MOORE) WILCOX; m W P TILLOTSON; Ref: 1850 Census Bradford Co PA p66, Pioneers of Bradford Co PA, Your Ancestors v10 #4 p1274.

MARY - b 1836 MA d/JONATHAN A & ABBA (-----) WILCOX of New Hartford, Litchfield Co CT; Ref: 1850 Census New Hartford CT p125 Dw# 185.

MARY - b 1837 NY d/JACOB & CAROLINE (-----) WILCOX of Sherburne, Chenango Co NY; Ref: 1850 Census Sherburne NY p249 Dw# 1624.

MARY - b 14 Oct 1837 Sandisfield, Berkshire Co MA d/CHAUNCEY & MARIANNE (POTTER) WILCOX; m SAMUEL WOODRUFF; Ref: Your Ancestors v12 #2 p1437, Desc of Wm Wilcoxson p223.

MARY - b ca 1838 Dover, Dutchess Co NY d/MARTIN & SARAH (-----) WILCOX; m ALBERT BROWN; Ref: Your Ancestors v4 #9&10 p585.

MARY - b 1838 NY d/BENJAMIN & HARRIET (-----) WILCOX of Lincklaen, Chenango Co NY; Ref: 1850 Census Chenango Co NY.

MARY - b 1838 VT d/ALONZO & ELIZABETH (-----) WILCOX of Orwell, Addison Co VT; Ref: 1850 Census Orwell VT Reel 920 p41.

MARY - m 03 Mar 1842 Warwick, Kent Co RI JOSEPH NASON; Ref: Arnold v1 p134.

MARY - b 1839 NY d/ALFRED & ABIGAIL (-----) WILCOX of Seneca Falls, Seneca Co NY; Ref: 1850 Census Seneca Falls NY p262 Dw# 1890.

MARY - b 1839 NY d/GEORGE & SARAH (-----) WILCOX of Harmony, Chautauqua Co NY; Ref: 1850 Census Harmony NY p267 Dw# 621.

MARY - b 10 Mar 1840 Cornwall, Litchfield Co CT; m ----- DENNING; m 24 Jun 1859 JOHN S JUDD; d Jul 1911 Bridgeport, Fairfield Co CT; Ref: Nutmegger v11 #3 p476.

MARY - b 1840 NY d/ISAIAH & LYDIA (-----) WILCOX of Columbus, Chenango Co NY; Ref: 1850 Census Columbus NY p279 Dw# 2126.

MARY - b 1840 VT d/JOSIAH & MARY (-----) WILCOX of Orwell, Addison Co VT; Ref: 1850 Census Orwell VT Reel 920 p41.

MARY - b 1840 CT d/LUCIUS & BELINDA S (DEMING) WILCOX of Cornwall, Litchfield Co CT; Ref: 1850 Census Cornwall CT p4 Dw# 61, See Lucius.

MARY - b 1841 VT d/OTIS & ABIGAIL (-----) WILCOX of Hancock, Addison Co VT; Ref: 1850 Census Hancock VT Reel 920 p64.

MARY - b 10 Sep 1841 d/ORRIN & HANNAH (HAMLIN) WILCOX of East Bloomfield, Ontario Co NY; d 1842; Ref: Your Ancestors v10 #3 p1249, Desc of Wm Wilcoxson p208.

MARY - b 1841/2 Halifax, Windham Co VT d/SAMUEL & MARTHA G (----) WILCOX; Ref: 1850 Census Halifax VT p131, Halifax Wilcox Fam mss.

MARY - b 1842 NY d/ J & SARAH (-----) WILCOX of Wheatland, Monroe Co NY; Ref: 1850 Census Wheatland NY p240 Dw# 268.

MARY - b 1842 NY d/ALANSON & ALMIRA (-----) WILCOX of Dayton, Cattaraugus Co NY; Ref: 1860 Census Dayton NY Reel 653 #726 p21.

MARY - b 1842 NJ d/----- & HENRIETTA (-----) WILCOX of Painesville, Lake Co OH; Ref: 1850 Census Painesville OH Reel 259 p182.

MARY - b 1843 d/CALVIN & ELIZA (-----) WILCOX of Black Brook, Clinton Co NY; Ref: 1850 Census, Florence Arnhart.

MARY - b 1844 NY d/EMERY & MARTHA (-----) WILCOX of Newport, Herkimer Co NY; Ref: 1850 Census Newport NY p173 Dw# 289.

MARY - b 1845 Chautauqua Co NY d/CHARLES W & EMILY (-----) WILCOX of Ripley, Chautauqua Co NY; Ref: 1850 Census Ripley NY p119 Dw# 259.

MARY - of Sherman, Chautauqua Co NY m 12 Jan 1868 HORACE GREELEY of NJ; Ref: 19th Cent Marriages Reported in Fredonia Censor p119.

MARY - b 1845 OH d/Rev MARTIN & MARTHA (-----) WILCOX of Madison, Lake Co OH; Ref: 1850 Census Madison OH Reel 259 p134.

MARY - b 1846 d/ALFRED & PHEBE (PERKINS) WILCOX of Groton, New London Co CT; Ref: 1850 Groton CT Census Reel 432 #49 p339.

MARY - b 1847 NY d/BIRDSEYE & LYDIA ANN (CALENDAR) WILCOX of Buffalo, Erie Co NY; Ref: 1850 Census Buffalo NY p237 Dw# 720, See Birdseye.

MARY - b 1848 NY d/CHARLES & REBECCA (-----) WILCOX of Lexington, Greene Co NY; Ref: 1850 Census Lexington NY p274 Dw# 50.

MARY - b 20 Feb 1849 Deep Cove, N B Canada d/WILLIAM & JANE (DRISCOLL) WILCOX; m EDWARD PREBLE GREEN s/WILLIAM & ELIZABETH (NEWTON) GREEN; ch WILLIAM EASTON, ALICE, HELEN UBERTA, LESLIE, GERTRUDE ALMA, HAROLD PAIGE, PERCY HARLAND; d 28 Nov 1931 Wood Island, N B Canada; Ref: Desc of Charles Dyer Wilcox pp 8,9.

MARY - m 17 Jun 1877 Woodstock, Windham Co CT ROBERSON EVANS ; Ref: Barbour's VR Brown Diary p145.

MARY - b Apr 1849 NY d/ISAAC & HESTER ANN (-----) WILCOX of Ithaca, Tompkins Co NY; Ref: 1850 Census Ithaca NY p227 Dw# 355.

MARY - b 1849 NY d/LYMAN & JOHANNAH (GUISLER) WILCOX of Sherman, Chautauqua Co NY; Ref: 1850 Census Sherman NY p276 Dw# 68, See Lyman.

MARY - b 1849 Jay, Essex Co NY d/HARVEY & SARAH (-----) WILCOX; Ref: 1850 Census Jay NY p204 Dw# 2914.

MARY - b 06 Mar 1850 Aurora, Dearborn Co IN d/JOHN KING & MEHITABLE SELINA (KELSEY) WILCOX; School teacher; Ref: Janet Armbrust.

MARY - b 1852 Lafayette, Onondaga Co NY d/ISAAC & NANCY (-----) WILCOX; Ref: Your Ancestors v13 #4 p1597.

MARY - b 1854 Simsbury, Hartford Co CT; d 20 Nov 1856; Ref: Rev Allen McLean Rec p17.

MARY - b 1854 NY d/AMOS P & ANN (-----) WILCOX of Jamestown, Chautauqua Co NY; Ref: 1860 Census Jamestown NY p725 Dw# 1302.

MARY - b 26 Jul 1855 d/SEYMOUR GOODALE & HELEN MARIA (HOWE) WILCOX of Rochester, Monroe Co NY; d 1855; Ref: Your Ancestors v10 32 p1225.

MARY - d/HIRAM & CYNTHIA E (LEETE) WILCOX of Victor, Ontario Co NY; m GEORGE O BROWN; Ref: Your Ancestors v10 #2 p1226.

MARY - b 1860 WI d/FRANCIS WILCOX; m 13 Sep 1878 Buffalo Co NE JAMES MATAMORE; Ref: Nebr Ancestree v8 #4 p129.

MARY - b 1861 Chautauqua Co NY d/ERASTUS B & ROXY (BUGBEE) WILCOX; m 11 Oct 1882 Cherry Creek, Chautauqua Co NY JAMES COX of Ellington, Chautauqua Co NY; m ED REED; d 1925; Ref: Wilcox Hist mss, 1870 Census Chautauqua Co NY p187, 19th Cent Marriages Reported in Fredonia Censor p119.

MARY - m 1878 Cazenovia, Madison Co NY FRANK CHAPHE who was b 01 Sep 1854 & d 04 Jul 1883 s/ALBERT HENRY & SUSAN (JILSON) CHAPHE; ch JOHN; Ref: Chaffee Gen pp 503, 560.

MARY A poss Mrs - b 1787 CT; Res Utica, Oneida Co NY; Ref: 1850 Census Utica NY p445 Dw# 875.

MARY A - b 17 Oct 1818 d/NORMAN & REBECCA (CASE) WILCOX of West Granville, Hampden Co MA; m HARVEY SPELLMAN; Ref: Your Ancestors v11 #4 p1380.

MARY A - m 14 Jan 1849 Jamestown, Chautauqua Co NY as his 2nd wife MERRICK SPURR; Res Wayne, Du Page Co IL 1850; Ref: Fenton Hist Society, Anna Waite, 1850 Census Wayne IL p202 Dw# 1431.

MARY A - m 29 Dec 1850 New Haven, New Haven Co CT JOHN H MYERS; Ref: Barbour's VR New Haven v6 p180.

MARY A - d/THOMAS & LYDIA (DIBBLE) WILCOX who Res Warren Co PA ca 1820; Ref: Fiske Card File.

MARY A - m 02 Aug 1853 Groton, New London Co CT GURDON HALL of Westerly, Washington Co RI; Ref: Barbour's VR Groton v1 p95.

MARY A - b 1838 NY d/DANIEL & MIRA (-----) WILCOX of Brookfield, Madison Co NY; Ref: 1850 Census Madison Co NY p57 Dw# 971.

MARY A - m ISAAC DAWLEY who was b 1837 & d 1893 s/ISAAC & HANNAH (HARVEY) DAWLEY; Ref: Dawley & Allied Lines mss.

MARY A - b 30 Sep 1844 Smyrna, Chenango Co NY d/HAZARD & FLAVILLA (PARSONS) WILCOX; m JOHN W INGALLS; Ref: Your Ancestors v3 #6 p397.

MARY A - b 1844 NY d/WILLIAM & NAOMI (-----) WILCOX of Harford, Cortland Co NY; Ref: 1850 Census Harford NY p425.

MARY A - d/NATHAN B & SUSAN (PRITCHARD) WILCOX; m OSCAR B LANE; Ref: Desc of Wm Wilcoxson p37.

MARY A - b 29 May 1850 d/ELON & MARY ELVIRA (BRYANT) WILCOX; Ref: Your Ancestors v3 #11&12 p471.

MARY A - b 1875 d/RAYMOND & PHEBE (WAITE) WILCOX; m 11 Aug 1896 Westerly, Washington Co RI JOHN M STONE; Res Ledyard, New London Co CT; Ref: Arnold v11 p48.

MARY ADELLA - b 18 Nov 1856 d/AUGUSTIN & MARIANA S (HOLCOMB) WILCOX; m ----- HAYDEN; d 08 Feb 1934; Ref: CT Bible Rec v18 pp522,523.

MARY ALBERTA - b 25 Oct 1883 d/EDWIN IVES & MARY ELLEN (MOFFAT) WILCOX of Montour, Tama Co IA; m JESSE G BRINKERHOFF; Ref: Your Ancestors v13 #3 p1672.

MARY ALICE - b 19 Apr 1848 d/JOHN WARREN & POLINA ALZINA (WEEKS) WILCOX of Oneida Co NY; m 25 Dec 1875 DANIEL B HOPKINS; Res MI; Ref: Gen of George Weekes p155.

MARY ALICE - b 05 Apr 1851 Tiverton, Newport Co RI d/HOLDER NELSON & BETSEY (HART) WILCOX; d 29 Jan 1858; Ref: NEH&GR Jan 1963 p20.

MARY ALICE - b 24 Apr 1856 NYC d/WILLIAM HENRY & ANNE HOLMES (GOODENOW) WILCOX; Ref: Wilcox-Meigs p99.

MARY AMANDA - b 27 Jan 1832 Killingworth, Middlesex Co CT d/BELA & AMANDA (GRUMBY) WILCOX; m 25 Apr 1867 JOHN WHEELER; Ref: Wilcox-Meigs p83, Barbour's VR Killingworth v2 p92.

MARY AMELIA - b 26 Feb 1856 MI d/FELIX AUGER & ELIZABETH (LITTLE) WILCOX; Ref: Your Ancestors v3 #11 & 12 p474.

MARY ANN - b ca 1765 d/JOSIAH & ELIZABETH (CURTIS) WILCOX; m 23 Aug 1787 L HART; Res East Berlin, Harford Co CT; Ref: Col Fam of US v5 p555, A Wilcox Book p18.

MARY ANN - b ca 1785 d/Maj ABRAHAM & ANNA (TILLINGHAST) HOXIE WILCOX; m 24 Mar 1805 RUSSELL MATTESON who was b 16 Apr 1787 & d 17 Jun 1820; ch ANN, PHOEBE, POLLY, LYRA/LYDIA; Ref: Your Ancestors v4 #7&8 p562.

MARY ANN - m 04 Dec 1823 Torrington, Litchfield Co CT JOHN H CHURCH of Bethlehem, Litchfield Co CT; Ref: Barbour's VR Torrington v1 p56.

MARY ANN - b 26 Sep 1804 Middletown, Middlesex Co CT d/SETH & MOLLY (-----) WILCOX; Ref: Barbour's VR Middletown v2 p194.

MARY ANN - b 02 Mar 1807 Stonington, New London Co CT d/SYLVESTER & MARVEL (BURTCH) WILCOX; Ref: Barbour's VR Stonington v4 p109, Hist of Stonington p661, C Douglass Alves Sr.

MARY ANN - b 29 Dec 1808 Sandisfield, Berkshire Co MA d/WILLIAM & LUCINDA (GIBBS) WILCOX; m LINUS SHEETS; d 20 Jan 1898; Ref: Sandisfield MA VR p73, Fiske Card File, Desc of Wm Wilcoxson pp244,245, Gifford Wilcox.

MARY ANN - m 30 Jun 1830 Stratford, Fairfield Co CT MINOR HIGLEY of Trumbull, Fairfield Co CT; Ref: Barbour's VR Stratford vA pp22,27.

MARY ANN - b 26 Jun 1817 RI d/WILLIAM & GULIELMA (ESTES) WILCOX; m OTIS PARKHURST; Ref: Snow-Estes Ancestry v2 p18, Your Ancestors v11 #2 p1345.

MARY ANN - b 20 Jun 1818 Killingworth, Middlesex Co CT d/NATHANIEL & FANNY (MANN) WILCOX; Ref: Wilcox-Meigs p84, Barbour's VR Killingworth v2 p103.

MARY ANN - b 14 Sep 1819 Richmond, Washington Co RI d/DANIEL & RUTH (GRIFFIN) WILCOX; m STEPHEN P STARR; Ref: Fiske Card File.

MARY ANN - m 08 Aug 1840 Ashville, Chautauqua Co NY FRANKLIN LONNEN of Mayville, Chautauqua Co NY who d ca 06 Jan 1869 diphtheria; 2ch d 1869 of diphtheria; Ref: 19th Cent Marriages Reported in Fredonia Censor p119, 19th Cent Death Notices Reported in Fredonia Censor p338, 10,000 VR Western NY p139.

MARY ANN - m 17 May 1843 Middletown, Middlesex Co CT JEDEDIAH WILCOX s/JOSEPH WILCOX; Ref: Barbour's VR Middletown v3 p504.

MARY ANN - m 29 Jun 1845 Ledyard, New London Co CT ROSWELL CHAPMAN; Ref: Barbour's VR Ledyard v1 p20.

MARY ANNE - b 1826 d/THOMAS & ELIZABETH (-----) WILCOX; m ca 1846 NELSON FENNER who was b 1823 NY; Res Ripley, Chautauqua Co NY; ch THEODORE; Ref: 1850 Census Ripley NY p114.

MARY ANN - b 1828 NY d/WHITMAN & LUCINDA (PARKER) WILCOX of Norwich, Chenango Co NY; Ref: 1850 Census_Norwich NY p179 Dw# 565, See Whitman.

MARY ANN - b 29 Jan 1830 d/EDWIN & SUSAN A (CHAPMAN) WILCOX; Ref: Chapman Fam Gen p137.

MARY ANN - b 1830; m HORACE C WALTER who was b 1829 & d 1894 Richfield Springs, Otsego Co NY; d 1915 bur Lake View Cem; Ref: Barber's NY & CT Records v1 p8.

MARY ANN - b 1833 s/DANIEL & PHOEBE (-----) WILCOX of Earlville NY ; Ref: Your Ancestors v4 #9&10 p583

MARY ANN - b 1833 CT d/SAMUEL & NANCY (----) WILCOX of Goshen, Litchfield Co CT; Ref: 1850 Census Goshen CT p96 Dw# 116.

MARY ANN - b 1837; d 1910 Mayville, Chautauqua Co NY; Ref: Tree Talks v24 #2 p92.

MARY ANN - b 1837 Great Valley, Cattaraugus Co NY d/SEYMOUR & SALLY (SARGENT) WILCOX; m JOHN BYRON HINMAN; d 1913; Ref: Dennis Davis, 1850 Census Great Valley NY p149 Dw# 64.

MARY ANN - d/LEWIS & MARIA (-----) WILCOX; d 03 Feb 1852 McLean, Tompkins Co NY; Ref: NYG&BR v105 p216.

MARY ANN - m 26 Sep 1852 RI DAVID J HEDLEY; Ref: Arnold v7 p503.

MARY ANN - b 1841 NY d/THOMAS S & ANN (-----) WILCOX of Davenport, Delaware Co NY; Ref: 1850 Census Davenport NY p129 Dw# 26.

MARY ANN - b 27 Aug 1841 d/NOAH & MARY (SHERMAN) WILCOX; m GEORGE CRANDALL; ch ELMER E; d 21 Jan 1926; Ref: Your Ancestors v4 #1&2 p495.

MARY ANN - b 1842 Ireland d/MICHAEL & MARY (-----) WILCOX of Vernon, Oneida Co NY; Ref: 1850 Census Vernon p85 Dw# 200.

MARY ANN - b 1845 CT d/RODNEY B & RACHEL (GREEN) WILCOX of Litchfield, Litchfield Co CT; Ref: 1850 Census Litchfield CT p284 Dw# 519, See Rodney B.

MARY ANN - b 1848 Wethersfield, Wyoming Co NY d/ALEXANDER & CAROLINE (-----) WILCOX; Ref: Your Ancestors v14 #3 p1669, 1850 Census Wethersfield NY p86 Dw# 1268.

MARY ANN - b 25 Dec 1855 IA; m 14 Apr 1877 HENRY H KENT; Res Chamberlain, Brule Co SD; ch LEWIS, MABEL, SIDNEY; d ca 1893; Ref: Hawkeye Heritage v16 #3 p164.

MARY ANN P - m 05 Sep 1832 New Haven, New Haven Co CT HARRY PRESCOTT; Ref: Barbour's VR New Haven v4 p146.

MARY AUGUSTA - b 10 Dec 1818 NYC d/OLIVER & SALLY (STANTON) WILCOX; m DAVID D MARVIN; m THOMAS C FANNING; Res Norwich, Chenango Co NY; Ref: Your Ancestors v3 #4 p350, NYG&BR April 1978 p94, Wilcox-Meigs p82, Cutter's New England Fam v1 p160.

MARY AZUBAH - b 21 Jan 1847 Litchfield, Herkimer Co NY d/DUDLEY & KEZIAH (TOWNSEND) WILCOX; m 26 Feb 1868 GEORGE S SLADE s/SAMUEL & ELSA (-----) SLADE; ch CLYDE T; d 06 Jan 1918 West Winfield, Herkimer Co NY; Ref: Your Ancestors v14 #1 p1617, DAR Record v357 p40, 1850 Census Litchfield NY p133 Dw# 282.

MARY B - b 1841 NY d/CLARK S & BEULAH ----- WILCOX of Lebanon, Madison Co NY; Ref: 1850 Census Lebanon NY p118 Dw# 1998.

MARY B - b 13 Dec 1843 Madison Co NY d/ALANSON CASE & CATHERINE (HUYCK) WILCOX of Lenox, Madison Co NY; m 20 Mar 1867 Oneida, Madison Co NY ALLEN S WHITMAN; Ref: Pioneers of Madison Co NY p280, 1850 Census Lenox NY p176 Dw# 221.

MARY B - b 03 Apr 1864 d/ORRIN B & SARAH (BURGESS) WILCOX; Res Pasadena, Los Angeles Co CA; Ref: Your Ancestors v3 #6 p398.

MARY BACON - b 06 Nov 1832 Middletown, Middlesex Co CT d/SAMUEL G & SARAH (-----) WILCOX; d 11 May 1833; Ref: Barbour's VR Middletown v3 p111.

MARY BELLE - b 15 Jun 1880 d/JONAS JESSE & HARRIET ELIZABETH (STEARNS) WILCOX; Ref: Gen of George Weekes p258.

MARY CARD - m 10 Jan 1811 Foster, Providence Co RI ASHER BENNETT Jr; Ref: Arnold v3 p31.

MARY CRITTENDEN - b 08 Aug 1866 Middletown, Middlesex Co CT d/WILLIAM WALTER & ELIZABETH SHEPHERD (CRITTENDEN) WILCOX; m 01 Oct 1890 HEMAN CHARLES WHITTLESEY who was b 04 Jan 1857 Newington, Hartford Co Ct s/HEMAN ALONZO WHITTLESEY; ch PERCIVAL WILCOX, WINIFRED HAMILTON; Ref: Gen of the Whittlesey Fam pp319,320, MUH p751.

MARY D - b ca 1805 Chenango Co NY d/SIMON GATES & ANNA (CARTWRIGHT) WILCOX; m SYLVANUS MOORE Jr; Ref: Hist of Tioga Co PA p730.

MARY D - b 1848 d/PRESERVED S & MARY G (DAVIS) WILCOX; d 30 Apr 1849 Westport, Bristol Co MA; Ref: Westport VR p293.

MARY E - b 1815; m 06 Sep 1856 Saybrook, Middlesex Co CT WILLIAM H LAY; Ref: Saybrook Colony VR p364.

MARY E - m 23 Oct 1850 Baldwinsville, Onondaga Co NY STEPHEN H PARSONS; Ref: 10,000 VR of Central NY p183.

MARY E - b 1831 OH d/OLIVER & ELEANOR (-----) WILCOX of Charlestown, Portage Co OH; Ref: 1850 Census Charlestown OH p159 Dw# 589.

MARY E - b 1832 Stanford, Delaware Co NY d/HARRY J & ----- (BROWN) WILCOX; Father b CT; m C ROSS WILLIAMS; Ref: Fiske Card File.

MARY E - b 1833 NY d/JOHN & ANN C (-----) WILCOX of Rushford, Allegany Co NY; Ref: 1850 Census Rushford NY p349 Dw# 66.

MARY E - b 26 Feb 1834 Lenox, Madison Co NY d/ALANSON & IRENE (JOHNSON) WILCOX; m WILLIAM V BOSWORTH; Ref: Pioneers of Madison Co NY p280.

MARY E - b 1836 NY d/WELCOME & HARRIET (-----) WILCOX of Wethersfield, Wyoming Co NY; Ref: 1850 Census Wethersfield NY p92 Dw# 1378.

MARY E - b 12 Sep 1838 d/AMOS & SOPHRONIA (HATFIELD) WILCOX of Wethersfield, Wyoming Co NY; m 1855 WILLIAM MILLS SLOCUM who was b 24 Nov 1835 Schuylerville, Livingston Co NY & d 13 Jan 1911 Perry, Wyoming Co NY s/WANTON & SARAH (AUSTIN) SLOCUM; ch SARAH JANE, JAMES MILLS, AMOS WANTON, MARY EVA; d 30 Apr 1907; Ref; Your Ancestors v14 #2 p1643, 1850 Census Wethersfield NY p86 Dw# 1269.

MARY E - b 1840 CT d/DANIEL & HARRIET (----) WILCOX of New London, New London Co CT; Ref: 1850 Census New London CT Reel 432 #49 p166.

MARY E - b 1841 NY d/MARTIN & SARAH/SALLY (-----) WILCOX of Dover, Dutchess Co NY; Ref: 1850 Census Dover NY p328 Dw# 269.

MARY E - b 1841 NY d/JACOB E & ANN C (-----) WILCOX of Worcester, Otsego Co NY; Ref: 1850 Census Worcester NY p177 Dw# 246.

MARY E - b 1843 d/WILLIAM S & SARAH E (DAY) WILCOX of Carlton, Orleans Co NY; d 1894; Ref: Your Ancestors v11 #1 p1320.

MARY E - b 1844 NY d/THURSTON & SARAH (-----) WILCOX of Greenwich, Washington Co NY; Ref: 1850 Census Greenwich NY p230 Dw# 463.

MARY E - b 1845 NY d/HANANIAH & NANCY E (-----) WILCOX of Dryden, Tompkins Co NY; Ref: 1850 Census Dryden NY p101 Dw# 652.

MARY E - b 08 Apr 1846 Taunton, Bristol Co MA d/ISAAC & MARY J (WETHERELL) WILCOX; Ref: Taunton VR.

MARY E - b 1846 NY Twin with MYRON E d/SHELDEN & MARY (-----) WILCOX of Danby, Tompkins Co NY; Ref: 1850 Census Danby NY p 56 Dw# 391.

MARY E - b 1847 NY d/HENRY W & EUNICE J (-----) WILCOX of Bergen, Genesee Co NY; Ref: 1850 Census Bergen NY p63 Dw# 872.

MARY E - b 1847 CT Twin with JULIA E d/AMOS & ELIZA JANE (MORLEY) WILCOX of Stonington, New London Co CT; Res Painesville, Lake Co OH; Ref: 1850 Census Stonington CT Reel 342 #48 p309, Your Ancestors v3 #2 p301.

MARY E - b 1848 NY d/HANEY N & AMANDA A (-----) WILCOX of Mexico, Herkimer Co NY; Ref: 1850 Census Mexico NY p77 Dw# 1183.

MARY E - b 1849 OH d/PELEG & MARGRETT (-----) WILCOX of Coe, Isabell Co MI; Ref: 1860 Census MI, Fiske Card File.

MARY E - b 1849 PA d/ISAAC & PHILANDA (-----) WILCOX; Res Le Roy, Bradford Co PA; Ref: 1860 Census Bradford Co PA p369.

MARY E - b Dec 1849 NY d/WILLIAM & JANE (-----) WILCOX of Petersburgh, Rensselaer Co NY; Ref: 1850 Census Petersburgh NY p195 Dw# 309.

MARY E - b 29 May 1850 d/DAVID HENRY & ADELIA A (HOPKINS) WILCOX of Cohocton, Steuben Co NY; d 1858; Ref: Your Ancestors v10 #1 p1200.

MARY E - b 20 Feb 1857 Stark Co IL; m 05 Apr 1885 Ft Calhoun, Washington Co NE WILLIAM H

EPLING; d 17 Dec 1928 Riverside, Riverside Co CA; Ref: 2nd Boat v4 #1 p7.

MARY E - m 25 Jun 1860 Bristol, Bristol Co RI ZWAR E JAMESON; Ref: Arnold v8 p576.

MARY E - b ca 1868 De Witt, Onondaga Co NY d/ORLANDO KING & MARY (WALTER) WILCOX; Ref: Erwin W Fellows.

MARY E - b 1876 Adrian, Lenawee Co MI d/CHARLES G & JEANETTE (MARVIN) WILCOX; m WILLIAM JERRELLS; Ref: Your Ancestors v11 #1 p1319.

MARY E - d/HARLOW G & MARY J (McEWEN) WILCOX; m GEORGE STEEL; Res NY & IL; Ref: Desc of Wm Wilcoxson p225.

MARY ELIZA - b 29 Dec 1804 d/MOSES & HULDAH (LORD) WILCOX; m HENRY WILLIAMS; Res Twinsburg, Summit Co OH; Ref: Lord Fam Gen p289.

MARY ELIZA - b 11 Aug 1869 d/HENRY FRANKLIN & LUCINDA HARRIET (BROWN) WILCOX; m 20 Sep 1890 ALBERT H SHEPARD; ch HELEN LUCINDA, HENRY MORTIMER, RACHEL LOUISE, MARY BARTH; Ref: Wilcox Excerpts v1 p3, Your Ancestors v13 #1 p1516.

MARY ELIZABETH - b 03 Jun 1816 Sandisfield, Berkshire Co MA d/SAMUEL & ELIZABETH (-----) WILCOX; Ref: Sandisfield VR p73, Fiske Card File.

MARY ELIZABETH - b 1819 d/IRA & LUCY (WILCOX) WILCOX; d 31 Jul 1838 Oxford, Chenango Co NY; Ref: Deaths from Otsego Co NY Newspapers v1 p91, Annals of Oxford NY p348,349, Your Ancestors v4 #1&2 p499.

MARY ELIZABETH - bpt 16 Sep 1821 Westbrook, Middlesex Co CT d/AMOS TODD & JEANNETTE (BUSHNELL) WILCOX; Adm to Church Mem 12 Nov 1834; m as his 3rd wife WILLIAM HENRY LAY who was b 1804 s/WILLIAM & LUCY (DEE) LAY; Ref: Westbrook 1st Cong Church Rec p198, Gen of the Whittlesey Fam p158.

MARY ELIZABETH - b 07 Sep 1830 Stonington, New London Co CT d/JEREMIAH & SABRINA A (BROWN) WILCOX; Ref: Barbour's VR Stonington v5 p79.

MARY ELIZABETH - b 21 Jul 1831 Griswold, New London Co CT d/HENRY & BETSEY (-----) WILCOX of

Preston, New London Co CT; Ref: Barbour's VR Preston v3 p155.

MARY ELIZABETH - b 08 Feb 1835 d/CHARLES & HARRIETT (ROBINSON) WILCOX; m ----- SPENCER; d 29 Apr 1914 Cleveland, Cuyahoga Co OH; Ref: 2nd Boat Jan 1987.

MARY ELIZABETH - b 23 May 1835 Norwich, New London Co CT d/WILLIAM BISSELL & MARY (KENYON) WILCOX; d 1837; Ref: Barbour's VR Norwich v5 p394, Esther Palmer Clark.

MARY ELIZABETH - b 09 Sep 1835 Madison, Lake Co OH d/RICHARD SELDEN & ELIZABETH (BOYNTON) WILCOX; Ref: Wilcox-Meigs p89, 1850 Census Madison OH Reel 259 p116.

MARY ELIZABETH - b 15 Nov 1837 d/GEORGE & ELIZABETH (GREENLEAF) WILCOX; m 13 Oct 1859 HENRY M MILES; ch FRANK C, GEORGE M, EVA, HENRY A, CLARKE, MARION E, NELLIE M, HAROLD M, CALISTA M; Ref: Gen of CT Fam v1 p245.

MARY ELIZABETH - b 27 Jun 1839 Madison, New Haven Co CT d/JOSEPH BENJAMIN & RUTH ELIZABETH (SCRANTON) WILCOX; m 21 Mar 1861 BENJAMIN R DOOLITTLE who was b 24 Oct 1830 & d 17 Mar 1892 Wallingford, New Haven Co CT; Ref: Wilcox-Meigs p108, Fam of Early Guilford p1214, Barbour's VR Madison v2 p30.

MARY ELIZABETH - b 30 Apr 1848 Vernon, Shiawassee Co MI d/MARVIN & MARIA (-----) WILCOX; m 21 May 1868 Marshall, Calhoun Co MI STEWART L MORLEY; ch A M; d 19 Jan 1901 Grand Ledge, Eaton Co MI; Ref: Flint MI Gen Quarterly v19 #1 p28.

MARY ELIZABETH - b 04 Feb 1863 d/GEORGE S & CLARA C (WILLIAMS) WILCOX; Ref: Your Ancestors v9 #3 p1152.

MARY ELIZABETH - b 08 Oct 1871 Wauwatosa, Milwaukee Co WI d/HENRY WILLIAM & MARY ELIZA (JONES) WILCOX; d 1909; Ref: Wilcox-Meigs p117.

MARY ELIZABETH - b 12 May 1876 IL d/FREDERICK WILLIAM & MARY ELIZABETH (MEAGHER) WILCOX of VT & Chicago, Cook Co IL; m 21 Jan 1897 LAMBERT J SCHMITZ; ch CHESTER LAMBERT; Ref: MUH p745.

MARY ELLA - b 22 Oct 1849 Surry, Cheshire Co NH d/Capt GEORGE & AURELIA (REED) WILCOX; m 1890

FRANCIS F FIELD; d 08 Jul 1899; Ref: Hist of Surry NH p949.

MARY ELLA - b 14 Jul 1857 d/DANIEL WILMARTH & MARTHA ANN (CHAPIN) WILCOX of Boston, Suffolk Co MA; Ref: Your Ancestors v3 #6 p400.

MARY ELLEN - b Oct 1838 Middletown, Middlesex Co CT d/ELISHA BACON & HEPZIBAH (CORNWELL) WILCOX; d 02 Mar 1840 bur Highland Cem; Ref: Hale Collection, Early Fam of Wallingford p333, Your Ancestors v3 #5 p379, Hist of Wallingford p939.

MARY ELLEN - b 12 Mar 1871 Troy, Rensselaer Co NY d/WORTHINGTON C & ELMIRA G (SPENCER) WILCOX; Ref: Wilcox-Meigs p106.

MARY ELLEN - b 06 Dec 1872 d/JOTHAM & LUCY (PRATT) WILCOX of Covert, Seneca Co NY; m JOHN W GREGG; d 24 Dec 1940; Ref: Cem Between the Lakes v2 p310.

MARY ELVIRA - b 11 Aug 1831 Austerlitz, Columbia Co NY d/CHAUNCEY & LOMIRA (IVES/CHAMBERLIN) WILCOX; Ref: Fiske Card File.

MARY EMILY - b 29 Dec 1804 Killingworth, Middlesex Co CT d/MOSES & HULDAH (LORD) WILCOX; m HIRAM WHEELER; Ref: Wilcox-Meigs p81, Your Ancestors v3 #2 p301, Barbour's VR Killingworth v2 p14.

MARY EMILY - b 07 Jun 1847 Painesville, Lake Co OH d/AARON & ELIZA JANE (MORLEY) WILCOX; d 25 Dec 1910; Ref: Wilcox-Meigs p98, 1850 Census Painesville OH Reel 259 p181.

MARY EMMA - b 1811 d/JESSE & CYNTHIA (-----) WILCOX of Carthage, Jefferson Co NY; d 1904; Ref: Early Settlers of NY p339.

MARY F - b 1830 RI d/STEPHEN S & SARAH L (ELMS) WILCOX of Lysander, Onondaga Co NY; Ref: 1850 Census Lysander NY p469 Dw# 135.

MARY F - b 05 Mar 1835 Newport, Sullivan Co NH d/CALVIN & DORCAS (FAXON) WILCOX; m Rev GEORGE F CHAPIN; Ref: Your Ancestors v3 #4 p350.

MARY F - b 1849 NY d/ISAIAH & ARMANDA (-----) WILCOX of Florence, Oneida Co NY; Ref: 1850 Census Florence NY p200 Dw# 144.

MARY F - b 1858 NY d/DANIEL T & POLLY M (COX) WILCOX of Ellington, Chautauqua Co NY; m 06 Jun 1875 FRANK ALFF who was b 1854 & d 1912; ch JOHN, DAISY, ZADIE, JESSIE; d 1910; Ref: Wilcox Hist mss, Cem Inscr, 19th Cent Marriages reported in Fredonia Censor p119, 1860 Census Ellington NY p109 Dw# 442.

MARY G - b 1835 VT d/TYLER & TEMPERANCE (FIFE) WILCOX of Halifax, Windham Co VT; Ref: 1850 Census Halifax VT p131.

MARY GOODRICH - b 1833 NY d/JUDSON & LAURA (GOODRICH) WILCOX of Catskill, Greene Co NY; Ref: 1850 Census Catskill NY p357 Dw# 322, See Judson.

MARY H - b 25 Feb 1833 Galesburg, Knox Co IL d/HENRY & MARY K (MEACHAM) WILCOX; d 11 Jun 1853; Ref: Wilcox-Meigs p101.

MARY H - b 22 Jun 1846 Plymouth, Luzerne Co PA d/ELIAS BROWN & NANCY E (MAXFIELD) WILCOX; m ALEXANDER FERGUSON; Ref: Your Ancestors v9 #2 p1126.

MARY H - b 23 Feb 1848 Madison, New Haven Co CT d/HORATIO & CAROLINE A (CADWELL) WILCOX; d 05 Dec 1852; Ref: Wilcox-Meigs p105, Fam of Early Guilford p1214.

MARY H - b 06 Dec 1859 Peoria, Peoria Co IL d/ERASTUS S & MARY T (HOTCHKISS) WILCOX; Ref: Wilcox-Meigs p119.

MARY HELEN - b 05 Feb 1879 d/JAMES DAVID & ANNA MARIE (ROBINSON) WILCOX; d 13 Apr 1880; Ref: Wilcox-Meigs p121, Desc of Wm Wilcoxson p144.

MARY HEPSIBAH - b 22 Oct 1893 d/STEPHEN MOULTON & MARY STEWART (SHEARMAN) WILCOX; Ref: Col Fam of US v5 p552.

MARY I - b 1831 NY d/CONSIDER & MARY (-----) WILCOX of Almond, Allegany Co NY; Ref: 1850 Census Almond NY p74 Dw# 777.

MARY I - b 1849 NY d/WILLIAM & ANN (-----) WILCOX of Stockbridge, Madison Co NY; Ref: 1850 Census Stockbridge NY p152 Dw# 223.

MARY J - b 1827 NY; Res Whitestown, Oneida Co NY; Ref: 1850 Census Whitestown NY p70 Dw# 115.

MARY J - b 1832 NY d/----- & HANNAH (-----) WILCOX of Petersburgh, Rensselaer Co NY; Ref: 1850 Census Petersburgh NY p180 Dw# 97.

MARY J - b 1836 NY d/RODMAN & MARY (-----) WILCOX of Ellicott, Chautauqua Co NY; Ref: 1860 Census Ellicott NY p754 Dw# 1514.

MARY J - b 1847 NY d/HIRAM & MARY (-----) WILCOX of Harford, Cortland Co NY; Ref: 1850 Census Harford NY p422 Dw# 1421.

MARY J - b 1848 NY d/CYRENUS & MARY A (-----) WILCOX of Fenner, Madison Co NY; Ref: 1850 Census Fenner NY p116 Dw# 1683.

MARY J - b Apr 1850 Stamford, Delaware Co NY d/JONATHAN & JANE A (-----) WILCOX; Ref: 1850 Census Stamford NY p194 Dw# 531.

MARY JANE - b 10 Mar 1822 d/RICHARD & ELIZABETH (LEWIS) WILCOX of Canton, Bradford Co PA; Ref: Your Ancestors v10 #4 p1273.

MARY JANE - of Litchfield, Litchfield Co CT m 23 Mar 1845 Waterbury, New Haven Co CT WILLIAM BOSSFORD of England; Ref: Barbour's VR Waterbury v3 p141.

MARY JANE - b ca 1825 Smithville, Chenango Co NY d/THURSTON & JANE (LOOMIS) WILCOX; m RANSOM YALE; Ref: Hist of Chenango Co NY p295.

MARY JANE - b 01 Jun 1830 Simsbury, Hartford Co CT d/CHESTER & ELIZABETH (ANDREWS) WILCOX; Ref: Your Ancestors v12 #1 p1408.

MARY JANE - b 25 Jun 1830 Marion, Wayne Co NY d/EARL & JANE (STEWART) WILCOX; m 29 Sep 1852 WILLIAM HARDIN who was b 19 Jul 1831 & d 25 Jan 1915 s/HIRAM & LUCINDA (CORBETT) HARDIN; ch JANE JOSEPHINE, MAHLAN DURFEE, JENNIE ESTELLE, HARRIET M, CORA; d Jul 1889 Martin, Allegan Co MI; Ref: Your Ancestors v10 #4 pp1293,1294.

MARY JANE - b 1839 NY d/HARMON & EUNICE (-----) WILCOX of Bergen, Genesee Co NY; Teacher; Ref: Your Ancestors v3 #2 p302, 1850 Census Bergen NY p45 Dw# 589, 1860 Census Bergen NY p985 Dw# 405.

MARY JANE - b 1842 OH/PA d/NATHAN BENJAMIN & SAMANTHA (BROOKS) WILCOX; m MOSES CUNNINGHAM; Ref: Dan Williams.

MARY JANE - b 1843 Deep River, Middlesex Co CT d/JONATHAN SAMUEL & DOLLY ANN (SOUTHWORTH) WILCOX; Ref: Fam of Early Guilford p1205.

MARY JANE - b 21 Apr 1850 d/JOTHAM & JANE ANN (-----) WILCOX; d Sullivan Co NY 23 Nov 1860 age 10yr 7mo 2da; Ref: Sullivan Co NY Graveyard Inscr Vol 10 p42.

MARY JANE - b Dec 1850 Plymouth, Marshall Co IN d/LEONARD & ELVIRA (-----) WILCOX; m 23 Dec 1865 WILLIAM KLINGER; Res Mishawaka, St Joseph Co IN; ch HATTIE; d 12 Oct 1902; Ref: Charlotte A Jacob-Hanson.

MARY JANE - m ca 1875 Jamestown, Chautauqua Co NY OTIS J NEWTON; Ref: Nutmegger v3 #4 p442.

MARY KATE - b 14 Jan 1859 d/JULIUS & MATTIE JANE (HOLTON) WILCOX of Warrenton, Warren Co N C; m 19 Sep 1883 FRANK PATTERSON HUNTER; ch MARY H, MATTIE C; Ref: Gen of CT Fam v1 245.

MARY KATHERINE - d/GEORGE HENRY & MARY M (YOUNGLOVE) WILCOX; m GEORGE DUNLAP; Res Northville, Wayne Co MI; Ref: Wilcox Excerpts v1 p5, Your Ancestors v13 #1 p1516.

MARY KATHERINE - b 17 May 1865 d/DAVID BAILEY & ANN ELIZABETH (OVENSHIRE) WILCOX; m WILLIAM T CONNER who was b ca 1865 & d 1939 s/MICHAEL & JANE (-----) CONNER; Res Plymouth, Wayne Co MI; ch HAZEL KATHERINE, ELIZABETH JANE; Ref: Wilcox Excerpts v1 p5.

MARY L - m 24 Dec 1834 Killingworth, Middlesex Co CT WYLLYS DUDLEY; Ref: Barbour's VR Killingworth v3 p385.

MARY L - b 09 Feb/Dec 1830 d/AZARIAH CLARK & RACHEL (VAN DEUSEN) WILCOX; Res probably NY; d 07 Feb 1836; Ref: Wilcox Excerpts v1 p2, Your Ancestors v13 #1 p1516.

MARY L - b ca 1845 Tioga Co PA d/JOHN DENNIS & ORRILLA (DIMMICK) WILCOX; m P R SHERMAN; Res MI; Ref: Hist of Tioga Co PA p732.

MARY L - b 1845 NY d/ERASMUS D & SARAH (-----) WILCOX of Vernon, Oneida Co NY; Ref: 1850 Census Vernon NY p97 Dw# 879.

MARY L - d/ROWLAND & ELIZABETH (VAN ETTEN) WILCOX; m ca 1825 WILLIAM BLAKE; Res Albany, Bradford Co PA; Ref: Pioneers of Bradford Co PA p309.

MARY L - b 09 Aug 1859 d/HENRY FRANKLIN & LUCINDA HARRIET (BROWN) WILCOX; d 26 Aug 1859; Ref: Wilcox Excerpts v1 p2.

MARY L - b 23 Sep 1885 d/JOHN D & AUGUSTA (STARK) WILCOX of Luzerne Co PA; d 1886; Ref: Hist of Luzerne Co PA p1455, Your Ancestors v9 #4 p1175.

MARY L - d 13 Feb 1900 Norwich, Chenango Co NY; Bur Sec 4 Lot 2; Ref: Norwich NY Cem Assoc Records p324.

MARY L A - b 28 Feb 1875; d 18 Feb 1885 Page Co IA bur North Grove Cem; Ref: Hawkeye Heritage v16 #4 p202.

MARY LAWTON - b 26 Aug 1863 d/GEORGE DAWLEY & MARY (LEACH) WILCOX Dighton, Bristol Co MA; Ref: Gen of Wm Tanner p110.

MARY LEORA - b 1850; d 1912 Napoli, Cattaraugus Co NY; Ref: Cem Inscr.

MARY LORINDA - b 03 Jul 1847 Shelburne Falls, Franklin Co MA d/ABRAHAM & LAURINDA (HARDY) WILCOX; Ref: Halifax VT Wilcox Fam mss, Your Ancestors v4 #9&10 p587.

MARY LOUISA - b 19 Aug 1859 d/HENRY FRANKLIN & LUCINDA H (BROWN) WILCOX; Ref: Your Ancestors v13 #1 p1516.

MARY LOVISA - b 03 Apr 1767 Gilsum, Cheshire Co NH d/OBADIAH & SARAH (TALCOTT) WILCOX; d 20 Jul 1798 Surry, Cheshire Co NH; Ref: Desc of Wm Wilcoxson p26, Hist of Surry NH pp381,945.

MARY LOVISA - b 02 Sep 1805 d/GAYLORD & ORINDA (CARPENTER) WILCOX of Surry, Cheshire Co NH; d 01 Oct 1806; Ref: Hist of Surry NH p946.

MARY LOVISA - b 21 Feb 1816 Surry, Cheshire Co NH d/ASA & LUCINDA (BEMIS) PHILLIPS WILCOX; d 09 Jan 1822/7 Typhoid Fever; Ref: Hist of Surry NH pp380,947.

MARY LOVISA - b 10 Jul 1828 Surry, Cheshire Co NH d/ASA & LUCINDA (BEMIS) PHILLIPS WILCOX; d 01 Jul 1838; Ref: Hist of Surry NH p947.

MARY LUANA - b 17 Mar 1863 Whitingham, Windham Co VT d/SILAS MASSENA HOWARD & CHLOE PRISCILLA (SHUMWAY) WILCOX; m 04 Jun 1883 FREDERICK DAVIS; d 05 Jun 1895; Ref: Iris W Baird.

MARY LUCAS - b 07 Jun 1801 d/NATHAN & MARY (CHENEVARD) WILCOX; d 30 Oct 1861; Ref: Your Ancestors v3 #9&10 p451.

MARY M - b 22 Aug 1821 Deerfield. Portage Co OH d/WILLIAM & LUCINDA (GIBBS) WILCOX; m 12 Nov 1845 LINUS SHEETS of Berlin, Portage Co OH; ch MARIA, NEWELL, CLARA, WARREN, EDDIE, ELLEN; d 21 Jan 1878; Ref: Hist of Portage Co OH p635, Desc of Wm Wilcoxson p244.

MARY M - b 1825 NY d/JOSIAH & ELEANOR (-----) WILCOX of Caneadea, Allegany Co NY; Ref: 1850 Census Caneadea NY p195 Dw# 202.

MARY M - d/PETER C & MARY (YOUKER) WILCOX of Oswego NY & Decatur, Van Buren Co MI; m_22 Feb 1853 JEDEDIAH MESSINGER; Ref: George Koppers.

MARY M - b 1851 PA d/O S & J C (-----) WILCOX; Res Le Roy, Bradford Co PA; Ref: 1860 Census Bradford Co PA p26.

MARY M - b 18 Aug 1876 d/MARINER & CORDELIA (CARD) WILCOX; Single; d 1941 bur Center Burlington Cem, Nova Scotia Canada; Ref: Desc of Charles Dyer Wilcox p14.

MARY MAMIE - b 19 May 1883 Panama, Chautauqua Co NY d/HENRY WILLIAM & LUCY (GLOVER) WILCOX; d 29 Jun 1887; Ref: A Wilcox Book p129.

MARY MARIA - b 19 Feb 1803 NY d/STEPHEN & PHOEBE (ROGERS) WILCOX; m 27 Dec 1821 Phelps, Ontario Co NY JAMES TAYLOR; Ref: LDS Fam Group Sheet.

MARY MATILDA - b 01 Aug 1821 E Guilford, New Haven Co CT d/TRUMAN NOYES & CHLOE (TODD) WILCOX; d Oct 1836; Ref: Wilcox-Meigs p88, Desc of Wm Wilcoxson p264.

MARY MATILDA - b 02 Apr 1839 Panama, Chautauqua Co NY d/GEORGE & SARAH (SPENCER) WILCOX; m 09 Jan

1859 Rockdale, Crawford Co PA ARTHUR JERVIS who was b 27 Sep 1829 Armstrong Co PA & d 1911 s/THOMAS R & JANE (HAUGHEY) JERVIS; ch DONNA NAOMI, COMMODORE S, GEORGE EMMETT, FRANK CLEMENT, JAMES ARTHUR, JENNIE, KATE BERNICE; d 09 Jan 1920; Ref: A Wilcox Book pp109,110.

MARY MATILDA - b 07 May 1843 NJ d/HORACE FRANKLIN & HENRIETTA FRANCES (SHEPARD) WILCOX; m 24 Nov 1869 FRANCIS D A CONGER Newark, Essex Co NJ; Ref: Wilcox-Meigs p90.

MARY MAY - b 18 Feb 1868 Lycoming Co PA d/GEORGE HENRY & ORRILLA ELIZABETH (FOOT/ROOT) WILCOX; m DAN COONEY who was b 20 Mar 1861 & d 03 Aug 1901; d 09 Oct 1914; Ref: Halifax VT Wilcox Fam mss.

MARY MEHITABEL - b 08 Nov 1860 d/JOHN HENRY OWEN & MARY (YOUNG) WILCOX; Ref: Your Ancestors v12 #2 p1436.

MARY MIRANDA - b 02 Mar 1844 Orangeville, Wyoming Co NY d/JAMES C & ORPHA JANE (SPINK) WILCOX; m 20 Apr 1863 AARON JONES; ch JENNIE L; Ref: Your Ancestors v4 #5&6 p542, Hist of Wyoming Co NY p236, 1850 Census Orangeville NY p35 Dw# 548.

MARY O - b 30 Mar 1860 d/GEORGE W & JOANNA ELIZABETH (ELLIS) WILCOX of Le Roy, Bradford Co PA; m JONATHAN BELLOWS; Ref: Your Ancestors v10 #4 p1274.

MARY OLIVA - b 02 Apr 1815 Sandisfield, Berkshire Co MA d/EBENEZER & MATILDA (HOSMER) WILCOX; Ref: Fiske Card File, Desc of Wm Wilcoxson p245.

MARY OLIVE - b 05 Feb 1812 Middlebury, Addison Co VT d/JULIUS & ELIZABETH (BROWN) WILCOX; m 01 Oct 1823 Deacon CYRUS PORTER who was b 21 Feb 1795 CT & d 01 Apr 1857 s/JOSEPH & SUSAN (LANGDON) PORTER of Farmington, Hartford Co CT; ch HENRY MARTIN, GEORGE LANGDON, ELIZA WILCOX, MARY BROWN, JULIUS WILCOX, SUSAN IDA, ELLA GRAVES, FLORA McDONALD; d 06 Sp 1884 East Liverpool, Columbiana Co OH; Ref: Gen of CT Fam v1 p245. 1850 Census Middlebury VT Reel 920 p148.

MARY OLIVE - b 1812 d/RICHARD & OLIVE (PORTER) WILCOX; m 08 May 1834 Berlin, Hartford Co CT

ALFRED NORTH; ch CATHERINE; Ref: Hist of Berlin p103, Barbour's VR Berlin v1 p55.

MARY OLIVIA - b 18 Mar 1858 d/HORACE HUBBARD & OLIVIA (RICHARDSON) WILCOX of Hancock Co IL & Butler Co KS; m 11 Mar 1880 JOHN ATLAS JONES; ch FLORA JOSEPHINE, CLAUDE J, LILLIE BLANCHE, JOHN ATLAS, OLLIE; Ref: Desc of Wm Wilcoxson p131.

MARY P - b 18 Apr 1821 Thetford, Orange Co VT d/AARON & TENCEY (HORSFORD) WILCOX; d 09 Oct 1862; Ref: Horsford-Hosford Fam p73.

MARY P - b 12 Sep 1840 d/JOSIAH S & MARY (ROOT) WILCOX of Orwell, Addison Co VT; m CHARLES WILLIAM WILCOX who was b Floyd, Oneida Co NY 25 Apr 1829 s/EZRA AARON & SARAH (DAVIS) WILCOX; ch WILLIAM STEVENS, MINNIE FRANCES; Ref: Cutter's Western NY v2 p741.

MARY R - b 1850 NY d/ANDREW J & ESTHER T (-----) WILCOX of Ellicott, Chautauqua Co NY; Ref: 1860 Census Ellicott NY p753 Dw# 1502.

MARY RUSSELL - b 1896 d/ALBERT & EFFIE (-----) WILCOX Tioga Co PA; Ref: PA DAR Records.

MARY S - d/STERLING OWEN & HARRIET (HAYES) WILCOX of Canton, Hartford Co CT; Ref: NYG&BR v78 p179.

MARY S - b 03 Mar 1813 Chester, Hampden Co MA d/ASA & RELIEF (COLTON) WILCOX; m EBENEZER WILLIAMS; m BRADFORD PALMER; Ref: Fiske Card File, Your Ancestors v3 #9&10 p452.

MARY S - b 13 Dec 1827 d/WILLARD DE RUYTER & SYBIL (GODFREY) WILCOX of De Ruyter, Madison Co NY & Homer, Cortland Co NY; m 18 Nov 1851 PERRY BURDICK MAXSON who was b 20 Jul 1826 Washington Co RI & d 07 Jan 1920 Emporia, Lyon Co KS s/PELEG & CLARISSA (BURDICK) MAXSON; Ref: Your Ancestors v12 #2 p1436, 1850 Census De Ruyter NY p292 Dw# 299.

MARY S - b 12 July 1831 Napoli, Cattaraugus Co NY d/LANSING H & MIRANDA (HOLMES) WILCOX; Teacher; Ref: Cutter's Western NY v1 p257, 1850 Census Napoli NY p63 Dw# 138, 1860 Census Napoli NY Reel 653 #726 p60.

MARY S - b 1837 CT d/ISAIAH & ANN (-----) WILCOX of Camillus, Onondaga Co NY; Ref: 1850 Census Camillus NY p260 Dw# 532.

MARY S - b 1840 IL d/HARLOW G & JEMIMA (NICHOLSON) WILCOX; Res Big Grove, Kendall Co IL; Ref: 1850 Census Big Grove IL, (See Harlow G).

MARY S - b 18 Jul 1842 Jackson Co IA d/JOHN 3rd & MARY MARIAH (CASWELL) WILCOX; d 02 Dec 1931; Ref: Desc of Wm Wilcoxson p123.

MARY S - b Dec 1849 NY d/ALFRED & ELIZA (-----) WILCOX of Hamilton, Madison Co NY; Ref: 1850 Census Hamilton NY p98 Dw# 1671.

MARY S - b 21 Jun 1865 Simsbury, Hartford Co CT d/APOLLOS & SARAH M (BABCOCK) WILCOX; m 05 Jun 1885 Naugatuck, New Haven Co CT WALTER L BENHAM who was b 1862; No ch; Ref: Naugatuck Cong Church Rec p138, Your Ancestors v12 #1 p1408.

MARY STANTON - b 08 Nov 1804 Foster, Providence Co RI d/STEPHEN & SUSANNAH (LEWIS) WILCOX; Ref: Arnold v3 p42, Your Ancestors v4 #1&2 p496.

MARY SUSAN - b 19 Oct 1861 Co NY d/JEFFERSON MONROE & MARY HARVEY (HUMASON) WILCOX of Fredonia, Chautauqua Co NY; m 30 Dec 1886 Lincoln, Lancaster Co NE WILLIAM HENRY ROBINSON who was b 03 Nov 1855 Greensburg, Westmoreland Co PA s/WILLIAM & MARIA MARGARET (KEMP) ROBINSON; Res Moorehead, Clay Co MN; ch FLORA HUMASON, WILLIAM WILCOX, ARCHBOLD HAMLINE, HELEN MARY; Ref: Colonial Fam of US v5 pp552,553, 19th Cent Marriages Reported in Fredonia Censor p119.

MARY SUSANNAH - b 18 Jan 1824 Madison, New Haven Co CT d/REUBEN & BETSEY (BARTLETT) WILCOX; m JOSIAH B GLADWIN of Guilford, New Haven Co CT; Ref: Fam of Early Guilford p1207, Barbour's VR Madison v1 p138, v2 p105.

MARY THERESA - b 26 Nov 1847 d/RENSELLAER & SARAH (REDFIELD) WILCOX; d 1848; Ref: Your Ancestors v13 #4 p1609.

MARY TREAT - b 29 Jun 1828 Berlin, Hartford Co CT d/ALSA & EMILY (TREAT) WILCOX; d 29 Jan 1833; Ref: MUH p756.

MARY V/POLLY - b 1794 Lancaster, Coos Co NH d/JEREMIAH WILCOX; Ref: Iris W. Baird.

MARY W - b ca 1820 Smithfield, Bradford Co PA d/STEPHEN & POLLY (ALLEN) WILCOX; m CALEB TRASK;

Ref: Halifax VT Wilcox Fam mss, Wilcox Genealogy p7.

MARY W - m 01 Jan 1832 Killingworth, Middlesex Co CT NATHAN W LOOMIS of Hartford, Hartford Co CT; Ref: Barbour's VR Killingworth v3 p382.

MARY W - d/WILBUR WILCOX; m 15 Oct 1898 Vernon, Tolland Co CT CHARLES A STONE who was b 09 Oct 1874 Hartford, Hartford Co CT & d 28 Jan 1926 Brooklyn NY; Ref: CT Bible Rec b9 p235.

MARY W - b 20 Jan 1898 IL d/SAMUEL WILCOX; Res CA; Ref: Your Ancestors v2 p254.

MARYETT - b 11 Apr 1830 Colesville, Broome Co NY d/DAVID & SARAH/SALLY (CRITTENDEN) WILCOX; m 31 Dec 1849 Binghamton, Broome Co NY ROBERT EMMET AUSTIN who was b 02 Apr 1827 Colesville, Broome Co NY & d 30 Nov 1913 Deland, Volusia Co FL; bur Oak Hill Cem Tama, Tama Co IA s/JOSEPH ADDISON SPENCER & TAMZON (BAKER) AUSTIN; ch WINFIELD SCOTT, CLIFFORD ST CLAIR, FRANK, CARRIE, MARYETT "METTA", GEORGE HENRY, ISABELLE, ARTHUR EUGENE, ROBERT EDWARD; d 19 Apr 1884 Tama IA bur Oak Hill Cem; Ref: Marjorie Stoner Elmore.

MARYETTE - b 1841 NY d/JOHN & ELIZA (-----) WILCOX of Westfield, Chautauqua Co NY; Ref: 1850 Census Westfield NY p143 Dw# 288.

MARYETTE - b 1846 NY d/MONROE & MALISSA (-----) WILCOX of Milford, Otsego Co NY; Ref: 1850 Census Milford NY p115.

MASON - b 13 Nov 1806 Stonington, New London Co CT s/JESSE & MEHITABLE (WILCOX) WILCOX; m 29 Nov 1827 LOUISA BROWN who was b 1803 & d 08 Aug 1854 Preston CT; m SALLY E ----- who was b 1798 & d 23 Jun 1882; Res Stonington & Preston, New London Co CT; ch HUMPHREY; d 21 Jan 1887; Ref: Hist of Stonington CT p661, Cem Records of New London Co CT v2 p29, 1850 Census Stonington CT Reel 432 #48 p256 Dw# 324, Barbour's VR Preston, v3 p104, Stonington v5 p18, C Douglass Alves Sr.

MASON A - b 25 Feb 1844 Newport, Sullivan Co NH s/ALBERT & CAROLINE KNOWLES (MASON) WILCOX; Ref: Your Ancestors v3 #4 p350.

MASON L - b 1846 NY s/CHAUNCEY G & WEALTHY (FOOTE) WILCOX of Cortland, Cortland Co NY; Ref:

1850 Census Cortland NY p367 Dw# 564, See Chauncey G.

MATILDA - b 21 May 1783 Middletown, Middlesex Co CT d/STEPHEN & MARY (KELSEY) WILCOX; m ----- PORTER; Ref: Barbour's VR Middletown v2 p202, CT Bible Rec v1 pp476-478, v9 pp435,436.

MATILDA - b 1788 d/JONATHAN & ELIZABETH (TODD) WILCOX of Guilford, New Haven Co CT; unmarried; d 22 Oct 1809; Ref: MUH p754, Fam of Early Guilford p1202, Your Ancestors v3 #2 p302.

MATILDA - b ca 1800 d/GEORGE & MARY (-----) WILCOX of Sodus, Wayne Co NY; m LAZARUS GRIFFIN/GRIFFITH; Ref: Your Ancestors v11 #1 p1319.

MATILDA - of Easton, Washington Co NY; m 12 Apr 1847 JOHN H HULL; Ref: NYG&BR v119 p36.

MATILDA - b 1831 PA d/ISAAC & FREELOVE (MADISON) WILCOX; Ref: Evangeline A Wilcox.

MATILDA - b 1839 d/WILLIAM S & SARAH E (DAY) WILCOX of Carlton, Orleans Co NY; d 1860; Ref: Your Ancestors v11 #1 p1320.

MATILDA - b 1863 Cattaraugus Co NY d/ELIHU & PHILOMELA (-----) WILCOX of Leon, Cattaraugus Co NY; Ref: Alice Wiatr.

MATILDA ANN - b 04 Dec 1811 Sandisfield, Berkshire Co MA d/EBENEZER & MATILDA (HOSMER) WILCOX; m her cousin WILLIAM CARYDON WILCOX s/SAMUEL & ELIZABETH (-----) WILCOX; Ref: Fiske Card File, Desc of Wm Wilcoxson p245.

MATILDA E - m 17 Jun 1830 Madison, New Haven Co CT ALEXANDER W HALL of Wallingford, New Haven Co CT; Ref: Barbour's VR Madison v1 p33.

MATILDA M - b 13 Nov 1819 RI d/MARTIN & MATILDA M (STILLMAN) WILCOX; Ref: NYG&BR v107 p193.

MATTHEW - b ca 1751 Richmond, Washington Co RI s/EDWARD & ESTHER (-----) WILCOX; m ----- WRIGHT; m RACHEL TILLOTSON who was b 1761 & d 13 Dec 1818; Res Onondaga Co NY; d 02 Nov 1833 bur Jamesville Cem; Ref: Onondaga's Rev Soldiers p35, Your Ancestors v12 #1 p1405.

MATTHEW - b 1791 s/WILLIAM & HANNAH (PEAT) WILCOX; m SUSANNA HOYT; Res Norwalk, Fairfield Co CT; War of 1812; Perhaps moved to Onodaga Co NY 1815; ch NELSON; Ref: Desc of Wm Wilcoxson p36.

MATTHEW - m 11 Jan 1835 Norwalk, Fairfield Co CT LYDIA MERRELL; Ref: Barbour's VR Norwalk v1 p19.

MATTHEW - b 1845 NY s/ANTHONY W & HARRIET (-----) WILCOX of Cherry Creek, Chautauqua Co NY; Ref: 1860 Census Cherry Creek NY p150 Dw# 788.

MATTHEW R - b Oct 1875 NY s/EUGENE A & MARY E (-----) WILCOX; Res Dane Co WI; Ref: 1900 Soundex.

MATTIE D - d/ALFRED DEFOREST & SYLVIA T (SCARRETT) WILCOX of Earlville, Chenango Co NY died age 13; Ref: Your Ancestors v12 #4 p1487.

MATTIE JULIUS - b 27 Oct 1865 Warrenton, Warren Co N C d/JULIUS & MATTIE JANE (HOLTON) WILCOX; d 11 Jun 1866; Ref: Gen of CT Fam v1 p245.

MAUDE - b 1876 Madison Co NY d/HARRISON & CATHERINE (SNYDER) WILCOX; m MATTHEW CAMP; Ref: Pioneers of Madison Co NY 281.

MAUD - b 1878 NY d/GEORGE S & MARY E (BENTON) WILCOX of Alma, Allegany Co NY; Ref: Carol A Cox.

MAUDE E - b 17 May 1878 Smithfield Twnshp, Bradford Co PA d/ELLIOTT URIAH & TIRZAH ELVIRA (SEYMOUR) WILCOX; d 10 Mar 1881; Ref: Wilcox Genealogy p20.

MAUD PHELENE - b 11 Feb 1874 Elm Island, prob Buffalo Co NE d/GEORGE HENRY & ORRILLA ELIZABETH (ROOT) WILCOX; m 14 Oct 1890 ELSWORTH GILBERT SHAW who was b 31 Jan 1866 Arcola, Allen Co IN & d 29 Jun 1945 Arthur, Arthur Co NE; d 29 Jan 1966 Brighton, Adams Co CO bur Arthur NE; Ref: Halifax VT Wilcox Fam mss.

MAURICE - b 15 May 1801 Berlin, Hartford Co CT s/DANIEL & MEHITABLE (WRIGHT) WILCOX; Res Great Barrington, Berkshire Co MA; Ref: Annals of Winchester CT p329,330.

MAURICE E - b 12 Apr 1881 s/ABEL J & MABEL A (TENNANT) WILCOX; Ref: Your Ancestors v3 #2 p301.

MAURICE HOLTON - b 10 Mar 1860 Warrenton, Warren Co N C s/JULIUS & MATTIE JANE (HOLTON) WILCOX; d 18 Mar 1879; Ref: Gen of CT Fam v1 p245.

MAURICE M - b 25 Oct 1874 Wyoming, Stark Co IL s/WILLIAM H & ELIZA P (KELLOGG) WILCOX; Ref: Wilcox-Meigs p120.

MAY - b 1869 d/WILLIAM H & MARY A (GREENE) WILCOX; m 1888 P J McKEE who was b 1860 & d 1910; Ref: Your Ancestors v9 #2 p1128.

MAY - b 1880 d/WILLIAM/WILLIE & ELLEN (KNOWLES) WILCOX; m FRANK KNOWLES; no ch; Ref: Desc of Wm Wilcoxson p197.

MAY ANGELIA - b 29 Jan 1874 Villanova, Chautauqua Co NY d/ALFRED JAMES & MARY ANGELIA (BABCOCK) WILCOX; m 06 Sep 1890 JAY WARREN WILCOX who was b 28 May 1868 Buffalo, Erie Co NY s/HARLOW MARTIN & MARILLA (JAY) WILCOX; Res Silver Creek Chautauqua Co NY; ch ALICE HAZEL, HERBERT, HARLOW MERLE, MARTELLA ANGELIA, DEXTER WARREN, LARRY MERLE, HULDAH MAY; d 25 Jan 1945; bur Villanova NY; Ref: Wilcox Hist mss, Marriage, Birth, & Death Records, Probate of Will.

MAY P - b 1871 Perry, Wyoming Co NY d/EDGAR UDAL & EMMA A (PRENTICE) WILCOX; d 29 Jun 1912 Rochester, Monroe Co NY; Ref: Your Ancestors v4 #5&6 p542.

MEHITABLE - b 22 Oct 1730 Middletown, Middlesex Co CT d/JANNA & RACHEL (BOARDMAN) WILCOX; m 14 Oct 1750/1 EBENEZER CHIPMAN; Ref: Nutmegger v13 #3 p389, Your Ancestors v4 #3&4 p524, Barbour's VR Middletown TR1 p22, v2 p205.

MEHITABLE - b poss 1750-53 Richmond, Washington Co RI d/BENJAMIN & ESTER (SHEFFIELD) WILCOX or RACHEL BENNET; m WOODWARD SANFORD; Ref: Desc of Charles Dyer Wilcox p v, Gen of RI Fam v2 p142, Samuel Gorton Desc v2 p587.

MEHITABLE - b 15 Jan 1771 Sandisfield, Berkshire Co MA d/ABEL & SUSANNAH (HALL) WILCOX; d 23 Oct 1805; Ref: Fiske Card File, Desc of Wm Wilcoxson p243.

MEHITABLE - b 1774 Stonington, New London Co CT d/EBENEZER & IANTHA (MASON) WILCOX; m 06 May 1798 Stonington CT JESSE WILCOX; ch IANTHA, EBENEZER, ELISHA, MASON, ELNATHAN F, SILAS, ELIAS; d 1868;

Ref: Barbour's VR Stonington v5 pp10,18, 1850 Census Stonington CT Reel 432 #48 p256, C Douglass Alves Sr.

MEHITABLE - b ca 1805 d/SAMUEL & MEHITABLE (WILLIAMS) WILCOX; m ALFRED PELTON; Res Clinton, Middlesex Co CT; 9 ch; Ref: Your Ancestors p256.

MEHITABLE - b ca 1810 d/OZIAL & NANCY (PAINE) WILCOX of Sandgate, Bennington Co VT; m ABEL GOWEY; Ref: Desc of Wm Wilcoxson p 169.

MEHITABLE - m 18 Dec 1842 Stonington, New London Co CT ELNATHAN N WILCOX; Ref: Barbour's VR Stonington v5 p109.

MEHITABLE - b 1849 Twin with JAMES d/ELNATHAN & JULIA (DENISON) WILCOX of Stonington, New London Co CT; Ref: 1850 Census Stonington CT Reel 432 #48 p256.

MELBOURNE - b 25 Jan 1842 Great Valley, Cattaraugus Co NY Twin with MELVIN s/SEYMOUR & SALLY (SARGENT) WILCOX; m 29 Dec 1859 AMANDA KEEN/KEAN who was b 1844 NY; d 09 Mar 1932; Ref: Dennis Davis, 1850 Census Great Valley NY p149 Dw# 64, 1860 Census Great Valley NY p368.

MELINDA - b 24 Feb 1796 Haddam, Middlesex Co CT d/LEVI & MARY (SPENCER) WILCOX; Ref: Desc of Wm Wilcoxson p132.

MELINDA - b 03 Apr 1805 Portsmouth, Newport Co RI d/WILLARD & HANNAH (GASKELL) WILCOX; Ref: Arnold v2 p167, Your Ancestors v11 #2 p1345.

MELINDA - b 1844 NY d/HAZZARD H & MARIAH (PALMER) WILCOX of Sherman, Chautauqua Co NY; Ref: 1850 Census Sherman NY p276 Dw# 67, See Hazzard H.

MELINDA L - b 1844_NY d/STEPHEN & AVAH (-----) WILCOX of Cazenovia, Madison Co NY;_Ref: 1850 Census Cazenovia NY p73 Dw# 1736.

MELISSA - b 21 Jun 1781 d/DANIEL & OLIVE (GASKILL) COOK WILCOX; Ref: Your Ancestors v11 #1 p1320.

MELISSA - b 04 Jul 1819 Somerset, Niagara Co NY d/EZRA AARON & SARAH (DAVIS) WILCOX; m EPHRAIM ELLIS; Ref: Colonial Fam of US v5 p555.

MELISSA - b 1829 NY d/EBER & RACHEL (-----) WILCOX of Cortlandville, Cortland Co NY; Ref: 1850 Census Cortlandville NY p370 Dw# 615.

MELISSA - b 1839 NY d/OZIAS WILCOX of Utica, Oneida Co NY; Ref: 1850 Census Utica NY p311 Dw# 25.

MELISSA - b 18 Jun 1842 d/ALBERT & EUNICE (NOBLE) WILCOX; m ----- BLAKE of Covington, Wyoming Co NY; Ref: Gen of Thomas Noble p484.

MELISSA - b 1847 OH d/SENECA & SAMANTHA (WILSON) WILCOX of Deerfield, Portage Co OH; Ref: 1850 Census Deerfield OH p188 Dw# 1039, See Seneca.

MELISSA ANN - b 09 Mar 1874 IL/NE d/ANDREW JACKSON & CARRIE HELEN (SARNES) WILCOX; m 08 Aug 1889 Western, Saline Co NE FRANCIS MARION PANTIER; d 03 Jan 1924 Pueblo, Pueblo Co CO; bur Mountain View Cem; Ref: Verna Betts.

MELISSA Z - b 1848 NY d/ALFRED SISSON & ALMENA COLE (WEAVER) WILCOX of Orangeville, Wyoming Co NY; m CHARLES PRENTICE; m GEORGE MATTESON; Ref: Your Ancestors v4 #5&6 p542, 1850 Census Orangeville NY p35 Dw# 544.

MELVIN - b 17 Jan 1833 Smyrna, Chenango Co NY s/HAZARD & FLAVILLA (PARSONS) WILCOX; d unmarried; Ref: Your Ancestors v3 #6 p397.

MELVIN - Twin with MELBOURNE - b 25 Jan 1842 Great Valley, Cattaraugus Co NY s/SEYMOUR & SALLY (SARGENT) WILCOX; m ELIZA -----; d 1926; Ref: Dennis Davis, 1850 Census Great Valley NY p149 Dw# 64.

MELVIN - b ca 1863 prob ME s/CHARLES DYER & MARY DUNN (CORBETT) WILCOX; d in western states or Yukon; Ref: Desc of Charles Dyer Wilcox p5.

MELVIN - b Apr 1895 s/ROSCOE & NELLIE (JOY) WILCOX; d 10 Dec 1917 bur Wood Island, N B Canada; Ref: Desc of Charles Dyer Wilcox p14.

MELVIN S - b 25 Oct 1841 s/DAVID & BETSEY (KELSEY) WILCOX of Newport, Sullivan Co NH; Ref: Your Ancestors v3 #6 p399.

MENZO - b 20 Dec 1832 Milford, Otsego Co NY s/JOHN & ABIGAIL W (WRIGHT) WILCOX; m 20 Dec 1858 PERMELIA WENTWORTH who was b 08 Apr 1839 Marshall,

Oneida Co NY & d 19 Jun 1918 d/DAVID M & MARIA A (HOWE) WENTWORTH; ch JOHN; d 27 Jun 1905 Milford NY; Ref: Your Ancestors v4 #7&8 pp565,566, Westcott Hist p388, 1850 Census Milford NY p119 Dw# 324.

MENZO J - b 20 Mar 1869 Tama, Tama Co IA s/LEWIS & RACHEL ANN (GLENN) WILCOX; m 24 Dec 1896 Toledo, Tama Co IA LULU MAY THORNE who was b 1876; d 14 Dec 1954 Tama IA Ref: Marjorie Stoner Elmore.

MERCIA - b 1833; m 05 Oct 1879 Villanova, Chautauqua Co NY NATHANIEL CROMPTON; Ref: Rev A J Wilcox's Marriage Record mss p13.

MERCY - b 09 Mar 1675/6 Middletown, Middlesex Co CT d/JOHN & ESTHER (CORNWELL) WILCOX; Ref: MUH p743, Cutter's CT Fam v2 p480.

MERCY - b 05 Sep 1719 Simsbury, Hartford Co CT Twin with NATHANIEL d/JOSEPH & ABIGAIL (THRALL) WILCOX; m 10 Nov 1737 GABRIEL CORNISH; Ref: Nutmegger v10 #2 p214, v13 #4 p660, Wilcox-Meigs p32, Your Ancestors v13 #3 p1567, Desc of Wm Wilcoxson p15.

MERCY/MARCY - b 06 Aug 1724 Westerly, Washington Co RI d/STEPHEN & MERCY (RANDALL) WILCOX; Ref: NEH&GR v15 pp65,66, Arnold v5 pt4 p144, Wilcox-Brown-Medbery p7.

MERCY - m 18 Jul 1762 Westerly, Washington Co RI DANIEL STANTON; Ref: Arnold v5 pt2 p69.

MERCY - m 23 Jul 1754 Richmond, Washington Co RI GEORGE TANNER; Ref: Arnold v5 pt6 p21.

MERCY - b 03 Dec 1764 Simsbury, Hartford Co CT d/SEDOTIA & MARCY (HUMPHREY) WILCOX; m ALEXANDER ALLEN who d 1816; Ref: Your Ancestors v11 #4 p1379, Barbour's VR Simsbury TM4 p190.

MERCY - b 23 Mar 1769 Westerly, Washington Co RI d/ISAIAH & SARAH (LEWIS) WILCOX; d 18 Sep 1789 Ref: Arnold v5 p145, Wilcox-Brown-Medbery p9.

MERCY - b 27 Nov 1774 Sharon, Litchfield Co CT Twin with ELIZABETH d/JONATHAN & SARAH (-----) WILCOX; Ref: Barbour's VR Sharon LR7 p308.

MERCY - b 1780 W Simsbury, Hartford Co CT d/WILLIAM & MERCY (CASE) WILCOX; d 1806 age 26; Ref: Early Settlers of W Simsbury p130.

MERCY - b 13 Jan 1793 Colchester, New London Co CT d/ASA & MERCY (RATHBONE) WILCOX; Ref: Barbour's VR Colchester v2 p135.

MERCY - b 29 Jun 1803 Winchester Litchfield Co CT d/DANIEL & MEHITABLE (WRIGHT) WILCOX; Res Great Barrington, Berkshire Co MA 1813; Ref: Annals of Winchester CT p329,330, Barbour's VR Winchester v2 p107.

MERCY A - m 26 Jan 1853 Vernon Co WI FRANKLIN COOLEY; wedding performed by Rev IRA WILCOX; Ref: Hist of Vernon Co WI p161.

MERCY S - b 1845 NY d/DUDLEY & KEZIAH (TOWNSEND) WILCOX of Litchfield, Herkimer Co NY; Ref: 1850 Census Litchfield NY p133 Dw# 282.

MERIBAH/MERIBE - b 17 May 1760 Southfield RI d/DANIEL & SILVIA (RUSSELL) WILCOX; m 10 Jun 1776 GIDEON THAYER who was b 05 Nov 1753 & d 20 Feb 1836 Lima, Livingston Co NY s/THOMAS & SUSANNA (BlAKE) THAYER; Res Mendon, Worcester Co MA, Owego, Tioga Co NY, Lima NY; ch SYLVIA, HOPPY?, WILLARD, DANIEL R, GIDEON; Ref: Hist of Wyoming Co NY p297 Arnold v2 p96, Your Ancestors v11 #1 p1320, #2 p1346.

MERIBAH - m 05 Feb 1784 Dartmouth, Bristol Co MA HUMPHREY WADY; Ref: Dartmouth VR p547.

MERIBAH - b 22 Aug 1802 Dartmouth, Bristol Co MA d/WILLIAM & RUTH (DURFEE) WILCOX; m ELLERY HICKS; Ref: Your Ancestors v10 #4 p1293.

MERIBAH/MERIBETH - b ca 1808/10 d/WILLIAM & GULIELMA (ESTES) WILCOX of Mendon, Worcester Co MA; m HORACE SOUTHWORTH; Ref: Your Ancestors v11 #2 p1345, Snow-Estes Ancestry v2 p18.

MERIDA/MERIBAH - b 03 Dec 1791 RI d/STEPHEN & SUSANNA (TILSON) WILCOX of Mendon, Worcester Co MA; m 05 Mar 1808 ARTEMUS PICKENING; Ref: Your Ancestors v11 #2 p1345.

MERRITT CRAWFORD - b 06 Jun 1842 Demopolis, Marengo Co AL s/LUCIUS & FRANCES A (CRAWFORD) WILCOX; m 1867 CAROLINE RICHARDSON d/WILLIAM & CAROLINE O (HEATON) RICHARDSON of Cortland Co NY; ch LUCIUS WILLIAM, MABEL MERRITT, CRAWFORD RICHARDSON; Ref: Your Ancestors v3 #11 pp1353,1354.

MERTIE - m CLARK STANBRO; Res Machais, Chautauqua Co NY; ch ROY L; Ref: Lois Barris.

MERTON - b 1872 Clockville, Madison Co NY s/ELISHA & ELIZABETH (HALL) WILCOX; Ref: Pioneers of Madison Co NY p281.

MERTON - b Sep 1891 Chautauqua Co NY s/PORTER B & MARY MAY (FROST) WILCOX; d be 1900; Ref: Wilcox Hist mss.

MICHAEL - b 1820 Ireland; m MARY ----- who was b 1818 Ireland; Res Vernon, Oneida Co NY; ch MARY ANN, MICHAEL; Ref: 1850 Census Vernon NY p85 Dw# 200.

MICHAEL - b 1846 Ireland s/MICHAEL & MARY (-----) WILCOX of Vernon, Oneida Co NY; Ref: 1850 Census Vernon NY p85 Dw# 200.

MICAJAH - b 1743 Dartmouth, Bristol Co MA s/STEPHEN & MARY (RICKETSON) WILCOX; d 18 Dec 1817 Stillwater NY; Ref: Your Ancestors v10 #3 p1268, Nutmegger v17 #1 p68.

MICAJAH STEPHEN - b 21 Mar 1807 Easton, Washington Co NY; m 25 Nov 1830 Phelps, Ontario Co NY LYDIA ANN CORY; d 1863 IL; Ref: Nutmegger v10 #3, LDS Fam Group Sheet.

MILA C - b ca 1831 d/WILLIAM & ESTHER S (COLE) WILCOX of Portland, Chautauqua Co NY; d age 7; Ref: Your Ancestors v12 #3 p1463.

MILDRED M - b 25 Oct 1891 d/FRANCIS & ELIZA A (BEACH) WILCOX; Res Wayne Co NY; Ref: Your Ancestors v10 #4 p1294.

MILES - b 08 Mar 1787 Torrington, Litchfield Co CT s/ASAHEL & MARY (COE) WILCOX; m 22 Oct 1807 Torrington CT JERUSHA BANCROFT; Res Chenango Co NY; ch EMELINE; Ref: Desc of Wm Wilcoxson p27, Barbour's VR Torrington v1 pp17,107.

MILES - b 1806; Stage driver; Res Cazenovia, Madison Co NY; d 23 Dec 1859 age 53; Ref: Pioneers of Madison Co NY p281, 1850 Census Cazenovia NY p68.

MILES - b 25 Jul 1818 s/ALLYN & CHLOE (WOODFORD) WILCOX; d 16 Apr 1819 age 9 mo; Ref: CT Bible Rec v15 pp254,255.

MILES - b 1830 NY s/DANIEL & PAMELA (-----) WILCOX of Litchfield, Herkimer Co NY; Farmer; Ref: 1850 Census Litchfield NY p126 Dw# 177.

MILFORD - b 1836 Chautauqua Co NY s/OLIVER C & MARIA (YALE) WILCOX; Ref: Your Ancestors v12 #3 p1463.

MILLENDA - b 25 Jan 1805 Ludlow, Windsor Co VT d/JONATHAN & EUNIS (-----) WILCOX; Ref: Fiske Card File.

MILLICENT HOPSON - b 13 Nov 1803 Killingworth, Middlesex Co CT Twin of WILLIAM d/ASA & DEBORAH (HOPSON) BRAINARD WILCOX; m 27 Aug 1827 ELIAS KIRTLAND STEVENS who was b 10 Apr 1794 & d 02 Sep 1865; d 18 Feb 1845 age 41y 3m 5d; Ref: Wilcox-Meigs p82, Your Ancestors v3 #3 p322, Barbour's VR Killingworth v3 p376, CT Bible Rec v20 pp282,285.

MILLY (MILLA) ANN - b 15 Dec 1795 E Guilford, New Haven Co CT d/ELIJAH & LOIS (FIELD) WILCOX; d 14 Apr 1825; Ref: Wilcox-Meigs p72, Fam of Early Guilford p1210.

MILO - b 1814 VT; m HARRIET ----- who was b 1814 VT & must have d be 1860; m SAMANTHA ----- who was b 1837 NY; Res Ellington, Chautauqua Co NY; ch by 1st wife; WORTHY, LOUISA, FLORENCE, TAYLOR, DARIUS; Ref: 1850 Census Ellington NY p159 Dw# 2193, 1860 Census Ellington NY p119 Dw# 525.

MILO - of OH; m 20 Aug 1848 ROXEY L WILCOX who was b 29 Mar 1821 d/OVID & ORPHA (WRIGHT) WILCOX of Granby, Hartford Co CT; Ref: Desc of Wm Wilcoxson p218, Barbour's VR Granby v1 p56, CT Bible Rec v18 pp520,521.

MILO - b 1829 Granby, Hartford Co CT; m 04 Jul 1850 Granby CT VESTA COWDRY who was b Hartland, Hartford Co CT; Ref: Barbour's VR Granby v1 pp252,253.

MILO - b 1830 NY s/HAZARD & BETSEY (-----) WILCOX of Georgetown, Madison Co NY; Ref: 1850 Census Georgetown NY p391 Dw# 268.

MILO - b 1855 NY s/ANTHONY W & HARRIET (-----) WILCOX of Cherry Creek, Chautauqua Co NY; Ref: 1860 Census Cherry Creek NY p150 Dw# 788.

MILO GEORGE - b 19 Sep 1837 Cleveland, Cuyahoga Co OH s/ISAAC ALMANZA & MARIETTE (OVIATT) WILCOX;

m 13 Mar 1856 Menard Co IL MARY/POLLY WELDON; m MARY PRUDENCE ASHLEY; d 11 Jul 1906 Butler, Bates Co MO; Ref: Verna Betts.

MILTON - b 27 Aug 1788 Simsbury, Hartford Co CT s/ROGER & ELIZABETH (CASE) WILCOX; Ref: Your Ancestors v12 #4 p1490, Barbour's VR Simsbury TM4 p302.

MILTON - b 1823 s/LAWRENCE & LAURA (PALMER) WILCOX; m MARGARET -----; ch CATHERINE, OMAR, LOUISA, ELIZABETH, MARTIN, ALANSON; Ref: Desc of Wm Wilcoxson p162.

MILTON - b Nov 1882 MI; Res Cherry Creek, Chautauqua Co NY in 1910; Ref: 1910 Census Chautauqua Co NY.

MILTON - s/FRANK E & MARY E (SULLIVAN) WILCOX of Port Chester, Westchester Co NY; d 25 Oct 1895; Ref: Cutter's Northern NY v2 p655.

MILTON JOHN - b 20 Feb 1812 W Winfield, Herkimer Co NY s/JOHN & SYBIL (GUILD) WILCOX; d 1818; Ref: Your Ancestors v3 #4 p352.

MILVILLE - b 1853 s/EZRA STILES & MARTHA (PETTIT) WILCOX; Res IA; Ref: Pioneers of Madison Co NY p218.

MINA - b 1813 NY d/JOHN & SARAH (-----) WILCOX of McDonough, Chenango Co NY; Ref: 1850 Census Chenango Co NY.

MINA C - b 1871 d/WILLIAM/WILLIE & ELLEN (KNOWLES) WILCOX; m FRANK COLEMAN; ch MARY ELLEN, MINNIE, WILLIAM, LEONARD, MAUDE, PAUL; d 1912; Ref: Desc of Wm Wilcoxson p196.

MINA MAUDE - b 07 Nov 1890 d/JAY EUGENE & KATE IDA (LOVELL) WILCOX; d 1902; Ref: FGS Seattle Gen Soc.

MINDWELL - b ca 1696 E Guilford, New Haven Co CT d/OBADIAH & SILENCE (MANSFIELD) WILCOX; m 20 Apr 1714 DANIEL HILL who was b 08 Jun 1692 & d 30 Jan 1745; ch REUBEN, JAMES, DANIEL, TIMOTHY, ABNER, MINDWELL, IRENA; d 03 Feb 1770; Ref: Wilcox-Meigs p26, Desc of Wm Wilcoxson pp8,15, Fam of Early Guilford p1208, Gen of CT Fam v2 p160, Hist of Surry NH p944.

MINDWELL - b 02 Jan 1713 Killingworth, Middlesex Co CT d/JOHN & HANNAH (SHAILOR) WILCOX; m 23 Oct 1733 NATHANIEL WILCOX who was b 01 Dec 1702 s/NATHANIEL & HANNAH (LANE) WILCOX; Ref: Desc of Wm Wilcoxson pp13,36, Bogue Fam p395, Wilcox-Meigs p31, Barbour's VR Killingworth v2 pp146,185.

MINDWELL - b 22 Sep 1734 Killingworth, Middlesex Co CT d/NATHANIEL & MINDWELL (WILCOX) WILCOX; m 25 Sep 1755 JOSEPH FARNUM; 9 ch Ref: Wilcox-Meigs p44, Desc of Wm Wilcoxson p20, Barbour's VR Killingworth v2 pp117,148.

MINDWELL - b 24 Oct 1742 Simsbury, Hartford Co CT d/JOSEPH & ELIZABETH (HUMPHREY) WILCOX; Ref: Wilcox-Meigs p49.

MINDWELL - b 11 May 1779 Conway, Franklin Co MA d/JOHN & MARY (-----) WILCOX; d 02 Aug 1816 age 36; Ref: Halifax VT Wilcox Fam mss.

MINDWELL - b ca 1820 Pompey, Onondaga Co NY d/CHESTER & AURELIA (SPERRY) WILCOX; m LEVI GIDDINGS; m JOHN POTTS; ch by 1st husband LEVI, MARSHALL; ch by 2nd husband JOHN AURELIA, CHARLOTTE; Ref: Your Ancestors v14 #2 p1645, #3 p1671.

MINER - m 10 Apr 1844 Voluntown, New London Co CT ALICE ANN CAREY; ch CALINDA M, HAMILTON M; Ref: Barbour's VR Voluntown v2 pp116,138.

MINER J - b 1829; m be 1856 SUSAN R -----; Res Saybrook, Middlesex Co CT; one son; Ref: Saybrook Colony VR p282.

MINERVA - b 11 Aug 1809 d/ALLYN & CHLOE (WOODFORD) WILCOX; Ref: CT Bible Rec v15 pp253,254.

MINERVA - b 1813 NY d/JOSEPH WILCOX of Tully, Onondaga Co NY; Ref: 1850 Census Tully NY p162 Dw# 168.

MINERVA - b ca 1827 Smithfield, Bradford Co PA d/STEPHEN & POLLY (ALLEN) WILCOX; Ref: Halifax VT Wilcox Fam mss.

MINERVA E - b 1830 S Canton, Hartford Co CT m 16 Oct 1850 Simsbury, Hartford Co CT SETH E CASE who was b 1824 Simsbury CT; Atty; Res New Britain, Hartford Co CT; Ref: Goodwin's Gen Notes p294,

Church Rec of Rev Allen McLean p23, Barbour's VR Canton v1 pp72,73.

MINERVA FRANCES - b 06 Aug 1882 Smithfield Twnshp, Bradford Co PA d/ELLIOTT URIAH & TIRZAH ELVIRA (SEYMOUR) WILCOX; m 25 Jan 1910 GEORGE WASHINGTON OVERACKER who was b 25 Apr 188? & d 21 Oct 19__; ch ELMER WILCOX, HELEN TIRZAH, ALBERT WILSON, ALICE FRANCES, FREDRICK KETTING, VIOLET MARIE, REXFORD EUGENE; d 01 Jan 1957 in auto accident Big Pond, Bradford Co PA bur Union Cem East Smithfield PA; Ref: Wilcox Genealogy pp20,53.

MINERVIA - b 1848 NY d/HANANIAH & NANCY E (-----) WILCOX of Dryden, Tompkins Co NY; Ref: 1850 Census Dryden NY p101 Dw# 652.

MINNIE - d/ASAPH CURTIS WILCOX; m CHARLES YOUNG; Res NY & Glenville, Freeborn Co MN; Ref: A Wilcox Book p10.

MINNIE - d/MARCELLUS & MARY J (WILCOX) WILCOX; m LEVI BOWEN; Ref: Desc of Wm Wilcoxson p65.

MINNIE - b 1857 Minneapolis, Hennepin Co MN d/WILLIAM OZIAS & MARTHA (STERNS) WILCOX; m ALBERT McMULLEN; 1 ch who died young; Ref: Bogue Fam p398.

MINNIE A - b 25 Apr 1867 Geneva, Ashtabula Co OH d/JOSEPH L & MARY S (IVES) WILCOX; m 31 Jul 1895 FRANK S BERRY; ch OLIVER, ZELLA; Ref: Bogue Fam p399.

MINNIE B - b Mar 1875 WI d/GEORGE & SUSAN (-----) WILCOX; Father b NY; Res Dakota, Waushara Co WI; Ref: 1900 Soundex Waushara Co WI.

MINNIE C - b 05 Mar 1859 Sunrise MN; m Waukesha, Waukesha Co WI BEN CLAYTON; ch DORA, BURNICE PHI, HOWARD GWYNIS; Ref: Jane Smith.

MINNIE ELLEN - b 1871 twin of MINA C d/WILLIAM/WILLIE & ELLEN (KNOWLES) WILCOX; m HENRY SEYMOUR GOTT; ch CARL, FERN KATHRYN; d 1950; Ref: Desc of Wm Wilcoxson p196.

MINNIE F - m 06 May 1884 Laona, Chautauqua Co NY BERT A RICE of Fredonia, Chautauqua Co NY; Infant son d 1885; Ref: 19th Cent Marriages Reported in Fredonia Censor p119, 19th Cent Death Notices Reported in Fredonia Censor p449.

MINNIE FRANCES - b ca 1873 Niagara Falls, Niagara Co NY d/CHARLES WILLIAM & MARY P (WILCOX) WILCOX; m 21 Jun 1893 EDWARD T WILLIAMS; Ref: Cutter's Western NY v2 p742.

MINNIE MAY - b 14 Oct 1875 d/THOMAS LITTLE & MARY M (SMITH) WILCOX; Ref: Desc of Wm Wilcoxson p126.

MINNIE MILDRED - b 14 Sep 1876 Elm Island prob Buffalo Co NE d/GEORGE HENRY & ORRILLA ELIZABETH (ROOT) WILCOX; d 1878; Ref: Halifax VT Wilcox Fam mss.

MINOR R - b ca 1820 s/ROWLAND & ELIZABETH (VANETTA) WILCOX; Res Albany, Bradford Co PA; Ref: Pioneers of Bradford Co PA.

MINTA - b 21 Aug 1872 Waters MI d/GEORGE & HARRIET ELVIRA (BACON) WILCOX; m 16 Apr 1889; d 06 Aug 1891 HENRY S WESTON; Ref: LDS Fam Group Sheet.

MIRA A - b 29 Aug 1861 d/ORRIN & ADELINE (-----) WILCOX; d 29 Oct 1862 Valois, Schuyler Co NY; Ref: Cem Between the Lakes v2 p319.

MIRA/MYRA DELIA/DELLA - b 31 Aug 1816 Detroit, Wayne Co MI d/CHARLES & ALMIRA (ROOD) WILCOX; m GEORGE DAVIS of Chicago, Cook Co IL who was b 31 Dec 1808; 8 ch; d 1906; Ref: Wilcox-Meigs p87, Desc of Wm Wilcoxson p260.

MIRANDA - of Granby, Hartford Co CT; m 30 Jul 1839 Farmington, Hartford Co CT VIRGIL CORNISH of Hartford, Hartford Co CT; Ref: Barbour's VR Farmington LR47 p100.

MIRANDA - of Westfield, Middlesex Co CT; m 20 Nov 1844 Middletown, Middlesex Co CT WILLIAM H HISLEY of Berlin, Hartford Co CT; Ref: Barbour's VR Middletown v3 p528.

MIRANDA - b 1822 NY d/SIMEON & EUNICE (-----) WILCOX of Independence, Allegany Co NY; Ref: 1850 Census Independence NY p159 Dw# 5.

MIRANDA/MELINDA - b 1837 NY d/REUBEN & ORRY (-----) WILCOX of McDonough, Chenango Co NY; Ref: 1850 Census Chenango Co NY, Your Ancestors v4 #11&12 p610.

MIRANDA - b 1852 d/DANIEL & ALMA/AMELIA (-----) WILCOX; d 05 Mar 1869; Ref: Your Ancestors v4 #9&10 p583.

MIRIAM - b 01 Jan 1769 Newport, Sullivan Co NH d/JESSE & THANKFUL (STEVENS) WILCOX; d 02 Jan 1769 age 1day Ref: Wilcox-Meigs p63, Nebr & Midwest Gen Rec v8 #1 pp22,23, Your Ancestors v3 #4 p349.

MIRIAM/MIRIEUM - b 24 Jan 1787 Newport, Sullivan Co NH d/JESSE & THANKFUL (STEVENS) WILCOX; m WORCESTER BALDWIN; d Benson, Rutland Co VT 23 Feb 1812 age 25y 1m; Ref: Nebr & Midwest Gen Rec v8 #1 p23. Your Ancestors v3 #4 p349.

MIRIAM - b 14 Dec 1804 Sandisfield, Berkshire Co MA d/GEORGE & SUSANNAH (HUMPHREY) WILCOX; Ref: Your Ancestors v12 #1 p1408, Desc of Wm Wilcoxson p223.

MOLLY - b 09 Feb 1766 Sandisfield, Berkshire Co MA d/EBENEZER & MARY (EDDY) WILCOX; Ref: Fiske Card File.

MOLLY - b 1769 d/JEHIEL & ABIGAIL (CRAMPTON) WILCOX; Ref: Desc of Wm Wilcoxson p28.

MOLLY - b 21 Feb 1779 Killingworth, Middlesex Co CT d/ELIJAH & MARY (FRENCH) WILCOX; m WILLIAM STORER; Ref: Wilcox-Meigs p80, Fam of Early Guilford p1206, Barbour's VR Killingworth v2 p14.

MOLLY - m Mar 1810 ----- LEONARD; Ref: VR of CT v7 p153.

MONROE - b 1824 NY s/----- & POLLY (-----) WILCOX; m MALISSA -----; Res Milford, Otsego Co NY; ch MARYETTE; Ref: 1850 Census Milford NY p115.

MONROE - b 1851 Stockton, Chautauqua Co NY s/HORACE W & JULIA (-----) WILCOX; Ref: Alice Wiatr.

MONROE P - b Aug 1883 WI s/EDWARD & MARIA (-----) WILCOX who were both b NY; Res Vilas Co WI; Ref: 1900 Soundex WI.

MORGAN L - b ca 1800 Ashford, Windham Co CT/NY s/STEPHEN & LOIS (CHAFFEE) WILCOX; m CAROLINE SATTERLEE who was b ca 1799; Res Granby, Oswego Co NY; ch ALMON/ALVIRA, LEROY, DWIGHT, HENRY, MORGAN; Ref: Your Ancestors v3 #9&10 p447, 1850 Census Granby NY p16 Dw# 243.

MORGAN L - b 1810 s/ENOCH & NANCY (WOODRUFF) WILCOX; m MARY ----- who was b 1815; Res South Bristol, Ontario Co NY; ch LOUISA; Ref: Your Ancestors v10 #1 p1202 #2 p1225.

MORRIS - b ca 1796 Whitestown, Oneida Co NY s/REUBEN & HANNAH (JOHNSON) WILCOX; m PHOEBE BROWN who was b 28 Jun 1799 & d 18 Apr 1883; Res Whitestown, Oneida Co NY; ch JOHN, JULIA W, poss THERESA; Ref: 1860 Census Whitestown NY p64 Dw# 872, Your Ancestors v4 #1&2 p500, #3&4 p523.

MORRIS - b 1835 NY s/ISAIAH & ARMANDA (-----) WILCOX of Florence, Oneida Co NY; Ref: 1850 Census Florence NY p200 Dw# 144.

MORRIS - s/LUCIUS C WILCOX; Res Angelo WI; Ref: Mrs. Dorothy Willis.

MORRISON D - b 1793; d 05 Dec 1831 in KY; formerly of Otsego Co NY; Ref: Deaths from Otsego Co Newspapers v1 p64.

MORTIMER - b 1829/30 s/PETER & HANNAH (RANSFORD) WILCOX; d 09 Mar 1835; Ref: Your Ancestors v10 #3 p1250, Desc of Wm Wilcoxson p207.

MORTIMER - b 1833 Fairport, Monroe Co NY s/LAWRENCE & LAURA (PALMER) WILCOX; m ELVIRA E NORTHRUP; ch MARY, JAMES H, HIRAM P; Ref: Desc of Wm Wilcoxson p162.

MORTIMER - s/LUCIUS C WILCOX; Res Angelo WI; Ref: Mrs Dorothy Willis.

MORTIMER - b 1839; m Jan 1862 Rochester, Oakland Co MI CHARLOTTE E HADLEY who was b 1843; Res Avon MI; Ref: Detroit Society of Gen Research Mag v54 #2.

MORTON - b 1820 Genesee Co NY s/LEVI & MARY (SPENCER) WILCOX; Ref: Desc of Wm Wilcoxson p133.

MOSES - b 31 Jul 1728 Middletown, Middlesex Co CT s/JOHN & MARY (BARNES) WILCOX; m 22 Mar 1753 DESIRE RANNEY; ch DESIRE, JOHN, JOSEPH, REUBEN, REUBEN; d 30 Jun 1784; Ref: NEH&GR v14 p138, Nutmegger v4 #3 p331, MUH p746, Barbour's VR Middletown v2 pp21,292.

MOSES - b 13 Dec 1732 Killingworth, Middlesex Co CT s/DAVID & MARY (HUTCHISON) WILCOX; m 30 Mar 1762 Harwinton, Litchfield Co CT THANKFUL

(SPENCER) BUNNELL of Farmington, Hartford Co CT who was b 1735 & d 25 Jan 1817; w/NATHANIEL BUNNELL; Res Harwinton, Litchfield Co CT; ch MOSES, OLIVE, OLIVE, TABITHA, AARON, SARAH; d 13 Aug 1803 bur Cem #27 Harwinton CT; Ref: Rev Soldiers Bur in Litchfield Co CT p125, Wilcox-Meigs p41, Desc of Abner & Lucy Wilcox p20, Barbour's VR Harwinton LR1 p20, LR2 p30, LR4 p634.

MOSES - b 13 Jun 1745 Middletown, Middlesex Co CT Twin with AARON s/JANNA & RACHEL (BOARDMAN) WILCOX; Ref: Your Ancestors v4 #3&4 p524, Barbour's VR Middletown TR1 p22.

MOSES - m 31 Jul 1765 Chatham, Middlesex Co CT HANNAH ROGERS; ch EPHRAIM; Ref: Barbour's VR Chatham v1 p14.

MOSES - b 02 Jul 1762 Goshen, Litchfield Co CT s/JOB WILCOX; Ref: Barbour's VR Goshen v1 p224.

MOSES - b 18 Dec 1762 Twin with AARON s/MOSES & THANKFUL (SPENCER) BUNNELL WILCOX Harwinton, Litchfield Co CT; Ref: Desc of Abner & Lucy Wilcox p20, Barbour's VR Harwinton LR1 p20, LR2 p30.

MOSES - of Colebrook, Litchfield Co CT m 1787 LYDIA LANCEY; Ref: Barbour's VR Rocky Hill, Hartford Co CT;

MOSES - b 01 Oct 1771 Middletown, Middlesex Co CT Twin with ELIAS s/ELIJAH & MARY (BUSHNELL) WILCOX; Ref: Barbour's VR Middletown v2 p28.

MOSES - b 18 May 1772 Middletown, Middlesex Co CT; Twin with AARON s/ABEL & MARY (HULL) WILCOX; m 09 Apr 1800 HULDAH LORD d/MARTIN & CONCURRENCE (SEWARD) LORD; Res Killingworth, Middlesex Co CT, 1810 Batavia, Genesee Co NY & Twinsburg, Summit Co OH 1823; ch CONCURRANCE SEWARD, WILLIAM LORD, MARY EMILY, CYNTHIA, HULDAH, EBENEZER HAYDEN, MOSES, AARON, HAYDEN, PHINEAS CALEB; d 07 Mar 1827 Twinsburg OH; Ref: Lord Fam Gen p289, Wilcox-Meigs p81, Our County & Its People Genesee Co NY p104, Barbour's VR Middletown v2 p14, Killingworth v2 pp43,133, Your Ancestors v3 #1 p280, #2 p301.

MOSES - b be 1775; Res Ashford, Windham Co CT; 4 daus; Ref: 1820 Census Ashford CT.

MOSES - b 1777; d 21 Sep 1827 Twinsburg, Summit Co OH; Ref: 19th Cent Death Notices Reported in Fredonia Censor p596, Index of Obits MA Cent

710

p4913, Gleanings from Christian Advocate & Journal & Zion's Herald p350.

MOSES - m 16 Apr 1801 Rocky Hill, Hartford Co CT MARY MILLER both of Middletown, Middlesex Co CT; Ref: Barbour's VR Rocky Hill v1 p68.

MOSES - b 27 Jun 1812 Killingworth, Middlesex Co CT s/MOSES & HULDAH (LORD) WILCOX; m ISABELLA FORSYTHE; Res Twinsburg, Summit Co OH; Ref: Lord Fam Gen p289, Wilcox-Meigs p81, Your Ancestors v3 #2 p301, Barbour's VR Killingworth v2 p14.

MOSES - b 18 Sep 1821 Lowville, Lewis Co NY s/ROSWELL & IRENE (NICHOLSON) WILCOX; d Jul 1835 Carthage, Jefferson Co NY; Ref: Early Settlers of NY p339, Cutter's Northern NY v2 p656, Desc of Wm Wilcox p65.

MOSES - b 1832 s/ALONZO BENJAMIN & HANNAH (SWIFT) WILCOX of Harpersfield, Delaware Co NY; d young; Ref: Your Ancestors v4 #7&8 p563.

MOSES - m 05 Jun 1837 Enfield, Hartford Co CT SUSAN F SAUN----; Ref: Hist of Enfield CT v2 p1814, Barbour's VR Enfield v4 p1814.

MOSES - m 01 Nov 1840 S Kingstown, Washington Co RI MARY C GARDINER; Ref: Arnold v5 pt2 p31.

MOSES - b 1847; d 18 Dec 1879 age 32 Evans, Erie Co NY; Ref: West NY Journal v14 #2 p63.

MOSES - b 1849 PA s/W E & SUSAN (-----) WILCOX; Res Le Roy, Bradford Co PA; Ref: 1860 Census Bradford Co PA p371.

MOSES BARBER - b 19 Feb 1839 s/WILLIAM B & IRENE (LARKIN) WILCOX of Putnam, Windham Co CT; Ref: Your Ancestors v4 #11&12 p609.

MOSES CASE - b 09 Aug 1781 Norfolk, Litchfield Co CT s/HOSEA Jr & ABIGAIL (-----) WILCOX; m 08 Nov 1807 PHEBE STARLING CROSBY who was b 12 Oct 1789 E Haddam, Middlesex Co CT & d 11 Jun 1875 Rome, Ashtabula Co OH; d 08 Feb 1866; Ref: Fiske Card File, Rev Soldiers bur in OH, Barbour's VR Norfolk v1 p3.

MOSES FIELD - b 29 Nov 1826 Gilsum, Cheshire Co NH s/ELEAZER & ESTHER (FIELD) WILCOX; m 15 May 1861 ELIZABETH A KEMP d/ERASTUS KEMP; d 15 Mar 1864 Gilsum NH; Ref: Hist of Sullivan NH p1055.

MOSES HAVENS - b 15 Aug 1858; m 08/18 Dec 1883 ESTELLA FISH MAYO who was b 05 Oct 1861 d/FRANK B & CATHERINE RATHBUN (FISH) MAYO; ch KATHERINE MAYO, ELIZA/ELIZABETH FRANCES, JULIA LOUISE, CLARENCE MAYO; Ref: Desc of Robert Burrows p120, Denison Gen p505.

MOSES S - b 11 Mar 1836 Harpersfield, Delaware Co NY s/ALONZO BENJAMIN & HANNAH (SWIFT) WILCOX; m LYDIA G BEARD; Res Jefferson, Schoharie Co NY; Ref: Your Ancestors v4 #7&8 p563, 1850 Census Harpersfield NY p158 Dw# 28.

MOSES T - b 11 Dec 1823 s/THOMAS & ELIZABETH (McCAIN) WILCOX of Hector, Schuyler Co NY; Ref: Your Ancestors v10 #4 p1274, 1850 Census Hector NY p 367 Dw# 128.

MUNSON - b 03 Feb 1820 Floyd, Oneida Co NY s/ELEAZER CURTIS & CYNTHIA (NOBLE) WILCOX; m 01 Jan 1848 WEALTHY A STONE; d 17 Oct 1873 York WI; Ref: A Wilcox Book p20, Gen of Thomas Noble p448.

MUNSON - m 18 Apr 1847 Bristol, Hartford Co CT Mrs HARRIET E MORTON; Ref: Barbour's VR Bristol v3 p34.

MURIEL E - b 1894 Wood Island, N B Canada d/EUGENE & HELEN UBERTA (GREEN) WILCOX; d 1913 bur Wood Island Cem; Ref: Desc of Charles Dyer Wilcox p25.

MYRA E - b 1869 Perry, Wyoming Co NY d/EDGAR UDAL & EMMA A (PRENTICE) WILCOX; Ref: Your Ancestors v4 #5&6 p542.

MYRON - b 1820 NY s/FRANCIS CLARK & LAURA (-----) WILCOX of Franklin, Delaware Co NY; Ref: 1850 Census Franklin NY p43 Dw# 226.

MYRON - b 1829 NY; Res Onondaga, Onondaga Co NY; Ref: 1850 Census Onondaga NY p270 Dw# 697.

MYRON - b 1847 Marion, Wayne Co NY s/CHARLES D & LOUISA (-----) WILCOX; Ref: Your Ancestors v10 #4 p1293.

MYRON ALFRED - b 1853 s/ALFRED SISSON & ALMENA COLE (WEAVER) WILCOX of Orangeville, Wyoming Co NY; m EMMA CRANDALL; Ref: Your Ancestors v4 #5&6 p542.

MYRON E - b 1846 NY Twin with MARY E s/SHELDEN & MARY (-----) WILCOX of Danby, Tompkins Co NY; Ref: 1850 Census Danby NY p56 Dw# 391.

MYRON HENRY - b 18 Oct 1840 s/RENSELLAER & SARAH (REDFIELD) WILCOX; Ref: Your Ancestors v13 #4 p1609.

MYRON JAMES - b 12 Nov 1859 Ticonderoga, Essex Co NY s/WILLIAM & CORNELIA P (TREADWAY) WILCOX; m 02 Apr 1890 ETTA MAY LILLIE of Putnam, Washington Co NY who was b 03 July 1867 d/DAVID & MARGARET (MAXWELL) LILLIE; ch KIRBY DAVID; Ref: Cutter's Northern NY v2 pp 655,656.

MYRON LA ROY - b 11 Jul 1844 s/JOHN WARREN & POLINA ALZINA (WEEKS) WILCOX of Oneida Co NY; m 15 Apr 1868 HELEN A SMALLEY; Res Brooklyn NY; Ref: Gen of George Weekes p155.

MYRON W - Enl 1861 from Saratoga Co NY; Disch & moved west; Ref: Hist of Saratoga Co NY p399.

MYRTA - b 1848 Deep River, Middlesex Co CT d/JONATHAN SAMUEL & DOLLY ANN (SOUTHWORTH) WILCOX; Ref: Fam of Early Guilford p1205.

MYRTICE - b 25 May 1878 Minneapolis, Hennepin Co MN d/JOHN FINLEY & EMMA (CLEMENT) WILCOX; m Dr WALTER T JOSLIN; 2 daus; Ref: Desc of Wm Wilcoxson p127.

MYRTILLA MAY - b 10 May 1849 d/JOHN WARREN & POLINA ALZINA (WEEKS) WILCOX of Oneida Co NY; m 17 May 1871 CYRUS H HAWKINS; Res NYC; Ref: Gen of George Weekes p155.

MYRTLE - b 1839 NY Twin with NANCY d/CHARLES & BARBARA (WILKS) WILCOX of Sardinia, Erie Co NY & MN; Ref: 1850 Census Sardinia NY p117 Dw# 1733, See Charles.

MYRTLE - b ca 1867 d/WILLIAM OZIAS & MARTHA (STERNS) WILCOX; Res Minneapolis, Hennepin Co MN; Ref: Bogue Fam p398.

MYRTLE - b 22 Oct 1871 Guthrie Center, Guthrie Co IA d/LEWIS ALLEN & SABINA McDONALD (HOPKINS) WILCOX; m FOX FREEMAN TRIPPY; Ref: Wilcox-Meigs pp117,118.

MYRTLE - b ca 1891 Farmington, Davis Co UT; m WILBUR WRIGHT; 4 ch; d 20 Aug 1929 Idaho Falls, Bonneville Co ID; Ref: Desc of Wm Wilcoxson p144.

MYRTLE - b 06 June 1899 Prob Cutler, Washington Co ME d/WILLIAM & ANNIE (PENCE) WILCOX; m ARTHUR RAMSDELL; Ref: Desc of Charles Dyer Wilcox p5.

--- N ---

N R - b 1865 NY; Res Oshkosh, Winnebago Co WI; ch WARREN, CHARLES; Ref: 1900 Soundex WI.

N W - m RUTH EMMA SAXTON who was b 1886 Luverne, Rock Co MN d/JOY HANDY & MATILDA (HERBERT) SAXTON; Ref: Nebr & Midwest Gen Rec v11 #3 p35.

NABBY - m 12 Sep 1819 Hopkinton, Washington Co RI JAMES W BROWN; Ref: Arnold v5 p28.

NABBY/ABIGAIL - b 04 Nov 1787 Newport, Sullivan Co NH d/JESSE & THANKFUL (STEVENS) WILCOX; m Nov 1806 STEPHEN HURD who was b 08 Jan 1787 & d 22 Dec 1865; ch infant, HOWARD, ABIGAIL, MARRIAM, EUNICE S, OWEN, NORMAN, ELIZABETH, JESSIE W, ALBION P, OWEN; d 28 Sep 1862; Ref: Nebr & Midwest Gen Rec v8 #1 p23, Your Ancestors v3 #4 p349.

NANCY - b be 1778 d/ELISHA & AMY (-----) WILCOX; m STEPHEN STRICKLAND who was b ca 1775; Res Wysox, Bradford Co PA; Ref: Pioneer Fam of Bradford Co PA p111.

NANCY - b 27 May 1784 Halifax, Windham Co VT d/STEPHEN & ELEANOR (EWING) WILCOX; m 05 Jun 1804 ASA PUTNAM of Guilford, Windham Co VT; Ref: Halifax Wilcox Fam mss, Fiske Card File.

NANCY - m be 1816 DEXTER WHIPPLE; Res Glen Falls, Saratoga Co NY Moreau Precinct; ch A P; Ref: Hist of Saratoga Co NY p511.

NANCY - m 26 Jan 1806 Stonington, New London Co CT BENJAMIN BABCOCK; Ref: Hist of Stonington CT p219.

NANCY - b 04 Jan 1787 Alford, Berkshire Co MA d/RUFUS & SARAH (ADAMS) WILCOX; m FREDERICK HAMLIN; ch FREDERICK Jr, LUCIUS, HOMER, JANE M; Ref: Your Ancestors v9 #3 p1154, Desc of Wm Wilcoxson pp200,201.

NANCY - b 15 Mar 1787 d/JESSE & NANCY/ANNE (PENDLETON) WILCOX; m JOSEPH SHEFFIELD; m SAMUEL TAYLOR; Ref: Hist of Stonington CT p660, C Douglass Alves Sr.

NANCY - b 03 Oct 1790 Westerly, Washington Co RI d/NATHAN & NANCY (LEWIS) WILCOX; m ----- STAFFORD; Res Danube, Herkimer Co NY; Ref: Will of Nathan Wilcox #18113 Herkimer Co Prob Rec, Arnold v5 p145.

NANCY - b 1793 Killingworth, Middlesex Co CT d/JOEL & ELIZABETH HAND (COAN) WILCOX; Ref: Wilcox-Meigs p80.

NANCY - bpt 30 Mar 1794 Bristol, Hartford Co CT d/BENJAMIN & PHILENA (ROWE) WILCOX; m 28 Nov 1822 Bristol, Hartford Co CT DAVID STEELE; Ref: Barbour's VR Bristol v1 p18, Your Ancestors v4 #9&10 p588.

NANCY - b Oct 1794 Stratford, Fairfield Co CT d/JOEL & SARAH (BOOTH) WILCOX; m CHARLES HILLS; Ref: Wilcox-Meigs p78, Stratford Gen p1347, Desc of Wm Wilcoxson p36.

NANCY - d 02 Sep 1796 Stonington, New London Co CT; Ref: Hale Coll of Cem #17 p171.

NANCY - b 01 Oct 1797 Westerly, Washington Co RI d/BENJAMIN & NANCY (THOMPSON) WILCOX; Ref: Arnold v5 p145, See Benjamin.

NANCY - b ca 1799 RI d/HAZARD & NANCY (MAXSON) WILCOX; m ca 1819 MATTHEW ROBINSON POTTER s/MATTHEW & MARY (BRAYMON) POTTER of Richmond, Washington Co RI; ch WILLIAM ZION, ABLERT STILLMAN, MARY ANN, CHARLES H, ABBY H, JOHN J L; Ref: Your Ancestors v12 #2 p1435.

NANCY - b ca 1800 d/ROBERT & SARAH (WILBUR) WILCOX of Lyme, New London Co CT; m ----- DANIELS; Ref: Your Ancestors v11 #3 p1352.

NANCY - b 31 Jan 1802 Danube, Herkimer Co NY d/ISAIAH & POLLY (PENDLETON) WILCOX; Ref: Wilcox-Brown-Medbery p11.

NANCY - m 19 Nov 1832 Stonington, New London Co CT LATHROP W WHEELER; Ref: Barbour's VR Stonington v5 p29.

NANCY - b 21 May 1808 d/JESSE & CYNTHIA (-----) WILCOX; d 21 Oct 1829 Carthage, Jefferson Co NY; Ref: Early Settlers of NY p339.

NANCY - b 17 May 1809 d/JOHN CLARK & DORCAS (HARRINGTON) WILCOX of Franklin, New London Co CT; m ISAAC STETSON; Ref: Your Ancestors v14 #2 p1658.

NANCY - b 22 Feb 1814 Charlestown, Washington Co RI d/JOSEPH & HULDAH (SHERMAN) WILCOX; Ref: Arnold v5 pt5 p28, See Joseph.

NANCY - m 02 Mar 1834 Stratford, Fairfield Co CT WILLIAM M PERRY of Sauguatuck, Fairfield Co CT; Ref: Barbour's VR Stratford vA p44.

NANCY - b 10 Dec 1814 Dover, Dutchess Co NY d/DANIEL & DEBORAH (ALLEN) WILCOX; d 11 May 1860; Ref: Your Ancestors v4 #7&8 p564, 1850 Census Dover NY p322 Dw# 189.

NANCY - b 27 Sep 1816 Stonington, New London Co CT d/PHINEAS & MERCY (TAYLOR) WILCOX; Ref: Barbour's VR Stonington v4 p29, See Phineas.

NANCY - b 1819 Cortland Co NY d/THOMAS JAMES & LUCY (-----) WILCOX; Parents moved to Dryden, Lapeer Co MI 1837; Ref: Detroit Soc Gen Magazine v54 #2.

NANCY - m Apr 1826 Mina, Chautauqua Co NY ISAAC STEADMAN; Ref: Notes on Settlement of Chautauqua Co NY p14.

NANCY - m 15 Feb 1838 Westerly, Washington Co RI IRA BURDEN; Ref: Arnold v11 p47.

NANCY - b 15 Nov 1821 McLean, Tompkins Co NY d/CLARK & SALLY (MAXSON) WILCOX; d 25 Nov 1830 McLean NY; Ref: NYG&BR v105 p216, Carol A Cox.

NANCY - d/NATHAN & NANCY (LEWIS) WILCOX m ----- WINEGAR; Res Danube, Herkimer Co NY; Ref: Will of Nathan Wilcox Bk G p182 #18113 Herkimer Co Probate Records.

NANCY - b 13 Aug 1823 Westerly, Washington Co RI d/GEORGE S & ANNA MARIE (BLIVEN) WILCOX; Ref: Arnold v5 pp27,145.

NANCY - b 1824; m 01 Mar 1843 Canton, Hartford Co CT WILLIAM HENRY HOSFORD who was b 1816 & d 06 Jan 1891 s/MOSES HOSFORD; ch WILLIAM HENRY, GEORGE

CHESTER, SYLVIA NANCY, ADDISON E; d 26 May 1873; Ref: Horsford-Hosford Fam pp171,172, Barbour's VR Canton v1 p18.

NANCY - b 01 Jan 1828 Stonington, New London Co CT; d 16 Sep 1848; Ref: Hale Coll Cem #20 p277.

NANCY - b 1837 NY d/OZIAL Jr & SYLVIA (STEVENS) WILCOX of Georgetown, Madison Co NY; Ref: 1850 Census Georgetown NY p387 Dw# 208, See Ozial Jr.

NANCY - d 25 Jul 1837; Ref: Deaths from NY Herald p551.

NANCY - b 28 Oct 1838 d/HAZARD & FLAVILLA (PARSONS) WILCOX of Smyrna, Chenango Co NY; m 24 Dec 1861 HENRY G GREEN of Earlville, Chenango Co NY who was b 19 Mar 1839 & d 01 Mar 1913; ch CORA ANNE, SARAH E M; d 12 Aug 1933; Ref: Cutter's Western NY v3 p1439, Your Ancestors v3 #6 p397.

NANCY - b 1839 NY Twin with MYRTLE d/CHARLES & BARBARA (WILKS) WILCOX of Sardinia, Erie Co NY & MN; Ref: 1850 Census Sardinia NY p117 Dw# 1733, See Charles.

NANCY - of Stonington, New London Co CT; m 14 Jul 1847 Groton, New London Co CT ANDREW CHEESEBOROUGH; Ref: Barbour's VR Groton v1 p83.

NANCY - d/DANIEL & PHOEBE (ARNOLD) WILCOX; m ERASTUS OVERTON; Ref: Desc of Wm Wilcoxson p240.

NANCY - b 1849 CT d/LODOWICK & SARAH (-----) WILCOX of Stonington, New London Co CT; Ref: 1850 Census Stonington CT Reel 432 #48 p257 Dw# 341.

NANCY ANN - m ca 1835 CT ROSWELL CHAPMAN who was b 5 May 1814 s/JOHN & BARTHENA (BUTTON) CHAPMAN; ch AMOS, EVERETT; Ref: Nutmegger v8 #1 p90.

NANCY ANN - b 1858 Sandgate, Bennington Co VT d/JAMES FRANKLIN & MARY ELIZABETH (NICHOLS) WILCOX; m CHARLES MONROE; 2 sons; d ca 1943; Ref: Desc of Wm Wilcoxson p171.

NANCY AURELIA - b 18 Jun 1843 Surry, Cheshire Co NH d/GEORGE & AURELIA M (REED) WILCOX; m 1868 JACKSON REED; d Keene, Cheshire Co NH 18 Oct 1920; Ref: Hist of Surry NH pp83,949.

NANCY - d/CHARLES & JULIA ANN (MERRILL) WILCOX of Lyme, Jefferson Co NY; m NORVAL ELIADA DOUGLAS; Ref: Your Ancestors v9 #2 p1128.

NANCY E - b 1845 NY d/JOHN S & ELIZA M (-----) WILCOX of Preston, Chenango Co NY; Ref: 1850 Census Preston NY p462 Dw# 2239.

NANCY L - m 01 Nov 1837 RI WILLIAM DAVIS; Ref: Arnold v7 p603.

NANCY LAY - b 28 Feb 1792 Killingworth, Middlesex Co CT d/NATHAN 2nd & ELIZABETH (ELIOT) WILCOX; m LINUS PIERSON; d 14 Jun 1878; Ref: Wilcox-Meigs p64, Your Ancestors v3 #7&8 p425, Barbour's VR Killingworth v2 p97.

NANCY M - b 02 Feb 1826 Middletown, Middlesex Co CT d/GUSTAVUS VASA & LUCY (LEE) WILCOX; m 09 Oct 1848 GILBERT D JOHNSON of Memphis, Shelby Co TN, merchant who was b 1823 Middletown CT; m 25 Jul 1878 O B SEYMOUR of Hartford, Hartford Co CT; Ref: Wilcox-Meigs p88, Barbour's VR Middletown v4 p124,125.

NANCY M - m 30 Jun 1846 Stonington, New London Co CT PELEG N NOYES; Ref: Barbour's VR Stonington v5 p151.

NANCY M - b 31 Jul 1860 d/JOSEPH EDWIN & EUNICE (GREGG) WILCOX of Newport, Sullivan Co NH; Ref: Your Ancestors v3 #6 p400.

NANCY SMITH - b 24 Mar 1857 Madison, New Haven Co CT d/MANFRED AUGUSTUS & NANCY SOPHRONIA (SMITH) WILCOX; m 12 Dec 1883 WILLIAM POTTER FOWLER who was b 07 Mar 1858 s/HORACE & ELIZA J (HILL) FOWLER; Ref: Wilcox-Meigs p111, Fam of Early Guilford pp493,1215.

NANCY T - m 31 Mar 1860 RI HENRY N MASON; Ref: Arnold v7 p583.

NAOMI - b 1811; d 05 Sep 1880 Evans, Erie Co NY; Ref: West NY Journal v14 #2 p63.

NAOMI - b 1854 PA d/HEZEKIAH R & POLLY (PARKHURST) WILCOX; Res Le Roy, Bradford Co PA; Ref: 1860 Census Bradford Co PA, See Hezekiah.

NATHAN - b 03 Dec 1716 Stonington, New London Co CT s/WILLIAM & DOROTHY GILBERT (PALMER) WILCOX; Ref: Hist of Stonington CT p659, Austin p423,

Barbour's VR Stonington v2 p50, Nutmegger v12 #3 p390, Your Ancestors v3 #1 p290.

NATHAN - b 05 May 1729 Stratford, Fairfield Co CT s/WILLIAM & ESTHER (BRINSMADE) WILCOX; m 16 May 1758/9 MARY BEACH who d 25 Jul 1775; m 15 Apr 1778 Mrs MARY MONROE a widow; ch NATHAN, JAMES, ABIJAH/WILLIAM, BEACH, SARAH, MARY; Ref: Wilcox-Meigs p60, Stratford Gen pp1346,1347, Desc of Wm Wilcoxson p37.

NATHAN - b 29 Mar 1730 Killingworth, Middlesex Co CT s/JOSEPH & REBECCA (HURD) WILCOX; m 14 Jan 1760 THANKFUL STONE; ch NATHAN, JOEL, THANKFUL; Ref: Wilcox-Meigs p61, Barbour's VR Killingworth v2 pp93,189.

NATHAN - b 06 Apr 1730 Stonington, New London Co CT s/WILLIAM & ELIZABETH (BROWN) WILCOX; m 25 Jan 1753 TABITHA PROSSER; ch NATHAN, WILLIAM, TABITHA, LUCY, PRUDENCE, DAVID, JOHN, JARED, DESIAH, MARTHA; Ref: Hist of Stonington pp660,661, ECM v1 p57, Barbour's VR Stonington v2 p48, v3 p190.

NATHAN - b 29 Apr 1730 Middletown, Middlesex Co CT s/FRANCIS & ABIGAIL (GRAVES) WILCOX; Ref: Fiske Card File, Barbour's VR Middletown LR2 p24.

NATHAN - b 30 Mar 1741 Killingworth, Middlesex Co CT s/THOMAS & MARTHA (-----) WILCOX; d 14 Dec 1755; Ref: Desc of Wm Wilcoxson pp20,44, Your Ancestors v4 #11&12 p611, Barbour's VR Killingworth v2 p160.

NATHAN - b 27 Jun 1742 Killingworth, Middlesex Co CT s/NATHANIEL & MINDWELL (WILCOX) WILCOX; Ref: Barbour's VR Killingworth v2 p148.

NATHAN - b 10 Apr 1743 Cromwell, Middlesex Co CT s/FRANCIS & RACHEL (WILCOX) WILCOX; m 18 Apr 1768 LOIS SAGE who was b 22 Aug 1743 & d 29 Nov 1830 d/JONATHAN & HANNAH (GIPSON) SAGE Middletown, Middlesex Co CT; ch RACHEL, LOIS, PERSIS; d 02 Apr 1774; Ref: Gen of CT Fam v3 p281, Your Ancestors v3 #11 & 12 p475, Barbour's VR Middletown v1 p127, v2 p223.

NATHAN - b ca 1744 s/THOMAS & ABIGAIL (OSBORNE) WILCOX Exeter, Washington Co RI; m 15 Jun 1764 Exeter RI MARY POTTER who was b ca 1746 d/JOSEPH POTTER of S Kingston, Washington Co RI; Res Exeter RI in 1774; 1 son & 1 dau; Ref: Arnold v5 pt3 p35,

1774 Census RI, Your Ancestors v3 #11&12 p472, See RIGR v2 #2 p97.

NATHAN - b ca 1747 Richmond, Washington Co RI s/WILLIAM & ELIZABETH (BAKER) WILCOX; m be 1772 REBECCA MOON who was b ca 1752 N Kingston, Washington Co RI d/EBENEZER & ELIZABETH (DAKE/DEAKE) MOON; Res Halifax, Windham Co VT; ch THOMAS, NATHAN Jr, STEPHEN, DAVID, ELSIE, RUTH, REBECCA, ABIGAIL, HANNAH, POLLY, SALLY, SUSAN, OLIVE, AMASA, BENJAMIN, ELIZABETH; d be 1823; Ref: Halifax Wilcox Fam mss, Samuel Gorton Desc v2 p586.

NATHAN - b 15 Nov 1753 Stonington, New London Co CT s/NATHAN & TABITHA (PROSSER) WILCOX; Ref: Hist of Stonington p661, Barbour's VR Stonington v3 p 190.

NATHAN - b 04/05 Nov 1758 Killingworth, Middlesex Co CT s/STEPHEN & MARY (PIERSON) WILCOX; m 15 Oct 1787 ELIZABETH ELIOT who was b 24 Aug 1768/9 & d 15 Jan 1840 Le Roy, Genesee Co NY; ch ELIZA, EUNICE/EMMA, NANCY LAY, NATHAN ELIOT, STEPHEN PIERSON, MABEL MARIAH, CATHARINE ANN, MARY, JARED ELIOT, CLARISSA, EMELINE; Rev War; d 23 Mar 1813 Le Roy NY; bur Ft Hill Cem; Ref: Wilcox-Meigs pp64,65, Tree Talks v12 #1 p25, 1810 Census Genesee Co NY p112, Tombstone Inscr Genesee Co NY p99, Cutter's New England Fam v1 p159, Your Ancestors v3 #3 p321 #7&8 p425, Barbour's VR Killingworth v2 pp38,97,159.

NATHAN - b ca 1760 s/JEHIEL & ABIGAIL (CRAMPTON) WILCOX; m PHOEBE MEIGS who was b 09 Sep 1772 & d 19 Nov 1803 d/ELIAS MEIGS; m ANNA WELD who was b 12 Jul 1764 & d 04 Oct 1843 d/JOSEPH WELD; Res E Guilford, New Haven Co CT; ch PHOEBE, ELIZA ANN; d 11 Feb 1829; Ref: Wilcox-Meigs p74, Fam of Early Guilford pp1210,1211, Desc of Wm Wilcoxson p28.

NATHAN Jr - b 02 Jul 1760 Stratford, Fairfield Co CT s/NATHAN & MARY (BEACH) WILCOX; m MARY MUNSON; Ref: Wilcox-Meigs p60, Stratford Gen p1347, Desc of Wm Wilcoxson p37.

NATHAN 3rd - b 16 Nov 1760 Killingworth, Middlesex Co CT s/NATHAN & THANKFUL (STONE) WILCOX; m 18 Nov 1779 RACHEL BENNET; ch LUTHER, CALVIN, BENJAMIN & DEBORAH twins, JEREMIAH, THANKFUL, PARDON, LYDIA, RACHEL, LUCY MILLER,

NATHAN; Ref: Wilcox-Meigs pp61,79, Barbour's VR Killingworth v2 pp38,83.

NATHAN - b 02 Jan 1763 Stonington, New London Co CT s/SIMEON & EUNICE (-----) WILCOX; Ref: Barbour's VR Stonington v3 p207.

NATHAN - b 07 Feb 1763 s/ELNATHAN & HANNAH (-----) WILCOX; m be 1791 SYLVIA HOPKINS who d 12 Feb 1813 d/EHUD & CHLOE (KING) HOPKINS; m ROXANNA TULLAR; m LEAH (HOLLENBECK) NOBLE d/DIRCK & MARY (-----) HOLLENBECK & w/SILAS NOBLE; Res East Bloomfield, Ontario Co NY & Oakland Co MI; ch LYMAN, CHLOE, EDWIN, JOHN, AMANDA, MARK, CALVIN, NEWTON; d 1844 Salem MI; Ref: Your Ancestors v9 #4 p1177, v10 #1 p1201, Edward D McCarthy, Desc of Wm Wilcoxson p204.

NATHAN - b ca 1768 Westerly, Washington Co RI; d 25 Jun 1845 age 77 Danube, Herkimer Co NY; Ref: Death Notices from Freewill Baptist Pub p365.

NATHAN Jr - b ca 1770 s/NATHAN & REBECCA (MOON) WILCOX; m 07 Feb 1808 Halifax, Windham Co VT VEODOCIA WHITING; Res Ellisburg, Jefferson Co NY; Ref: Halifax Wilcox Fam mss.

NATHAN - b 30 May 1774 Newport, Sullivan Co NH s/JESSE & THANKFUL (STEVENS) WILCOX; m 03 Jun 1798 Lempster, Sullivan Co NH LUCY HURD who was b 27 Apr 1772; Res Orwell, Addison Co VT; ch FANNY, MARIA; d 03 Jun 1825 Orwell VT; Ref: Your Ancestors v3 #4 pp349,350, Wilcox-Meigs p63, NH VR, Nebr & Midwest Gen Rec v8 #1 p23.

NATHAN - b 16 Aug 1774 Exeter, Washington Co RI s/JOB & MARY (GATES) WILCOX; m RUTH TILLINGHAST who was b 1773 & d 01 Oct 1827; d Sep 1827 Pawtucket, Providence Co RI; Ref: Arnold v19 p242, Cutter's Western NY v3 p1436, Your Ancestors v4 #11&12 p609.

NATHAN - b 25 Aug 1776 Chester, Hampden Co MA s/ELISHA & ABIGAIL (RANNEY) WILCOX; m MARY CHENEVARD who was b 13 Nov 1775 & d 08 Nov 1843; ch MARY LUCAS, ABIGAIL RANNEY, CHARLES ELISHA, JULIA MARIE, ELIZABETH PRISCILLA, NATHAN HENRY, EDWARD HORATIO, GEORGE; d 27 Jul 1848; Ref: Your Ancestors v3 #9&10 p451.

NATHAN - b ca 1777 CT; m NANCY ----- who was b ca 1795 CT; Res Pownall, Bennington Co VT; Ref: CT Nutmeggers Who Migrated p264.

NATHAN - b 1777; Res Middletown, Middlesex Co CT; Mechanic; d 24 Feb 1848 age 71; Ref: Barbour's VR Middletown v4 pp68,69.

NATHAN - b 1778 Guilford, New Haven Co CT; Ref: Gen Helper Sep/Oct 1981 p39.

NATHAN - b 01 Jun 1780 Killingworth, Middlesex Co CT s/SIMEON & LUCRETIA (KELSEY) WILCOX; Ref: Wilcox-Meigs p67, Barbour's VR Killingworth v2 p88.

NATHAN - b 29 May 1781 Sturbridge, Worcester Co MA s/DANIEL & HANNAH (-----) WILCOX; Ref: VR of Sturbridge MA p143.

NATHAN - b 03 May 1783 Westerly, Washington Co RI s/DANIEL & PRUDENCE (WILCOX) WILCOX; Ref: Arnold v5 p145, C Douglass Alves Sr.

NATHAN - b 1784 CT; m HANNAH ----- who was b 1790 CT; Res Stonington, New London Co CT; ch BENJAMIN; Ref: 1850 Census Stonington CT Reel 432 #48 p268 Dw# 486.

NATHAN - served in War of 1812 from NY; Res Virgil IL; Ref: Index of Awards from NY p538.

NATHAN - b ca 1799 N Stonington, New London Co CT; m 25 Feb 1821 Voluntown, New London Co CT SYBEL HANCOCK; d 15 Jun 1849 age 50; Ref: Barbour's VR Voluntown v2 p29 v3 p60.

NATHAN - of Middletown, Middlesex Co CT; m 09 Feb 1824 Wallingford, New Haven Co CT POLLY IVES; ch CAROLINE C, EBENEZER C, JOHN T; Ref: Barbour's VR Middletown v4 p30, Wallingford v7-1 p79.

NATHAN - m be 1825 MARIA -----; Res Herkimer Co NY; ch MARY; Ref: NY NSDAR Rec v4 p158.

NATHAN - b 31 Mar 1799 Middletown, Middlesex Co CT s/LUTHER & HULDAH (PULSIFER) WILCOX; Ref: Barbour's VR Middletown v3 p23, See Luther.

NATHAN - b 12 May 1799 Killingworth, Middlesex Co CT s/NATHAN 3rd & RACHEL (BENNET) WILCOX; Ref: Wilcox-Meigs p79, Barbour's VR Killingworth v2 p83.

NATHAN - b 1800 NY; m MERCY L ----- who was b 1807 NY; Res Petersburgh, Rensselaer Co NY; ch

SIMEON, MARINDA, CALVIN, SUSAN E, HARRIET, WARREN; Ref: 1850 Census Petersburgh NY p195 Dw#310.

NATHAN - m 16 Jan or 09 Jun 1802 New Bedford, Bristol Co MA ELIZABETH COREY; Ref: New Bedford MA VR p596, VR of Freetown MA.

NATHAN - b 1802 NY poss s/AMOS & MARY (-----) WILCOX of Orange Co NY; m ca 1824 SUSAN -----; Res Le Roy, Bradford Co PA; ch WILLIAM B, G C, AMANDA, HENRY E, DEBORAH, CELESTIA, ELMER; Ref: 1850 Census Bradford Co PA p68, Your Ancestors v9 #4 p1176.

NATHAN - m 23 Oct 1831 Hopkinton, Washington Co RI SOPHIA CHURCH; ch NATHAN ASA GATES; Ref: Arnold v5 pp28,53, v17 p186.

NATHAN - b 1804 NY; m REBECCA ----- who was b 1802 NY; Res Minisink, Orange Co NY; ch SARAH, WILLIAM, HOWELL, ISAAC, RANSOM, IRA; Ref: 1850 Census Minisink NY p265 Dw# 337.

NATHAN - b 1816 s/THOMAS & LYDIA (DALRYMPLE) WILCOX; d 06 Jan 1837 Hinesburg, Windham Co VT; Ref: VT VR, See Thomas.

NATHAN - b 1820 CT; Res Stonington, New London Co CT; Ref: 1850 Census Stonington CT Reel 432 #48 p320 Dw# 323.

NATHAN - b 1829 s/GEORGE S & ELIZA (-----) WILCOX; Res Stonington, New London Co CT; Sailor; Ref: 1850 Census Stonington CT Reel 432 #48 p236 Dw# 48.

NATHAN - b 1831 NY; Res Paris, Oneida Co NY; Ref: 1850 Census Paris NY p225 Dw# 1643.

NATHAN - b 17 Nov 1833 Charlestown, Washington Co RI s/JOSEPH & HULDAH (SHERMAN) WILCOX; Ref: Arnold v5 pt5 p28, See Joseph.

NATHAN - b 1835 NY s/CHARLES & REBECCA (-----) WILCOX of Lexington, Greene Co NY; Ref: 1850 Census Lexington NY p274 Dw# 50.

NATHAN - b 1837; m SARAH J ----- who was b 12 Mar 1840 & d 10 Jan 1888 Page Co IA; d 15 Sep 1910 Page Co IA bur North Grove Cem; Ref: Hawkeye Heritage v16 #4 p202.

NATHAN - b ca 1840 s/HARRINGTON & CHARITY (RATHBUN) WILCOX; Res Smithville, Chenango Co NY; Ref: Hist of Chenango Co NY p304.

NATHAN - b 1847 PA s/LEVI C WILCOX; Res Le Roy, Bradford Co PA; Ref: 1850 Census Bradford Co PA p66.

NATHAN ASA GATES - b 23 Dec 1832 Hopkinton Washington Co RI s/NATHAN & SOPHIE (CHURCH) WILCOX; Ref: Arnold v5 pt7 p28,53.

NATHAN B - b 27 Aug 1815 s/BEACH & ANNA (BEEBE) WILCOX of Brookfield, Fairfield Co CT; m SUSAN PRITCHARD; ch WILLIAM B, MARY A, NATHAN F, SUSAN E; Ref: Desc of Wm Wilcoxson p37.

NATHAN B - b 17 Oct 1828 Westerly, Washington Co RI s/GEORGE S & ELIZA (-----) WILCOX; Ref: Arnold v5 p145.

NATHAN BENJAMIN - b 1806 NY prob s/ELNATHAN WILCOX; m 23 May 1824 Huntsburg, Geauga Co OH SAMANTHA BROOKS; Res Geauga Co OH, Fayetteville, Washington Co AR; ch ELIZABETH, ------, JAMES HARVEY, HORACE E, SHERMAN, LAURA, ANNA ELIZABETH, DAVID, MARY JANE, ANDREW JACKSON; Shoemaker; Served in Mexican War; d 30 Apr 1873 Clarksville, Red River Co TX; Ref: Dan Williams.

NATHAN BURTON - b 09 Jan 1848 Middlebury [now Akron] Summit Co OH s/DAVID GILBERT & HANNAH (WHITNEY) WILCOX; m 1888 IDA COLE; ch BERTHA, GRACE, HARRY; d 1925; Ref: Gifford Wilcox, Desc of Wm Wilcoxson p128.

NATHAN E - m 17 Sep 1837 Redding, Fairfield Co CT HANNAH W BANKS; Ref: Barbour's VR Redding v1 p142.

NATHAN E - m 12 Dec 1841 Redding, Fairfield Co CT POLLY FAIRCHILD; Ref: Barbour's VR Redding v1 p150.

NATHAN E - b 1819; m 10 Jun 1850 Norwalk, Fairfield Co CT POLLY SELLECK who was b 12 Feb 1812 Delaware Co NY d/JESSE & ELIZABETH (BENNETT) SELLECK; Res Danbury, Fairfield Co CT; Ref: Nutmegger v16 #4 p665.

NATHAN ELIOT - b 09 Apr 1794 Killingworth, Middlesex Co CT s/NATHAN 2nd & ELIZABETH (ELIOT) WILCOX; d 30 Sep 1814; Ref: Wilcox-Meigs p64, Your

Ancestors v3 #7&8 p425, Barbour's VR Killingworth v2 p97.

NATHAN F - b 04 Jun 1847 s/NATHAN B & SUSAN (PRITCHARD) WILCOX; Ref: Desc of Wm Wilcoxson p37.

NATHAN G - Res Voluntown, New London Co CT 1852; ch BETSEY A; Ref: Barbour's VR Stonington v6 p15.

NATHAN HENRY - b 30 Oct 1811 s/NATHAN & MARY (CHENEVARD) WILCOX; d 07 May 1828; Ref: Your Ancestors v3 #9&10 p451.

NATHAN I - b 1838 NY s/HENRY & LOUISA (-----) WILCOX of Parish, Oswego Co NY; Ref: 1850 Census Parish NY p4 Dw# 50.

NATHAN L - b 1779 NY; Res Manlius, Onondaga Co NY; Boatman; Ref: 1850 Census Manlius NY p61 Dw# 924.

NATHAN P - b 10 Apr 1766 Westerly, Washington Co RI s/ISAIAH & SARAH (LEWIS) WILCOX; m 17 Feb 1790 NANCY LEWIS d/HEZEKIAH LEWIS, Res Danube, Herkimer Co NY; ch NATHAN, ISAIAH N, HEZEKIAH LEWIS, AMANDA (WILCOX) SIMMS, NANCY (WILCOX) STAFFORD, BETSY (WILCOX) DAWLEY, NANCY (WILCOX) WINEGAR, RHODA (WILCOX) REED, HOLMES D, LARNER; d 29 Oct 1842 Herkimer Co NY; Ref: Hist of Herkimer Co NY p123, Arnold v5 pp70,145, Will Book G p182 Herkimer Co NY, Deed Book v21 p216, Wilcox-Brown-Medbery p9.

NATHAN PENDLETON - b 03 May 1804 Danube, Herkimer Co NY s/ISAIAH & POLLY (PENDLETON) WILCOX; m 09 Oct 1828 LURANCIE RICHARDSON d/WILLIAM & SARAH (NORTON) RICHARDSON; Res Nunda, Livingston Co NY; Architect & builder of Baptist Church Nunda NY; ch THOMAS JEFFERSON, NATHAN PENDLETON; d 24 Apr 1833 age 29; Widow m WILLIAM WILLIAMS of Smithport, McKean Co PA; Ref: Wilcox-Brown-Medbery pp11,16.

NATHAN PENDLETON - b 16 May 1832 Nunda, Livingston Co NY s/NATHAN PENDLETON & LURANCIE (RICHARDSON) WILCOX; m 06 Oct 1856 Coventry, Chenango Co NY CELESTINE BIRGE d/JOHN & NANCY (LITTLE) BIRGE; Res Olean, Cattaraugus Co NY, Nicholson, Wyoming Co PA; Hardware Merchant; ch WILLIAM ALONZO, CLARA BIRGE, HENRY PENDLETON, ANNA JANET; Ref: Wilcox-Brown-Medbery pp16,23,24.

NATHAN R - m 22 Mar 1835 Killingly, Windham Co CT HANNAH D KINGSBURY; Ref: Barbour's VR Killingly v1 p93.

NATHAN W - b ca 1828 s/PETER C & MARY (YOUKER) WILCOX of Herkimer Co NY; m IRENE FREEMAN; Ref: George Koppers.

NATHANIEL - b 02/29 Aug 1668 Killingworth, Middlesex Co CT s/JOSEPH & ANN (SHEATHER) WILCOX; m 21 Nov 1695 HANNAH LANE who was b 21 Dec 1668 & d 21 Dec 1727 d/ROBERT & SARAH (PICKETT) LANE; ch SARAH, THOMAS, NATHANIEL, DANIEL, JONATHAN; d 13 Jun 1712/3 Killingworth CT; Ref: Nutmegger v11 #2 p209, Wilcox-Meigs pp30,31, Desc of Wm Wilcoxson pp12,28,36, Bogue Fam p394, Cutter's Northern NY v2 p656, Cutter's New England Fam v1 p159, Your Ancestors v4 #11&12 p611, Barbour's VR Killingworth v1 p81, Torrey's Marriage Rec microfilm.

NATHANIEL - b 19 Jul 1700 Killingworth, Middlesex Co CT s/NATHANIEL & HANNAH (LANE) WILCOX; m 23 Oct 1733 MINDWELL WILCOX who was b 02 Jan 1713/14 d/JOHN WILCOX; ch MINDWELL, EBENEZER, NATHANIEL, JOHN, MABEL, JOEL, JERUSHA; d 10 Nov 1762; Ref: Nutmegger v11 #3 p390, Wilcox-Meigs p44, Your Ancestors v4 #11&12 p611, Barbour's VR Killingworth v2 pp146,148, Desc of Wm Wilcoxson p 20.

NATHANIEL - b 01 Dec 1702 Twin with DANIEL Killingworth, Middlesex Co CT; Ref: Desc of Wm Wilcoxson p36.

NATHANIEL - b 05 Sep 1719 Simsbury, Hartford Co CT Twin with MERCY s/JOSEPH & ABIGAIL (THRALL) WILCOX; m 23 Dec 1748 RACHEL MOSES who d 1807; ch NATHANIEL, JOSEPH, RACHEL, SETH, SARAH, TEMPERANCE; d 1791; Ref: Wilcox-Meigs p32, Nutmegger v10 #2 p214, Early Settlers of W Simsbury pp127,128, Your Ancestors v13 #3 p1567, Desc of Wm Wilcoxson p15.

NATHANIEL 2nd - m 24 Nov 1748 Goshen, Litchfield Co CT ABIGAIL HURLBUTT; ch RUTH,JONAH, ABNER, JESSE; Ref: Barbour's VR Goshen v1 pp259,260,271,273.

NATHANIEL - b 28 Sep 1723 Middletown, Middlesex Co CT s/ISRAEL & MARY (NORTH) WILCOX; Ref: Nutmegger v4 #3 p331, Barbour's VR Middletown LR2 p11.

NATHANIEL - b 27 Jun 1742 Killingworth, Middlesex Co CT s/NATHANIEL & MINDWELL (WILCOX) WILCOX; d 14 Dec 1755 or in Colonial Wars 1762; Ref: Wilcox-Meigs p44, Desc of Wm Wilcoxson p20, Barbour's VR Killingworth v2 p70..

NATHANIEL - b af 1743 W Simsbury, Hartford Co CT s/NATHANIEL & RACHEL (MOSES) WILCOX; d 1776 Rev War; Ref: Early Settlers of Simsbury CT p128, Fiske Card File.

NATHANIEL - int to marry 08 Oct 1787 Spencer, Worcester Co MA BETSEY PEASE; Res Brookfield, Worcester Co MA; Ref: Fiske Card File.

NATHANIEL - b 06 Jan 1759 Killingworth, Middlesex Co CT s/HIEL & DEBORAH (GILLETT) WILCOX; m JOANNA McGONIGLE who was b 17 Nov 1771 & d 23 Nov 1836; (Your Ancestors gives wife as JOANNA MALLORY who was b 17 Nov 1771 & d 23 Nov 1836 d/OLIVER & MARGARET (-----) MALLORY); Res Hillsdale, Columbia Co NY; ch HENRY, OLIVER, JOSEPH, MARGARET, JEHIEL, ANNA, JOHN, SARAH, THOMAS; Rev War; d 14 Feb 1837 Lexington, Greene Co NY; Ref: Desc of Wm Wilcoxson p59, Wilcox-Meigs pp65,83,84, Your Ancestors v4 #11&12 p612.

NATHANIEL - b 10 Aug 1764 Berlin, Hartford Co CT s/DANIEL Jr & SUSANNAH (PORTER) WILCOX; Ref: Hist of Berlin CT p89.

NATHANIEL - b 25 Nov 1769 Killingworth, Middlesex Co CT or Newport, Sullivan Co NH s/JESSE & THANKFUL (STEVENS) WILCOX; d 21 Jun 1805 Killingworth CT; Ref: Wilcox-Meigs p63, Nebr & Midwest Gen Rec v8 #1 pp22,23.

NATHANIEL - b be 1775; Res Conway, Franklin Co MA; Ref: 1820 Census Franklin Co MA p8.

NATHANIEL - m 26 Nov 1788 Lanesborough, Berkshire Co MA ABIGAIL HURLBUT; Ref: Fiske Card File.

NATHANIEL - Int to marry 26 Sep 1801 Ashfield, Franklin Co MA EASTER WALKER; Res Charlemont, Franklin Co MA; Ref: Fiske Card File.

NATHANIEL - b 18 Mar 1781; d 12 Aug 1823 Berkshire, Tioga Co NY; bur Jenkintown Cem; Ref: Cem Records of Tioga Co NY.

NATHANIEL - d 13 Nov 1782 Killingworth, Middlesex Co CT; Ref: Barbour's VR Killingworth v2 p71.

NATHANIEL - b 1783 RI; m ca 1802 Chenango Co NY LUCY LEWIS who was b 1781 RI d/SAMUEL LEWIS Jr; Res Voluntown, New London Co CT & Preston, Chenango Co NY; ch REBECCA, NATHANIEL, GATES, SALLY, ISAAC, ELI, SAMUEL; Ref: Hist of Chenango Co NY p261, Fiske Card File, 1850 Census Preston Chenango Co NY.

NATHANIEL - b 03 Nov 1783 Killingworth, Middlesex Co CT s/EBENEZER & MARY (NETTLETON) WILCOX; m 07 Apr 1813 FANNY MANN; ch JOHN, FREDERIC WILLIAM, MARY ANN, WILLIAM, NATHANIEL HENDERSON; Ref: Desc of Wm Wilcoxson p59, Wilcox-Meigs pp66,84, Barbour's VR Killingworth v2 pp43,81,103.

NATHANIEL - b 23 Apr 1789 Halifax, Windham Co VT s/STEPHEN & ELINOR (EWING) WILCOX; m 07 Dec 1809 BETSEY BOLSTER; ch JOEL; Ref: VT VR, Halifax Wilcox Fam mss.

NATHANIEL - m be 1848 FANNY H -----; Res Oxford, Chenango Co NY; ch HARRIETT ELIZA; Ref: VR of Chenango Co NY p227.

NATHANIEL - b 09 Jun 1835; d 12 Oct 1861 Tioga Co NY; Ref: Tioga County Cemeteries.

NATHANIEL B - 1833 purchased lots 45 & 46 Twnshp 1 Range 15 in Chautauqua Co NY; Ref: Chautauqua Co Deed Book v13 pp94,95.

NATHANIEL B - b 1823 W Greenwich, Kent Co RI; m 02 Sep 1849 Voluntown, New London Co CT JULIA PALMER who was b 1829 Exeter, Washington Co RI; Res Griswold, New London Co CT; Ref: 1850 Census Griswold CT Reel 432 #49 p31 Dw# 129, Barbour's VR Voluntown v3 p2.

NATHANIEL BROWN - s/ROBERT & DEBORAH (BROWN) WILCOX; m HANNAH AUGUSTA GARDNER: Ref: Your Ancestors v11 #3 p1352.

NATHANIEL GREEN - b ca 1805 s/BENAJAH HUMPHREY & EUNICE (FANCHER) WILCOX of Simsbury, Hartford Co CT; Ref: Your Ancestors v12 #1 p1407.

NATHANIEL HENDERSON - b 01 Mar 1825 Killingworth, Middlesex Co CT s/NATHANIEL & FANNY

(MANN) WILCOX; Ref: Wilcox-Meigs p84, Barbour's VR Killingworth v2 p103.

NATHANIEL PORTER - b 10 Aug 1764 Middletown, Middlesex Co CT s/DANIEL & SUSANNAH (PORTER) WILCOX; d 12 Mar 1765; Ref: Barbour's VR Middletown v2 p150.

NELLIE - d/HENRY & SARAH (BOWERS/POWERS) WILCOX; Res Eden, Erie Co NY; grndau of JEHIEL & CHLOE (NICHOLS) WILCOX; Ref: Eden Town Historian.

NELLIE - b 20 Jul 1864 d/AUSTIN WILCOX; Ref: CT Bible Rec v15 p254.

NELLIE - d/LUTHER H & JEWELL (TRIPP) WILCOX; Res Springwater, Livingston Co NY; Ref: Your Ancestors v10 #2 p1224.

NELLIE - b 1874 MI d/GEORGE & HARRIET ELVIRA (BACON) WILCOX; m 24 May 1892 Standish, Arenac Co MI WILLIAM ARTHUR McCLELLAN who was b 1871 & d 02 Feb 1934; Res Waters MI; d 28 Nov 1943; Ref: LDS Record of Edith Rose Smith.

NELLIE - b 10 Mar 1889 Danbury, Fairfield Co CT d/JAMES AUGUSTUS & LILLIAN (COWEN) WILCOX; m ----- BULLARD d 12 Dec 1918; Ref: Desc of Wm Wilcoxson p259.

NELLIE A - b 12 Dec 1874 De Witt, Onondaga Co NY d/ORLANDO KING & MARY (WALTER) WILCOX; m FRANK ABBOTT; Ref: Erwin W Fellows.

NELLIE CASE - b 27 Apr 1876 Cambridge, Middlesex Co MA d/JONATHAN BRENTON SHAW & FANNY ELLEN (IRONS) WILCOX; m ARTHUR STOCKWELL; ch DOROTHY; Ref: Desc of Robert Burrows v2 p1482.

NELLIE H - b 11 Dec 1851 Brooklyn NY d/JAMES & CLARISSA H (GRISWOLD) WILCOX; d 21 Nov 1857; Ref: Wilcox-Meigs p105.

NELLIE L - d/ELIJAH W & LYDIA (STRAIGHT) WILCOX of Winfield, Herkimer Co NY; m JOHN WHOLAHAN or J J WHITAKER; Ref: Your Ancestors v3 #6 p402, Desc of Wm Wilcoxson p240.

NELLIE M - b 24 Jul 1853 Peterboro, Hillsboro Co NH d/GEORGE & MARY ANN (MORRISON) WILCOX; Res Antrim, Hillsboro Co NH; Ref: Hist of Hancock NH v2 p1023.

NELLIE MARGARET - b 20 May 1864 MI d/FREDERICK WILLIAM & MARGARET (BOGARDUS) WILCOX; d 01 Dec 1871 Clinton, Middlesex Co CT; Ref: Your Ancestors v2 p257.

NELLIE THORNE - b 15 Oct 1876 Heyworth, McLean Co IL d/CHAUNCEY HILL & HESTER ANN (FRYE) WILCOX; m 20 Feb 1898 Heyworth IL ROY M HOYT who was b 26 Jul 1874 Lincoln, Lancaster Co NE & d 21 May 1942 Clinton, Iroquois Co IL s/ORRIN ACEL & EUNICE A (COBB) HOYT; Res Clinton IL; ch CLARA MARGUERITE, REBA JOSEPHINE, MILDRED VERNE, MABEL HESTER, HUBERT EARL, HELEN ELIZABETH; d 17 Oct 1973 La Mesa, San Diego Co CA; Ref: Carolin C Janzen.

NELSON - b 27 Aug 1788 Simsbury, Hartford Co CT s/ROGER & ELIZABETH (CASE) WILCOX; Ref: Wilcox-Meigs p85.

NELSON - b 05 Jul 1815 s/EBENEZER & JAEL (HANCHETT) WILCOX of Canada; d in infancy; Ref: Desc of Wm Wilcoxson p124.

NELSON - b 1816 s/MATTHEW & SUSANNA (HOYT) WILCOX; m POLLY BATES; ch AGNES, OPHELIA S, AMANDA M, ANTOINETTE, MARIA D; Ref: Desc of Wm Wilcoxson p37.

NELSON - of Norwalk, Fairfield Co CT; m 16 Sep 1833 Wilton, Fairfield Co CT POLLY -----; Ref: Barbour's VR Wilton v1 p15.

NELSON - b 1817 NY s/AARON & ELECTA (-----) WILCOX of Bainbridge, Chenango Co NY; Ref: 1850 Census Chenango Co NY.

NELSON - s/LODOWICK & FANNY (COTTRELL) WILCOX; m 26 Sep 1852 Stonington, New London Co CT HARRIET H NOYES who was b 02 Feb 1824 & d 23 Jan 1913; ch FRANCES MARIA, JOHN CALVIN, ASA CLINTON, PHEBE ELLEN; Ref: Denison Gen p461, Barbour's VR Stonington v6 p16.

NELSON - b 1825 NY s/----- & Climena (-----) WILCOX; m ABIGAIL ----- who was b 1813 NY; Res Hamilton, Madison Co NY; ch CHARLES E, CLARISSA E; Ref: 1850 Census Hamilton NY p102 Dw# 1740.

NELSON - b 1828 NY; Res Paris, Oneida Co NY; Ref: 1850 Census Paris NY p226 Dw# 1643.

NELSON - m 12 Feb 1851 Lorain Co OH SUSAN C WALKER; Ref: Marriages Lorain Co OH p119.

NELSON - m 29 May 1869 Goodhue Co MN ROXANA FAIRCHILD; Ref: Red Wing MN Argus 20 Jan 1870 issue p4 col 3.

NELSON - b 1835 NY; m MATILDA ----- who was b 1839 NY; Res Rome, Oneida Co NY; Ref: 1860 Census Oneida Co NY p21 Dw# 138.

NELSON - b 1844 NY s/ASHER & LUCY (-----) WILCOX of Truxton, Cortland Co NY; Ref: 1850 Census Truxton NY p153 Dw# 387.

NELSON - b 09 Mar 1857 prob Jackson Co IA s/ABNER THORP & LYDIA A (CHANDLER) WILCOX; m 1879 MARY L MILLER; Res Chadron, Dawes Co NE; ch NOBLE E, BERT, BESSIE C; d 24 Feb 1919; Ref: Desc of Wm Wilcoxson p125.

NELSON - m be 1882 MARY LANG; Res Eagle Grove, Wright Co IA; ch BERT ABNER; Ref: Hawkeye Heritage v113 #1 p15.

NELSON B - b 1841 NY s/JOHN & FIDELIA (-----) WILCOX of Lafayette, Onondaga Co NY; Ref: 1850 Census Lafayette NY p216 Dw# 375.

NELSON CHAPMAN - b 01 Jan 1836 Whitestown, Oneida Co NY s/REUBEN Jr & LOUISA (CHAPMAN) WILCOX; Res Eau Claire, Eau Claire Co WI 1856; m 14 Mar 1861 Gerry, Chautauqua Co NY FRANCES A BLANCHARD who was b Gerry NY 1837 & d 13 May 1868 Eau Claire WI d/MOULTON BLANCHARD; m 28 June 1870 Mrs ANGELINE (TEWKESBURY) BELLINGER; ch ROY P, NELSON J, THORP J; d 21 Mar 1906; Ref: Hist of Eau Claire Co WI pp899,900, Hist of Chippewa Valley WI p560, Your Ancestors v4 #3&4 p523, Chapman Gen p176, 19th Cent Death Notices Reported in Fredonia Censor p596.

NELSON F - b 1825 CT s/LYMAN & ELIZABETH (WHEELER) WILCOX; Res Stonington, New London Co CT; Ref: 1850 Census Stonington CT Reel 432 #48 p309 Dw# 166.

NELSON GRAVES - b 28 Nov 1853 s/JULIUS & SARAH ANN (NICHOLS) WILCOX; d Feb 1856; Ref: Gen of CT Fam v1 p245.

NELSON GRAVES - b 06 May 1856 s/JULIUS & SARAH ANN (NICHOLS) WILCOX; d 15 Jul 1856; Ref: Gen of CT Fam v1 p245.

NELSON J - b 1803 s/Dr JEREMIAH & SUSANNAH (WILCOX) WILCOX m 07 Jun 1829 Foster, Providence Co RI OLIVE HERRINGTON d/EPHRAIM HERRINGTON; Ref: Arnold v3 p31, Your Ancestors v4 #3&4 p520.

NELSON J - b 27 Jan 1875 Eau Claire, Eau Claire Co WI s/NELSON CHAPMAN & ANGELINE (TEWKESBURY) WILCOX; Ref: Hist of Eau Claire Co WI p900.

NELSON OTIS - b 06 Aug 1847 Bennington, Bennington Co VT s/Dr SILAS & SUSAN/SUSANNAH (EDSON) WILCOX; m FANNY MARIA NOBLE who was b 10 Jul 1867 Bennington VT d/WILLIAM BOLTWOOD & ANN (JACKSON) NOBLE; ch HENRY SILAS, WILLIE NOBLE, HATTIE EDSON; Ref: Gen of Thomas Noble p541, Your Ancestors v12 #4 p1490.

NELSON OZIAL - b 1826 NY s/OZIAL Jr & SYLVIA (STEVENS) WILCOX; Res Georgetown twnshp, Madison Co NY; Ref: Desc of Wm Wilcoxson p169, 1850 Census Georgetown NY p387 Dw# 208.

NELSON PLIMPTON - b 31 Jul 1857 Stamford, Bennington Co VT; m 23 Dec 1886 LUCY BELLE POLAND; ch ESTELLA MAUDE, NELLIE PEARL, ANNA ALICE, HAZEL RAE, MATTIE MAY, LENA MILDRED, CLARENCE ERWIN, ELSIE LOU; d 16 Mar 1920; Ref: Halifax VT Wilcox Fam mss.

NETTIE - m 05 Nov 1875 BELUS CALKINS Jr; Res Varysburgh, Wyoming Co NY; Ref: Hist of Wyoming Co NY p269.

NEWCOMB - m MIRANDA STEARNS; Res Naples, Ontario Co NY; ch LORING P; Ref: Fiske Card File.

NEWCOMB - b 1796 s/ISAAC & NANCY (NEWCOMB) WILCOX; m 18 Nov 1815 Pawling, Dutchess Co NY HANNAH SPRAGUE; ch NANCY, CORNELIA, ISAAC, GILBERT A, BENONI, NEWCOMB, JOHN, CHARLES; Ref: Your Ancestors v9 #2 p1125 #3 p1151.

NEWEL - m POLLY HUTCHINSON who was b 22 Dec 1790 & d 29 Aug 1884 bur Lot 327 Old Riverside Cem Onondaga Co NY; ch CHARLES & prob others; Ref: Vorhees Records v1 p39,40.

NEWEL - b ca 1800 NY; m MARTHA -----; Res Granby, Oswego Co NY; ch MARTHA, GEORGE, PHILURA; Ref: 1850 Census Granby NY p9 Dw# 125.

NEWELL - b 1825 NY s/----- & BETSEY (-----) WILCOX; Res Streetsborough, Portage Co OH; Ref: 1850 Census Streetsborough OH p37 Dw# 119.

NEWELL D - b 15 May 1819 Deerfield Portage Co OH s/WILLIAM & LUCINDA (GIBBS) WILCOX; m 16 Dec 1841 AMELIA N HALL of Palmyra, Portage Co OH who was b 1817; Res Edinburgh, Portage Co OH; ch WILLIAM WALLACE; d 01 Mar 1881; Ref: Hist of Portage Co OH p635, 1850 Census Edinburgh OH p228, Desc of Wm Wilcoxson p245.

NEWMAN - b 1837 NY s/CHARLES & REBECCA (-----) WILCOX of Lexington, Greene Co NY; Ref: 1850 Census Lexington NY p274 Dw# 50.

NEWTON - b 22 Dec 1794 s/DANIEL & ESTHER (MERRITT) WILCOX; d Simsbury, Hartford Co CT 28 Sep 1841; Ref: Rev Allen McLean Rec p12, Your Ancestors v11 #3 p1353, CT Bible Rec v11 p551.

NEWTON - b 20 Feb 1812 W Winfield, Herkimer Co NY s/JOHN & SYBIL (GUILD) WILCOX; m EMILY JONES; Ref: Your Ancestors v3 #4 p352.

NEWTON PELEG - b 27 May 1844 Litchfield, Herkimer Co NY s/RODNEY & EMILY (DAVIS) WILCOX; m 12 Nov 1866 Avilla, Noble Co IN MARY E HILL; ch GLEN AVERY, JOSEPH E, MABEL H, CHARLES N; d 29 Jul 1902; Ref: Your Ancestors v14 #1 p1617.

NICHOLAS - b England 1614; came to St Christophers aboard the ship *Matthew* 25 May 1635; Ref: NEH&GR v14 p353.

NINA - b 1889 NY d/GEORGE S & MARY E (BENTON) WILCOX of Alma, Allegany Co NY; Ref: Carol A Cox.

NINA IRENE - b 16 May 1894 Bennington Co VT d/WILLIE OZIAL & ADDIE (MOREY) WILCOX; m WILLIAM CRANDALL; 2 ch; Ref: Desc of Wm Wilcoxson p172.

NOAH - b 29 Jul 1746 Stonington, New London Co CT s/WILLIAM & THANKFUL (-----) WILCOX; Ref: Barbour's VR Stonington v3 p203.

NOAH - b 1756; Res Washington Co RI; d af 1833; Ref: Arnold v12 p371.

NOAH - m 15 Nov 1789 of Richmond, Washington Co RI MARTHA ALBRO of N Kingston, Washington Co RI; ch JOHN, ALICE, ELIZABETH, HANNAH, NOAH; Ref: Arnold v5 pt6 p21, Your Ancestors v3 #11&12 p472.

NOAH - b 11 Jun 1788 Stratford, Fairfield Co CT s/GIDEON & ANNA (HANFORD) WILCOX; m ESTHER HOYT; Res Norwalk, Fairfield Co CT; Ref: Wilcox-Meigs p79, Stratford Gen p1347, Desc of Wm Wilcoxson p36.

NOAH - b 1789 N Stonington, New London Co CT s/DANIEL & HANNAH (WILBUR) WILCOX; JOSHUA BABCOCK appointed guardian; Ref: Will of Daniel Wilcox probated 1803.

NOAH - m 1801 Sunderland, Bennington Co VT ----- MILES; Ref: New England Exodus v1 #1 p15.

NOAH - of Colchester, Chittenden Co VT; Served in War of 1812; Ref: VT Roster War of 1812 p455.

NOAH - b 19 Jun 1816 Richmond, Washington Co RI s/NOAH & MARTHA (ALBRO) WILCOX; m 1838 MARY SHERMAN d/SAMUEL W SHERMAN; ch MARY ANN, NOAH SAMUEL, GEORGE W, SARAH E, JOHN T; d 01 Apr 1883; Ref: Your Ancestors v3 #11&12 p472 v4 #1&2 p495.

NOAH - b 1829; m Aug 1864 Ceres, Allegany Co NY LYDIA A BISSELL who was b 1846; Ref: West NY Journal v3 #4 p168.

NOAH - b 10 Feb 1837 Griswold, New London Co CT s/THOMAS & SALOME (-----) WILCOX; Ref: 1850 Census Griswold CT Reel 432 #49 p31 Dw# 131, Barbour's VR Griswold v1 p250.

NOAH POST - of Haddam, Middlesex Co CT s/JOHN & RACHEL FLORILLA (POST) WILCOX; m 01 May 1850 Haddam CT SARAH/SALLY MARIA WILCOX; ch CHARLES C; Ref: Your Ancestors v4 #1&2 p497, Desc of Wm Wilcoxson p130, Barbour's VR Haddam v1 p61.

NOAH SAMUEL - b Feb 1844 s/NOAH & MARY (SHERMAN) WILCOX; d 1932; Ref: Your Ancestors v4 #1&2 p495.

NOBLE - b 08 Apr 1803 Granville, Hampden Co MA s/ELEAZER CURTIS & CYNTHIA (NOBLE) WILCOX; m 18 Feb 1828 LOIS CLARK who was b 16 Mar 1799 & d 23 Aug 1851 d/OLIVER & EUNICE (WEEKES) CLARK & w/OLIVER MARKHAM; m 01 Feb 1852 LOIS SHATTUCK; Res Stittville, Oneida Co NY; d 10 Oct 1882; Ref: A Wilcox Book p19, Gen of Thomas Noble p447, Geo Weekes Gen p140.

NOBLE - b 21 Mar 1855 s/ABNER THORP & LYDIA A (CHANDLER) WILCOX of Jackson Co IA; d 1937 near

Marquette, Clayton Co IA; Desc of Wm Wilcoxson p125.

NOBLE EDMUND - b 25/26 Sep 1822 Manlius, Onondaga Co NY s/DAVID & ASENETH (NOBLE) WILCOX; m 13 Mar 1845 ANNA M MABIE; Res Kirkville, Onondaga Co NY; ch WILLIAM W, DARWIN D; d 13 Apr 1901 bur Kirksville Cem; Ref: Hist of Onondaga Co NY p421, Gen of Thomas Noble p615, Your Ancestors v3 #11&12 p474, Gifford Wilcox, Desc of Wm Wilcox pp126,129, 1850 Census Manlius NY p28 Dw# 417.

NOLAN PREBLE - b 1865 Wood Island, N B Canada s/ABEL & HANNAH AMELIA (GREEN) WILCOX; drowned 27 Jun 1869; Ref: Desc of Charles Dyer Wilcox p24.

NORA - b 31 Oct 1865 Clinton, Middlesex Co CT d/EDWARD AUGUSTUS & EMMA A (BAILEY) WILCOX; Ref: Your Ancestors v2 p257.

NORA E - b 07 Jan 1871 d/THOMAS LITTLE & MARY M (SMITH) WILCOX; d in infancy; Ref: Desc of Wm Wilcoxson p126.

NORMAN/NORMOND - b 08 Mar 1775 Simsbury, Hartford Co CT s/SEDOTIA & MERCY (HUMPHREY) WILCOX; m 16 Mar 1797 Barkhamsted, Litchfield Co CT REBECCA CHASE; Res West Granville, Hampden Co MA; ch NORMAN, GAMALIEL, HORACE, MARY A; Ref: Nutmegger v12 #1 p248, v13 #2 p288, Your Ancestors v11 #4 pp1379,1380.

NORMAN - b 11 Apr 1798 Middletown, Middlesex_Co CT s/BENJAMIN & RACHEL (WILCOX) WILCOX; Ref: Barbour's VR Middletown v3 p88.

NORMAN - b 30 Aug 1802 s/ALLYN & CHLOE (WOODFORD) WILCOX; d 24 Dec 1802; Ref: CT Bible Rec v15 pp254,255.

NORMAN - b ca 1812 CT s/NORMAN & REBECCA (CHASE) WILCOX; m EUNICE MORSE; d 03 Apr 1896 OH; Ref: Nutmegger v13 #2 p288.

NORMAN - m 25 Dec 1823 Middletown, Middlesex Co CT OLIVE G WILCOX; ch CORNELIA MARIA; Ref: Barbour's VR Middletown; v3 pp145,148.

NORMAN - b 27 Apr 1816 s/RALPH & BETSEY (NOONEY) WILCOX; d 30 Mar 1817; Ref: Your Ancestors v3 #9&10 p452.

NORMAN - b 1836 NY s/AMOS & SOPHRONIA (HATFIELD) WILCOX of Wethersfield, Wyoming Co NY; Ref: Your Ancestors v14 #2 p1643, 1850 Census Wethersfield NY p86 Dw# 1269.

NORMAN - b 1839 NY s/CHARLES & REBECCA (-----) WILCOX of Lexington, Greene Co NY; Ref: 1850 Census Lexington NY p274 Dw# 50.

NORMAN H - b 1818; m CAROLINE A -----; m CANDICE -----; Res Montua, Portage Co OH; ch by 1st wife WALLACE W; ch by 2nd wife EDWIN; Ref: 1850 Census Montua OH p57 Dw# 68, OH Cem Records p57.

NORMAN M - b 1809 s/SOLOMON & LYDIA (PARDEE) WILCOX; m 1828 ANNA M NEWTON; ch EDWIN F; d 1855; Ref: Your Ancestors v3 #7&8 pp427,428.

NORRIS - s/JACOB & RACHEL (PORTER) WILCOX of Berlin, Hartford Co CT; m HARRIET HART d/JESSE HART; ch KATHERINE; Ref: Hist of Berlin p94, Barbour's VR Berlin v1 p6.

NORTH - b 15 Mar 1855 s/EBON NORTH & MARIE LOUISE (COLE) WILCOX; m Dec 1885 San Francisco, CA ALICE L PRESCOTT; ch MARION NORTH; d 17 Nov 1923 Ann Arbor, Washtenaw Co MI; Ref: Desc of Wm Wilcoxson p260.

NORTON - b 1843 Smyrna NY; d 07 Feb 1847 Smyrna, Chenango Co NY; Ref: VR of Chenango Co NY p321.

NOYES - b Nov 1812 Bergen, Genesee Co NY s/PITMAN & ELIZABETH (WILCOX) WILCOX; d Feb 1819; Ref: Fam of Early Guilford p1202.

--- O ---

O G - m E -----; Res Oswego, Oswego Co NY; ch WILLIAM HENRY, JOHN, JOSIAH; Ref: Tree Talks v10 #3 p176.

O R - b 1791-1800; Res Ripley, Chautauqua Co NY; 3 sons & 4 daus; Ref: 1840 Census Chautauqua Co NY.

O R - b 1813 PA; m LOUISE ----- who was b 1823 NY; Res Greene, Chenango Co NY; Butcher; ch ALVAH; Ref: 1850 Census Greene NY p328 Dw# 223.

OBADIAH - b ca 1648 Stratford, Fairfield Co CT s/WILLIAM & MARGARET (-----) WILCOX; m ca 1668 MARY GRISWOLD who was b 28 Jan 1650 Wethersfield, Hartford Co CT & d 07 Aug 1670 d/MICHAEL & ANNE (-----) GRISWOLD; m by 1676 LYDIA ALLING who was b 26 Dec 1656 New Haven, New Haven Co CT d/JOHN & ELLEN (BRADLEY) ALLING; m by 1690 SILENCE MANSFIELD who was b 24 Oct 1664 New Haven CT d/JOSEPH & MARY (-----) MANSFIELD & who later m GEORGE CHATFIELD; Res Killingworth, Middlesex Co & E Guilford, New Haven Co CT; ch by 2nd wife MARY, LYDIA, OBADIAH, EBENEZER; ch by 3rd wife TIMOTHY, JOHN, JOSEPH, MINDWELL, SILENCE, EPHRAIM, JANNA, JEMIMA, THANKFUL; d 1713; Will probated 01 Nov 1714; Ref: Wilcox-Meigs pp25,26, Desc of Wm Wilcoxson p8, Bogue Fam p394, Stratford Gen p1346, Cutter's New England Fam v1 p159, Fam of Early Guilford p1208, New Haven Fam v1 p5, Torrey's Marriage Rec microfilm. Hist of Surry NH pp943,944.

OBADIAH - b 14 Dec 1679 E Guilford, New Haven Co CT s/OBADIAH & LYDIA (ALLING) WILCOX; d be 1689; Ref: Wilcox-Meigs p26, Desc of Wm Wilcoxson p8, Fam of Early Guilford p1208.

OBADIAH - b 15 Apr 1719 E Guilford, New Haven Co CT s/JOHN & DEBORAH (PARMELEE) WILCOX; m 12 Oct 1743 Hebron, Tolland Co CT LYDIA WILCOX who was b 12 Apr 1716/19 Hebron CT & d 16 Jan 1796 d/EBENEZER WILCOX; Res Gilsum, Cheshire Co NH; ch LYDIA, OBADIAH, ELEAZER, DEBORAH; d 26 Aug 1771; Ref: Wilcox-Meigs p50, Desc of Wm Wilcoxson pp15,25,26, CT Nutmeggers Who Migrated p264, Fam of Early Guilford pp1208,1209, Barbour's VR Guilford v2 pp14,58,80,102, Hist of Surry NH pp945,946.

OBADIAH - b 12 Jul 1724 Hebron, Tolland Co CT s/EBENEZER & MARTHA (GAYLORD) WILCOX; m 26 Feb 1749/50 SARAH TALCOTT who was b 03 Mar 1734/5 & d 21 Sep 1809 Surry, Cheshire NH d/Capt JOHN & LUCY (BURNHAM) TALCOTT; ch OBADIAH, JOHN, LUCY, ASA, SARAH, ANNE, MARTHA, PHOEBE, MARY LOUISA/LOVISA, GAYLORD, EUNICE, LYDIA, PRUDENCE, LUCINDA; d 20 Feb 1810 Surry NH; Ref: Wilcox-Meigs p50, CT VR v1 pp53,77, CT Nutmeggers Who Migrated p264, Barbour's VR Hebron v1 pp53,77, v2 pp254,255,257, Desc of Wm Wilcoxson pp15,25, Hist of Surry NH pp76,944,945.

OBADIAH - b 25 Jan 1746/47 Guilford, New Haven Co CT s/OBADIAH & LYDIA (WILCOX) WILCOX; Ref:

Wilcox-Meigs p51, Desc of Wm Wilcoxson p26, Fam of Early Guilford p1209, Barbour's VR Guilford v2 p80.

OBADIAH - b 02 Jan 1750/1 s/OBADIAH & SARAH (TALCOTT) WILCOX; m 03 Sep 1774 Surry, Cheshire Co NH HANNAH MERRIAM who later m JACOB HAYWARD Jr of Acworth, Sullivan Co NH & d 24 Nov 1839 d/Lt JOHN MERRIAM; Res Surry NH; ch OBADIAH, MARY JOHN; Rev War; d 21 Nov 1797; Ref: Nutmegger v10 #3, Wilcox-Meigs p50, Barbour's VR Hebron v1 p57, Desc of Wm Wilcoxson p25, Hist of Surry NH p946.

OBADIAH - b 06 Jan 1776 Surry, Cheshire Co NH s/OBADIAH & HANNAH (MERRIAM) WILCOX; m be 1800 MARGARET BAXTER; ch PHILO; Ref: Hist of Surry NH p946.

OBADIAH - b 23 Dec 1781 Torrington, Litchfield Co CT s/ASAHEL & MARY (COE) WILCOX; Ref: Desc of Wm Wilcoxson p27, Barbour's VR Torrington v1 p107.

OBADIAH - b 1775-1784 s/EPHRAIM & DIADAMA (FRENCH) WILCOX; m 04 Dec 1806 Rockingham, Windham Co VT MARY (POLLY) MILLER; Res Barton, Orleans Co & Westminster, Windham Co VT; 1 son in 1800; d 1806; Ref: Your Ancestors v4 #5&6 p545, 1800 Census Orleans Co VT p101, NEH&GR v54 p258, Fiske Card File.

OBADIAH W - of Hartland, Hartford Co CT; m 15 Sep 1840 E Granby, Hartford Co CT MARY ANN COMBS/COWLES; Res Hartford, Hartford Co CT & Springfield, Hampden Co MA; Ref: Cong Church Records E Granby CT, Barbour's VR Granby v1 p33.

OCTAVIA A - b 1857 d/WILLIAM & AVINA (BARKER) WILCOX; d 1875; Ref: Jane Smith.

OCTAVUS S - b 30 Mar 1864 s/CHARLES & ESTHER (CEASE) WILCOX; m 12 May 1891 MAMIE E YOUNG; Res Nanticoke, Luzerne Co PA; Ref: Your Ancestors v9 #3 p1151.

OLGA MARY - m 07 Nov 1936 Stockbridge, Berkshire Co MA RALPH M HARDEN who was b Mar 24 1880 Gardner, Kennebec Co ME; Ref: Wilcox Excerpts v1 p4.

OLIN JEFFERSON - b 16 Jun 1849 NY s/JEFFERSON MONROE & MARY HARVEY (HUMASON) WILCOX; m 03 May 1899 Lincoln, Lancaster Co NE CARRIE A LEONARD; Res Fredonia, Chautauqua Co NY & Lincoln NE; ch

JEFFERSON LEONARD; d 24 Nov 1905 Lincoln NE; Ref: Col Fam of US v5 p552.

OLIVE - b 16 Oct 1751 d/DANIEL & SARAH (WHITE) WILCOX Middletown, Middlesex Co CT; d 01 Nov 1771; Ref: MUH p749, Cutter's CT Fam v2 p657, Hist of Berlin CT p89, Barbour's VR Middletown v1 p102.

OLIVE - b 16 Oct 1764 Harwinton, Litchfield Co CT d/MOSES & THANKFUL (SPENCER) BUNNELL WILCOX; Ref: Barbour's VR Harwinton LR1 p20 LR2 p30.

OLIVE 2nd - b 16 Sep 1766 Harwinton, Litchfield Co CT d/MOSES & THANKFUL (SPENCER) BUNNELL WILCOX; m 09 Nov 1786 BENONI JOHNSON; Ref: Barbour's VR Harwinton LR2 p30 LR4 p632.

OLIVE/OLLIE - b 01 Nov 1776 Middletown, Middlesex Co CT d/GILES & RACHEL (DOWD) WILCOX; m 21 Apr 1796 AMOS CHURCHILL Jr who was b 14 Apr 1775; Res Wallingford, New Haven Co CT; ch OLIVE; Ref: Early Fam of Wallingford p332, Barbour's VR Middletown v2 p160, Your Ancestors v3 #5 p379, Hist of Wallingford p938.

OLIVE - b 14 Jan 1778 Middletown, Middlesex Co CT d/JOSIAH & HULDAH (SAVAGE) WILCOX; m 22 Dec 1800 JAMES BOOTH who was b 1776 & d 02 Jan 1859; ch HORACE; d 16 Feb 1847; Ref: MUH p752, Hist of Berlin CT p99, Barbour's VR Middletown, v2 p221.

OLIVE - d/JANNA & CANDACE (GOODELL) WILCOX d 18 Sep 1811 Ludlow, Windsor Co VT; Ref: Goodell mss VT State Library.

OLIVE - b 5 Jan 1781 Halifax, Windham Co VT d/NATHAN & REBECCA (MOON) WILCOX; m 09 Jan 1810 WILLIAM CARPENTER of Marlboro, Windham Co VT; Ref: Halifax Wilcox Fam mss.

OLIVE - b ca 1795 E Guilford, New Haven Co CT d/JOSEPH & OLIVE (DOWD) WILCOX; m 23 Dec 1832 ABRAHAM CADWELL who was b 05 Aug 1791 & d 1874; Res Saybrook, Middlesex Co CT; d Dec 1864; Ref: Wilcox-Meigs p73, Cutter's CT Fam v4 p1769, Fam of Early Guilford p1211.

OLIVE - b 13 Jul 1797 RI d/STEPHEN & SUSANNA (TILLSON) WILCOX; Ref: Arnold v2 p173, Your Ancestors v11 #2 p1345.

OLIVE - d/PELEG Jr & THANKFUL (WILCOX) WILCOX of Lebanon, Madison Co NY; m JARAH L LILLIBRIDGE; ch VERNON W; d af 1846; Ref: Verna Betts.

OLIVE - b 10 May 1800 Harwinton, Litchfield Co CT d/AARON & LOIS (PHELPS) WILCOX; d young; Ref: Your Ancestors v3 #1 p279.

OLIVE - b 08 Mar 1802 d/JOHN & SUSANNAH (NICHOLS) WILCOX of Smyrna, Chenango Co NY; m WILLIAM KNOWLES; Ref: Your Ancestors v3 #4 p348.

OLIVE - b 09 May 1803 Middletown, Middlesex Co CT d/SAMUEL & LOIS (GRAVES) WILCOX; Ref: Barbour's VR Middletown v2 p224, See Samuel.

OLIVE - b ca 1805 d/THOMAS WILCOX; m SHELDING GUERNSEY; Res Milltown, Bradford Co PA; Ref: Pioneers of Bradford Co PA p309.

OLIVE - b 07 Mar 1807 Harwinton, Litchfield Co CT d/AARON & LOIS (PHELPS) WILCOX; m FREDERICK COLLINS; Ref: Your Ancestors v3 #1 p279.

OLIVE - d/HEZEKIAH & ABIAH (CLARK) WILCOX of Herkimer, Herkimer Co NY; m ISAAC BUCKLIN who was b 30 Mar 1816 s/SIMEON & MARY (SOUTHWICK) BUCKLIN; ch SIMEON, DARIUS, ROBERT; Ref: Your Ancestors v3 #6 p402.

OLIVE - moved from Bloomfield, Richmond Co NY to Oakland Co MI 1833; Ref: Yesteryears v23 #92 p81.

OLIVE - m 30 Jul 1835 Westfield, Chautauqua Co NY ROBERT M LOWRY; Res Mayville, Chautauqua Co NY; Ref: West NY Journal v10 #1, 19th Cent Marriages Reported in Fredonia Censor p119.

OLIVE - b ca 1820 d/OTHANIEL & ANN/NANCY (TILLINGHAST) WILCOX; m JAMES TEFFT; Res RI; ch JOHN T, CHARLES; Ref: Westcott Hist p108, Your Ancestor v3 #1 p277.

OLIVE - b 1839 IL d/HARLOW G & JEMIMA LEWIS (NICHOLSON) WILCOX; Res Big Grove, Kendall Co IL; Ref: 1850 Census Kendall Co IL.

OLIVE - m 28 Dec 1869 Goodhue Co MN GAIUS B PARKER; Ref: Red Wing Argus 20 Jan 1870 p4 col 3.

OLIVE - b 1845 PA d/WEALTHY WILCOX; Res Le Roy, Bradford Co PA; Ref: 1850 Census Bradford Co PA p68.

OLIVE - b be 1855 d/ABRAHAM & NANCY ANN (McLAIN) WILCOX; Res MI or IN; Ref: Wilcox Excerpts v1 p17.

OLIVE - b 06 Oct 1883 d/FREDERICK DUNBAR & JULIA (LOVENGUTH) WILCOX of Camden, Oneida Co NY; m 03 Jun 1908 Hamilton, Madison Co NY CHARLES ELMER CLARKE who was b 26 Aug 1878 Brookfield, Madison Co NY s/ELMER J & MARY AMELIA (BROWNING) CLARKE; ch FLOYD WILCOX; Ref: Your Ancestors v14 #3 p1672.

OLIVE ALMIRA - d/JANNA & CANDACE (GOODELL) WILCOX; d 1832 Ludlow, Windsor Co VT; Ref: Goodell mss VT State Library.

OLIVE B - m 03 Nov 1853 Butternuts, Otsego Co NY LOVETT VAN HORN; Ref: Marriages from Otsego Newspapers v3 p3.

OLIVE G - m 25 Dec 1823 Middletown, Middlesex Co CT NORMAN WILCOX; Ref: Barbour's VR Middletown v3 p148.

OLIVE HAZZARD - b 19 Oct 1812 Foster, Providence Co RI; d/STEPHEN & SUSANNAH (LEWIS) WILCOX; Ref: Arnold v3 p42, Your Ancestors v4 #1&2 p496.

OLIVE JANET - b 18 Mar 1811 VT d/ASHER SMITH & OLIVE (STURDEVANT) WILCOX of Shaftsbury, Bennington Co VT; m 23 Oct 1831 Bedford, Lawrence Co IN ALEXANDER CLARK who was b 01 Mar 1810 Benson, Rutland Co VT & d 17 Feb 1856 Huron, Lawrence Co IN; d 07 Feb 1854 Huron IN; Ref: Patricia Wetmore.

OLIVER - b 11 Oct 1747 Tiverton, Newport Co RI s/EPHRAIM & MARY (-----) WILCOX; Ref: Arnold v8 p56.

OLIVER - b ca 1750; m 12 Jul 1772 N Stonington, New London Co CT MARY STEWART; Ref: ECM v1 p61.

OLIVER - b 05 Mar 1753 Goshen, Litchfield Co CT s/GIDEON & MARY (BLANCHARD) WILCOX; m 10 Jan 1773 REBECCA DOOLITTLE; Ref: ECM v5 p21, Barbour's VR Goshen v1 p270, See Gideon.

OLIVER - b 05 Apr 1753 Middletown, Middlesex Co CT s/JONATHAN & DINAH (ORVIS) WILCOX; Ref: Barbour's VR Middletown v2 p11, See Jonathan.

OLIVER - b 24 Feb 1763 Middletown, Middlesex Co CT s/JONATHAN & RACHEL (LEWIS) WILCOX; Ref: Barbour's VR Middletown v2 p181.

OLIVER Col - b 10 Feb 1772 Alford, Berkshire Co MA s/SYLVANUS & JUSTINA/CHESTINA (CURTIS) WILCOX; m BETSEY SPRAGUE d/SILAS SPRAGUE; m LUNA JONES who was b 1786 & d 1862; Res Buffalo, Erie Co NY; ch HESTER MALVINA d 1817/1831 Buffalo NY; Ref: Your Ancestors v9 #4 p1177, Desc of Wm Wilcoxson pp190,200.

OLIVER - b 26 Jun 1773 Westerly, Washington Co RI s/ISAIAH & SARAH (LEWIS) WILCOX; m RUBY ----- who was b 1772 & d 25 May 1839; ch EPHRAIM C; d 03 Dec 1853 Westerly RI; Ref: Arnold v5 p145, Westerly RI & Its Witnesses p301, Wilcox-Brown-Medbery p10.

OLIVER - b 11 Nov 1779 Newport, Sullivan Co NH s/JESSE & THANKFUL (STEVENS) WILCOX; m 01 Sep 1807 SALLY STANTON who was b 19 Oct 1786 & d 1843 d/ADAM STANTON; Res Norwich, Chenango Co NY; ch ALBERT OLIVER, EDWIN, ELIZABETH STANTON, HENRIETTA, MARY AUGUSTA, GILES BUCKINGHAM, HAMILTON, STANTON, WILLIAM HENRY; d 24 Jan 1837; Ref: NYG&BR Apr 1978 p94, Your Ancestors v3 #4 pp349,350, Deaths from NY Herald p551, Nebr & Midwest Gen Rec v8 #1 p23.

OLIVER - b 1780 MA; m MARIE -----; Res Elbridge, Onondaga Co NY; Ref: 1850 Census Onondaga Co NY.

OLIVER - b 1781 CT; m ELEANOR ----- who was b 1782 CT; ch EMILINE C, GEORGE W, MARY E; Res Charlestown, Portage Co OH; Ref: 1850 Census Charlestown OH p159 Dw# 589.

OLIVER - b 12 Feb 1783 Hebron, Tolland Co CT s/JEHIEL & LYDIA (MACK) WILCOX; Ref: Barbour's VR Hebron v2 p261, Wilcox-Meigs p69.

OLIVER - m 24 Dec 1806 Bolton, Tolland Co CT ELEANOR HAMMOND; Ref: Fiske Card File.

OLIVER - b 10 Jun 1788 s/ISAAC & MARTHA (EVANS) BURDICK WILCOX; of Easton, Washington Co NY; m 2nd

CALISTA (TAYLOR) BURDICK; Ref: Your Ancestors v4 #5&6 p541.

OLIVER - b 1799; Came to Chautauqua Co 1809; 1835 Owned Lot 56 Hanover Twnshp 5 Range 10; Res Arkwright, Chautauqua Co NY; 4 sons & 4 daus incl HELEN; d 09 Jan 1881 Laona, Chautauqua Co NY; Ref: 1830,1840 Census Chautauqua Co NY, Deed Book 16 p298, 19th Cent Death Notices Reported in Fredonia Censor p596.

OLIVER - Res Lyme, Jefferson Co NY; Served in War of 1812; Ref: Index of Awards NY p538.

OLIVER - b 1794 Litchfield, Herkimer Co NY s/JOHN & MARY (CROSBY) WILCOX; m HANNAH -----; ch HENRIETTA; d 1850 OH; Ref: Jane Smith.

OLIVER - b 08 May 1795 Lexington, Greene Co NY s/NATHANIEL WILCOX; m 18 Mar 1818 Austerlitz, Columbia Co NY CYNTHIA BEEBE d/ROSWELL & ANNIE (GOTT) BEEBE; Res Middletown, Middlesex Co NY; ch HORATIO R, FRANKLIN AUGUSTUS; d 1857; Ref: Hist of Orange Co NY, Wilcox-Meigs p102, Your Ancestors v4 #11&12 p612.

OLIVER - b ca 1809 s/ JOSIAH & HANNAH (-----) WILCOX; m 2nd 30 May 1852 Portsmouth, Newport Co RI CHRISTIANIA GRENNELL who was b 1833 d/ MOSES & HANNAH (-----) GRENNELL; Res Tiverton, Newport Co RI; Ref: Arnold v4 pt1 p48.

OLIVER - b 1814 NY; m ELIZA -----; Res Eaton, Madison Co NY; ch HELLEN M, ALBERT O; Ref: 1850 Census Eaton NY p350 Dw# 370.

OLIVER - b 1823 NY s/CHARLES & BARBARA (WILKS) WILCOX of Sardinia, Erie Co NY & MN; Ref: 1850 Census Sardinia NY p117 Dw# 1733, See Charles.

OLIVER - b 29 Apr 1823 Bloomfield, Ontario Co NY s/EDWIN & CANDACE (GILBERT) WILCOX; d 24 Aug 1852; Ref: Edward McCarthy.

OLIVER - b Mar 1833 NY; m HANNAH -----; Res Hanover, Chautauqua Co NY; Ref: 1910 Census Chautauqua Co NY.

OLIVER - b 1836/7 Cattaraugus Co NY s/HORACE J & RACHEL (-----) WILCOX; m ORRILLA ----- who was b 1829; Res in household of ISAIAH & NANCY WRIGHT Collins, Erie Co NY; m 1865 LEFA ANN (-----) HOWE

743

w/GEORGE HOWE; Res Persia, Cattaraugus Co NY; ch EMMA B, CLARA A,ETHELBERT adpt; Ref: Alice Wiatr.

OLIVER - b 1847 NY s/ROSWELL & OLIVIA (-----) WILCOX of Sardinia, Erie Co NY; Ref: 1850 Census Sardinia NY p117, Dw# 1732.

OLIVER - b 1858 s/SAMUEL & LAURA (STARK) WILCOX of Simsbury OH; Ref: Your Ancestors v9 #2 p1126.

OLIVER - b 1879 s/WILLIAM/WILLIE & ELLEN (KNOWLES) WILCOX; d young; Ref: Desc of Wm Wilcoxson p197.

OLIVER B - b 1828 s/JERAULD & AMELIA (DARLING) WILCOX; d 1832; Ref: Your Ancestors v11 #3 p1371.

OLIVER BARKUS - b 16 May 1818 Sandisfield, Berkshire Co MA s/SAMUEL & ELIZABETH (-----) WILCOX; Ref: Sandisfield VR p73, Fiske Card File.

OLIVER C - m ELIZABETH -----; Res Chautauqua Co NY; ch AARON, ALFRED, ABRAHAM; d 1836; Ref: Land Records v20 pp349,360.

OLIVER C - b 1799 Simsbury, Hartford Co CT s/AARON & IRANA (BARNARD) WILCOX; m 02 Oct 1823 at Pomfret, Chautauqua Co NY MARIA YALE who was b 1799 in VT; Res Sheridan & Arkwright, Chautauqua Co NY; ch CYNTHIA, DELIA, CAROLINE, HELEN, AZARIAH, MILFORD, ANN M, HARRISON; Ref: 1830 Census, 1860 Census Sheridan NY p486 Dw# 1012, Your Ancestors v12 #2 p1438, #3 p1463, West NY Journal v7 #2 p62, 19th Cent Marriages Reported in Fredonia Censor p244.

OLIVER C - b 07 Jun 1848 s/ELON & MARY ELVIRA (BRYANT) WILCOX; Ref: Your Ancestors v3 #11&12 p471.

OLIVER L - will Probated 1880 Niagara Co NY; File W43; Ref: West NY Journal v6 #3 p131.

OLIVER LATHROP - b 26 Jun 1809 Glen, Montgomery Co NY s/SYLVANUS & SARAH (JOHNSTON) WILCOX; m 02 Oct 1833 ADALINE SHULER who was b 13 Aug 1811 & d 10 Sep 1892 d/JOHN & HANNAH (BUCK) of Florida NY; Res Montgomery Co NY & Gasport, Niagara Co NY; ch GEORGE A, AVERY HUBBARD; d 07 Mar 1880; Ref: Your Ancestors v9 #3 p1153, Desc of Wm Wilcoxson p191.

OLIVER LEROY - b 06 Sep 1865 Farmington, Davis Co UT s/JAMES DAVID & ANNA MARIA (ROBINSON) WILCOX; Ref: Desc of Wm Wilcoxson p144.

OLIVER LEWIS - b 17 Jan 1821 s/RICHARD & ELIZABETH (LEWIS) WILCOX of Canton, Bradford Co PA; Ref: Your Ancestors v10 #4 p1273.

OLIVER PERRY - b 06 Sep 1865 s/JAMES DAVID & ANNA MARIA (ROBINSON) WILCOX; Ref: Wilcox-Meigs p121.

OLIVER S - b ca 1775; m SARAH ----- who was b 1776 & d 01 Apr 1823; Res Peterboro, Madison Co NY af 1802; ch OLIVER S; Ref: Pioneers of Madison Co NY p282.

OLIVER S Jr - b 1814 Peterboro, Madison Co NY; Res Eaton, Madison Co NY; d 26 Apr 1880; Ref: Pioneers of Madison Co NY p282.

OLIVER SAMUEL - b 25 Jan 1773 prob Stratford, Fairfield Co CT s/SAMUEL & ANNE (CLARK) WILCOX; Ref: Wilcox-Meigs p59, Stratford Gen p1347.

OLIVER W - m 21 Feb 1836 Dartmouth, Bristol Co MA HARRIET VINCENT; Res Westerly, Washington Co RI; Ref: Dartmouth VR p547.

OLIVIA - b 1852 d/HORATIO R & SARAH M (KINSLEY) WILCOX; m 1875 JAMES WHITING SLAWSON Middletown, Orange Co NY; Ref: Hist of Orange Co NY, Wilcox-Meigs p121.

OLY - b 1835 NY s/THOMAS R & LOUISA (-----) WILCOX of Belfast, Allegany Co NY; Ref: 1850 Census Belfast NY p266 Dw# 56.

ORA - b 15 Jul 1852 Guthrie Center, Guthrie Co IA d/LEWIS ALLEN & SABINA McDONALD (HOPKINS) WILCOX; m ----- GLOZIER; Ref: Wilcox-Meigs p117.

ORA L - b 1835 NY d/HENRY & LOUISA (-----) WILCOX of Parish, Oswego Co NY; Ref: 1850 Census Parish NY p4 Dw# 50.

ORA S - b 1885 d/GILBERT H & EVA (BROWN) WILCOX; Ref: Desc of Wm Wilcoxson p240.

ORAMUS/ORAMON - b 1838 NY s/ALANSON & ALMIRA (-----) WILCOX of Dayton, Cattaraugus Co NY; d 01 May 1899 bur Sec A 3 Pinehill Cem Gowanda, Erie

Co NY; Ref: 1860 Census Dayton NY Reel 653 #726 p21, Alice Wiatr.

ORANDA/ORMANDA - b 16 Jul 1750 Killingworth, Middlesex Co CT s/GILES & LYDIA (WARD) WILCOX; d 08 Aug 1752; Ref: Wilcox-Meigs p65, Your Ancestors v3 #9&10 p449, Texas Society DAR Roster v4 p2287.

OREMUS - b 1856 Genesee Co NY s/RUSSELL & MARIAH (BURBEE) WILCOX; Ref: Your Ancestors v14 #3 p1669, See Russell.

OREN - m 31 Jun 1809 Hawley, Franklin Co MA ABIGAIL JENKINS; Ref: Fiske Card File.

ORESTES - b 1803 prob Simsbury, Hartford Co CT; d 28 Nov 1829; Ref: Rev Allen McLean Rec p8.

ORIGEN ABBEY - b 01 Dec 1840 Erie Co NY s/JOHN ABBE & FANNY OSBURN (MANTER) WILCOX; m 23 Aug 1868 Sardinia, Erie Co NY CLARA JANE EMERSON who was b 24 Mar 1848 & d 29 Mar 1907 Porterville, Tulare Co CA; ch MAMIE JESSIE, JOHN ALFRED, FREDERICK EMERSON, HARRY ABBE, ALICE EDNA, GUY FAY, GRACE ADELINE, & a dau who d; d 20 Apr 1919 Porterville CA; Ref: Jane Smith.

ORIGEN ELEAZER - b 13 Nov 1836 Ashford, Cattaraugus Co NY s/JEREMIAH& MELINDA (ABBEY) WILCOX; d 05 Apr 1838 Ashford NY bur Springville, Erie Co NY; Ref: Jane Smith.

ORLANDA - b 1842 NY d/JOHN & MARY ANN (-----) WILCOX of Parish, Oswego Co NY; Ref: 1850 Census Parish NY p5 Dw# 67.

ORLANDO - b 20 Apr 1795 Killingworth, Middlesex Co CT s/JOHN & MARGARET (KELSEY) WILCOX; 2nd m 09 Aug 1837 Madison, New Haven Co CT CHARLOTTE LEE who was b 02 Mar 1808 d/JONATHAN & MINDWELL (HILL) LEE; Ref: Your Ancestors v2 p255, Wilcox-Meigs pp70,71, Fam of Early Guilford p763, Gen of CT Fam v2 p419, Barbour's VR Madison v1 p75, CT Bible Rec v16 pp363,365.

ORLANDO - b 10 Mar 1819 Danbury, Fairfield Co CT s/AUGUSTUS & FANNY (BENEDICT) WILCOX; m 19 Oct 1841 Danbury CT SARAH B BENJAMIN; ch CHARLES HENRY, ARTHUR BENJAMIN, HERBERT EUGENE, EMILY NORTH, JAMES AUGUSTUS; d 23 Dec 1858; Ref: Desc of Wm Wilcoxson p259, Barbour's VR Danbury v3 p112.

ORLANDO - b 1826 CT; d 26 Mar 1859 Columbia Co NY; Ref: Hale Collection.

ORLANDO B - b 30 Sep 1831 Bennington, Bennington Co VT s/ROMULUS WILCOX; m NANCY ELIZABETH NOBLE who was b 07 Nov 1832 Hannibal, Oswego Co NY d/HORACE LEVINS & AMANDA ELIZA (HASKINS) NOBLE; Res Sextonville, Richland Co WI; ch HORACE NOBLE, IDA AMANDA; Ref: Desc of Thomas Noble p465.

ORLANDO BLISS - b 23 Dec 1812 Newport, Sullivan Co NH s/ASA & SYBIL (BLISS) WILCOX; m LYDIA ALLEN who was b 1827 OH d/LYMAN MARSHALL & ELIZABETH (FOOTE) ALLEN; Res Painesville, Lake Co OH; ch CHARLES ASA, FRANKIE EUGENIA, JASPER, ELIZABETH; Ref: Bogue Fam pp397,398, 1850 Census Painesville OH Reel 259 p197, Your Ancestors v3 #5 p378.

ORLANDO BLODGETT - b 19 Aug 1867 s/ORLANDO BOLIVAR & MARY LOUISE (FARNSWORTH) WILCOX; m 29 Jun 1898 JESSIE (COOKE) GILPIN d/WILLIAM HARVEY COOKE of Bethlehem PA; Res Washington DC; Ref: Wilcox-Meigs p104, 1880 Census Camp Verdi AZ.

ORLANDO BOLIVAR Gen - b 16 Apr 1823 Detroit, Wayne Co MI s/CHARLES & ALMIRA (ROOD) POWERS WILCOX; m 01 Oct 1852 MARIE LOUISE FARNSWORTH who was b 15 Dec 1831 & d 15 Apr 1873 d/CHANCELLOR ELON FARNSWORTH; m 24 Nov 1881 JULIA ELIZABETH (Mc REYNOLDS) WYETH who was b 24 Nov 1841, w/CHARLES JONES WYETH of Detroit, MI; Res MI, NY, VA, CA, AZ, Washington DC; Graduate of USMA West Point NY 01 Jul 1847 & was 8th in his class; Awarded Cong Med of Honor for Battle of Bull Run, Commanding Officer of AZ Military Dist; Willcox AZ named for him; Retired April 1887; ch MARIE LOUISE, ELON FARNSWORTH, CORA FARNSWORTH, ALMIRA, GRACE NORTH, CAROLINE B, ORLANDO BLODGETT, CHARLES McALLISTER, JULIAN PARSONS; d 10 May 1907 Coburg, Ontario Canada; Ref: 1880 Census Camp Verdi, Yavapai Co AZ p459, Wilcox-Meigs pp87,103,104, Willcox AZ Museum, Desc of Wm Wilcoxson p260, Dict of Am Biography v10 p283.

ORLANDO G - b 1833 NY s/WILLIAM & NAOMI (-----) WILCOX of Harford, Cortland Co NY; Ref: 1850 Census Harford NY p425.

ORLANDO KING - b 02 Sep 1823 De Witt, Onondaga Co NY s/ABEL & ACHSA (KING) WILCOX; m ca 1861 MARY WALTER; ch GEORGE W, ORLANDO KING, ARDELLA E, MARY

E, EMMETT A, NELLIE A, SAMUEL TILDEN, HUBERT; d 19 May 1888; Ref: Erwin W Fellows.

ORLANDO KING - b ca 1865 NY s/ORLANDO KING & MARY (WALTER) WILCOX; m FRANCES BOYD 1909; Res Chattanooga, Marion Co TN; Ref: Erwin W Fellows.

ORLANDO PHILIP - b 06 Feb 1854 MI s/ABRAHAM & NANCY (McLAIN) WILCOX; m 20 Mar 1878 Angola, Steuben Co IN JANET KNAPP who was b 09 Jun 1860 Angola IN & d 24 May 1942 Mansfield, Wright Co MO d/LESLIE & POLLY (LAMBERT) KNAPP; Res Wright Co MO; ch CHARLES ELMER, CELIA VILLA EVELYN, ARCHIE PAUL; d 20 Mar 1934; Ref: Wilcox Excerpts v1 p18.

ORPHA - b 07 Jun 1788 d/SADOCE & ROXY (HAYSE) WILCOX; d 25 Apr 1866 age 78; Ref: CT Bible Rec v18 pp520,522, See Sadoce.

ORPHA - b 1839 NY d/STEPHEN D & ALMINA (-----) WILCOX of Manlius, Onondaga Co NY; Ref: 1850 Census Manlius NY p18 Dw# 268.

ORPHA - b 29 Jan 1846 prob Hancock Co IL d/HORACE HUBBARD & OLIVIA (RICHARDSON) WILCOX of Clifford twnshp, Butler Co KS; m 04 Jul 1869 WILLIAM HENRY LAWRENCE; Ref: Desc of Wm Wilcoxson p131.

ORPHA MARIE - b 1892 d/CLINTON & MATTIE MAE (WILBUR) WILCOX; m EARL FINLEY; ch NANCY, SALLY; Ref: Desc of Wm Wilcoxson p196.

ORREN - b ca 1788 W Simsbury, Hartford Co CT s/AMOS & ANNA (CASE) WILCOX; Ref: Early Settlers of W Simsbury p134.

ORRIN - b 11 Feb 1782 Middletown, Middlesex Co CT s/JACOB & RACHEL (PORTER) WILCOX; Ref: MUH p749, Barbour's VR Middletown v2 p343.

ORRIN - b 07 Apr 1801 East Bloomfield, Ontario Co NY s/SMITH & MARTHA (TURNER) WILCOX; m HANNAH HAMLIN who was b 29 Nov 1800 & d 09 Mar 1872; Res Orleans Co NY & Disco, Macomb Co MI 1853; ch ALBERT N, WELLINGTON, LOIS, MARTHA ELVIRA, ELIZABETH A, CHARLOTTE MARIA, ELISHA, MARY; d 01 Dec 1872 Utica, Macomb Co MI; Ref: Your Ancestors v10 #3 p1249, Desc of Wm Wilcoxson pp207,208.

ORRIN/ORIN - b 1820 Cortland Co NY s/THOMAS JAMES & LUCY (-----) WILCOX; Parents moved to

Dryden, Lapeer Co MI 1837; Ref: Detroit Soc Gen Magazine v54 #2.

ORRIN - b 1820 NY; m POLLY M ----- who was b 1821 NY; Res Georgetown, Madison Co NY; ch POLLY A; Ref: 1850 Census Georgetown NY p391 Dw# 270.

ORRIN - b 1821 CT s/JEDEDIAH & BETSEY (WILCOX) WILCOX; m ADELINE SQUIRE; Res Hector, Tompkins Co NY & Valois, Schuyler Co NY; ch ADELINE M, MIRA A, WALTER R; d 14 May 1882 Washington DC; bur Valois NY Cem; Ref: Cem of Between the Lake Country v2 p319, Your Ancestors v12 #4 p1490, 1850 Census Hector NY pp359,360 Dw# 15.

ORRIN - of New Marlboro, Berkshire Co MA m 23 Mar 1845 Norfolk, Litchfield Co CT E HAWKS of Canaan, Litchfield Co CT; Ref: Barbour's VR Norfolk v2 p25.

ORRIN - b 1832 OH s/EDWIN & ELIZA (-----) WILCOX of Edinburgh, Portage Co OH; Ref: 1850 Census Edinburg OH p227 Dw# 1639.

ORRIN - of Farmington, Hartford Co CT m ELLEN M FOOTE who was b 1850 d/LUCIUS & SARAH (BARBER) FOOTE; ch EMMA, HENRY; Ref: Foote Fam Gen p384.

ORRIN - b 1843 NY s/THOMAS S & ANN (-----) WILCOX of Davenport, Delaware Co NY; Ref: 1850 Census Davenport NY p129 Dw# 26.

ORRIN/ORSEN - b 1843 CT s/ABRAHAM & LOIS (-----) WILCOX of New Hartford, Litchfield Co CT; Ref: 1850 Census New Hartford CT p125 Dw# 182.

ORRIN - of Suffield, Hartford Co CT; m 15 Dec 1879 Holyoke, Hampden Co MA NETTIE C BENHAM; Ref: Barbour's VR Suffield NB1 p428.

ORRIN - b 1871 Collins, Erie Co NY s/JOHN G & ROXY (COWDRY) WILCOX; Ref: Alice Wiatr.

ORRIN - b 20 Aug 1878 MI s/GEORGE & MARY A (FIRST) WILCOX; d 1882 Sebewa MI; Ref: Your Ancestors v3 #7&8 p423.

ORRIN A - m MARY B WATERMAN who was b 28 Nov 1868 & d 17 Apr 1909 Stonington, New London Co CT d/JAMES WILLIAMS & PRUDENCE ELIZABETH (BAILEY) WATERMAN; ch HELEN M; Ref: Desc of Robert Waterman v1 p576.

ORRIN B - b 1816; ch was bur 05 May 1850; d 14 Apr 1850 Baldwinsville, Onondaga Co NY; Bur Riverside Cem Baldwinsville 16 Apr 1850; Ref: Tree Talks v24 #1 p49, 10,000 VR of Central NY p264 Vorhees Rec v1 p96.

ORRIN B Dr - b 01 Mar 1833 Smyrna, Chenango Co NY s/HAZARD & FLAVILLA (PARSONS) WILCOX; m 24 Jun 1863 SARAH BURGESS of Richfield, Otsego Co NY who was b 18 Mar 1838 & d 08 Mar 1865; m LIZZIE WADSWORTH who was b 21 Nov 1840 West Winfield, Herkimer Co NY d/JOEL & SARAH (GOODIER) WADSWORTH; ch by 1st wife MARY B, ch by 2nd wife SARAH F, EARL WADSWORTH; Res Cedarville, Herkimer Co NY, Earlville Chenango Co NY; d 1895; Ref: Cutters Western NY v3 p1439, Your Ancestors v3 #6 pp397,398.

ORRIN E - b 19 April 1830 Smithfield twnshp, Bradford Co PA s/STEPHEN & POLLY (ALLEN) WILCOX; m ESTHER A HARKNESS who was b 16 Jul 1831 & d 28 Feb 1905 d/WILLIAM & CLARISSA (-----) HARKNESS of Springfield PA; Civil War Pvt Co G 64th NY Rgt; Wounded at Spottsylvania & disch 14 Jul 1865; ch JOHN L, IRENE CHARLOTTE, CLARA; d 02 Oct 1908; Both bur Union Cem East Smithfield PA Ref: Halifax VT Wilcox Fam mss, Wilcox Genealogy pp7,11.

ORRIN FRED - b 18 Sep 1866 Paw Paw, Van Buren Co MI s/CALVIN & ROSANNA M (STUYVESANT) WILCOX; m 25 Sep 1887 La Porte, La Porte Co IN MYRTILLA JANE SWARTZELL; d 17 Mar 1948 Wayne Co MI; Ref: George Koppers.

ORRIN/ORIN S - b 1839 NY s/THURSTON & SARAH (-----) WILCOX of Greenwich, Washington Co NY; Ref: 1850 Census Greenwich NY p230 Dw# 463.

ORRIN/ORIN WILLIE - b 14 May 1898 Sandgate, Bennington Co VT; m HELEN PISTELL; m JENNIE THOMPSON of Shaftsbury, Bennington Co VT; 1 dau by 1st wife; ch by 2nd wife HARLEY ORIN; Ref: Desc of Wm Wilcoxson p172.

ORSON - b 1805 s/ENOCH & NANCY (WOODRUFF) WILCOX of E Bloomfield, Ontario Co NY; m TERESA COOLEY; Ref: Your Ancestors v10 #1 p1202.

ORSON CHARLES - b 15 Oct 1881 Farmington, Davis Co UT s/JAMES DAVID & ANNA MARIA (ROBINSON) WILCOX; m ROSE ADELINE FEHR; Ref: Wilcox-Meigs p121, Desc of Wm Wilcoxson p144.

ORSOVA - b 28 Dec 1853 d/HORACE HUBBARD & OLIVIA (RICHARDSON) WILCOX of Hancock Co IL & Butler Co KS; d 06 Jun 1883; Ref: Desc of Wm Wilcoxson p131.

ORTON - b Mar 1866 s/HENRY HOPSON & ELIZABETH (LADD) WILCOX; Ref: Your Ancestors v3 #3 p319.

ORVILLE - b 1792 W Simsbury, Hartford Co CT s/WILLIAM & MERCY (CASE) WILCOX; m widow/CHESTER GIDDINGS; Ref: Early Settlers of W Simsbury p130.

ORVILLE - b 15 Aug 1817 s/LILLIBRIDGE & ANNA (HOXSIE) WILCOX; d 15 Feb 1821 Earlville, Chenango Co NY; Ref: Chenango Co Cem Records mss p9, Your Ancestors v3 #4 p347.

ORVILLE - b 09 Sep 1824 Lenox, Madison Co NY s/ALANSON & IRENE (JOHNSON) WILCOX; Ref: Pioneers of Madison Co NY p280.

ORVILLE - b 1826 VT; m SARAH ----- who was b 1826 NH; Res Orwell, Addison Co VT; Ref: 1850 Census Orwell VT Reel 920 p44 Dw# 174.

ORVILLE - b 03 Mar 1861 Wood Island, N B Canada s/ABEL & HANNAH AMELIA (GREEN) WILCOX; m ELLA LYONS; d 20 Apr 1907; bur Wood Island Cem; Ref: Desc of Charles Dyer Wilcox p24.

ORVILLE G - b 1847 CT s/ABRAHAM & LOIS (-----) WILCOX of New Hartford, Litchfield Co CT; Ref: 1850 Census New Hartford CT p125 Dw# 182.

OSBURN - b 1842 NY s/DANIEL & ELVIRA E (-----) WILCOX of Varick, Seneca Co NY; Ref: 1850 Census Varick NY p58 Dw# 862.

OSCAR - b 1829 NY s/JACOB & CAROLINE (-----) WILCOX of Sherburne, Chenango Co NY; Ref: 1850 Census Sherburne NY p249 Dw# 1624.

OSCAR - b 1830; m 25 Feb 1849 Lorain Co OH LURA GILETT/GILLETTE who was b OH; Res Avon, Lorain Co OH; ch HORACE; Civil War; d 1884; Ref: 1850 Census Lorain Co OH, Carol Wood, Marriages Lorain Co OH p119.

OSCAR - b 02 Mar 1832 Dover, Dutchess Co NY s/MARTIN & SARAH (-----) WILCOX; m AMANDA VINCENT; Ref: Your Ancestors v4 #9&10 p585, 1850 Census Dover NY p328 Dw# 269.

OSCAR - b 1841 s/WILLARD & ANNE/AMY (BROWN) WILCOX of Lansing, Tompkins Co NY; d 11 Mar 1844; Ref: Your Ancestors v14 #1 p1631.

OSCAR - b 1842 NY s/ELISHA & ELIZABETH (WILCOX) SHIPPEN WILCOX of Dover, Dutchess Co NY; Ref: 1850 Census Dover NY p311 Dw# 4, See Elisha.

OSCAR - b 1845 VT s/HARLOW & SALLY (-----) WILCOX; Res Cambridge, Lamoille Co VT; Ref: 1860 Census Cambridge VT p108 Dw# 223.

OSCAR - b 1846 NY s/CHARLES & ELIZA (-----) WILCOX of Skaneateles, Onondaga Co NY; Ref: 1850 Census Skaneateles NY p463.

OSCAR - b 1847 NY s/ISAIAH & POLLY A (-----) WILCOX of Columbus, Chenango Co NY; Ref: 1850 Census Columbus NY p280 Dw# 2131.

OSCAR - b 1850 NY s/ASA & HARRIET (STEVENS) WILCOX of Hamilton twnshp, Madison Co NY; Ref: Desc of Wm Wilcoxson p169.

OSCAR E - b 02 Feb 1847 Columbus, Chenango Co NY s/ISAIAH & POLLY ANN (-----) WILCOX; Ref: VR Chenango Co NY p33.

OSCAR F - b 1831 NY s/ALANSON & ALMIRA H (-----) WILCOX; m ca 1855 LUCY ----- who was b 1835 NY; Res Dayton, Cattaraugus Co NY; ch CLARENCE, GEORGIA; d prob 19 Jan 1891 bur Pinehill Cem Gowanda, Erie Co NY; Ref: 1860 Census Dayton NY Reel 653 #726 p21, Your Ancestors v13 #4 p1609, Alice Wiatr.

OSWALD LEWIS - b 20 Oct 1896 MI s/FRED & MARY (OSWALD) WILCOX; m Cape Girardeau, Cape Girardeau Co MO ELLEN WILSON; Ref: Wilcox Excerpts v1 p6.

OTHANIEL - b 06 Jul 1782 s/ROBERT & CATHERINE (TRIPP) WILCOX; m be 1810 Exeter, Washington Co RI ANN /NANCY TILLINGHAST who was b 15 Oct 1786 & d 1872 d/JOHN & ANNE (THITMAN) TILLINGHAST; ch MARY, CHARLES T, ANNA, KATHERINE, AMANDA/BRIDGET, OLIVE; d 13 Aug 1868; Ref: Westcott Hist p108, Arnold v6 pt3 p64, Your Ancestors v3 #1 p277.

OTHANIEL - m 16 May 1825 Providence, Providence Co RI PATIENCE SANDS; Ref: Arnold v7 p512.

OTIS - b 1814 VT; m ABIGAIL ----- who was b 1819 MA; Res Hancock, Addison Co VT; ch MARY,

ALMIRA, LORIN, GEORGE, AGNES; Ref: 1850 Census Hancock VT Reel 920 p64 Dw# 57.

OTIS - b 1837 NY s/TYLER WILCOX; Res Halifax, Windham Co VT; Ref: 1850 Census Halifax VT p131 Dw# 219, Halifax Wilcox Fam mss.

OTIS EVELIN - b 17 Feb 1809 ch/ISAAC WILCOX; Ref: CT Bible Rec v1 p476.

OVID/OVIL - b 03 Mar 1790 Granby, Hartford Co CT s/SADOCE/SEDOTIA & ROXEY (HAYSE) WILCOX; int to m 23 Sep 1816 Granville, Hampden Co MA ORPHA WRIGHT who was b 07 Jun 1788; ch RICHARDSON, SAPHRONIA, ROXEY, JAMES, AUGUSTIN, ELIZA ANN; d 02 Jan 1862 age 73; Ref: Desc of Wm Wilcoxson p218, Barbour's VR Granby TM1 p25, CT Bible Rec v18 pp520,522.

OWEN - b 1842 NY s/CHARLES & REBECCA (-----) WILCOX of Lexington, Greene Co NY; Ref: 1850 Census Lexington NY p274 Dw# 50.

OWEN - b 1844 Lafayette, Onondaga Co NY s/FREEMAN & HULDAH (-----) WILCOX; Ref: Your Ancestors v13 #1 p1513, 1850 Census Lafayette NY p224 Dw# 513.

OZIAL/OZIEL - b 25 Jan 1729 Killingworth, Middlesex Co CT s/THOMAS & MARTHA (-----) WILCOX; d 27 Feb 1787; Ref: Wilcox-Meigs p43, Desc of Wm Wilcoxson p43, Your Ancestors v4 #11&12 p611, Barbour's VR Killingworth v2 p160.

OZIAL/OZIEL - b 10 Aug 1759 Lee, Berkshire Co MA s/PETER & JERUSHA (-----) WILCOX; m 10 Oct 1782 Lee MA LOIS GOODRICH; d Feb/Mar 1787 Sheffield, Berkshire Co MA; Ref: Desc of Wm Wilcoxson p59, Lee MA VR p171, Fiske Card File, Janet Armbrust.

OZIAL - b 1774; m ca 1794 NANCY PAINE; ch JOEL, AMELIA, ERMINA, OZIAL Jr, MEHITABLE, JOHN, ASA, JOSEPH RUGGLES, ANNIS, JOHN AUSTIN; d 15 Mar 1856 Sandgate, Bennington Co VT; Ref: VT VR, Desc of Wm Wilcoxson pp169,170.

OZIAL Jr - b 1807 Sandgate, Bennington Co VT s/OZIAL & NANCY (PAINE) WILCOX; m SYLVIA STEVENS who prob d before 1860; Res Georgetown twnshp, Madison Co NY; ch NELSON OZIAL, FRANKLIN, NANCY, AUSTIN, LYMAN, WARREN, JULIA A, CALEB, SARAHA, SHUBAL, JAMES, SARAH; Ref: Desc of Wm Wilcoxson p169, 1850 Census Georgetown NY p387 Dw# 208.

OZIAL/OZIEL - of Killingworth, Middlesex Co CT; m 20 Feb 1826 Guilford, New Haven Co CT LUCY LEETE d/JARED LEETE; Res Genesee Co NY; Ref: Fiske Card File, Barbour's VR Guilford v2 p288.

OZIAS - b 16 Sep 1730 Middletown, Middlesex Co CT s/JOHN & MARY (BARNES) WILCOX; m 31 Oct 1758 Washington, Litchfield Co CT MABEL GOULD who was b 19 Nov 1732 & d 26 Sep 1774 Middletown CT d/JOHN & MEHITABLE (COOK) GOULD; ch AMOS, ELIPHALET, ASA, EBENEZER, BENJAMIN, CYRUS, LUCY, OZIAS, MABEL, SETH; Ref: MUH pp746,747, Barbour's VR Middletown v2 pp21,322, Fam of Early Guilford p506.

OZIAS - m Mrs MARY (ATWATER) JOHNSON who was b 12 Feb 1727 Wallingford, New Haven Co CT & d 1780 w/THOMAS JOHNSON; Ref: Fam of Ancient New Haven v1 p66.

OZIAS - b 1765; m BETSY ----- who was b 1776 & d 23 Aug 1831 age 55 New Hartford, Oneida Co NY; d 4 Dec 1838 age 73; Ref: Fiske Card File.

OZIAS - b 21 Apr 1766 Middletown, Middlesex Co CT s/OZIAS & MABEL (GOULD) WILCOX; Ref: Barbour's VR Middletown v2 p322.

OZIAS - m 30 May 1782 Cromwell, Middlesex Co CT MARY LUSK; Ref: ECM v2 p95.

OZIAS/ORIAS - b 1785 NY; m -----? who was b 1788 NY; Res Utica, Oneida Co NY; ch MARTHA, EMMA, HARRIETT, HENRY, MELISSA, MARIAH, CATHERINE, HELEN; Ref: 1850 Census Utica NY p311 Dw# 25.

OZIAS - b 19 Mar 1796 NY s/EZRA & PHOEBE (WOODRUFF) WILCOX; m Mar 1826 SUSAN/SALLY MOULTON/ MORRISON who was b 21 Jun 1804 & d 10 Mar 1874 d/SALMON & SUSANNAH (JOHNSON) MOULTON; ch JEFFERSON MONROE, JERMAINE W, SUSAN MOULTON, SOPHIA CONVERSE; d 11 Mar 1876 Turin, Lewis Co NY; Ref: 10,000 VR of Central NY p264, Col Fam of US v5 p556, Wilcox-Meigs p97.

OZIAS - b 1802-1810; Res Frankfort, Herkimer Co NY; 2 daus; Ref: 1810 Census Herkimer Co NY p155.

OZIAS [see WILLIAM OZIAS] - b 30 Mar 1824 Crown Point, Essex Co NY s/ASA & SYBIL (BLISS) WILCOX; m M L STEARNS; Ref: Fiske Card File.